ENTERPRISE ARCHITECTS

Other books by Svyatoslav Kotusev:

THE PRACTICE OF ENTERPRISE ARCHITECTURE
A Modern Approach to Business and IT Alignment

ENTERPRISE ARCHITECTS
The Agents of Digital Transformation

Svyatoslav Kotusev

Copyright © 2024 by Svyatoslav Kotusev

All rights reserved.

No part of this publication may be reproduced, distributed, or transmitted in any form or by any means, including photocopying, recording, or other electronic or mechanical methods, without the prior written permission of the publisher, except in the case of brief quotations embodied in critical reviews and certain other noncommercial uses permitted by copyright law.

All trademarks used herein are the property of their respective owners. The use of any trademark in this text does not vest in the author or publisher any trademark ownership rights in such trademarks, nor does the use of such trademarks imply any affiliation with or endorsement of this book by such owners.

Although every precaution has been taken to verify the accuracy of the information contained herein, the author and publisher assume no responsibility for any errors or omissions. No liability is assumed for damages that may result from the use of information contained within.

First published in 2024 by SK Publishing, Melbourne, Australia 3000

ISBN (Kindle): 978-1-7636486-0-9
ISBN (ePub): 978-1-7636486-1-6
ISBN (Paperback): 978-1-7636486-2-3
ISBN (Hardcover): 978-1-7636486-3-0

 A catalogue record for this book is available from the National Library of Australia

ACM Computing Classification System (2012): Applied computing ~ Enterprise architectures

Printed in the United States of America

10 9 8 7 6 5 4 3 2 1

Visit https://kotusev.com

Contents

Contents v
Complete Table of Contents vii
Foreword xix
Preface xxiii
PART I: Introduction to Enterprise Architects 1
Chapter 1: Digital Transformation 3
Chapter 2: Digital Transformation Initiatives 21
Chapter 3: Architectural Planning 41
Chapter 4: Welcome, Enterprise Architects 63
Chapter 5: Enterprise Architects in Context 85
PART II: Enterprise Architects in Depth 99
Chapter 6: Resources of Enterprise Architects 101
Chapter 7: Instruments of Enterprise Architects 117
Chapter 8: The Catalog of Enterprise Architecture Artifacts 145
Chapter 9: Using Enterprise Architecture Artifacts 175
Chapter 10: Basic Activities of Enterprise Architects 197
Chapter 11: Leading the Development of Plans 225
Chapter 12: Ensuring Adherence to Plans 247
Chapter 13: The Work of Enterprise Architects 271
Chapter 14: The Profession of Enterprise Architects 293
PART III: Enterprise Architects in Organizations 309
Chapter 15: The Archetype of Enterprise Architects 311
Chapter 16: The Archetype of Solution Architects 345
Chapter 17: Architecture Positions in Organizations 373
Chapter 18: Challenges of Enterprise Architects 393
Chapter 19: Other Aspects of Enterprise Architects 421
Afterword 433
Notes 435
References 475
Index 497
About the Author 507

Complete Table of Contents

Contents v

Complete Table of Contents vii

Foreword xix
    Materials for This Book xx
    Acknowledgments xxi

Preface xxiii
    The Subject of This Book xxiii
    This Book and "The Practice of Enterprise Architecture" xxiv
    The Features of This Book xxv
        Based on Original Research and Empirical Evidence xxv
        Descriptive and Analytical Attitude xxv
        Dispassionate and Factual View xxv
        Both Practical and Conceptual Perspective xxv
        Systematic and Comprehensive Approach xxvi
        Introduces Novel Conceptualizations xxvi
        Addresses the Organizational, Not Technical Side xxvi
        Focuses on Doing Work, Not Getting Certified xxvi
        Placed in the Context of the Existing Literature xxvii
    The Intended Audience of This Book xxvii
    The Teaching Pack for This Book xxvii
    The Structure of This Book xxviii
    A Note on the Used Terminology xxix
    Staying Updated with Research Products xxx

PART I: Introduction to Enterprise Architects 1

Chapter 1: Digital Transformation 3
    Development and Progress of Information Technology 3
    Digital Transformation in Organizations 5
    Drivers of Digital Transformation 6
        Different Types of Transformation Drivers 7

Business Strategy as a Transformation Driver	9
Comprehensive Motivational Context	10
Technical Challenges of Digital Transformation	12
Virtually Unlimited Choice of Technical Options	13
Enormous Complexity of Information Technology Landscapes	13
Critical Cybersecurity Risks, Threats and Vulnerabilities	14
Organizational Challenges of Digital Transformation	14
Tight Coupling of Information Systems and Business Activities	14
Multitude of Conflicting Interests, Ideas and Considerations	15
Normative Regulations, Obligations and Restrictions	18
The Overall Context of Digital Transformation	18
Chapter Summary	20

Chapter 2: Digital Transformation Initiatives 21

Digital Transformation Initiatives in Organizations	21
Ideation of Digital Transformation Initiatives	21
Implementation of Digital Transformation Initiatives	22
Stakeholders of Digital Transformation Initiatives	24
Different Types of Digital Transformation Initiatives	26
The Hierarchy of Digital Transformation Initiatives	29
Implementation of Hierarchical Digital Transformation Initiatives	30
Execution of Digital Transformation Projects	34
Generic Project Delivery Process	34
Waterfall and Agile Delivery Methodologies	35
Challenges of Implementing Digital Transformation Initiatives	37
Chapter Summary	39

Chapter 3: Architectural Planning 41

The Notion of Architectural Planning	41
Stakeholders of Architectural Planning	43
The Technical Side of Architectural Planning	45
The Organizational Side of Architectural Planning	46
Architectural Planning in Its Full Complexity	48
Organizational Domains Relevant to Architectural Planning	50
The Stack of Organizational Domains	51
Differences Between Organizational Domains	52
Coverage of Organizational Domains in Architectural Solutions	55
Architectural Planning of Hierarchical Initiatives	57
Architectural Solutions for Projects, Programs and Strategies	57
Architectural Planning of Projects, Programs and Strategies	58

Chapter Summary 61

Chapter 4: Welcome, Enterprise Architects 63
  Enterprise Architects as Specialized Professionals 63
    Competencies and Occupation of Enterprise Architects 63
    Enterprise Architects as Practitioners of Enterprise Architecture 64
    Enterprise Architects as Actors of Organizational Enterprise Architecture Practice 66
    Enterprise Architects as Internal Consultants 67
    Enterprise Architects as City Planners 69
  Enterprise Architects at Work 70
    Enterprise Architects Do Not Work Like Traditional Architects 70
    How Do Enterprise Architects Work? 70
    Work in the Process of Initial Ideation 71
    Work During the Conception Phase 72
    Work During the Planning Phase 73
    Work During the Execution Phase 74
    Agreed Plans Trump Perfect Plans 75
  Two Hats of Enterprise Architects 76
    The Hat of Technology Experts 77
    The Hat of Change Agents 78
    Enterprise Architects as Ambidextrous Personalities 79
    Enterprise Architects, Senior Techies and Change Activists 81
  Chapter Summary 82

Chapter 5: Enterprise Architects in Context 85
  Enterprise Architects in the Organizational Environment 85
    Enterprise Architects in the Organizational Structure 85
    Enterprise Architects in the Ecosystem of Organizational Positions 87
    Enterprise Architects in the Context of Strategy Execution 89
  What Organizations Employ Enterprise Architects? 90
  The Value of Enterprise Architects for Organizations 91
    Costs and Benefits of Enterprise Architects 91
    Value Propositions of Enterprise Architects 92
  Who Enterprise Architects Are Not 93
    Not Enterprise Strategists 93
    Not Chief Technologists 94
    Not Universal Transformers 94
    Not System Architects 94
    Not Supreme Draftsmen 95
    Not Systems Thinkers 95
    Not Omniscient Masterminds 96

Not Almighty Wizards 96
Not the Smartest Guys 96
Not Grumbling Loafers 97
Chapter Summary 97

PART II: Enterprise Architects in Depth 99

Chapter 6: Resources of Enterprise Architects 101
Resources Possessed by Enterprise Architects 101
Knowledge of Enterprise Architects 101
General Business-Related Knowledge 102
General IT-Related Knowledge 102
Industry-Specific Business-Related Knowledge 103
Industry-Specific IT-Related Knowledge 103
Organization-Specific Business-Related Knowledge 104
Organization-Specific IT-Related Knowledge 104
The Taxonomy of Knowledge of Enterprise Architects 105
Skills of Enterprise Architects 106
Communication Skills 106
Collaborative Attitude 107
Innovative Mindset 107
Disciplined Thinking 108
The Framework of Skills of Enterprise Architects 109
Experience of Enterprise Architects 110
Anticipating Long-Term Consequences 111
Realizing the Effects of Scale 111
Considering Entire System Lifecycles 112
Seeing the Pitfalls of Technologies 112
Detecting Hype, Puffery and Fashions 112
Applying Lessons from Practice 113
The Pyramid of the Resources of Enterprise Architects 113
Chapter Summary 114

Chapter 7: Instruments of Enterprise Architects 117
Instruments Employed by Enterprise Architects 117
Two Functions of Enterprise Architecture Artifacts 117
Documenting the Existing Situation 118
Capturing Architectural Solutions 119
Duality of Enterprise Architecture Artifacts 121
Explicit Duality 122
Implicit Duality 123

Different Types of Enterprise Architecture Artifacts 124
    Different Orientations: Actualities and Plans Artifacts 125
    Different Affiliations: Initiative-Specific and General Artifacts 127
    Different Objects: Solutions, Structures and Rules Artifacts.................................. 129
    Different Viewpoints: IT-Focused and Business-Focused Artifacts........................ 132
The CSVLOD Taxonomy for Enterprise Architecture Artifacts 135
    Considerations (Business-Focused Rules) 135
    Standards (IT-Focused Rules)... 136
    Visions (Business-Focused Structures) 136
    Landscapes (IT-Focused Structures).. 136
    Outlines (Business-Focused Solutions) 137
    Designs (IT-Focused Solutions).. 137
    Resulting Taxonomy 138
Other Instruments of Enterprise Architects 140
    Modeling Languages... 140
    Software Tools 140
    Analytical Techniques 141
    Auxiliary Artifacts 142
Chapter Summary... 143

Chapter 8: The Catalog of Enterprise Architecture Artifacts 145
Popular Enterprise Architecture Artifacts 145
Considerations.. 146
    Principles and Policies 146
    Architecture Strategies... 147
    Analytical Reports and Conceptual Data Models 148
    Other Considerations 149
Standards... 150
    Technology Reference Models 150
    Technology Inventories and Technology Roadmaps.. 151
    IT Principles and Guidelines.. 152
    Patterns and Logical Data Models 153
    Other Standards... 155
Visions 155
    Target States and Roadmaps... 155
    Business Capability Models.. 157
    Process Maps and Value Chains 158
    Other Visions 159
Landscapes 160
    Landscape Diagrams and Asset Inventories 160
    System Portfolio Models and Landscape Maps.. 161

IT Roadmaps and Asset Roadmaps 163
Other Landscapes 164
Outlines 165
Solution Overviews 165
Solution Briefs and Solution Options 166
Other Outlines 167
Designs 168
Solution Designs and Preliminary Solution Designs 168
Other Designs 169
Summary of Popular Enterprise Architecture Artifacts 170
Mapping of Enterprise Architecture Artifacts to Organizational Domains 170
Enterprise Architecture on a Page 172
Chapter Summary 173

Chapter 9: Using Enterprise Architecture Artifacts 175

The Use of Enterprise Architecture Artifacts by Enterprise Architects 175
Using EA Artifacts for Documenting the Existing Situation 175
Specifics of Using EA Artifacts for Documenting the Existing Situation 176
Choosing Suitable EA Artifacts for Documenting the Existing Situation 176
Using EA Artifacts for Capturing Architectural Solutions 179
Specifics of Using EA Artifacts for Capturing Architectural Solutions 179
Specifics of Using EA Artifacts for Hierarchical Transformation Initiatives 181
Mutual Influence of Architectural Solutions for Different Initiatives 182
Choosing Suitable EA Artifacts for Capturing Architectural Solutions 184
Examples of Using EA Artifacts for Capturing Architectural Solutions 186
Digital Channels Strategy 186
Data Analytics Strategy 187
Intra-Initiative Guidance and Inter-Initiative Influence 188
Architectural Context Formed by Architectural Decisions 190
Overarching Transformational Context 192
Digitalization Initiatives in the Transformational Context 194
Chapter Summary 196

Chapter 10: Basic Activities of Enterprise Architects 197

Activities Performed by Enterprise Architects 197
Two Contexts of Activities 198
Five Activities of Enterprise Architects 199
Activities in Different Contexts 200
Analyzing the External Environment 201
Meaning and Goals 201

  Context of Fulfillment 202
  Means of Fulfillment 203
  Relevant Enterprise Architecture Artifacts 204
  Additional Concerns 205
 Studying the Internal Environment 207
  Meaning and Goals 207
  Context of Fulfillment 209
  Means of Fulfillment 210
  Relevant Enterprise Architecture Artifacts 210
  Additional Concerns 213
 Providing Advisory Services 214
  Meaning and Goals 214
  Context of Fulfillment 215
  Means of Fulfillment 219
  Relevant Enterprise Architecture Artifacts 220
  Additional Concerns 222
 Chapter Summary 223

Chapter 11: Leading the Development of Plans 225
 Leading the Development of Plans as a Distinct Activity 225
 Meaning and Goals 227
 Context of Fulfillment 228
 Means of Fulfillment 229
  Planning Meetings as Technical Means 229
  Planning Process as Logical Means 231
 Relevant Enterprise Architecture Artifacts 236
  Artifact Templates 238
  Presentation Packs 239
  Decision Papers 241
 Additional Concerns 243
 Chapter Summary 245

Chapter 12: Ensuring Adherence to Plans 247
 Ensuring Adherence to Plans as a Distinct Activity 247
  Difficulties of Achieving Adherence Without Managerial Authority 248
  Leveraging Architecture Governance Bodies for Achieving Adherence 248
 Meaning and Goals 250
 Context of Fulfillment 252
 Means of Fulfillment 254
  Individual Approaches as Personal Means 254

  Governance Procedures as Organizational Means 256
  Combining Different Means of Achieving Adherence 258
 Relevant Enterprise Architecture Artifacts 260
  Compliance Checklists 261
  Exception Forms 262
  Amendment Forms 264
 Additional Concerns 265
  Revising the Existing Plans 266
  Deviating from Plans 266
  Exploring Beyond Plans 267
  Finding the Right Balance 267
 Chapter Summary 268

Chapter 13: The Work of Enterprise Architects 271
 The Occupation of Enterprise Architects as the Unity of Five Activities 271
  Logical Relationships Between Different Activities 271
  Sequential Relationships Between Different Activities 272
  Dynamic Interplay Between Different Activities 273
  Activities of Enterprise Architects in Different Lifecycle Phases of Initiatives 274
  The Value Stream of the Activities of Enterprise Architects 276
 The Work of Enterprise Architects in Organizations 278
  The Work of Enterprise Architects in the Organizational Context 278
  The Work of Enterprise Architects in the Initiative Context 279
  The Work of Enterprise Architects in Its Entirety 279
 The Schedule of Enterprise Architects 281
  The Daily Timetable of Enterprise Architects 281
  The Schedule of Enterprise Architects and the Pipeline of Initiatives 284
 Enterprise Architects as the Advocates of Technical Interests 285
  Enterprise Architects as Initiative Stakeholders 287
  Enterprise Architects as Driver Proponents 289
  Technical Rationalization Initiatives 289
 Chapter Summary 291

Chapter 14: The Profession of Enterprise Architects 293
 The Job of Enterprise Architects as a Separate Profession 293
  Is the Job of Enterprise Architects a Profession? 293
  The Integrative Framework of the Profession of Enterprise Architects 295
  Art, Craft and Science in the Profession of Enterprise Architects 296
 The Historical Evolution of Enterprise Architects 299
  The Past of Enterprise Architects 300
  The Present of Enterprise Architects 301

The Future of Enterprise Architects 303
Different Understandings of Enterprise Architects 304
    Enterprise Architects as a Profession 304
    Enterprise Architects as an Archetype 304
    Enterprise Architects as a Position 305
    Other Understandings of Enterprise Architects 305
    Different Understandings of Enterprise Architects and the Structure of This Book .. 306
Chapter Summary 308

PART III: Enterprise Architects in Organizations 309

Chapter 15: The Archetype of Enterprise Architects 311

Enterprise Architects as a Distinct Archetype of Architects 311
Resources of Enterprise Architects 313
    Knowledge 314
    Skills 314
    Experience 315
Instruments of Enterprise Architects 315
    Considerations, Standards, Visions and Landscapes 315
    Outlines and Designs 316
Activities of Enterprise Architects in the Organizational Context 316
    Analyzing the External Environment 316
    Studying the Internal Environment 317
    Providing Advisory Services 317
    Involvement in the Initial Ideation of Digital Transformation Initiatives 318
Activities of Enterprise Architects in the Initiative Context 318
    The Implementation Process of High-Level Transformation Initiatives 319
    Activities During the Conception Phase 321
    Activities During the Planning Phase 323
    Activities During the Execution Phase 325
    Activities During the Revision Phase 326
    Activities Along the Initiative Implementation Process 327
The Work of Enterprise Architects 329
Organization-Centric Work of Enterprise Architects 330
    Intertwined, Implicit and Inarticulate High-Level Transformation Initiatives 330
    Organization-Centric View of Digital Transformation 331
    Enterprise Architects in the Organization-Centric View 334
    Activities of Enterprise Architects in the Organization-Centric View 335
    The Work of Enterprise Architects in the Organization-Centric View 337
Domain Specialization of Enterprise Architects 339
The Integrative Framework of the Archetype of Enterprise Architects 342

    Chapter Summary 343

Chapter 16: The Archetype of Solution Architects 345
    Solution Architects as a Distinct Archetype of Architects 345
    Resources of Solution Architects 347
        Knowledge 347
        Skills 348
        Experience 348
    Instruments of Solution Architects 349
        Considerations, Standards, Visions and Landscapes 349
        Outlines and Designs 349
    Activities of Solution Architects in the Organizational Context 350
        Analyzing the External Environment 350
        Studying the Internal Environment 350
        Providing Advisory Services 351
        Involvement in the Initial Ideation of Digital Transformation Initiatives 351
    Activities of Solution Architects in the Initiative Context 352
        The Implementation Process of Digital Transformation Projects 352
        Activities During the Concept Step 358
        Activities During the Decision Step 359
        Activities During the Design Step 360
        Activities During the Delivery Step 362
        Activities Along the Project Implementation Process 364
    The Work of Solution Architects 366
    Domain Specialization of Solution Architects 367
    The Integrative Framework of the Archetype of Solution Architects 369
    Enterprise Architects and Solution Architects 370
    Chapter Summary 371

Chapter 17: Architecture Positions in Organizations 373
    Specific Positions for Architects in Organizations 373
    Vertical Tier-Based Specialization of Architects 374
        One-Tier Architecture Functions 374
        Two-Tier Architecture Functions 376
        Three-Tier Architecture Functions 378
    Horizontal Area-Based Specialization of Architects 380
        Domain-Centric Architecture Functions 380
        Business-Centric Architecture Functions 381
        Combined Architecture Functions 383
    The Spectrum of Architecture Functions 385

Interactions Between Specialized Architects 388
    Offering Advice 388
    Supervising Decisions 388
    Co-Planning Transformations 389
    Providing Drivers 389
    Seeking Synergies 389
    The Work of Architects as Teamwork 390
Chapter Summary 391

Chapter 18: Challenges of Enterprise Architects 393

Engagement Between Enterprise Architects and Business Leaders 393
    Alternatives for Business Leaders Seeking Digitalization 394
    Involvement of Enterprise Architects at Different Stages of Initiative Formation 396
    Early Involvement as a Practical Imperative for Enterprise Architects 399
    Reputation as a Critical Resource of Enterprise Architects 400
    General Approaches for Starting Engagement with Business Leaders 402
Individual Challenges of Enterprise Architects 404
    Challenges of Technology Experts 405
    Challenges of Change Agents 406
Organizational Challenges of Enterprise Architects 407
    Challenges of Managerial Understanding 408
    Challenges of Managerial Desire 410
    Challenges of Managerial Distance 415
Chapter Summary 418

Chapter 19: Other Aspects of Enterprise Architects 421

Career Paths of Enterprise Architects 421
How to Become an Enterprise Architect? 423
What Enterprise Architects Should Know About... 426
    Modeling Languages 426
    Software Tools 426
    Enterprise Architecture Frameworks 427
    Professional Certifications 428
Conundrums of Enterprise Architects 429
    Reasoning Through Superficiality 429
    Deciding Under Uncertainty 429
    Influencing Without Power 430
    Enterprise Architects as an Intriguing Profession 431
Chapter Summary 431

Afterword **433**

Notes **435**

References **475**

Index **497**

About the Author **507**

Foreword

The profession of enterprise architects, as someone who drives digital transformation and merges business and IT in organizations, arguably represents one of the hallmarks of the 21st century. As more and more companies become affected by the ever-growing digitalization trends, the prominence of this profession in the industry obviously increases. Today, no complex organization of a considerable size can expect to prosper in its digital transformation endeavors without employing specialized enterprise architects.

However, despite their evident importance, the role, work and personality of enterprise architects can hardly be considered well-studied, thoroughly described or widely comprehended. To many, architects still remain largely a mystery and their profession — a kind of arcane witchcraft[1]. There is no consensus as to what their job implies[2] and even practicing architects themselves often struggle to explain their own role[3]. This state of affairs, though, is far from surprising in view of the fact that the literature on enterprise architects, and especially serious one, is badly scarce. Except for superficial, five-minutes-to-read online articles, existing sources of information about architects and their occupation are very limited[4].

Indeed, the available practitioner books devoted specifically to enterprise architects, not to the discipline of enterprise architecture at large, can be counted literally on the fingers of one hand[5]. In terms of their content, these books offer witty jokes, enlightening lessons and practical advice on virtually all aspects of life[6], entertaining stories featuring fictional enterprise architects at work[7], self-help career development guidelines[8], depictions of someone suspiciously resembling software architects[9] or, contrary to the promising titles, actually tell next to nothing on the subject[10]. None of these books even attempts to provide a *systematic* description of enterprise architects from which interested readers can learn who they are, what they do and how they behave.

Interestingly, the situation with the industry literature on enterprise architects, as individual actors, differs radically from that with enterprise architecture, as an organizational practice. Whereas the latter comprises about a hundred books of varying quality and multiple "definitive" sources irresponsibly promoting nobody's fake "best practices" (e.g. TOGAF, Zachman and other frameworks), the former is characterized by acute shortage and has no sources that can be regarded, even falsely, as definitive.

In the academic world, empirical research on enterprise architects has not been particularly extensive and fruitful either[11]. For instance, the vast majority of scientific publications about architects addressed their competencies, skills and other passive attributes[12], but only a few studies tried to analyze their behavior and activities in organizations[13]. Overall, the existing body of scholarly writings barely constructs a consistent evidence-based picture of enterprise architects and their work[14].

Paradoxically, enterprise architects objectively exist as a notable industry phenomenon, and have existed in some form for much longer than most people tend to think, possibly since the very first business information system built circa 1950[15], but their solid understanding and concomitant reflection in the literature are still absent. In this light, it is rather amusing to see various calls for the professionalization of architects[16], when no one can meaningfully articulate exactly what their profession involves, as well as speculations about how their role should change in the future[17], when no one can clearly formulate what their role is right now.

At the same time, conceptually, the occupation of enterprise architects is extremely sophisticated, multifaceted and rich with nuances. In the literature, for their extraordinarily broad skill sets, architects are frequently compared to jacks-of-all-trades[18], superhumans[19] and even five-legged sheep[20]. To elucidate different facets of their job, various authors often resort to ingenious metaphors such as management consultants[21], city planners[22], wedding planners[23], diplomats[24], translators[25], salesmen[26] and tour guides[27]. Therefore, their "business" is anything but simple, allows numerous interpretations and defies simplistic definitions. Describing the work of enterprise architects in its full complexity represents a daunting task.

In these settings, I set out to close an inexcusable gap in the literature and write a long-overdue, comprehensive book about enterprise architects. Initially, I conceived this new book largely as a supplement to my first book *The Practice of Enterprise Architecture: A Modern Approach to Business and IT Alignment*. I also envisioned the resulting book to be somewhere around 200–250 pages and consisting of approximately 6–8 chapters. However, as more and more intricacies of architects' work unfolded in my mind during the writing process, the book became more and more detailed and inexorably grew in size. Eventually, it took twice more time than I planned to finish writing, while the book itself turned out to be twice thicker than I expected, and some worthy materials have been left out for the next editions to avoid "scope creep". To my own astonishment, the job of individual enterprise architects proved to be even more difficult to explain adequately than the mechanism of enterprise architecture practices. Now, I rightfully regard this book as an equal companion, rather than a mere addition, to my first book.

The book is admittedly less straightforward than some people may wish, but this is arguably an inevitable consequence of the fact that the occupation of enterprise architects is itself far from straightforward. Due to its variability and versatility, their work is not amenable to simple descriptions and any possible "abridged versions" are likely to be incomplete in some important aspects or miss certain essential points. This book also does not propose any universal, step-by-step prescriptions that can be followed by aspiring practitioners to succeed. Architects do many different things in many different ways in many different circumstances, depending on the context in which they find themselves. Their actions are very organization-, position- and even task-specific, they cannot be reduced to formulaic approaches. Any opposite claims are likely to be deceptive and only create dangerous illusions. So, please prepare to appreciate complexity and enjoy the reading!

Materials for This Book

The foundation for this book is laid by the ongoing research in enterprise architecture of Australian origin conducted by the author systematically in different forms since 2013. As part of this research effort, to date, nearly 3000 publications on enterprise architecture and information systems planning have been studied and more than 200 interviews with practicing architects from dozens of organizations have been taken and analyzed. However, of the whole extensive material base accumulated over the years, the following sources were particularly relevant to this book:

- Rereading of about 170 publications related specifically to enterprise architects and about 50 publications related to their education, including practitioner books, academic articles, conference papers, industry reports and web pages
- A series of 32 broad interviews with architects of various titles from different Australian organizations that covered their day-to-day activities, communication patterns, utilized artifacts and other aspects of their occupation
- A series of 30 in-depth interviews with architects of various titles from different Australian companies that addressed specifically their engagement, collaboration and interactions with business managers at different levels
- A number of formal and informal conversations with experienced architects where the main conceptual models resulting from the analysis were discussed, validated and confirmed

All in all, this book stands upon a sound empirical grounding that embraces architects of manifold denominations from organizations of disparate sizes representing diverse industry sectors, though the bulk of the underlying dataset has Australian provenance. The content of the book is substantiated, for the most part, by the primary data collected directly by the author and, where appropriate, by the secondary data provided by the available literature on the subject.

Acknowledgments

As a firm advocate of the research approach that can be succinctly called "from practitioners to practitioners", the center of my attention is practitioners as both privileged carriers of original knowledge and ultimate consumers of research findings. Hence, for the very possibility of creating this book, I am indebted, above all, to numerous practicing architects who generously agreed to be interviewed and share their knowledge, experiences and best practices with me, and eventually with the broader architecture community. All these people fairly deserve to be acknowledged here for their valuable contribution to my research initiatives, especially the participants of the interviews immediately connected to the book's subject. However, because generally accepted research ethics guarantees total anonymity to all participators, I can only name those architects who explicitly permitted me to thank them in person for their input. These architects are Alex Burnett, Ali Motahari, Anthony Popple, Chong Ng, Chris Kempster, Craig Childs, Craig Watson, Cristian Southall, David Whyte, Frank Fu, Gary Franks, Ghouse Mohammed, Jeff Warke, Jon Stubing, Karen Modena, Luke Toop, Malcolm Cook, Marc Campbell, Mark Ames, Maurice Loillet, Minnie Tabilog, Neil Spragg, Nick Browne, Nick Sheridan, Nilesh Kevat, Paul Monks, Paul Sagor, Peter King, Pramod Fanda, Robert Cheung, Russell Bailey, Sam Lees, Sam Zamani, Sean Smith, Stefan Ziemer, Stewart Pitt, Suren Gunasekera, Sylvia Githinji, Vivek Pande and Wayne Hepenstall. It is to them and other anonymous participants of my studies that I am the most grateful!

Svyatoslav Kotusev (kotusev@kotusev.com)
Melbourne, Australia
June 2024

Preface

This preface opens the book, puts it within the broader context of literature, frames its informational contents and provides a basic introduction to its substance. In particular, this preface starts with explaining the subject of this book and its relationship to the book *The Practice of Enterprise Architecture*. Then, this preface describes the distinctive features of this book and its intended audience. Lastly, this preface presents the structure of this book and clarifies some important terminological issues.

The Subject of This Book

The main subject of this book are people who are now generally known in the industry as "enterprise architects". However, this term itself is rather ill-defined, open to diverse interpretations and surrounded by different expectations as to what exactly these people ought to do. Without attempting to propose a strict, clear-cut definition of the term "enterprise architects" acceptable to everyone, it would be fair to say that the core subject of this book is specialized professionals responsible for planning IT in the best interests of business, thereby promoting digital transformation in organizations. Put it simply, this book is about modern information systems planners, irrespective of their preferred title. In particular, the book intends to provide a comprehensive coverage of their personality and occupation in all relevant aspects, including their resources, instruments and activities, as well as their complex interplay in operation.

At the same time, business planning, digital transformation, enabling technologies and technical best practices for designing information systems are not the subject of this book. Even though the book touches on all these topics to the extent that is necessary for understanding the job of enterprise architects, its real subject stays somewhat apart from these topics and concentrates specifically on dedicated experts able to bring all these topics together. From this standpoint, the subject of this book can be formulated as specialists capable of merging business planning with the design of information systems using the most suitable technologies and best practices, causing digital transformation.

It is also important to realize that this book describes architects concerned with planning "ordinary" information systems deployed in organizations to support their business capabilities, e.g. custom websites, mobile apps, backend platforms, configurable vendor products and cloud-based solutions. Its descriptions do not apply to more narrow-focused architects of highly specific IT systems with unique demands and planning approaches, such as aviation systems, medical devices, equipment controllers, search engines, social networks, or simply super complex, multimillion-lines-of-code software systems that represent major engineering challenges on their own[1].

xxiii

This Book and "The Practice of Enterprise Architecture"

This book is complementary to the sibling book *The Practice of Enterprise Architecture: A Modern Approach to Business and IT Alignment*[2]. Fundamentally, both books address the same broader subject called enterprise architecture (EA). However, these books adopt disparate "optics" and offer quite different perspectives on this subject. Whereas *The Practice of Enterprise Architecture* presents enterprise architecture top-down from an organizational point of view, this book presents it bottom-up from the viewpoint of individual architects. While the former centers mainly around organizational decision-making processes and various artifacts as their essential tools, the latter centers around separate transformation initiatives served by enterprise architects along their lifecycle. Together, they provide a rich and deep, "binocular" outlook on enterprise architecture.

Conceptually, the relationship between *The Practice of Enterprise Architecture* and this book is analogous to the relationship between macroeconomics and microeconomics respectively. Both macroeconomics and microeconomics clearly relate to economics, but approach the subject from different angles. Namely, macroeconomics analyzes the behavior of a national economy as a whole, while microeconomics — the behavior of separate economic actors. However, because a national economy consists of numerous economic actors and its behavior is determined by the individual behavior of all these actors, macroeconomics and microeconomics are tightly connected. Exactly the same with enterprise architecture: an organizational practice of enterprise architecture is composed of the activities of multiple enterprise architects performing their jobs, making the "macro" and "micro" views of the subject inextricably bound. Like macroeconomics and microeconomics describe different but linked aspects of economics, *The Practice of Enterprise Architecture* and this book describe different but linked aspects of enterprise architecture.

Even though the two books are coupled and supplementary to each other, they are independent in the sense that either book can be read end-to-end separately from the other. In other words, the books can be studied in any sequence without incurring the loss of meaning. To achieve self-sufficiency, their contents partly overlap, but only to the extent necessary to tell uninterrupted, coherent stories about their primary subjects and enable a "seamless" reading experience. Specifically, to present a continuous narrative about enterprise architects, this book includes a concise description of popular EA artifacts, their properties and taxonomy, as well as some other notions thoroughly discussed in *The Practice of Enterprise Architecture*.

Moreover, the two books are fully compatible and consistent in terms of their style, approach and key concepts. For instance, both of them follow the same tradition of evidence-based, descriptive research uniting theory and practice. Although they cover different subjects with many "native", subject-specific concepts, the books also share a set of common concepts with identical meaning that represent logical "integration points" between them, e.g. general types and narrow subtypes of artifacts and architecture governance bodies.

However, for the sake of strict terminological consistency within each book, not all terms are perfectly consistent across the books. For this reason, some concepts are the same for both books, but named differently or described somewhat differently to better fit into the context of the respective narrations. In these cases, the cross-book correspondence between the related terms and concepts is clarified in explanatory comments.

The Features of This Book

Its subject and attitude make this book quite a unique product on the bookshelves. On the one hand, historically, this book represents the first deliberate attempt to provide a comprehensive, research-based discussion of enterprise architects and their trade through both conceptual and practical lenses. On the other hand, this book intends to capture, analyze and describe the actual behavior of architects at work observed in the industry, rather than trying to invent, propose or recommend some new ways of working. By virtue of its distinctive approach, this book has a number of specific features distinguishing it from an "average" book in the area of management and IT.

Based on Original Research and Empirical Evidence

This book is based primarily on a methodical analysis of the empirical evidence gathered by the author from practicing enterprise architects and covering various aspects of their occupation. All the source materials underpinning it are completely original and authentic. This book does not try to "repack" mainstream ideas and does not build upon any existing models, but rather starts from the basics and constructs an entirely fresh view of enterprise architects and their work ensuing directly from the collected data. All the key models, observations and conclusions presented in this book are produced by the author out of first-hand evidence as part of persistent research efforts.

Descriptive and Analytical Attitude

This book is analytical and descriptive in nature. It aims to analyze the role of enterprise architects in its full complexity with all the major variations of this role identified in the industry without attempting to artificially simplify it. This book also provides a purely descriptive account of architects and their job without making any normative prescriptions. In particular, this book avoids any speculations as to what architects should do, how they should behave or what their role in organizations must be, but only depicts realistically how they actually perform in practice. For this reason, it propagates no superficial step-wise instructions or naive "how-to" recipes for guiding their activities, but calls for a deeper understanding of the overall meaning, general approach and contextual character of their work.

Dispassionate and Factual View

This book intends to clearly illuminate the profession of enterprise architects in its current form from a factual perspective, without trying to entertain, motivate or envision the future. It can hardly be regarded as a source of inspirational thoughts, innovative ideas or unachievable ideals for practitioners to be striven for. Instead, the sole objective of this book is to accurately inform its readers about the present industry situation with enterprise architects based on the best available evidence in a dispassionate, value-neutral fashion. This book takes the existing situation for granted and does not judge it as good or bad, satisfactory or unsatisfactory, nor does it prophesy its further development or propose a "desirable" way forward.

Both Practical and Conceptual Perspective

This book is both theoretical and practical simultaneously. On the one hand, it includes many high-level conceptual models reflecting different aspects of enterprise architects and their job in an abstract manner. On the other hand, in given contexts, these models are immediately translatable into the down-to-earth language of practice, e.g. concrete actors, tasks, documents and decisions. In line with this approach, this book also avoids any theoretical discussions having no tangible practical manifestations as well as any practical illustrations having no broader theoretical generalizations. Therefore, this book maintains a strong linkage between theory and practice, covers both the "big picture" and its smaller details and can be considered generic and specific at the same time.

Systematic and Comprehensive Approach

This book adopts a holistic perspective and provides a systematic and comprehensive treatment of enterprise architects. It attempts to embrace all significant aspects of their environment, occupation and personality, and to explain connections between these aspects. On the one hand, this book considers architects as unique organizational actors with their own specific resources, instruments and activities and describes how those are interrelated to enable their productive performance. On the other hand, it intends to present an exhaustive, all-encompassing description of architects covering all important facets of their profession. Essentially, this book endeavors to integrate all the available information about enterprise architects into a single logical "story".

Introduces Novel Conceptualizations

This book introduces brand new theoretical conceptualizations of enterprise architects and their work, which resulted squarely from the analysis of first-hand empirical evidence. Due to the lack of solid theoretical models relevant to architects, especially trustworthy and empirically validated ones, there is simply no foundation upon which a serious discussion of their job can be based. For this reason, this book lays the very foundation for discussing architects from scratch, grounded directly in the data collected "from the fields". This foundation consists of multiple novel conceptual models, patterns and frameworks portraying architects from different viewpoints and provides the necessary theoretical apparatus for analyzing their conduct.

Addresses the Organizational, Not Technical Side

This book is non-technical in character and highlights the organizational side of the occupation of enterprise architects. It does *not* discuss specific technologies, technical best practices, principles of robust system design or approaches to structuring complex IT landscapes; these topics are widely discussed in many other sources[3]. Instead, this book accentuates specifically the place of enterprise architects in the organizational context, their niche in the organizational ecosystem and their role in organizational decision-making processes. Accordingly, it cannot teach aspiring architects, for example, how to select the most suitable technologies, make proper technical choices or build large-scale IT systems, but rather how to behave in organizations to facilitate their digital transformation.

Focuses on Doing Work, Not Getting Certified

This book is not a certification guide, unrelated to any certification programs and describes how enterprise architects actually do their daily work, regardless of their previous education, diplomas or titles. It does not explain how to take tests, pass exams, fulfill certification requirements, obtain "black belts" or stockpile professional credentials; these issues are addressed in some other sources[4]. Instead, this book concentrates exclusively on the practical matters composing the occupation of architects in organizations, their real tasks, challenges and ways of overcoming them. In short, it cannot assist the readers in getting certified, but it can assist them in getting the job done and turning into accomplished enterprise architects.

Placed in the Context of the Existing Literature

This book is placed in the context of the available literature on enterprise architects and, where appropriate, amply refers to topical publications. In particular, references to other sources with explanatory comments are generally included in four different cases. First, references to other publications are provided when some information in the book is taken verbatim from these original publications. Second, references are provided when similar ideas have already been expressed earlier by other authors. Third, references to other publications are provided when certain notable ideas in these publications patently contradict the established empirical facts. And lastly, references are provided to connect the ideas formulated in the book with broader research streams and position them in the overarching context of organizational theory. The text of this book contains numerous references to other sources, which explain the relationship between the ideas expressed in the book and the existing body of knowledge.

The Intended Audience of This Book

This book is aimed at a wide readership, including practitioners, academics, students and all other people interested in concerted planning of business and IT as part of digital transformation efforts in organizations. It does not require any previous theoretical knowledge or practical experience as enterprise architects, though some general understanding of business and IT is highly desirable.

First, this book can be helpful to novice and seasoned enterprise architects, as well as to IT managers and other senior specialists involved in systems planning. It is written in plain language appealing to pragmatic practitioners and addresses mostly the questions of immediate relevance to practice. To newbie architects, this book offers reasonable actionable suggestions to start doing the work and paves the path to succeeding in the profession. To veteran architects, this book provides a comprehensive kit of reference models and "tools for thinking" that allow them to better understand various aspects of their own job.

Second, this book can be beneficial for academics and researchers of the phenomenon of enterprise architects. It consolidates the available theoretical knowledge and provides an array of reliable, evidence-based conceptual models explaining the personality and occupation of architects that can be "borrowed" as the foundation for further studies. Moreover, it contains a rich bibliography and, whenever it is appropriate, explains the relationship between the presented ideas and earlier publications, putting the narrative in the context of the extant literature.

Third, this book can be valuable to students interested in the role of enterprise architects and their teachers. It is written in a sequential manner, does not require any prior knowledge of the subject and can provide a sound introduction to the profession of architects for beginners. It can also be used by lecturers for developing curricula and teaching courses about enterprise architects to undergraduate and postgraduate students in universities.

The Teaching Pack for This Book

This book goes with a complementary teaching pack on enterprise architecture intended for universities and other parties carrying out educational activities. The teaching pack comprises a collection of resources that can be instrumental in organizing full-fledged academic programs for undergraduate and postgraduate students, as well as short-term courses and trainings for practitioners. The teaching pack is based on the contents of this book and *The Practice of Enterprise Architecture*, closely linked to their structure and, in some cases, provides explicit references to relevant book chapters and sections. Specifically, it includes a set of lectures as MS PowerPoint presentations corresponding to book chapters, tests with single and multiple choice questions for lectures and some other helpful teaching materials.

The teaching pack is freely available to educators on request to the author at kotusev@kotusev.com. The materials of the teaching pack can be either used "as-is" or tailored for particular needs and audiences, though always with the explicit acknowledgment of original authorship and references to the source in any convenient form. For example, the teaching pack can be reorganized for university courses of varying lengths (e.g. one or two semesters), adapted to the demands of practitioners with different backgrounds and levels of knowledge or even translated into other languages. However, the teaching pack must not be distributed to third parties without notifying the author.

The Structure of This Book

This book consists of nineteen consecutive chapters organized into three separate parts. Part I (Introduction to Enterprise Architects) provides a general introduction to enterprise architects and the overall context in which they operate. In particular, Chapter 1 (Digital Transformation) introduces the very notion of digital transformation, different types of transformation drivers that stimulate the respective efforts and the most typical technical and organizational challenges associated with them. Chapter 2 (Digital Transformation Initiatives) describes digital transformation initiatives in organizations, their initial origination, implementation lifecycle and stakeholder groups, their typology, hierarchy and nuances of execution at different levels. Chapter 3 (Architectural Planning) discusses architectural planning with its technical and organizational sides, different domains relevant to architectural planning and the planning of hierarchical digitalization initiatives. Chapter 4 (Welcome, Enterprise Architects) introduces enterprise architects as the agents of digital transformation, explains the specifics of their role in organizations, describes their work in change initiatives and discusses the two hats that they wear. Lastly, Chapter 5 (Enterprise Architects in Context) explains the place of enterprise architects in the organizational structure, ecosystem and environment, their costs, benefits and value propositions for organizations, as well as who they are definitely not.

Part II (Enterprise Architects in Depth) provides a very detailed coverage of enterprise architects as specialized professionals from various angles. In particular, Chapter 6 (Resources of Enterprise Architects) covers resources possessed by enterprise architects and describes in detail all the major classes of their resources: knowledge, skills and experience. Chapters 7, 8 and 9 together cover instruments employed by enterprise architects. Initially, Chapter 7 (Instruments of Enterprise Architects) introduces different categories of instruments of enterprise architects including EA artifacts, the CSVLOD taxonomy for organizing them and some other instruments. Then, Chapter 8 (The Catalog of Enterprise Architecture Artifacts) presents a comprehensive catalog of EA artifacts corresponding to the six general types defined by the CSVLOD taxonomy: Considerations, Standards, Visions, Landscapes, Outlines and Designs. Finally,

Chapter 9 (Using Enterprise Architecture Artifacts) describes in great detail the use of EA artifacts by architects for documenting the existing situation and capturing architectural solutions, as well as the architectural context formed by these artifacts. Chapters 10, 11 and 12 together cover activities performed by enterprise architects. First, Chapter 10 (Basic Activities of Enterprise Architects) introduces different types of activities of enterprise architects with their contexts and thoroughly describes their three basic activities: analyzing the external environment, studying the internal environment and providing advisory services. Next, Chapter 11 (Leading the Development of Plans) continues the discussion of the activities of enterprise architects and describes in great detail their central activity: leading the development of plans. Lastly, Chapter 12 (Ensuring Adherence to Plans) finishes the discussion of the activities of enterprise architects and describes in great detail their closing activity: ensuring adherence to plans. Chapter 13 (The Work of Enterprise Architects) provides an integral view of the work of enterprise architects in different contexts in terms of their activities, describes their working schedule and explains their advocacy of technical interests. In conclusion, Chapter 14 (The Profession of Enterprise Architects) discusses the profession of enterprise architects with its features, the historical evolution of their profession over decades and different understandings of architects prevalent in the industry.

Part III (Enterprise Architects in Organizations) covers various aspects of enterprise architects related to their work in organizations. In particular, Chapter 15 (The Archetype of Enterprise Architects) describes Enterprise Architects as a major archetype of architects driving high-level digitalization efforts with the specifics of their resources, instruments, activities and work in different contexts. Chapter 16 (The Archetype of Solution Architects) describes Solution Architects as another major archetype of architects serving separate digitalization projects with the specifics of their resources, instruments, activities and work in different contexts. Chapter 17 (Architecture Positions in Organizations) discusses concrete positions in architecture functions through the lens of the archetypes of Enterprise Architects and Solution Architects with their dependence on the size and structure of organizations. Chapter 18 (Challenges of Enterprise Architects) analyzes the problem of achieving effective engagement between enterprise architects and business leaders with the ensuing individual and organizational challenges faced by architects. Finally, Chapter 19 (Other Aspects of Enterprise Architects) discusses the career paths of enterprise architects with the associated difficulties, the role of modeling languages, software tools, EA frameworks and professional certifications in their job, as well as the central conundrums of architects.

A Note on the Used Terminology

The industry discourse around enterprise architects traditionally suffers from vague and inconsistent terminology, where the same concepts are named differently by different authors and the same terms refer to different things in different organizations. In this terminological mess, among other discrepancies, the central controversy surrounds the very term "enterprise architects", which has multiple divergent interpretations in the literature along at least two different lines[5]. The first line of dispute concerns the *role* of enterprise architects and the exact scope of their responsibilities, e.g. whether they participate in the implementation of IT solutions and communicate with project teams. The second line of dispute concerns the *variety* of architects and their relation to enterprise architects, e.g. whether architects focusing on separate business units and organization-wide technology domains are really enterprise architects. Any serious discussion of enterprise architects and their work requires, first of all, reaching absolute clarity on these controversial but crucial questions.

In this book, these two questions about the role and variety of enterprise architects are clearly resolved in the following way: basically, as a profession, enterprise architects are understood in the broadest reasonably possible sense, embracing all duties and variations typical for architects, and then more concrete archetypes and positions for architects are presented as narrow *specializations* within the overarching profession. In other words, enterprise architects represent a *collective image* of all kinds of architects, while different kinds of architects (e.g. domain-specific enterprise and solution architects) are introduced separately as their prominent subtypes. The book's narrative, thus, descends from the generic view of all architects (Parts I and II) to more nuanced views of particular specializations of architects (Chapters 15, 16 and 17 in Part III), as outlined previously in the book structure.

Besides the foundational resolutions regarding the term "enterprise architects" and related notions explained above, smaller terminological issues are addressed in this book by explicitly defining all the key terms (**bolded** when first introduced) and consistently sticking to them throughout the text. Furthermore, for better coherence, the titles of the most pivotal concepts permeating the narration are capitalized. These concepts include different hats of enterprise architects (e.g. Technology Experts and Change Agents), major archetypes of architects (e.g. Enterprise Architects and Solution Architects) as well as general types and narrow subtypes of EA artifacts (e.g. Standards and Target States).

Another important terminological caveat relates specifically to the prevalence of the term "digital transformation" on the pages of this book. On the one hand, this term sounds overly pretentious and grandiose. As it is fairly noticed by many observers, not every change is a transformation[6]. On the other hand, this term is also not particularly meaningful and arguably redundant. In most contexts, it seems virtually synonymous with any productive use of IT[7]. And yet, despite these problems, presently this buzzword has become an integral part of the widely accepted mainstream jargon that can hardly be eschewed. For this single reason, this book unenthusiastically adopts the term "digital transformation", though uses it largely interchangeably with "IT-supported change". In short, numerous references to digital transformation represent mostly a tribute to the industry hype and do not bear much special meaning.

Staying Updated with Research Products

The collection of research products accompanying this book is periodically updated with new additions, e.g. books, articles, posters, teaching materials, their new versions or editions. To stay informed of the author's latest deliverables, the readers are welcome to:

- Visit the author's official website: https://kotusev.com
- Connect with the author on LinkedIn: https://www.linkedin.com/in/kotusev
- Follow the author on Twitter (now X): https://twitter.com/kotusev

PART I: Introduction to Enterprise Architects

Part I of this book provides a general introduction to enterprise architects and the overall context in which they operate. This part discusses different aspects of digital transformation in organizations, the role, personality and activities of enterprise architects as its leading agents, the meaning of architectural planning as the central duty that they perform and their place in the organizational environment.

Part I consists of five consecutive chapters. Chapter 1 introduces the very notion of digital transformation, different types of transformation drivers that stimulate the respective efforts and the most typical technical and organizational challenges associated with them. Chapter 2 describes digital transformation initiatives in organizations, their initial origination, implementation lifecycle and stakeholder groups, their typology, hierarchy and nuances of execution at different levels. Chapter 3 discusses architectural planning with its technical and organizational sides, different domains relevant to architectural planning and the planning of hierarchical digitalization initiatives. Chapter 4 introduces enterprise architects as the agents of digital transformation, explains the specifics of their role in organizations, describes their work in change initiatives and discusses the two hats that they wear. Lastly, Chapter 5 explains the place of enterprise architects in the organizational structure, ecosystem and environment, their costs, benefits and value propositions for organizations, as well as who they are definitely not.

Chapter 1: Digital Transformation

This chapter provides the necessary background for this book by introducing digital transformation and other basic notions. In particular, this chapter begins with discussing the historical evolution of IT, its ever-growing influence on the business of organizations and the modern phenomenon of digital transformation. Then, this chapter describes different drivers of digital transformation in organizations, explains the role of business strategy in digitalization efforts and introduces the concept of motivational context. Finally, this chapter analyzes various technical and organizational challenges of digital transformation faced by organizations and their numerous practical implications.

Development and Progress of Information Technology

Since its inception in the 1940s, electronic **information technology (IT)**, or information and communication technology (ICT), has been evolving very rapidly and its historical progress seems truly impressive. Virtually every year IT delivers to the market some new high-potential innovations capable of improving or even reshaping the business of many companies[1]. Unsurprisingly, during the recent decades, IT has become one of the primary drivers of change in organizations, if not the single most important driver.

Over the course of its development, IT went through a series of successive epochs with certain distinctive attributes and features. On the one hand, each epoch is characterized by specific technologies, buzzwords and trendsetters prominent during the respective time periods. On the other hand, each epoch is also characterized by its own dominant *philosophy* defining the overall perceived role and place of IT in business. Although the division of the entire IT chronicle into different periods and milestones can be subject to interpretation, key epochs in its evolution are arguably evident and indisputable.

Initially, as early business computers were mere calculating machines with limited capacity, IT engendered a primitive **epoch of process automation**. In this epoch, electronic computers were generally regarded only as a means of automating routine clerical tasks in offices and repetitive production processes in factories. Replacing human labor with computers allowed organizations to cut their operating costs and increase their throughput, but without affecting fundamentally their approaches to doing business[2]. The process automation epoch peaked around the 1960s and is associated with cumbersome mainframes, magnetic tapes and teleprinters.

Then, empowered by dramatic enhancements in computing, storage and networking capabilities, the world of IT entered a qualitatively new **epoch of strategic systems**. In this epoch, information systems became widely respected as instruments of strategic differentiation and sources of sustainable competitive advantage. Building complex IT systems allowed organizations to reform their business models, offer innovative services and communicate in novel ways with their customers, suppliers and partners[3]. The strategic systems epoch reached its climax during the 1980s and is associated with personal computers, relational databases and interorganizational networks.

Next, precipitated by the global expansion of the Internet, IT stepped into a more advanced **epoch of electronic business**. In this epoch, information systems turned into a prerequisite for conducting most business activities and an enabler of completely new profit-making models. Constructing IT systems connected to the Internet allowed organizations to serve their customers remotely, partly or fully migrate their businesses online and engage in electronic commerce, or e-commerce[4]. The electronic business epoch reached its pinnacle near the turn of the century and is associated with websites, hosting platforms and Internet service providers.

Finally, boosted by further developments at all frontiers of technology, relatively recently IT arrived at the present **epoch of digital transformation**. In this epoch, information systems became integral to any business endeavors and penetrated almost all aspects of personal and social life. Using diverse but interlinked IT systems allowed organizations to reinvent themselves and profoundly reconsider the meaning of their business and the way it is done[5]. The digital transformation epoch is currently at its zenith and associated with various mobile devices, big data analytics and ubiquitous Internet connectivity.

To summarize, historically IT progressed gradually through different epochs with a steadily increasing impact on organizations, from purely operational to more strategic and even disruptive, fueled by the continuous emergence of new, more powerful technologies. The approximate timeline of major epochs and milestones in the evolution of IT and its business influence with the underlying technological innovations is shown in Figure 1.1.

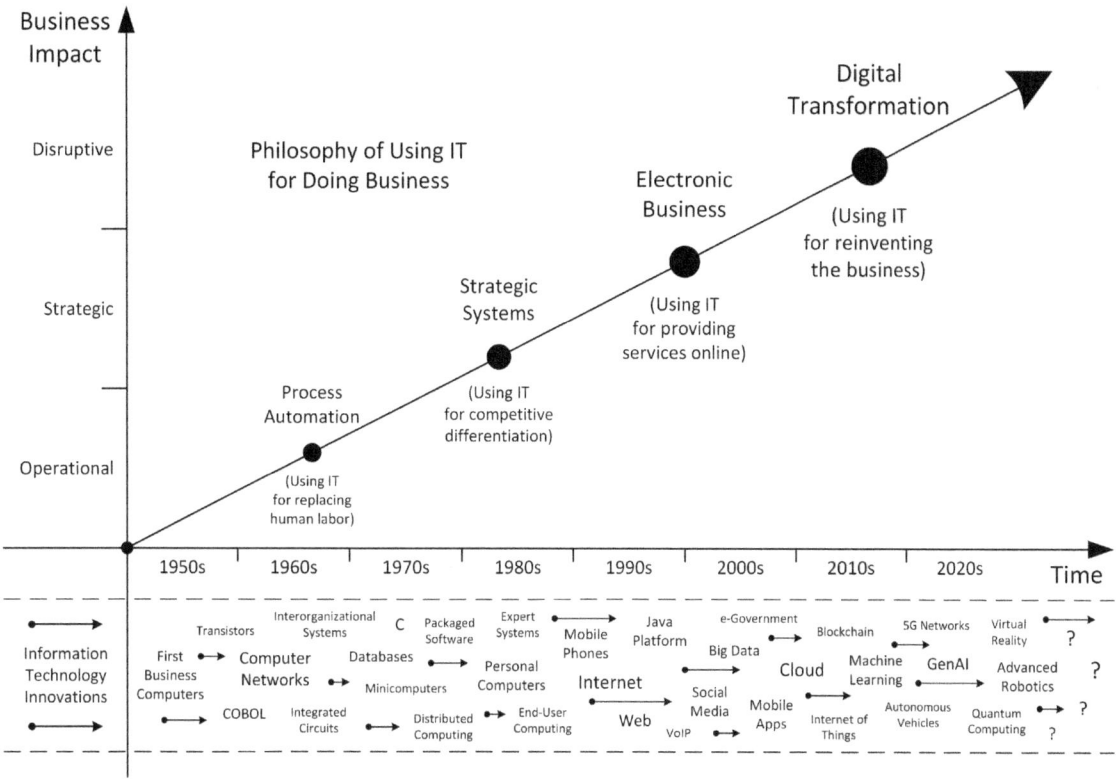

Figure 1.1. Major epochs and milestones in the development and business impact of IT

Besides its broad meaning as a new era and philosophy in the history of IT, digital transformation has a pretty concrete practical meaning when applied to organizations and their business activities.

Digital Transformation in Organizations

Being admittedly a rather vague term, **digital transformation**, or simply digitalization, in the organizational context generally involves introducing some or the other advanced information systems and technologies to improve or enable the business[6]. Although this term itself is relatively new, the very phenomenon of digitalization is quite old as IT has been increasingly transforming organizations and the way they operate for decades[7]. Hence, digital transformation actually began much earlier than the term was coined — it has been taking place and gradually intensifying since the birth of IT.

In a competitive business environment, digital transformation represents a constant objective and never-ending pursuit for organizations[8]. Digitalization often, but not necessarily, implies innovating with IT in one of the following ways:

- Further optimizing internal business processes and operations, reducing their costs, risks and variability, increasing their speed, reliability and efficiency by means of leveraging the recent fruits of progress in IT

- Developing new business products, services or market offerings with a digital component that were made possible by the latest developments of technology or their widespread adoption in society
- Inventing trailblazing business models that exploit the capabilities of breakthrough advancements in IT to provide novel ways of serving customers, adding value and generating revenue

At its disposal, digital transformation has an immensely rich and diversified arsenal of technologies, products and tools spawned by the decades of active IT evolution (see Figure 1.1). The contents of this arsenal range from tried and proven technologies that stood the test of time (e.g. the TCP protocol and relational databases) to bleeding-edge ones with poorly understood perils and consequences (e.g. generative artificial intelligence and quantum computing). This arsenal also includes completed ready-to-use solutions (e.g. packaged and cloud-based software products) as well as general-purpose instruments that can be used to create any solutions (e.g. programming languages and frameworks). The former category, in turn, includes generic solutions applicable to most industries, such as enterprise resource planning (ERP) and customer relationship management (CRM) platforms, as well as industry-specific solutions with narrow applicability, such as hospital information systems (HIS) and learning management systems (LMS).

Progressing with digital transformation in organizations requires exerting considerable efforts. **Digital transformation efforts**, or digitalization efforts, are deliberate organizational activities intended to carry out digital transformation. These activities represent the coordinated work of multiple people to accomplish the desired changes in the organization by deploying and embracing the necessary IT solutions, where an **IT solution** can be defined simply as an information system, or a set of related systems, addressing a particular business need[9]. In practice, digital transformation efforts are typically initiated in response to specific drivers.

Drivers of Digital Transformation

Digitalization efforts in organizations have numerous driving forces that set them in motion. Drivers of digital transformation, or simply **transformation drivers**, are certain conditions, factors or circumstances that motivate organizations to change their business with IT. Transformation drivers answer the question of *why* digitalization is desired by the organization to improve its position in the competitive environment. These drivers can stem from a variety of objective and subjective sources, be real or imaginary. For example, they can be dictated by current business predicaments, suggested by global industry-wide trends or inspired by the revelations of individual visionaries, gurus and thought leaders, possibly fueled by the capabilities of new technologies.

All drivers of digital transformation in organizations are strongly associated with specific people standing behind them whose vested interests they represent. Proponents of transformation drivers, or simply **driver proponents**, are organizational actors who identify, own and advocate the respective drivers. Driver proponents can come from any business units, functional areas and administrative levels of the company. As organizations are normally directed by business leaders, who better understand their operations, markets and clientele, most transformation drivers are promoted from the business side. However, some drivers can also arise from the IT side and have IT leaders as their sole proponents.

Because the representatives of different parts of the organization have unique viewpoints and inconsistent interests, different managers tend to see different transformation drivers and prioritize them differently. As a result, different drivers are often backed by different groups of proponents understanding their importance and pushing them to the fore.

Different Types of Transformation Drivers

Drivers of digital transformation can be very diverse from the standpoint of their origin, attitude and nature. Although they can be classified in numerous ways[10], for the purposes of further discussion, all transformation drivers can be loosely grouped into six general types: deliberate intentions, emergent opportunities, operational problems, ad hoc demands, permanent imperatives and technical concerns[11].

First, **deliberate intentions** represent various business-related transformation drivers resulting from conscious attempts to plan future business development in advance. This category of drivers comprises all clearly formulated aims, aspirations, courses of action and other scenarios produced by means of rational upfront planning within the organization. Examples of transformation drivers that reflect deliberate intentions include the plans to double the turnover in a specific product line, increase the presence in a particular market segment and extend the scope of business activities to new geographic regions.

Second, **emergent opportunities** represent various transformation drivers of a business nature associated with some unexpected possibilities for growing the business opening in the environment that can be seized by the organization[12]. This category embraces all newly uncovered market niches, demands for new offerings and other insights as to how the business can be expanded inspired by unfolding external circumstances. Examples of transformation drivers that can be viewed as emergent opportunities include the idea to make use of the latest release of ChatGPT to create a pioneering product, the need for radically novel services attributed to abrupt pandemic-related lifestyle changes and the potential to enter new markets suddenly made vacant by recent geopolitical upheavals.

Third, **operational problems** represent various business-side transformation drivers that ensue from some current unsatisfactory conditions inside the organization. This category encircles all known issues, existing bottlenecks and pain points in business operations that deserve attention and need to be addressed. Examples of transformation drivers that belong to operational problems include systematic delays in order delivery, frequent outages in production and manual error-prone handling of documentation in supply chains.

Fourth, **ad hoc demands** represent various transformation drivers of business origin arising from some unanticipated changes in the external environment that require immediate reaction. This category of drivers covers all urgent customer needs, threatening competitor moves and tightening regulatory amendments. Examples of transformation drivers related to ad hoc demands include insistent customer requests for new product functionality, the launch of innovative services by industry rivals and updates in legislation imposing new obligations on all market players.

Fifth, **permanent imperatives** represent various business-side transformation drivers inherent to the adopted business model or the nature of competition in the industry that are persistent and, unlike other drivers, do not change over time. This category encompasses all constant objectives, fundamental capabilities and essential operations without pursuing or perfecting which organizations cannot expect to survive in the market. Examples of transformation drivers that can be classified as permanent imperatives include cutting the costs of operations in retail, increasing passenger safety in transportation and automating production processes in manufacturing.

Lastly, **technical concerns** represent all transformation drivers from the IT side, regardless of their origin and character. This category comprises all sorts of technology strategies, optimization opportunities and necessary upgrades dictated by purely technical considerations, rather than business needs. Examples of transformation drivers belonging to technical concerns include migrating applications to the cloud platform, streamlining the IT landscape structure and introducing critical security enhancements.

The six types of transformation drivers discussed above provide comprehensive coverage of conditions that stimulate digitalization in organizations. To better understand the differences and similarities between them, these drivers can be classified along a number of dimensions clarifying their properties. First, of the six transformation drivers, only technical concerns represent IT-specific drivers, while all the other five are business-side drivers. Second, of the five business-side transformation drivers, only permanent imperatives represent *constant* drivers, whereas the remaining four are *variable* drivers. Finally, the four variable business-side transformation drivers can be further organized based on their origin and attitude. Specifically, deliberate intentions and operational problems originate primarily from the *internal* situation in the organization, when emergent opportunities and ad hoc demands — from the *external* environment. Also, deliberate intentions and emergent opportunities arise from *proactive* thinking about what could be done, but operational problems and ad hoc demands — from *reactive* tracking of what needs to be done. These dimensions can be used to construct a logical taxonomy for transformation drivers explaining many of their features. The resulting taxonomy of drivers of digital transformation in organizations is presented in Figure 1.2.

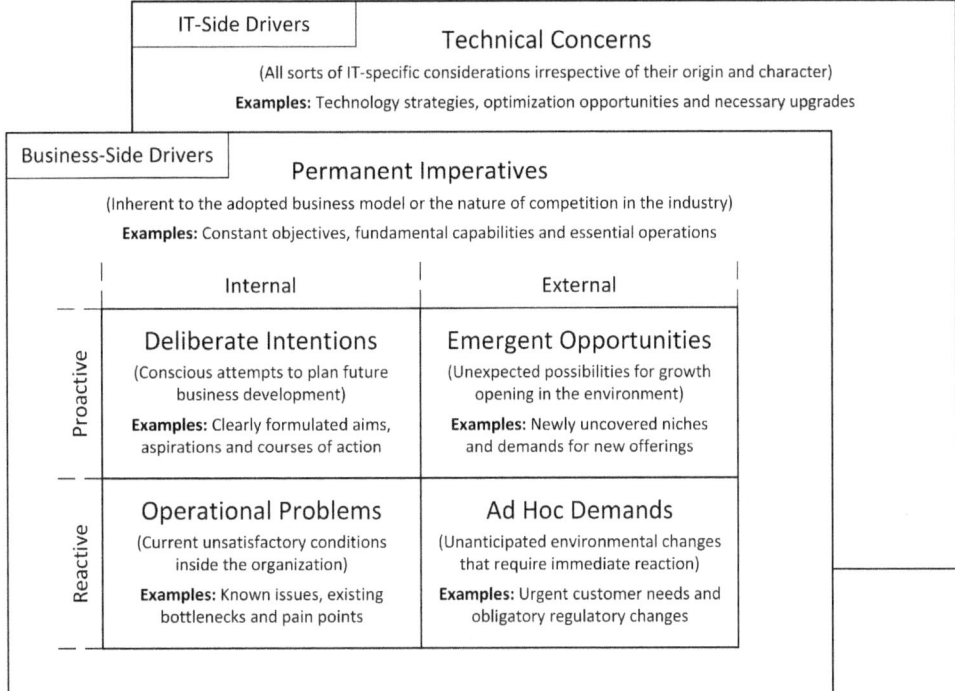

Figure 1.2. Different types of drivers of digital transformation

Even though the classification of transformation drivers summarized in Figure 1.2 is imperfect and somewhat arbitrary, it helps organize multifarious drivers of digitalization in a meaningful manner and make sense of them. Interestingly, most of these drivers are practically unrelated to business strategy, which is often regarded as the prime cause of any organizational transformations.

Business Strategy as a Transformation Driver

A corporate **business strategy**, at least in a narrow sense, can be understood as an official written statement about what the organization wants to accomplish in the future and what the organization intends to undertake to achieve that. Strategy often includes a unifying mission, a long-term vision, inspiring values, general goals, specific objectives and key performance indicators (KPIs). Business strategy is owned by C-level executives and endorsed by the board of directors. It is typically considered as a supreme guiding document that sets the global decision-making context and frames all lower-level activities in the whole organization.

Ideally, everything that organizations do, including their digitalization endeavors, should be driven by their business strategies. In practice, however, business strategies rarely provide a clear foundation for taking action, especially in matters of digital transformation. For instance, strategies can be vague, ambiguous and allow different interpretations, e.g. "become number one" or "provide best services". Strategies can be purely aspirational and consist of sheer motivational slogans, e.g. "get closer to the customer" or "leverage synergies". Strategies can comprise various business objectives and indicators offering no actionable hints for IT, e.g.

"increase market share by X%" or "grow revenue to $Y". Strategies can focus on the business aspects that are changing, but neglect some of the more fundamental pillars that remain the same, e.g. emphasize new capabilities instead of core ones. Elements of strategy related to partnerships, mergers and acquisitions can be market-sensitive, deliberately obscure and surrounded by secrecy. Owing to management turnover and political churn, strategies can be unstable, volatile and reverse their direction several times a year. Even worse, in privately held companies, formal business strategies can be simply absent altogether[13].

For all these reasons, top-level business strategy on its own usually represents a rather *weak* driver of digital transformation, even when it meets the widely accepted SMART (specific, measurable, achievable, relevant and time-bound) criteria[14]. Although business strategy is indubitably valuable or even necessary as a general background for digitalization, it tends to be too abstract to offer any specific prescriptions on what to do in terms of actually improving the business with IT. Consequently, except for small, primitive organizations where business strategy can be fairly concrete, it cannot be viewed as a direct transformation driver analogous to the six drivers discussed earlier (see Figure 1.2).

Moreover, of the six types of transformation drivers, only deliberate intentions, as certain future plans developed in the organization upfront, are conceptually similar to business strategy and kindred to it. It is these drivers that result from processes highly resembling strategizing in a classic sense, e.g. analysis of facts, evaluation of alternatives and calculation of risks. For this reason, deliberate intentions are normally formulated by business leaders based on their organizational strategy, or even derived from it, and can be interpreted as its immediate *continuation*. Basically, deliberate intentions embody strategic plans at the next level of detail down below corporate strategy, often local plans of individual business units, converting this strategy into more actionable suggestions as to what needs to be done to implement it.

At the same time, all other drivers of digital transformation are fundamentally unrelated to business strategy and present in organizations irrespective of what their declared strategies are. Namely, emergent opportunities are provided to organizations by the external environment and cannot be foreseen beforehand and planned for as part of strategy. Operational problems exist in organizations objectively and do not depend on their future direction reflected in strategy. Ad hoc demands are constantly incoming from the external environment in a completely random, strategy-detached fashion. Permanent imperatives are strategy-neutral by definition and imposed by the immanent specifics of a particular industry or business model. And finally, technical concerns arise from technology-related considerations having nothing to do with business strategy.

As it turns out, business strategy, as an organization-wide guiding manifest, neither itself represents a direct transformation driver that can be put into action, nor even determines most of the actual drivers that lead to action. Nevertheless, strategy definitely influences digitalization efforts indirectly, by shaping deliberate intentions as lower-level, more local and actionable plans.

Comprehensive Motivational Context

Taken together, all transformation drivers with the groups of their proponents present in the organization form its global **motivational context** within which all digitalization activities take place. This context contains all the existing stimuli for changing the business with IT, or reasons for investing in IT, and all interests in transforming the company. The motivational context frames and propels digital transformation efforts in the organization by "explaining" why these efforts are necessary or beneficial.

Because of all transformation drivers constituting the motivational context only deliberate intentions are derived straight from business strategy, the whole context is influenced but not entirely defined by strategy. In other words, the motivational context is partially connected to business strategy and loosely aligned with its directives. For this reason, it generally facilitates the realization of strategy, though also introduces some other motives irrelevant to its realization but necessary to run the business.

Logically, the motivational context is situated "under" corporate strategy and provides a more granular view of what needs to be improved or fixed in different parts of the organization. In contrast to strategy governed at the chief executive level, for most of the real transformation drivers, their proponents are business leaders located *one or a few levels below* the C-level in the administrative hierarchy, who are more knowledgeable about how the business actually operates in its various aspects. The concept of motivational context, its relationship to business strategy and role in digitalization efforts are depicted schematically in Figure 1.3.

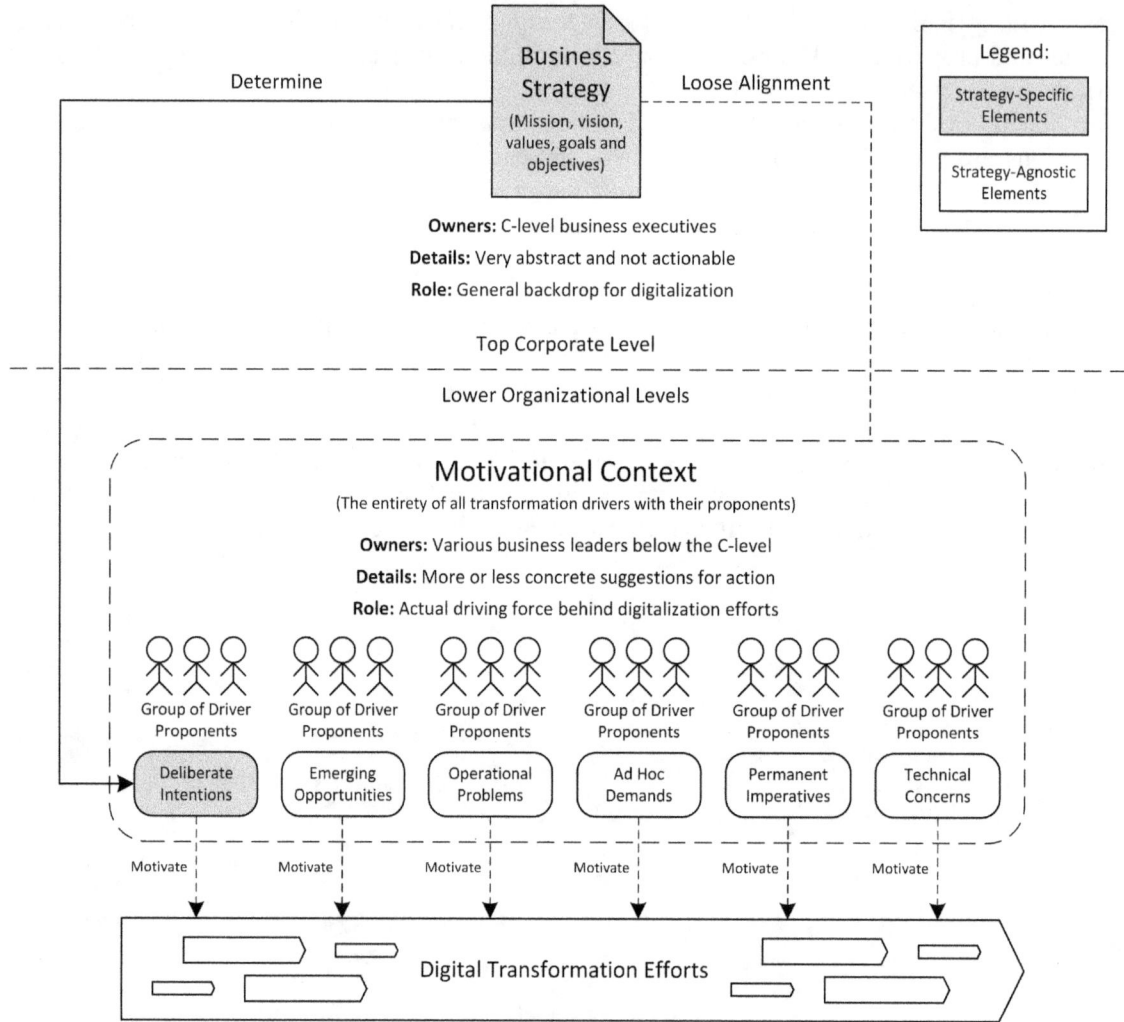

Figure 1.3. Motivational context and its relationship to business strategy

The fact that far from all digital transformation endeavors in organizations ensue from their business strategies has a number of implications for understanding digitalization processes. Most importantly, this fact suggests that digital transformation can thrive even in organizations *without* a meaningful business strategy, being motivated by other, strategy-independent drivers. However, as complex undertakings, digitalization efforts face multiple challenges of both technical and organizational nature making their successful completion a rather non-trivial matter.

Technical Challenges of Digital Transformation

Despite its tremendous value, vast opportunities for innovation and other compelling drivers spurring digitalization (see Figure 1.3), an introduction of new IT systems into the organizational fabric is associated with a number of difficulties of technical origin. **Technical challenges of**

digital transformation aggregate numerous IT-specific choices that need to be made, puzzles to be solved and problems to be tackled during the construction of information systems in organizations. These challenges are relatively narrow in their scope and lie solely within the realm of technology. They relate primarily to the selection of suitable systems, their proper integration into the existing IT environment and ensuring their security (not to mention the traditional issues of detailed system design and development, which are not considered architectural and, therefore, are out of the scope of this book and omitted here).

Virtually Unlimited Choice of Technical Options
Modern information systems and technologies are incredibly diverse and come in all "colors and flavors". Commercial off-the-shelf (COTS) products alone represent dozens of classes of systems providing a broad spectrum of functional capabilities (e.g. accounting, production, logistics and sales management), and each of these classes typically includes multiple solutions from different vendors with their own features[15]. Bespoke applications can be developed to realize almost any imaginable business functionality based on tens of technologies at each layer of the technology stack. Nowadays, information systems can be deployed, partly or wholly, essentially anywhere from smart mobile devices of their end users to dedicated mainframe servers in corporate data centers to third-party cloud hosting services.

In short, the current IT environment offers plenty of technical options for implementing any information system. Every single business idea or need can be addressed with many possible IT solutions with their unique advantages and shortcomings. For multi-component solutions, these options multiply and grow exponentially with the number of their components. Moreover, as the market of technologies and products is continually evolving, these options never stay constant and evolve accordingly with completely new options periodically emerging. The combination of variety and variability of the available options complicates the selection of appropriate solution implementation approaches, which impedes digital transformation in organizations.

Enormous Complexity of Information Technology Landscapes
Information systems in organizations rarely "live" alone in isolation or vacuum, but are usually interwoven into extensive corporate IT landscapes. IT landscapes of large companies often consist of hundreds, if not thousands, of very diverse systems and applications. Some of these systems can be brand new and based on the latest technologies, while others can be decades old and use long-obsolete software and equipment. Some of them can address current business needs, some can run for historical reasons, whereas others could be obtained from previous corporate mergers and acquisitions that occurred in the distant past. These systems and applications also tend to be *interlinked* and exchange information, often in unobvious, hard-to-elicit ways, rendering IT landscapes extremely entangled, inflexible and brittle, especially when no one knows exactly how they work[16].

New information systems in organizations, thus, are not constructed as "greenfield" projects from scratch, but rather built upon the foundation and within the context of the surrounding IT landscape, which has a number of important implications for their structure and design. First, new systems can potentially benefit from reusing the available application capabilities, data sources and hardware infrastructure. Second, these systems should be somehow connected to the existing systems to compose an integrated IT platform. Third, new systems should try to preserve the technical consistency, homogeneity and simplicity of the IT landscape, e.g. avoid introducing new but unnecessary technologies, vendors and approaches. And lastly, these systems bear the risk of causing disruption or breaking the normal functioning of routine business and IT operations due to the landscape modifications that they bring, particularly if they replace some of the older systems. All in all, introducing new information systems into complex IT landscapes is associated with various opportunities, problems and constraints, and poses a difficult technical task that complicates digital transformation efforts, especially in organizations with a long business history and a rich IT legacy.

Critical Cybersecurity Risks, Threats and Vulnerabilities
Ubiquitous connectivity to the Internet exposes organizations to all sorts of security risks and threats incoming from an increasingly hostile cyber environment. Anonymous hackers and cybercriminals are eager to ruin their critical IT infrastructure, thieve and sell the identities, bank card numbers or personal correspondence of their clients, or simply bring corporate websites down with distributed denial-of-service (DDoS) attacks. No company can feel secure from malicious software infecting the computers of its employees, gaining access to their accounts, stealing their confidential data or encrypting their working files for ransom. Unsurprisingly, cybersecurity and privacy have recently turned into a perpetual "headache" for IT executives[17].

The introduction of new information systems, especially externally facing ones, inevitably opens the organization up to new risks, dangers and vulnerabilities. Poorly designed or improperly implemented IT systems can lead, for example, to the leakage of business-critical information out of the firm to adversary parties, to its irreversible destruction or other grave consequences. Potentially, each insecure system can cost companies substantial amounts of money, severe legal troubles as well as their reputation in the market, if not business survival. The criticality of cybersecurity issues represents another technical factor that prevents an easy realization of any digitalization aspirations in organizations.

Organizational Challenges of Digital Transformation

In addition to the purely technical challenges described above, digital transformation is also associated with a plexus of more intricate difficulties of organizational character. **Organizational challenges of digital transformation** reflect various conceptual questions about the desirable synergy between information systems and business activities in the overall organizational and environmental context. These challenges are very broad in their scope, expand far beyond the realm of technology and have no clearly delineated boundaries. They relate mostly to the operational and strategic interdependencies between business and IT, the appropriateness of some or the other solutions for the organization and their compliance with regulatory norms and requirements (not to speak of the classic problems of interpreting the external environment and defining organizational strategy, which are out of the scope of this book and not discussed here).

Tight Coupling of Information Systems and Business Activities
Information systems in organizations are inextricably tied to their business operations. The sole purpose of introducing IT systems is to enable or facilitate some business activities and most of these activities today cannot be performed without the underlying system support. For this reason, the business and IT parts of the organization should evolve *synchronously in concert*.

Moreover, the productive use of information systems requires coherent and harmonious changes in multiple business aspects, e.g. roles, responsibilities, tasks, processes, decision-making procedures, incentive schemes, information accessibility and even departmental structures. Beneficial effects for organizations result not from the systems themselves, but from a *synergistic combination* of modifications in their business and IT elements.

The practical unity of business and IT in modern organizations has critical implications for their digitalization efforts. Specifically, for every use of IT, it necessitates devising complex and multifaceted organizational changes that go hand in hand with the deployment of information systems. These changes may include, for example, optimizing business processes to fully utilize the functionality of new systems, training employees to work with these systems properly, defining the respective duties with their performance indicators and restructuring existing business units according to the operational shifts caused by the automation.

This interdependence of business and IT at the operational level also leads to their interdependence at the strategic level, where long-term business goals have to correlate with far-reaching technology choices[18]. On the one hand, specific business directions normally require corresponding IT capabilities. On the other hand, available technical capabilities often create profitable business opportunities. The overall congruence between business and IT at the operational and strategic levels of organizations constitutes the notion of **business and IT alignment**[19] and represents a perennial concern for their managers[20].

Furthermore, innovating with IT also requires initiative, enthusiasm and creativity from both the business and IT sides of the organization and represents a "two-way street", where new business opportunities can stimulate the invention of pioneering IT solutions and, conversely, new capabilities of technology can inspire breakthrough business insights regarding their commercial application. Put it simply, IT-enabled business innovations are driven simultaneously by business and IT. The necessity of bringing business and IT viewpoints together for generating new ideas for the use of IT and developing integrated change scenarios with business and IT components traditionally poses a major challenge for organizations and their digital transformation endeavors.

Multitude of Conflicting Interests, Ideas and Considerations

By their nature, organizations are very complex and heterogeneous structures. Except for the smallest of them, organizations comprise a ramified, multilevel hierarchy of diverse and semi-autonomous business units, such as functions, divisions or even full-fledged lines of business, where each unit has its own specific tasks and managers accountable for their fulfillment[21].

Collectively, the appointed managers of all business units promulgate and assert **business interests** intended to benefit the organization in terms of revenue, profits, new products, time-to-market, service quality, customer satisfaction and process execution. However, these managers tend to adopt fragmented, unit-centric worldviews, typically aligned with their functional areas (e.g. supply chains, production, marketing, sales or service), and concentrate on their own goals, problems and needs, which are often inconsistent with those of other managers. Also, managers occupying different levels of the corporate hierarchy have different scopes of concern, planning horizons and outlooks on the organization, ranging from global, long-term and strategic ones down to local, short-term and operational ones, which further diversifies their perspectives[22].

This mix of "horizontal" and "vertical" differentiation in points of view results in pronounced **conflicts of interests** between business leaders in organizations, when managers of different areas and levels pursue different objectives[23]. Because of their conflicting interests, different groups of managers usually have quite different opinions on what is good for the organization and exactly what should be done (not to mention possible conflicts between the organizational and personal interests of managers as individuals, which are not discussed in this book[24]).

At the same time, IT represents a separate major functional area with its own unique specifics, intricacies and concerns. Information systems in organizations tend to be durable, long-living entities. After their introduction, they become integral parts of the organizational organism and then often exist in the landscape for as long as 10–15 years before being decommissioned or replaced[25]. Information systems are laborious to modify, upgrade and integrate with each other. In the world of IT, many implemented decisions are surprisingly difficult to revert and roll back. As a result, IT landscapes are typically clumsy, highly inertial and slow to change. Information systems are also far from being free for organizations, but expensive to develop, expensive to support and, in some cases, even expensive to remove. Furthermore, each new system adds an extra burden to the organization by increasing its landscape complexity, reducing overall flexibility and bringing additional risks. Mindlessly introducing more and more systems quickly deteriorates the quality of the organizational IT estate, inflates operating expenses and eventually leads to disaster. Shortsightedly constructed systems often do a disservice to organizations and put them in a disadvantageous position.

These and other intrinsic properties of information systems engender a special class of **technical interests** familiar to all IT professionals. Prominent technical interests include, for example, simplicity and modularity, reuse and lack of duplication, engineering neatness, correctness and elegance, maintainability, extensibility and some other "-ilities". However, most of these interests are alien and largely incomprehensible to the business audience. Business managers barely understand the repercussions of neglecting them and seldom appreciate their importance in its full worth. This is not surprising, though, as IT-specific worries are fundamentally different from typical business concerns and may have no apparent impact on the organization, especially in the short term. Simply put, business and technical interests lie in almost orthogonal dimensions.

Therefore, the presence of IT in organizations introduces another layer of interests to an already complex mosaic of contradictory interests existing within the community of business leaders, aggravating the ensuing conflicts. The conflicts of interests between various organizational actors representing different functional areas and administrative levels are illustrated in Figure 1.4.

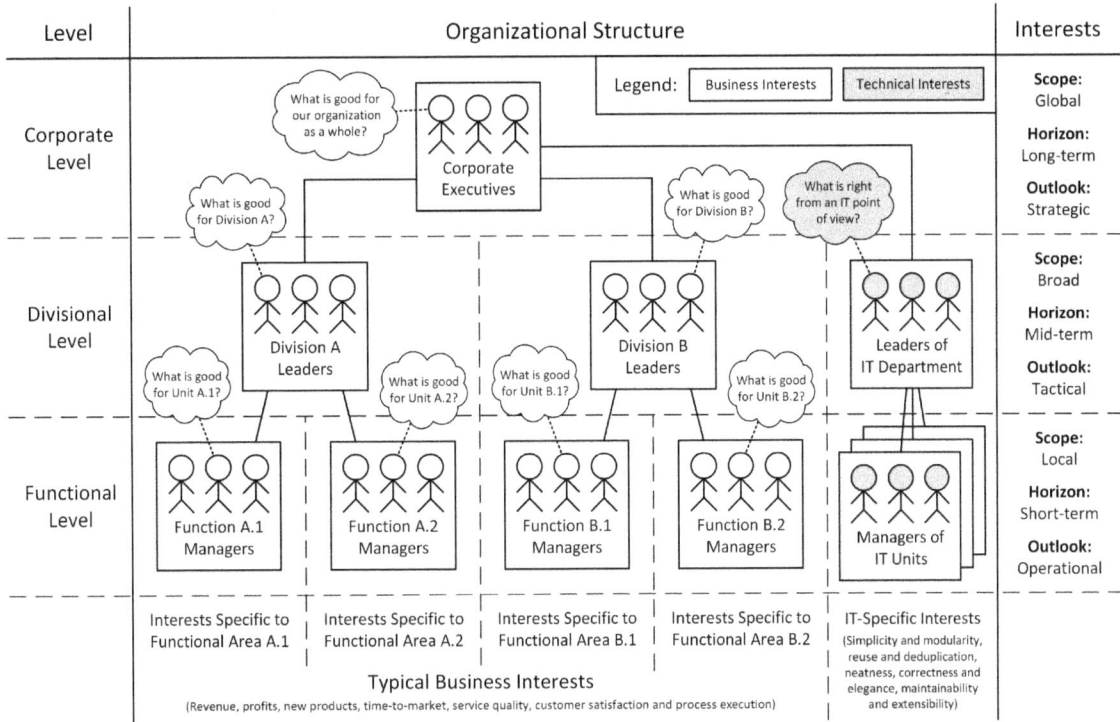

Figure 1.4. Conflicts of interests between different organizational actors

Because of the multiplicity of disparate interests and concerns present in organizations, their digital transformation ambitions can advance forward only if they satisfy the considerations of all constituencies. As organizations imply functional specialization, these considerations span spatially from narrow subject area-specific issues to overarching corporate matters. As organizations tend to be permanent entities intending to exist for very long, potentially infinite periods of time, these considerations also stretch temporally from today's demands to the distant future.

For these reasons, any decision to introduce IT-enabled changes requires great wisdom to properly assess their value, cost and other consequences for the organization and its individual subunits over different time horizons. For example, some changes may benefit only specific business units, but not the entire company. Some changes may be tactically desirable, but strategically futile. Other changes may, on the contrary, promise significant strategic contribution, but ignore pressing operational needs. Or, the resulting systems may seem perfectly valuable now as well as in the future, but prohibitively difficult for IT to own and maintain. In these circumstances, trying, for instance, to chase every fleeting opportunity or react to each business idea and whim of customers with new digitalization efforts can hardly be the right approach for the company in the long run. Oppositely, aiming these efforts exclusively at the five-year enterprise-wide vision is not a particularly good idea either. In short, there is no single answer in organizations about the best way to go.

To summarize, due to numerous conflicting concerns, organizations in their digitalization journeys cannot simply respond to all transformation drivers promoted by some proponents, but need a more selective and balanced approach to steering their course. Finding the right trade-off between various local and global, operational and strategic, business and technical interests advocated by different organizational actors, as shown in Figure 1.4, while also taking into account both value- and cost-related considerations, represents a classic problem for organizations and an inherent challenge for their digitalization aspirations.

Normative Regulations, Obligations and Restrictions

Owing to the criticality of information in modern society, both information handled by IT systems and technologies involved in its processing are increasingly becoming the subject of legislative regulation and various **normative acts**. On the one hand, most countries have long enacted national laws intended to control the collection, storage and transfer of personal, commercial and other sensitive data in a digital form, e.g. Personal Information Protection and Electronic Documents Act (PIPEDA) in Canada. International industry bodies publish somewhat similar complementary standards for securing information assets as well, e.g. ISO/IEC 27001. Besides that, corporate legislation in many countries obliges organizations to log certain activities and retain their digital traces for the purposes of potential audit and criminal investigation, e.g. Sarbanes–Oxley Act (SOX) in the United States. Critical IT solutions in sensitive industries, like finance, can also be shaped by more specific compliance requirements dictated and verified by local regulators, e.g. Australian Prudential Regulation Authority (APRA).

On the other hand, for the sake of national security, some countries impose legislative bans on software and hardware equipment of foreign origin in their governmental organizations and state-owned enterprises, e.g. espionage suspicions over Huawei and Kaspersky. Or, the use of certain technologies can also be heavily regulated because of their potential dangers to society, e.g. different legal status of cryptocurrencies and self-driving cars in different jurisdictions. Moreover, some especially hazardous IT innovations could even be prohibited preemptively, e.g. public calls for banning the further development of artificial intelligence (AI). Failure to comply with the applicable laws, regulations and normative acts may lead to negative consequences for organizations, including substantial fines[26].

The existence of a relevant legislative base with stringent requirements for organizations, in addition to other challenges of digital transformation, also puts the respective efforts into the regulatory context. The need for compliance limits the possible opportunities for designing IT-enabled products and services and imposes certain constraints on what companies can and cannot do in terms of their business conduct. Hence, the necessity to align their digitalization plans with the current and anticipated restrictions of the regulatory environment represents yet another organizational challenge of digital transformation.

The Overall Context of Digital Transformation

The rapidly evolving technology market constantly offers new ventures for organizations to leverage the latest advances in IT in their business activities that can be realized only through purposeful digital transformation efforts. These efforts are motivated by multiple competing transformation drivers partly linked to business strategy (see Figure 1.3). However, they face very diverse technical and organizational challenges originating from both the internal and external environments that complicate digitalization endeavors in organizations. The overall context of digital transformation and its key challenges associated with introducing new information systems in the organizational business and IT landscape are illustrated in Figure 1.5.

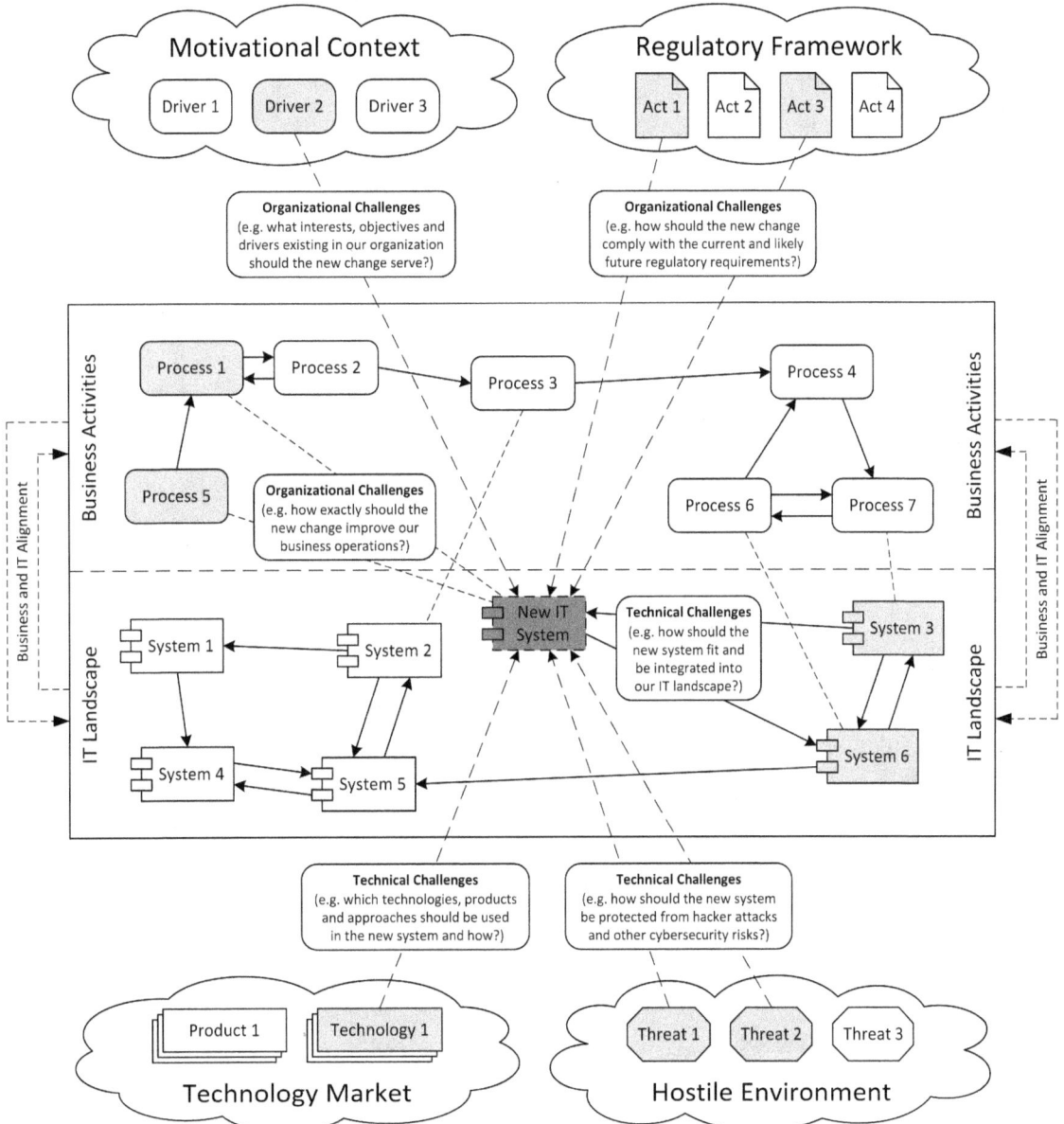

Figure 1.5. The context and key challenges of digital transformation in organizations

Although the challenges of digital transformation are exemplified in Figure 1.5 for an elementary business change with one IT system, they are generally valid and relevant to all digitalization efforts, it is only their severity that varies with the breadth, depth and other specifics of the intended transformation. For instance, for larger-scale transformation efforts, these challenges stay conceptually the same, but multiply greatly in quantitative terms with the growth in the number of involved components, so that they can easily become overwhelming and insurmountable. To restrain and localize the challenges associated with digitalization, the respective efforts in organizations are normally structured into separate transformational initiatives representing limited chunks of transformation with a more or less clear scope, boundaries and impact.

Chapter Summary

This chapter discussed the historical development of IT and its increasing impact on the business of organizations, introduced the notion of digital transformation and different types of transformation drivers in organizations, described various technical and organizational challenges of digitalization and presented the overall context of digital transformation. The key message of this chapter can be summarized in the following essential points:

- Since its inception, IT has continuously progressed through the four successive epochs of process automation, strategic systems, electronic business and digital transformation with an ever-growing influence on the business of organizations
- Although this phenomenon is old and the term is vague, digital transformation in the organizational context implies introducing some or the other advanced information systems and technologies to improve or enable the business
- All drivers of digital transformation in organizations have specific proponents and can be classified into deliberate intentions, emergent opportunities, operational problems, ad hoc demands, permanent imperatives and technical concerns
- Business strategy provides predominantly a general backdrop for organizational digitalization efforts, but is typically too symbolic, abstract, volatile, secretive and distant from IT to serve as an actionable transformation driver on its own
- The motivational context represents the entirety of all transformation drivers with their proponents existing in the organization, partly depending on its top-level business strategy, and motivates all organizational digitalization efforts
- Technical challenges of digital transformation lie solely within the realm of technology and relate primarily to the selection of suitable systems, their proper integration into the existing IT environment and ensuring their security
- Organizational challenges of digital transformation transcend the realm of technology and relate mostly to the operational and strategic interdependencies between business and IT, the appropriateness of some or the other solutions for the organization and their compliance with regulatory norms and requirements
- Digital transformation efforts in organizations happen in a very complex context with multiple competing transformation drivers and diverse technical and organizational challenges of the internal and external origin

Chapter 2: Digital Transformation Initiatives

The previous chapter introduced the notion of digital transformation and different types of transformation drivers motivating the respective efforts in organizations. This chapter focuses specifically on digital transformation initiatives and presents the conceptual framework necessary for understanding their realization. In particular, this chapter starts with explaining the meaning of digital transformation initiatives, their initial ideation, implementation process and stakeholders in organizations. Next, this chapter discusses different types of digital transformation initiatives, their nested hierarchy and the specifics of their implementation at different hierarchical levels. Lastly, this chapter analyses the technical and organizational challenges associated with digital transformation initiatives at different levels of their hierarchy.

Digital Transformation Initiatives in Organizations

Nowadays, pursuing digital transformation is imperative for the competitive survival of organizations in the market. Their digitalization, however, does not happen automatically on its own along with the progress in technology, but only through implementing specific transformational initiatives.

Digital transformation initiatives, or simply IT initiatives, represent concrete organizational change initiatives with business and IT components, where new information systems are being introduced in organizations to enable or enhance their business. These initiatives organize their digitalization efforts into meaningful, coherent and manageable pieces of change. Each transformation initiative has one or many goals that it is trying to achieve. **Initiative goals** specify exactly what should be accomplished as part of the initiative and can be accompanied by precise quantitative metrics to measure the extent of their achievement, e.g. process execution time, net sales revenue or customer retention rate.

As discussed earlier, digitalization in organizations unfolds within the global motivational context, which is influenced by business strategy and aggregates all the existing drivers that stimulate the respective transformation efforts (see Figure 1.3). In this context, each individual digitalization initiative is motivated, directly or indirectly, by one or many, often disparate transformation drivers, e.g. deliberate intentions, operational problems and ad hoc demands (see Figure 1.2). These drivers explain why the initiative is needed, define the ultimate goals of the initiative, largely determine the benefits of its implementation for the organization and justify the associated expenses[1].

Ideation of Digital Transformation Initiatives

All digitalization initiatives in organizations stem from specific ideas about what needs to be done to enhance the business with IT. Accordingly, **initial ideation** is an organizational process of creating ideas and insights for IT-backed business improvements. The seminal ideation process implies analyzing the organization with its motivational context and producing suppositions as to what changes in its business and IT landscape can be the most advantageous in light of the existing transformation drivers. These changes can have different effects on the organization, vary greatly in magnitude and range in their innovativeness from routine process automation to genuine competitive inventions.

As input, the process of initial ideation takes business strategy and the whole set of more concrete transformation drivers. As output, it gives rise to vague suggestions for new change initiatives that can potentially be launched to respond to these drivers. For this reason, the overall meaning of this process can be best summarized as *drivers-to-ideas*.

The initial ideation of digitalization initiatives embodies *generating* during which numerous thoughts of varying quality are put forward for consideration. As organizations are constantly evolving, this process is fundamentally continuous, though it can run unevenly over different periods, possibly peaking in its intensity at opportune moments along the yearly planning or budgeting cycle. The process of initial ideation and its relationship to resulting digital transformation initiatives are shown schematically in Figure 2.1.

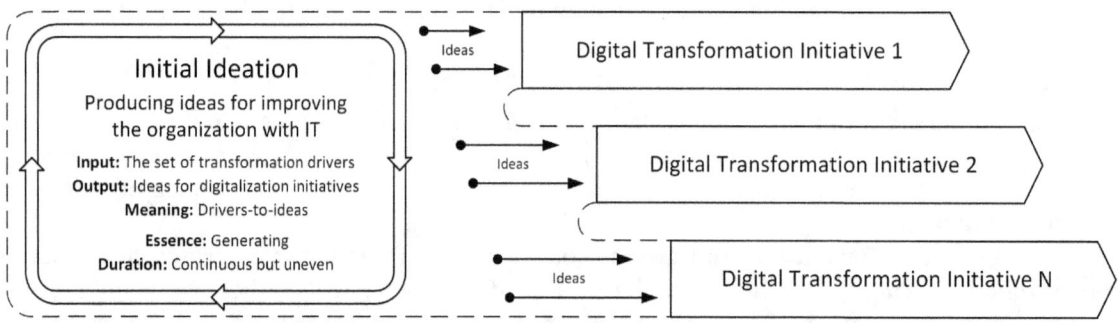

Figure 2.1. The initial ideation of digital transformation initiatives

After their ideation, the best ideas for digitalization are turned into actual transformation initiatives to be implemented, where these ideas are subjected to closer scrutiny, then elaborated in more detail and finally get materialized.

Implementation of Digital Transformation Initiatives

To effect any organizational changes, ideas converted into digitalization initiatives must be implemented by completing certain tasks and actions. The implementation process of digital transformation initiatives, or simply the **initiative implementation process**, is a sequence of activities that need to be performed to materialize the intended modifications in the business and IT sides of the organization. Although implementing digitalization initiatives involves many diverse activities, these activities can generally be grouped into three consecutive lifecycle phases with increasing commitment, exertion and funding demands: conception, planning and execution.

The opening **conception phase** of the initiative implementation process implies giving more careful thought to the original ideas that engendered change initiatives and coming to a deeper understanding of what needs to be accomplished and how. Even though these efforts clearly belong to specific initiatives, it is still a preliminary, *pre-initiative* phase as at this stage it is difficult to talk about initiatives as such; there are no formalized initiatives yet, only some precursory discussions. In fact, early ideas and aspirations may or may not develop into full-fledged initiatives, depending on whether they are deemed promising after their more thorough examination. Because discussing nascent initiatives is a largely informal and not particularly laborious task, it typically does not require any special funding.

As input, the conception phase takes raw ideas for digitalization initiatives incoming from the process of initial ideation and the subset of transformation drivers that motivated them (see Figure 2.1). As output, it provides more refined notions of initiatives with their goals, purposes and scopes. For this reason, the overall meaning of this phase can be best summarized as *idea-to-concept*. The conception phase embodies *envisioning* during which the intentions and contours of initiatives are formulated and delineated more precisely. Although all digitalization initiatives begin their existence with conception, which often happens rather quickly, the exact boundaries of this lifecycle phase can hardly be defined.

The next **planning phase** of the initiative implementation process implies thinking about how initiatives should be materialized and making all the necessary plans, arrangements and other preparations to ensure their successful execution. These plans and arrangements can cover all the pertinent aspects of initiatives, e.g. business, technical, legal, sourcing, financing and other resources. As the development of plans is a non-trivial exercise of noticeable size, it is likely to require some seed funding to sponsor the respective activities.

As input, the planning phase takes the abstract concepts of initiatives resulting from their conception. As output, it creates pretty detailed outlines of desired changes and scenarios of their practical realization. Hence, the overall meaning of this phase can be best summarized as *concept-to-plan*. The planning phase embodies *deciding* during which all the principal decisions regarding initiatives are settled. This lifecycle phase usually occupies a relatively small fraction of the total initiative implementation time.

The concluding **execution phase** of the initiative implementation process implies acting according to the prepared plans and arrangements to materialize initiatives and cause beneficial organizational effects. These actions can result in both tangible changes in organizations (e.g. enhanced business operations) and changes in their policies (e.g. refocused investment priorities). Unlike all the preceding inexpensive preparations, they require substantial funding to pay the bills for the involved workforce, licenses and equipment.

As input, the execution phase takes the existing plans for initiatives produced as part of their planning. As output, it applies actual modifications to the business and IT landscape, thereby delivering what was envisioned in the plans. For this reason, the overall meaning of this phase can be best summarized as *plan-to-delivery*. The execution phase embodies *doing* during which the developed plans are followed, the previous decisions get realized and all the "visible" work takes place. This lifecycle phase normally takes the bulk of the initiative implementation time.

Therefore, all digital transformation initiatives emerge, at first, as mere ideas out of the ideation process, then are reformulated as clearer concepts, elaborated into more concrete plans and finally get executed, turning into reality. The generic initiative implementation process with its three major phases discussed above is presented in Figure 2.2.

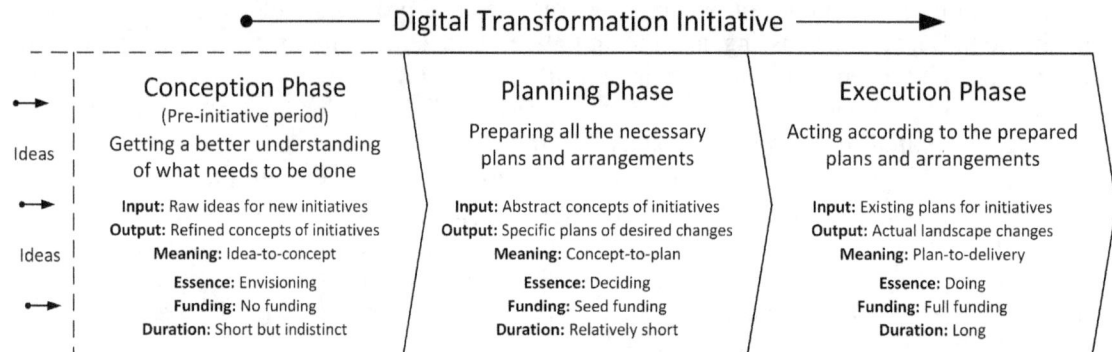

Figure 2.2. The implementation process of digital transformation initiatives

Of course, the initiative implementation process depicted in Figure 2.2 with the three clear-cut, strictly sequential phases of conception, planning and execution represents a certain simplification of the organizational reality as, in practice, the boundaries between these phases can be blurred and various non-linear, iterative features can also be present. Notwithstanding its apparent simplicity, this three-phase process provides a convenient reference model of the implementation lifecycle of digital transformation initiatives that will be used further in this book with the necessary refinements introduced where appropriate. However, because the conception phase belongs to the pre-initiative period and is not always relevant, this phase will be omitted in further discussions unless it is particularly important in a specific context.

Stakeholders of Digital Transformation Initiatives

Stakeholders of digital transformation initiatives, or simply **initiative stakeholders**, are organizational actors pursuing certain interests in these initiatives and participating in their implementation processes. Initiative stakeholders typically represent various units and areas of the organization impacted by initiatives or contributing to their realization. As digitalization initiatives consist of business and IT components, the circle of their stakeholders normally includes some members of both business and IT communities.

Initiative stakeholders can also vary in the degree of their influence, involvement and commitment to initiatives and range from their principal owners, whose vital interests are at stake, to rather peripheral people, whose daily work is somehow affected by these initiatives. As for their roles in the initiative implementation process, stakeholders are usually not homogeneous and take somewhat different parts in different lifecycle phases of digital transformation initiatives (see Figure 2.2). On this basis, a number of distinct but possibly overlapping subgroups of initiative stakeholders can be articulated.

Most importantly, **initiative sponsors** are a subset of stakeholders promoting the very need to implement initiatives. It is these people who generate ideas for change, launch initiatives, define their goals and provide the necessary funding from the budgets they control. Unsurprisingly, initiative sponsors are the most powerful of all initiative stakeholders having a veto right over all decisions related to their initiatives. These stakeholders are very active during the conception phase of initiatives, but can be less involved in their detailed planning, sometimes acting only as approvers of key decisions, and even less so in their subsequent execution. Often, initiative sponsors come from the proponents of transformation drivers that motivate digitalization efforts in the organization (see Figure 1.3).

Another noteworthy subset of stakeholders are **initiative executors**, who immediately participate in the execution of digital transformation initiatives. Initiative executors perform all the necessary work to make the desired transformation actually happen. Typically, they are among the least powerful initiative stakeholders whose concerns are taken into account and respected, but not considered decisive for the course of initiatives. As opposed to initiative sponsors, these stakeholders may not take any part in the conception of initiatives, but actively contribute to their planning and carry out their execution. Classic examples of initiative executors are project managers and other members of project teams discussed later in this chapter.

This heterogeneity of the stakeholder audience creates a potential for serious conflicts of interests even within a single digitalization initiative. As initiative stakeholders represent different organizational units, levels and areas, their interests with respect to achieving the goals of the initiative often collide (see Figure 1.4). Even worse, because each initiative can be motivated by multiple transformation drivers with each driver having its own proponents, the circle of initiative stakeholders can be fragmented and comprise different factions or coalitions of supporters interested in its implementation for their own reasons, which leads to far more profound contradictions around the very goals of the initiative. In these situations, different constituencies not simply pursue different interests regarding the same goals, but see entirely different goals, provoking acute conflicts at the most basic level.

Besides that, the interests of initiative sponsors and initiative executors, as two different parties playing disparate roles in the initiative implementation process, are not identical and do not always match. While initiative sponsors are interested in attaining the stated goals of the initiative with whatever approaches, initiative executors are interested in using proper approaches towards whatever goals. Or, speaking metaphorically, initiative sponsors are seeking to arrive at the right destination by any route, when initiative executors are seeking to follow the best route to any destination. For this reason, initiative executors can be largely indifferent to ends, whereas initiative sponsors — to means.

As a result, initiative stakeholders often vary greatly in terms of their interests and allegiance to the goals of the initiative. For instance, some stakeholders, especially initiative sponsors, can be strongly devoted to specific goals, which are sometimes not shared by other members pursuing their own goals. At the same time, other stakeholders, especially initiative executors, can pursue certain "neutral" interests unrelated to any particular goals. Initiative stakeholders with their interests and major subgroups of initiative sponsors and initiative executors mapped to the relevant lifecycle phases of digital transformation initiatives are shown in Figure 2.3.

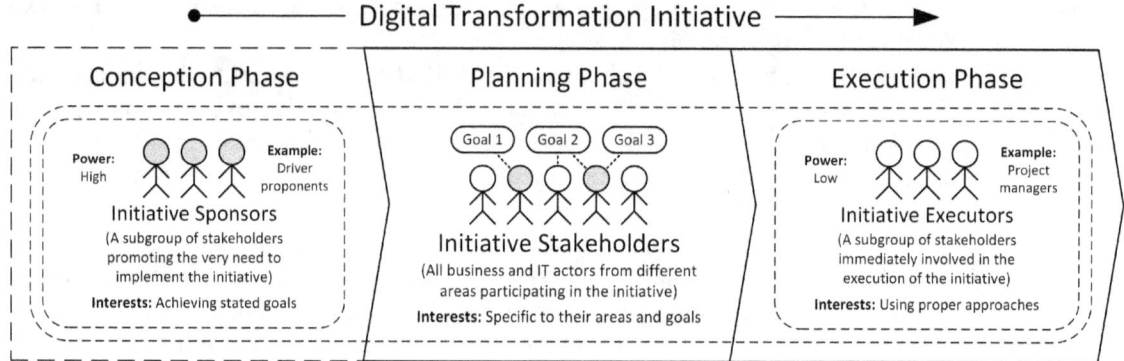

Figure 2.3. Stakeholders of digital transformation initiatives with their subgroups

Although the mapping of different subsets of stakeholders to the three lifecycle phases of digitalization initiatives presented in Figure 2.3 is rather loose, it clarifies exactly what categories of stakeholders are engaged more actively in the initiative implementation process at its different stages as well as what their typical interests are.

Different Types of Digital Transformation Initiatives

Digital transformation initiatives are intentional and concerted undertakings that require considerable investments of organizational resources. Although all digitalization initiatives imply modifying both business and IT aspects of organizations, they can vary greatly in their scale, magnitude and "caliber". Their size, in turn, determines many of their salient features in the context of digital transformation.

Specifically, depending on their scope and impact on the organization, all digital transformation initiatives can be loosely separated, in order of their significance, into projects, programs and strategies. Albeit the practical boundaries between these notions can be blurred, this simple classification helps capture and reflect the common properties of transformation initiatives of different sizes.

Projects represent relatively small digitalization initiatives[2]. They are characterized by a limited and clearly delineated scope and result in strictly localized changes in the organization and its IT landscape, normally separate IT solutions. Projects are typically motivated by one or a few closely related drivers and ensuing goals. Their stakeholders tend to form rather small and cohesive teams of people, often from the same business area, united by these drivers and goals.

Projects have a well-understood structure with concrete constituent components and relationships between them. They are executed as one-shot pieces of work within bounded timeframes usually taking up to 6–12 months, preferably shorter. Examples of projects that can be initiated in organizations include:

- Creating a new IT system to automate some steps of the procurement process and decrease its dependence on the human factor
- Extending a mobile app to provide additional functionality and more powerful visualization capabilities to customers

- Developing an analytical system to forecast future peaks in market demand based on previous sales statistics

By virtue of their definite structure, the costs of new projects can be assessed fairly accurately. Benefits anticipated from their implementation are also reasonably predictable, which often allows preparing detailed business cases, applying discounted cash flow (DCF) analysis and calculating precise return on investment (ROI).

Programs represent larger digital transformation initiatives. Their scope may be not exactly clear upfront, though still controllable, leading to considerable but not pervasive changes in the organization and its IT landscape, possibly several IT solutions[3]. Programs are often motivated by a number of different, loosely tied drivers and goals centered around a common pivotal theme. Their stakeholders are pretty wide circles of people from various business areas, sometimes with diverging opinions about the importance of these drivers and goals.

Programs have only an approximate structure with abstract logical components and their interrelationships. They are executed step-by-step as series of multiple related projects over long periods of time, but within a more or less foreseeable horizon of, say, 1–3 years. Examples of programs that can be launched in organizations include:

- Consolidating all elements of the corporate IT platform for inbound logistics to achieve end-to-end process automation
- Integrating all user-facing mobile apps to enable seamless customer experience and real-time data interchange
- Building an enterprise data warehouse with accompanying applications to be able to analyze many aspects of the market situation

Because their structure is not very well defined, potential costs and outcomes of new programs can only be evaluated tentatively, sometimes as an order of magnitude. For this reason, the respective business cases and ROI estimations can be rough at best.

Finally, **strategies** represent global, organization-wide digitalization initiatives. Their scope can be very broad and largely uncertain, causing fundamental changes in how the organization does its business and employs IT, beyond individual IT solutions. Strategies can be motivated by a hierarchy of first- and second-order drivers and goals bundled under a common transformational agenda. Their stakeholders comprise multiple diverse groups of people that are often dispersed across the organization, isolated from each other and focused on completely different drivers and goals.

Strategies may have no formal structure altogether, but provide only general suggestions as to where and which way to go, what approaches and technologies to use. They are materialized through executing the right programs and projects aligned with their imperatives, as well as by establishing an overall decision-making framework reflecting their philosophy. Strategies are oriented mainly towards the long-term future relevant to the horizon of 3–5 years ahead, often having no specific timelines or completion dates. Examples of strategies that can be enacted in organizations include:

- Striving for a unified enterprise-wide platform for all operations in all points of presence to leverage economies of scale
- Embracing a mobile-first attitude to position handheld devices as the primary sales and customer communication channel

- Becoming a data-driven company where decisions are backed by the best available evidence from all sources

Due to their vague scope and conceptual nature, it is typically impossible to assess the costs of realizing strategies with any confidence or precision, but only to speculate about the associated expenditures. All business consequences of pursuing strategies also cannot be anticipated in advance and their benefits for organizations can only be formulated in qualitative terms. Standard financial methods and investment valuation techniques are usually found inapplicable to strategies, motivating the search for more sophisticated ways of their evaluation, e.g. real options[4].

As the borders between projects, programs and strategies in practice are debatable and rather indistinct, these three types of initiatives should be better viewed merely as dense clusters of transformation initiatives with similar features in the continuous spectrum of possible digitalization initiatives of various scales. The full spectrum of digital transformation initiatives with projects, programs, strategies and their key properties is shown in Figure 2.4.

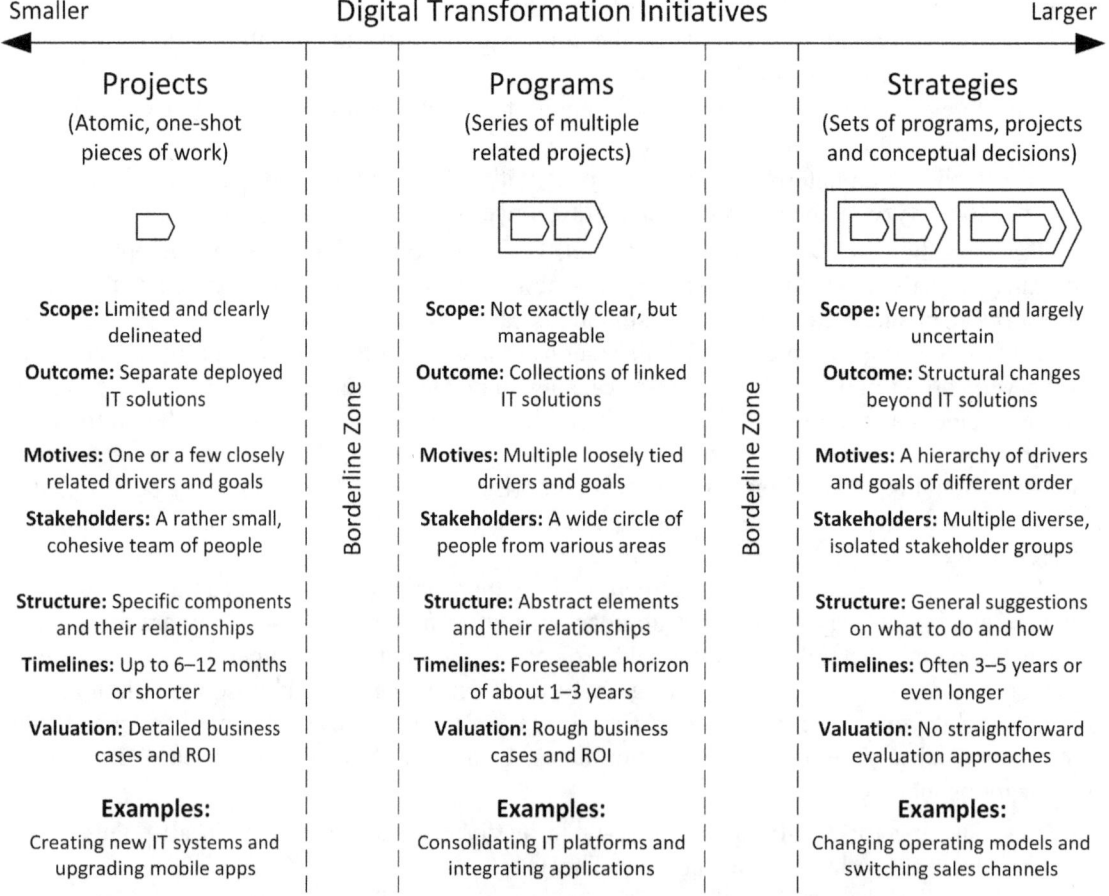

Figure 2.4. The size spectrum of digital transformation initiatives

Even though the classification of all transformation initiatives into projects, programs and strategies presented in Figure 2.4 is admittedly rather loose, it is reasonably accurate, realistic and explanatory. Moreover, because of its simplicity, intuitive appeal and consistency with common industry terminology, this classification is very convenient for illustrating various concepts relevant to digitalization efforts in organizations. For this reason, it will be used further in this book as a general conceptual framework for discussing digital transformation initiatives.

The Hierarchy of Digital Transformation Initiatives

As programs consist of smaller projects and strategies comprise other programs and projects, digital transformation initiatives in organizations evidently form an **initiative hierarchy**, where higher-level initiatives are composed of lower-level ones. In other words, transformation initiatives can be viewed as a nested set, where strategies represent highest-level initiatives, programs — mid-level initiatives, and projects — lowest-level initiatives. Metaphorically, strategies can be compared to trunks, programs — to branches, and projects — to leaves.

However, the initiative hierarchy can start descending from progenitor initiatives at any level, not only from top-level strategies. In other words, lower-level initiatives can be perfectly detached as separate roots of the hierarchy and do not necessarily belong to any higher-level "parent" initiatives. For example, projects can be launched either on their own, or as part of broader transformation programs or strategies. Likewise, programs can be either initiated independently, or descend from some higher-order strategies.

From this perspective, all digital transformation initiatives in the hierarchy can be divided into autonomous and derivative ones. **Autonomous initiatives**, or standalone initiatives, are *independent* initiatives forming the roots of the hierarchy that have no parents and are launched on their own. These initiatives are always induced directly by the global motivational context aggregating various transformation drivers. The goals of autonomous initiatives are wholly determined by the underlying drivers that motivated them with larger initiatives generally having more drivers (see Figure 2.4).

By contrast, **derivative initiatives**, or subordinate initiatives, are *dependent* initiatives composing the hierarchy that are strongly affiliated with their parents and launched as part of them. Unlike autonomous initiatives, they are spawned by their parent initiatives and link to the motivational context only indirectly. Accordingly, their goals are determined mostly by the goals of their parents from which they descend. In other words, the goals of derivative initiatives typically represent lower-level *subgoals* of their parent initiatives. Like initiatives themselves, initiative goals at different levels are also hierarchical. By providing certain motives that induce new initiatives and define their goals, their parents' goals serve for derivative initiatives exactly the same purpose as transformation drivers do for autonomous initiatives. Essentially, for derivative initiatives, their parent initiatives constitute their own, local motivational context.

Various combinations of autonomous and derivative initiatives at different hierarchical levels form separate "families" of initiatives somehow related to each other and to the common motivational context. The hierarchy of digital transformation initiatives with strategies, programs and projects illustrating the possible patterns of their composition and their connection to the motivational context is presented in Figure 2.5.

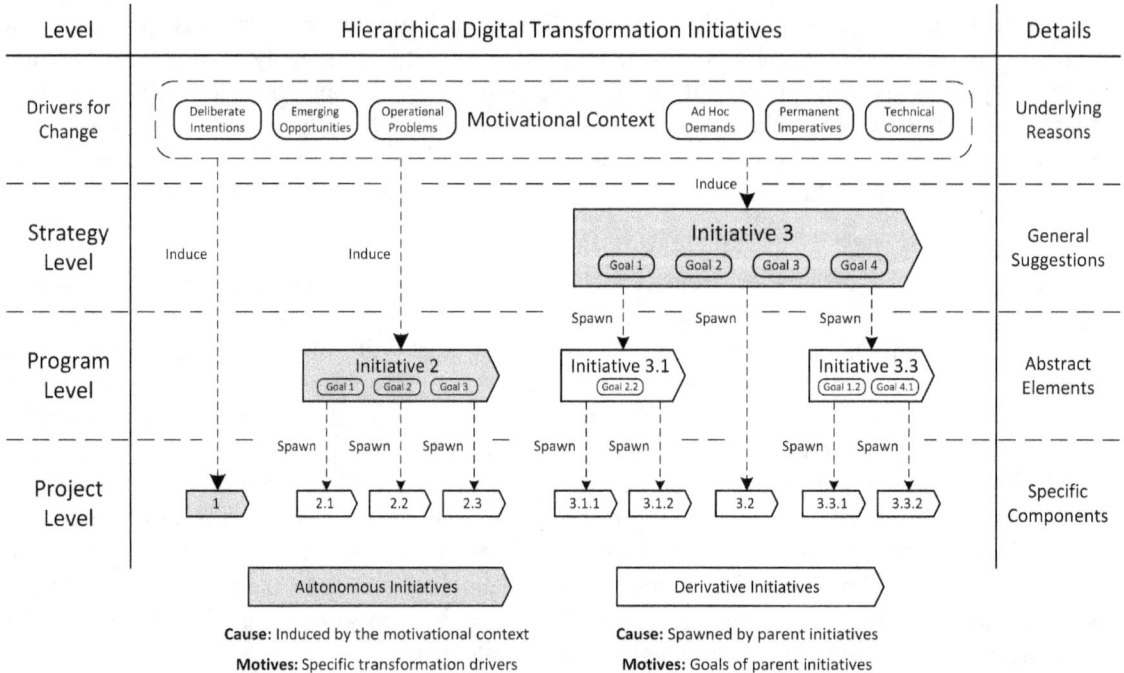

Figure 2.5. The hierarchy of digital transformation initiatives in the motivational context

As shown in Figure 2.5, some digitalization initiatives can be totally independent projects with their own drivers (e.g. Initiative 1) or projects descending from autonomous programs (e.g. Initiatives 2.1), from derivative programs (e.g. Initiative 3.1.1) or even squarely from top-tier strategies (e.g. Initiative 3.2). Other initiatives can be standalone programs (e.g. Initiative 2), subordinate programs (e.g. Initiative 3.1) or overarching strategies (e.g. Initiative 3).

Implementation of Hierarchical Digital Transformation Initiatives

As digitalization initiatives in organizations are hierarchical in nature, their implementation activities reflect their nested structure and also take into account the specifics of transformation initiatives at different levels of their hierarchy. Most importantly, implementing any higher-level initiative requires implementing all the lower-level initiatives constituting it. For example, programs are implemented by implementing all their projects, whereas strategies — through the implementation of all the associated programs and projects. In short, digital transformation initiatives are implemented recursively.

However, specifically from the standpoint of their execution, of the three types of transformation initiatives, only projects are executed in a "physical" sense, while programs and strategies are executed mainly through converting their abstract suggestions into lower-level, more detailed planning decisions for derivative initiatives. Namely, projects are usually executed by constructing new information systems and embedding their use into regular business operations. By contrast, programs are executed by initiating the necessary projects and shaping their structure. In a similar vein, strategies are executed by ideating the right programs and projects and influencing their composition.

At the root of the initiative hierarchy, autonomous transformation initiatives are launched based on completely new ideas for digitalization arriving from the process of initial ideation (see Figure 2.1). Then, for strategies and programs, when executing these initiatives, their intentions serve as seminal ideas for their descending initiatives from which their implementation processes begin (see Figure 2.2). In this case, the ideation of derivative initiatives ensues from the goals of their parents. In other words, subordinate initiatives are launched based on the existing intentions for digitalization reflected in their parents' plans, bypassing the initial ideation process.

Consequently, in the hierarchy of digital transformation initiatives, the execution of high-level initiatives occurs essentially *during* the conception and planning of their descendants. In some sense, these two processes are equivalent to each other and represent simply views from opposite sides on precisely the same activities. For instance, proper execution at the strategy level manifests itself in proper planning at the program and project levels. Likewise, executing programs in the right way means planning the right projects. Only the execution of projects, as lowest-level initiatives in the hierarchy, requires taking "real" actions to change the organizational business and IT landscape.

However, for the sake of convenience and conceptual consistency, the execution of projects can also be interpreted as launching and controlling subordinate delivery efforts at a lower delivery level. This **delivery level** represents a virtual sub-level of the project level where all tangible modifications are introduced into the corporate landscape as part of the project execution, e.g. installing hardware devices, deploying software packages, redefining business roles and changing operational procedures. In this light, the corresponding activities carried out at the delivery level can be aggregated into the special **delivery phase** of the project implementation process, which is identical to the execution phase, but highlights its practical side. As in the case of the conception phase (see Figure 2.2), the delivery level is relevant only in specific contexts and will often be omitted in further discussions.

These relationships between the different hierarchical levels of transformation initiatives in terms of their conception, planning and execution also suggest important relationships between the circles of their stakeholders (see Figure 2.3). As the conception of derivative programs and projects takes place as part of the execution of their parent initiatives in accordance with their intentions, they are sponsored largely by their parents' executors. In other words, the initiative executors of parent initiatives typically turn into the primary initiative sponsors for their descendants, e.g. program-level executors become project-level sponsors. Generally, in the initiative hierarchy, the executors of higher-level initiatives tend to be among the major sponsors of lower-level ones. Only autonomous, parentless digitalization initiatives conceived independently based on some transformation drivers (see Figure 2.5) are sponsored exclusively by the respective driver proponents.

Besides the differences in their ideation, execution and stakeholder aspects discussed above, the implementation processes of projects, programs and strategies also differ significantly from an administrative perspective. Because implementing projects involves actual system construction at the delivery level, it necessitates allocating material organizational resources, like money and labor, through established bureaucratic procedures. For this reason, projects are formalized administratively as separate units of work, well-defined in terms of their scope and usually have official project charters or statements of work specifying their exact content. The initiation of new projects always sets in motion certain organizational mechanisms necessary for enabling their implementation, e.g. budgeting, staffing, vendor negotiations and tenders. By contrast, as higher-level transformation initiatives themselves do not imply any hands-on activities, they can remain administratively invisible to the rest of the organization and exist only unofficially in the minds of their sponsors as unwritten decisions to launch particular projects in the future. Their implementation does not require any formal procedural support and, from an administrative point of view, manifests itself only at the project level, when their derivative projects are initiated one by one[5].

To summarize, the implementation of hierarchical digitalization initiatives represents a multilevel exercise, where high-level initiatives merely guide lower-level planning efforts, possibly staying invisible from an administrative standpoint, and only projects actually modify the organizational landscape and engage some administrative mechanisms. The relationship between the motivational context, initial ideation and different lifecycle phases of strategies, programs and projects described above is illustrated in Figure 2.6.

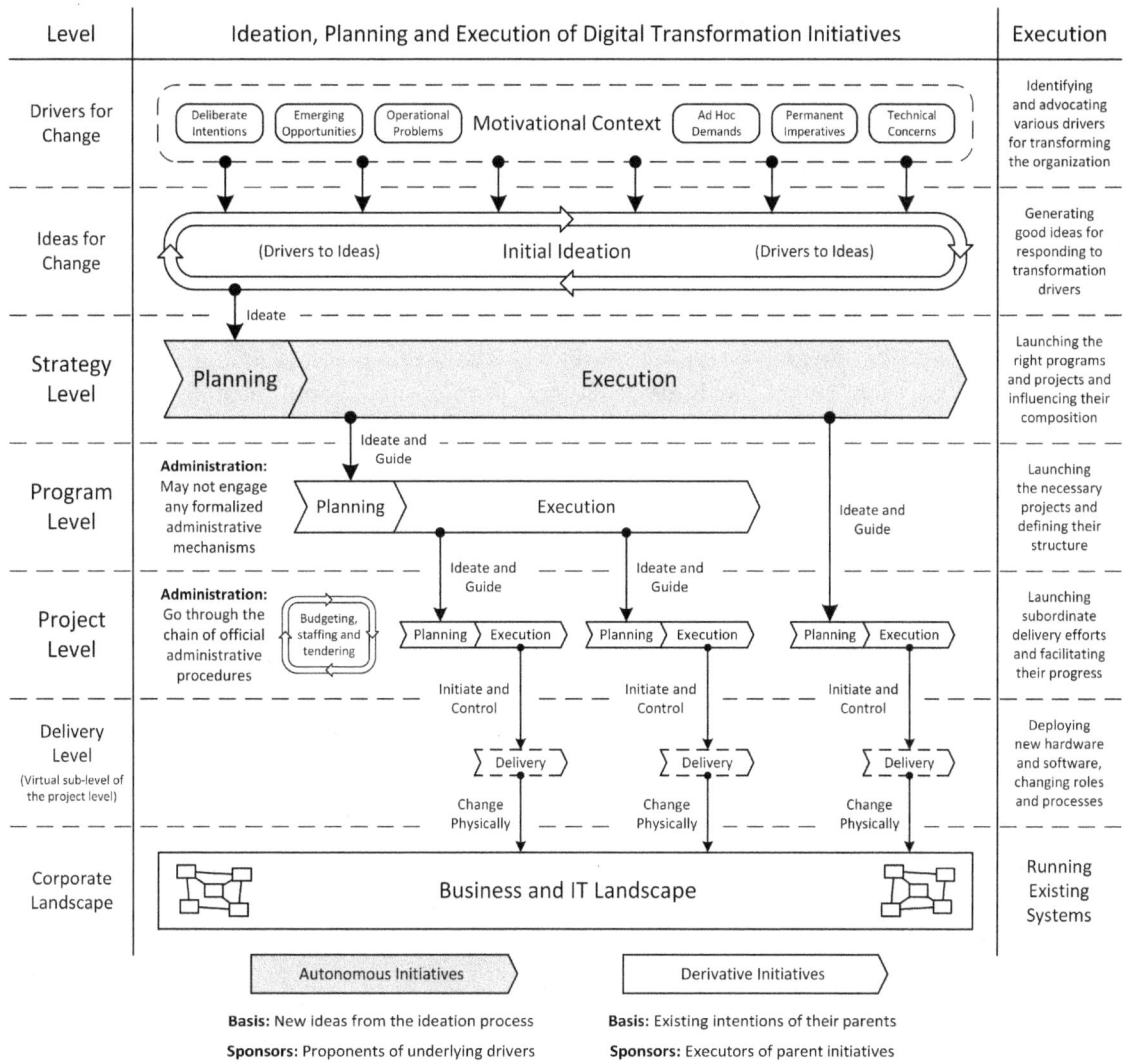

Figure 2.6. Implementation of hierarchical digital transformation initiatives

As shown in Figure 2.6, higher-order digital transformation initiatives never touch the organizational landscape directly. Instead, they "trickle down" via a sophisticated transmission mechanism, where the execution of higher-level initiatives drives the ideation, conception and planning of lower-level ones, forming a descending cascade of initiatives. Eventually, all these initiatives turn into material landscape changes through implementing concrete projects. In spite of certain simplifications analogous to those acknowledged earlier for Figure 2.2, Figure 2.6 adequately explains the relationships between the different lifecycle phases of digitalization initiatives at different levels of their hierarchy.

Execution of Digital Transformation Projects

As discussed above, the execution of digitalization projects differs in principle from the execution of higher-level transformation initiatives because it involves physical landscape modification efforts performed at the bottom delivery level (see Figure 2.6). In organizations, these efforts are normally structured into some systematic processes, often using specific delivery methodologies.

Generic Project Delivery Process

The process of project delivery, or simply the **project delivery process**, defines a repeatable sequence of actions that should be accomplished within the delivery phase to execute the project by developing new information systems according to its existing plans. Although this process can be organization-, department- and even project-specific, its overall meaning can be best represented by three successive steps: building, testing and deployment.

The first **building step** of the project delivery process implies creating the information systems specified in the plans with all their internal components. This step includes procuring hardware equipment, writing software code, configuring databases, preparing virtual, physical and cloud infrastructure, purchasing required licenses and taking other actions necessary to construct the systems.

The second **testing step** of the project delivery process implies checking the quality and trying to use the new information systems. This step comprises all sorts of testing approaches (e.g. unit, integration, functional, usability, performance, stress and acceptance) and other quality assurance measures intended to guarantee that the developed systems meet the needs of their users.

The final **deployment step** of the project delivery process implies rolling the resulting information systems out for their use in production. This step involves making the systems available to all their users, training the users to work with them, changing their tasks to leverage new system capabilities, reshaping the respective business processes and eventually institutionalizing the use of these systems as part of established organizational routines.

The three-step process of project delivery is performed by specially assembled, multidisciplinary **project teams**. They are usually headed by dedicated project managers and include various members specialized in relevant aspects of IT, e.g. business analysts, software developers, database administrators, infrastructure engineers, security experts, system testers and possibly some external vendor representatives. Project teams are typically rather small and cohesive, but temporary and formed on an ad hoc basis for the demands of concrete projects. The generic process of project delivery carried out by project teams within the delivery, or execution, phase of digital transformation projects is shown in Figure 2.7.

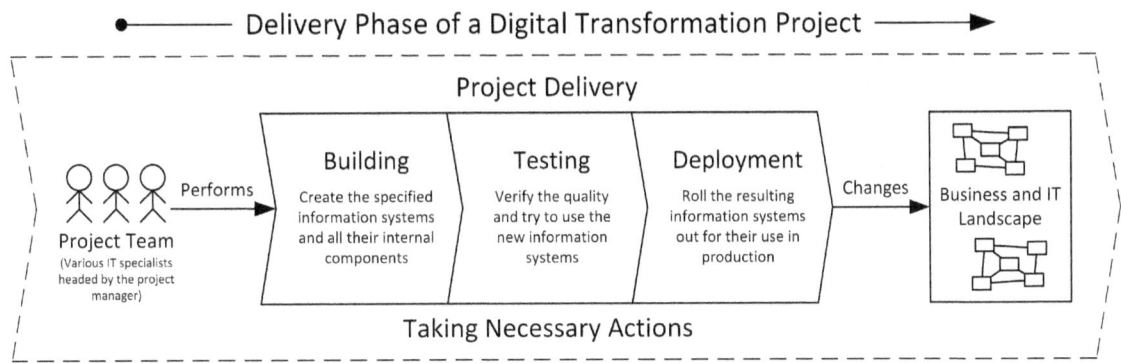

Figure 2.7. The generic process of project delivery fulfilled by project teams

The high-level project delivery process presented in Figure 2.7 accurately reflects the general logical flow of activities that take place within the delivery phase on the way to project execution. In reality, however, this flow can be embodied differently, often iteratively, in concrete delivery methodologies adopted in organizations for executing projects.

Waterfall and Agile Delivery Methodologies

Over the long history of system and software engineering, numerous detailed methodologies have been proposed to deliver IT projects. For simplicity, the whole variety of these methodologies can be reduced to two classic contrasting families of approaches that largely define the current professional discourse in this field: waterfall and agile.

On the one hand, **waterfall methodologies** represent a family of deterministic, disciplined and "heavyweight" approaches to project delivery[6]. These approaches are characterized by strictly sequential, step-wise project lifecycles that progress linearly from design to development to testing to deployment, resulting in "big bang" deliverables in the form of entire information systems. They imply significant upfront planning, rely on careful analysis, try to capture all requirements in advance and tend to create voluminous supporting documentation. Waterfall methodologies have been in the industry since the early days of software engineering. The most prominent branded methodologies leaning towards the waterfall attitude originated and matured during the 1990s–2000s and include, for instance, Rational Unified Process (RUP) and earlier Rapid Application Development (RAD)[7].

On the other hand, **agile methodologies** represent a family of adaptive, loose and "lightweight" approaches to project delivery[8]. These approaches are characterized by iterative project lifecycles that progress spirally release by release, producing incremental deliverables in the form of small pieces of new system functionality. They do not require substantial forward planning, leverage rapid feedback, adapt to changing requirements and generate little or no intermediate documents (importantly, some high-level planning actually happens for all projects as part of their planning phase, as shown in Figure 2.2, irrespective of their delivery approach, but these plans are too abstract to guide their delivery activities on a day-to-day basis). Agile methodologies entered the industry in the late 1990s, when web-based IT systems became prevalent. The most famous labeled methodologies that can be classified as agile emerged and flourished during the 2000s–2010s and include, among others, Scrum, Extreme Programming (XP), Crystal and earlier Dynamic Systems Development Method (DSDM)[9].

Due to their inherent strengths and weaknesses, neither waterfall nor agile methodologies are universal and can work effectively for all projects[10]. Instead, the choice of an appropriate delivery methodology is project-specific and contingent on numerous factors such as the clarity of scope, requirements and priorities, the presence of external dependencies, immutable constraints, strict regulatory and safety requirements, revertability of design decisions, ease of redeployment, as well as some other circumstances. For example, an isolated, non-security-critical web application that can be redeployed in one click to make its latest updates instantly available to end users can be best delivered with agile methodologies. By contrast, a high-load payment processing system that integrates with many other IT systems and requires purchasing expensive hardware components definitely demands more thoughtful treatment associated with waterfall methodologies. Without diving into further details, the following simple rule of thumb can be formulated: agile methodologies tend to work better for software application projects, whereas waterfall methodologies — for hardware infrastructure projects[11].

Moreover, all well-known waterfall and agile methodologies represent merely coherent sets of prescriptive guidelines proposed by someone in the industry as recommended means for delivering information systems. In practice, however, because of the uniqueness of each project and other complexities of the real world, these methodologies can be regarded only as *naive archetypes* of approaches none of which is likely to work successfully in its pure form, exactly as described[12]. For this reason, various delivery methodologies should be considered more as collections of ideas to pick from, while the concepts of waterfall and agile — as idealized antagonistic antipodes that are not incompatible, but allow all sorts of mixed variations and gradients between "black and white". In fact, most projects in organizations combine some elements of both the waterfall and agile philosophies in different proportions to compose more balanced methodologies[13]. As a rule, the more reversible the project decisions, the more agile features its delivery methodology may contain, and vice versa.

Consequently, the division between waterfall and agile should be viewed as a continuous spectrum of possible delivery methodologies between the two opposite extremes of absolute rigidity and total flexibility. The differences between waterfall and agile methodologies for project delivery, as well as the spectrum of their possible hybrids, are summarized in Figure 2.8.

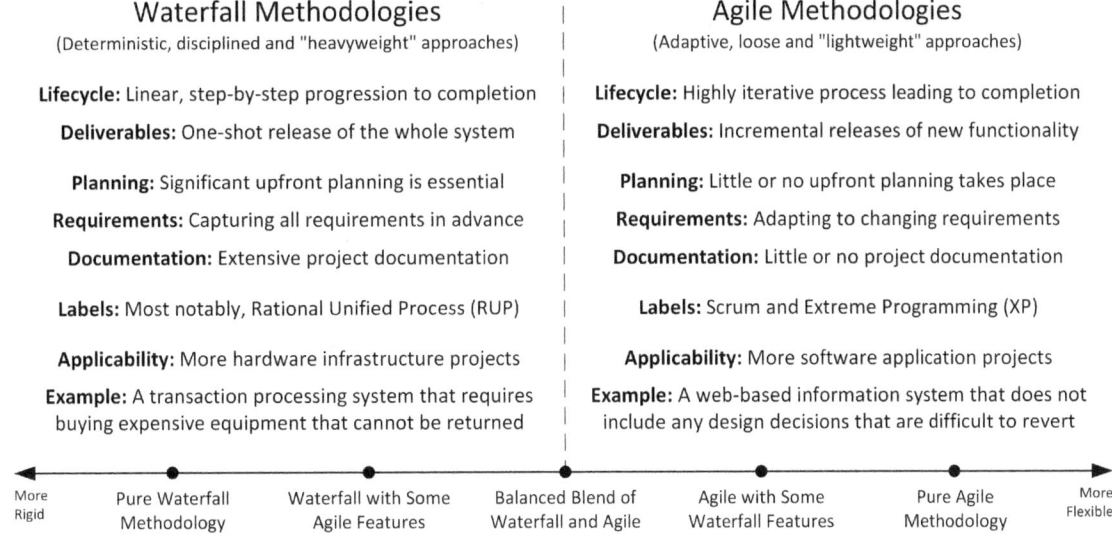

Figure 2.8. Waterfall and agile methodologies for project delivery

Selecting suitable delivery methodologies is crucial for succeeding with system development efforts and coping with the common challenges of software engineering, e.g. ever-changing requirements, unrealistic estimations and quality issues. These methodologies are, however, irrelevant to higher-level challenges accompanying digital transformation initiatives in organizations.

Challenges of Implementing Digital Transformation Initiatives

As noted earlier, the typical technical and organizational challenges of digital transformation generally affect all digitalization efforts in organizations, regardless of their magnitude (see Figure 1.5). However, owing to significant differences in the properties of different types of transformation initiatives attributed to their size and position in the initiative hierarchy (see Figure 2.5), these challenges are distributed unevenly across their spectrum. Specifically, the severity of technical and organizational challenges associated with particular digitalization initiatives is determined by two main factors respectively: technical granularity and stakeholder diversity.

First, **technical granularity** represents the extent to which the IT-specific details of transformation initiatives should be elaborated. This factor necessitates diving directly into low-level technicalities, making numerous minute design decisions and dealing with difficult technology choices, integration problems and security threats. For these reasons, the factor of technical granularity complicates digitalization initiatives from the IT side and increases their technical challenges.

Second, **stakeholder diversity** represents the quantity and variety of stakeholders and their interests that should be satisfied by transformation initiatives (see Figure 1.4). This factor strengthens the contradictions about the desired initiative outcomes and ways of their achievement, intensifies disputes within the stakeholder community and renders finding a reasonable balance between the existing interests much trickier. For these reasons, the factor of stakeholder diversity complicates digitalization initiatives from the business side and amplifies their organizational challenges.

Therefore, technical granularity and stakeholder diversity are the key determinants of the challenges accompanying digital transformation initiatives. These factors can be used as two independent measurement scales to assess the magnitude of technical and organizational challenges for change initiatives at different levels of the initiative hierarchy.

At the bottom of the initiative hierarchy, projects represent the most local and down-to-earth digitalization initiatives. Because they are executed physically by introducing new information systems into the corporate IT landscape (see Figure 2.7), projects demand a thorough elaboration in terms of IT-specific details, rank high on the technical granularity scale and face technical challenges of digital transformation in full. At the same time, by virtue of their clear motives, limited scope and narrow audience (see Figure 2.4), projects involve relatively few stakeholders with conflicting interests, rank low on the stakeholder diversity scale and encounter fairly mild organizational challenges on the way to their realization.

In the middle of the initiative hierarchy, programs represent rather broad and abstractive digitalization initiatives. Even though they are not executed physically in a way similar to projects (see Figure 2.6), they still require making many IT-related choices touching the details of technology. Because of their multiple motives, considerable scope and wide stakeholder circle (see Figure 2.4), they also have to wade through various conflicts of interests between their participants. Accordingly, programs rank average on both the technical granularity and stakeholder diversity scales and experience moderate technical and organizational challenges of digital transformation.

At the top of the initiative hierarchy, strategies represent the most comprehensive and abstract digitalization initiatives. As they are never executed in a physical sense but only spawn derivative programs and projects, strategies imply purely conceptual IT-related decisions very distant from their details, rank low on the technical granularity scale and bear only a modest burden of technical challenges. However, due to the plurality of their motives, extensive scope and multifarious constituencies (see Figure 2.4), strategies involve numerous stakeholders with mutually incompatible interests and goals, rank high on the stakeholder diversity scale and face tremendous organizational challenges during their implementation[14].

Generally, with regard to the challenges associated with digitalization initiatives at different hierarchical levels, the factors of technical granularity and stakeholder diversity work in opposite directions. On the one hand, higher-level initiatives tend to be more conceptual, stay farther from any IT-specific details and, thus, be less affected by technical challenges. On the other hand, higher-level, larger initiatives also tend to have more stakeholders, include more conflicting interests and, thus, be more affected by organizational challenges. In short, with the increase in the level and size of initiatives, their technical challenges diminish, while organizational challenges mount. The dependence of technical and organizational challenges on the level of digital transformation initiatives is illustrated schematically in Figure 2.9.

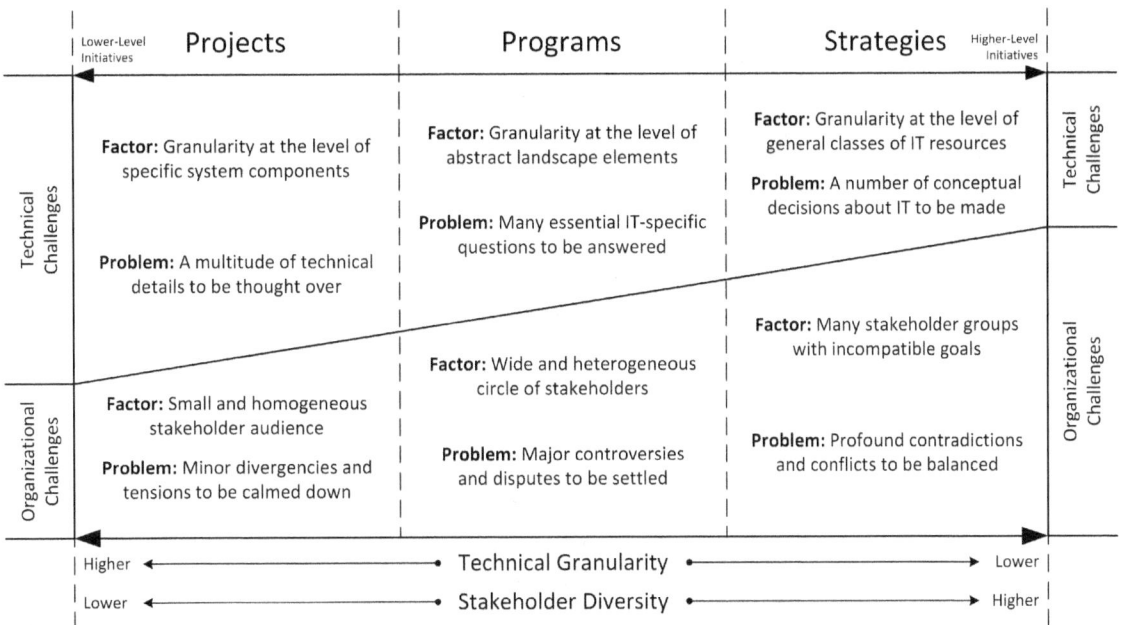

Figure 2.9. Challenges of implementing digitalization initiatives at different levels

Although the proportion of technical and organizational challenges for projects, programs and strategies varies greatly, their "total" volume stays roughly the same for all transformation initiatives across the size spectrum, as demonstrated in Figure 2.9. These challenges are unavoidable, cannot be ignored by organizations as nonexistent or dealt with haphazardly in an ad hoc fashion, but demand systematic treatment via meaningful architectural planning.

Chapter Summary

This chapter introduced digital transformation initiatives with their initial ideation, phased implementation process and different stakeholder groups, discussed the hierarchy of transformation initiatives and their implementation at different levels, described the project delivery process with waterfall and agile delivery methodologies and explained the challenges of implementing different types of digitalization initiatives. The core message of this chapter can be summarized in the following major points:

- Digital transformation initiatives are concrete change initiatives with business and IT components that structure organizational digitalization efforts into meaningful, coherent and manageable pieces of change with specific goals
- Initial ideation is a continuous organizational process of generating ideas for new digitalization initiatives based on the current motivational context the overall meaning of which can be best summarized as drivers-to-ideas
- The initiative implementation process is a sequence of activities that need to be performed to materialize the intended change with three phases: conception (idea-to-concept), planning (concept-to-plan) and execution (plan-to-delivery)

- Initiative stakeholders are organizational actors pursuing certain interests in digitalization initiatives and participating in their implementation processes, where initiative sponsors promote the very need to implement these initiatives and initiative executors immediately participate in their execution
- Digital transformation initiatives can be classified based on their size into projects (atomic pieces of work), programs (series of related projects) and strategies (sets of programs and projects), forming a three-level nested initiative hierarchy
- Autonomous initiatives are independent initiatives that have no parents and are launched on their own, whereas derivative initiatives are dependent initiatives that are strongly affiliated with their parents and launched as part of them
- In the hierarchy of strategies, programs and projects, high-level initiatives are executed by launching lower-level derivative initiatives and only projects are executed physically at the delivery level by constructing new information systems
- Project delivery process is a sequence of actions with three steps, building, testing and deployment, performed by multidisciplinary project teams to develop new IT systems based on the existing plans following waterfall or agile methodologies
- Technical challenges of initiatives are determined by their technical granularity (highest for projects, lowest for strategies), while organizational challenges — by their stakeholder diversity (lowest for projects, highest for strategies)

Chapter 3: Architectural Planning

The previous chapter discussed digital transformation initiatives, their implementation processes and accompanying challenges. This chapter introduces the concept of architectural planning as the necessary organizational response to the challenges of digital transformation. In particular, this chapter begins with explaining the meaning of architectural planning with its primary and secondary stakeholders and disparate technical and organizational sides. Then, this chapter describes the organizational domains relevant to architectural planning, their representation as a multilayer stack and the conceptual differences between them from a planning perspective. Finally, this chapter discusses the specifics of multilevel architectural planning of hierarchical digitalization initiatives in organizations.

The Notion of Architectural Planning

Succeeding with digital transformation endeavors in organizations portends many business benefits, but requires coping with diverse challenges of a technical and organizational nature that hinder the implementation of the respective initiatives (see Figure 1.5). These challenges, in turn, can hardly be overcome without practicing disciplined architectural planning.

Architectural planning is the overall process of developing optimal architectural solutions for digital transformation initiatives addressing both their technical and organizational challenges. Architectural planning represents a complicated *organizational* effort that unites all the relevant actors, activities, documents and other elements necessary to work out reasonable courses of action for IT-driven business transformations. Due to its inherent complexity, this effort demands a well-coordinated collaboration of multiple participants from the business and IT sides of the organization.

In the organizational mechanism, architectural planning is accomplished during the planning phase of the initiative implementation process (see Figure 2.2) and constitutes a major part of this phase. As digitalization initiatives of disparate sizes experience analogous challenges (see Figure 2.9), architectural planning equally applies to projects, programs and strategies (see Figure 2.4). Besides that, numerous implicit manifestations of architectural planning in a broader sense spread far beyond the planning phase of specific change initiatives and pervade many other, more general IT-related decision-making processes in organizations.

Architectural planning does not deal with all possible planning decisions pertaining to transformation initiatives, but only with architectural decisions. **Architectural decisions** represent a broad class of planning decisions relevant specifically to the *structure* of the organizational business and IT landscape. For example, various decisions about financing (e.g. whether to use own funds or borrowed money), sourcing (e.g. where to find IT staff with the required skills) and procurement (e.g. from which supplier to purchase the necessary equipment) are not considered architectural and lie out of the scope of architectural planning. In other words, architectural planning concentrates on the very *substance* of transformation and determines what is to be done as part of the initiative, i.e. how exactly the organization should be changed from business and IT viewpoints.

In the context of architectural planning, **architectural solutions** for digital transformation initiatives should be understood specifically as comprehensive sets of coherent architectural decisions covering all business and IT aspects of these initiatives in their wholeness (importantly, this term should *not* be confused with IT solutions as physical information systems arising from initiatives, as discussed earlier). Architectural solutions for transformation initiatives define both the actions necessary to implement these initiatives and their expected beneficial consequences. Simply put, they explain what will be done as part of initiatives as well as why it is good for the organization. Finalized solutions indicate both the desire and readiness of the organization to execute the initiative.

Developed architectural solutions for digitalization initiatives are captured and documented in material architectural plans. **Architectural plans** are tangible deliverables reflecting the resulting planning decisions made during the architectural planning of digital transformation initiatives. As architectural solutions for transformation initiatives address both their technical and organizational facets, the corresponding plans also consist of technical components (e.g. changes in the composition of the IT landscape) and organizational components (e.g. changes in the conduct of business activities). Similarly to architectural decisions, these plans represent only a subset of the entire collection of plans that can be prepared for initiatives, e.g. financial plans, procurement schedules and outsourcing agreements.

Depending on the nature and scope of the respective initiatives, architectural plans can take a variety of different forms and contain very diverse information. For example, they can be embodied, among others, in the following formats:

- For projects — rather detailed blueprints of specific IT solutions depicting the structure of their internal system components as well as the relationship between these components and business operations that they automate
- For programs — relatively abstract investment schedules outlining the desired future spendings on new IT systems, their anticipated impact on the business of the organization and their contribution to its long-term objectives
- For strategies — highly conceptual imperatives, rules and suggestions for prospective information systems with the justification of their necessity from a business point of view and their linkage to the organizational strategic context

After being produced by means of architectural planning within the planning phase of transformation initiatives, architectural plans guide the subsequent activities during their execution phase — either the launching of derivative initiatives at lower levels, or the physical delivery efforts of project teams (see Figure 2.6 and Figure 2.7). As a result, architectural solutions developed for these initiatives materialize and turn into reality. The logical relationship between the planning and execution phases of digital transformation initiatives, architectural planning, architectural decisions, solutions and plans is shown in Figure 3.1.

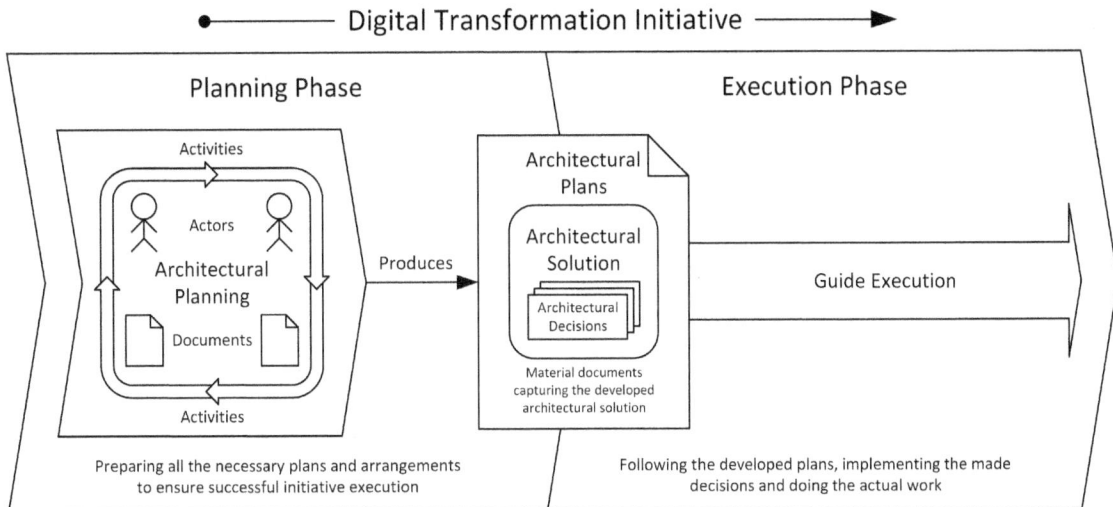

Figure 3.1. Architectural planning, decisions, solutions and plans in the initiative context

As a complex organizational activity, architectural planning involves multiple actors cooperating to develop optimal architectural solutions for digitalization initiatives. All these actors can be viewed as stakeholders of architectural planning.

Stakeholders of Architectural Planning

Stakeholders of architectural planning are a broad subgroup of initiative stakeholders having certain interests specifically in architectural decisions and participating in the architectural planning of digital transformation initiatives, thereby shaping their architectural solutions. Because most stakeholder interests relate, in one way or another, to the landscape structure, the vast majority of initiative stakeholders, if not all of them, actually become the stakeholders of architectural planning and get involved in the respective processes. Although every employee can possibly turn into a stakeholder of some transformation initiative, all potential stakeholders of architectural planning can be loosely separated into primary and secondary ones.

Primary stakeholders of architectural planning include business representatives of all functional areas and corporate levels, from C-level management all the way down the administrative hierarchy (see Figure 1.4). These people are responsible for operating the organization, serving customers, generating profits and producing other valuable outcomes. They are both the patrons and final "consumers" of resulting organizational changes, standing behind all business-side transformation drivers (see Figure 1.2). For this reason, these stakeholders typically constitute a powerful subgroup of initiative sponsors and represent key decision-makers, who have the "last word" and whose interests are paramount in architectural planning (see Figure 2.3). Even though their specific positions and even functional specializations are virtually innumerable, primary stakeholders can be loosely clustered based on their level in the corporate hierarchy, which determines the scope and time horizon of their concerns, into three categories:

- **Business executives** — top-tier business managers accountable for different aspects of the whole organization with an outlook of 3–5 years or longer and interested in adding maximum strategic value with each transformation initiative
- **Business managers** — mid-level business leaders responsible for specific business functions or units with a horizon of about 2–3 years and interested in gaining maximum tactical value for their own areas
- **Business specialists** — rank-and-file business staff performing concrete business processes and routine daily tasks with a short-term perspective of 1–2 years and interested in improving their particular operations

Secondary stakeholders of architectural planning include various IT representatives. These people usually belong to the subgroup of initiative executors and rarely become the sponsors or ultimate beneficiaries of digital transformation (see Figure 2.3). Nevertheless, their concerns often influence the success of change initiatives and, thus, cannot be neglected. Moreover, at times, they can promote purely technical concerns as independent, full-fledged IT-side transformation drivers. Although IT representatives of different profiles can have different interests in matters of digitalization, the three most typical groups of secondary stakeholders of architectural planning can be articulated:

- **Subject-matter experts** — all sorts of specialists with deep but narrow expertise in specific technologies, products or subject areas (e.g. telephony equipment, SAP ERP or cybersecurity) interested in their proper utilization or treatment
- **Project team members** — all IT specialists involved in project delivery (e.g. software developers, infrastructure engineers and project managers, see Figure 2.7) interested in ensuring the practical feasibility of the proposed action plans
- **Operations specialists** — all IT representatives responsible for keeping information systems up and running and interested in ensuring their operational stability and the overall resilience of the corporate IT infrastructure

All these and other groups of actors can be the stakeholders of digital transformation initiatives and take part in their architectural planning. However, concrete lists of stakeholders are always initiative-specific and depend on the nature, size and impact of the respective initiatives. For example, the proportion of business executives, managers and specialists among the initiative stakeholders certainly varies for strategies, programs and projects as larger initiatives require the involvement of more senior decision-makers. Or, members of project teams come as stakeholders mainly for projects as higher-level transformation initiatives are purely conceptual and their execution does not imply any direct changes in the organizational landscape. Potential groups of stakeholders with their basic interests in the context of architectural planning are shown in Figure 3.2.

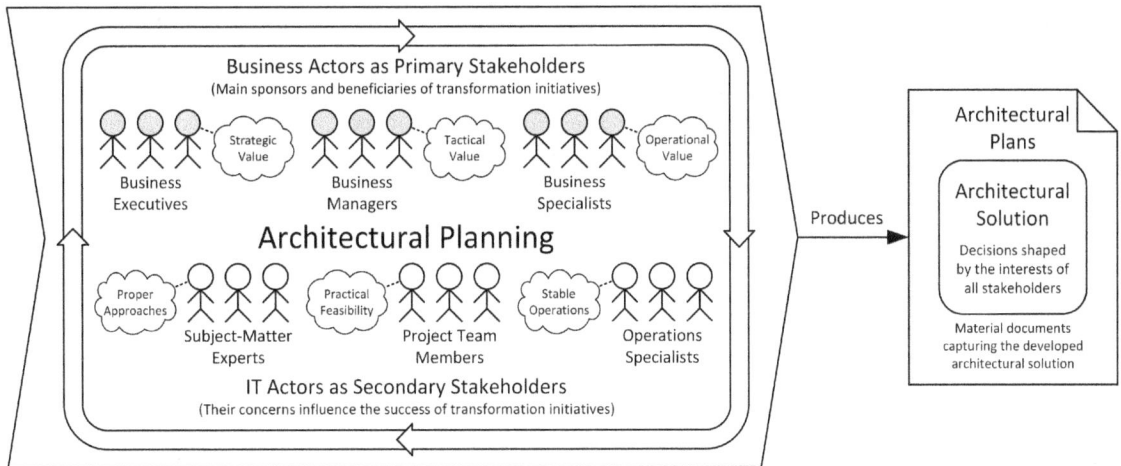

Figure 3.2. Potential stakeholders of architectural planning and their typical interests

Architectural planning deals with technical and organizational challenges of digital transformation. On the one hand, addressing technical challenges requires deciding on the *means* of transformation and making *factual* judgments based on a simple criterion of fitness-for-purpose. On the other hand, addressing organizational challenges requires deciding on the *ends* of transformation and making *value-laden* judgments that imply defining the ultimate purpose itself[1]. Due to the disparate character of these challenges, as well as of their solutions, the meaning of architectural planning can be best understood if its technical and organizational sides are first analyzed separately.

The Technical Side of Architectural Planning

Technical challenges of digital transformation can be attributed to the complexity of the external IT environment and the internal IT landscape, e.g. an overwhelming multitude of available products and technologies, entangled interconnections between numerous landscape components and ever-increasing sophistication of cybersecurity threats (see Figure 1.5). These challenges all refer to some or the other IT-specific design choices united by the common motive of producing adequate, robust and fit-for-purpose information systems, which is familiar to and shared by all IT experts.

Accordingly, the corresponding technical components of architectural solutions for digital transformation initiatives, or simply **technical solutions**, represent consistent sets of purely technical planning decisions regarding the *structure* of the proposed changes in the corporate IT landscape. For example, a technical solution for a digitalization initiative may include, but is not limited to, the following decisions:

- What new systems, or classes of systems, will be installed into the IT landscape
- What technologies will be used to construct them, how and why
- Which legacy systems will be replaced or removed from the landscape
- Where the necessary input information will be obtained and in what formats
- Where the resulting output will be sent to and which protocols will encrypt it
- How potential outages will be handled and where data backups will be stored

Because IT provides the very means of digital transformation, technical solutions naturally cover more the *actionable* part of the respective initiatives and define mostly *what* needs to be done to implement them, though they also explain the technology-specific rationales and benefits of the planned actions. As these solutions determine only the ways of achieving certain business aims, their correctness can be judged based on factual premises using the criterion of efficiency, i.e. whether a solution fully meets the business needs with minimum possible resources. Put it simply, technical solutions can be considered optimal if they offer optimal means to given ends.

The solution space of potential technical solutions for any digitalization initiative is bounded and lies within the tight overlap of business requirements and technology capabilities. Obviously, technical solutions should implement the requested functionality and satisfy other business demands. At the same time, they can only be built with existing technologies and cannot provide what is technically impossible. This combination of business and technology constraints on technical solutions makes their solution space rather narrow and fixed.

Due to the clarity of the ultimate goal, relative unambiguity of requisite criteria and limited solution space, technical challenges of digital transformation highly resemble traditional *engineering* tasks and can be tackled largely by analytical means. Consequently, technical solutions can be mostly designed by individual experts with broad IT competence, or small groups of complementary specialists, based on stipulated business requirements. To do that, the following question should be meaningfully answered: "What solution is feasible technically?" For instance, an IT expert can study the technology market and select the most suitable technologies for the stated business problem, idea or need, examine the current IT landscape and find the best approach to integrate the new system, analyze security risks and devise appropriate protective measures. In this case, the quality of the resulting solution wholly depends on the talent and proficiency of its creator and is determined, more or less objectively, by its technical attributes, cost efficiency, alignment with requirements and adherence to acknowledged best practices.

In summary, the technical side of architectural planning implies developing technical solutions to technical challenges of digital transformation. As these solutions are engineering by their nature and require deep IT expertise, effective architectural planning must involve competent IT professionals capable of designing decent technical solutions on behalf of the organization.

The Organizational Side of Architectural Planning

Organizational challenges of digital transformation can be attributed to the complexity of the relationship between business and IT over different time horizons, e.g. a wide variety of ways of achieving synergy between business activities and information systems, debatable relative advantages of some or the other IT solutions on the whole, multiplied by various regulatory complications (see Figure 1.5). Unlike technical challenges, these challenges are inherently multidisciplinary. They do not belong to any single field or area of expertise, but always combine many disparate aspects (e.g. strategic, tactical, operational, financial and legal) and motives specific to different functional areas.

Therefore, the corresponding organizational components of architectural solutions for digital transformation initiatives, or simply **organizational solutions**, are also multi-aspect, or multidimensional, and aggregate certain business planning decisions regarding the overall *value* of these initiatives for organizations based on the entirety of all their aspects. For example, an organizational solution for a digitalization initiative may include, but is not limited to, the following decisions:

- What processes will be automated and which capabilities will be uplifted
- How business departments should be restructured and which roles will be affected
- What strategic contribution and operational improvements will be achieved
- When the initiative and its major components can be delivered
- What efforts and expenditures are necessary to implement and support it
- What operational, regulatory and security risks will be accepted

Because positive changes in the way of doing business represent the very purpose of digital transformation, organizational solutions naturally cover more the *motivational* part of the respective initiatives and explain mostly *why* they are needed in the current motivational context (see Figure 1.3), though they also define the business actions that should be taken to implement them. As these solutions determine the aims of transformation initiatives, their correctness cannot be judged based on any objective factual premises, but only subjectively, depending on the adopted system of values, i.e. whether a solution pursues what is *deemed* valuable for the company. For this reason, organizational solutions can be considered optimal if they are believed to be optimal.

Their intrinsic "arbitrariness" makes organizational solutions much more open-ended than technical solutions. While the solution space of possible technical solutions is always limited and strictly bound to concrete business requirements, for organizational solutions this space encompasses essentially all imaginable business ideas, or whatever business people may wish. Interestingly, in some cases, the most optimal organizational solution can be simply to alter manual work processes without touching any IT systems or even to leave everything as it is, do not introduce any changes and cancel the initiative.

Since each of the organizational aspects and functional areas is characterized by its own objectives, preferences and constraints, which are often inconsistent with those of others, organizational challenges pose the problem of multicriteria optimization, where a solution should be optimized along many dimensions at the same time, e.g. provide both instantaneous and long-term benefits in all areas as soon as possible and for the lowest price. As in organizations these dimensions are "owned" and advocated by different actors, organizational challenges of digital transformation require reaching a *political* compromise on what solution is desired and can be resolved only via *negotiations* between multiple constituencies — stakeholders representing different corporate levels and functional areas with their own views, interests, motives and opinions (see Figure 3.2). These negotiations are further complicated by a virtually unlimited solution space of organizational solutions.

For this reason, organizational solutions cannot be designed by any one person in a similar way to technical solutions, but only developed collaboratively, through intense dialog with the involvement of all relevant parties, based on the balance of their interests, though within the possibilities and constraints of technology. To do that, the following question should be meaningfully answered: "What solution is desirable organizationally?" For instance, stakeholders of a digital transformation initiative can schedule a series of meetings to discuss possible initiative implementation options taking into account everyone's considerations and eventually come up with the best mutually acceptable solution[2]. In this case, the quality of the resulting solution can only be assessed subjectively, by the extent to which a reasonable trade-off between different interests has been achieved[3].

To summarize, the organizational side of architectural planning implies developing organizational solutions to organizational challenges of digital transformation. As these solutions are political in principle and require searching for compromise, effective architectural planning must be participative and involve the representatives of different groups of interest to reach a consensus solution.

Architectural Planning in Its Full Complexity

The technical and organizational sides of architectural planning discussed above are by no means separate or incompatible, but present only different perspectives on the very same activity. Furthermore, either of these sides can be clearly interpreted from the standpoint of the other. Namely, the desired engineering qualities of a technical solution can be viewed merely as another aspect of a broader organizational solution to be negotiated among its stakeholders, whereas the political acceptability of an organizational solution for its stakeholders can be viewed merely as another "business requirement" for a technical solution to be met by its designers.

Technical and organizational solutions also actually refer to different sides of the very same architectural solution and are inseparable from each other. Needless to say, most solution options have both technical and organizational consequences. For instance, the functional capabilities of a technical solution are determined by what is desirable to the organization, but the attractiveness of an organizational solution, in turn, depends on its price ensuing from the costs of implementing these capabilities. And yet, technical solutions can be designed by IT experts, but organizational solutions must be reached collectively.

For these reasons, architectural planning implies a very intricate *interplay* of engineering and political activities, while any architectural solution for a digital transformation initiative always represents a complex compromise between various technical features (e.g. functionality, throughput, reliability and security) and organizational qualities (e.g. business impact, strategic value, immediate and delayed costs). The planning process, thus, involves finding an optimal trade-off between all these parameters and composing the whole architectural solution as the unity of disparate engineering and political components[4]. The overall meaning of architectural planning with its technical and organizational sides and their interrelationship discussed above is depicted schematically in Figure 3.3.

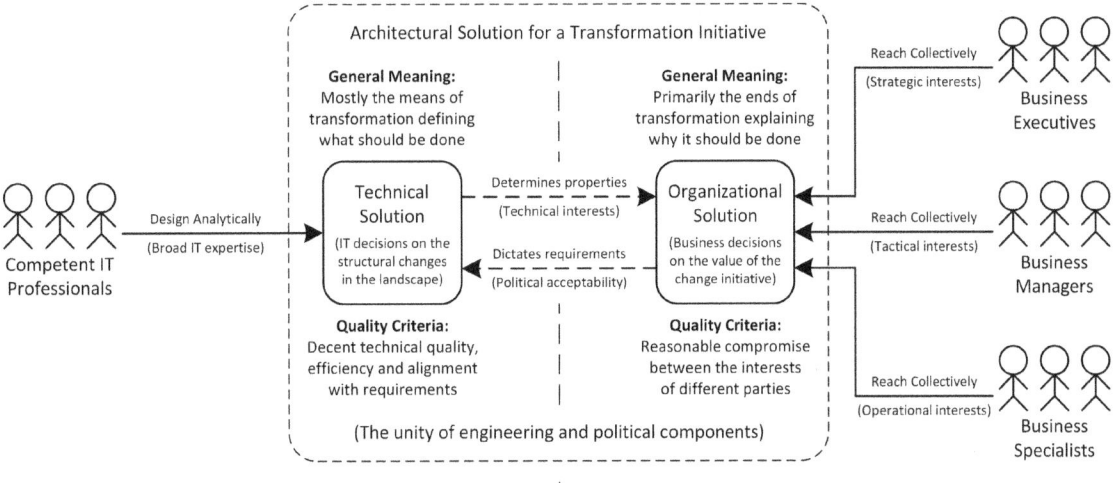

Figure 3.3. Architectural planning with its technical and organizational sides

As shown in Figure 3.3, architectural planning, as a complex socio-technical effort, cannot be accomplished by a single person or a small group of people, but only collaboratively with the involvement of members of multiple diverse occupational communities. On its technical side, the presence of IT professionals with proper qualifications is essential for designing technical solutions that determine their physical structure. On its organizational side, the presence of business representatives of different profiles is essential for shaping organizational solutions that determine their fitness for the organization.

Although technical and organizational solutions are disparate in their qualities and methods of development, both of them are integral parts of architectural solutions for digital transformation initiatives. As IT supplies the means of transformation, technical solutions are necessary to define exactly how these means will be applied to transform the organization. As the ends of transformation are determined by the anticipated increments of business value, organizational solutions are necessary to motivate, justify and fund the transformation in light of the existing drivers. Without achieving certainty on both their means and ends in the form of elaborate technical and organizational solutions, digitalization initiatives in organizations cannot be launched[5].

Organizational Domains Relevant to Architectural Planning

Architectural solutions for digitalization initiatives with their technical and organizational components comprise numerous planning decisions touching various business and IT aspects of organizations (see Figure 3.3). Different aspects of organizations affected by digital transformation and addressed in architectural solutions are usually called domains. In the context of architectural planning, **organizational domains** represent coherent, logically distinct areas of concern relevant to digital transformation initiatives and their architectural solutions. Jointly, these domains fully cover the organization with its IT landscape from all viewpoints necessary and sufficient for composing comprehensive technical and organizational solutions for change initiatives.

Although there is no single right or best way to split the organization and its IT infrastructure into separate domains[6], in practice six different domains pertinent to architectural planning are typically distinguished: business, applications, data, integration, infrastructure and security[7]. Each of these domains spotlights a rather narrow subset of concepts, objects and entities from the entire organizational system.

Specifically, the **business domain** encompasses everything that belongs to the business side of the organization. This domain includes, for example, business geographies, locations and points of presence, business structures, departments and units, business capabilities, value streams and operations, business processes, tasks and roles, supply chains, cash flows and customer experience.

The **applications domain** embraces all software systems, applications and their components that support the execution of business activities in the organization. This domain includes end-user applications, enterprise systems and batch processing jobs, offline programs, online websites and mobile apps, programming tools, frameworks and libraries, bespoke software, vendor products and cloud-based software as a service (SaaS).

The **data domain** comprises all logical data entities that the organization operates with and their physical storage. This domain includes conceptual data objects, their structures and representation formats, relational, graph and key–value databases, master data sources, synchronous replicas and archival backup copies, transactional datastores, data warehouses and reporting dashboards, cloud buckets, data lakes and big data.

The **integration domain** covers all integration platforms, mechanisms and approaches used in the organization to interconnect different IT systems and data sources. This domain includes application programming interfaces (APIs) and invocation formats, interaction protocols and remote procedure calls (RPCs), integration buses and message-oriented middleware as well as extract, transform, load (ETL) and extract, load, transform (ELT) data manipulation tools.

The **infrastructure domain** encompasses all underlying hardware infrastructure and system software necessary to host information systems in the organization. This domain includes physical servers, disk arrays and network equipment, virtual containers, orchestration engines and hypervisors, operating systems, virtual machines and utility programs, resource scheduling, monitoring and alerting tools, closed-circuit television (CCTV), telephony and cabling, data centers, private clouds and external cloud-based infrastructure as a service (IaaS).

Lastly, the **security domain** comprises all software, devices and equipment intended to protect the organization from cybersecurity threats, risks and breaches. This domain includes network firewalls, traffic filters and analyzers, authentication approaches, identity and access management services, cryptographic protocols, secure channels and virtual private networks (VPNs), intrusion detection and prevention systems, honeypots and anti-malware.

The six organizational domains outlined above reflect dissimilar categories of issues that should be taken care of as part of architectural planning. These domains, however, are pretty high-level and somewhat notional as their boundaries can be rather blurred. Moreover, each of them can be further separated into more narrow subdomains. For example, the applications domain can be decomposed into mobile apps, web-based applications, backend systems and batch processing, whereas the data domain can be subdivided into operational databases, master data management, data warehousing and real-time analytics. Besides that, for young, cloud-native organizations relying solely on SaaS solutions and other applications deployed in the public cloud and having no own hosting infrastructure, the very infrastructure domain can be largely irrelevant.

The Stack of Organizational Domains

The six major domains of organizations — business, applications, data, integration, infrastructure and security — are strongly intertwined as each element from any domain can be somehow bound to one or many elements from other domains. Nonetheless, taken together, they can be roughly viewed as a multilayer **domain stack**, where its higher layers are buttressed by its lower layers. Namely, the business domain represents the top layer of the stack, which is built upon all the other IT-related layers. The applications domain automates business operations and activities from the business domain. The data domain provides information to be processed by applications and systems from the applications domain. The integration domain offers the means of interlinking various applications and data sources from the applications and data domains. The infrastructure domain hosts all applications, databases and integration platforms from the respective domains. And finally, the security domain permeates all the above domains by embedding the necessary security measures into their elements. The six organizational domains relevant to architectural planning and the relationships between them in the form of a multilayer stack are illustrated in Figure 3.4.

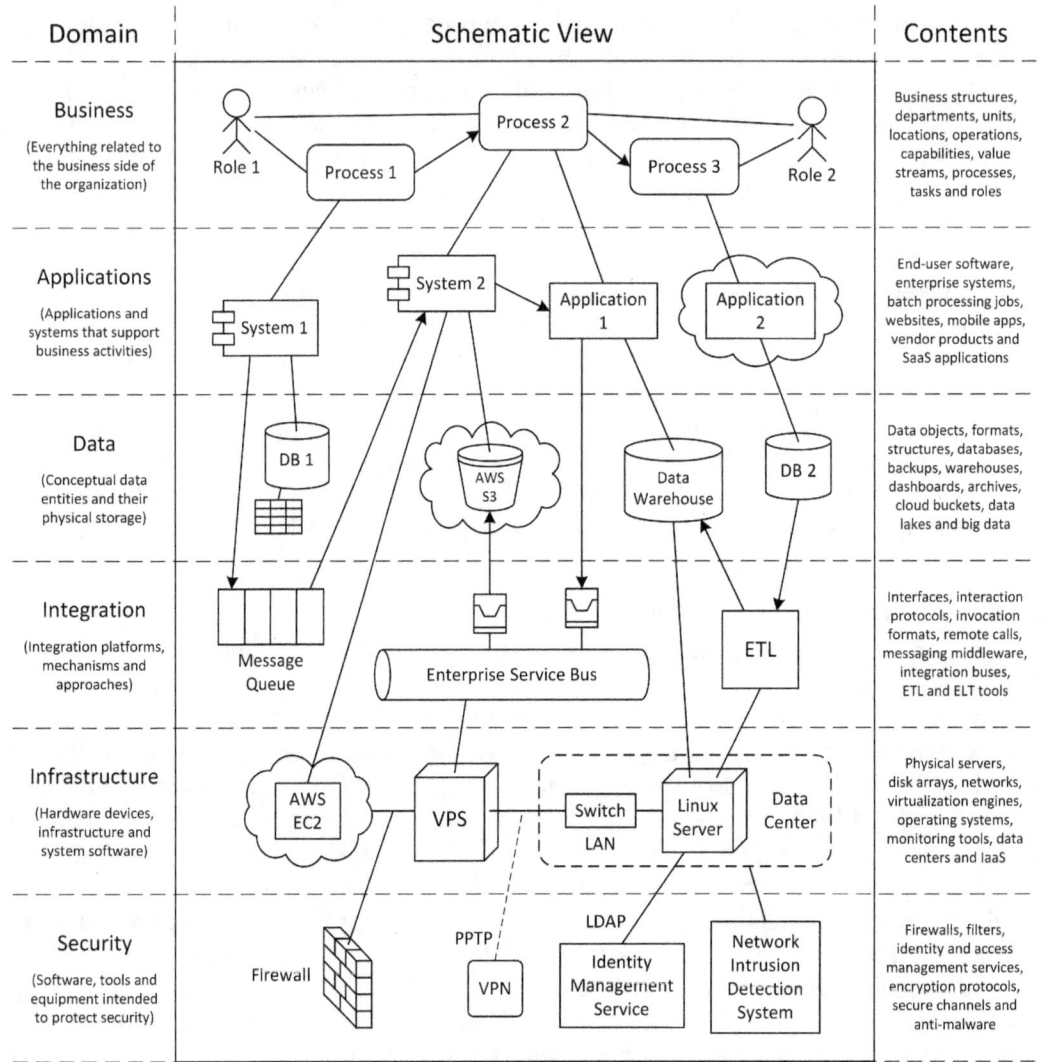

Figure 3.4. The stack of the six organizational domains relevant to architectural planning

In this interpretation as an ordered stack, different organizational domains can be regarded largely as separate layers of the corporate landscape, descending from the topmost layer of business activities down to the middle layers of business applications and data to the bottom layers of technical infrastructure and security.

Differences Between Organizational Domains

The six key domains constituting the stack depicted above represent disparate facets of organizations that have little or nothing in common. Unsurprisingly, these domains have very different properties in the context of architectural planning. Specifically, the six organizational domains can be classified in at least three different ways helping better understand their distinctive features.

First, from the perspective of their relationship to technology, all organizational domains can be divided into technical domains and non-technical domains. **Technical domains** are technology-specific and directly relate to some or the other technologies. Their comprehension requires highly specialized knowledge and simply cannot be achieved by an ordinary business manager. All organizational domains except business evidently represent technical domains and, in many contexts, can even be viewed collectively as a single IT domain. For instance, software systems, database engines, integration platforms, hardware equipment and security devices all clearly refer to the underlying technologies and can hardly be understood adequately without the appropriate education.

By contrast, **non-technical domains** are technology-neutral and unrelated to any particular technologies. Their adequate understanding does not require any specialized knowledge or expertise, but only general business background and outlook. Of the six "classic" organizational domains, only the business domain can be considered fully non-technical, though logical aspects of information from the data domain also belong to this category. Obviously, such notions as customer needs, business processes, product characteristics, profits and losses have nothing to do with technology. The main differences between technical and non-technical domains described above are summarized in Table 3.1.

Classification	Technical domains	Non-technical domains
Technology	Closely related to concrete technologies	Have nothing to do with technology
Knowledge	Highly specialized technical knowledge	General business knowledge and outlook
Six domains	All except business (the IT domain)	Only the business domain

Table 3.1. Technical and non-technical domains

Second, from the perspective of their relevance to business functionality, all organizational domains can be grouped into functional domains and non-functional domains. **Functional domains** define the ultimate functionality provided by information systems and determine what the business can and cannot do. Because these domains directly shape available business capabilities, they can also be called *business-enabling* domains. Planning decisions pertaining to these domains have pronounced business implications and are immediately relevant to business leaders. Of the six organizational domains, the business, applications and data domains can be regarded as functional. For example, business managers should clearly realize how their business processes will be organized, what IT systems they will use and which information will be accessible to them.

By contrast, **non-functional domains** provide the necessary foundation for information systems, but do not determine what the business can do from a functional point of view. Because these domains do not shape business capabilities directly, they can also be called *business-supporting* domains. Planning decisions related to these domains do not have apparent business consequences and are not particularly relevant to business leaders. Of the six organizational domains, the integration, infrastructure and security domains can be viewed as non-functional. For example, business managers are unlikely to be interested in exactly how their systems are integrated, where they are hosted and how they are protected, as long as they exchange the right information, are accessible and secure. The main differences between functional and non-functional domains described above are summarized in Table 3.2.

Classification	Functional domains	Non-functional domains
Functionality	Define the functionality of IT systems	Provide the foundation for IT systems
Capabilities	Shape available business capabilities	Do not shape business capabilities directly
Audience	Immediately relevant to business leaders	Mostly irrelevant to business leaders
Six domains	Business, applications and data	Integration, infrastructure and security

Table 3.2. Functional and non-functional domains

Lastly, from the perspective of their standing in the landscape, all organizational domains can be separated into substantive domains and non-substantive domains. **Substantive domains** constitute the very substance of the corporate landscape in terms of its major constituents and largely define its fundamental structure. Metaphorically, they can be compared to hard bones of the landscape that form its overall skeleton. In light of digitalization, substantive domains usually represent the prime cause for change initiatives in organizations. In other words, it is an unsatisfactory condition in these domains that tends to initiate new transformation efforts. They determine whether organizations "do the right things".

Of the six organizational domains, the business, applications and infrastructure domains can be considered substantive. For instance, the core landscape structure is typically viewed roughly as the set of business processes supported by software applications deployed on hardware infrastructure[8]. Also, change initiatives in organizations are most often motivated either by the desire to enhance business operations with new information systems (i.e. the conjunction of the business and applications domains), or by the desire to supply new IT infrastructure in anticipation of future application needs (i.e. the infrastructure domain). Some initiatives combine both these components and include, first, deploying new infrastructure and then introducing new applications with the accompanying improvements in business processes.

By contrast, **non-substantive domains** are necessary for the functioning of the corporate landscape, but do not represent its central substance. Metaphorically, they can be compared to soft tissues of the landscape that cover its basic skeleton. With regard to digital transformation, these domains relatively rarely become the prime stimuli for any change efforts, but mostly control that all initiated changes are implemented properly. They determine, for the most part, whether organizations "do things in the right way".

Of the six organizational domains, the data, integration and security domains can be considered non-substantive. For example, they tend to get much less visibility in the landscape structure than substantive domains. Also, it is rather uncommon for organizations to launch new initiatives motivated primarily by the need for changes in some of these domains, though such initiatives occasionally happen, e.g. creating a data warehouse, replacing an integration bus and installing a new traffic filtering appliance. Instead, non-substantive domains are more often affected, or disturbed, by modifications occurring in substantive domains and intend to ensure that the respective aspects are adequately addressed, e.g. new applications access the appropriate data sources and are duly integrated, while new IT infrastructure is protected from hostile interventions. The main differences between substantive and non-substantive domains described above are summarized in Table 3.3.

Classification	Substantive domains	Non-substantive domains
Landscape	Constitute the substance of the landscape	Necessary for the landscape functioning
Metaphor	Hard bones forming the landscape skeleton	Soft tissues covering the landscape skeleton
Initiatives	Cause new transformation initiatives	Ensure proper implementation of initiatives
Motive	Doing the right things	Doing things in the right way
Six domains	Business, applications and infrastructure	Data, integration and security

Table 3.3. Substantive and non-substantive domains

The differences between the six organizational domains from the standpoint of their relationship to technology, their relevance to business functionality and their standing in the landscape summed up in Table 3.1, Table 3.2 and Table 3.3 respectively have important implications for their treatment as part of architectural planning.

Coverage of Organizational Domains in Architectural Solutions

Generally, architectural solutions for digital transformation initiatives span the full stack of organizational domains, from business to security (see Figure 3.4). However, because their technical and organizational components involve quite different kinds of planning decisions (see Figure 3.3), these components cover different domains.

On the technical side of architectural planning, the respective solutions aggregate all technical planning decisions on the structure of new information systems. Therefore, technical solutions potentially cover all technical domains (see Table 3.1) as it is these domains that represent different layers of the technology stack of IT systems, from applications to security, and determine their technical quality in the eyes of IT professionals. Furthermore, designing adequate technical solutions requires achieving a sufficient level of depth in their coverage.

On the organizational side of architectural planning, the corresponding solutions combine all business planning decisions concerning the value of change initiatives for organizations. For this reason, organizational solutions potentially cover all functional domains (i.e. business, applications and data, see Table 3.2) as it is these domains that determine the business and IT capabilities of proposed solutions, their benefits and costs, and ultimately their political acceptability among different groups of business stakeholders. Even though organizational solutions also embrace such technical domains as applications and data, these domains are covered at a relatively basic level and exposed mostly from their business-facing sides, e.g. core application functionality and data analysis capabilities respectively.

While technical and organizational solutions for digitalization initiatives jointly encompass all six domains, the initiatives themselves are usually caused by the demands incoming specifically from substantive domains, rather than non-substantive ones (see Table 3.3). Technical and organizational solutions for digital transformation initiatives and the associated domains of organizations are shown schematically in Figure 3.5.

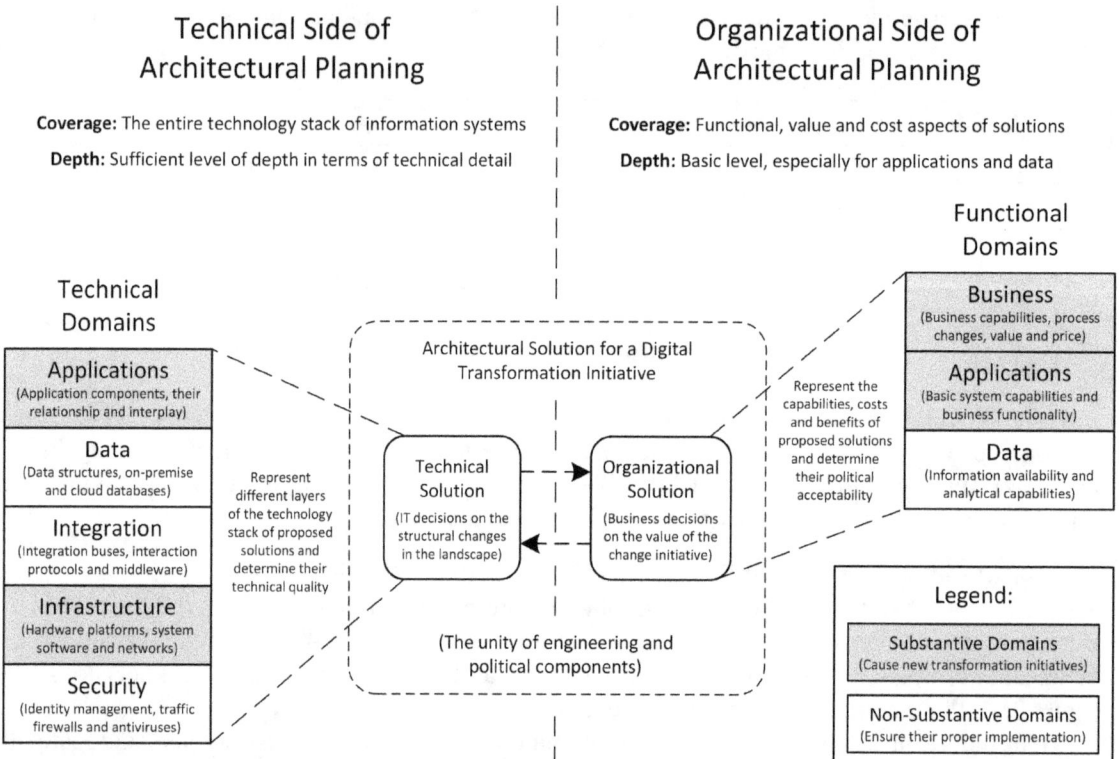

Figure 3.5. Technical and organizational solutions for initiatives and the associated domains

The generic view presented in Figure 3.5 applies to rather complex transformation initiatives and their architectural solutions that affect all six domains of organizations. However, many solutions can be simpler and modify only some organizational domains, leaving the others intact. For example, small business apps querying information directly from the existing databases and deployed on the existing infrastructure essentially touch only the business and applications domains. Also, as initiatives themselves are more often motivated by the necessity of modifications in substantive domains, some of these domains are more likely to be covered in architectural solutions, whereas non-substantive domains are more likely to be absent. For instance, most architectural solutions impact the business, applications or infrastructure domains, but many of them do not deal seriously with data, integration and security.

One noteworthy exception to the generalized situation reflected in Figure 3.5 are change initiatives that affect only non-functional domains (see Table 3.2) and have no business, applications and data elements, e.g. infrastructure initiatives building new hosting environments and connectivity arrangements. Organizational components of their architectural solutions comprise non-functional rather than functional domains and their stakeholder circles include primarily IT leaders instead of the business audience, as for regular initiatives (see Figure 3.2). Such initiatives and solutions represent a somewhat special, simplified planning scenario as in this case both their technical and organizational components are developed by people with IT background, which makes their collaboration much easier.

Architectural Planning of Hierarchical Initiatives

Similarly to technical and organizational challenges, the general logic of architectural planning with its technical and organizational sides applies to all digitalization initiatives in organizations. Hence, technical and organizational solutions have to be developed for change initiatives of all sizes at all levels of their hierarchy (see Figure 2.5). Projects, programs and strategies all consist of engineering components, which can be designed analytically by skilled IT professionals, and political components, which must be reached collectively through negotiations with broad stakeholder participation (see Figure 3.3). The content of these components in terms of covered organizational domains is also basically identical for all transformation initiatives (see Figure 3.5). And yet, some important aspects of architectural solutions and their planning do differ for different types of initiatives.

Architectural Solutions for Projects, Programs and Strategies

Even though the very pattern of technical and organizational solutions in its generic form stays perfectly valid for all transformation initiatives, the specific contents of these components can vary greatly in their granularity for initiatives at different hierarchical levels, from fine details to sheer generalities. The seniority of stakeholders involved in their development can vary accordingly, from ordinary staff to top-tier business executives (see Figure 3.2).

On the one extreme, at the bottom of the initiative hierarchy, architectural solutions for small projects tend to describe in detail concrete system modules, database tables, process steps and profit figures. Their stakeholders may include, say, local business leaders, line managers, subject-matter experts and even some operational specialists. On the opposite extreme, at the top of the initiative hierarchy, architectural solutions for enterprise-wide strategies focus predominantly on abstract classes of computing resources, logical types of information, highest-level business capabilities and conceptual benefits. Their stakeholder circle is typically limited to only senior executives, vice presidents and their deputies. Examples of technical and organizational solutions for different types of digital transformation initiatives with their key properties are provided in Figure 3.6.

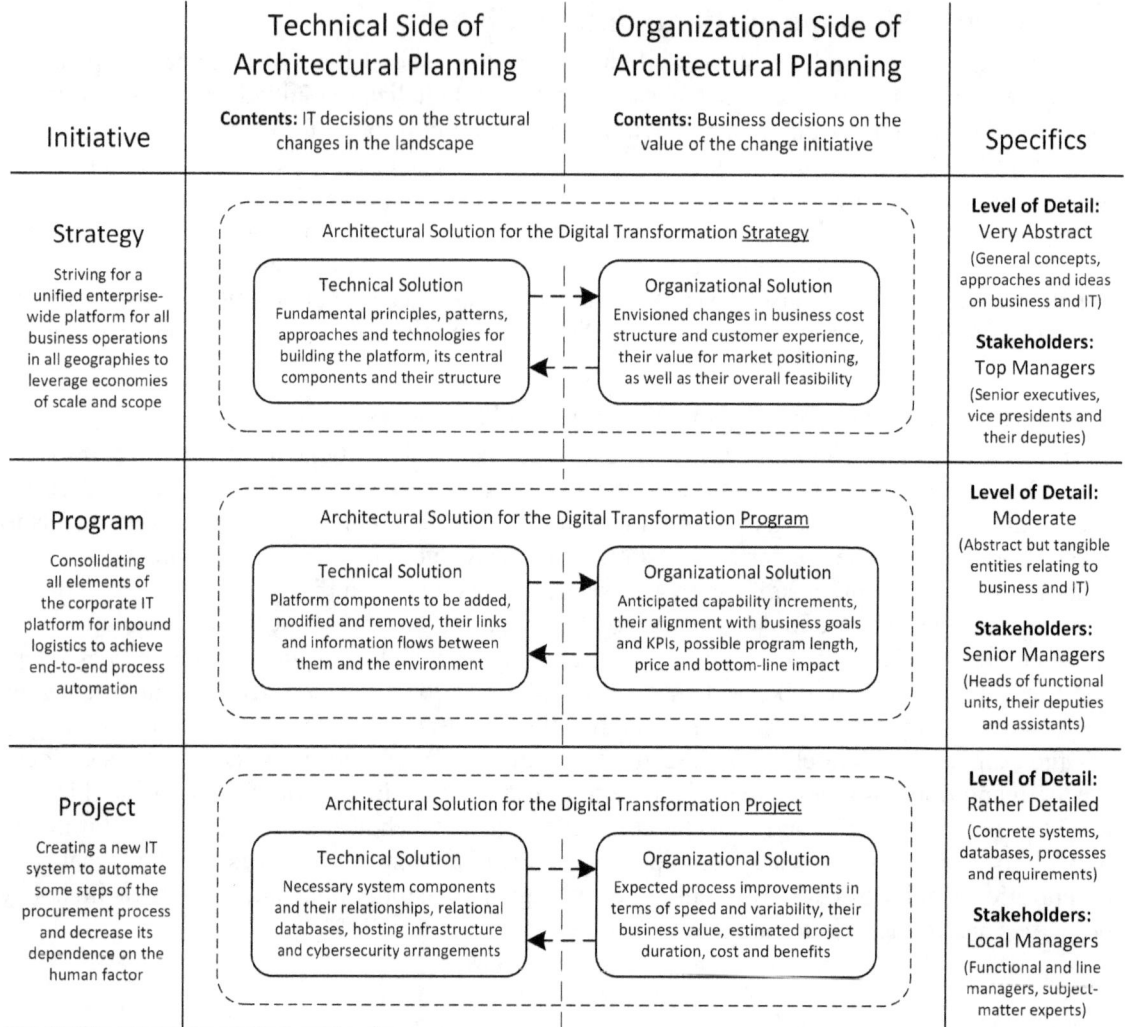

Figure 3.6. Technical and organizational solutions for change initiatives at different levels

Although the nature of challenges associated with developing technical and organizational solutions for different types of digital transformation initiatives is substantially the same, the architectural planning of transformation initiatives at different hierarchical levels has some notable specifics.

Architectural Planning of Projects, Programs and Strategies

Architectural solutions with technical and organizational constituents, and thus architectural plans as their material reifications, exist for all sorts of digital transformation initiatives (see Figure 3.6). As the execution of higher-level initiatives is exercised in the planning of their lower-level descendants (see Figure 2.6), architectural solutions for projects, programs and strategies are obviously linked by parent–child relationships (however, projects and programs can also be implemented independently, without being spawned by any higher-order initiatives, as shown in Figure 2.5). Specifically, architectural plans for strategies influence the architectural planning of their derivative programs and projects. Likewise, program-level architectural plans guide the architectural planning of their subordinate projects.

This linkage of higher- and lower-level plans relates to both the technical and organizational sides of architectural planning, e.g. technical and organizational solutions for programs mold technical and organizational solutions for their projects respectively. On the technical side, higher-level solutions gravitate towards defining fundamental principles, overarching patterns and technology choices, while lower-level solutions align their more detailed system structures with these principles, patterns and choices. On the organizational side, higher-level solutions lean towards defining global objectives, general directions and conceptual approaches and lower-level solutions then align their more specific business changes with these objectives, directions and approaches. In short, higher-order technical and organizational solutions provide certain *decision premises* for developing the respective "downstream" solutions[9].

Potential suggestions, requirements and constraints imposed by "parent" architectural solutions further complicate architectural planning as they add additional concerns that need to be taken into account. On the one hand, technical solutions designed by IT professionals, besides addressing regular business requirements dictated by the corresponding organizational solutions, should also conform to the requirements of higher-level technical solutions. On the other hand, organizational solutions reached collectively by their stakeholders, besides being determined by the corresponding technical solutions, should also stick to the imperatives of higher-level organizational solutions.

Except for the granularity of the respective solutions and the seniority of the stakeholders involved in their development (see Figure 3.6), as well as the relative magnitude of technical and organizational challenges that have to be surmounted (see Figure 2.9), essentially the same process of architectural planning is carried out at every layer of the hierarchy, but at lower levels this process is performed within the framework of decisions made earlier at higher levels. The technical and organizational sides of linked architectural planning of digital transformation initiatives at different hierarchical levels are depicted schematically in Figure 3.7.

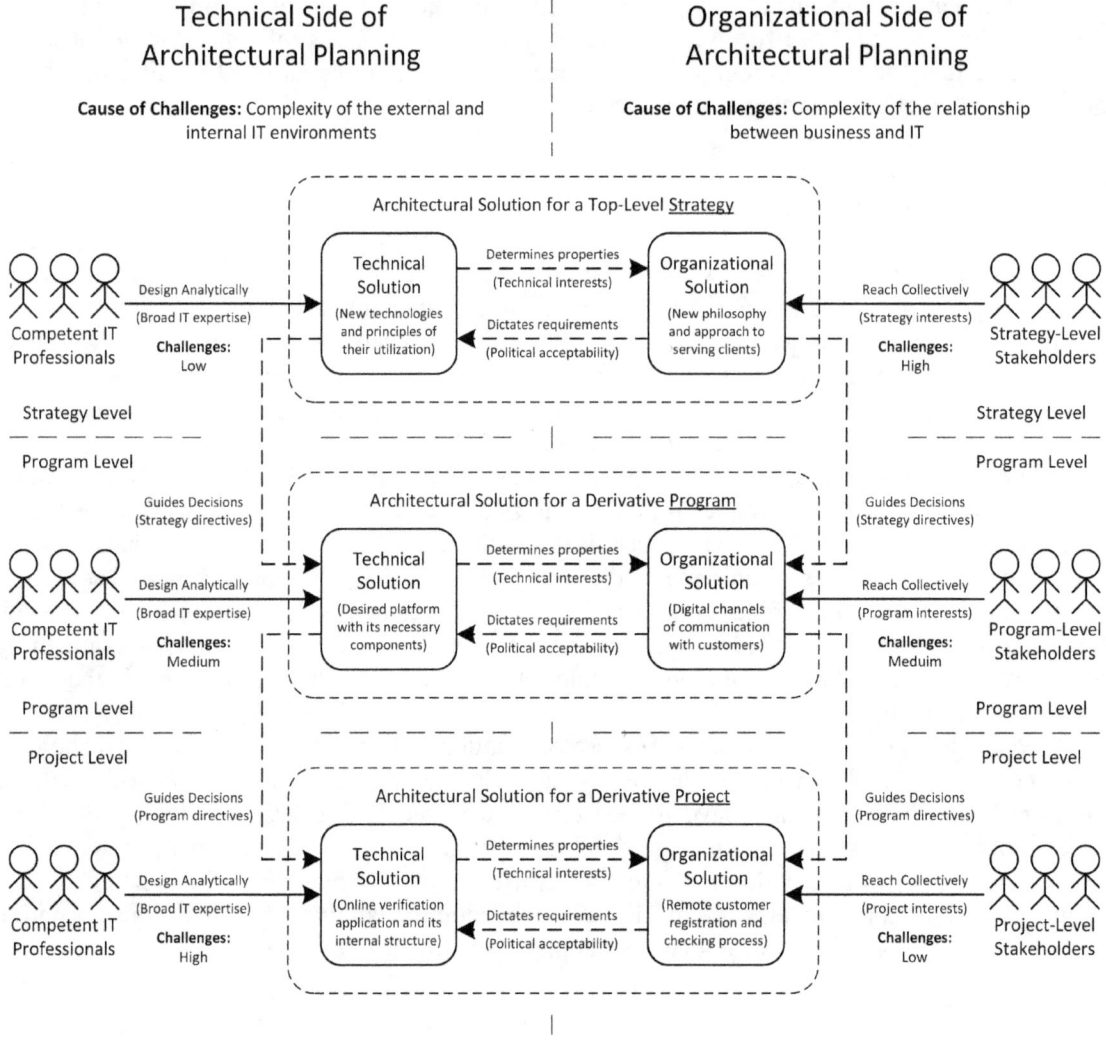

Figure 3.7. Linked architectural planning of transformation initiatives at different levels

As it is evident from the diversity of the associated challenges, as well as from the intricacy of their solutions, succeeding with digitalization endeavors presents difficult problems for organizations. All digital transformation initiatives, irrespective of their level and size, need technical and organizational solutions that can be put together only via meaningful architectural planning.

However, the respective planning activities are far from trivial, fairly sophisticated and unthinkable without specialists possessing a rich hodgepodge of pertinent competencies and skills necessary to make them happen. These competencies are vital but unusual; they cannot be acquired quickly or easily, but take time and effort to master. For this reason, sensible architectural planning in organizations can hardly be conducted properly by ordinary managers or mere techies assigned to the task, but requires well-qualified experts devoted specifically to this kind of work on a permanent basis[10]. The widespread demand for such dedicated experts across the industry has engendered a separate full-fledged profession of enterprise architects. Enterprise architects are responsible exclusively for leading the architectural planning of digitalization initiatives and ensuring their success.

Chapter Summary

This chapter introduced the notion of architectural planning with its stakeholders, technical and organizational sides, described the organizational domains relevant to architectural planning with their multilayer stack, conceptual differences and relationship to technical and organizational solutions, and discussed the specifics of architectural planning of hierarchical initiatives with linked architectural solutions. The key message of this chapter can be summarized in the following essential points:

- Architectural planning is a complex, multi-aspect organizational effort of developing optimal architectural solutions for digital transformation initiatives addressing both their technical and organizational challenges
- Architectural solutions for digitalization initiatives represent comprehensive sets of architectural decisions covering all business and IT aspects of these initiatives in their wholeness, which can be documented in material architectural plans
- Stakeholders of architectural planning are initiative stakeholders who shape architectural solutions for change initiatives, including business representatives as primary stakeholders and IT representatives as secondary stakeholders
- The technical side of architectural planning addresses technical challenges of digitalization, covers the actionable part of change initiatives, involves traditional engineering exercises and develops technical solutions
- The organizational side of architectural planning addresses organizational challenges of digitalization, covers the motivational part of change initiatives, requires reaching political compromises and develops organizational solutions
- Architectural planning deals with six interrelated organizational domains, which can be conveniently represented together as a multilayer domain stack: business, applications, data, integration, infrastructure and security
- The six organizational domains can be classified into technical and non-technical ones, functional and non-functional ones, substantive and non-substantive ones, and have different relationship to technical and organizational solutions
- Architectural planning equally applies to strategies, programs and projects, but differs in the seniority of involved stakeholders and the granularity of resulting solutions, with architectural solutions for hierarchical initiatives being linked

Chapter 4: Welcome, Enterprise Architects

The previous chapter discussed architectural planning as a multifaceted socio-technical activity with all the associated difficulties. This chapter introduces enterprise architects who carry out architectural planning in organizations, propelling their digital transformation. In particular, this chapter starts with explaining the competencies and occupation of enterprise architects, their place in the context of enterprise architecture practice and other distinctive features of their role. Next, this chapter describes enterprise architects at work, including their contribution to the initial ideation of digitalization initiatives and their activities during different phases of their implementation. Lastly, this chapter discusses the complex personality of enterprise architects and the two hats of Technology Experts and Change Agents that they wear in organizations.

Enterprise Architects as Specialized Professionals

Succeeding with digital transformation initiatives in organizations requires addressing the accompanying technical and organizational challenges with disciplined architectural planning (see Figure 3.1). Because of the inherent complexity of this activity, architectural planning cannot be delegated to random people, but needs to be driven by properly qualified experts prepared to deal with its numerous difficulties.

Enterprise architects, or simply architects, are specialized professionals responsible for *leading* architectural planning in organizations, thereby enabling the success of their digitalization aspirations. For their capacity to unlock the business potential of IT and exploit it to transform the way organizations operate, architects are widely recognized and praised in the mainstream media as the agents of digital transformation[1].

Presently, enterprise architects are prevalent across the industry, form a distinct professional community and constitute a large family of kindred organizational positions with similar duties containing the keyword "architect" in their titles, e.g. "platform architect", "insurance architect", "transformation architect" and "principal architect". Architects possess all the relevant knowledge and abilities necessary for putting together optimal architectural plans for digitalization initiatives and effecting their implementation. Enterprise architects and various aspects of their work in organizations represent the primary subject of this book.

Competencies and Occupation of Enterprise Architects

Enterprise architects combine quite an exotic blend of expertise, qualities and skills. Although most architects come from IT departments with a strong background in technology, their competence extends far beyond purely technical questions[2]. The sphere of their mastery is hard to delineate precisely as it is rather broad and encompasses such disparate areas as technical proficiency, communicative skills, systemic thinking, business savvy and even political shrewdness[3]. A partial list of capabilities of enterprise architects includes the following competencies:

- A comprehension of the external IT environment, available technologies and vendor products with the ability to pick the most suitable solutions for addressing particular organizational needs
- An aptitude for communicating with business leaders and understanding their concerns with the necessary skills to work out a common way forward optimal from both business and IT viewpoints and advocate it
- An understanding of the internal IT landscape, deployed IT assets and utilized technologies with the ability to integrate new information systems into this environment while reusing existing capacities
- Knowledge of the regulatory base, pertinent national laws, industry standards and security requirements with practical experience in designing IT solutions compliant with these laws, standards and requirements
- A grasp of the situation as a whole and interdependencies between all its individual components, factors and features with the propensity for holistic decision-making taking into account all these elements

Concrete actions, responsibilities and contacts of enterprise architects in organizations are also very difficult to enumerate as they are extremely diverse, position-specific and context-dependent[4]. Generally, in their everyday work, architects study the IT environment, keep abreast of the swiftly evolving technology market, advise others on various IT-related issues and, most importantly, participate in all sorts of digital transformation initiatives as their chief planners handling the associated challenges (see Figure 1.5). By ensuring adequate architectural planning as part of digitalization efforts and facilitating the development of appropriate technical and organizational solutions for the respective initiatives (see Figure 3.7), architects unfold their potential and enable their success[5]. The role of enterprise architects as the leaders of architectural planning and enablers of digital transformation is shown in Figure 4.1.

Figure 4.1. Enterprise architects as lead planners and enablers of digital transformation

Basically, enterprise architects are the only organizational actors concentrating specifically on architectural planning. In their job, they routinely use different tools from the copious arsenal of the discipline of enterprise architecture.

Enterprise Architects as Practitioners of Enterprise Architecture

Enterprise architects are practitioners and central characters of the complex discipline commonly known today as **enterprise architecture (EA)**[6]. The EA discipline purports to address the problem of business and IT alignment in organizations by means of using special documents called EA artifacts. **EA artifacts** describe various aspects of the relationship between business and IT, promote communication between disparate business and IT communities and support architectural planning as part of digital transformation initiatives. Consequently, practicing enterprise architecture in organizations tends to boost their digitalization efforts[7].

EA artifacts are the primary instruments of enterprise architects essential to their occupation. As native EA practitioners, architects actively employ various EA artifacts for a number of purposes, most importantly, for communicating with different stakeholders during architectural planning (see Figure 3.2), capturing the resulting architectural solutions and representing the produced architectural plans (see Figure 3.1).

EA artifacts that proved helpful in the industry are very diverse as they cover different facets of transformation initiatives and pertain to initiatives of different scales (see Figure 2.4), though the correspondence between them can be rather loose. For example, architectural solutions for smaller projects can be documented in EA artifacts often called solution overviews that provide high-level mixed-format descriptions of IT solutions with their logical components from a business point of view. Architectural solutions for larger transformation programs can be partly reflected in target states that present abstract graphical depictions of the specific configuration of the organization in terms of business and IT. Finally, architectural solutions for global digitalization strategies can be captured in architecture strategies that contain conceptual directions for the organization from the standpoint of the relationship between business and IT.

Schematic graphical examples of popular EA artifacts that can be used by enterprise architects to represent architectural plans for different types of digital transformation initiatives are exhibited in Figure 4.2, whereas more detailed descriptions of these and many other artifacts are provided later in Chapter 8 (The Catalog of Enterprise Architecture Artifacts).

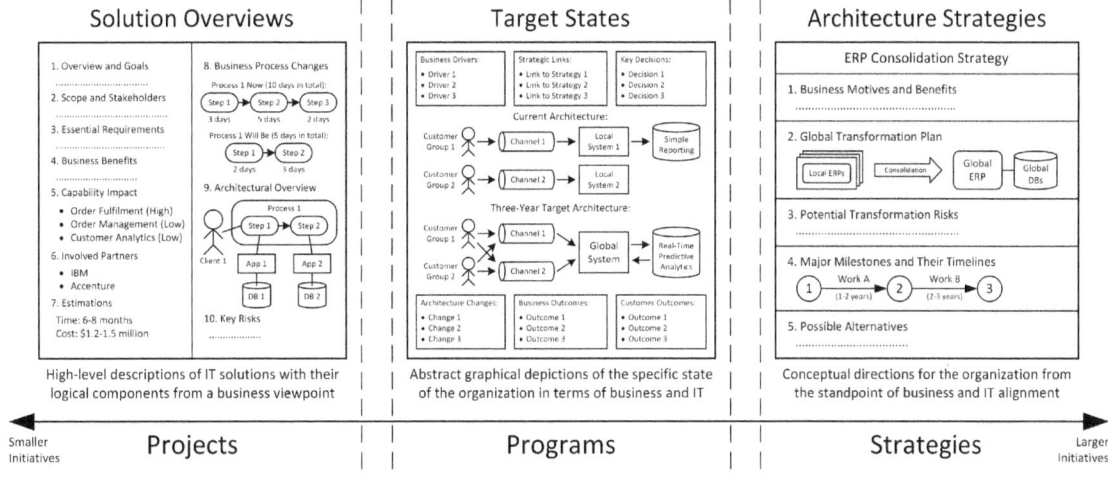

Figure 4.2. Examples of EA artifacts that can be used to represent architectural plans

Using EA artifacts, such as those exemplified in Figure 4.2, helps enterprise architects bridge the communication gaps between different groups of stakeholders, reach mutual understanding and address many of the typical challenges of digital transformation. Besides EA artifacts, in their daily work, architects also apply many other useful instruments, techniques and approaches from the rich EA toolkit.

Enterprise Architects as Actors of Organizational Enterprise Architecture Practice

Organizationally, enterprise architects operate in the institutional framework of an EA practice. The practice of enterprise architecture, or simply an **EA practice**, is an organizational practice of disciplined architectural planning that makes use of various EA artifacts (see Figure 4.2) for improving communication between business and IT stakeholders and facilitating the respective planning efforts. EA practices are embedded in organizations administratively as one form of their legitimate decision-making mechanisms. Conceptually, they translate transformation drivers from the motivational context of the organization into architectural plans for its digitalization initiatives.

Enterprise architects are the key actors of an EA practice and the principal owners of all EA artifacts. Besides architects and artifacts, an EA practice also embraces other organizational actors involved in architectural planning activities, supporting software tools, systematic planning processes and ancillary organizational arrangements intended to promote productive collaboration of all its participants. Various processes, routines and other elements of an EA practice are tightly integrated with regular administrative mechanisms enabling the implementation of transformation initiatives at different levels of their hierarchy, especially projects (see Figure 2.6).

One particularly noteworthy constituent of an EA practice is **architecture governance bodies** — official decision-making committees responsible for carrying out necessary governance procedures and endorsing significant architectural decisions. These committees include enterprise architects together with various business and IT leaders to examine proposed planning decisions and sanction their implementation. Governance committees with their authorization procedures are institutionalized in organizations as part of their EA practices and represent very important pillars pivotal for their functioning. The contents of an EA practice and its place in the overall organizational context are shown in Figure 4.3.

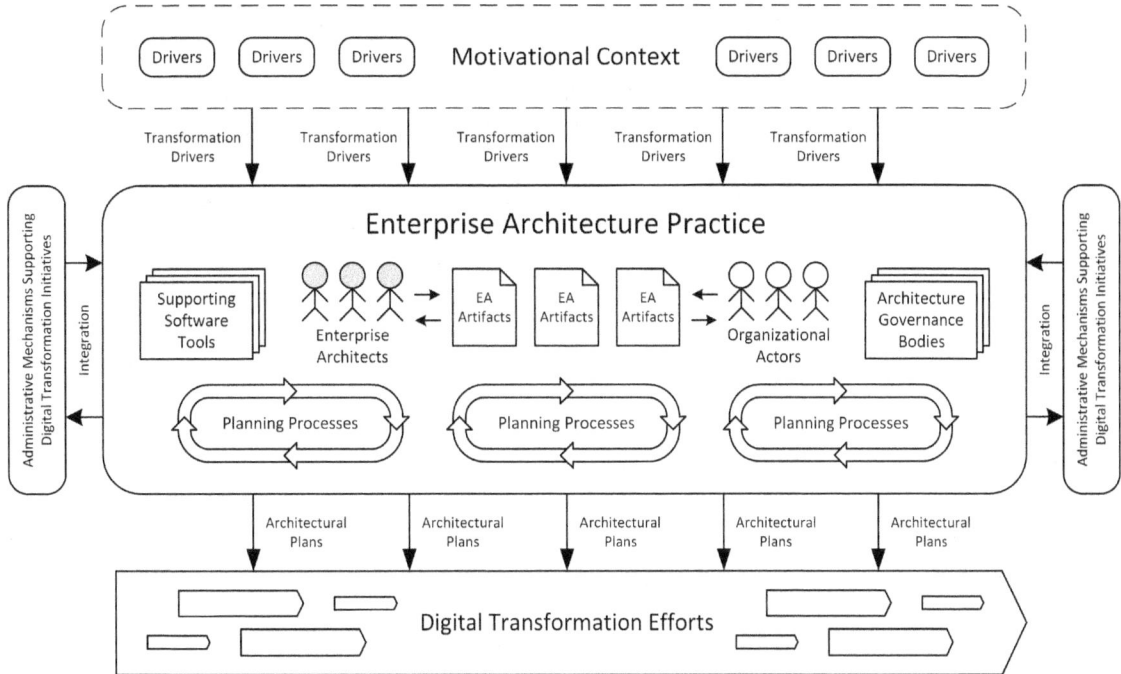

Figure 4.3. An EA practice with enterprise architects in the organizational context

As leading actors of an EA practice, enterprise architects steer its internal decision processes and sit in architecture governance bodies. The nature of their duties in organizations, however, is not operational or managerial, but mainly expert and consultative.

Enterprise Architects as Internal Consultants

The occupation of enterprise architects is pretty unusual as it typically does not imply any operational and managerial responsibilities. Unlike ordinary specialists, architects normally do not perform any routine, repetitive tasks constituting regular operating processes running in organizations on a day-to-day basis. Unlike business and IT managers, they do not wield power or official management authority to be able to assign tasks to other employees, allocate organizational resources, enforce the execution of decisions, recruit, promote and fire people. In short, architects have no routine work, no subordinates and no budgets.

Instead, enterprise architects act largely as independent experts and contribute to the organization primarily by applying their unique competencies in connecting business and IT. Due to the lack of any operational and managerial duties on their part, architects in many respects highly resemble traditional *management consultants*, who provide intelligent advice, but bear little or no accountability for the ultimate outcomes and consequences. For this reason, with a few exceptions, a final say in decision-making procedures always belongs to real managers burdened with responsibility, whereas architects can only influence the resulting decisions by promoting their ideas, sharing their opinions and voicing their concerns[8].

In a position of mere consultants, the authority of enterprise architects in organizations can only be unofficial, based on their reputation and credibility in the eyes of managers. Such informal authority cannot be simply granted to them administratively, but has to be deserved by own deeds and earned by "talking sense". Essentially the only actual power that architects can possess and leverage is "soft" power exerted by persuasion, logical reasoning and strong arguments. Thus, from the standpoint of authority and power, their relationships with managers are very unequal[9].

As consultants, enterprise architects are called for help by other organizational actors and invited to lead the architectural planning of digitalization initiatives by their sponsors (see Figure 2.3). Generally, architects cannot intervene in any decision-making processes at their own discretion and cannot do anything unless they are asked for it by responsible managers. Unsurprisingly, in the organizational ecosystem, the community of architects is often viewed as an *internal consultancy* that offers architectural advisory services to a wide circle of customers from the rest of the organization[10].

For managers, cooperation with enterprise architects is usually optional and occurs mostly of their own volition. **Voluntary interactions** with architects are initiated personally by managers at their will, according to their pragmatic interests. These interactions are not regulated formally and sought after because the participation of architects is considered advantageous by managers and conducive to the success of their endeavors. For example, business leaders may wish to discuss with architects their ideas about a new transformation initiative to ensure their feasibility and then engage them in its planning to maximize the chances of its smooth implementation. Simply put, voluntary interactions happen because managers *want* to involve architects.

However, in some situations, managers may be obliged to cooperate with enterprise architects without or even contrary to their desire. **Mandatory interactions** with architects are imposed by administrative mechanisms constituting an EA practice, such as architecture governance bodies (see Figure 4.3), via established organizational routines that require their presence, most notably, during the implementation of change initiatives at different levels. These interactions are more formal and take place as part of institutionalized decision-making processes regardless of the will of their participants. For example, standard project approval procedures can include a separate sign-off by architects to guarantee that proposed projects are secure and grant them veto rights on certain classes of decisions. In short, mandatory interactions happen because managers *must* deal with architects. The relationship between enterprise architects and managers in terms of their power, activities and interactions discussed above is summarized in Figure 4.4.

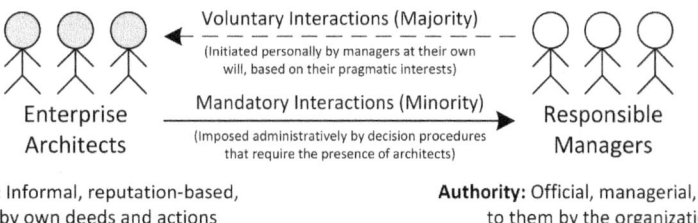

Figure 4.4. Enterprise architects as internal management consultants

As it is evident from the character of interrelations between enterprise architects and managers shown in Figure 4.4, the former can conduct architectural planning only on behalf of the latter, who possess full decision-making power. In other words, organizational managers can *choose* to entrust the mandate to lead architectural planning to professional architects, or delegate this task to them. Only by being empowered with this mandate from management can architects be respected and treated seriously in the organization as chief planners of its digital transformation efforts.

Enterprise Architects as City Planners

Besides resembling management consultants in some aspects of their occupation, enterprise architects can also be compared metaphorically to *city planners*[11]. In this interpretation, organizations can be viewed as cities, where their different business areas correspond to separate urban districts, while specific information systems supporting these areas — to individual buildings constituting the respective districts[12]. Analogously to city planners mapping out various elements of transport, communication and utility infrastructure, roads and streets, quarters and buildings, enterprise architects deal with the composition of business capabilities, processes, applications, databases, integration, hosting and network infrastructure[13].

In fact, cities the evolution of which city planners guide and organizations the digitalization of which enterprise architects drive have much in common from the standpoint of their planning. Specifically, the commonalities between them include, but are not limited to, the following important properties:

- Both cities and organizations represent very large, extremely complex and self-evolving entities whose development is fundamentally endless, continuous, path-dependent, has no ultimate destination and cannot be planned in every detail
- Both cities and organizations have multiple heterogeneous stakeholder groups and no single optimal way to evolve, their future direction is determined by the interests, opinions and concerns of diverse constituencies, often conflicting ones

- Both cities and organizations have some technical side that refers to the means of their evolution as well as some "value" side that refers to the ends of their evolution, necessitating their mutual adjustment

In this light, enterprise architects have to cope with many of the same conceptual difficulties that city planners do, though in relation to organizational, rather than urban, landscapes. This resemblance between the two occupations makes their work somewhat similar in technology-agnostic matters[14].

Enterprise Architects at Work

As discussed earlier, enterprise architects in organizations can be regarded largely as internal consultants engaged by managers, because of their reputation as competent experts, to lead the architectural planning of digitalization initiatives using various EA artifacts. Their planning activities, however, are rather special and differ substantially from conventional planning exercises.

Enterprise Architects Do Not Work Like Traditional Architects

For most people, the very word "architect" is strongly associated with traditional building architects[15]. However, it is important to realize that in the case of enterprise architects, this word essentially represents only a loose, and even partly misleading, metaphor that does *not* actually indicate any practical similarity between enterprise architects and classic architects. In fact, enterprise architects and traditional architects plan disparate objects and face radically different challenges dealing with which requires different mindsets, habits and approaches to planning.

Unlike buildings, organizations are *not* static entities that can be carefully planned using rigorous analytical methods and then constructed exactly as intended. On the contrary, they closely resemble living organisms that gradually evolve, or grow, over time as a result of countless planning decisions made every day by their managers at all corporate levels[16]. As explained previously, in terms of their planning, organizations can be fairly compared to vibrant cities whose sprawl can be controlled only through flexible, politicized decision-making adaptive to changing realities and opinions[17].

Moreover, decision processes in organizations are incredibly complex, inscrutable and surprisingly frequently exhibit various signs of randomness, irrationality and unreason[18]. Organizations are teeming with uncertainty, ambiguity, incomplete information, shifting priorities, conflicting interests and fluidity of actors. For these reasons, organizational decisions often somehow "happen" largely by virtue of coincidental circumstances, rather than get deliberately "made" in a thought-out manner[19]. In these settings, neither enterprise architects nor anyone else, including senior executives, can really plan enterprises and their transformations in the same sense as traditional architects design buildings.

How Do Enterprise Architects Work?

Because organizations evolve by making tons of planning decisions and acting on them, the only practicable way to shape their structure and the structure of their change initiatives is to influence these decisions and ensuing actions. Accordingly, enterprise architects try to *influence decision-making processes* at different levels and stages in order to guide the evolution of the organization in the right direction, towards achieving the desired outcomes[20]. These efforts require interacting with numerous stakeholders, understanding their interests, proposing the best mutually satisfactory way forward and then advocating adherence to this path.

In fact, the work of enterprise architects in organizations covers all logical stages of digital transformation initiatives and actually begins even *before* any specific initiatives are articulated. Namely, it starts with identifying organizational motives for digitalization and converting them into the right initiatives and ends with planning and executing these initiatives in the right way. In other words, architects gather existing thoughts and ideas for using IT, help distinguish the most promising ideas and then assist in their proper materialization. Although explicit architectural planning driven by architects takes place only during the planning phase of transformation initiatives (see Figure 3.1), the core intention of architectural planning — matching technically feasible and organizationally desirable solutions (see Figure 3.3) — implicitly permeates virtually all stages of their work.

Work in the Process of Initial Ideation

Conceptually, the work of enterprise architects begins with taking part in the very origination of ideas for new digital transformation initiatives (see Figure 2.1). In the first place, architects by all available means cultivate their reputation as valuable partners to win respect in managerial circles and gain informal authority necessary for influencing planning decisions (see Figure 4.4). By helping business and IT leaders with their advice on the use of technology, architects build up their communication network across the organization and keep in touch with various decision-makers.

Being in constant contact with managers, enterprise architects dive into their motivational context and recognize their drivers, needs and desires (see Figure 1.3). Along with that, they also identify managers' ideas for digitalization, propose their own, perhaps better ideas or collectively produce truly innovative ideas and then funnel these ideas into coherent IT-backed transformation initiatives of different scales, e.g. small projects, larger programs or global strategies. In other words, architects continually "scan" the organization for emerging motives, demands and ideas for using IT and aid management in framing them correctly as concrete change initiatives.

In this way, with the assistance of enterprise architects, autonomous transformation initiatives are generated through the initial ideation process directly from the motivational context, whereas their lower-level derivative initiatives, in turn, are spawned later based on their intentions (see Figure 2.6). The activities of enterprise architects in the process of initial ideation that result in new digitalization initiatives in organizations are shown in Figure 4.5.

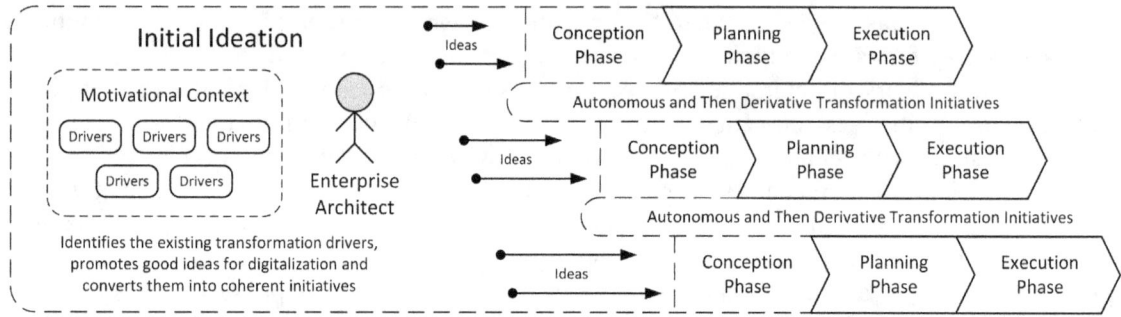

Figure 4.5. Activities of enterprise architects resulting in the origination of new initiatives

Then, if their further assistance in materializing transformation initiatives and their possible descendants is requested by managers, the work of enterprise architects on these initiatives continues, though unevenly, for their entire implementation period and embraces all their lifecycle phases, from conception to planning to execution (see Figure 2.2). Within each phase, architects perform quite different kinds of activities with varying intensity and deal with different subgroups of initiative stakeholders.

Work During the Conception Phase

During the pre-initiative conception phase, enterprise architects communicate with potential initiative sponsors to better understand what should be done and then formulate the very concept of a new initiative with its goals, desired impact and scope. For autonomous initiatives originating straight from the motivational context, their sponsors are likely to be the proponents of the underlying transformation drivers, who discuss with architects these drivers and various ideas for responding to them with IT. For derivative initiatives descending from some higher-level parents, their sponsors are likely to be the executors of the parent initiatives, who discuss with architects the goals of these initiatives and current intentions for their achievement.

In this phase, using their deep knowledge of IT, enterprise architects help initiative sponsors conceive the right initiatives that can best meet their genuine needs with the available resources. Because these efforts imply marrying business ends and IT means and, at a high level, face the same familiar technical and organizational challenges, they involve many elements of architectural planning and, on this basis, can be regarded as **architectural pre-planning**. Unlike full-fledged architectural planning, "lightweight" pre-planning activities are mostly oral and do not produce any formalized, written plans for initiatives. Nevertheless, they create a common view of the situation, establish some verbal agreements on foundational premises and result in relative certainty on a number of fundamental questions about initiatives, e.g. what approximately has to be done, how and why.

The purpose of architectural pre-planning is not to develop any architectural solutions themselves, but only to do a basic feasibility study, assure that satisfactory solutions for initiatives *exist in principle* and outline their possible solution space for future planning exercises, e.g. ascertain that the hoped-for business improvements can indeed be achieved with IT for an affordable price using a particular class of technologies. Hence, the architectural planning of digitalization initiatives actually starts implicitly from the moment of their conception.

Architectural pre-planning carried out by enterprise architects within the conception phase of digital transformation initiatives is shown in Figure 4.6.

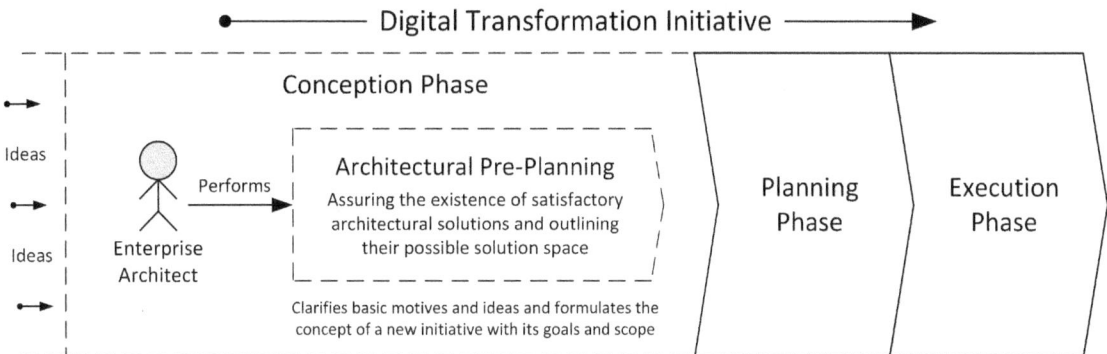

Figure 4.6. Architectural pre-planning fulfilled by enterprise architects

By confirming the hypothetical existence of architectural solutions acceptable to all parties, architectural pre-planning asserts that initiatives are promising and deserve to proceed further to their detailed planning. As architectural pre-planning is very abstract and notional, the conception phase usually does not require much exertion on the part of enterprise architects.

Work During the Planning Phase

By contrast, the succeeding planning phase, which starts immediately after the overall concept of the initiative is shaped, is a "high season" for enterprise architects as it is this phase that includes the fulfillment of their key responsibility — leading architectural planning (see Figure 4.1) — in the most explicit form. The activities of architects in the planning phase roughly follow a certain logical flow, or process. The process of architectural planning, or simply the **architectural planning process**, is an approximate sequence of actions that should be accomplished to produce architectural plans for a digital transformation initiative. For any initiative, be it a broad strategy, a mid-size program or a small project, at a high level, this process contains three successive steps orchestrated by architects: discussion, elaboration and approval.

First, the discussion step implies communicating with the full circle of initiative stakeholders (see Figure 3.2), studying in more detail their perspectives, aims and demands, collecting their thoughts, suggestions and opinions. Next, the elaboration step embodies the climax of architectural planning and involves developing initial proposals regarding the desired future course of action with both technical and organizational components, presenting these plans to the stakeholders, gathering their feedback, reacting to it and adjusting the plans to address their concerns, thereby converging the technical and organizational solutions (see Figure 3.3). Finally, the approval step includes reaching agreement on the proposed course of action among all the parties, completing the resulting architectural plans and their formal endorsement.

Each of these steps is loosely structured, highly iterative and requires *intense* communication between architects and initiative stakeholders. In short, enterprise architects practice "planning by talking". To facilitate communication and represent the preliminary and finalized architectural plans during different steps of the planning process, architects select and use suitable EA artifacts from their toolkit (see Figure 4.2). The high-level process of architectural planning conducted by enterprise architects within the planning phase of digital transformation initiatives is shown in Figure 4.7, whereas a more detailed discussion of this process is provided later in Chapter 11 (Leading the Development of Plans).

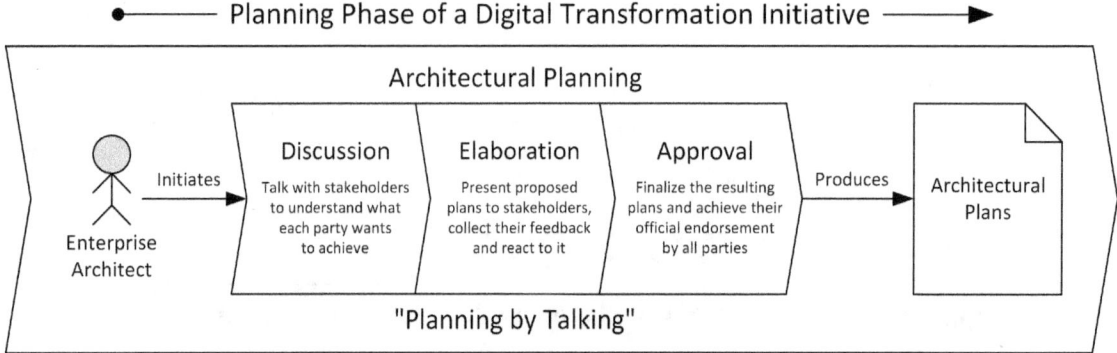

Figure 4.7. The high-level process of architectural planning led by enterprise architects

However, planning-related activities in organizations do not stop right after some plans are created, but expand further to control compliance with these plans and possibly revise them in the face of changing circumstances. Any plans are largely worthless unless they are respected by their executors and followed up by their creators. For this reason, besides leading the architectural planning of digitalization initiatives, enterprise architects are also responsible for monitoring the realization of developed plans.

Work During the Execution Phase

Once the mutually agreed architectural plans for transformation initiatives are produced and all the concomitant issues are settled, the execution phase begins. For strategies and programs, it implies launching lower-level derivative initiatives ensuing from their plans (see Figure 2.6), whereas for projects — introducing tangible changes in the landscape structure by building, testing and deploying new information systems described in their plans by project teams (see Figure 2.7), according to a certain project delivery methodology, e.g. waterfall or agile (see Figure 2.8). This phase is normally a lengthier one, but much less strenuous and requires relatively modest exertions on the part of enterprise architects. Namely, at the commencement of the execution phase, the role of architects in the initiative implementation process switches from being lead planners to that of *chief supervisors*, who exercise architectural oversight over all the "downstream" decisions and actions.

Architectural oversight is the whole set of administrative measures in an EA practice intended to ensure adherence to the approved architectural plans for digital transformation initiatives during their execution. Similarly to architectural planning, architectural oversight represents a complex organizational activity that includes all the relevant actors, committees, routines and other elements necessary to follow the enacted courses of action for IT-driven business transformations. Nonetheless, most of the respective tasks are the direct responsibility of enterprise architects. These tasks can be performed by architects in various ways either individually by personal communication, or through special organizational arrangements, like formal endorsement procedures fulfilled by architecture governance bodies as part of an EA practice (see Figure 4.3). Existing architectural plans in the form of concrete EA artifacts underpin the corresponding efforts by providing an authoritative source of reference against which the adequacy of decisions made as part of the initiative execution can be evaluated.

When exercising architectural oversight, enterprise architects become the principal proponents of the developed plans by reminding their stakeholders, in particular initiative executors, of what agreements have been reached and why they are deemed desirable for the organization. By inducing, persuading and sometimes even enforcing the initiative executors to adhere to the existing plans, architects move the organization closer to the envisioned future and to the attainment of its objectives. The activities of enterprise architects within the planning and execution phases of digital transformation initiatives are shown in Figure 4.8.

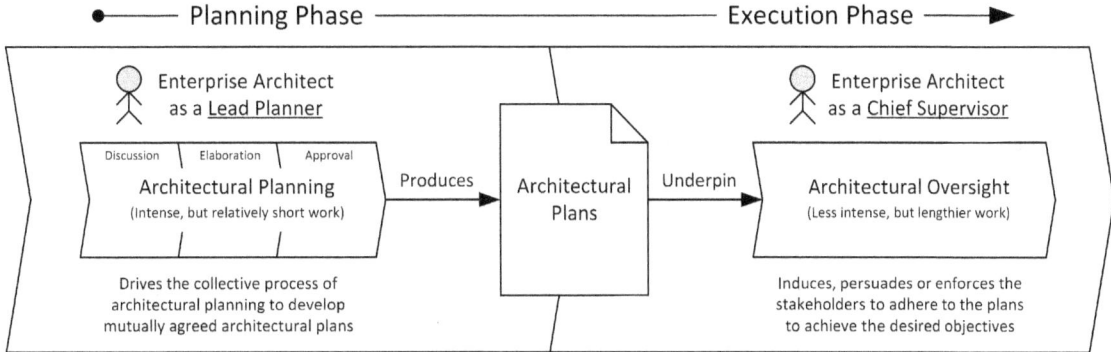

Figure 4.8. Activities of enterprise architects in the key phases of transformation initiatives

Importantly, since both architectural planning and oversight are inherently *cooperative* activities that necessitate the active involvement of many organizational actors, enterprise architects do *not* perform these activities on their own, but rather organize and guide them by coordinating the respective efforts[21]. Because of the immanent difficulties associated with the attempts to unite diverse and independent actors under a common plan and make all of them stick to it, the occupation of architects, in many respects, can be fairly compared with "herding cats"[22]. Planning and supervisory work that enterprise architects do, thus, barely resembles rigorous engineering and construction exercises, but represents primarily people-centric *communication* activities the core meaning of which is to devise a mutually acceptable course of action, get everyone to approve it and then follow it.

Agreed Plans Trump Perfect Plans
As organizations consist of multiple actors with different interests, priorities and opinions (see Figure 1.4), developing a consensus view as to what needs to be done or achieved is crucial for ensuring effective collective action[23]. Interestingly, the objective rationality of any plans does not necessarily guarantee their universal acceptance among their stakeholders without which their execution can hardly be particularly successful. Furthermore, as discussed earlier, in the context

of architectural planning cogent criteria of quality assessment exist only for technical solutions, while the rationality of organizational solutions is always subjective (see Figure 3.3).

For this reason, in organizational settings, general agreement on plans and their widespread support are usually far more important than their formal "correctness" (even when this term can be applied). Unless they are widely agreed upon, even the most "optimal", "perfect" or "best" plans have little or no chance of being successfully implemented[24]. Basically, unanimous, conscious and genuine stakeholder agreement with the resulting plans represents the single most critical success factor of architectural planning efforts as well as the only reasonable criterion of their rationality[25].

One of the ensuing consequences of this fact is that architectural plans cannot be imposed by enterprise architects on their stakeholders, but only produced *collaboratively* with them. All plans created by architects without sufficient stakeholder participation, no matter how competent, are typically not taken seriously, ignored and shelved[26]. Architectural plans that have not been agreed upon are not even plans, but mere trinkets. Therefore, enterprise architects should always seek maximum stakeholder involvement and convergence of their opinions on the developed plans.

Two Hats of Enterprise Architects

The basic introduction provided above explained what enterprise architects generally do in organizations (see Figure 4.1), approximately how they approach it (see Figure 4.5 to Figure 4.8) and what kind of instruments they use (see Figure 4.2). This discussion, however, barely explains who enterprise architects *are* in terms of their personalities, competencies and abilities, so that they are capable of leading architectural planning and propelling digital transformation.

Indeed, digitalization initiatives are challenging undertakings and their proper architectural planning represents a rather sophisticated task with multifarious sub-activities largely obscure to outsiders. Also, enterprise architects, as the leading actors in the respective planning processes, possess an unusually broad and peculiar combination of competencies, skills and expertise that can hardly be summarized into something intelligible. As a result, neither the activities nor the resources of architects are easily explainable to the general public.

In fact, the profession of enterprise architects is quite unique in its kind and has no close analogs among other, more conventional professions. There are arguably no expressive metaphors that can adequately capture the essence of their job in its full complexity with reasonable accuracy. For instance, the straightforward analogy to traditional architects is obviously flawed due to the dynamic and somewhat messy nature of organizations, as explained earlier. The two other popular metaphors of enterprise architects as city planners and management consultants introduced previously are perfectly appropriate, but these metaphors weakly reflect the personality of architects as individuals with their pursuits. Namely, the metaphor of city planners characterizes more the object of their planning (i.e. organizations as cities whose further development needs to be planned), whereas that of management consultants — only their power relations with managers (i.e. architects as consultants invited by managers to serve their interests); neither of these metaphors describes architects themselves and the substance of their work. Unsurprisingly, to many, the very profession of enterprise architects seems shadowy, mysterious and shrouded with secrecy. Moreover, the meaning and purpose of their job are often difficult to elucidate not only to laypersons, but even to experienced IT specialists[27].

At the highest level of abstraction, the occupation of enterprise architects can arguably be best explicated and understood if decomposed into two separate constituents representing different "hats" that architects wear in organizations: Technology Experts and Change Agents[28]. Each of these two hats aggregates certain duties, tasks and actions that architects perform as part of their job as well as the relevant knowledge, skills and EA artifacts necessary for accomplishing them. Although these hats are conceptually different, mutually independent and logically complete, both of them must be worn by architects for the successful fulfillment of their responsibilities as information systems planners and enablers of digital transformation. Most of the resources, instruments and activities of enterprise architects, as well as the challenges they face in their work, can be clearly attributed to one of these two hats.

The Hat of Technology Experts

Wearing the hat of **Technology Experts** implies being very knowledgeable in IT, capable of addressing technical challenges of digital transformation, operating on the technical side of architectural planning and designing technical solutions for concrete transformation initiatives (see Figure 3.3). Technology Experts are authoritative mavens in IT-specific questions and foremost "go-to" specialists when a competent opinion on technology is sought. Their broad and deep technical expertise makes them indispensable for organizations in the matters of selection of appropriate technologies, products and approaches.

The primary resource of Technology Experts is their extensive IT background, knowledge and experience. Technology Experts have been working for many years in various positions in IT departments, dealt with numerous technologies and solved diverse IT-related problems. Their knowledge is not confined to specific technical "enclaves", but rather spans across different subdomains of IT, from applications and data to infrastructure and security (see Figure 3.4), at least at a certain level sufficient for their sound conceptual understanding. Their vast experience has taught them many lessons on how to (and not to) use technology in organizations. On the whole, the knowledge and competencies of Technology Experts are highly specialized and belong predominantly to "hard" skills.

The key instruments of Technology Experts are all sorts of IT-focused EA artifacts that can be used for reflecting technical solutions for transformation initiatives and storing other valuable information of technical nature. In their format, they often resemble traditional engineering drawings and documentation understandable only to educated techies. Typical examples of these artifacts are solution designs, landscape diagrams, asset inventories and technology reference models.

The practical activities of Technology Experts in organizations include mostly advising on IT-related issues and designing technical solutions. On the one hand, they act as trusted advisors on technology and attend various meetings and discussions where solid IT expertise is demanded. On the other hand, they design technical solutions for digital transformation initiatives to provide the necessary functionality and meet other requirements with minimal costs.

By and large, all the activities of Technology Experts are IT-centric and imply leveraging their specialized knowledge, in one way or another, to help their organizations make the best possible technical choices. In their mindset and behavior, Technology Experts closely resemble classic engineers proficient in technicalities incomprehensible to others.

The Hat of Change Agents

Wearing the hat of **Change Agents** implies being very communicable, capable of addressing organizational challenges of digital transformation, operating on the organizational side of architectural planning and helping reach organizational solutions for concrete transformation initiatives (see Figure 3.3). Change Agents are skillful intermediaries and negotiators able to bring diverse stakeholders together, arrange a constructive dialog between them, facilitate the development of mutually acceptable planning decisions by coordinating their activities and then "sell" these decisions for execution[29]. In short, they are professional enthusiasts, "cat herders" and catalysts of change. Their proficiency in interacting with different constituencies makes them indispensable in the matters of orchestrating complex, multi-aspect organizational transformations. Importantly, because enterprise architects are not endowed with managerial authority (see Figure 4.4), being Change Agents involves only conceiving, drafting and advocating change initiatives, but not managing their implementation, which is the responsibility of true managers, e.g. appointed project and program managers.

The resources of Change Agents comprise various pertinent skills and some knowledge. Although their skills are pretty diverse, they revolve mainly around effective communication and teamwork, e.g. "groping" the common language, explaining ideas in simple words and delivering exciting presentations. One of the most critical elements of their skill set is the ability to deal with conflicts of interests in a diplomatic manner, by finding the foundation for consensus between diverging points of view, e.g. opinions of the representatives of different parts of the organization (see Figure 1.4), initiative sponsors and executors (see Figure 2.3). The knowledge base of Change Agents can be very broad but shallow as its purpose is only to understand the terminology, objectives and concerns of different stakeholders sufficiently enough to feel relatively on par with them during conversations. In terms of specific subject areas, their knowledge tends to mirror the subject areas of the relevant audiences and stakeholder groups, usually covering some or the other spheres of the business. Overall, the abilities and competencies of Change Agents are rather generic and belong mostly to "soft" skills.

The principal instruments of Change Agents are various business-focused EA artifacts that can be used for reflecting organizational solutions for transformation initiatives and discussing them with their stakeholders. For this purpose, they normally provide simplistic, intuitive visualizations easily understandable and appealing to different audiences with mixed backgrounds. Illustrative examples of these artifacts are solution overviews, target states, business capability models and architecture strategies (see Figure 4.2).

The practical activities of Change Agents encompass all the actions required to produce commonly agreed organizational solutions in the heterogeneous stakeholder environment. In particular, they typically include communicating with different stakeholders, figuring out their interests and drivers, putting together optimal architectural plans and achieving their wide acceptance. It is these activities that constitute "planning by talking", i.e. developing future plans through discussing what needs to be accomplished and how best to realize this change (see Figure 4.7).

Generally, all the activities of Change Agents are people-centric and imply using their communicative abilities to help organizations progress with their transformation efforts[30]. In their attitude and behavior, Change Agents can be compared to politicians promoting reforms among different social strata of the population.

Enterprise Architects as Ambidextrous Personalities

The two hats worn by enterprise architects described above — Technology Experts and Change Agents — introduce the highest-level conceptualization of their occupation and provide the most basic understanding of what their work in organizations is all about. These hats also offer catchy metaphors that neatly capture who architects are and what they do. The properties and positions of the two hats of enterprise architects in the context of architectural planning are shown schematically in Figure 4.9.

Technical Side of Architectural Planning

Challenges: Technical challenges caused by the complexity of the external and internal IT environments

Organizational Side of Architectural Planning

Challenges: Organizational challenges caused by the complexity of the relationship between business and IT

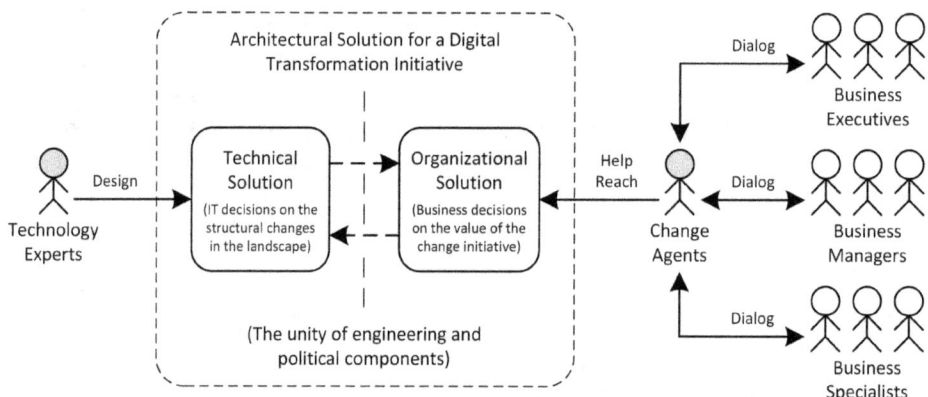

Resources: Extensive knowledge of various technology domains and rich practical experience with IT

Skills: Predominantly highly specialized "hard" skills

Instruments: IT-focused EA artifacts useful for capturing technical solutions and storing IT-related information

Activities: Providing advisory services and designing technical solutions for digitalization initiatives

Focus: IT-centric, exclusively on technology issues

Objective: Help organizations make the best possible technical choices and decisions

Meaning: Competent IT professionals capable of finding optimal engineering approaches and solutions

Analogy: Engineers knowledgeable in technicalities

Resources: Strong communication and teamwork abilities, as well as some subject area knowledge

Skills: Mostly generic and universal "soft" skills

Instruments: Business-focused EA artifacts useful for capturing organizational solutions and enabling their discussion

Activities: Interacting with stakeholders and facilitating the development of organizational solutions

Focus: People-centric, mainly on stakeholder interests

Objective: Help organizations progress with their transformation efforts

Meaning: Proficient communicators capable of finding politically acceptable planning decisions

Analogy: Politicians promoting reforms among the people

Figure 4.9. Two hats of enterprise architects in the context of architectural planning

As it is evident from the juxtaposition of the hats of Technology Experts and Change Agents presented in Figure 4.9, these hats are disparate in virtually every aspect and wearing them implies different, non-overlapping resources, instruments and activities. And yet, the very essence of the job of enterprise architects is in wearing both hats, rather than either one of them. It is this peculiar mixture of resources, instruments and activities that allows architects to design decent solutions responding to technical challenges and, at the same time, also push these solutions politically through organizational challenges, thereby driving digital transformation[31].

In the same sense in which architectural solutions for digital transformation initiatives represent the unity of their technical and organizational components, enterprise architects represent the unity of Technology Experts and Change Agents capable of developing both of the two solution components and composing integral solutions. In other words, architects have a *double identity*, i.e. possess two consistent identities of Technology Experts and Change Agents simultaneously. Hence, their profession is *dual* in nature, requires "ambidextrous" individuals and combines pronounced engineering and political elements[32].

Enterprise Architects, Senior Techies and Change Activists

Interestingly, putting on any one of the two hats does not make a person an agent of digital transformation. On the one hand, senior techies wearing only the hat of Technology Experts can neither orchestrate complex changes in an organizational sense, nor settle the inherent conflicts of interests between different parties involved in the interlacement of business and IT to enable the transformation[33]. For this reason, their role in digitalization efforts is limited only to serving as assistants, consultants or "subcontractors" to real agents of change.

On the other hand, change activists wearing only the hat of Change Agents do not understand technology well enough to propose any concrete IT solutions for broader organizational discussion and protect technical interests during political negotiations. The absence of serious IT background and expertise renders them helpless in the questions of digital transformation, whereas acting as mere intermediaries between IT specialists and business decision-makers proved rather ineffectual in practice.

Therefore, it turns out that only full-fledged enterprise architects wearing both hats, by virtue of their ability to propose technical solutions and also assist in reaching organizational ones, can act as forceful agents of digital transformation. The relationship between enterprise architects, senior techies and change activists discussed above is shown in Figure 4.10.

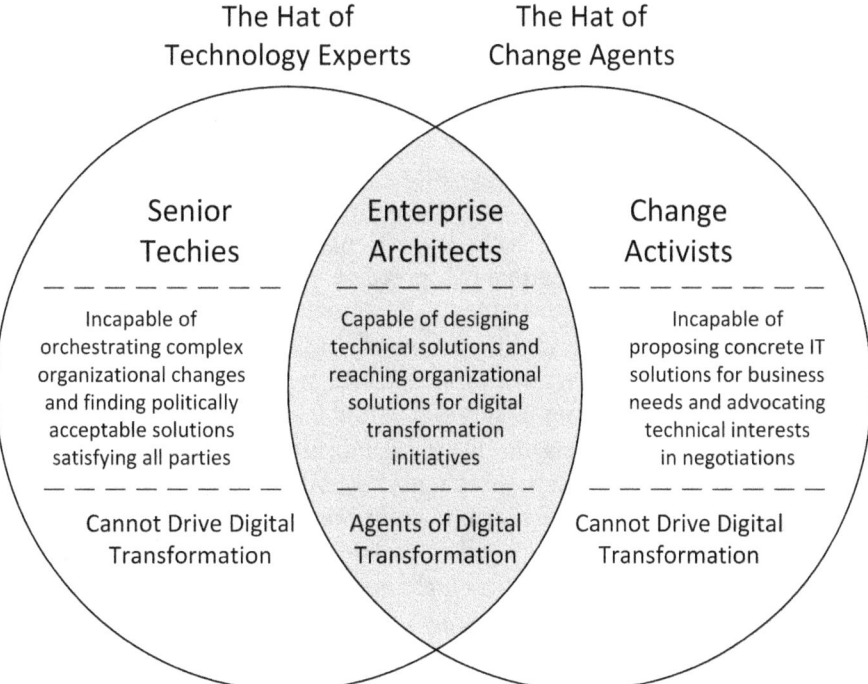

Figure 4.10. Enterprise architects, senior techies and change activists

The synergistic conjunction of the qualities of Technology Experts and Change Agents, which can hardly be found in any other organizational positions, empowers enterprise architects to drive end-to-end architectural planning as part of digital transformation initiatives. Namely, they can propose the very idea of an architectural solution, engineer the solution itself, present it to their business counterparts, represent technical interests in political negotiations and eventually amend the solution to gratify all the stakeholders.

The hats of Technology Experts and Change Agents offer a reasonably accurate, expressive and intuitive abstraction of the work of enterprise architects in organizations that can be used to elucidate the meaning of their profession to the general audience. Moreover, the two-hat model also provides an overall context and powerful conceptual framework for a more detailed analysis of the resources, instruments, activities and other attributes of enterprise architects. This model will be used further in this book as the basis for explaining various facets of their occupation.

Chapter Summary

This chapter introduced enterprise architects as specialized architectural planners with their competencies, occupation and specific features, described their work in the initial ideation of digitalization initiatives and during different phases of their implementation, and explained the nature of their personality through the two hats of Technology Experts and Change Agents. The core message of this chapter can be summarized in the following major points:

- Enterprise architects are specialized industry professionals responsible for leading architectural planning as part of digitalization efforts in organizations, for which they are widely recognized as the agents of digital transformation
- Enterprise architects typically emerge from IT departments, but their competence extends far beyond technology and encompasses, among other areas, communication skills, systems thinking, business savvy and political sagacity
- Enterprise architects are practitioners of the EA discipline and actively use various EA artifacts for communicating with stakeholders during architectural planning, capturing architectural solutions and representing architectural plans
- Enterprise architects operate in the institutional context of an EA practice, where they steer internal decision-making processes, sit as members in architecture governance bodies and participate in their formal governance procedures
- Enterprise architects have no official authority to make any decisions on behalf of the organization and can only influence decisions by advising real managers endowed with power, acting largely as internal management consultants
- The work of enterprise architects in organizations spans from the ideation to completion of change initiatives, where they, first, help generate good ideas for initiatives, then perform their architectural pre-planning, lead their architectural planning and, finally, exercise architectural oversight over their execution
- Enterprise architects carry out architectural planning by talking with different initiative stakeholders and debating proposed planning decisions, roughly following the three successive steps: discussion, elaboration and approval

- Enterprise architects wear the hat of Technology Experts, who are knowledgeable in IT and capable of designing technical solutions, as well as the hat of Change Agents, who are communicable and capable of reaching organizational solutions

Chapter 5: Enterprise Architects in Context

The previous chapter introduced enterprise architects as the agents of digital transformation and many of their distinctive attributes. This chapter presents enterprise architects in the broader organizational, managerial and environmental context. In particular, this chapter begins with describing the place of enterprise architects in the organizational structure, position ecosystem and strategy-to-execution chain, as well as in the industry in general. Then, this chapter discusses the value of employing enterprise architects for organizations by analyzing their financial costs, general benefits and specific value propositions. Finally, this chapter debunks popular misconceptions about enterprise architects and explains who they are certainly not.

Enterprise Architects in the Organizational Environment

In the organizational context, enterprise architects work as part of an EA practice that provides an overarching institutional framework for their activities with the necessary processes, procedures, tools and governance bodies (see Figure 4.3). The view of architects simply as actors of an EA practice, however, does not explain many important aspects of their relationship to the surrounding organizational environment and their specific place within this environment, most notably, in the organizational administrative structure, in the overall ecosystem of organizational positions and in the logical chain of strategy execution.

Enterprise Architects in the Organizational Structure

Organizations, at least large ones, typically comprise a number of primary business units (e.g. lines of business, business functions or geographic divisions) and supporting corporate functions (e.g. finance, accounting, human resources and IT) common to all these units and serving their needs. In this generic organizational structure, enterprise architects most often reside inside an IT function, specifically within a dedicated architecture function that represents its narrow sub-function, along with delivery and support.

An **architecture function** is a specialized organizational function implementing an EA practice with all its various constituents. It is responsible for architectural planning and other associated tasks relevant to digital transformation and business and IT alignment[1]. This function provides an official "home" for all enterprise architects employed by the organization. However, in highly decentralized organizations, architects can be distributed more locally according to the business structure.

The size of architecture functions in terms of the number of enterprise architects is approximately proportional to the number of IT staff working for organizations, both insourced and outsourced, so that they form a relatively small but constant fraction of their IT labor force. Currently, on average, architects often constitute around 4–5% of the total IT headcount, which roughly amounts to one architect for every 20–25 employees of the IT department[2]. As organizations vary greatly in their scale, so do their architecture functions. For instance, the smallest architecture functions obviously consist of only a single architect, whereas the largest ones can easily comprise hundreds of architects.

Administratively, architecture functions in organizations usually represent special sub-units of their IT departments reporting, directly or indirectly, to their chief IT executives[3]. They are known in the industry under different, sometimes peculiar titles, e.g. IT strategy and planning, strategy and architecture, architecture and digitalization, enterprise IT architecture and ICT architecture.

Externally, as a shared corporate function, an architecture function offers its architectural planning and advisory services organization-wide, to all primary business units as well as to other supporting functions. Basically, managers of any organizational unit can request the assistance of enterprise architects, as internal consultants (see Figure 4.4), in addressing their business needs or transforming their activities with IT. In some sense, an architecture function can be regarded as the proper entry point to the realm of IT for the rest of the organization.

Internally, within an IT function, an architecture function closely interacts with a delivery function, but much less so with a support function. A delivery function employs project teams who execute transformation projects by developing new information systems based on their architectural plans incoming from enterprise architects. A support function hosts operations teams who, in turn, maintain the developed systems handed over to them by project teams in a stable, operational mode, staying relatively distant from architects. The most typical place of enterprise architects in the corporate structure of a large organization is depicted in Figure 5.1.

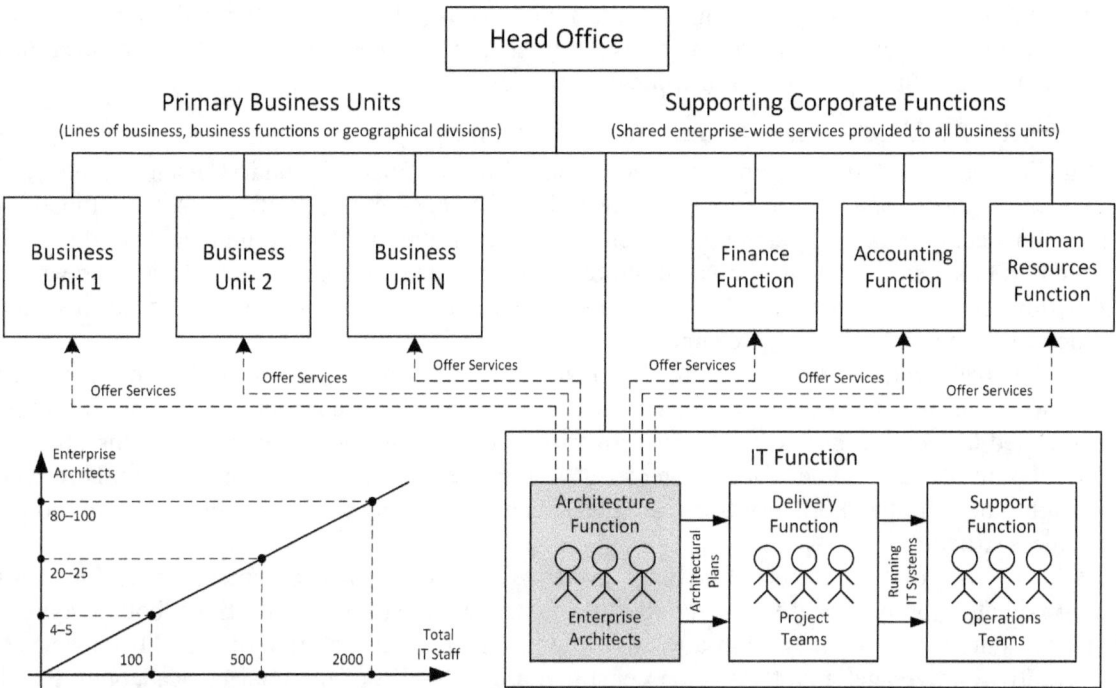

Figure 5.1. The typical place of enterprise architects in the organizational structure

Due to their unusual abilities and duties, enterprise architects occupy a rather special niche in the organizational ecosystem, standing somewhere in between the typical business and IT positions.

Enterprise Architects in the Ecosystem of Organizational Positions

The organizational ecosystem includes multiple positions at different levels of the administrative hierarchy, which can usually be related to either business or IT "hemispheres". Most of the respective actors have some knowledge and perception of IT, as well as certain needs and interests associated with information systems. As discussed earlier, all these actors represent potential stakeholders of digital transformation initiatives and other IT-related planning decisions (see Figure 3.2). However, because of their insufficient competence or preoccupation with other activities, these actors themselves are mostly incapable of conducting adequate architectural planning to enable the successful implementation of digitalization initiatives.

For instance, top business executives, such as chief executive officers (CEOs), chief operating officers (COOs) and other C-level officers, are normally accountable for developing overall business strategy, setting global long-term objectives and working on other corporate issues. They may realize the strategic role of IT in general and even judge the business value of particular IT platforms, but their awareness of technologies is usually limited to their basic capabilities and obviously insufficient to propose any concrete architectural solutions, let alone design them in greater detail.

Middle business managers (e.g. heads of business departments and their deputies) are responsible for ensuring the normal functioning of their units in an operational sense and creating local development plans. These managers may appreciate the importance of IT for the activities of their units and even understand specific information systems they deal with, but they are certainly not competent enough in technical matters to engineer these systems beyond suggesting their high-level functional requirements.

Ordinary business specialists, like sales representatives, market analysts or human resources managers, run daily business operations and perform routine tasks. They might be rather knowledgeable in the specifics of applications they use in their jobs, but are also not capable of designing any architectural solutions, except for specifying their functional requirements. Put it simply, business-side actors concentrate on business issues and cannot plan digital transformation initiatives because their understanding of IT is very shallow.

On the IT side of the organization, the situation is somewhat different as the necessary IT background is present. However, here, other factors come into play. For instance, senior IT executives, such as chief information officers (CIOs), chief technology officers (CTOs) and chief digital officers (CDOs), are accountable for developing corporate technology strategy and dealing with other global IT-related questions. These executives are typically competent in IT and capable of planning digitalization initiatives, but they work at a very high level, are burdened with a wide circle of concerns (e.g. organization of the IT department, staff sourcing, project delivery, system support, vendor relationships, cybersecurity, etc.) and can rarely afford to focus their attention specifically on architectural planning[4].

Mid-level IT managers (e.g. heads of IT units, operations and development) are responsible for their own specific functions, their uninterrupted fulfillment and continuous improvement. They may also understand IT well enough to lead architectural planning, but their constant preoccupation with managerial duties and operational issues usually prevents them from devoting a considerable portion of their time and energy to planning efforts.

Lastly, rank-and-file IT specialists, like software developers, database administrators or infrastructure engineers, concentrate on accomplishing their respective tasks within the stipulated timeframes and according to certain quality standards. These specialists are proficient with their particular technologies or at their concrete tasks, but most often have insufficient knowledge, broad-mindedness and experience to approach the problem of architectural planning at large. Interestingly, even people occupying typical positions in IT departments can hardly act as architectural planners owing to either their inadequate competence or their busyness with other matters[5].

These organizational positions can also be analyzed for their ability to drive architectural planning and digital transformation through the lens of the two hats of enterprise architects (see Figure 4.9). On the one hand, business leaders can, and often do, wear the hat of Change Agents, but they obviously cannot act as Technology Experts. On the other hand, IT leaders can, and often do, wear the hat of Technology Experts, which makes them kindred to architects[6], but because of the broad, operational or simply different focus of their work, they can seldom act effectively as Change Agents. In short, business and IT leaders tend to wear only one of the two hats and, for this reason, cannot lead architectural planning to enable digitalization[7]; it is only enterprise architects who wear both hats simultaneously, acting as true agents of digital transformation (see Figure 4.10).

Therefore, enterprise architects fill a separate vacant niche in the rich ecosystem of organizational positions. With their unusual competencies and exclusive concentration on architectural planning, they stand apart from all other positions, fulfilling a unique and indispensable function in the ecosystem. Simply put, architects do what nobody else in the organization does. Logically, as a cohesive professional community, they inhabit the middle levels of the corporate hierarchy, fitting somewhere between business and IT[8]. The niche of enterprise architects in the organizational ecosystem is shown schematically in Figure 5.2.

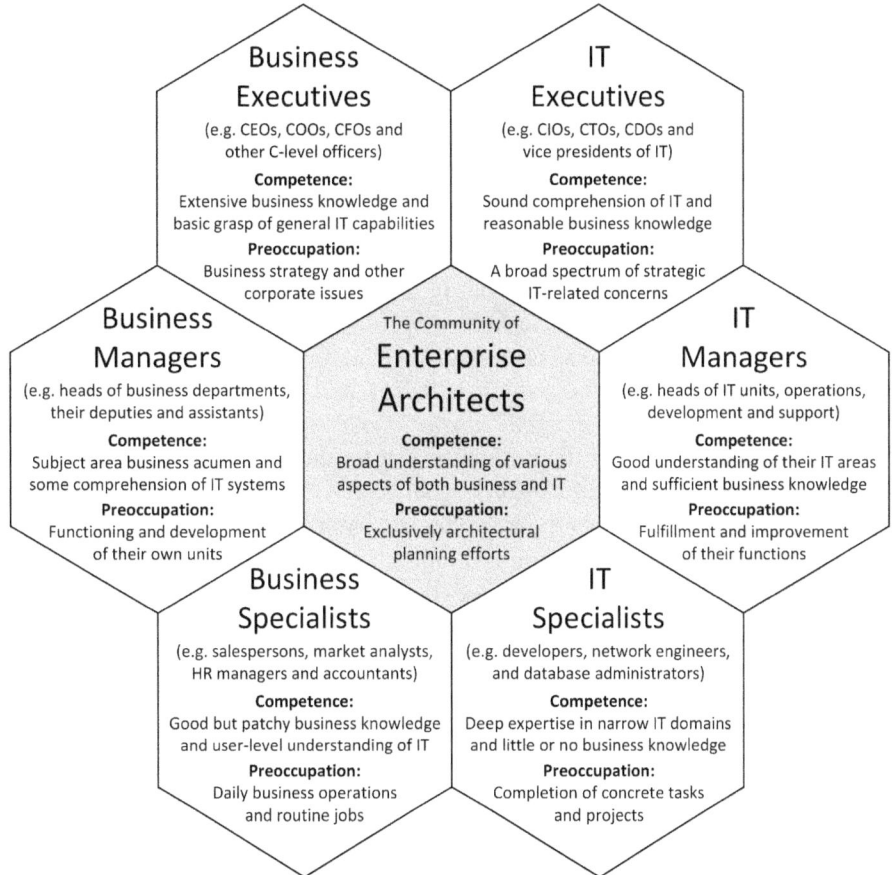

Figure 5.2. The niche of enterprise architects in the organizational ecosystem

As demonstrated in Figure 5.2, different functions in organizations are realized by different actors. For example, corporate strategic planning is fulfilled by business executives, local business planning — by business managers, control of IT units — by IT managers, physical implementation of digitalization initiatives — by IT specialists, while their architectural planning — by enterprise architects. Architects are positioned uniquely in the organizational ecosystem, so that they can serve as the chief agents of digital transformation and principal planners of concrete IT-driven change initiatives, facilitating the execution of business strategy in IT-related aspects.

Enterprise Architects in the Context of Strategy Execution

Being mid-level intermediaries between business and IT, enterprise architects enable the effective realization of business strategy in terms of digitalization and other IT-dependent issues. From the viewpoint of strategy execution, architects help convert abstract business considerations of senior management into specific actionable prescriptions for IT professionals constructing new information systems[9].

On the one hand, enterprise architects actively interact with various business leaders acting as the proponents of transformation drivers, many of which represent deliberate intentions derived from top-level business strategy (see Figure 1.3). These drivers, in turn, induce new transformation initiatives of different sizes (see Figure 2.5), where the respective driver proponents become their key sponsors as well as the primary stakeholders of their architectural planning. In this way, via communicating with business leaders, architects turn business strategy into concrete change initiatives and architectural solutions conducive to its execution.

On the other hand, enterprise architects also collaborate with project teams who eventually develop new information systems and modify the organizational business and IT landscape (see Figure 2.7). By proposing architectural solutions for specific transformation projects congruent with the interests of business leaders standing behind business strategy, they promote the implementation of the right projects in the right way. In this way, via communicating with project teams, architects achieve the alignment of project-level activities with strategic business goals.

Continually interacting with the communities of both business leaders and project teams allows enterprise architects to perform the *translation* of high-level business plans into material information systems supporting them[10]. From assisting in the initial ideation of initiatives aligned with business strategy (see Figure 4.5) to supervising project teams that deliver the necessary IT systems (see Figure 4.8), they facilitate proper decision-making along the entire "value chain" of strategy realization. By connecting business planners and IT implementers, the community of architects provides an intermediate link between strategy planning and execution, though predominantly in IT-related matters. The conceptual role of enterprise architects in the execution of business strategy is shown in Figure 5.3.

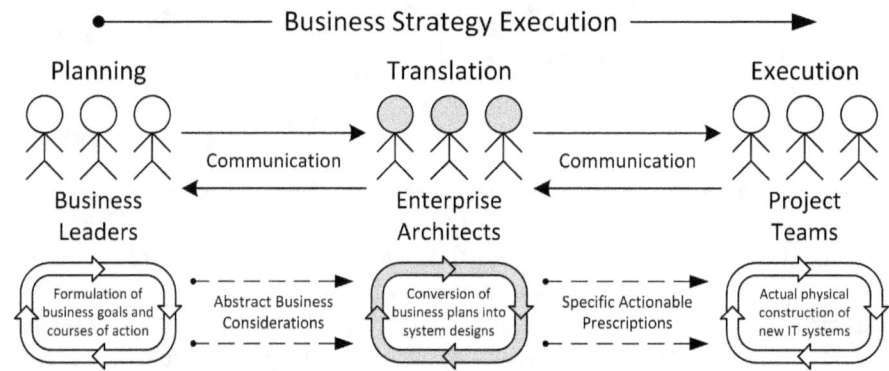

Figure 5.3. The role of enterprise architects in the execution of business strategy

As illustrated in Figure 5.3, on a logical corporate strategy execution path, enterprise architects sit right between business leaders and project teams, helping translate business thoughts into IT actions. From a functional perspective in the broader organizational organism, architects can be best viewed as the conductors of business strategy execution through digitalization opportunities.

What Organizations Employ Enterprise Architects?

Enterprise architects are normally employed by large organizations having at least 30–50 people in their IT departments and at least tens of information systems in their IT landscapes. It is these organizations where separate, full-time positions for driving digital transformation and leading architectural planning become truly necessary. By contrast, in smaller companies and especially startups, opening dedicated positions for architects usually does not pay off as the respective duties can be easily fulfilled on a part-time basis by their IT leaders, also wearing the hat of Technology Experts. For this reason, in many organizations, the role of architects can exist *informally*, without bearing the title "architect"[11].

Enterprise architects are rather universal and, for the most part, industry-neutral professionals. As the agents of digitalization, they are demanded in organizations from virtually all industry sectors irrespective of their specifics. Unsurprisingly, architects can be found in many public and private, commercial and non-profit organizations, e.g. banks, retailers, manufacturers, universities, hospitals, city councils and government agencies.

However, in many digitally native companies, like Google, Facebook and Netflix, specialized enterprise architects are often unnecessary[12]. In these companies, their business leadership typically comes with a solid technical background, deeply understands technology and is perfectly capable of making sound IT-related decisions without outside assistance. In other words, business leaders of digital companies act as Technology Experts themselves and need no architects to think about the use of IT.

Furthermore, besides "end-user" organizations, enterprise architects are often also employed by various providers of IT-related business-to-business (B2B) services, such as IT consultancies, system integrators, hardware, software and cloud vendors. When working in these companies, architects visit their client organizations as temporary external advisors to assist them with the digital transformation of their businesses[13].

Generally, enterprise architects are highly demanded across the industry[14]. Their job market is traditionally characterized by a persistent shortage of talent and a limited availability of candidates with the necessary qualifications[15]. For this reason, architects represent precious employees for organizations that are difficult to attract, hire and retain[16], leaving many architecture functions understaffed[17].

The Value of Enterprise Architects for Organizations

Like all employees, enterprise architects are recruited by organizations to bring business value and contribute to their prosperity. However, due to the highly conceptual character of their work and the intangible nature of its outcomes, their value for organizations is rather elusive and surprisingly difficult to explain[18], let alone quantify[19]. ROI in architects is nearly impossible to calculate or measure. Nevertheless, architects can be analyzed from the standpoint of their costs, benefits and value propositions.

Costs and Benefits of Enterprise Architects

One way to approach the problem of evaluating enterprise architects is to examine the costs and benefits of their employment for organizations. On the one hand, the cost side of this equation is a simple one as the costs of hiring architects for organizations are transparent and very easy to reckon. These costs correspond to their regular base salary, plus some concomitant expenses. For example, in the United States, the average salary of an architect in 2024 constitutes about 120–180 thousand dollars per year[20].

On the other hand, the profit side of the equation is much more puzzling as the benefits of employing enterprise architects for organizations are very uncertain. Better architectural planning, as well as the extent to which the presence of architects boosts digital transformation, can hardly be assessed objectively or converted into dollars. Instead, they can only be "felt" subjectively by business and IT leaders and other organizational actors. Moreover, because the respective efforts are collective in nature and represent teamwork whose outcomes depend on the active participation of multiple people, the personal contribution of a particular architect to their success is difficult to estimate. For these reasons, the salary of architects is usually fixed and cannot be based on their individual performance. Also, owing to the intangibility of their "products", they are often among the first candidates to be laid off when organizations need to cut their operating costs.

Interestingly, in many cases, the value of enterprise architects for organizations can arguably be best made evident and understood through their *absence*. As no other actors in the organizational ecosystem are capable of addressing the need for architectural planning as part of digitalization endeavors in the way architects do, the lack of professional architects renders organizations clumsy and inert in terms of managing their IT investments, aligning them with their business plans and taming the complexity of their system landscapes, thereby exposing the glaring demand for architects. Without specialized architects, or with their acute shortage, IT landscapes quickly deteriorate, become desolate and deserted[21].

Value Propositions of Enterprise Architects

Another way to look at the value of enterprise architects for organizations is to articulate their specific value propositions. Generally, the employment of architects is associated with all sorts of advantages in the efficiency and effectiveness of using IT for doing business. Despite the wide variety of beneficial effects that architects bring to organizations, all these effects can arguably be reduced to three core value propositions: robust decisions, translation capability and strategic linkage.

First, **robust decisions** represent the organizational capacity for making sound planning decisions that can be characterized as thought-out, well-rounded, future-proof and cost-effective. By applying their rich expertise in technology and related areas, architects contribute to the overall collective intelligence with regard to the utilization of IT for business purposes, serving all units and functions of the organization (see Figure 5.1). For example, they can find the most optimal approaches for meeting current needs with the available IT assets, technologies and resources while avoiding possible risks and complications for the company in the long run. This capacity for robust decisions can be thought of as *technical wisdom* in organizations.

Second, **translation capability** represents the organizational capacity for translating ideas, plans and needs from the realm of business into the realm of IT, and back. By leveraging their broad knowledge and developed communication skills, architects act as bilingual interpreters between the business and IT audiences speaking different languages and unable to understand each other, uniting otherwise disjointed business and IT "halves" of the organization (see Figure 5.2). For example, they can convert business desires into the IT-talk meaningful to techies and technical system capabilities into the language of money appealing to business managers, enabling the company to work as one[22]. Because of its potential for bringing together and merging business and IT viewpoints, translation capability can be thought of as a *horizontal linkage* in organizations.

Lastly, **strategic alignment** represents the organizational capacity for putting all digital transformation initiatives into the strategic context and connecting them to some long-term aspirations. By applying their "big picture" thinking abilities, architects help bridge the gulf between the top-level goals and lower-level tactics of their practical realization, providing a medium for IT-supported strategy execution to the organization (see Figure 5.3). For example, they can select technologies, solutions and implementation approaches best suitable for the company in light of its global objectives[23]. In virtue of its potential for bringing together and sewing strategy and implementation, strategic alignment can be thought of as a *vertical linkage* in organizations. The three main value propositions of enterprise architects described above are summarized in Table 5.1.

Value proposition	Robust decisions	Translation capability	Strategic alignment
Practical meaning	Making sound planning decisions satisfying the criteria of quality and cost	Translating business talks into the arcane language of technology, and vice versa	Converting strategic goals into implementation-level steps, options and choices
Metaphorical view	Technical wisdom	Horizontal linkage	Vertical linkage

Table 5.1. Three core value propositions of enterprise architects

The three concrete value propositions of enterprise architects presented in Table 5.1 offer a certain elucidation of the "added value" that they bring to organizations. Nonetheless, their occupation is associated with multiple persistent misbeliefs deforming its substance.

Who Enterprise Architects Are Not

In part, because of the industry hype and excitement around enterprise architects and, in part, because the meaning of their job is very difficult to pin down conceptually and explain in simple terms, their profession in the mainstream discourse is generally surrounded by gossip and often subjected to weird interpretations. Architects themselves frequently become the heroes of various "urban legends" that inadequately present their personality and activities in organizations, explicitly or implicitly. In some cases, the role of enterprise architects is downplayed and their entire work is unfairly reduced to only certain aspects of their occupation[24]. In other cases, their role is, on the contrary, overstated and they are ascribed with superhuman abilities untypical to mere mortals of flesh and blood[25].

To distinguish reality from fiction, it is necessary to clarify who enterprise architects are definitely not. The most prominent misconceptions about enterprise architects are dispelled below, while some other important nuances of the terminological ambiguity of the title "enterprise architect" are discussed later in Chapter 14 (The Profession of Enterprise Architects).

Not Enterprise Strategists

Enterprise architects should not be taken for enterprise strategists who develop business strategy for the whole organization and define its long-term strategic goals[26]. Although architects often lead strategy-level digitalization initiatives, these initiatives are driven by the higher-order vision and objectives set for them in a top-down fashion by senior business managers. In other words, architects consider business strategy with the ensuing elements of the motivational context largely as a given foundation for all digital transformation efforts. Enterprise-wide strategy is formulated by C-level executives and their deputies at the highest "floors" of the organization, where architects typically have no access, nor do they have the necessary competencies to contribute to its development. For this reason, the purview of enterprise architects is limited only to making the existing strategy happen with the best possible use of IT resources and innovations.

Not Chief Technologists

Enterprise architects should not be confused with chief technologists who simply understand and master all relevant domains of IT. Indeed, architects wear the hat of Technology Experts and are very competent in technical matters, which explains their popular public image as senior technologists. However, though it is not completely untrue, the perception of architects as mere technologists represents a misguiding *half-truth* that drastically truncates their role and overshadows the other essential part of their occupation — leading IT-enabled business change. In addition to being accomplished Technology Experts, architects also wear another hat of Change Agents, which allows them to invent new applications of IT in business, introduce technology in organizations and drive their digital transformation efforts aligned with strategic goals. Without the second half of their role as Change Agents, enterprise architects would have never risen to prominence, formed a separate profession and deserved a dedicated book.

Not Universal Transformers

Enterprise architects should not be viewed as universal transformers capable of guiding any kind of organizational transformation or executing business strategies in all their aspects[27]. Architects specialize specifically in *digital* transformations, as those that imply introducing IT in organizations, and, therefore, can actually contribute to the execution of their strategies only in IT-related matters (see Figure 5.3). In a word, their core subject area is IT. For this reason, with some situational exceptions, architects cannot, for example, define desired product portfolios and price ranges, select target markets and customer segments, plan marketing and promotional campaigns, design supply and production chains, choose legal and organizational structures, devise employee training programs and incentive schemes, and do many other things that might be required to implement corporate business strategy. Put it simply, enterprise architects do not deal with all planning decisions necessary for strategy execution, but only with the decisions concerning IT.

Not System Architects

Enterprise architects should not be mixed up with system architects and other IT specialists of their kind, such as software architects, technical architects and system designers, who concentrate exclusively on designing individual information systems from a purely technical point of view. Although these specialists are also "architects" of a sort[28], their personalities, perspectives and duties in organizations are, in fact, disparate from those of enterprise architects. In their personalities, system architects are deep techies of narrow specialization distant from any business issues. In their perspectives, they are limited only to the internals of separate IT systems, but do not consider the organizational IT landscape as a whole, let alone its connection with business capabilities. In their duties, they are responsible solely for defining detailed system structures based on given functional and non-functional requirements, preselected technology stack and other architectural plans. Organizationally, system architects typically belong to delivery, not architecture, functions (see Figure 5.1), join concrete digitalization projects when they are already in flight and work on their delivery as senior members of project teams (see Figure 2.7). Because of the narrowness of their technical expertise and outlook, lack of business knowledge, communication skills and other necessary qualities, they cannot lead architectural planning as enterprise architects do, but can only contribute to the process as competent subject-matter experts (see Figure 3.2). Surprisingly, notwithstanding the apparent consonance of enterprise and system architects, their abilities and roles in organizations are actually very different and practically unrelated[29].

Not Supreme Draftsmen

The work of enterprise architects, as well as the practice of enterprise architecture in general, is strongly associated with creating various pictures, diagrams and models. Accordingly, architects are often portrayed largely as well-trained draftsmen capable of drawing "correct" diagrams with proper software tools, graphical notations, modeling languages and meta-models, particularly by those who advertise these tools and languages[30]. However, in practice, architectural diagrams provide only the means of communication used by architects, whereas the real product of their activities is *better planning decisions*. Viewing architects as draftsmen, thus, falsely shifts the focus from ends to means. Besides that, the most crucial criterion of good diagrams is their comprehensibility to the target audience, not their adherence to specific modeling "standards", which greatly reduces the actual importance of any diagramming tools, languages and conventions in the work of architects. More importantly, diagramming evidently represents only one of the numerous facets of their occupation that by no means adequately characterizes it in its entirety and barely reflects its basic purpose. In short, the image of enterprise architects as superior draftsmen has some grain of truth, but is misleading on the whole.

Not Systems Thinkers

Because corporate landscapes consist of large systems of systems of interrelated business and IT elements, the practice of enterprise architecture is also closely associated with systems thinking, while enterprise architects, as its key actors, are sometimes regarded primarily as systems thinkers[31]. Although systemic thinking indeed represents one of the notable skills of architects, its overall significance in the context of their occupation should not be exaggerated as it does not convey accurately the spirit of what they actually do in organizations. As collectivities of cooperating people, organizations implement group decision-making with the involvement of multiple actors. In these settings, the quality of resulting organizational decisions can be increased predominantly by improving *inter-actor communication*, but no individual thinking on its own can seriously change the situation for the better[32]. Considering architects, above all, as systems thinkers distorts the substance of their work and de-emphasizes their truly paramount role as communicators, intermediaries and liaisons between different parties. In other words, placing their systems thinking abilities over their communicative abilities would be a mistake as successful architects are much more talkers than thinkers. Again, although it is not entirely untrue, the perception of enterprise architects mainly as systems thinkers is detrimental to their reputation in organizations as well as to their profession in general.

Not Omniscient Masterminds

As digitalization cuts through all layers of the business and IT landscape, enterprise architects should ideally understand the whole organization end-to-end, including all aspects of its business and IT. However, as ordinary people not endowed with any supernatural abilities and subject to the same cognitive limitations as all human beings, they cannot know everything and cannot understand any areas better than their specialized subject-matter experts[33]. Obviously, architects cannot understand how the business works better than business managers responsible for running it. For example, customer needs, market opportunities, competitive pressures and other similar questions clearly fall within the zone of competence of business representatives out of reach to architects. For this reason, all business-side transformation drivers dictating how the organization should be changed are exogenous to architects and largely taken by them for granted. Even from the IT side, despite being experienced technology professionals, architects cannot appreciate the latest features and capabilities of specific programming languages, cloud platforms and network devices better than hands-on software developers and hardware engineers working with these technologies on a full-time daily basis. To summarize, because of the inherent functional specialization of employees in organizations, architects cannot understand narrow subject areas of IT, let alone of business, better than dedicated specialists assigned to these areas. Instead of faking competence and playing an omniscient "Mr. Know-it-all", enterprise architects organize *participative planning* with the involvement of genuine subject-matter experts from different fields as stakeholders to leverage and benefit from their expertise.

Not Almighty Wizards

Sometimes, enterprise architects are envisioned as "designers of organizations" who "architect enterprises" in a literal sense, as if they were potent sorcerers, or demiurges, capable of modifying organizations at their will based on some blueprints with the wave of a magic wand[34]. Organizations, however, cannot be modified in this manner not only because architects have no official managerial power to be able to command transformation, but also because *no one* can actually transform them with that ease. As extremely complicated, organic entities driven by decentralized and partly chaotic group decision-making processes, organizations in principle cannot be designed or "architected" by any separate individuals, even by their CEOs. In reality, any complex organizational change requires persistent work and, more importantly, a *political consensus* of powerful organizational actors that this change should be carried out. For this reason, architects do not make changes happen magically, but build strong coalitions of supporters to begin implementing changes and then protect these coalitions from dissolving as these changes unfold to finish them. Hence, enterprise architects are not almighty wizards transmogrifying organizations, but astute politicians winning the hearts and minds of decision-makers to accomplish organizational transformations.

Not the Smartest Guys

Enterprise architects are extremely intelligent and broadly educated people with considerable practical experience in the industry. By virtue of their typical engineering or similar background, they also often have a very well-developed sense of logic, deduction and reasoning. From the viewpoint of their "scientific" rationality, many decisions and actions of business managers, especially those trained in humanities, may seem rather strange and unreasonable, if not foolish.

However, architects are far from the only clever people in organizations and definitely not the smartest guys in the room. Business leaders are also very talented, not silly and often have their own valid reasons for some or the other "bizarre" choices that may be unknown or not fully comprehensible to architects. Moreover, in the organizational world of ambiguity, uncertainty and volatility, strict cause-and-effect logic from the world of technology may not always be applicable. For this reason, mature architects treat their business colleagues as equally intelligent peers, do not try to question or underestimate their competence and respect their opinions, even when they find these opinions unfounded or irrational. Enterprise architects lead architectural planning and digital transformation efforts not because they have the highest IQ and are smarter than everybody else in the organization, but merely because of their unique combination of knowledge and skills that puts them in a better position to handle this task.

Not Grumbling Loafers

Historically, in many organizations, enterprise architects deserved a bad reputation as idle people residing in "ivory towers", who only loaf around, draw curious but arcane diagrams, lament that their brilliant ideas are ignored and their advice is not taken by anyone seriously[35]. This reputation usually stems from the *lack of engagement* between architects and business representatives, which does not allow them to exert any real influence on decision-making[36]. By contrast, successful architects seek to dive deep into the business context, establish their communication networks in management circles, grow their reputation as valuable business partners and use their informal authority to shape decisions. They are respectable and busy people whose consultations are in high demand across the company and whose weekly calendar is full of various meetings. Effective architects not just draw diagrams, but promote the visions depicted there to business leaders, so that these diagrams cause action and eventually turn into reality. They do not speculate or goof around, they induce organizational change and actuate digital transformation.

Chapter Summary

This chapter discussed the place of enterprise architects in the organizational structure, their niche in the organizational ecosystem, their role in strategy execution and their overall standing in the industry, explained the costs, benefits and value propositions of enterprise architects for organizations and clarified who enterprise architects are not. The key message of this chapter can be summarized in the following essential points:

- Organizationally, enterprise architects typically reside in specialized architecture functions, which belong to IT sub-functions, report to chief IT executives and offer their services to all primary business units and other corporate functions
- Conceptually, the community of enterprise architects occupies the middle levels of the administrative hierarchy, placing right in the center between business executives, managers and specialists and IT executives, managers and specialists
- Strategically, enterprise architects provide a conduit between strategy planning and execution by converting abstract business considerations of senior leaders into specific actionable prescriptions for IT professionals building new systems

- Enterprise architects are highly demanded by large organizations from all industry sectors (except digitally native companies) and various IT service providers, whereas in small organizations their role is often fulfilled part-time by IT leaders
- While the costs of enterprise architects are perfectly transparent and equal to their salary, their benefits for organizations are much less certain, highly subjective and intangible, and often can be best understood through their absence
- Beneficial effects of enterprise architects for organizations can be summarized in three core value propositions: robust decisions (technical wisdom), translation capability (horizontal linkage) and strategic alignment (vertical linkage)
- Enterprise architects should not be confused with enterprise strategists and chief technologists, universal transformers and system architects, supreme draftsmen and systems thinkers, omniscient masterminds and almighty wizards

PART II: Enterprise Architects in Depth

Part II of this book provides a very detailed coverage of enterprise architects as specialized professionals from various angles. This part discusses different types of resources, instruments and activities of enterprise architects, the work of architects in organizations as an integration of all their properties and their profession as a whole in the broader occupational, historical and terminological contexts.

Part II consists of nine consecutive chapters. Chapter 6 covers resources possessed by enterprise architects and describes in detail all the major classes of their resources: knowledge, skills and experience. Chapters 7, 8 and 9 together cover instruments employed by enterprise architects. Initially, Chapter 7 introduces different categories of instruments of enterprise architects including EA artifacts, the CSVLOD taxonomy for organizing them and some other instruments. Then, Chapter 8 presents a comprehensive catalog of EA artifacts corresponding to the six general types defined by the CSVLOD taxonomy: Considerations, Standards, Visions, Landscapes, Outlines and Designs. Finally, Chapter 9 describes in great detail the use of EA artifacts by architects for documenting the existing situation and capturing architectural solutions, as well as the architectural context formed by these artifacts. Chapters 10, 11 and 12 together cover activities performed by enterprise architects. First, Chapter 10 introduces different types of activities of enterprise architects with their contexts and thoroughly describes their three basic activities: analyzing the external environment, studying the internal environment and providing advisory services. Next, Chapter 11 continues the discussion of the activities of enterprise architects and describes in great detail their central activity: leading the development of plans. Lastly, Chapter 12 finishes the discussion of the activities of enterprise architects and describes in great detail their closing activity: ensuring adherence to plans. Chapter 13 provides an integral view of the work of enterprise architects in different contexts in terms of their activities, describes their working schedule and explains their advocacy of technical interests. In conclusion, Chapter 14 discusses the profession of enterprise architects with its features, the historical evolution of their profession over decades and different understandings of architects prevalent in the industry.

Chapter 6: Resources of Enterprise Architects

Previously, Chapter 4 introduced enterprise architects and provided a high-level overview of their competencies and abilities. This chapter concentrates specifically on the resources of enterprise architects and describes the main classes of their resources in great detail. In particular, this chapter starts with discussing general categories of knowledge of enterprise architects and specific elements of knowledge within each category. Next, this chapter discusses broad groups of skills of enterprise architects and narrow clusters of skills within each group. Lastly, this chapter describes the practical experience of enterprise architects with its manifestations and summarizes the discussion of their resources by presenting the pyramid of resources.

Resources Possessed by Enterprise Architects

Enterprise architects are complex personalities that, at the highest level, can be best summarized in their two hats of Technology Experts and Change Agents (see Figure 4.9). As part of their daily work in organizations, they carry out a wide variety of activities and fulfill a rich set of responsibilities associated with wearing these hats. To be able to fulfill these responsibilities with a due degree of efficacy, architects need specific resources.

Resources of enterprise architects represent their inalienable possessions, or qualities, that enable their capabilities, allow them to do their job in organizations and successfully lead architectural planning by wearing the hats of Technology Experts and Change Agents. Architects accumulate their resources gradually, over the course of their entire careers, starting from their most junior pre-architecture positions and up to their maturation as accomplished professionals. Moreover, because this occupation demands continuous self-development, even seasoned architects constantly learn new lessons, perfect their mastery and "sharpen their axe", further ramping up their resources.

Although the resources of enterprise architects are rather diversified and acquirable by different means, they can be loosely structured into three major classes: knowledge, skills and experience[1]. Some of these resources belong more to Technology Experts and others — to Change Agents.

Knowledge of Enterprise Architects

The first broad class of the resources of architects is their vast knowledge and erudition. **Knowledge of enterprise architects** aggregates everything that they know expressly, as articulate facts about technology, their organization and its environment. Knowledge represents an *explicit* form of information that can be readily codified, externalized and learned by studying written or other recorded materials. It can also be exchanged between architects via oral communication or by means of creating shared document repositories. For this reason, compared with other types of architects' resources, knowledge can be viewed as the most accessible, superficial and easily acquirable asset.

In terms of its content, knowledge possessed by enterprise architects is rather extensive and encompasses diverse areas relevant to the use of information systems in organizations. However, for explanatory purposes, all knowledge of architects can be conveniently organized according to two orthogonal dimensions into an intuitive knowledge taxonomy. On the one hand, knowledge can be loosely classified into business-related and IT-related. Business-related knowledge covers business aspects of organizations and their environment, whereas IT-related knowledge embraces various facets of technology and its use. Business-related knowledge is necessary for wearing the hat of Change Agents and interacting with various business representatives. IT-related knowledge is vital for wearing the hat of Technology Experts and designing information systems.

On the other hand, all knowledge of enterprise architects can also be classified into general, industry-specific and organization-specific. General knowledge is absolute and applies to all industries and organizations, industry-specific knowledge relates only to particular industry sectors, while organization-specific knowledge relates exclusively to concrete organizations. This two-dimensional classification scheme yields six different categories of knowledge of architects.

General Business-Related Knowledge

First, **general business-related knowledge** refers to what doing business is all about and how organizations generally work in their different aspects. This category of knowledge includes, but is not limited to:

- Classic business disciplines — standard fields of knowledge usually studied in MBA programs and familiar to most businesspersons, like economics, marketing, accounting and finance
- Organization theory — the basics of organizational structure, behavior and decision-making, governance, leadership and management, personalities, teamwork and motivation
- Business analysis tools — various instruments, techniques and approaches used for business analysis and decision-making, such as ROI, net present value (NPV), SWOT analysis and other strategy frameworks
- Legislative context — national and supranational laws and normative acts that regulate the collection, use and sharing of personal, commercial and other sensitive information by organizations, e.g. GDPR in the European Union[2] and analogous privacy laws in other countries[3]

This knowledge is prerequisite for making sense of the business and comprehending the surrounding organizational reality. Possessing it is important for enterprise architects to feel comfortable and confident during their conversations with business managers of all ranks and specializations.

General IT-Related Knowledge

Second, **general IT-related knowledge** refers to what is usually meant under the umbrella term "IT background" and implies a broad understanding of foundational theoretical and practical aspects of IT. This knowledge covers, among many other things:

- Computer science — the underlying principles of computing and programming, hardware and software, algorithms, data structures and network protocols, applications, databases and operating systems

- Technology landscape and market — main classes of technologies, systems and solutions across all subdomains of IT, their capabilities, purposes and features, as well as their major vendors and popular offerings on the market
- System design principles — approaches, patterns and best practices for constructing robust IT systems, meeting functional and non-functional requirements, achieving high availability, scalability, maintainability and security
- IT management practices — approaches to project management (e.g. PMBOK[4] and PRINCE2[5]), service management (e.g. ITIL[6]) and IT governance (e.g. COBIT[7]), system development methodologies (e.g. Scrum[8]), testing and other quality assurance techniques for IT solutions, version control and build automation, continuous integration, deployment and other DevOps practices

This knowledge constitutes elementary IT literacy and provides an overall framework for interpreting all other information about technology. It allows enterprise architects to orientate in the complex world of IT and approach the problem of designing technical solutions for digital transformation initiatives with due gumption.

Industry-Specific Business-Related Knowledge

Third, **industry-specific business-related knowledge** encompasses everything that concerns the specifics of doing business in a particular industry sector. This category of knowledge comprises, but is not limited to:

- Industry concepts and practices — common industry notions, terms, approaches, business models, best practices and ways of conducting operations, as well as the industry-wide trends in their development
- Competitive environment — current and emerging leaders, their sources of competitive edge, principal competitive drivers, factors and resources, as well as the general nature of competition in the industry
- Industry regulations — national and international laws, legislative acts and their requirements that apply to all organizations in the industry, as well as various standards, norms and recommendations issued by industry consortia, e.g. HIPAA for healthcare[9] in the United States and PCI DSS for payments globally[10]
- Industry reference models — reference models describing, at a high level, generic business activities characteristic or typical for all companies operating in the industry sector, e.g. eTOM for telecom[11], BIAN for banking[12], ACORD for insurance[13] and SCOR for supply chains[14]

This knowledge is necessary for a more nuanced understanding of the business, its difficulties and opportunities. Possessing it helps enterprise architects better grasp the interests and objectives of business stakeholders, establish more trustful relationships with them and eventually build a deeper partnership between business and IT.

Industry-Specific IT-Related Knowledge

Fourth, **industry-specific IT-related knowledge** covers everything about the application of IT and the use of information systems in a particular industry sector. This knowledge includes, but is not limited to:

- Standard ways of using IT — industry-standard approaches for utilizing technology in the respective business models and accepted best practices in addressing common sector-specific problems with IT, e.g. RFID in logistics
- Niche IT solutions — existing vendors and their products addressing business needs and automating operations essential to the industry sector, their distinctive features, relative advantages and disadvantages, e.g. LMS platforms in education
- Technological innovations — technology trends, breakthrough innovations and their promising applications specific to the industry sector capable of reshaping the entire competitive landscape
- Data exchange formats — standardized data structures, formats and conventions enabling effective intra-industry information sharing and electronic integration between trading partners, e.g. HL7 for healthcare[15], LEDES for legal[16], AIDX for aviation[17] and railML for railways[18]

This knowledge is beneficial for appreciating the particularities of IT support in specific types of organizations and leveraging the collective technical wisdom of the industry. It allows enterprise architects to find more suitable technology solutions to relevant business problems and adopt proven industry approaches instead of "reinventing the wheel".

Organization-Specific Business-Related Knowledge

Fifth, **organization-specific business-related knowledge** refers to the actual business and decision-making arrangements in the current organization. This category of knowledge covers, among other things:

- Business activities — geographical locations and points of presence, services, products and lines of business, partners and customers, costs and revenue streams, operations, processes and tasks, as well as their unique organizational specifics
- Strategic context — top-level business strategy and more tangible transformation drivers from the motivational context, as well as the overall competitive position of the organization on the market and its key competitors
- Stakeholder context — senior executives, heads of business units and other decision-makers, their drivers, interests and concerns, power and influence, reporting and authority structure, as well as who makes what kind of decisions
- Business terminology — the general language used by business managers, the genuine meaning of specific terms in specific contexts and different interpretations of the same terms by different audiences

This knowledge represents a requisite "entrance ticket" for enterprise architects to any meetings with business stakeholders without which architectural planning cannot take place. It is crucial not only for understanding the contents of concrete business discussions, but even for figuring out with whom these discussions should be held and who else needs to be involved.

Organization-Specific IT-Related Knowledge

Lastly, **organization-specific IT-related knowledge** refers to the structure of the corporate IT landscape and respective management practices in the current organization. This knowledge includes, but is not limited to:

- Utilized technologies — the overall technology portfolio of the organization at all layers of the stack as well as the expertise accumulated within the IT department in using and supporting these technologies
- Existing IT assets — deployed instances of information systems, applications, databases, integration platforms, hardware infrastructure and data centers, as well as their capabilities in terms of serving the business
- Current landscape structure — relationships between different IT assets and business activities, the logical flow of information through the elements of the IT landscape, its opportunities and bottlenecks
- Adopted practices of IT management — institutionalized approaches to IT project management, IT service management, operations support, equipment procurement and other IT-related decision-making procedures

This knowledge is critical for realizing current IT capabilities, constraints and opportunities for reuse. Possessing it allows enterprise architects to make the best use of the available IT resources in digital transformation initiatives and ensure the proper integration of new information systems into the corporate IT environment.

The Taxonomy of Knowledge of Enterprise Architects

Arranging all knowledge of architects according to two independent dimensions, as described above, helps make sense of what they need to know to perform their job. The six categories of knowledge of enterprise architects organized into the two-dimensional knowledge taxonomy are summarized in Figure 6.1.

	General Knowledge	Industry-Specific Knowledge	Organization-Specific Knowledge
Business-Related Knowledge	Classic Business Disciplines; Organization Theory; Business Analysis Tools; Legislative Context	Industry Concepts and Practices; Competitive Environment; Industry Regulations; Industry Reference Models	Business Activities; Strategic Context; Stakeholder Context; Business Terminology
IT-Related Knowledge	Computer Science; Technology Landscape and Market; System Design Principles; IT Management Practices	Standard Ways of Using IT; Niche IT Solutions; Technological Innovations; Data Exchange Formats	Utilized Technologies; Existing IT Assets; Current Landscape Structure; Adopted Practices of IT Management

Figure 6.1. Six categories of knowledge of enterprise architects

The knowledge taxonomy presented in Figure 6.1 offers a concise structured view of what exactly enterprise architects should know to succeed in their occupation, which is irreducible in principle to any single sphere of competence.

Skills of Enterprise Architects

The second broad class of the resources possessed by architects is their special skills and knacks. **Skills of enterprise architects** encompass all the practical abilities, behavioral and mental habits that they have mastered or adopted to fulfill their responsibilities in organizations. Skills represent a *tacit* form of information that can hardly be codified and obtained by reading, but only learned by doing in practice. As skills reside largely in a subconscious "muscle memory", they can be exchanged between architects either by watching their colleagues in action and replicating what they do, or through active coaching, mentorship and apprenticeship relations. Although skills cannot be acquired as straightforwardly as explicit knowledge, they can still be developed via circulating within the community of architects and imitating their behavior[19].

In terms of their content, all the skills of enterprise architects can be loosely organized into four major groups: communication skills, collaborative attitude, innovative mindset and disciplined thinking[20]. Most of these skills are necessary for wearing the hat of Change Agents and being capable of reaching optimal organizational solutions.

Communication Skills

Communication skills represent the proficiency of enterprise architects in communicating with very diverse audiences and groups of stakeholders, ranging from senior business executives to junior IT technicians[21]. Developed communicative skills are essential for architects and constitute one of their core capabilities. In the context of their work and responsibilities, communication skills can be decomposed into several rather specific abilities:

- Listening and understanding — the ability to hear the views, opinions and concerns of different people, understand their situations, considerations and motives and appreciate their unique perspectives on the subject
- Adapting the language — the ability to choose the right words, tone and terminology for communicating with various audiences, or to speak like a "native" in different stakeholder circles
- Conveying ideas — the ability to formulate, express and present ideas in a form accessible and appealing to the intended audience, whether with or without formal presentations, and make sure that these ideas are clearly understood
- Visualizing information — the ability to create intuitive diagrams, charts and models that illustrate ideas and concepts in such a way that they can be easily grasped even by laypersons, similar to those demonstrated in Figure 4.2
- Building relationships — the ability to establish trustful, empathetic and long-lasting partnership relationships with stakeholders and turn into a desired guest at every IT-related meeting or discussion
- Sticking to etiquette — the overall adherence to the norms of office communication etiquette, selection of appropriate modes and means of

communication, as well as the ability to properly organize and appoint formal and informal meetings

As enterprise architects practice "planning by talking" (see Figure 4.7), their ability to communicate with others efficiently is paramount for their occupation. Basically, excellent communication skills can be fairly regarded as the *single most important quality* of architects without which this profession is simply inconceivable[22].

Collaborative Attitude

A **collaborative attitude** represents the aptitude of enterprise architects for acting as effective team players. Because significant decisions in organizations are normally made collectively, architects often find themselves to be part of some or the other team, so that teamwork actually constitutes the bulk of their activities. For this reason, they benefit from a number of personal traits, skills and qualities necessary for being genuine team members and facilitating constructive team-wide cooperation:

- Brainstorming ability — the capacity for generating interesting ideas and possible solutions to the problem at hand, as well as stimulating creative thinking in other team members
- Negotiation skills — the proficiency in identifying commonalities among different viewpoints and overlaps between different interests, and then finding mutually acceptable decisions and trade-offs
- Consensus seeking — an aspiration for reaching consensus, widespread agreement and sincere support of the proposed planning decisions and courses of action among all members of the team
- Conflict resolution — a flair for resolving difficult conflicts of interests between different stakeholders, reconciling discrepancies in opinions, settling down disagreements and bringing together diverging points of view
- Pliability and flexibility — readiness to concede, put aside their own personal opinion and wholeheartedly commit to the agreed group decisions for the sake of the common good
- Political sagacity — an understanding of the political aspects of the decision-making context and leveraging this understanding for achieving more coherent team decisions

A strong collaborative attitude allows enterprise architects to contribute to any collective efforts and, by their presence, add value to group decision-making sessions. The organizational reality rarely rewards individualism and the profession of architects is definitely not the one where being individualistic can be a virtue[23].

Innovative Mindset

An **innovative mindset** represents the ability of enterprise architects to promote innovation in organizations. As noted earlier, today technology has turned into the primary driver of change and the latest developments in IT constantly open new opportunities for their application in business (see Figure 1.1). In the current technological context, architects are naturally positioned to act as the chief advocates of IT-enabled business improvements and transformations. Fulfilling this role demands from architects the possession of certain proclivities, habits and qualities:

- Appreciation of novelty — a personal preference and penchant for novelty, being not afraid of changes and readiness to accomplish them, as well as the ability to inspire others with exciting new ideas
- Proactive learning — the habit of persistent learning, seeking and consuming new information, studying the latest technologies, their capabilities and possible applications, as well as the overall curiosity of mind
- Technology evangelism — an inclination for advertising the power of IT, praising emerging technologies, accentuating their potential advantages over old ones and promoting their organizational adoption
- Out-of-the-box thinking — an aptitude for generating unorthodox ideas and finding unconventional solutions, being capable of envisioning transformative, rather than incremental, changes
- Matching capability — the ability to match opening technology opportunities with existing business needs and see where new technologies can be applied for the maximum business impact
- Change leadership — an aspiration to induce and lead change, persuade others of their necessity, cope with the resistance in conservative circles and turn oneself into a genuine thought leader

The very gist of digital transformation is persistently searching for novel ways of using IT in business settings, and it is the innovative mindset of enterprise architects, manifested in their willingness to explore new horizons, experiment with ideas and invent ingenious solutions, that turns them into productive transformers of organizations[24].

Disciplined Thinking

Disciplined thinking represents the capacity of enterprise architects to reason in an orderly manner duly taking into account and balancing all relevant factors. Organizations are complex socio-technical systems with multifarious interrelated and constantly interacting entities, where any changes in their separate elements are likely to affect some other elements, cause a ripple across the broader system and also somehow influence its future behavior. While their technical elements are associated with concreteness, objectivity and precision, their social elements possess exactly the opposite properties — immateriality, subjectivity and vagueness. Understanding organizations and conceiving their change require a mature thinking discipline to be able to grasp the links and causal relationships between their disparate business and IT elements spanning conceptual, spatial and temporal boundaries[25]. Specifically, the disciplined thinking of architects involves the following constituents:

- Analytical abilities — an aptitude for comprehensively analyzing the situation, logically relating known facts, "joining the dots", identifying potential inconsistencies and missing pieces of the puzzle
- Problem-solving skills — the ability to approach complicated problems, decompose them into smaller sub-problems, diagnose their root causes and untangle possible interdependencies between them

- Engineering mindset — the proficiency in formal analysis and synthesis, working with numerical equations and figures, designing and describing the structure of complex, multi-component systems
- Systems thinking — the propensity to consider socio-technical systems holistically, recognizing the connections between the whole and its parts, causes and their effects, present conditions and their future consequences
- Zooming capability — the ability to think at multiple different levels of abstraction at the same time, freely zoom in and out, switching the focus from the entire "forest" down to the details of individual "trees" and back[26]
- Ambiguity tolerance — a comfortable acceptance of uncertainties abounding in the business world, exploring vagueness, dealing with ambiguity and acknowledging its presence as normal for organizational life

Modern organizations embody intricate interlacements of business and IT elements that require well-thought-out, concerted changes. Unless enterprise architects can adequately comprehend their structure in its full complexity, optimal planning decisions on their further evolution can hardly be made.

The Framework of Skills of Enterprise Architects

For presentational purposes, the four groups of skills of enterprise architects discussed above can be loosely organized into four partly overlapping categories. First, communication skills and collaborative attitude can be viewed as *behavioral* skills of architects that are more externally facing, social, people-oriented and influence their observable conduct. Second, an innovative mindset and disciplined thinking can be viewed as *mental* skills that are more internally facing, private, ideas-oriented and determine their decision preferences. Third, an innovative mindset and communication skills characterize enterprise architects more as "knowledge intrapreneurs", who generate pioneering ideas and disseminate them across the organization, thereby pushing it forward. Fourth, disciplined thinking and collaborative attitude characterize them more as "corporate integrators", who are concerned with consistency and harmony of the whole organization as a mechanism or collectivity. All the skills of enterprise architects organized according to the framework described above are summarized in Figure 6.2.

	Collaborative Attitude	Communication Skills
Behavioral Skills	Brainstorming Ability Negotiation Skills Consensus Seeking Conflict Resolution Pliability and Flexibility Political Sagacity	Listening and Understanding Adapting the Language Conveying Ideas Visualizing Information Building Relationships Sticking to Etiquette
Mental Skills	**Disciplined Thinking** Analytical Abilities Problem-Solving Skills Engineering Mindset Systems Thinking Zooming Capability Ambiguity Tolerance	**Innovative Mindset** Appreciation of Novelty Proactive Learning Technology Evangelism Out-of-the-box Thinking Matching Capability Change Leadership
	Enterprise Architect as "Corporate Integrator"	Enterprise Architect as "Knowledge Intrapreneur"

Figure 6.2. Four groups of skills of enterprise architects

The skills framework presented in Figure 6.2 offers a concise structured view of what exactly enterprise architects should be able to do, or how they have to think and behave, to succeed in their occupation.

Experience of Enterprise Architects

The third broad class of the resources of architects is their overall experience and sapience. **Experience of enterprise architects** aggregates all the observations made and lessons learned over the course of their working life regarding all aspects of business and IT. Architects, like all people, tend to acquire much of what they know in a practical sense from their own personal experience. Accumulating experience develops practical wisdom and professional intuition that allow seeing as obvious many of the things imperceptible to newbies, which are difficult or impossible to discern without sufficient experiential background. For example, by virtue of their considerable experience, chess grandmasters intuitively distinguish good and bad moves, positions and patterns on the chessboard that beginners simply cannot see[27]. In a similar vein, veteran enterprise architects, unlike novice IT specialists, often "feel" that some solutions are unlikely to work out successfully, when other solutions may succeed.

Furthermore, because of the inherent complexity and ambiguity of the world, many regularities and causal relationships can only be observed, recognized and grasped over time. In the same sense in which large objects can only be seen from a distance, some fundamental principles and far-reaching conclusions take a lot of time to comprehend. Learning certain precious lessons requires being active in the industry long enough to appreciate them. The practical value of experience, thus, grows increasingly with its temporal length.

Enterprise architects also greatly benefit from the variety of their experience. Being in many different situations, organizations and industries, dealing with different technologies, products and solutions all enriches their worldview and gives them a better understanding of what works and what does not work in practice. The importance of diversified, long-term experience for architects is difficult to overemphasize[28]. Albeit their experience does not lie solely within the province of IT, it is arguably more relevant to wearing the hat of Technology Experts and being capable of designing sound technical solutions.

Experience represents a *heuristic* form of information that can be gained only by working, acting, sensing and reflecting. It cannot be obtained quickly, but rather takes significant time, often measured in years and decades, to gather. There are no shortcuts to getting the necessary experience. Experience also cannot be easily transferred, exchanged or shared between architects. For these reasons, of all the resources of enterprise architects, their experience can be regarded as the most personal, scarce and "expensive" one[29].

Although experience undoubtedly plays an important role in the decision preferences of enterprise architects and its "imprint" can often be noticed even in concrete planning decisions, the exact influence of experience on decision-making can hardly be formalized. Nonetheless, specifically in the context of their job in organizations, several distinct applications of experience can be clearly articulated.

Anticipating Long-Term Consequences

Full repercussions of many IT-related planning decisions unfold gradually over the passage of time, are manifested mostly in the long run and simply cannot be observed and understood immediately after these decisions have been made. For this reason, some choices that proved successful in the short term may eventually turn out detrimental, while solutions that initially seemed effective may no longer look as such after a few years.

Substantial experience is necessary for enterprise architects to recognize the potential presence of unobvious but negative long-term effects, or side effects, of planning decisions and develop a sufficient sense of perspective to be able to foresee these effects. Whereas junior IT specialists tend to think in relatively short time horizons of, say, less than 1–2 years, experienced architects may have a habit of looking much farther in the future, possibly up to 5–10 years ahead or even longer.

Realizing the Effects of Scale

Consequences of architectural decisions are often also manifested at scale and cannot be evaluated fully in pilot projects, isolated landscape areas or test environments with limited numbers of instances. For example, some ways of structuring IT landscapes may prove perfect for a landscape with a dozen information systems, but turn out ineffective for a landscape with a hundred systems and sheerly disastrous for the one with a thousand systems.

Significant industry experience tends to raise awareness of the issues of size, contribute to the formation of "large-scale" thinking and teach enterprise architects to ask the question of whether a proposed solution can still be effective if scaled by one or two orders of magnitude[30]. For instance, to experienced architects, the solution can look acceptable not when it has demonstrated its efficiency at a single site, but only if it can be deployed at tens of locations where the company is currently operating and is potentially extendable to hundreds of new locations that might emerge in the future.

Considering Entire System Lifecycles

As the duration of the end-to-end lifecycle of information systems in organizations often approaches 10–15 years, all implications of this lifecycle are difficult to comprehend without having commensurable practical experience in the industry. In particular, experience might be required to start thinking of systems in terms of their complete lifecycles, from introduction to retirement, rather than only in terms of their development projects the timelines of which are typically measured in months, not years.

Adopting this "historic" view, in turn, is beneficial for understanding the full organizational ramifications of the decisions to create new IT systems, as well as for estimating their total costs and risks, which enables enterprise architects to make wiser planning decisions. Moreover, thinking about entire system lifecycles also prompts architects to treat quite seriously various "secondary" design issues related to maintainability, extensibility, portability and inevitable obsolescence of information systems. For example, an experienced architect can raise valid questions about decommissioning the system beforehand, at the time of its introduction, to prevent possible problems with data and functionality migration for the organization in the future[31].

Seeing the Pitfalls of Technologies

The choices of technologies to be deployed at scale are especially critical as they demand long-term commitment from organizations, their use can be pervasive across the IT landscape and, once adopted, they are usually much more difficult to get rid of than individual information systems. Strong reliance on specific technologies also binds organizations to the respective technology vendors and makes them highly dependent on vendors' future behavior and their product strategies, posing major risks for organizations in the long run.

Rich practical experience in dealing with multiple technologies and vendors allows enterprise architects to judge them more objectively and intuitively see various pitfalls, hidden dangers and "red flags" during the selection of technology products unnoticeable to newbies. For example, the foresight of architects can help their organizations stay out of the potential trouble of getting stuck in the situation of vendor lock-in, suffering from vendors' technology wars, politically motivated service rejections or cross-border information sharing restrictions. Or, they can ensure the choice of a "matching" vendor, whose product philosophy and development trajectory truly align with the organization's future vision and expectations, by sorting out fake pretenders, who only imitate such alignment by applying superficial renovations to their crooked products[32].

Detecting Hype, Puffery and Fashions

The mainstream IT and managerial discourse is teeming with fads and buzzwords. These fads and buzzwords are transient in nature: they tend to come suddenly, excite interest, raise hype and then quickly go, leaving little or no persistent effect. Like waves of fashion, they change every several years, occasionally returning back to the stage under novel labels. Notwithstanding their shallow and passing character, fascination with fads can corrupt decision-making and inflict long-lasting damage to organizations.

Considerable experience allows enterprise architects to properly interpret the industry rhetoric and distinguish fashions from fundamentals, "flavors of the month" from genuine trends, marketing promises from responsible statements, inflated expectations from actual results, thereby avoiding costly mistakes for their companies. When inexperienced enthusiasts may mindlessly rush to adopt the latest "hot" technology, paradigm or approach (e.g. service-oriented architecture (SOA) in the 2000s or its next incarnation as microservices recently), a seasoned architect can make a more sober assessment of its applicability and say, "No, wait, it is unlikely to work in our conditions".

Applying Lessons from Practice
IT represents a very sophisticated field of knowledge where far from all fair judgments can be derived from pure logic by means of reasoning; some of them require a well-developed professional intuition shaped and substantiated by previous empirical observations. Not every aspect of technologies and their use is reflected in documentation and manuals, much important information about them lies elsewhere in the realm of praxis.

Extensive practical experience educates enterprise architects in this sense and endows them with certain occupational wisdom and gut feelings inaccessible to newbies. This wisdom comprises countless hard-won lessons accumulated over their careers (e.g. never to use version 1.0 of any software or technology in the production environment) that eventually help them make more robust and future-proof planning decisions. Unlike novice IT specialists, experienced architects can "see" good and bad ideas, patterns and solutions, even when the rationales behind them cannot always be clearly explained.

The Pyramid of the Resources of Enterprise Architects

The three major classes of resources possessed by enterprise architects can be conveniently summarized as a **pyramid of resources** with three layers, which can be viewed as a comprehensive competency framework for their profession[33]. In this pyramid, knowledge, as the most surface and readily available resource of architects (but in no case the least important one), represents its topmost layer. Experience, as the most profound and least accessible asset, is at the foundation of the pyramid. Following this logic, skills can be placed in the middle of the pyramid, between knowledge and experience. The resulting pyramid of the resources of enterprise architects is shown in Figure 6.3.

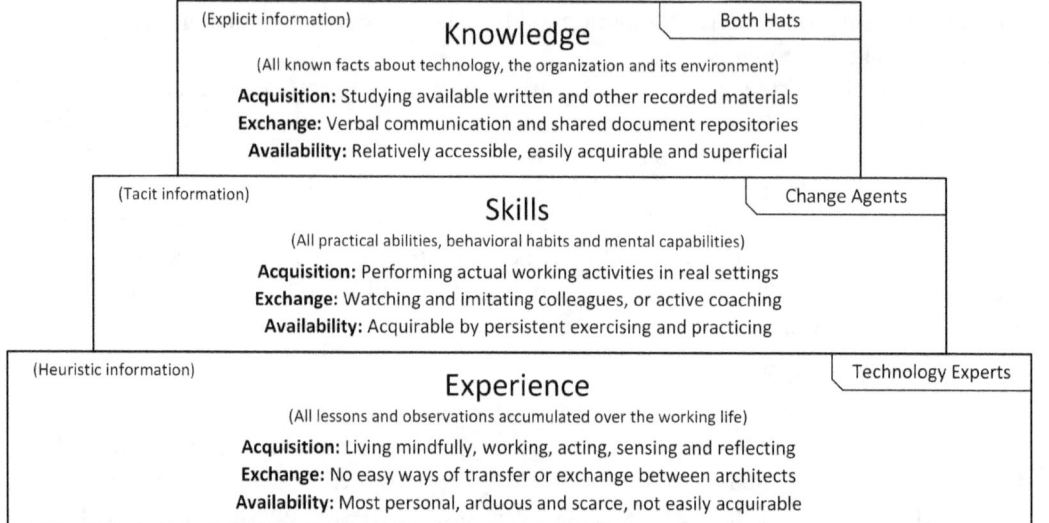

Figure 6.3. The pyramid of the resources of enterprise architects

The three-layer pyramid presented in Figure 6.3 structures all the resources of enterprise architects necessary for leading architectural planning in organizations and wearing the hats of Technology Experts and Change Agents. This pyramid also explains the differences between these resources in terms of their acquisition, exchange and availability.

Chapter Summary

This chapter discussed six categories of knowledge of enterprise architects and their taxonomy, described four groups of skills of enterprise architects and their framework, discussed the experience of enterprise architects with its role and applications in their work and presented the pyramid of the resources of enterprise architects. The core message of this chapter can be summarized in the following major points:

- All resources of enterprise architects can be structured into three major classes with different properties, means of acquisition and exchange: knowledge (explicit information), skills (tacit information) and experience (heuristic information)
- Knowledge of enterprise architects is very broad and can be classified into six different categories based on its subject area (business or IT) and applicability (general, industry-specific or organization-specific)
- Communication skills represent the proficiency of enterprise architects in dealing with diverse audiences and include listening, understanding, adapting, conveying ideas, visualizing information, building relationships and some other skills
- A collaborative attitude represents the aptitude of enterprise architects for acting as effective team players and implies brainstorming ability, negotiation skills, consensus seeking, conflict resolution, pliability, flexibility and political sagacity

- An innovative mindset represents the ability of enterprise architects to promote innovation and includes an appreciation of novelty, proactive learning, technology evangelism, out-of-the-box thinking, matching capability and change leadership
- Disciplined thinking represents the capacity of enterprise architects to reason in an orderly manner and embraces analytical abilities, engineering mindset, problem solving, systems thinking, zooming capability and ambiguity tolerance
- Experience of enterprise architects is extensive, diversified and conducive to anticipating long-term consequences, realizing the effects of scale, considering entire system lifecycles, seeing the pitfalls of technologies and detecting hype
- The three resources of enterprise architects can be organized as a three-layer pyramid, where, based on the relative easiness of their acquisition, knowledge can be placed at the top, skills — in the middle, and experience — at the bottom

Chapter 7: Instruments of Enterprise Architects

Previously, Chapter 4 provided a basic overview of EA artifacts as the primary instruments used by enterprise architects in their job. This chapter begins a detailed discussion of the instruments of enterprise architects and focuses specifically on EA artifacts and other categories of their instruments. In particular, this chapter starts with explaining the two major functions of EA artifacts in the work of enterprise architects and the critical property of their duality in its explicit and implicit forms. Then, this chapter describes different types of EA artifacts with their features and presents a comprehensive CSVLOD taxonomy for organizing artifacts in a meaningful way. Finally, this chapter discusses various secondary instruments of enterprise architects helpful in their occupation, including modeling languages, software tools, analytical techniques and auxiliary artifacts.

Instruments Employed by Enterprise Architects

The primary responsibility of enterprise architects in organizations is leading the architectural planning of digital transformation initiatives, which implies dealing with numerous technical and organizational decisions as Technology Experts and Change Agents (see Figure 4.9). Although architects generally practice "planning by talking" (see Figure 4.7), architectural planning processes, as complex collective efforts, cannot be carried out by chatting only and the agreements reached as their outcomes cannot stay purely verbal. Furthermore, effective planning decisions cannot be made by people based on their memory, intuition and imagination alone. For these reasons, architects leverage various instruments to support architectural planning and other activities from their repertoire.

Instruments of enterprise architects represent all the special documents, techniques and means that help them perform their duties in organizations, cooperate with others and lead architectural planning by wearing the hats of Technology Experts and Change Agents. As noted earlier, architects are practitioners of enterprise architecture and most of the documents that they create and use in their job are commonly known as EA artifacts (see Figure 4.2). These artifacts are "hammers and chisels" of architects with which they shape digitalization initiatives. Various EA artifacts with the accompanying modeling, storage and analytical approaches constitute the bulk of their professional instrumentation. Some of them belong more to the toolkits of Technology Experts and others — to those of Change Agents.

Two Functions of Enterprise Architecture Artifacts

EA artifacts are versatile and powerful instruments that are used by enterprise architects in many different ways and serve multiple practical purposes in their work during all phases of digitalization initiatives, from conception to execution. In the most general sense, artifacts facilitate collaboration, knowledge exchange and information analysis in various contexts occurring within digital transformation endeavors and their architectural planning[1]. In a narrower sense, however, all their usage scenarios can be reduced to two distinct functions that they fulfill in architects' occupation: documenting the existing situation in the organization and capturing architectural solutions for initiatives changing this situation.

Documenting the Existing Situation

The function of **documenting the existing situation** implies recording in EA artifacts certain objective facts about the organization and its IT landscape relevant to architectural planning. In this function, artifacts can vary in their coverage of different segments of the corporate landscape. On the one hand, EA artifacts can encompass different scopes of the landscape with the appropriate levels of granularity, e.g. local, broad and global. On the other hand, EA artifacts can describe different layers of the landscape loosely corresponding to the stack of organizational domains (see Figure 3.4), e.g. business activities and operations, supporting applications and information systems, underlying infrastructure and technology platforms.

Embraced landscape areas form a continuous scope spectrum, varying from rather narrow fragments to the entire landscape of the organization. Various strata of the landscape can also be viewed as a spectrum ranging from the topmost layer of forefront business activity to the bottommost layer of deeply technical infrastructure. Due to their orthogonality, these two spectra can be combined into a continuous two-dimensional **space of descriptive representations**, where all their variations can be placed based on their relevance to different scopes and layers of the corporate landscape. Possible coverage of different landscape scopes and layers in the space of descriptive representations by EA artifacts is illustrated in Figure 7.1.

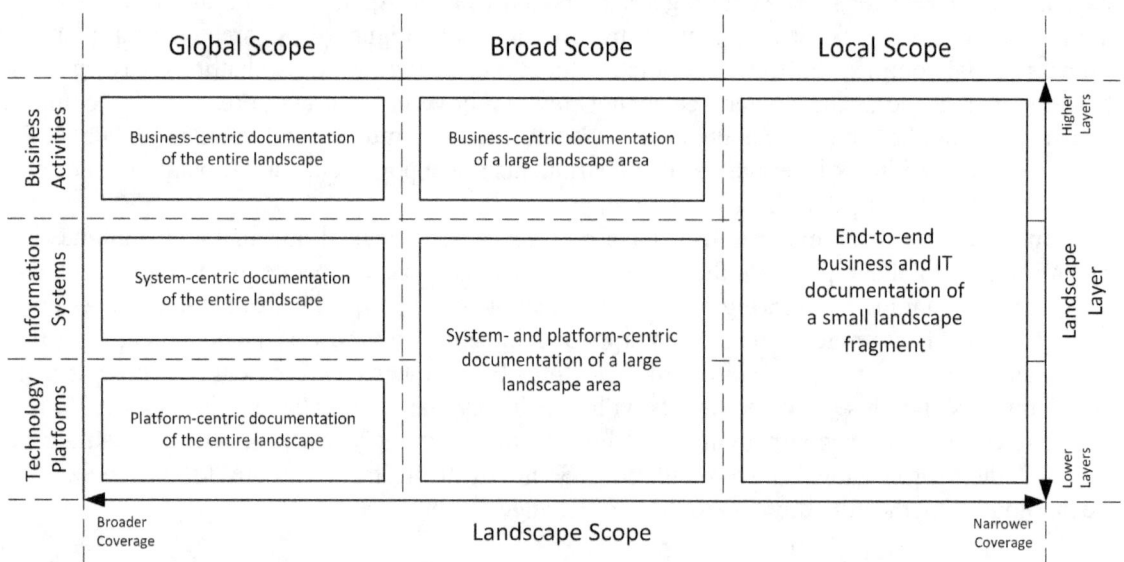

Figure 7.1. Possible coverage of the space of descriptive representations by EA artifacts

When serving the function of documenting the existing situation, EA artifacts are employed by enterprise architects to preserve and share knowledge on the current environment by materializing this knowledge, turning it into a durable form and making it available to whoever seeks it. Additionally, because artifacts structure and formalize information, they enable the application of various analytical techniques for its in-depth "slicing and dicing". The storage approaches and representation formats of EA artifacts fulfilling this function are optimized accordingly for continuous accumulation, long-term retention, searchability and analysis of information.

In the organizational context, for the purposes of documenting the existing situation, EA artifacts can be modified — created or updated — by enterprise architects essentially anytime to capture important facts on the business and IT landscape. These artifacts can then be studied by any actors, including architects themselves, as reliable reference materials on the current environment, either during the architectural planning of specific transformation initiatives, or for general decision-making purposes when the respective knowledge is required. Documenting the existing situation imposes no obligations on anyone and has no implications for the future whatsoever. The use of EA artifacts by enterprise architects for documenting the existing situation is shown schematically in Figure 7.2.

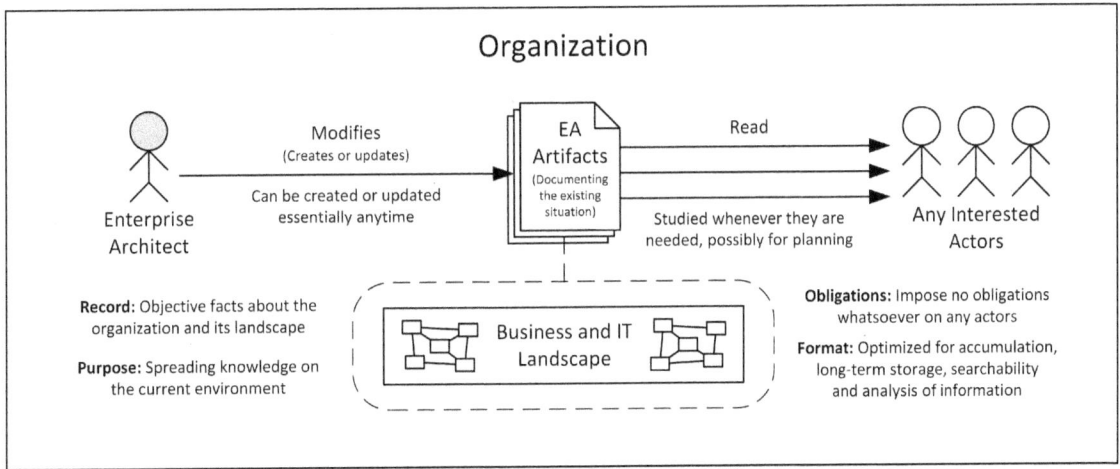

Figure 7.2. The use of EA artifacts by architects for documenting the existing situation

Documenting the existing situation is a very important function of EA artifacts conducive to disciplined architectural planning. However, it represents only their secondary function which does not directly address the planning process itself.

Capturing Architectural Solutions

The function of **capturing architectural solutions** implies recording in EA artifacts various planning decisions constituting architectural solutions for digital transformation initiatives (see Figure 3.1). It is artifacts capturing architectural solutions that represent architectural plans. In this function, EA artifacts can vary in their coverage of different facets of architectural solutions with their technical and organizational components at different levels (see Figure 3.6).

On the one hand, because any non-trivial change initiatives involve many diverse architectural decisions, individual EA artifacts can capture some or all decisions that constitute their architectural solutions. First, they can record separate architectural decisions related to initiatives pertaining to their technical or organizational side, e.g. the decision to adopt a particular technology or to uplift a specific business capability. Second, they can reflect complete technical or organizational solutions for initiatives with all the constituting decisions, i.e. the sets of all IT decisions or business decisions relevant to initiatives. Finally, they can describe whole architectural solutions with both their technical and organizational components, i.e. all architectural decisions defining change initiatives.

On the other hand, because digitalization initiatives vary greatly in their scale and belong to different levels of the initiative hierarchy (see Figure 2.5), individual EA artifacts tend to reflect architectural decisions, or entire solutions, for initiatives at a specific hierarchical level, where highest-level decisions relate to global strategies, while lowest-level decisions — to local projects. Generally, some artifacts capture architectural solutions for higher-level transformation initiatives, or simply higher-level architectural solutions, whereas other artifacts — lower-level architectural solutions.

Digitalization initiatives of different calibers form a continuous size spectrum and occupy the corresponding levels in the initiative hierarchy — the lowest project level, the middle program level or the highest strategy level. Various elements of their architectural solutions can also be viewed as a spectrum ranging from purely technical elements to purely organizational ones. Due to their orthogonality, these two spectra can be combined into a continuous two-dimensional **space of architectural solutions**, where all their constituents can be placed based on their relevance to technical and organizational components and to different hierarchical levels. Possible coverage of different solution components and levels in the space of architectural solutions by EA artifacts is illustrated in Figure 7.3.

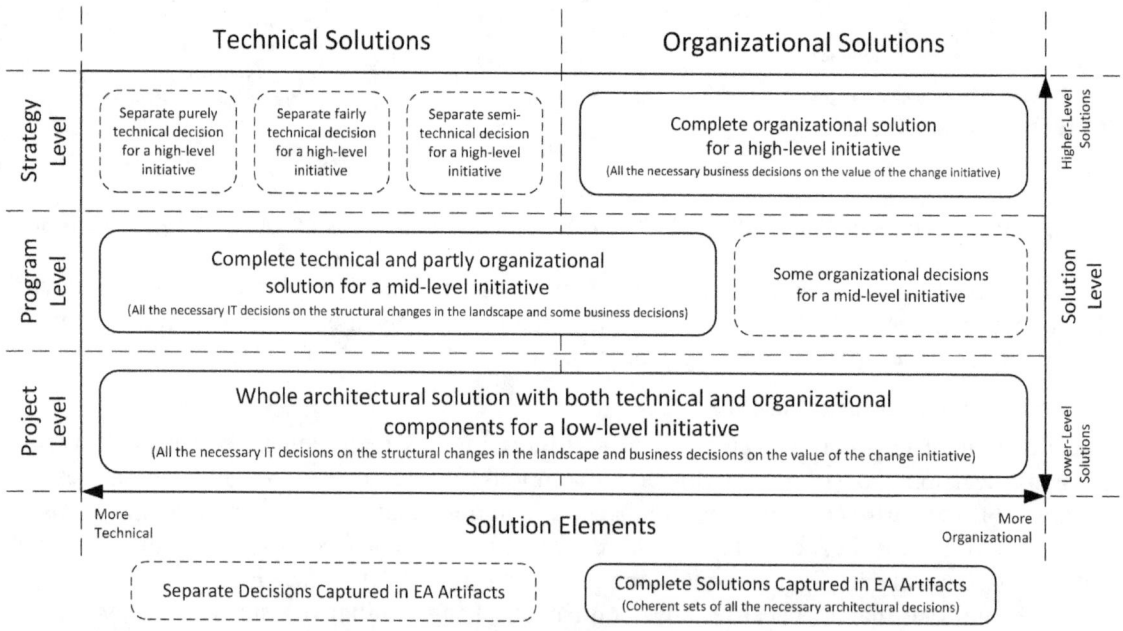

Figure 7.3. Possible coverage of the space of architectural solutions by EA artifacts

When serving the function of capturing architectural solutions, artifacts are employed by enterprise architects to facilitate the collaborative process of architectural planning by supporting constructive conversations with different stakeholders, promoting more rational choices and documenting the resulting agreements. The storage approaches and representation formats of EA artifacts fulfilling this function are optimized accordingly for productive teamwork and effective cooperation with the involvement of many parties.

For the purposes of capturing architectural solutions, EA artifacts can be modified — developed from scratch or refined — by enterprise architects only in the initiative context, as part of the architectural planning of particular transformation initiatives within their planning phase, to materialize, first, preliminary architectural solutions put forward for discussion and then finalized solutions endorsed by stakeholders (see Figure 4.7). After being produced, they are referred to in the course of the execution phase of these initiatives by their executors and underpin architectural oversight (see Figure 4.8). Capturing architectural solutions, thus, obliges all initiative stakeholders to stick to the agreed plans and always has actionable implications for the future. The use of EA artifacts by enterprise architects for capturing architectural solutions is shown schematically in Figure 7.4.

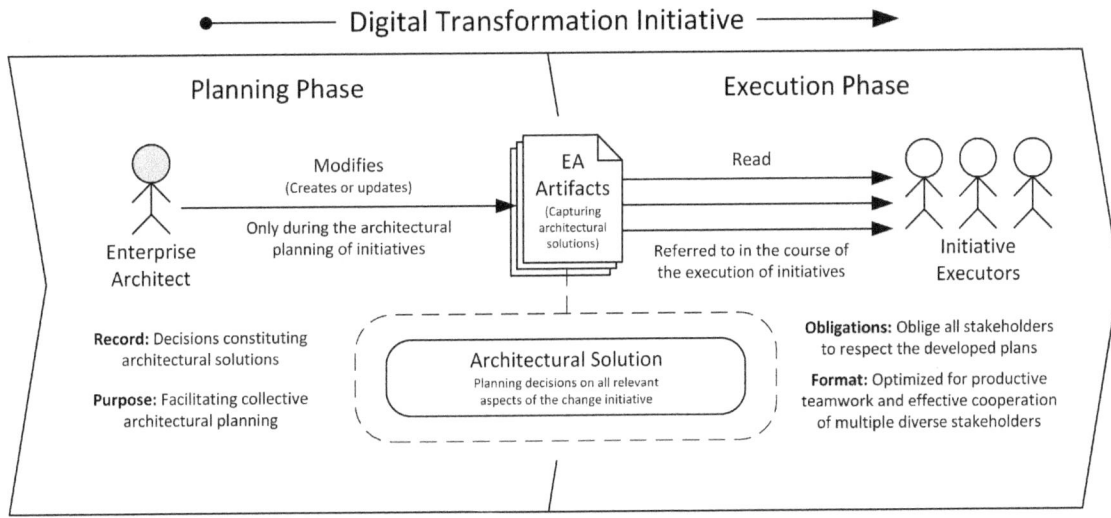

Figure 7.4. The use of EA artifacts by architects for capturing architectural solutions

The capacity of EA artifacts for performing their functions, and especially capturing architectural solutions, rests upon their ability to bridge the communication gaps between different stakeholder groups participating in digitalization efforts and their architectural planning.

Duality of Enterprise Architecture Artifacts

Conceptually, EA artifacts should be best viewed as the means of *communication and knowledge sharing* between different organizational actors from diverse business and IT communities. To be able to provide a communication medium for the representatives of these disparate communities, they must possess the property of duality. Generally, the **duality of EA artifacts** implies that the information contained in these artifacts is relevant to the business and IT audiences simultaneously, addresses the information needs of both these audiences and is presented in a way convenient for both of them[2]. It is this property of duality that makes EA artifacts helpful as communication devices and allows enterprise architects to use them for supporting intercommunity collaboration[3].

Specifically in the context of their function in architectural planning, the duality of EA artifacts can be interpreted more narrowly as their ability to capture both technical and organizational components of architectural solutions for digital transformation initiatives (see Figure 7.3), where technical components are particularly relevant to IT representatives and organizational components — to various business stakeholders. Depending on the way that technical and organizational solutions are reflected in EA artifacts, their duality can be explicit or implicit. Although both forms of duality facilitate cross-community interactions, they use rather different mechanisms to unite technical and organizational constituents into coherent architectural solutions.

Explicit Duality

The idea of **explicit duality** implies structuring EA artifacts into different sections, where some of these sections focus solely on technical solutions and other sections concentrate on organizational solutions. In other words, with explicit duality, technical and organizational solutions are described in different sections of the same artifact. The mechanism of explicit duality can be vividly illustrated based on the example of solution overviews — EA artifacts that provide high-level descriptions of IT solutions with their logical components from a business standpoint (see Figure 4.2). Solution overviews comprise multiple chapters covering various aspects of IT solutions and most of these chapters can be clearly related to either technical solutions (e.g. system structure, utilized technologies and involved vendors) or organizational solutions (e.g. business requirements, anticipated benefits and process impact). Each of these chapters is not particularly informative on its own, but together they form holistic architectural solutions for digitalization projects. An exemplary solution overview with its different sections demonstrating the concept of explicit duality is shown in Figure 7.5.

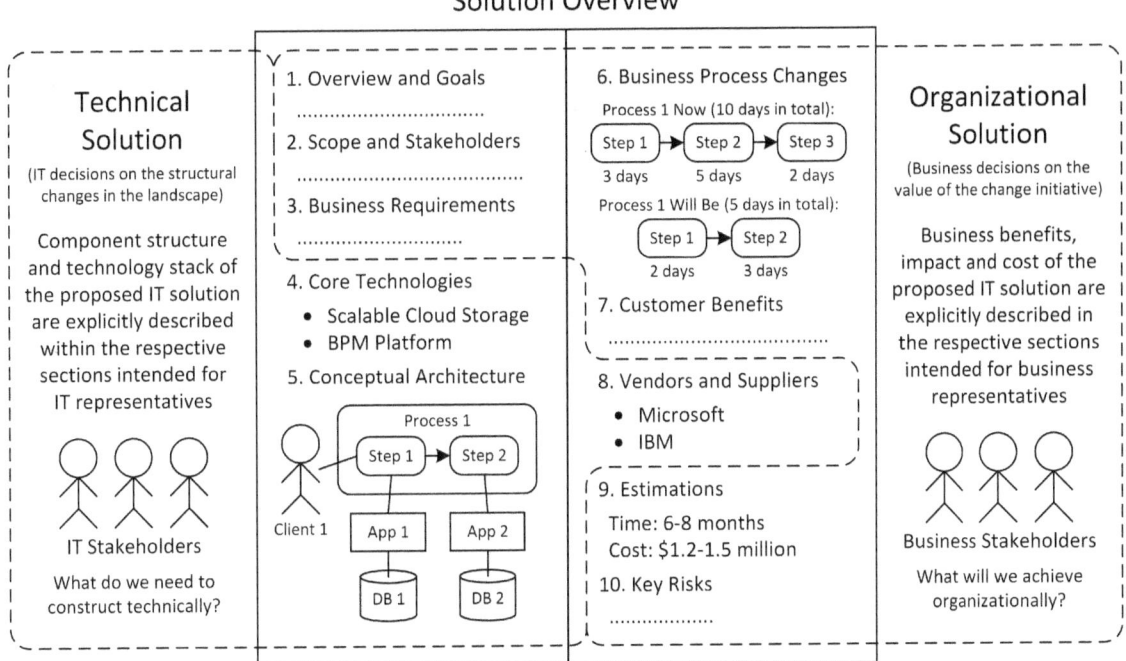

Figure 7.5. The concept of explicit duality of EA artifacts

Explicit duality provides enterprise architects with a straightforward approach to satisfying disparate information demands of the business and IT audiences with the same EA artifacts. An alternative, somewhat more sophisticated but probably also more potent way of getting business and IT representatives "on the same page" is offered by implicit duality.

Implicit Duality

The idea of **implicit duality** implies using in EA artifacts certain descriptions that allow flexible interpretation and have both technical and organizational meaning, so that they define technical and organizational solutions at the same time. Put it simply, with implicit duality, technical and organizational solutions are tacitly reflected in the same sections of artifacts. The mechanism of implicit duality can be clearly illustrated based on the example of target states — EA artifacts that provide abstract graphical views of the specific functional configuration of the organization (see Figure 4.2). Visual diagrams constituting the substance of target states are highly conceptual and convey somewhat different messages to different audiences. For this reason, their interpretation from an IT viewpoint renders technical solutions (e.g. what kind of systems should be developed), while their reading from a business perspective — organizational solutions (e.g. how business operations will be improved). Hence, these diagrams on their own can describe entire architectural solutions for digitalization programs with their technical and organizational components. An exemplary target state with its powerful diagrams demonstrating the concept of implicit duality is presented in Figure 7.6.

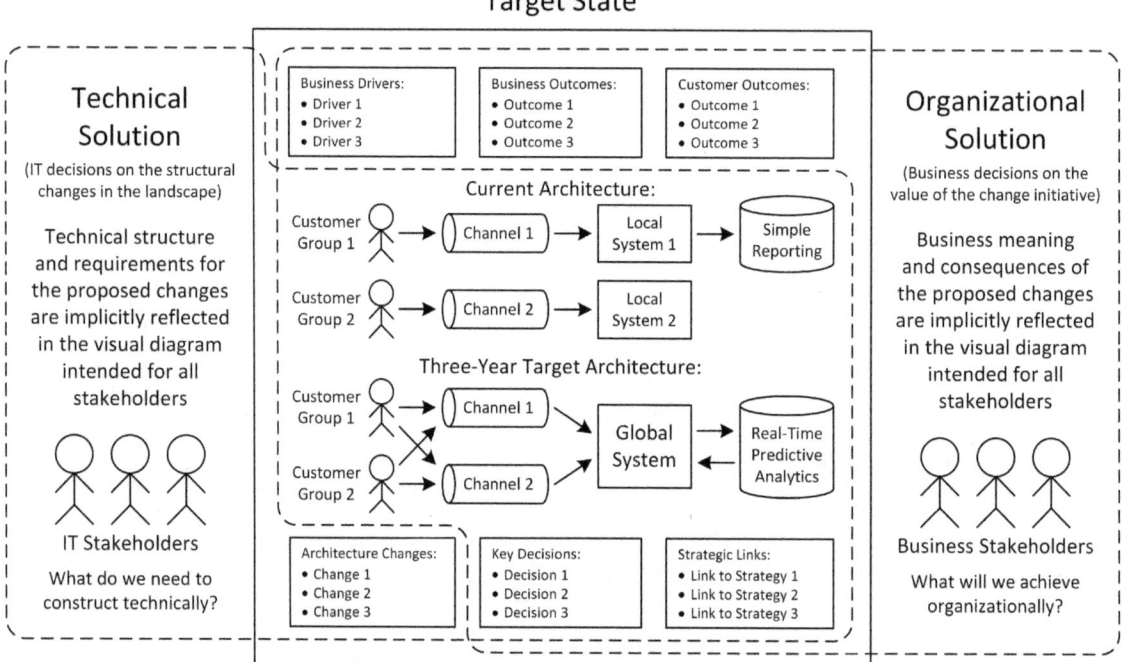

Figure 7.6. The concept of implicit duality of EA artifacts

For enterprise architects, duality represents arguably the single most important property of EA artifacts without which their utility as the means of communication cannot be realized. The mechanisms of explicit and implicit duality illustrated in Figure 7.5 and Figure 7.6 respectively offer two different approaches to achieving this property, though in practice they are often used in conjunction, resulting in mixed approaches. For instance, some elements of the target state shown in Figure 7.6 (e.g. architecture changes and business outcomes) still relate exclusively to either technical or organizational solutions, i.e. this artifact actually combines implicit duality with some degree of explicit duality.

Different Types of Enterprise Architecture Artifacts

Specific EA artifacts that proved useful in the toolkits of enterprise architects across the industry are numerous and very diverse in their features. For example, only from the standpoint of their informational contents, these artifacts can vary greatly in the following properties:

- Organizational domains — EA artifacts can cover any combinations of domains, from business and applications to infrastructure and security (see Figure 3.4)
- Subject of description — EA artifacts can focus on disparate subjects, e.g. individual entities, relationships between different entities or rules for all entities
- Organizational scope — EA artifacts can range in their coverage from entire organizations to separate business areas to narrow landscape sectors

- Level of detail — EA artifacts can range in their granularity from very high-level overarching abstractions to rather low-level meticulous details
- Temporal state — EA artifacts can describe the current state, future states for any time horizons, transitions between any of these states and can even be stateless, i.e. do not refer to any specific points in time
- Logical affiliation — EA artifacts can relate to organizations or their parts as well as to particular projects, programs or strategies running in organizations
- Representation format — EA artifacts can be represented in textual, graphical and tabular formats, or as a mixture of some or all of these formats

Informational contents of EA artifacts largely define their purposes, practical applicability and usage scenarios in the work of enterprise architects. Although their concrete use cases are very content-specific, all artifacts can be organized according to a number of basic properties that determine their ability to serve their two major functions: documenting the existing situation and capturing architectural solutions (see Figure 7.2 and Figure 7.4 respectively). Namely, the whole set of EA artifacts regularly employed by architects in practice can be meaningfully classified along four distinct, though not completely independent dimensions: temporal orientation, initiative affiliation, described objects and presented viewpoints.

Different Orientations: Actualities and Plans Artifacts

First and most importantly, based on their *orientation* in time, all EA artifacts can be loosely separated into actualities and plans[4]. On the one hand, **actualities EA artifacts** focus on the current situation and describe what actually is in the organization right now. These artifacts provide, in some form or the other, accurate views of the present state of affairs, but do not try to look into the future, make suggestions or prescribe anything. The very notion of time horizon is inapplicable to them. Typical examples of EA artifacts that can be related to actualities include:

- Technology inventories listing all technologies utilized across the IT landscape
- Asset inventories listing all applications and databases deployed in the landscape
- System portfolio models showing what IT systems support various business areas

From a functional point of view, actualities EA artifacts are obviously aimed to be used by enterprise architects for documenting the existing situation in the organization (see Figure 7.2). At the same time, due to their concentration solely on current realities, they are unsuitable for capturing architectural solutions for change initiatives.

On the other hand, **plans EA artifacts** focus on the future and describe intentions as to what should be achieved in the organization. These artifacts provide either explicit descriptions of what future is desired at a specific moment in time (e.g. concrete target states to be reached), or more general suggestions on the future way of working (e.g. rules to be followed from now on). Their horizon can span anywhere from the short-term to the long-term to the indefinite future. Typical examples of EA artifacts that can be related to plans include:

- Solution overviews providing conceptual views of IT solutions to be constructed
- Technology roadmaps describing the desired evolution of adopted technologies
- IT principles defining how the organization needs to work from an IT perspective

Functionally, plans EA artifacts are naturally intended to be used by enterprise architects for capturing architectural solutions for all sorts of digital transformation initiatives and representing their architectural plans (see Figure 7.4). However, owing to their pronounced future orientation, they are not suitable for documenting the existing situation.

Because a single EA artifact can describe any temporal states (e.g. both the current and future states, as well as the transition between them), the border between actualities and plans is undoubtedly blurred and many hybrids of these categories can be found in practice. For example, depictions of the IT landscape in its current form can also highlight some planned changes in its structure. Or, descriptions of the desired target state can be contrasted with the present situation, as illustrated in Figure 7.6. In these cases, EA artifacts can fulfill both functions, though to varying extents.

For this reason, the separation of EA artifacts into actualities and plans, as well as their functional applicability, should be viewed more as a continuous spectrum between the two opposite extremes of pure archetypes. Nevertheless, the vast majority of artifacts that proved helpful in the industry tend to gravitate to either actualities or plans. The differences between actualities and plans EA artifacts, their suitability for the two main functions and the spectrum of their possible mixes are summarized in Figure 7.7.

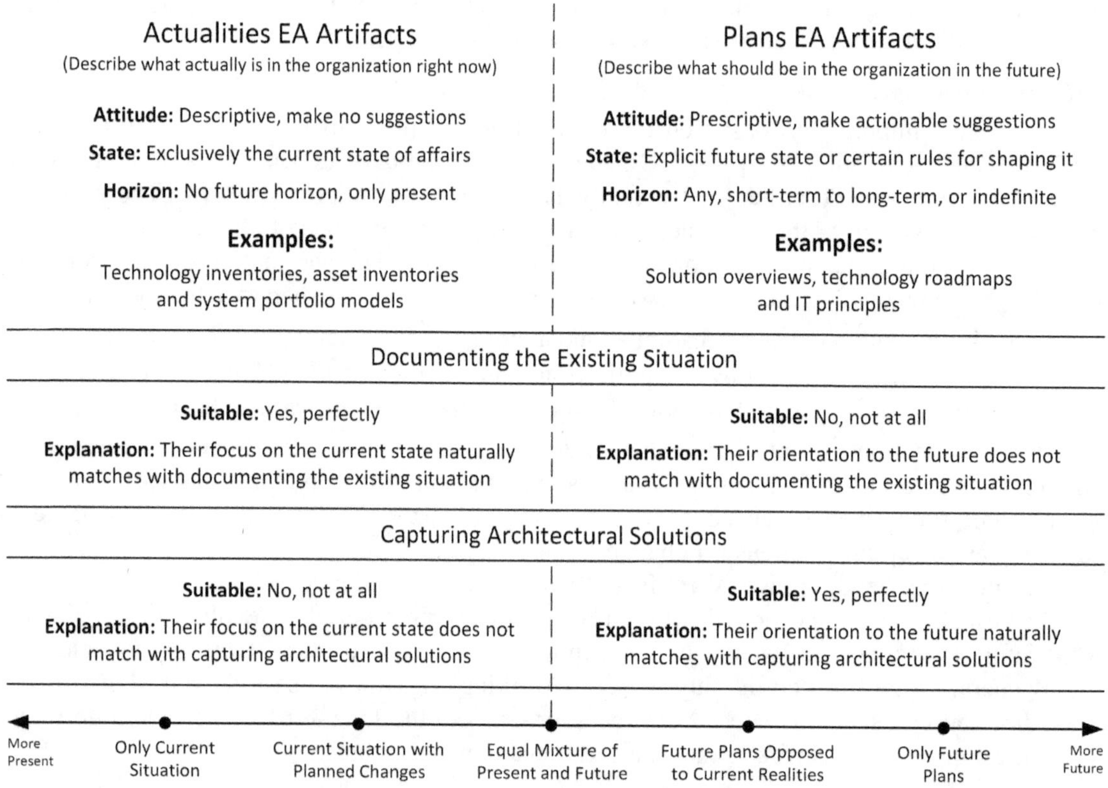

Actualities EA Artifacts	Plans EA Artifacts
(Describe what actually is in the organization right now)	(Describe what should be in the organization in the future)
Attitude: Descriptive, make no suggestions	**Attitude:** Prescriptive, make actionable suggestions
State: Exclusively the current state of affairs	**State:** Explicit future state or certain rules for shaping it
Horizon: No future horizon, only present	**Horizon:** Any, short-term to long-term, or indefinite
Examples: Technology inventories, asset inventories and system portfolio models	**Examples:** Solution overviews, technology roadmaps and IT principles

Documenting the Existing Situation

Suitable: Yes, perfectly	**Suitable:** No, not at all
Explanation: Their focus on the current state naturally matches with documenting the existing situation	**Explanation:** Their orientation to the future does not match with documenting the existing situation

Capturing Architectural Solutions

Suitable: No, not at all	**Suitable:** Yes, perfectly
Explanation: Their focus on the current state does not match with capturing architectural solutions	**Explanation:** Their orientation to the future naturally matches with capturing architectural solutions

More Present ← Only Current Situation — Current Situation with Planned Changes — Equal Mixture of Present and Future — Future Plans Opposed to Current Realities — Only Future Plans → More Future

Figure 7.7. Actualities and plans EA artifacts

Actualities and plans clearly correspond to the two key functions of EA artifacts: documenting the existing situation and capturing architectural solutions respectively.

Unsurprisingly, both these types of artifacts are indispensable instruments in the toolkit of any enterprise architect.

Different Affiliations: Initiative-Specific and General Artifacts

Second, based on their *affiliation* with digital transformation initiatives, all EA artifacts can be divided into initiative-specific and general ones[5]. On the one hand, **initiative-specific EA artifacts** are tied to concrete digitalization initiatives. These artifacts describe different facets of the respective initiatives, i.e. projects, programs or strategies. They are produced within these initiatives, used during their implementation but then archived after their completion. The lifespan of initiative-specific EA artifacts is always limited and bounded by the duration of the initiatives they are created for. Typical examples of EA artifacts that can be classified as initiative-specific include:

- Solution options comparing alternative IT solutions that can be built by projects
- Target states defining the ultimate landscape structure pursued by programs
- Architecture strategies setting the overall direction for digitalization strategies

From a functional standpoint, initiative-specific EA artifacts are used by enterprise architects for capturing architectural solutions for transformation initiatives. In this function, their exclusive affiliation with particular initiatives affords two notable features. First, initiative-specific artifacts allow architects to capture complete technical and organizational solutions, or even full architectural solutions, for change initiatives (see Figure 7.3). Second, they allow architects to thoroughly describe these initiatives in isolation from other initiatives and, to some extent, from the rest of the organization. However, for the same reason, these artifacts do not allow them to describe comprehensively the integration of change initiatives into the body of the organization.

As for documenting the existing situation, because of their limited lifetime and transient character, initiative-specific EA artifacts are largely unsuitable for the long-term accumulation and storage of knowledge. Nonetheless, archived versions of these artifacts can be rather valuable as one form of landscape documentation. For example, they can retain archival descriptions of information systems at the time of their construction that are often found helpful for detailed studies of the landscape's internals. In short, their practical utility for architects is determined by the following qualities: highly focused, but localized and temporary.

On the other hand, **general EA artifacts** exist independently of any digitalization initiatives. These artifacts describe or relate to entire organizations or their large areas, e.g. lines of business, business functions or divisions. They are developed once, constantly used in different contexts and periodically updated together with the evolution of the organization, often as part of the implementation of transformation initiatives. Basically, general EA artifacts have an "infinite" lifespan as they may lose their relevance and get discarded only in relatively rare and special circumstances, for instance, when they are found unhelpful, their maintenance does not pay off or the organization itself changes radically. Typical examples of EA artifacts that can be regarded as general include:

- Technology reference models describing the stack of recommended technologies
- Logical data models defining the detailed structure of important business objects
- Asset roadmaps depicting the projected lifecycles of IT assets in the landscape

Functionally, similarly to their initiative-specific counterparts, general EA artifacts can also be used by enterprise architects for capturing architectural solutions for transformation initiatives, though with their own strengths and limitations. Specifically, as they focus broadly on the organization itself, these artifacts allow architects to describe planned changes from individual initiatives in the full organizational context, thereby integrating them into the organizational organism, harmonizing them with the changes from other initiatives and maintaining overall organizational coherence. At the same time, they cannot concentrate on concrete initiatives to describe them in due detail and usually capture only separate architectural decisions, rather than complete solutions (see Figure 7.3). For this reason, in matters of capturing architectural solutions, general EA artifacts complement initiative-specific ones. Besides that, as they are long-living in nature, these artifacts are used by architects for documenting the existing situation and preserving current-state knowledge as well. In short, their practical applicability is determined by the following qualities: comprehensive and durable, but lacking focus.

Interestingly, as digitalization initiatives get larger in their duration and scope and grow into protracted, multiyear transformation strategies encompassing vast organizational areas, the borderline between initiative-specific and general EA artifacts becomes somewhat indistinct. In this case, temporary initiative-specific artifacts typical for time-bound projects and programs essentially turn into permanent ones associated with long-lasting strategies and start to resemble general artifacts in their features, e.g. evolve along with the progress in strategy implementation and transformation of the affected areas of the organization.

On the whole, the longer and more extensive initiatives, the more properties of general EA artifacts their initiative-specific artifacts tend to possess, which also influences their functional utility for enterprise architects. The differences between initiative-specific and general EA artifacts, their suitability for the two main functions and the spectrum of possible initiative variations are summarized in Figure 7.8.

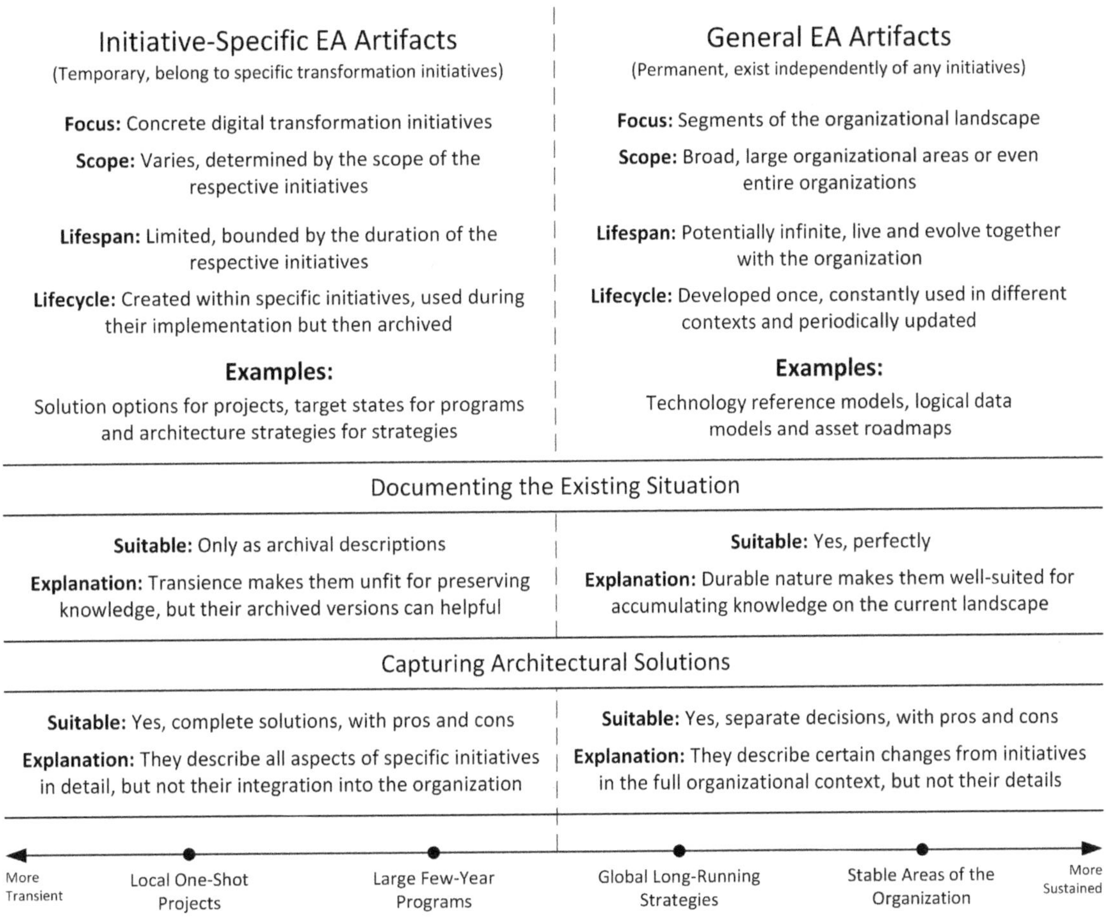

Figure 7.8. Initiative-specific and general EA artifacts

Initiative-Specific EA Artifacts (Temporary, belong to specific transformation initiatives)	General EA Artifacts (Permanent, exist independently of any initiatives)
Focus: Concrete digital transformation initiatives	**Focus:** Segments of the organizational landscape
Scope: Varies, determined by the scope of the respective initiatives	**Scope:** Broad, large organizational areas or even entire organizations
Lifespan: Limited, bounded by the duration of the respective initiatives	**Lifespan:** Potentially infinite, live and evolve together with the organization
Lifecycle: Created within specific initiatives, used during their implementation but then archived	**Lifecycle:** Developed once, constantly used in different contexts and periodically updated
Examples: Solution options for projects, target states for programs and architecture strategies for strategies	**Examples:** Technology reference models, logical data models and asset roadmaps
Documenting the Existing Situation	
Suitable: Only as archival descriptions	**Suitable:** Yes, perfectly
Explanation: Transience makes them unfit for preserving knowledge, but their archived versions can helpful	**Explanation:** Durable nature makes them well-suited for accumulating knowledge on the current landscape
Capturing Architectural Solutions	
Suitable: Yes, complete solutions, with pros and cons	**Suitable:** Yes, separate decisions, with pros and cons
Explanation: They describe all aspects of specific initiatives in detail, but not their integration into the organization	**Explanation:** They describe certain changes from initiatives in the full organizational context, but not their details

◄── More Transient — Local One-Shot Projects — Large Few-Year Programs — Global Long-Running Strategies — Stable Areas of the Organization — More Sustained ──►

Figure 7.8. Initiative-specific and general EA artifacts

The separation of EA artifacts into initiative-specific and general has many implications for their circulation in organizations and usage by enterprise architects. Because of their complementarity, architects actively use both these classes of artifacts in their daily work.

Different Objects: Solutions, Structures and Rules Artifacts

Third, depending on the *objects* of their description, all EA artifacts can be loosely separated into solutions, structures and rules[6]. **Solutions EA artifacts** describe specific IT solutions in the organizational context, i.e. individual information systems in the surrounding landscape. They cover narrow organizational scopes, but provide a significant level of detail, distinguishing concrete business tasks and process steps, system components and use cases, data entities and communication interfaces, hardware devices and security appliances. Although these artifacts generally embrace all six organizational domains, more often they emphasize specifically substantive domains as those constituting the core of most IT solutions, i.e. business, applications and infrastructure (see Table 3.3). For instance, solutions EA artifacts can explain exactly how a specific information system automates business operations, interacts with the surrounding IT environment and is structured internally from its key building blocks. To provide such granular descriptions, they normally use mixed presentation formats, combining textual narratives, graphical diagrams and sometimes tables. Typical examples of EA artifacts that can be related to solutions include:

- Solution briefs providing very abstract conceptual views of IT solutions
- Preliminary solution designs providing high-level technical views of IT systems
- Solution designs providing detailed technical specifications of IT systems

From a functional point of view, solutions EA artifacts are used by enterprise architects for capturing architectural solutions. Owing to their high granularity but narrow scope, in this function they are perfectly suitable specifically for projects, but not for higher-level transformation initiatives (see Figure 7.3). Potentially, solutions EA artifacts can also be employed by architects for documenting the existing situation in detail in local landscape areas (see Figure 7.1). However, because maintaining detailed descriptions and keeping them up to date is very time-consuming, in practice they are seldom used for this purpose.

Structures EA artifacts describe high-level structures of the organization or its parts, i.e. compositions of large segments of the corporate landscape. In comparison with solutions, structures encompass broader organizational scopes, but offer more abstract views, concentrating mostly on major elements of the business and IT environment such as geographic regions, customer groups, business capabilities, main information systems, data repositories and infrastructural arrangements, as well as change initiatives modifying them. However, they also focus more on substantive domains as those forming the core landscape framework. For instance, structures EA artifacts can depict the relationship between business locations, manufacturing activities, underlying IT platforms and information flows. In their descriptions, they tend to rely predominantly on graphical presentation formats, often in the form of rich pictorial visualizations. Typical examples of EA artifacts that can be related to structures include:

- Value chains providing structured views of the value-adding business activities
- Process maps providing high-level hierarchical views of business processes
- Landscape maps providing structured graphical views of the IT landscape

Functionally, structures EA artifacts can be used by enterprise architects for capturing architectural solutions. Due to their abstractness and wide coverage, in this function they are more appropriate for high-level transformation initiatives, especially for programs (see Figure 7.3). As structures EA artifacts are not particularly detailed and can be relatively easily maintained current, they are also very useful to architects for the purposes of documenting the existing situation in the business and IT landscape with a broad or even global scope (see Figure 7.1).

Rules EA artifacts describe universal rules defining the organization or its divisions, i.e. common "rules of the game" for all organizational decision-making. While solutions and structures in their descriptions refer to more or less specific, tangible and countable instances (e.g. concrete capabilities, initiatives, processes, systems and databases), rules formulate purely conceptual imperatives that may apply to an indefinite number of instances, or even to all instances of a particular kind. Although these artifacts can cover any organizational domains, comparatively more frequently they highlight specifically non-substantive domains as those concerned more with the proper ways of doing things than with the things themselves, i.e. data, integration and security (see Table 3.3). For instance, rules EA artifacts can prescribe how certain sensitive classes of data should be treated in the organization or how all information systems in its IT landscape should be constructed. For expressing their suggestions, they use mostly textual presentation formats, often complemented with simple graphical illustrations. Classic examples of EA artifacts that can be related to rules include:

- Principles defining how the company needs to work in terms of business and IT
- Policies defining global information handling requirements for IT systems
- Guidelines defining recommended practices for using specific technologies

From a functional perspective, rules EA artifacts are used by enterprise architects primarily for capturing architectural solutions. Because of their vast scope and pervasive influence on the organization, in this function they are more suitable for very high-level transformation initiatives, especially for strategies (see Figure 7.3). Even though rules EA artifacts are easily maintainable and potentially fit also for documenting the existing situation on a global scale (see Figure 7.1), for their focus on imperatives rather than instances, they tend not to reflect any definite state of the corporate landscape, whether current or future. For this reason, they are capable of serving this function for architects, but only to the extent to which knowledge about the current environment is contained there or can be deduced from their descriptions.

Due to the differences in their levels of abstraction and covered organizational scopes, from the standpoint of architectural planning, solutions, structures and rules EA artifacts are of different relevance to the three types of digital transformation initiatives — projects, programs and strategies. Namely, solutions, as the most detailed and narrowly scoped EA artifacts, naturally match mostly with local projects. Structures, as pretty abstract EA artifacts of a broader scope, are more "proportionate" to larger transformation programs. Finally, rules, as the most conceptual and overarching EA artifacts, highly correlate with comprehensive digitalization strategies. Unsurprisingly, when solutions, structures and rules represent architectural plans, they more often reflect architectural solutions for projects, programs and strategies respectively.

Even though there might be no strict correspondence between different types of EA artifacts and digitalization initiatives, especially when both the proposed classifications themselves are somewhat loose, the very idea of *commensurability* of artifacts and initiatives helps better understand the applicability of various artifacts as means of capturing architectural solutions for projects, programs and strategies. The differences between solutions, structures and rules EA artifacts, their suitability for the two main functions and the spectrum of their possible variations are summarized in Figure 7.9.

Solutions EA Artifacts
(Describe specific IT solutions in the organizational context)

Scope: Narrow, limited to separate IT solutions or systems

Instances: Detailed, e.g. process steps, system components and IT devices

Domains: More substantive domains, like business, applications and infrastructure

Format: Text, diagrams and some tables

Examples:
Solution briefs, preliminary solution designs and solution designs

Structures EA Artifacts
(Describe high-level structures of the organization or its parts)

Scope: Broad, often cover large areas of the organization

Instances: Abstract, e.g. business and IT capabilities and information systems

Domains: Mostly substantive domains, i.e. business, applications and infrastructure

Format: Usually large visual diagrams

Examples:
Value chains, process maps and landscape maps

Rules EA Artifacts
(Describe general global rules defining the organization or its units)

Scope: Very broad, often relate to the entire organization

Instances: Do not refer to any particular instances, only to broad categories

Domains: More non-substantive domains, such as data, integration and security

Format: Often text with simple diagrams

Examples:
Principles, policies and guidelines

Documenting the Existing Situation

Suitable: Yes, potentially, for small areas
Explanation: They can document in detail separate landscape fragments, but their maintenance is very time-consuming

Suitable: Yes, perfectly, for large areas
Explanation: They can describe extensive parts of the corporate landscape and be relatively easily maintained

Suitable: Possibly, for very large areas
Explanation: Even though they are easily maintainable, they often do not reflect any definite state of the landscape

---

Capturing Architectural Solutions

Suitable: Yes, mainly for projects
Explanation: Narrow scope and high granularity make them perfectly appropriate for small initiatives

Suitable: Yes, more for programs
Explanation: Abstractness and broad scope make them particularly fit for medium-sized initiatives

Suitable: Yes, more for strategies
Explanation: Vast scope and pervasive influence make them particularly fit for very large change initiatives

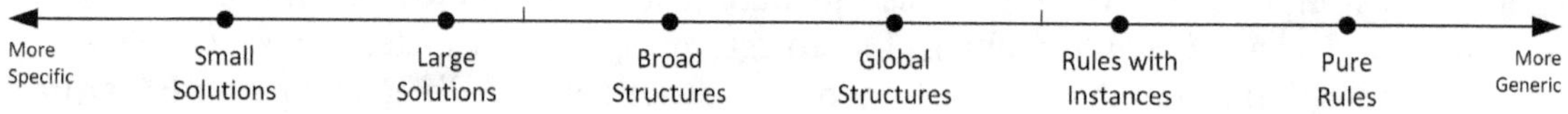

◄──── More Specific ── Small Solutions ── Large Solutions ── Broad Structures ── Global Structures ── Rules with Instances ── Pure Rules ── More Generic ────►

Figure 7.9. Solutions, structures and rules EA artifacts

Solutions, structures and rules fulfill quite diverse practical functions and each of these functions is important for steering the course of digital transformation. Therefore, all three types of EA artifacts can be found in the toolkits of enterprise architects.

Different Viewpoints: IT-Focused and Business-Focused Artifacts

Lastly, depending on the *viewpoints* they present, all EA artifacts can be loosely divided into IT-focused and business-focused ones[7]. On the one hand, **IT-focused EA artifacts** are technical in nature and use highly IT-specific language and terminology, routinely referring to systems, databases, interfaces, servers, firewalls and technologies. Usually, they cover various technical domains, but in some cases can touch the domain of business as well (see Table 3.1). IT-focused artifacts can be formal, voluminous and full of sheer technicalities incomprehensible to non-experts. They are associated with "hard" engineering-style descriptions or drawings, often using specialized modeling conventions and notations. Because of their strong technical "flavor", these artifacts are relevant primarily to IT representatives of different profiles. Typical examples of EA artifacts that can be classified as IT-focused include:

- Landscape diagrams depicting the connections between IT systems and databases
- Patterns describing standard solutions to the common problems of system design
- IT roadmaps showing scheduled change projects in particular technology areas

From a functional point of view, IT-focused EA artifacts are used by enterprise architects both for documenting the existing situation and for capturing architectural solutions. In the former scenario, these artifacts document the corporate landscape from the IT side, accentuating its technical constituents (see Figure 7.1). In the latter scenario, they capture mostly technical components of architectural solutions for transformation initiatives (see Figure 7.3). IT-focused EA artifacts are owned by enterprise architects wearing the hat of Technology Experts and helpful for designing technical solutions.

On the other hand, **business-focused EA artifacts** are technology-neutral and use plain business language and terminology, often talking about markets and customers, products and services, business capabilities and processes, their automation and data availability. Normally, they cover the business domain and, at a high level, some other domains, especially functional ones, e.g. applications and data (see Table 3.2). Unlike their IT-focused counterparts, business-focused artifacts tend to be brief, largely informal and contain only the most essential summary information. They are associated with "soft" marketing-style descriptions or pictures, typically using appealing presentation formats and intuitively understandable graphical symbols. By virtue of their non-technical character, these artifacts are directly relevant to business managers of various denominations. Typical examples of EA artifacts that can be regarded as business-focused include:

- Business capability models providing hierarchical views of business capabilities
- Conceptual data models defining the basic structure of prominent business entities
- Roadmaps showing envisioned digitalization projects in particular business units

Functionally, business-focused EA artifacts also fulfill both functions for enterprise architects. When documenting the existing situation in the organization, these artifacts describe the corporate landscape from the business side, highlighting its business elements and their IT support (see Figure 7.1). When capturing architectural solutions for transformation initiatives, they capture mostly their organizational components (see Figure 7.3). Business-focused EA artifacts are owned by enterprise architects wearing the hat of Change Agents and helpful for reaching organizational solutions.

As EA artifacts can combine diverse pieces of business- and IT-related information, their separation into IT-focused and business-focused categories should certainly be viewed as a continuous spectrum between the two opposite extremes. Furthermore, because possessing the property of duality, explicitly or implicitly (see Figure 7.5 and Figure 7.6), is necessary for EA artifacts to serve as the means of communication between business and IT communities, the majority of artifacts, in fact, gravitate to the middle of the spectrum, though from different sides.

However, some EA artifacts belonging to the ends of the spectrum that cannot be considered dual have also found their use in practice. For instance, on the IT-focused extreme, certain artifacts describing IT landscapes from a purely technical perspective proved valuable for enterprise architects and other people from IT circles. On the business-focused extreme, many important documents, like business strategies, business plans and business cases, are used in organizations, but they are usually not regarded as EA artifacts. The differences between IT-focused and business-focused EA artifacts, their suitability for the two main functions and their relationship to the property of duality are summarized in Figure 7.10.

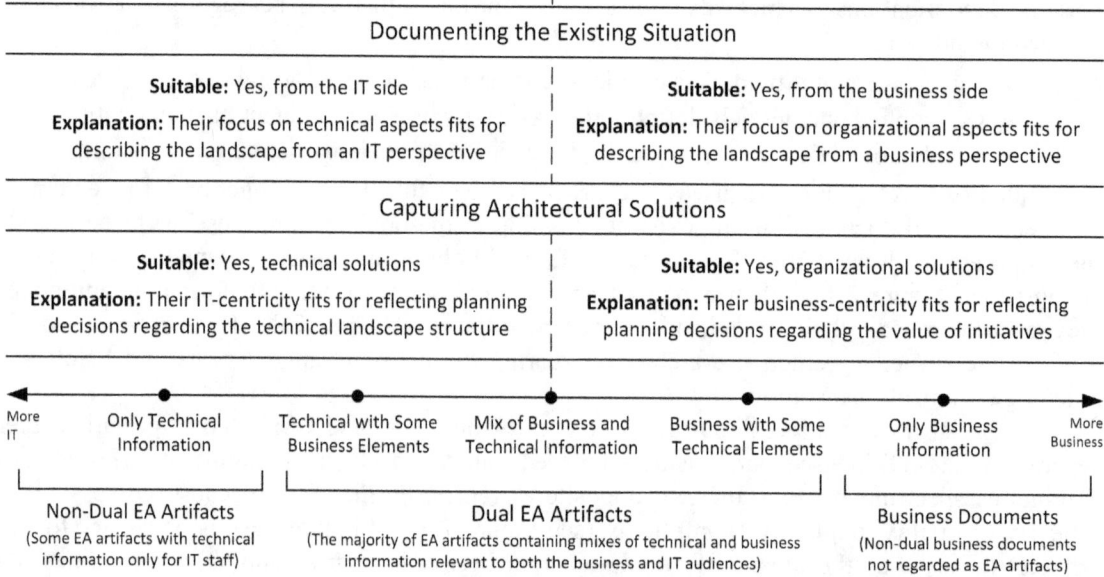

Figure 7.10. IT-focused and business-focused EA artifacts

IT-focused and business-focused EA artifacts are equally necessary for recording architectural decisions pertaining to digital transformation initiatives as well as germane facts on the organizational environment. In their practice, enterprise architects work with both these types of artifacts.

The CSVLOD Taxonomy for Enterprise Architecture Artifacts

Temporal orientation (see Figure 7.7), initiative affiliation (see Figure 7.8), described objects (see Figure 7.9) and presented viewpoints (see Figure 7.10) all represent important dimensions along which EA artifacts can be classified and which determine their practical functions and other features in the context of architectural planning and the work of enterprise architects. These four classifications can be combined into an integrative taxonomy for EA artifacts that provides a comprehensive view of their most salient properties.

Specifically, described objects (solutions, structures and rules from Figure 7.9) and presented viewpoints (IT-focused and business-focused from Figure 7.10) are orthogonal dimensions that characterize, first, *what* EA artifacts describe and, second, *how* they describe, respectively. The intersection of these dimensions, what and how, produces six general types of EA artifacts, where each of these types also strongly correlates with the two remaining dimensions — temporal orientation (actualities and plans from Figure 7.7) and initiative affiliation (initiative-specific and general from Figure 7.8).

In this typology, all business-focused rules EA artifacts can be collectively titled as Considerations since all these artifacts provide some general overarching business *considerations* defining architectural decision-making in the organization. All IT-focused rules EA artifacts can be jointly titled as Standards as all these artifacts represent some IT-specific technical *standards* shaping the designs of all information systems in the organization. All business-focused structures EA artifacts can be collectively titled as Visions because all these artifacts provide some abstract business *visions* of the organization in light of its futurity. All IT-focused structures EA artifacts can be jointly titled as Landscapes since all these artifacts describe some significant parts of the organizational *landscape* from a technical point of view. All business-focused solutions EA artifacts can be collectively titled as Outlines as all these artifacts represent some succinct *outlines* of specific IT solutions explaining their business meaning. And lastly, all IT-focused solutions EA artifacts can be jointly titled as Designs because all these artifacts describe some detailed technical *designs* of specific information systems[8].

Considerations (Business-Focused Rules)

First, **Considerations** describe global conceptual rules and fundamental considerations important for business and pertinent to IT. They are dual EA artifacts relevant to both business executives and enterprise architects (see Figure 7.5 and Figure 7.6). Considerations normally either do not refer to specific points in time or focus on the long-term future. They are typically expressed in simple intuitive formats, often as brief written statements, sometimes with inelaborate visualizations. In their temporal orientation, Considerations can be clearly classified as plans. They are usually general artifacts, but can also relate to specific digitalization initiatives. Illustrative examples of EA artifacts that belong to Considerations include principles and architecture strategies.

From a functional point of view, Considerations are used by enterprise architects for capturing architectural solutions by recording planning decisions on how the organization needs to work or what it wants to achieve from a business and IT perspective. In particular, they help capture organizational and some technical elements of high-level architectural solutions for large-scale transformation initiatives, e.g. changes in business models, communication channels and value propositions. As for documenting the existing situation, Considerations typically contain little or no information from which the current landscape structure can be deduced.

Standards (IT-Focused Rules)

Second, **Standards** describe global technical rules, norms, patterns and best practices relating to information systems. They are mostly not dual EA artifacts and relevant predominantly to enterprise architects and other IT representatives. Standards usually either do not refer to specific points in time or focus on the current state. They can be expressed in various formats, often using strict notations. In their temporal orientation, Standards can be viewed primarily as plans and partly as actualities. They are nearly always general artifacts and very rarely belong to specific transformation initiatives. Illustrative examples of EA artifacts that belong to Standards include technology reference models and guidelines.

Functionally, Standards can be used by enterprise architects for capturing architectural solutions and, in some cases, also for documenting the existing situation. In the former scenario, they reflect architectural decisions on how all IT systems should be constructed and help capture technical and possibly some organizational elements of high-level architectural solutions for large-scale transformation initiatives, e.g. changes in the technology portfolio, provision of IT services and ways of applying technologies. In the latter scenario, Standards document the current approaches to system implementation and technologies utilized in the organization.

Visions (Business-Focused Structures)

Third, **Visions** provide high-level conceptual descriptions of the organization from a business perspective. They are dual EA artifacts relevant to both business leaders and enterprise architects. Visions often focus on the long-term future up to 3–5 years ahead. They are typically expressed in brief informal formats, often as large but simple one-page diagrams. In their temporal orientation, Visions can be categorized mainly as plans. They can either be general artifacts or relate to specific transformation initiatives. Illustrative examples of EA artifacts that belong to Visions include business capability models and roadmaps.

From a functional standpoint, Visions are used by enterprise architects for capturing architectural solutions by recording planning decisions on what IT should provide to the organization in the long run. Specifically, they help capture organizational and some technical elements of mid-level architectural solutions for medium-sized transformation initiatives, e.g. changes in business capabilities, production activities and information availability. As for documenting the existing situation, Visions typically offer only very abstract views of the business and IT landscape suitable solely for introductory purposes.

Landscapes (IT-Focused Structures)

Fourth, **Landscapes** provide high-level technical descriptions of the organizational IT landscape. They are mostly not dual EA artifacts and relevant predominantly to enterprise architects and other IT representatives. Landscapes focus mainly on the current state, sometimes looking into the future. They are typically expressed in strict formats, often as complex one-page diagrams using formal modeling notations. In their temporal orientation, Landscapes can be viewed primarily as actualities and partly as plans. They are usually general artifacts, but some of them can also belong to specific transformation initiatives. Illustrative examples of EA artifacts that belong to Landscapes include asset inventories and landscape diagrams.

Functionally, Landscapes can be used by enterprise architects for documenting the existing situation and, in some cases, also for capturing architectural solutions. In the former scenario, Landscapes document the current structure of the IT landscape in terms of its software and hardware components, their relationship to each other and to business operations. In the latter scenario, they reflect architectural decisions on the future landscape evolution and help capture technical and possibly some organizational elements of mid-level architectural solutions for medium-sized transformation initiatives, e.g. changes in the landscape composition, underlying IT infrastructure and system interaction schemes.

Outlines (Business-Focused Solutions)

Fifth, **Outlines** provide high-level descriptions of separate IT solutions from a business point of view. They are dual EA artifacts relevant to both business managers and enterprise architects. Outlines usually focus on the mid-term future up to 1–2 years ahead. They are typically expressed as a mix of textual descriptions and simple diagrams. In their temporal orientation, Outlines can definitely be classified as plans. Outlines are always initiative-specific artifacts and do not exist outside of the context of concrete transformation initiatives. Illustrative examples of EA artifacts that belong to Outlines include solution briefs and solution overviews.

From a functional point of view, Outlines are used by enterprise architects for capturing architectural solutions by recording planning decisions on how approximately specific information systems should be implemented. In particular, they help capture organizational and some technical elements of low-level architectural solutions for small transformation initiatives, e.g. changes in business processes, automation of tasks, their costs and timelines. As for documenting the existing situation, Outlines can offer only archival descriptions of conceived IT solutions.

Designs (IT-Focused Solutions)

Finally, **Designs** provide detailed technical and functional descriptions of separate IT systems with their internal structure. They are dual EA artifacts relevant to both enterprise architects and project teams. Designs normally focus on the short-term future up to one year ahead. They are typically expressed as a mix of text, tables and complex diagrams, can be voluminous and often use formal modeling notations. In their temporal orientation, Designs can definitely be categorized as plans. Similarly to Outlines, Designs are always initiative-specific artifacts and cannot exist independently of concrete transformation initiatives. Illustrative examples of EA artifacts that belong to Designs include solution designs and preliminary solution designs.

From a functional standpoint, Designs are used by enterprise architects for capturing architectural solutions by recording planning decisions on how exactly specific IT systems should be constructed. Specifically, they help capture technical and possibly some organizational elements of low-level architectural solutions for small transformation initiatives, e.g. system components, logical structure and functional behavior. As for documenting the existing situation, Designs can offer only archival descriptions of deployed IT systems.

Resulting Taxonomy

Considerations, Standards, Visions, Landscapes, Outlines and Designs (CSVLOD) form the six-cell **CSVLOD taxonomy for EA artifacts** and represent major classes of instruments constituting the toolkit of enterprise architects. IT-focused artifacts — Standards, Landscapes and Designs — are employed by architects acting as Technology Experts, while business-focused ones — Considerations, Visions and Outlines — by architects acting as Change Agents. The CSVLOD taxonomy for EA artifacts with their most important properties is shown in Figure 7.11[9].

Chapter 7: Instruments of Enterprise Architects

		How EA Artifacts Describe? (Viewpoints)	
		IT-Focused	Business-Focused
What EA Artifacts Describe? (Objects)	**Rules**	*Technology Experts* **Standards** (IT-specific technical standards shaping the designs of all IT systems) **Content:** Global technical rules, norms, patterns and best practices relevant to information systems **Orientation:** Primarily plans, partly actualities **Affiliation:** Almost always general, seldom initiative-specific *Documenting the Existing Situation* Document the current approaches and utilized technologies *Capturing Architectural Solutions* Record decisions on how all IT systems should be implemented to capture technical and possibly organizational solutions for large-scale transformation initiatives	*Change Agents* **Considerations** (General overarching business considerations defining decision-making) **Content:** Global conceptual rules and fundamental considerations important for business and relevant to IT **Orientation:** Always plans **Affiliation:** Usually general, sometimes initiative-specific *Documenting the Existing Situation* Contain little or no information on the current landscape *Capturing Architectural Solutions* Record decisions on how the organization needs to work from a business and IT perspective to capture organizational and partly technical solutions for large-scale transformation initiatives
	Structures	*Technology Experts* **Landscapes** (Descriptions of the organizational landscape from the technical side) **Content:** High-level technical descriptions of the organizational IT landscape **Orientation:** Primarily actualities, partly plans **Affiliation:** Usually general, sometimes initiative-specific *Documenting the Existing Situation* Document the current structure of the IT landscape *Capturing Architectural Solutions* Record decisions on the future landscape evolution to capture technical and possibly organizational solutions for mid-size transformation initiatives	*Change Agents* **Visions** (Abstract business visions of the organization in light of its futurity) **Content:** High-level conceptual descriptions of the organization from a business perspective **Orientation:** Mainly plans **Affiliation:** Can be general or initiative-specific *Documenting the Existing Situation* Offer only very abstract views of the corporate landscape *Capturing Architectural Solutions* Record decisions on what IT should provide to the organization in the long run to capture organizational and partly technical solutions for mid-size transformation initiatives
	Solutions	*Technology Experts* **Designs** (Detailed technical designs of specific information systems) **Content:** Detailed technical and functional descriptions of separate IT systems with their internal structure **Orientation:** Always plans **Affiliation:** Always initiative-specific *Documenting the Existing Situation* Offer only archival descriptions of deployed IT systems *Capturing Architectural Solutions* Record decisions on how exactly specific IT systems should be constructed to capture technical and possibly organizational solutions for small transformation initiatives	*Change Agents* **Outlines** (Brief outlines of specific IT solutions explaining their business meaning) **Content:** High-level descriptions of separate IT solutions from a business point of view **Orientation:** Always plans **Affiliation:** Always initiative-specific *Documenting the Existing Situation* Offer only archival descriptions of conceived IT solutions *Capturing Architectural Solutions* Record decisions on how approximately specific IT systems should be implemented to capture organizational and partly technical solutions for small transformation initiatives

Figure 7.11. The CSVLOD taxonomy for EA artifacts

The CSVLOD taxonomy summarized in Figure 7.11 covers the whole diversity of regular EA artifacts that proved useful in the work of enterprise architects. This taxonomy characterizes artifacts, first of all, in terms of the objects they describe, viewpoints they present and functions they serve. It also explains many of their other prominent features and attributes relevant in the context of architectural planning, e.g. temporal orientation, initiative affiliation and presentation format. The CSVLOD taxonomy offers an intuitive and powerful framework for thinking about EA artifacts that neatly captures their overall meaning.

Other Instruments of Enterprise Architects

Whereas different types of EA artifacts from the CSVLOD taxonomy represent the primary instruments of enterprise architects, some other helpful means can be viewed as their secondary instruments. Most of these instruments, though, indirectly relate to EA artifacts and support their creation and storage, or complement their usage. The secondary instruments of architects can be classified mainly into modeling languages, software tools, analytical techniques and auxiliary artifacts.

Modeling Languages

Because most EA artifacts, and especially solutions and structures (see Figure 7.9), include some graphical visualizations, they can potentially make use of formal **modeling languages** that offer standardized ways of drawing various diagrams, charts and models. Specifically, all modeling languages and notations relevant to enterprise architects can be loosely organized into three broad groups:

- EA-specific languages — specialized modeling languages designed for representing the relationship between business and IT at a relatively high level of abstraction, e.g. current ArchiMate and obsolescent ARIS[10]
- Process-centric languages — specialized modeling languages developed for depicting sequential business processes and functional flows in their details, e.g. modern BPMN and antiquated IDEF0[11]
- System-oriented languages — specialized modeling languages intended for describing low-level technical structures of separate information systems, e.g. established UML and emerging C4[12]

Each of these groups of modeling languages has some value and application scenarios in the occupation of enterprise architects. However, because business leaders uneducated in modeling are capable of understanding only intuitive visualization approaches, but not sophisticated diagramming notations, the practical applicability of formal modeling languages is largely limited only to IT-focused EA artifacts produced solely for the specialist audience (see Figure 7.10).

Software Tools

Nowadays, most EA artifacts and other documents in organizations exist only in an electronic form. At the same time, modern IT landscapes tend to be extremely complicated and comprise numerous interrelated physical and logical elements the information of which is difficult to handle manually. For these reasons, in their daily work, enterprise architects actively employ various **software tools** to create and manage EA artifacts with the associated information on the landscape structure. Specifically, all software tools relevant to architects can be loosely grouped into four major categories:

- Office tools — standard productivity applications included in the Microsoft Office suite, most notably PowerPoint, Visio, Word and Excel, as well as their various commercial, open-source and cloud-based analogs
- Storage tools — all sorts of general-purpose information storage and knowledge management systems, e.g. enterprise portals, corporate wikis, content databases and file repositories
- EA-specific tools — complex software products for EA practices with their own internal architectural repositories, powerful modeling, storage and analytical capabilities, e.g. Software AG Alfabet, Avolution ABACUS and Ardoq[13]
- Specialized tools — diverse software for tracing and discovering different aspects of the IT environment, e.g. project-tracking, license management, IT asset management, IT service management and infrastructure monitoring systems

Each of these categories of software tools has its use in the job of enterprise architects. For instance, actualities EA artifacts serving architects for documenting the existing situation, for which they should be optimized for accumulation, search and analysis of information (see Figure 7.2), can be better maintained in EA-specific or other tools with specialized repositories providing these capabilities. On the contrary, plans EA artifacts used for capturing architectural solutions, for which they should be optimized for teamwork and collaboration of multiple parties (see Figure 7.4), can be better created with widespread office tools enabling their easy distribution, demonstration and editing.

Because enterprise architects practice "planning by talking", which involves giving numerous presentations to the stakeholder audience, MS PowerPoint, or one of its equivalents, is particularly important for their pursuits. In some sense, PowerPoint can be fairly regarded as the single most important software application in their toolkit.

Analytical Techniques

As part of architectural planning efforts, enterprise architects have to process mentally large volumes of diverse information about the business and IT landscape normally contained in EA artifacts. To facilitate this task, they tend to apply various **analytical techniques** that aid them in organizing their thinking, structuring thought processes and arriving at some conclusions. Specifically, helpful analytical approaches and methods routinely leveraged by architects include, but are not limited to, the following techniques:

- Gap analysis — analyzing exactly what needs to be done in order to migrate from the current state to the desired future state in terms of necessary changes in the business and IT landscape
- Impact analysis — analyzing probable immediate and longer-term consequences and ripple effects for business and IT that can result from modifying specific parts or components of the corporate landscape
- Application portfolio assessment — assessing the existing portfolio of applications for their actual business value by contrasting their pros (e.g. practical utility) versus their cons (e.g. maintenance costs)

- Strategic fitness assessment — assessing the available IT assets for their alignment with business and IT strategies and their ability to obstruct, support or enable the realization of particular strategic goals

These and many other, less prominent analytical techniques play an important role in the occupation of enterprise architects. However, different techniques are used in different situations and associated with different types of EA artifacts, sometimes very closely. For example, gap analysis is strongly connected to plans EA artifacts, especially those that imply substantial but concrete changes in the business and IT landscape, such as Visions and Outlines. By contrast, application portfolio and strategic fitness assessments hinge on actualities EA artifacts that refer to specific IT assets deployed in the organization, like Landscapes and some Standards.

Auxiliary Artifacts

In addition to the six general types of EA artifacts defined by the CSVLOD taxonomy (see Figure 7.11) and a number of instruments related to these artifacts described above, some other artifacts that can be considered auxiliary also belong to the toolkit of enterprise architects. **Auxiliary artifacts** are various architectural or semi-architectural documents that have some connection to EA practices and the work of architects in organizations. Often, these artifacts are custom, situation-specific and can be created when necessary for particular tasks, meetings or demands, but make little or no sense in other contexts. Unlike regular EA artifacts, they may have no consistent meaning even within the same organization, represent merely interim derivatives from "real" artifacts, relate to architectural planning rather loosely or target an EA practice itself. Although auxiliary artifacts can be extremely diverse, all these artifacts can be roughly separated into four distinct categories: ad hoc papers, communication materials, item registers and meta-EA artifacts. The four categories of auxiliary artifacts with their descriptions and typical examples are presented in Table 7.1.

Category	Description	Examples
Ad hoc papers	Temporary artifacts created to accomplish certain tasks, conduct some assessments or formalize the results of performed analysis	Comparative tables, relational matrices, miscellaneous reports and whitepapers
Communication materials	Disposable artifacts produced solely for communication purposes, often for concrete meetings with specific audiences	Slide decks, executive summaries, decision papers, handout leaflets and wall posters
Item registers	Durable artifacts established to reliably record some important items of mostly technical information for future reference	Operational risk registers, security vulnerability registers and architecture debt registers
Meta-EA artifacts	Permanent artifacts intended to regulate and govern different aspects of the functioning of EA practices in organizations (see Figure 4.3)	Process definitions, standardized templates, various checklists, exception and amendment forms

Table 7.1. Four categories of auxiliary artifacts

Each of the categories of auxiliary artifacts listed in Table 7.1 has its use in the job of enterprise architects. For instance, ad hoc papers are usually written by architects on demand, when some form of study, inquiry or evaluation needs to be carried out. Communication materials are typically prepared by architects before their formal meetings with initiative stakeholders to be presented and discussed during these meetings. Item registers can be set up by architects whenever certain valuable information has to be organized, stored and later retrieved. And lastly, meta-EA artifacts are used by architects to align their own behavior with the rules and policies of the organizational EA practice as part of which they work. Regular EA artifacts forming the CSVLOD taxonomy are described in detail in the next chapter, while some auxiliary artifacts will be introduced later in this book when they are relevant.

Chapter Summary

This chapter discussed EA artifacts as the key instruments of enterprise architects and the two main functions of artifacts in their work, explained the explicit and implicit duality of EA artifacts and introduced different types of EA artifacts with the CSVLOD taxonomy for organizing them, as well as some other important instruments of enterprise architects. The key message of this chapter can be summarized in the following essential points:

- EA artifacts are the primary instruments of enterprise architects that facilitate collaboration, knowledge exchange and information analysis in many different ways during digital transformation efforts and their architectural planning
- The first function of EA artifacts in the work of enterprise architects is documenting the existing situation, which implies recording objective facts about the organization and its IT landscape relevant to architectural planning
- The second function of EA artifacts in the work of enterprise architects is capturing architectural solutions, which implies recording various planning decisions constituting architectural solutions for digitalization initiatives
- The duality of EA artifacts represents their ability to address the information needs of both the business and IT audiences, either explicitly by structuring their content into different sections, or implicitly through their interpretive flexibility
- EA artifacts that proved helpful for enterprise architects are numerous, diverse and differ in their temporal orientation (actualities or plans), initiative affiliation (initiative-specific or general), described objects (solutions, structures or rules) and presented viewpoints (IT-focused or business-focused)
- Based on their objects and viewpoints, all EA artifacts can be classified using the CSVLOD taxonomy into six general types that determine their major properties: Considerations, Standards, Visions, Landscapes, Outlines and Designs
- Secondary instruments in the toolkit of enterprise architects include modeling languages, software tools, analytical techniques and auxiliary artifacts, such as ad hoc papers, communication materials, item registers and meta-EA artifacts

Chapter 8: The Catalog of Enterprise Architecture Artifacts

The previous chapter discussed different types of EA artifacts and introduced the CSVLOD taxonomy for their organization. This chapter continues the discussion and describes specific EA artifacts that belong to the six general types defined by the CSVLOD taxonomy: Considerations, Standards, Visions, Landscapes, Outlines and Designs. In particular, this chapter starts with providing a rich overview of all widely used EA artifacts related to each general type with their typical informational contents, unique features and suitability for documenting the existing situation and capturing architectural solutions. Next, this chapter explains the relationship between all these artifacts and the six organizational domains relevant to architectural planning. Lastly, this chapter introduces "Enterprise Architecture on a Page" as a convenient graphical catalog of common EA artifacts with their most essential properties.

Popular Enterprise Architecture Artifacts

EA artifacts represent the principal instruments of enterprise architects that they use, first, for documenting the existing situation in the organization (see Figure 7.2) and, second, for capturing architectural solutions for digital transformation initiatives (see Figure 7.4). The whole diversity of regular artifacts that proved helpful in practice can be neatly organized according to the CSVLOD taxonomy into the six general types — Considerations, Standards, Visions, Landscapes, Outlines and Designs — that determine, among other properties, their practical applicability and functional utility in the work of architects (see Figure 7.11).

Each of the six general types of EA artifacts from the CSVLOD taxonomy actually embraces numerous artifacts with similar attributes and features. The toolkit of enterprise architects, thus, comprises a vast array of artifacts that can potentially be employed in different circumstances. However, because some EA artifacts are used more frequently than others, the most popular of these artifacts can be further grouped into a limited number of narrow subtypes within their general types defined by the CSVLOD taxonomy.

Narrow subtypes of EA artifacts accurately describe their informational contents, temporal orientation, initiative affiliation and other unique properties, though always with certain situation-specific variations. More importantly, from a functional point of view, these subtypes determine the typical usage scenarios of the respective artifacts and their capacity for serving the two major functions: first, their ability to document different segments of the organizational landscape (see Figure 7.1) and, second, their ability to capture either separate architectural decisions or complete solutions at different levels of the initiative hierarchy (see Figure 7.3). As many EA artifacts have no consistent or commonly accepted titles across the industry and can be referred to under different labels in different companies by different architects, further in this book these artifacts are discussed under their most popular or most explanatory titles[1].

Considerations

The general type of Considerations unites all business-focused rules EA artifacts, which provide general overarching business considerations defining architectural decision-making in the organization. Considerations are used by enterprise architects predominantly for capturing high-level architectural solutions, mostly their organizational components, for large-scale digitalization initiatives. Popular artifacts related to this general type include Principles, Policies, Architecture Strategies, Analytical Reports and Conceptual Data Models.

Principles and Policies

Arguably the most exemplary subtypes of Considerations are Principles and Policies, both of which outline how the organization needs to work in the most general terms. **Principles** (also known as maxims) are specific Considerations defining global high-level guidelines relevant to all decision-making and planning in the organization. Principles often include four distinct components, or some of their variations: concise titles, statements clarifying their exact meaning, rationales explaining their motivation and implications expounding their consequences for organizations and their IT landscapes. The lists of Principles are usually maintained independently of any digitalization initiatives, though individual Principles in these lists often relate to concrete initiatives and initiative-specific sets of Principles can also be created. As pronounced plans in their temporal orientation, Principles are used by enterprise architects for capturing top-level architectural decisions leaning towards the organizational side. All lower-level architectural solutions developed in the organization are expected to align with the established Principles (see Figure 3.7). As for documenting the existing situation, Principles do not contain any reliable knowledge about the current landscape.

A closely related sibling of Principles is Policies. **Policies** (can be called cloud policies, information exchange policies, etc.) are specific Considerations defining overarching normative prescriptions relevant to certain aspects of organizational decision-making. Policies are formulated as plain written statements explaining what the organization must or must not do concerning its IT systems and information processing. They can be either produced internally based on peculiar organizational needs, or derived from externally imposed legislative acts or requirements of industry regulators. Like Principles, the lists of enacted Policies usually exist independently of any transformation initiatives, though in some cases they can also be initiative-specific. In a similar fashion, Policies serve enterprise architects for capturing highest-level architectural decisions pertaining mostly to organizational solutions, so that all solutions developed "below" have to comply with their instructions. Likewise, they offer no information on the current landscape structure for documentation purposes. The schematic graphical representations of Principles and Policies are shown in Figure 8.1.

Principle 1: Standardized Business Processes
Statement: ....
Rationale: ....
Implications: ....
Principle 2: Single Customer View
Statement: ....
Rationale: ....
Implications: ....
Principle 3: Business Continuity
Statement: ....
Rationale: ....
Implications: ....

External	National Privacy Policies	Policy 1: Personal Data Must Be Stored Onshore Description: ....
		Policy 2: Destroy Personal Data When Not Needed Description: ....
	Sarbanes-Oxley Policies	Policy 3: Log All Accesses to Accounting Systems Description: ....
		Policy 4: Retain Audit Trails and Emails for 5 Years Description: ....
Internal	Data Security Policies	Policy 5: No Sensitive Data on Mobile Devices Description: ....
		Policy 6: Store Credit Cards in Encrypted Formats Description: ....
	Data Exchange Policies	Policy 7: Do Not Share Key Data with Third Parties Description: ....
		Policy 8: Share Client Data with Trusted Partners Description: ....
	Cloud Hosting Policies	Policy 9: Use Only the PCI DSS Compliant Cloud Description: ....
		Policy 10: Do Not Store Health Data in the Cloud Description: ....

Figure 8.1. Principles and Policies

Principles and Policies enjoyed broad industry adoption as simple but powerful EA artifacts that allow enterprise architects to reflect the most basic architectural decisions regarding the corporate business and IT landscape.

Architecture Strategies

Another prominent subtype of Considerations is Architecture Strategies, which point out approximately where the organization needs to go. **Architecture Strategies** (also known as technology strategies, strategic papers, governance papers and many other names) are specific Considerations defining abstract conceptual directions for the organization in terms of the relationship between business and IT. Architecture Strategies can address various aspects of organizations and their IT platforms, ranging from the overall way of doing business in the digital world to the productive use of concrete technologies in the given organizational settings. They can also be rather diverse in their informational contents and specify, for example, long-term ends that should be achieved and means of their attainment, fundamental decisions made about the future and their rationales, recommended approaches that should be applied and their implications, anticipated timelines for realizing the stated objectives and potential risks on the way.

Architecture Strategies can be general or initiative-specific EA artifacts. In the former case, they refer to separate business areas or even to the whole organization. In the latter case, they relate to major transformation initiatives with global impact and far-reaching consequences. However, because of the prolonged nature of such initiatives, they often exhibit certain features of general artifacts, e.g. exist for a few years being periodically updated according to the current status of these initiatives until their completion. Architecture Strategies are used by enterprise architects for capturing very high-level architectural solutions with their technical and organizational components. They provide the foundation for launching lower-level change initiatives and shape their architectural solutions. From the standpoint of documenting the existing situation, Architecture Strategies tend to include little or no meaningful information about the current landscape. The schematic graphical representations of Architecture Strategies (general and initiative-specific ones) are shown in Figure 8.2.

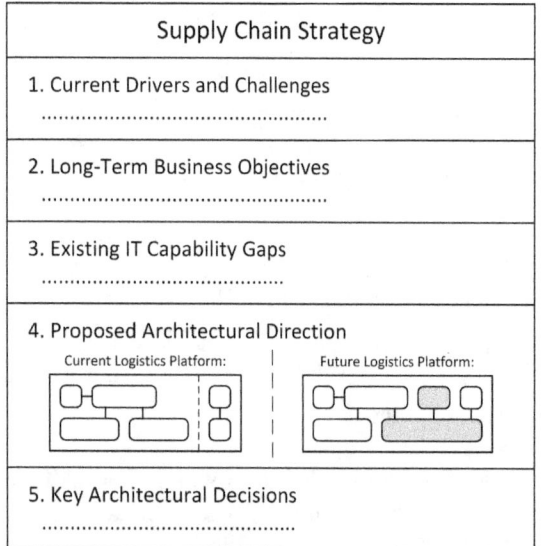 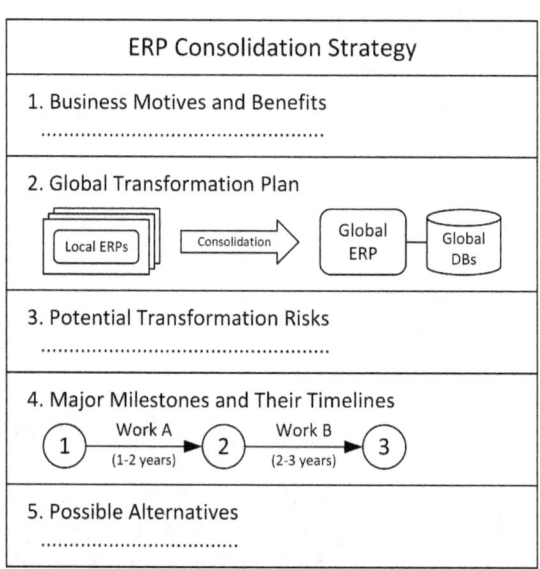

Figure 8.2. Architecture Strategies (general strategies and initiative-specific strategies)

Architecture Strategies are important EA artifacts at the disposal of enterprise architects as they allow them to record different kinds of architectural decisions for guiding the long-term evolution of the organizational business and IT landscape.

Analytical Reports and Conceptual Data Models

Less widely used subtypes of Considerations are Analytical Reports and Conceptual Data Models, which suggest what breakthrough technologies the organization needs to embrace and what information it needs to possess. **Analytical Reports** (also known as whitepapers, position papers and some other names) are specific Considerations providing executive-level analyses of relevant technology trends and their potential impact on the organization. They can take various forms, use any presentation formats and incorporate different elements of well-known techniques for environmental analysis, such as SWOT analyses, technology radars and hype cycles. Analytical Reports are general EA artifacts that are periodically updated to keep up with the progress in technology, often on a yearly basis, and do not depend on concrete transformation initiatives. Analytical Reports are used by enterprise architects roughly for capturing overarching architectural decisions in the matters of technical and organizational ramifications of adopting, or not adopting, particular technologies and reacting to general technology-related challenges and pressures. All other architectural solutions in the organization should align with their suggestions. For documentation purposes, Analytical Reports contain, at best, only some vague information about the current landscape.

Conceptual Data Models (CDMs, also known as corporate data models, data reference models, information maps and many other names) are specific Considerations providing abstract definitions of the key data entities vital for the business of the organization and their relationship. They are normally materialized as simple visual diagrams using straightforward, intuitive notations to describe main data objects, their essential attributes and interconnections. Conceptual Data Models are general EA artifacts that are linked to the organization as a whole and exist independently of its transformation initiatives. They serve enterprise architects for capturing high-level architectural decisions on the information aspects of organizational solutions. All lower-level architectural solutions developed in the organization should align their data structures with Conceptual Data Models. As for documenting the existing situation, Conceptual Data Models potentially carry very valuable knowledge on the composition of corporate information assets, but this knowledge is accurate only to the extent to which their idealized picture matches the actual imperfect realities. The schematic graphical representations of Analytical Reports (in the form of technology radars) and Conceptual Data Models are shown in Figure 8.3.

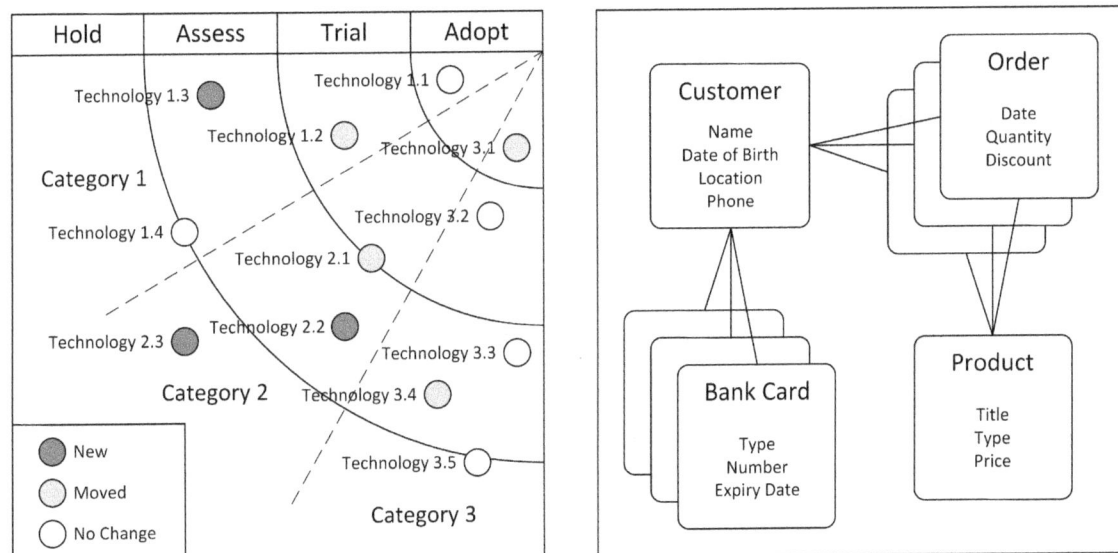

Figure 8.3. Analytical Reports and Conceptual Data Models

Analytical Reports and Conceptual Data Models are rather narrow-purposed EA artifacts, but they are helpful to enterprise architects in situations when architectural decisions about technology adoption and information structuring have to be made.

Other Considerations

In addition to the five major EA artifacts introduced above, some other useful accessory documents can also be loosely related to Considerations. Other Considerations that can be employed by enterprise architects include, for example, the following artifacts:

- **Business motivation models** — structured descriptions of strategic business goals and various transformation drivers motivating digitalization, i.e. formalized materializations of the motivational context of the organization (see Figure 1.3)
- **Strategy maps** — structured graphical mappings of strategic business goals and the underlying means of their achievement at different organizational levels enabling transparent means-to-ends traceability

These and similar artifacts can help architects understand the motivational context, develop organizational components of very high-level architectural solutions for digitalization initiatives and link them to business strategy and associated transformation drivers.

Standards

The general type of Standards unites all IT-focused rules EA artifacts, which represent IT-specific technical standards shaping the designs of all information systems in the organization. Standards are used by enterprise architects for capturing technical components of high-level architectural solutions for large-scale transformation initiatives and, in some cases, also for documenting the existing situation in terms of system implementation approaches and technologies. Popular artifacts related to this general type include Technology Reference Models, Technology Inventories, Technology Roadmaps, IT Principles, Guidelines, Patterns and Logical Data Models.

Technology Reference Models

One of the most important subtypes of Standards are Technology Reference Models, which define the technology "stance" of the organization. **Technology Reference Models** (TRMs, also known as technology portfolio models, technology standards, technology maps and many other names) are specific Standards providing structured graphical representations of the technology portfolio of the organization. They depict all technologies used in the entire organization on a single page organizing them in a logical manner, often aligning with different layers of the technology stack, e.g. frontend applications, backend systems, data storage, hosting infrastructure and security mechanisms. Technology Reference Models can vary in their structure, composition, granularity and other details. They also typically apply some or the other color-coding schemes and conventions to indicate the status of technologies in the IT landscape (e.g. emerging, active, supported and deprecated) and, thereby, determine their introduction needs and reuse prospects.

Technology Reference Models are general EA artifacts belonging to the whole organization, rather than to concrete transformation initiatives. Mixing actualities and plans in their temporal orientation allows them to serve enterprise architects effectively for both documenting the existing situation and capturing architectural solutions. In the first function, Technology Reference Models document the current IT environment from the viewpoint of utilized technologies and provide an authoritative source of knowledge on the subject. In the second function, they capture top-level architectural decisions on the technical side related specifically to the selection of technologies. Accordingly, all lower-level architectural solutions developed in the organization should align their technology choices with Technology Reference Models. The schematic graphical representations of Technology Reference Models (two different variations) are shown in Figure 8.4.

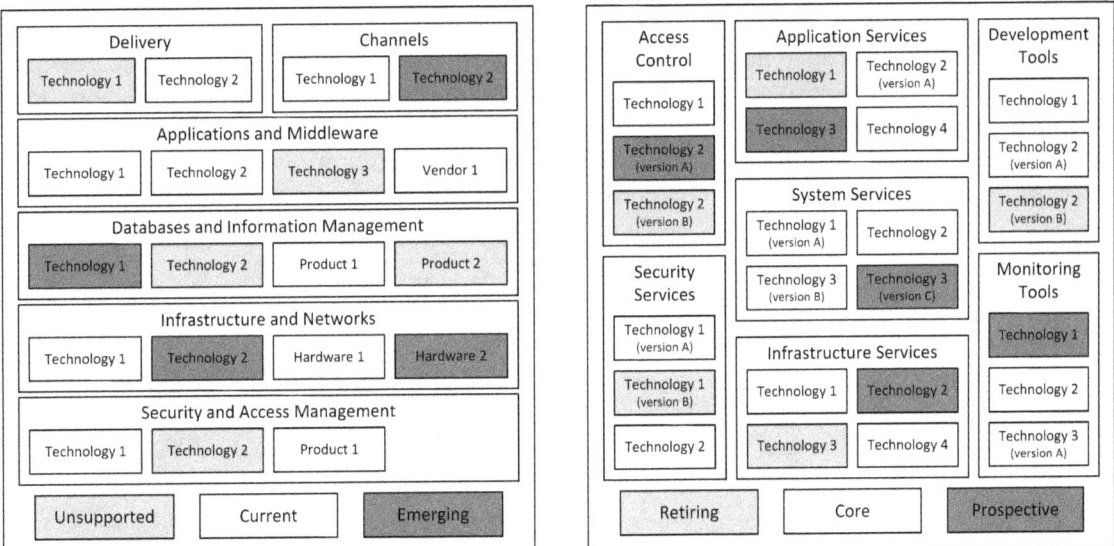

Figure 8.4. Technology Reference Models (two different variations of models)

Technology Reference Models are very useful and multifunctional EA artifacts that allow enterprise architects to control the corporate technology portfolio by representing its current condition and reflecting architectural decisions on its future evolution.

Technology Inventories and Technology Roadmaps

Two related but less popular subtypes of Standards also dealing with technologies and their usage in the organization are Technology Inventories and Technology Roadmaps. **Technology Inventories** (also known as technology registers, technology catalogs and some other names) are specific Standards providing structured catalogs of technologies with their key properties, attributes and features. Put it simply, Technology Inventories present comprehensive lists of technologies deployed in the organization with detailed descriptive information about them, e.g. their vendors, licensing terms, inception dates, technical functions, owner contacts, known issues and costs of maintenance. They also specify the status of these technologies for the purposes of their potential reuse in new digitalization initiatives. Technology Inventories are general EA artifacts encompassing the entire organization, which fulfill exactly the same functions as Technology Reference Models. Namely, they are used by enterprise architects both for documenting the existing technological environment and for capturing highest-level technology-related architectural decisions. All lower-level architectural solutions in the organization should base their technology selection on Technology Inventories.

Technology Roadmaps (also known as product roadmaps, vendor roadmaps and some other names) are specific Standards providing structured graphical views of the lifecycles of technologies with their phases. Technology Roadmaps show the anticipated future of technologies found in the corporate IT landscape, or different versions of these technologies, in terms of their projected lifecycle stages (e.g. introduction, usage, decline and decommissioning) and their timelines. Essentially, they elaborate on the temporal dimension of Technology Reference Models and Technology Inventories discussed above. Technology Roadmaps are general EA artifacts tracing the prospects of technologies in the whole organization. Although they also serve enterprise architects for documenting the existing IT environment, their primary function is capturing the technology aspects of high-level architectural solutions. All lower-level architectural solutions in the organization should follow the suggestions of Technology Roadmaps in their technology choices. The schematic graphical representations of Technology Inventories and Technology Roadmaps are shown in Figure 8.5.

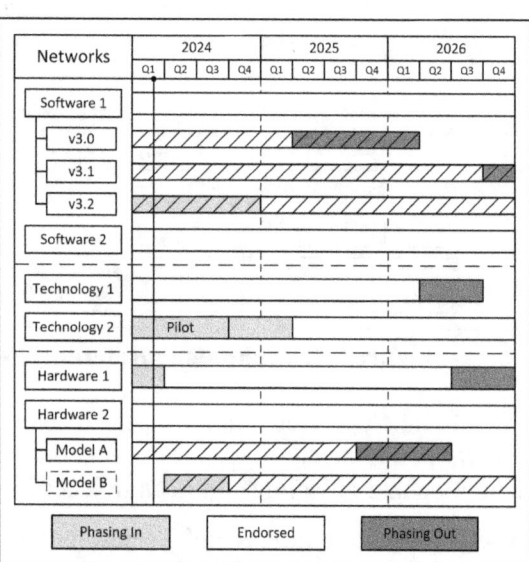

Figure 8.5. Technology Inventories and Technology Roadmaps

Technology Inventories and Technology Roadmaps offer alternative EA artifacts for enterprise architects to manage the evolution of the organizational IT landscape from a technological perspective.

IT Principles and Guidelines

Other noteworthy Standards are IT Principles and kindred Guidelines, both of which shape the way information systems in the organization are constructed. **IT Principles** (also known as simply principles) are specific Standards defining global high-level IT-centric guidelines relevant to all IT-related decisions and plans in the organization. In their idea, format and structure, IT Principles closely resemble regular Principles (see Figure 8.1), can also include titles, statements, rationales and implications, but capture purely technical imperatives having little or no direct relevance to business. For convenience, they are often classified according to different domains of IT, e.g. applications, infrastructure and security. Analogously to Principles, organizational sets of IT Principles are typically general EA artifacts, seldom initiative-specific. IT Principles are used by enterprise architects for capturing top-level architectural decisions pertaining predominantly to technical solutions. All lower-level architectural solutions in the organization should align with their directives. From the standpoint of documenting the existing situation, IT Principles do not reflect any actual knowledge about the current landscape.

A close "relative" of IT Principles is Guidelines. **Guidelines** (also known as simply standards) are specific Standards providing detailed IT-specific implementation-level prescriptions applicable to narrow technology areas or domains. Guidelines in many respects highly resemble IT Principles, but contain much lower-level, very fine-grained recommendations as to how exactly to use particular technologies, products or approaches. They are often clustered around concrete classes of technology or spheres of expertise (e.g. mobile apps, websites, data warehouses and system hosting) and can have varying strictness (e.g. mandatory, recommended and optional). Usually, Guidelines are general EA artifacts, but they can also be developed for specific initiatives if needed. Guidelines serve enterprise architects for capturing technical elements of mid-level architectural solutions. All lower-level technical solutions in the organization should adhere to their prescriptions. Like IT Principles, they offer no credible information on the current landscape structure for documentation purposes. The schematic graphical representations of IT Principles and Guidelines are shown in Figure 8.6.

Category	IT Principle		Category	Guideline	Strictness
Applications	IT Principle 1: Prefer Open Source Solutions Description:		Server Deployment Standards	Guideline 1: Run Applications as OS Services Description:	Mandatory
	IT Principle 2: Log All Main Operations Description:			Guideline 2: Store Deployment Packages in VCS Description:	Optional
Data	IT Principle 3: Use Scalable Storage Description:		Network Protocol Standards	Guideline 3: Prefer REST Over SOAP Description:	Recommended
	IT Principle 4: Backup All Permanent Data Description:			Guideline 4: Avoid Using UDP Multicast Description:	Optional
Integration	IT Principle 5: Use Middleware for Integration Description:		Data Encryption Standards	Guideline 5: Use 256-Bit Encryption Keys Description:	Recommended
	IT Principle 6: Avoid Binary Integration Protocols Description:			Guideline 6: Store MD5 Hashes of Passwords Description:	Mandatory
Infrastructure	IT Principle 7: Host in the Cloud Description:		Interface Design Guidelines	Guideline 7: Place Menu in the Top Right Corner Description:	Recommended
	IT Principle 8: Dedicated Server for Each System Description:			Guideline 8: Use Web-Safe Colours Description:	Optional
Security	IT Principle 9: Isolate Externally Facing Systems Description:		Secure Coding Guidelines	Guideline 9: Initialize Variables to Safe Defaults Description:	Mandatory
	IT Principle 10: Secure by Default Description:			Guideline 10: Validate All Incoming Data Description:	Mandatory

Figure 8.6. IT Principles and Guidelines

IT Principles and Guidelines are important EA artifacts that allow enterprise architects to record various universal and technology-specific architectural decisions on the technical structure of the IT landscape.

Patterns and Logical Data Models

Somewhat less popular subtypes of Standards are Patterns and Logical Data Models, which define reusable solution components and detailed data structures respectively. **Patterns** (also known as reference architectures) are specific Standards providing generic reusable solutions to commonly occurring problems in the design of information systems. They describe logical building blocks embodying proven ways of addressing typical technical challenges from which new IT systems can be constructed and also include some contextual information regarding their applicability, e.g. what problems they solve, when they should be used, their rationales and limitations. Patterns tend to be general EA artifacts and their catalogs are normally maintained in organizations independently of any transformation initiatives, though sometimes they can also be created for specific initiatives. Patterns are used by enterprise architects for capturing technical aspects of high-level architectural solutions, particularly those dealing with integration, infrastructure and security. All lower-level technical solutions developed in the organization are expected to reuse the respective approaches to constructing IT systems. As for documenting the existing situation, Patterns cannot be viewed as a reliable reflection of the current landscape texture.

Logical Data Models (also known as canonical data models, data schemas and some other names) are specific Standards providing logical or even physical platform-specific definitions of common data entities and their relationship. They are usually materialized as rather complex diagrams often using specialized modeling notations to describe relevant data objects, their fields and attributes, keys and links between each other. Logical Data Models are typically general EA artifacts, but they can also be developed for specific transformation initiatives if necessary. They serve enterprise architects for capturing data-related elements of mid-level architectural solutions, more from their technical side. All lower-level architectural solutions in the organization should align their data formats with Logical Data Models. For documentation purposes, Logical Data Models potentially contain very useful knowledge on the exact structure of major business objects, but the accuracy of this knowledge depends on the degree of correspondence between ideal data types that they depict and real table definitions in existing databases. The schematic graphical representations of Patterns and Logical Data Models are shown in Figure 8.7.

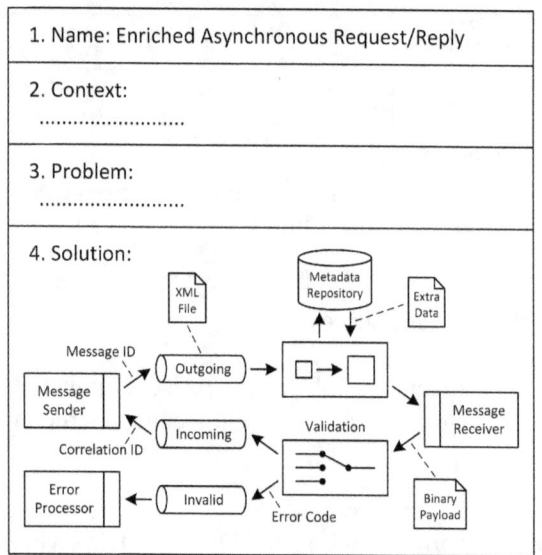
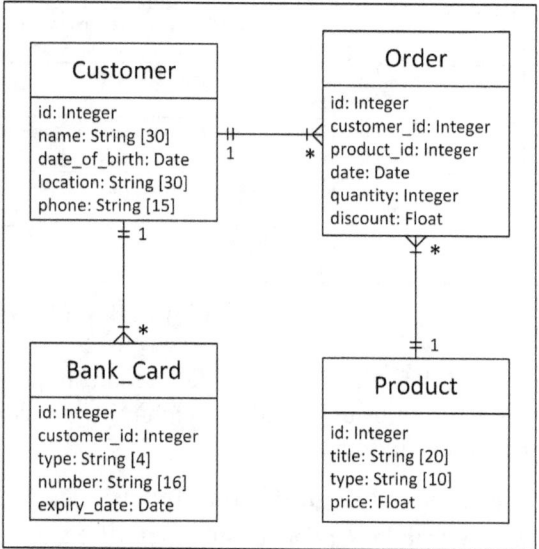

Figure 8.7. Patterns and Logical Data Models

Patterns and Logical Data Models are not so widely applicable EA artifacts, but they are indispensable for enterprise architects in circumstances when architectural decisions about uniform problem solutions and detailed data structures have to be recorded.

Other Standards

In addition to the seven notable EA artifacts described above, some other, less frequently used Standards also deserve to be mentioned. Other Standards that can be employed by enterprise architects include, for example, the following artifacts:

- **Interface definitions** — formal specifications of common remote call interfaces, invocation protocols, message types, formats and payloads existing and evolving in the organization independently of specific information systems
- **IT architecture strategies** — IT-oriented counterparts of business-focused Architecture Strategies (see Figure 8.2) defining conceptual directions for purely technical landscape layers, such as integration, infrastructure and security
- **IT analytical reports** — IT-oriented analogs of regular Analytical Reports (see Figure 8.3) evaluating various technology trends of no relevance directly to the business, e.g. programming languages, database platforms and development tools

These and similar EA artifacts can help architects grasp the technology environment, capture technical components of high-level architectural solutions for transformation initiatives and drive the technological evolution of the corporate IT landscape.

Visions

The general type of Visions unites all business-focused structures EA artifacts, which provide abstract business visions of the organization in light of its futurity. Visions are used by enterprise architects primarily for capturing mid-level architectural solutions, mostly their organizational components, for medium-sized digitalization initiatives. Popular artifacts related to this general type include Target States, Roadmaps, Business Capability Models, Process Maps and Value Chains.

Target States and Roadmaps

Two essential subtypes of Visions are Target States and Roadmaps, which describe what future is desired and how to get there. **Target States** (also known as target architectures, future state architectures and some other names) are specific Visions providing high-level graphical descriptions of the specific state of the organization in terms of business and IT. Target States usually materialize as intuitive visualizations, often rather large ones, depicting what the desired long-term future looks like from the standpoint of the relationship between business and IT, sometimes in the form of simple business application portfolios. This envisioned future is often contraposed to the current situation to clarify the substance and meaning of anticipated changes. Target States can be general or initiative-specific EA artifacts. In the former case, they typically focus on separate business areas and continuously evolve in tandem with these areas and their development strategies. In the latter case, they are produced for particular digitalization initiatives having definite timeframes and ultimate destinations. Target States, in principle, are used by enterprise architects for capturing mid-level architectural solutions with both their technical and organizational components, though in different proportions. They represent important drivers for lower-level transformation initiatives and provide an overall context that forms their architectural solutions. As for documenting the existing situation, Target States may or may not contain systematic information on the current landscape structure.

A natural companion of Target States is Roadmaps defining concrete steps towards the future. **Roadmaps** (also known as capability roadmaps, application roadmaps and some other names) are specific Visions providing structured graphical views of IT initiatives having direct business value for the organization. Roadmaps show planned digitalization initiatives, usually projects, with their expected timelines, commencement and completion dates. These initiatives are often color-coded based on their status, magnitude, price tag or other pertinent properties and organized logically into a number of tracks corresponding to different business areas, functions or capabilities. Besides the initiatives themselves, Roadmaps can also present relevant contextual information, e.g. transformation drivers motivating the initiatives, current and desired future states in terms of information systems. Like Target States, Roadmaps can be general as well as initiative-specific EA artifacts. General Roadmaps usually relate to particular business units or capability areas and "live" with them, whereas initiative-specific ones are developed to steer individual digitalization initiatives, typically programs or strategies. Roadmaps, thus, serve enterprise architects for capturing both technical and organizational components of mid-level architectural solutions. As they specify concrete pieces of work scheduled for implementation, Roadmaps provide, in the most explicit form, the existing intentions based on which lower-level derivative initiatives are launched (see Figure 2.6). Similarly to Target States, they may not carry any structured knowledge about the current landscape for documentation purposes. The schematic graphical representations of Target States (initiative-specific ones) and Roadmaps (general ones) are shown in Figure 8.8.

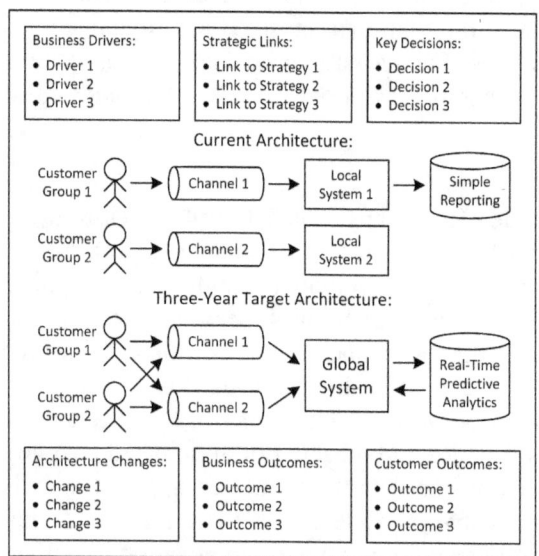
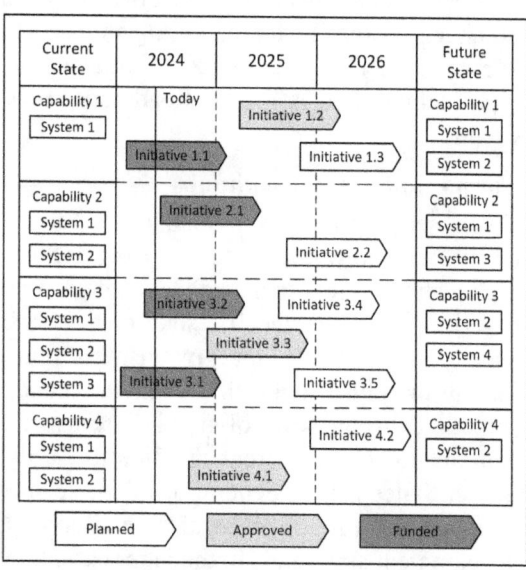

Figure 8.8. Target States and Roadmaps

Target States and Roadmaps are the "bread and butter" of enterprise architects as it is these EA artifacts that are utilized, in some form or the other, to reflect the most important architectural decisions for the vast majority of change initiatives of considerable size, larger than separate projects.

Business Capability Models

Another very important subtype of Visions is Business Capability Models, which help represent the business of the organization and concentrate improvement efforts. **Business Capability Models** (BCMs, also known as business capability maps, capability reference models and some other names) are specific Visions providing structured graphical views of organizational business capabilities, their relationship and hierarchy. On one page, Business Capability Models decompose the business of the whole organization into a nested set of independent business capabilities, where each capability abstracts all the underlying resources necessary for its fulfillment, e.g. people, processes, know-how, physical facilities and information systems. They also apply a rich variety of color-coding schemes and mappings, first, to figure out where and what kind of improvements are required and, second, to visualize these conclusions. Besides that, Business Capability Models can exhibit lots of other supplementary information to support decision-making, e.g. business goals, objectives, customers and suppliers. They can vary greatly in many properties, such as their logical structure and informational contents, granularity and level of depth, color-coding and mapping approaches, and range from very simple to rather sophisticated ones.

Business Capability Models are always general EA artifacts that coevolve slowly with the business of the organization and are fundamentally detached from concrete transformation initiatives. Functionally, they are used by enterprise architects mostly for capturing high-level architectural decisions belonging predominantly to organizational solutions. An understanding of capabilities that need to be uplifted provided by Business Capability Models often serves as the foundation for launching lower-level initiatives and also influences their architectural solutions. From the standpoint of documenting the existing situation, they offer a very conceptual view of the current landscape that communicates only a basic notion of what the organization does as part of its business, but lacks any material details. The schematic graphical representations of Business Capability Models (simple and complex ones) are shown in Figure 8.9.

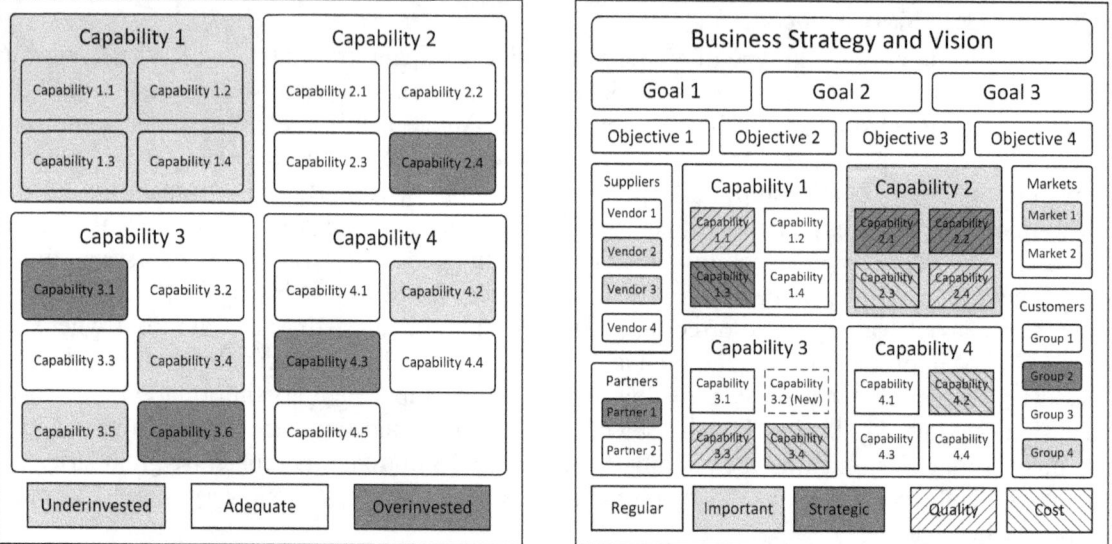

Figure 8.9. Business Capability Models (simple models and complex models)

Business Capability Models proved to be very useful EA artifacts that help enterprise architects analyze the organization and record architectural decisions about global improvements required in its different business areas.

Process Maps and Value Chains

Two alternative but less popular subtypes of Visions also intended to structure the business of the organization and accentuate priorities are Process Maps and Value Chains. **Process Maps** (also known as business process models, process architectures and some other names) are specific Visions providing structured graphical views of high-level business processes, their relationship and hierarchy. Similarly to Business Capability Models, they break down the business of the organization into a number of top-level, end-to-end business processes, or value streams (e.g. explore-to-mine, produce-to-sell, order-to-deliver and hire-to-retire), and their constituting lower-level subprocesses. Likewise, Process Maps apply various color-coding patterns and mapping approaches to understand and indicate which business processes need to be added, modified, revamped or eliminated. By focusing specifically on executable processes, they offer a somewhat more material view of the business than Business Capability Models. Process Maps are general EA artifacts aggregating process change requirements from all digitalization initiatives in the organization. They are used by enterprise architects for capturing high-level architectural decisions on the organizational side, spawning lower-level initiatives and shaping their architectural solutions. As for documenting the existing situation, Process Maps convey only a basic conception of what kind of business processes the organization runs, omitting any of their details.

Value Chains (also known as value streams, value reference models and some other names) are specific Visions providing structured graphical representations of the added value chain of the organization or its lines of business. They demonstrate the progression of activities performed by the business to deliver its goods and services to the market, classifying them into primary activities (e.g. production, marketing and sales) and supporting activities (e.g. accounting, finance and human resource management). Value Chains also apply color-coding and mapping approaches similar to those used in Business Capability Models and Process Maps to localize and articulate desired organizational improvements. One of the notable specifics of Value Chains is that they typically describe a single line of business, so that multi-profile companies tend to create separate Value Chains for each of their businesses, e.g. crude oil, oil refinement and petrochemistry. Accordingly, they are general EA artifacts linked to the respective lines of business. Value Chains serve enterprise architects for capturing mostly organizational aspects of high-level architectural solutions, motivating lower-level transformation initiatives and influencing their architectural solutions. For documentation purposes, Value Chains contain only very abstract depictions of organizational business activities that lack any physical details. The schematic graphical representations of Process Maps and Value Chains are shown in Figure 8.10.

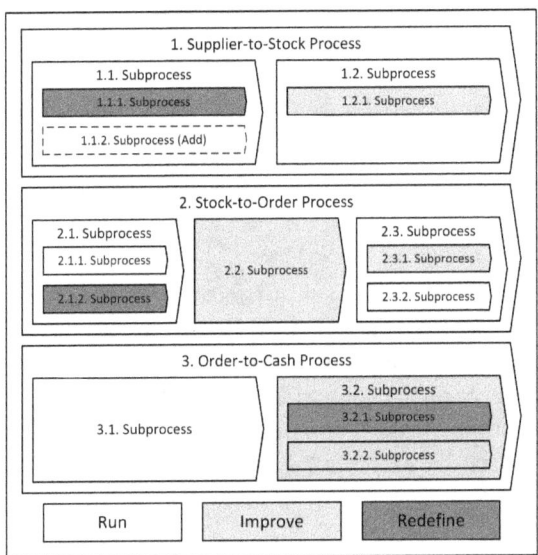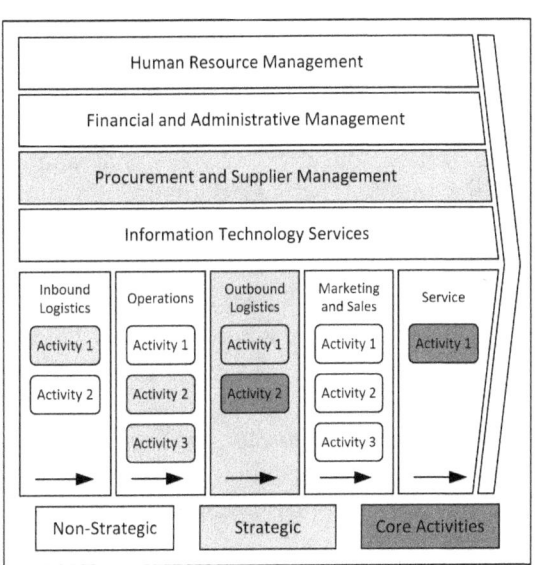

Figure 8.10. Process Maps and Value Chains

Analogously to Business Capability Models, Process Maps and Value Chains allow enterprise architects to reflect architectural decisions on the necessary organizational improvements, though from somewhat different angles and viewpoints.

Other Visions

In addition to the five prominent EA artifacts discussed above, some other, more unusual Visions are also worth referencing. Other Visions that can be employed by enterprise architects include, for example, the following artifacts:

- **Industry reference models** — generic models of the business in particular industries adapted to the needs of the organization or enriched with additional organization-specific details[2]

- **Core diagrams** — explicit one-page depictions of the organization in terms of its main business processes, data classes and their relationship reflecting the standardization and integration requirements of the adopted operating model[3]
- **Business model canvases** — abstract views of the organizational business model with its key elements: partners, activities, resources, value propositions, customer relationships, channels, customer segments, cost structure and revenue streams[4]
- **Context diagrams** — high-level graphical descriptions of the current operational flows of the organization that explain on a single page how the business works, what its major elements are and how they interact with each other
- **Organizational structures** — structured descriptions of which business units are responsible for particular activities, where they are located, what business capabilities they implement and what outputs they generate
- **Product catalogs** — structured descriptions of what products the organization produces, where they are produced, what source materials are required for these products and who eventually consumes them

These and similar EA artifacts can help architects understand the business of the organization, develop organizational and partly technical components of high- to mid-level architectural solutions for digitalization initiatives and guide digital transformation efforts.

Landscapes

The general type of Landscapes unites all IT-focused structures EA artifacts, which describe significant parts of the organizational landscape from a technical point of view. Landscapes are used by enterprise architects for documenting the existing situation in terms of available IT assets and their relationships and, in some cases, also for capturing technical components of mid-level architectural solutions for medium-sized transformation initiatives. Popular artifacts related to this general type include Landscape Diagrams, Asset Inventories, System Portfolio Models, Landscape Maps, IT Roadmaps and Asset Roadmaps.

Landscape Diagrams and Asset Inventories

Probably the most classic subtypes of Landscapes are Landscape Diagrams and Asset Inventories, which document the structure and composition of the IT landscape respectively. **Landscape Diagrams** (also known as relational diagrams, system interaction models, integration contexts and many other names) are specific Landscapes providing technical depictions of the landscape structure in terms of its components, their connections and interactions. Landscape Diagrams are materialized as graphical "boxes and arrows" schemes of different scopes and granularities, often pretty large and complex ones, typically describing the corporate IT landscape in its current state. They can either concentrate on particular layers of the IT landscape, such as systems, databases and infrastructure, or combine all these elements together. Landscape Diagrams are usually general EA artifacts strongly attached to different landscape areas, though in some cases they can also be created for specific transformation initiatives. As pronounced actualities in their temporal orientation, Landscape Diagrams are used by enterprise architects mainly for documenting the existing IT environment and form a powerful knowledge base on the landscape structure. When they happen to record some planning decisions, they capture mostly technical, structural aspects of mid-level architectural solutions, so that lower-level solutions have to stick to their suggestions.

Asset Inventories (also known as asset registers, system registries and some other names) are specific Landscapes providing structured catalogs of IT assets with their essential properties, attributes and features. Asset Inventories list all available IT assets constituting the organizational landscape and contain detailed information on these assets, e.g. their purpose, technology stack, introduction date, business owners, IT owners, reported problems and overall "health". They also indicate, in one way or another, the status of IT assets from the standpoint of their organizational fitness and reusability in future IT solutions. Asset Inventories are fundamentally general EA artifacts unrelated to any transformation initiatives. Similarly to Landscape Diagrams, they serve enterprise architects chiefly for documenting the existing IT environment and offer a comprehensive centralized repository of knowledge on the landscape composition. However, they are also used partly for capturing technical elements of mid-level architectural solutions that refer to the choice of appropriate building blocks for new information systems, influencing lower-level solutions. The schematic graphical representations of Landscape Diagrams and Asset Inventories are shown in Figure 8.11.

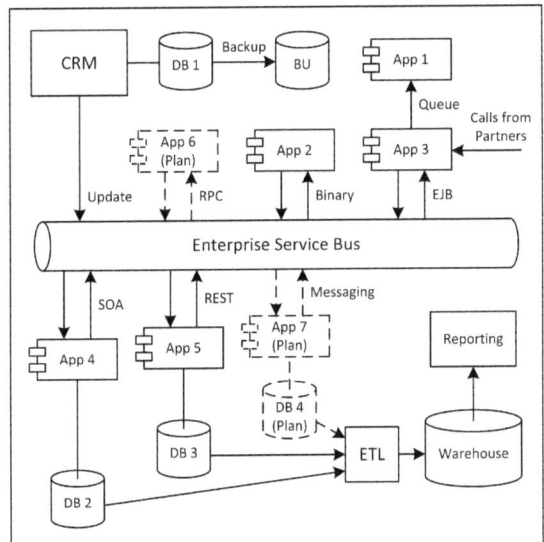

Figure 8.11. Landscape Diagrams and Asset Inventories

Landscape Diagrams and Asset Inventories are standard EA artifacts from the toolkit of enterprise architects indispensable for gaining an in-depth understanding of the IT landscape and sharing this knowledge across the organization.

System Portfolio Models and Landscape Maps

Two other subtypes of Landscapes addressing specifically the relationship between business and IT are System Portfolio Models and Landscape Maps. **System Portfolio Models** (also known as application portfolios, applications-to-capabilities mappings, capability models with system overlays and many other names) are specific Landscapes providing structured high-level mappings of core information systems to relevant business capabilities. System Portfolio Models present very abstract, condensed one-page views of the entire business and IT landscape, distinguishing only the most important systems. In their structure, they mirror Business Capability Models (see Figure 8.9) and show which systems support each of the capabilities. System Portfolio Models also color-code information systems based on their status in the landscape (e.g. strategic, current, obsolescent and legacy) to outline their future prospects. System Portfolio Models are always general EA artifacts that encompass the whole organization. Functionally, they serve enterprise architects for documenting the existing situation and, to a lesser extent, for capturing architectural solutions. In the first function, System Portfolio Models document the highest-level composition of the current IT landscape and offer a valuable source of contextual knowledge on the internal environment. In the second function, they capture mostly technical, system-centric elements of high-level architectural solutions. All lower-level solutions developed in the organization should take into account their suggestions regarding the reuse and reliance on certain information systems.

Landscape Maps (also known as landscape models, application landscapes and some other names) are specific Landscapes providing structured high-level mappings of key IT systems to relevant functional and organizational areas. On a single page, they explain how various information systems deployed in the organization relate to its different lines of business, divisions, geographies, functions, operations or activities. Like System Portfolio Models, Landscape Maps offer top-level summary views of the overall business and IT landscape and color-code information systems to indicate their condition, adequacy or status, though with a particular emphasis on centralization and decentralization issues. In the same manner, Landscape Maps, being general EA artifacts, combine both the functions of documenting the existing situation and capturing architectural solutions, i.e. store knowledge on the current landscape structure and also reflect high-level architectural decisions on systems reuse and consolidation, providing certain guidance to lower-level architectural solutions. The schematic graphical representations of System Portfolio Models and Landscape Maps are shown in Figure 8.12.

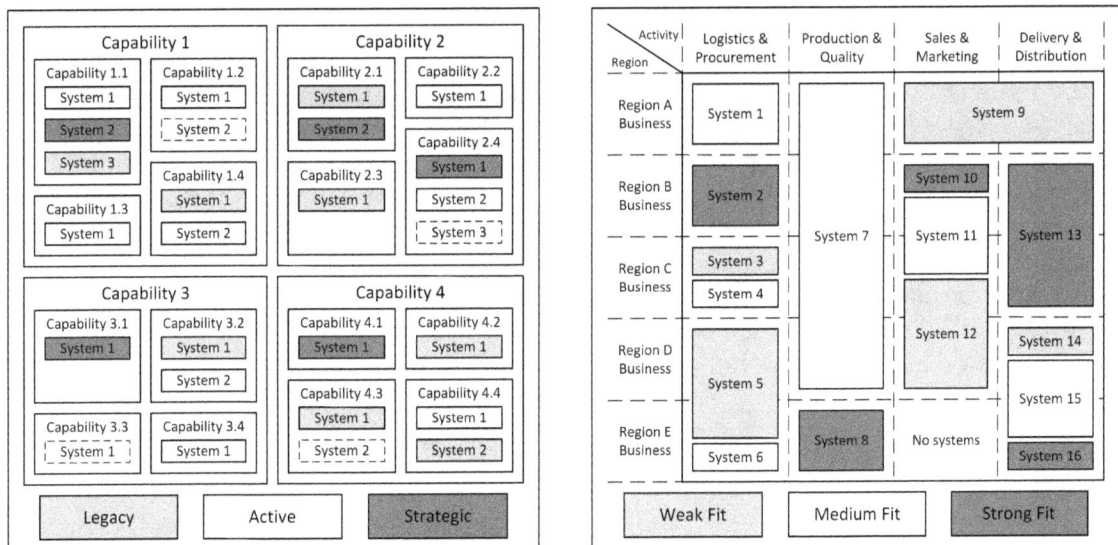

Figure 8.12. System Portfolio Models and Landscape Maps

System Portfolio Models and Landscape Maps are very useful EA artifacts as they allow enterprise architects to depict the entire business and IT landscape holistically on just one page and record far-reaching architectural decisions about its further development.

IT Roadmaps and Asset Roadmaps

Two less typical subtypes of Landscapes that look more into the future of the corporate IT landscape are IT Roadmaps and Asset Roadmaps. **IT Roadmaps** (also known as platform roadmaps, infrastructure roadmaps and some other names) are specific Landscapes providing structured graphical views of IT initiatives of a purely technical nature having no visible business impact. Analogously to business-focused Roadmaps (see Figure 8.8), they show scheduled change initiatives, usually projects, with their approximate implementation timelines. IT Roadmaps often also color-code these initiatives to indicate their status, criticality or funding needs, structure them into different tracks corresponding to their subdomains of technology and possibly provide some additional contextual information. IT Roadmaps can be general or initiative-specific EA artifacts. In the former case, they relate to different areas of the organizational IT infrastructure and coevolve with them. In the latter case, they are produced to support particular digitalization initiatives, like programs and strategies, from an infrastructural perspective. Accordingly, IT Roadmaps are used by enterprise architects for capturing primarily technical components of mid-level architectural solutions. As they itemize concrete pieces of work to be implemented, IT Roadmaps explicitly specify the existing intentions based on which lower-level derivative initiatives are launched. For documentation purposes, they may not carry any systematic knowledge about the current landscape.

Asset Roadmaps (also known as asset plans, system roadmaps and some other names) are specific Landscapes providing structured graphical views of the lifecycles of IT assets with their milestones. Asset Roadmaps explain exactly what is supposed to happen in the future with each IT asset existing in the organization in terms of its projected lifecycle phases, e.g. when it is going to be developed, maintained, upgraded and retired. They are usually organized around different business areas or asset classes, e.g. systems, databases and infrastructure equipment. In many respects, Asset Roadmaps highly resemble Technology Roadmaps (see Figure 8.5), but deal with physical instances of IT assets instead of abstract technologies. Asset Roadmaps are general EA artifacts that keep track of organizational IT assets and trace their prospects. Although they are also helpful to enterprise architects for the purposes of documenting the current composition of the IT landscape, their main function is capturing mid-level architectural decisions on the technical side, particularly concerning the utilization of available assets. All lower-level architectural solutions in the organization should respect their suggestions on the lifecycles of IT assets. The schematic graphical representations of IT Roadmaps (general ones) and Asset Roadmaps are shown in Figure 8.13.

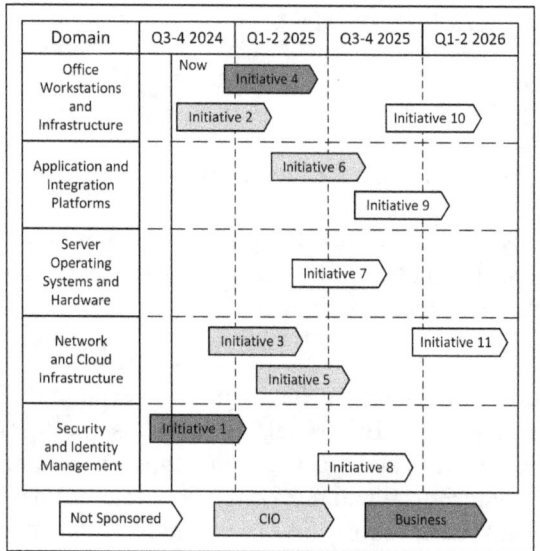
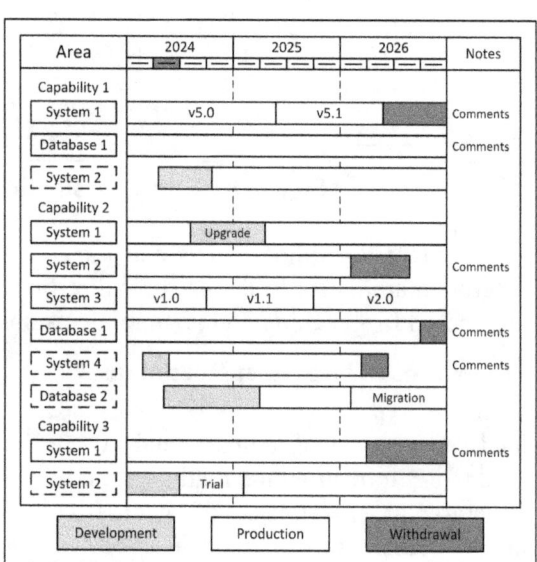

Figure 8.13. IT Roadmaps and Asset Roadmaps

IT Roadmaps and Asset Roadmaps are the most prominent EA artifacts focusing intentionally on the future of the IT landscape from its technical side that help enterprise architects control its evolution.

Other Landscapes

In addition to the six major EA artifacts presented above, some other, rather exotic Landscapes can also be found helpful in practice. Other Landscapes that can be employed by enterprise architects include, for example, the following artifacts:

- **Extended inventories** — catalogs of the clusters of interrelated IT assets fulfilling specific functions with their comprehensive textual and diagrammatic descriptions, resembling a blend of Asset Inventories and Landscape Diagrams

- **Data portfolio models** — structured high-level mappings of all essential data entities to relevant business capabilities, i.e. data-centric equivalents of System Portfolio Models
- **Infrastructure portfolio models** — structured high-level mappings of all core infrastructure components to relevant business capabilities, i.e. infrastructure-centric equivalents of System Portfolio Models
- **Information inventories** — structured catalogs of logical pieces of information possessed in any form, including structured databases, unstructured documents, file storages and even paper archives, with their properties and features
- **IT target states** — IT-oriented analogs of business-focused Target States (see Figure 8.8) defining the desired long-term future state for purely technical landscape layers, such as integration, infrastructure and security
- **IT capability models** — IT-oriented counterparts of Business Capability Models (see Figure 8.9) providing structured graphical representations of all organizational IT capabilities, their relationship and hierarchy

These and similar EA artifacts can help architects comprehend the complexity of the existing IT landscape, develop technical components of mid-level architectural solutions for transformation initiatives and manage landscape development.

Outlines

The general type of Outlines unites all business-focused solutions EA artifacts, which represent succinct outlines of specific IT solutions explaining their business meaning. Outlines are used by enterprise architects solely for capturing low-level architectural solutions, mostly their organizational components, for small digitalization initiatives. Popular artifacts related to this general type include Solution Overviews, Solution Briefs and Solution Options.

Solution Overviews

The most notable subtype of Outlines is Solution Overviews, which describe the substance of individual IT solutions from a business point of view. **Solution Overviews** (also known as solution architectures, conceptual architectures, solution outlines and many other names) are specific Outlines providing high-level descriptions of IT solutions with their logical components highlighting their business aspects. Solution Overviews typically explain what information systems constitute IT solutions, who their intended users are, how these systems relate to business processes, where the necessary data comes from and other questions relevant to the business audience. In other words, they describe both the conceptual technical structure of IT solutions and their integration into business activities and information flows within the organization. Besides describing IT solutions themselves, Solution Overviews usually contain various supplementary information about the solutions, e.g. business goals, solution scope, basic requirements, expected benefits, associated risks, substantiated estimates of time, cost and effort. Also, they can explain exactly how IT solutions align with higher-level architectural decisions reflected in other EA artifacts, like Principles (see Figure 8.1), Target States and Roadmaps (see Figure 8.8).

Solution Overviews are always initiative-specific EA artifacts created for particular digitalization initiatives and not existing outside of their context. Functionally, they are used by enterprise architects for capturing organizational and abstract technical components of low-level architectural solutions, normally for projects. Fairly detailed planning decisions recorded in Solution Overviews, in turn, shape even lower-level architectural solutions for the same initiatives. As they get archived after the completion of initiatives, for the purposes of documenting the existing situation, Solution Overviews can provide only the original descriptions of IT solutions at the time of their implementation. The schematic graphical representations of Solution Overviews (two different variations) are shown in Figure 8.14.

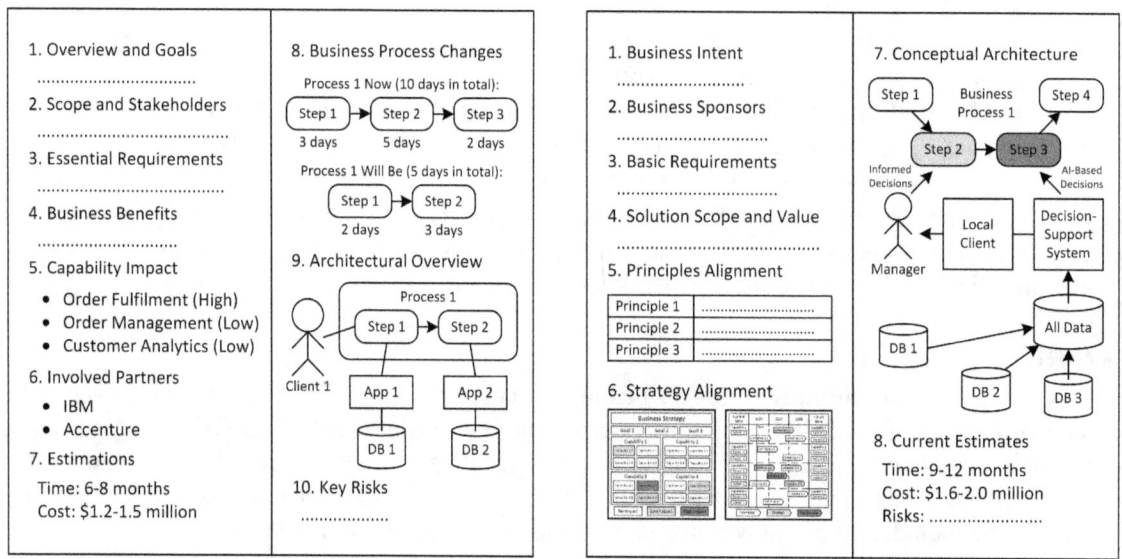

Figure 8.14. Solution Overviews (two different variations of overviews)

Solution Overviews are very important EA artifacts that allow enterprise architects to capture both technical and organizational components of architectural solutions during the architectural planning of transformation projects.

Solution Briefs and Solution Options

Somewhat less widely applicable subtypes of Outlines are Solution Briefs and Solution Options, which present very conceptual business descriptions of separate IT solutions and available options for their implementation. **Solution Briefs** (also known as concept briefs, solution proposals, investment cases and many other names) are specific Outlines providing very high-level sketches of IT solutions emphasizing their business contribution to the organization. Solution Briefs describe the general idea of IT solutions, their potential business impact and value, as well as their likely conceptual structure. Typically, they also contain rough guesswork-based time and cost estimations and other contextual information about the solutions. Basically, Solution Briefs can be viewed as more abstract, higher-level Solution Overviews. Solution Briefs are always initiative-specific EA artifacts developed for individual digitalization initiatives. They are used by enterprise architects for capturing rather low-level architectural solutions, typically for projects, mainly from the organizational side. Planning decisions recorded in Solution Briefs, in turn, influence lower-level architectural solutions for the same initiatives. As for documenting the existing situation, they can offer only archival descriptions of implemented IT solutions.

A quite different approach to describing IT solutions is embodied by Solution Options. **Solution Options** (also known as options papers, solution assessments and some other names) are specific Outlines providing lists of possible high-level implementation options for IT solutions with their pros and cons. Solution Options describe at a high level multiple different IT solutions capable of addressing the specified business need, i.e. alternative ways of solving the same business problem with IT. For each available option, they also explain the advantages, disadvantages, costs and risks of the respective IT solution, possibly using some formal scoring schemes to facilitate the comparison of options. Solution Options are always initiative-specific EA artifacts produced for particular digitalization initiatives. They are used by enterprise architects for capturing organizational and basic technical components of low-level architectural solutions, normally for projects. Alternative possibilities reflected in Solution Options then influence lower-level architectural solutions for the same initiatives. For documentation purposes, they contain almost no valuable information on the current landscape. The schematic graphical representations of Solution Briefs and Solution Options are shown in Figure 8.15.

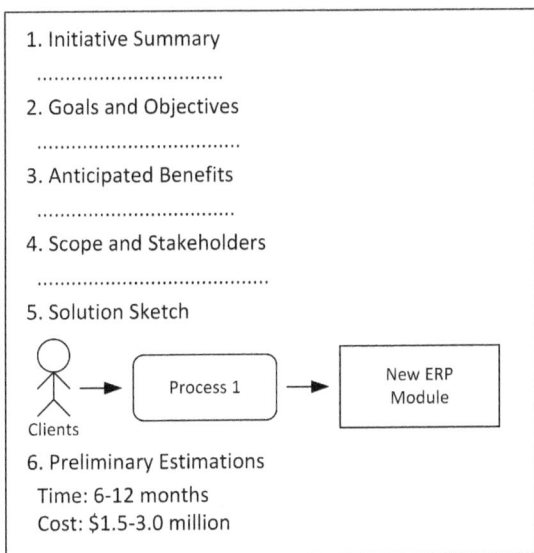
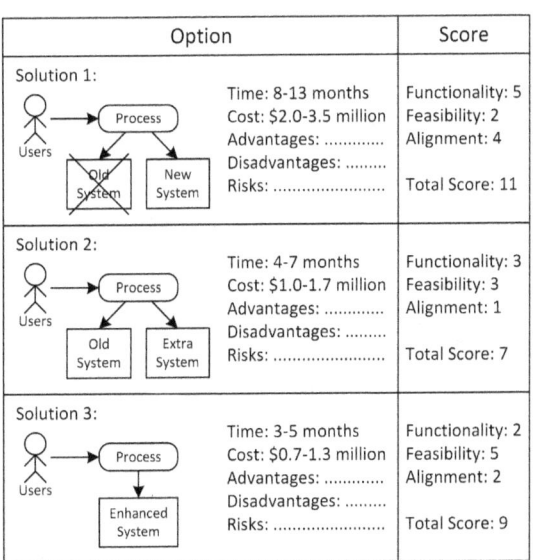

Figure 8.15. Solution Briefs and Solution Options

Solution Briefs and Solution Options are EA artifacts that are not always appropriate, but they help enterprise architects when it is necessary to capture preliminary and potential architectural solutions during the architectural planning of transformation projects.

Other Outlines
In addition to the three renowned EA artifacts described above, some other, less popular Outlines are also worthy of attention. Other Outlines that can be employed by enterprise architects include, for example, the following artifacts:

- **Architectural directions for Outlines** — formalized architectural requirements and decision premises applicable to specific IT solutions, e.g. pre-made technology choices and pre-selected implementation approaches
- **Solution diagrams** — simple, intuitively understandable, one-page graphical descriptions of IT solutions conveying their overall meaning to a wide audience in a single diagram
- **Analytical papers** — comparative analyses of suitable technologies or products for concrete IT solutions with their pros and cons, resembling technology-centric Solution Options and initiative-specific Analytical Reports (see Figure 8.3)
- **Process models** — separate detailed models of business processes associated with specific IT solutions and describing their anticipated impact on business tasks and operations

These and similar EA artifacts can help architects communicate with the sponsors of IT solutions, develop organizational and partly technical components of low-level architectural solutions for digitalization projects and move them towards completion.

Designs

The general type of Designs unites all IT-focused solutions EA artifacts, which describe detailed technical designs of specific information systems. Designs are used by enterprise architects exclusively for capturing low-level architectural solutions, mostly their technical components, for small digitalization initiatives. Popular artifacts related to this general type include Solution Designs and Preliminary Solution Designs.

Solution Designs and Preliminary Solution Designs

Two essential subtypes of Designs are Solution Designs and Preliminary Solution Designs, which contain detailed and high-level technical descriptions of separate IT solutions. **Solution Designs** (also known as detailed designs, physical designs, solution definitions and many other names) are specific Designs providing detailed technical and functional specifications of IT systems with their physical components. Solution Designs thoroughly cover all layers of the information systems stack, from business and software to hardware and security. They can describe, for example, what applications constitute IT solutions, what business tasks they automate, what data objects they process, how these applications interact with each other, where they are hosted and how they are protected from unauthorized access. They can also explain how IT systems conform to higher-level technical decisions reflected in Standards, like Technology Reference Models (see Figure 8.4), IT Principles and Guidelines (see Figure 8.6). Solution Designs are always initiative-specific EA artifacts created for individual digitalization initiatives. They are used by enterprise architects for capturing predominantly technical components of lowest-level architectural solutions for projects. Unlike other general types of EA artifacts that merely influence lower-level architectural solutions, planning decisions recorded in Solution Designs immediately guide the actual delivery efforts of project teams (see Figure 2.7). As for documenting the existing situation, archived Solution Designs offer accurate technical descriptions of IT systems at the time of their construction that can be valuable for future reference.

Very similar but much less prevalent EA artifacts are Preliminary Solution Designs. **Preliminary Solution Designs** (also known as preliminary solution architectures, logical designs and some other names) are specific Designs providing high-level technical and functional descriptions of IT systems with their physical components. Like regular Solution Designs, they cover all standard layers of the IT stack and explain exactly how information systems are structured technically, though at a higher abstraction level. Basically, Preliminary Solution Designs can be viewed as less elaborate and detailed Solution Designs. They are also initiative-specific EA artifacts used by enterprise architects for capturing primarily technical components of very low-level architectural solutions for projects. Planning decisions reflected in Preliminary Solution Designs eventually guide project delivery efforts. For documentation purposes, they provide archival descriptions of deployed IT systems that can be helpful. The schematic graphical representations of Solution Designs and Preliminary Solution Designs are shown in Figure 8.16.

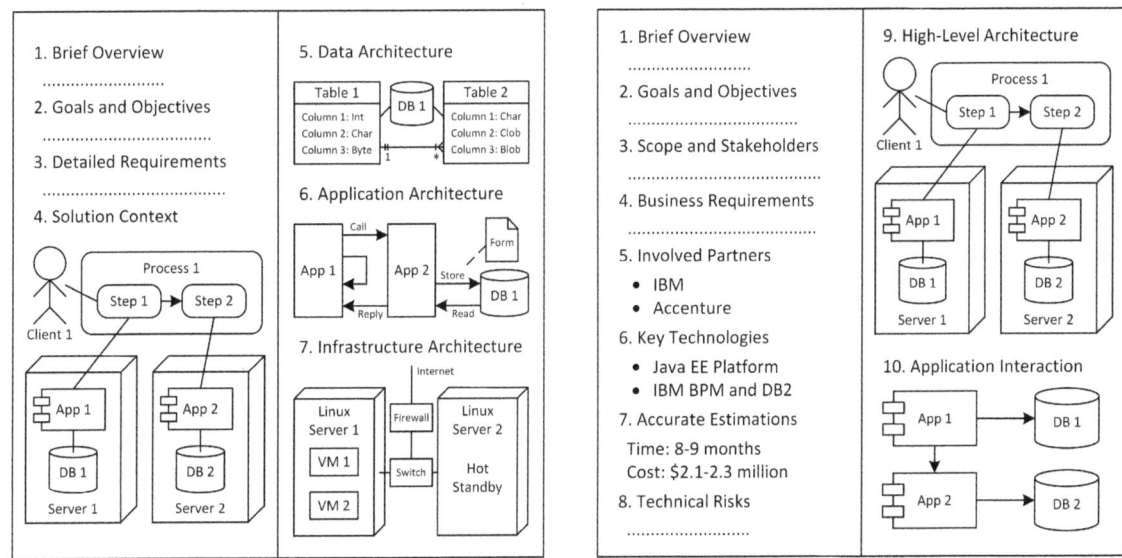

Figure 8.16. Solution Designs and Preliminary Solution Designs

Solution Designs and Preliminary Solution Designs are the necessary instruments of enterprise architects that allow them to control the delivery-level activities of project teams constructing new information systems.

Other Designs

In addition to the two typical EA artifacts discussed above, some other, more rarely used Designs are also worth mentioning. Other Designs that can be employed by enterprise architects include, for example, the following artifacts:

- **Architectural directions for Designs** — formalized architectural requirements and decision premises applicable to specific IT systems, e.g. prescribed infrastructure deployment patterns and mandatory table structures for databases

- **Mini-designs** — simplified, shortened or ad hoc technical designs for projects that do not require full-fledged Designs, e.g. minor, architecturally insignificant projects or projects delivered with agile methodologies (see Figure 2.8)
- **Business requirements documents** — separate documents with detailed functional, non-functional and architectural requirements for IT systems, serving largely as formal contracts between organizations and their delivery partners
- **Release designs** — bundled technical designs of multiple projects delivered during the same release cycle by the same partner and modifying the same part of the landscape, also formalizing the relationships with external delivery partners
- **Supplementary materials** — technology-specific ancillary materials for certain types of projects complementary to their general-purpose Designs, e.g. ERP configuration documents or XML-based settings files for middleware

These and similar EA artifacts can help architects communicate with project teams as key initiative executors, develop technical components of very low-level architectural solutions for transformation projects and support their execution.

Summary of Popular Enterprise Architecture Artifacts

As it is evident from the overview of popular EA artifacts provided above, these artifacts are very diverse and address a broad spectrum of needs related to architectural planning. In fact, the toolkit of enterprise architects includes rich paraphernalia of EA artifacts that can be used in different situations and circumstances. These artifacts can be summarized by mapping them to organizational domains and putting them all together on a single page.

Mapping of Enterprise Architecture Artifacts to Organizational Domains

Because each EA artifact has a definite logical structure, representation format and informational contents, all artifacts can be associated with one or more of the six organizational domains that they tend to describe (see Figure 3.4). Some EA artifacts are strongly associated with particular domains, whereas others can have a rather weak domain affiliation.

In case of a strong association, EA artifacts belong to certain domains essentially by their definition. Most notably, the very idea of such artifacts as Conceptual Data Models and Logical Data Models automatically confines them specifically to the domain of data. Following the same logic, Business Capability Models, Process Maps and Value Chains are tightly bound to the business domain. Basically, these EA artifacts are domain-specific, "native" to their own domains and their sensible analogs for other domains are difficult to imagine. Or, as a more sophisticated example, the very concept of mapping IT systems to business activities embodied in System Portfolio Models and Landscape Maps firmly links these artifacts to the domains of business and applications.

By contrast, in case of a weak association, EA artifacts can cover various organizational domains without being specific to them. In other words, these artifacts are potentially applicable to multiple domains exactly in the same way. And yet, from a practical point of view, they can be suitable for describing some domains more than others, resulting in a loose domain affiliation. For example, such EA artifacts as Principles, IT Principles, Guidelines and Landscape Diagrams are largely universal, domain-neutral and can theoretically address almost any of the six domains or their combinations. However, in practice, IT Principles and Guidelines seldom touch the domain of business, while Principles, on the contrary, more often focus on functional domains (see Table 3.2). The resulting mapping of popular EA artifacts to the six organizational domains with an indication of the strength of their association is depicted in Figure 8.17.

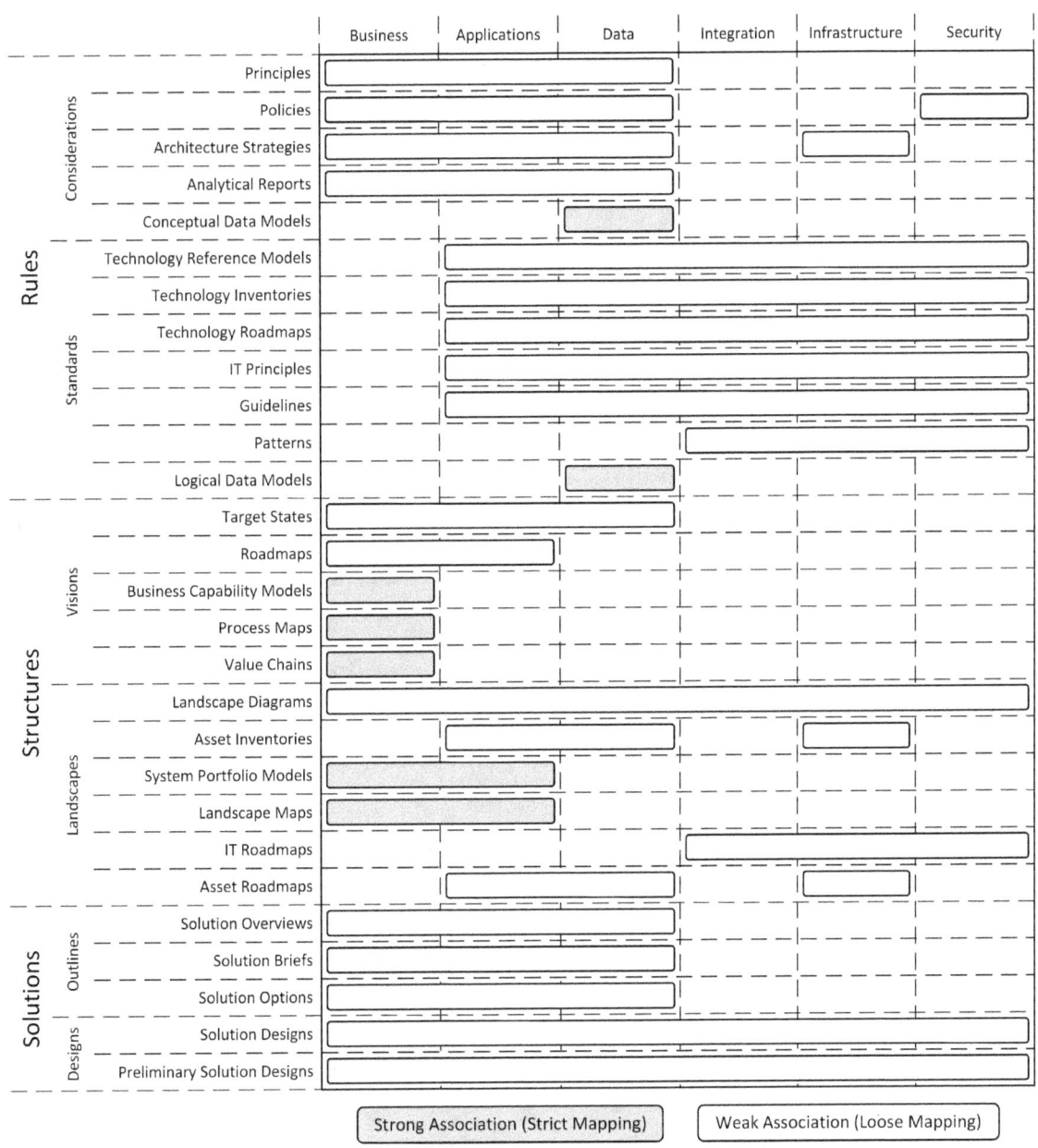

Figure 8.17. Mapping of EA artifacts to the six organizational domains

The domain mapping of EA artifacts provided in Figure 8.17 clarifies exactly which facets of organizations and transformation initiatives are usually described in various artifacts from the arsenal of enterprise architects. For better visibility, these artifacts can also be summarized graphically on one page.

Enterprise Architecture on a Page

In the overview of EA artifacts presented in this chapter, each artifact is accompanied by a schematic graphical representation demonstrating what it typically looks like (see Figure 8.1 to Figure 8.16). All these artifacts with their pictorial icons can be organized around the overarching CSVLOD taxonomy (see Figure 7.11), put on a single page and color-coded according to their relative popularity to construct a comprehensive reference model of instruments available to enterprise architects. The resulting graphical view of the catalog of EA artifacts can be called simply **Enterprise Architecture on a Page**[5]. The full version of Enterprise Architecture on a Page is freely available to download at https://eaonapage.com. A simplified schematic view of Enterprise Architecture on a Page is shown in Figure 8.18.

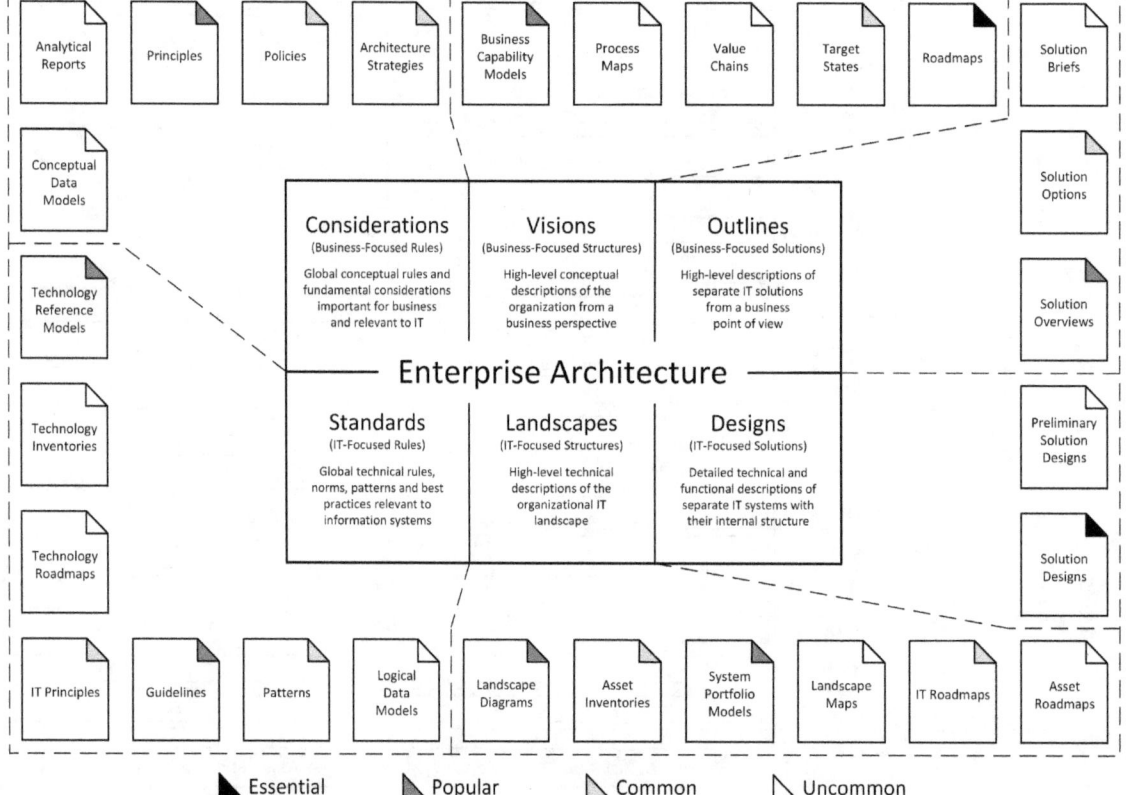

Figure 8.18. Enterprise Architecture on a Page (schematic view only)

Enterprise Architecture on a Page offers an intuitive visual overview of EA artifacts that proved useful in the industry. It can be used as a convenient sense-making device or a tool for thinking about enterprise architecture. It can be freely distributed and used as a common reference point for EA-related discussions. It can be printed, used as a poster and pinned on the wall. It can be helpful to various people dealing with enterprise architecture including aspiring and practicing architects in organizations as well as EA lecturers and students in universities. Enterprise Architecture on a Page can be downloaded at https://eaonapage.com.

Chapter Summary

This chapter explained the relationship between the general types of EA artifacts and their narrow subtypes, described in detail the most widely used subtypes of EA artifacts related to each general type, presented their mapping to the six organizational domains and introduced Enterprise Architecture on a Page as their intuitive graphical catalog. The core message of this chapter can be summarized in the following major points:

- Each of the six general types of EA artifacts from the CSVLOD taxonomy embraces numerous artifacts with similar properties, but some of these artifacts are more popular than others and can be grouped into consistent subtypes
- Considerations cover all business-focused rules EA artifacts the most popular subtypes of which include Principles, Policies, Architecture Strategies, Analytical Reports and Conceptual Data Models
- Standards cover all IT-focused rules EA artifacts the most popular subtypes of which include Technology Reference Models, Technology Inventories, Technology Roadmaps, IT Principles, Guidelines, Patterns and Logical Data Models
- Visions cover all business-focused structures EA artifacts the most popular subtypes of which include Target States, Roadmaps, Business Capability Models, Process Maps and Value Chains
- Landscapes cover all IT-focused structures EA artifacts the most popular subtypes of which include Landscape Diagrams, Asset Inventories, System Portfolio Models, Landscape Maps, IT Roadmaps and Asset Roadmaps
- Outlines cover all business-focused solutions EA artifacts the most popular subtypes of which include Solution Overviews, Solution Briefs and Solution Options
- Designs cover all IT-focused solutions EA artifacts the most popular subtypes of which include Solution Designs and Preliminary Solution Designs
- Some EA artifacts are strongly associated with specific organizational domains by their logical structure, whereas other artifacts can have only a weak domain affiliation manifested solely in their typical practical use
- Enterprise Architecture on a Page offers a convenient one-page visual catalog of the most popular EA artifacts with their key properties that can be freely downloaded at https://eaonapage.com and publicly distributed

Chapter 9: Using Enterprise Architecture Artifacts

The two previous chapters discussed the general types and narrow subtypes of EA artifacts respectively. This chapter concludes the discussion of EA artifacts and describes their practical use by enterprise architects for different purposes. In particular, this chapter begins with explaining the specifics of using EA artifacts for documenting the existing situation and the selection of suitable artifacts for this purpose. Then, this chapter explains the complex specifics of using EA artifacts for capturing architectural solutions, discusses the selection of suitable artifacts for this purpose and provides some illustrative examples of their usage scenarios. Finally, this chapter introduces the concept of architectural context formed by EA artifacts and explains its relationship to digital transformation initiatives of different types.

The Use of Enterprise Architecture Artifacts by Enterprise Architects

EA artifacts are very diverse in terms of their temporal orientation, initiative affiliation, described objects and presented viewpoints and can be organized into six general types according to the CSVLOD taxonomy (see Figure 7.11). Toolkits of enterprise architects include a wide variety of specific artifacts representing different general types that can be concisely summarized as Enterprise Architecture on a Page (see Figure 8.18). Each EA artifact has its own unique usage scenarios in the work of architects enabled by its informational contents and other properties.

However, from the standpoint of their practical use by enterprise architects, the main borderline lies specifically between actualities and plans EA artifacts as it is this dichotomy that largely determines their functional applicability (see Figure 7.7). Actualities artifacts are employed by architects primarily for documenting the existing situation in the organization (see Figure 7.2), while plans artifacts — for capturing architectural solutions for digitalization initiatives (see Figure 7.4). Importantly, because EA artifacts can combine in different proportions the elements of both actualities and plans, the correspondence between these types and fulfilled functions is not perfect, i.e. many actualities artifacts also record planning decisions and many plans artifacts also record objective facts.

Using EA artifacts by enterprise architects for either function implies both actively modifying and passively studying them. On the one hand, architects modify artifacts to write down some valuable information in them. Modifying EA artifacts can mean either creating new artifacts from scratch or updating existing artifacts with new information. On the other hand, architects also study available artifacts to consume the information contained in them. Working with EA artifacts for documenting the existing situation and capturing architectural solutions has substantial differences.

Using EA Artifacts for Documenting the Existing Situation

For documenting the existing situation in the organization, enterprise architects employ mostly actualities EA artifacts that focus exclusively on the current state and also some plans EA artifacts that reflect the current landscape only peripherally, partly or conditionally. The practical use of these artifacts has certain specifics and requires choosing the right instruments based on their fitness for purpose.

Specifics of Using EA Artifacts for Documenting the Existing Situation

As business and IT landscapes of large organizations are very complicated, extensive and stratified, they require multiple descriptive representations. At the same time, EA artifacts themselves are very diverse and can concentrate on different scopes and layers of the landscape. For these reasons, in practice, corporate landscapes cannot be described fully in all their details and aspects, but only the most important viewpoints on their structure can be presented in various artifacts.

As discussed earlier, for the purposes of documenting the existing situation, EA artifacts can be modified by enterprise architects virtually anytime, whenever some information on the current landscape needs to be documented (see Figure 7.2). In this scenario, the documentation process is pretty straightforward and routine. It starts from new facts about the landscape being uncovered by architects or communicated to them by other actors. Then, architects create new or update existing EA artifacts to record these facts, converting them into a material form. To ensure the high quality of the resulting artifacts, they can opt to demonstrate these artifacts to knowledgeable people for their validation and approval or to other architects to make sure that the respective descriptions are readable and intelligible. After EA artifacts documenting the existing situation are produced, they can be freely looked up and studied by any actors, often by their own creators, to gain knowledge of the landscape structure[1].

Choosing Suitable EA Artifacts for Documenting the Existing Situation

Among the multitude of EA artifacts available to enterprise architects, the primary candidates for documenting the existing situation in the organization are actualities artifacts perfectly suitable for this purpose by virtue of their focus on the current state. However, some categories of plans EA artifacts, despite their future orientation, can also partially serve this purpose with certain nuances, limitations and caveats.

First, plans EA artifacts with systematized factual information on the current landscape, such as Technology Roadmaps and Asset Roadmaps, explicitly document the existing situation, though it is not their main function, and can thus be used by architects in the same way as regular actualities. Second, plans artifacts with high-level structured views of the organization, like Process Maps and Value Chains, also depict basically the existing situation, though these depictions are very abstract and lack concrete tangible instances. Third, plans artifacts with intended data definitions — Conceptual Data Models and Logical Data Models — tend to strongly overlap with the existing situation, though their ideal structures seldom match the actual ones in every detail. And lastly, plans artifacts with the descriptions of separate IT solutions, most notably Solution Overviews and Solution Designs, turn into granular snapshots of the existing situation at the moment when these solutions are deployed, but, as archived artifacts, they gradually lose their descriptive accuracy as the corporate landscape evolves over time. All these categories of EA artifacts are relevant to documenting the existing situation in the organization, albeit with important nuances, unlike genuine actualities.

As discussed earlier, the variety of all possible landscape descriptions can be seen as a continuous two-dimensional space of descriptive representations, where all their variations can be placed based on their relevance to different landscape scopes and layers (see Figure 7.1). At the same time, all EA artifacts can be classified into solutions, structures and rules, and this classification highly correlates with the scope of their coverage (see Figure 7.9). All artifacts can also be roughly separated into IT-focused and business-focused ones, which largely determines their fitness for describing various business and IT elements of the landscape (see Figure 7.10). This linkage of EA artifacts and landscape segments allows mapping specific artifacts discussed previously to the space of descriptive representations, so that their approximate positions on this "map" indicate their appropriateness for documenting different scopes and layers of the corporate landscape. The resulting mapping of popular EA artifacts to the space of descriptive representations with their temporal orientation, the most typical information contained in them and associated caveats is depicted in Figure 9.1 (their complementary mapping to the six organizational domains is shown in Figure 8.17).

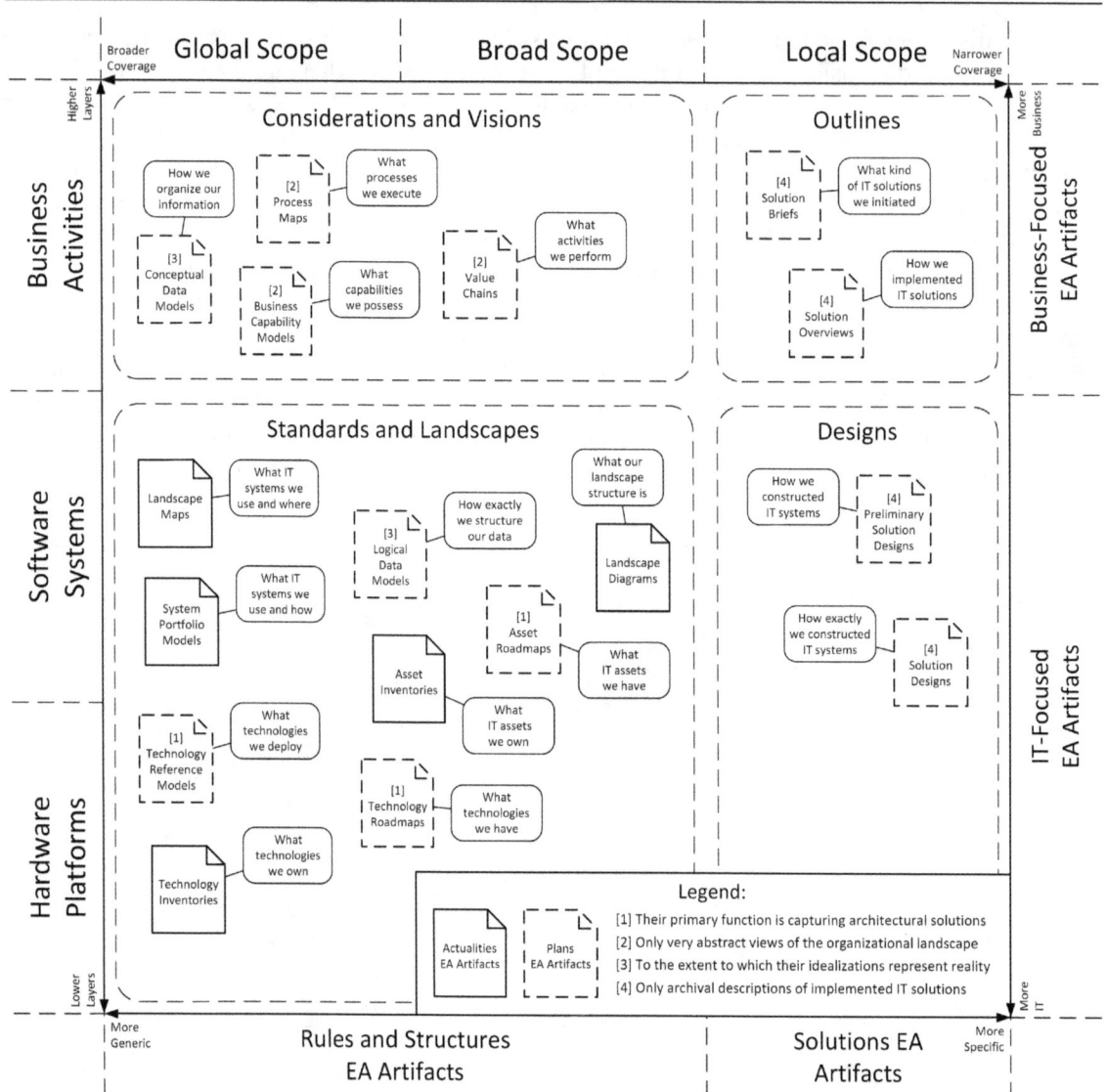

Figure 9.1. Mapping of EA artifacts to the space of descriptive representations

The map of EA artifacts presented in Figure 9.1 helps choose the most suitable instruments for documenting the existing situation based on target landscape segments. Importantly, in this function, actualities artifacts can be both studied and updated by enterprise architects at any time, whereas most plans artifacts can only be passively studied as they are intended for a different purpose and reflect the current situation only inadvertently.

Interestingly, the mapping of EA artifacts to the space of descriptive representations also demonstrates that organizational landscapes are *not* covered by artifacts evenly. Instead, the mapping reveals notable differences in coverage of different landscape zones by different types of artifacts. These differences can be reduced to two general observations about documenting the existing situation. First, enterprise architects do not maintain any detailed local-scope descriptions of the current landscape, but refer to archived solutions EA artifacts when such descriptions are needed. As it requires significant efforts on the part of architects, their maintenance is typically considered too burdensome and impractical.

Second, enterprise architects usually also do not maintain any precise business-centric descriptions of the current state, like task-level process models. Because operational processes are owned by business managers, their changes are not controlled by architects and can hardly be accurately mirrored in EA artifacts in the long run. For this reason, in search of current-state business knowledge, architects either resort to very abstract views provided mostly by Visions, or go directly to business representatives for pertinent information and possibly some up-to-date business documentation. Therefore, true actualities EA artifacts maintained by architects, in fact, cover mainly large scopes of the corporate landscape at a high level from the IT side, while other information should be sought elsewhere and is available only with limitations.

Using EA Artifacts for Capturing Architectural Solutions

For capturing architectural solutions for digitalization initiatives, enterprise architects employ predominantly plans EA artifacts that concentrate specifically on the future and also some actualities EA artifacts that reflect proposed future changes to the current landscape. As discussed earlier, architectural solutions represent comprehensive sets of planning decisions relevant to initiatives and architectural plans nail down these decisions in a material form (see Figure 3.1). Accordingly, all EA artifacts that capture architectural solutions for change initiatives constitute their architectural plans. The practical use of these artifacts has certain specifics and requires selecting the appropriate instruments based on their fitness for purpose.

Specifics of Using EA Artifacts for Capturing Architectural Solutions

As digitalization initiatives are multifaceted undertakings that have to cope with disparate technical and organizational challenges, they require complex, multi-aspect architectural solutions. At the same time, EA artifacts are themselves very diverse and can focus on different elements of architectural solutions, technical or organizational. For these reasons, most architectural solutions cannot be reflected adequately in their entirety in single artifacts, but only in multiple artifacts presenting them from different viewpoints and highlighting their various technical and organizational aspects. Digital transformation initiatives are usually too complex and imply too many heterogeneous decisions to be described all in one document in a meaningful manner. Simply put, any non-trivial architectural solution ordinarily requires more than one EA artifact to fully capture all its technical and organizational elements.

For instance, even architectural solutions for moderate projects tend to materialize in at least two EA artifacts: Solution Designs covering mostly their technical components and Solution Overviews accentuating their organizational components. On the opposite end of the spectrum, large transformation strategies may require, for example, Architecture Strategies to describe their overall intent, Target States to depict what the desired outcome looks like and Roadmaps to propose concrete steps towards this outcome, combined with the concomitant changes in Technology Reference Models, System Portfolio Models and Conceptual Data Models to reflect their technology, systems and information-related elements respectively. As a rule, technical solutions for digitalization initiatives are captured in IT-focused EA artifacts (Standards,

Landscapes and Designs), while organizational solutions — in business-focused ones (Considerations, Visions and Outlines) (see Figure 7.11).

As discussed earlier, for the purposes of capturing architectural solutions, EA artifacts can be modified by enterprise architects only as part of architectural planning taking place within the planning phase of digital transformation initiatives (see Figure 7.4). Generally, architectural solutions for change initiatives can be captured, with their own benefits and limitations, in both initiative-specific and general EA artifacts (see Figure 7.8). However, due to the fundamental differences in their lifecycles, these classes of artifacts are handled quite differently by architects during architectural planning efforts. Namely, initiative-specific EA artifacts are *created* specifically to capture the elements of architectural solutions, whereas general ones are merely *updated* to reflect their elements. The very process of architectural planning and the role of different artifacts in this process are discussed in great detail later in Chapter 11 (Leading the Development of Plans).

Then, in the course of the execution phase of initiatives, both initiative-specific and general EA artifacts are equally used, in one way or another, to guide their execution, i.e. launch derivative initiatives or fulfill project delivery. The logical relationship between architectural planning, architectural solutions, architectural plans and different types of EA artifacts is shown in Figure 9.2.

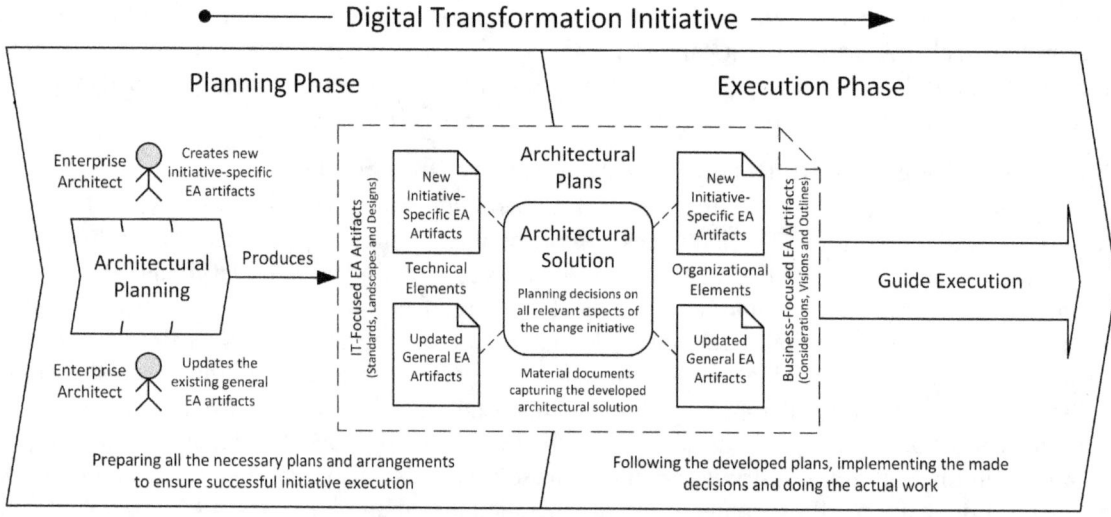

Figure 9.2. Architectural planning, solutions, plans and different types of EA artifacts

As demonstrated in Figure 9.2, technical and organizational elements of architectural solutions for digital transformation initiatives can be reflected in both initiative-specific and general EA artifacts. Whereas initiative-specific artifacts always capture architectural solutions for single initiatives, general ones can incorporate the elements of architectural solutions for many different, potentially unrelated initiatives at the same time.

Specifics of Using EA Artifacts for Hierarchical Transformation Initiatives

As discussed earlier, digital transformation initiatives in organizations form a nested hierarchy of strategies, programs and projects (see Figure 2.5). In this context, corresponding to the three types of digitalization initiatives, initiative-specific EA artifacts can be further subdivided into strategy-, program- and project-specific ones.

As hierarchical initiatives are implemented recursively, so that the execution of higher-level initiatives is manifested in the proper planning of lower-level ones, strategy-specific EA artifacts direct the planning of derivative programs and program-specific artifacts, in turn, drive the planning of subordinate projects. In other words, initiative-specific EA artifacts are created as part of the architectural planning of transformation initiatives at different levels to guide the execution of these initiatives by guiding the planning of their descendants or, in the case of project-specific artifacts, their physical delivery by project teams. Thereby, these artifacts convert architectural solutions for higher-level initiatives into architectural solutions for lower-level ones (see Figure 3.7) and, eventually, into the actual changes in the business and IT landscape.

However, planning decisions from higher-level initiatives can be translated into lower-level initiatives also through general EA artifacts. For example, the updates introduced into these artifacts as a result of the architectural planning of a transformation strategy or program can then influence planning at the project level. In this scenario, architectural solutions for higher-order initiatives get reflected in general artifacts to shape lower-level architectural solutions. The usage of initiative-specific and general EA artifacts in the implementation of hierarchical digital transformation initiatives is illustrated in Figure 9.3.

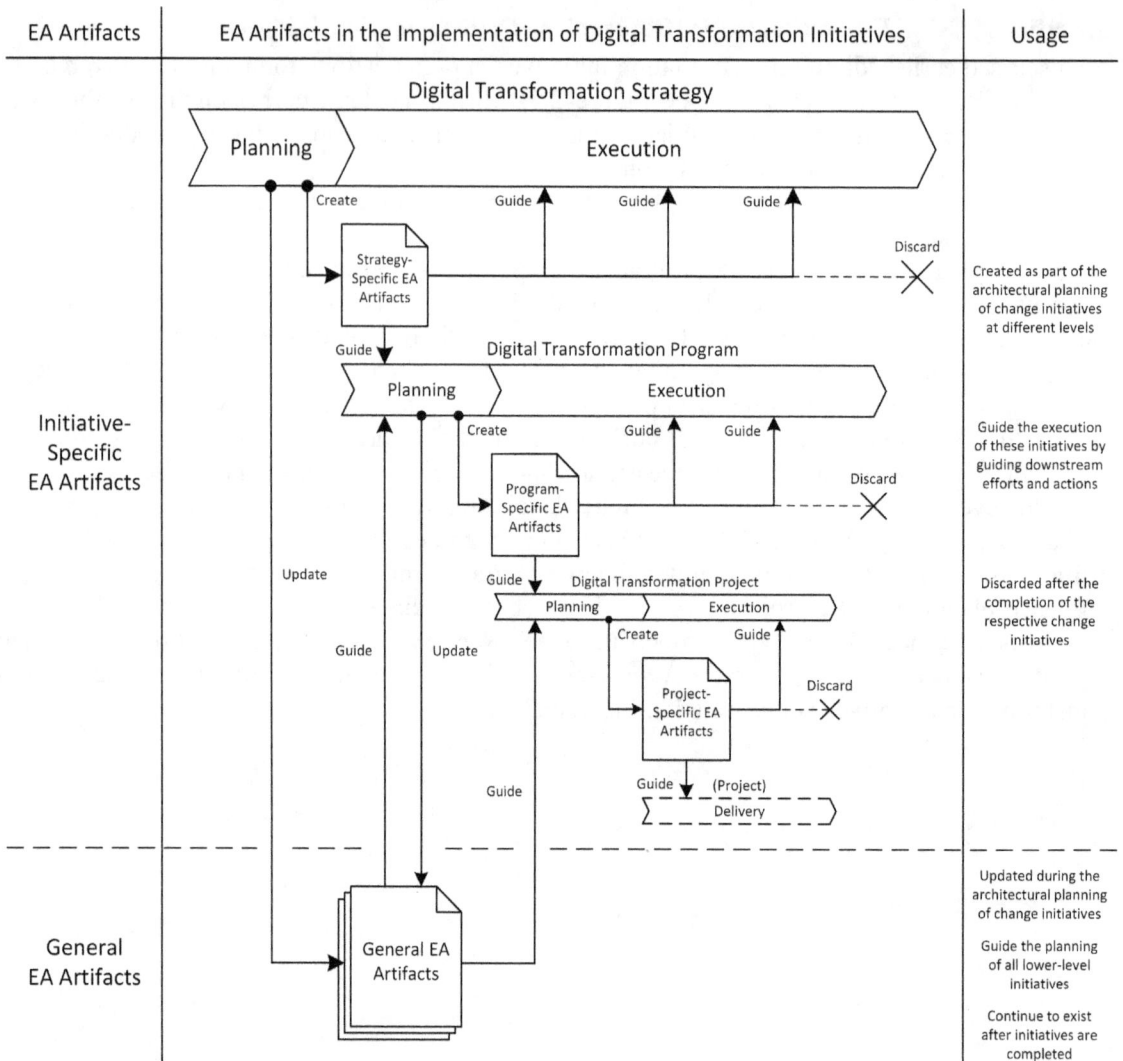

Figure 9.3. Initiative-specific and general EA artifacts in the hierarchy of initiatives

As shown in Figure 9.3, the implementation of hierarchical transformation initiatives implies creating multiple initiative-specific EA artifacts with varying lifespans at different levels of the initiative hierarchy as well as updating long-living general artifacts for capturing necessary architectural solutions and converting them into lower-level solutions for descending initiatives.

Mutual Influence of Architectural Solutions for Different Initiatives

As demonstrated in Figure 9.2 and Figure 9.3, architectural solutions for digital transformation initiatives resulting from their architectural planning can be equally captured in both initiative-specific and general EA artifacts. Importantly, because general artifacts do not belong to concrete initiatives and can be updated as part of any of them, they typically record numerous planning decisions incoming from multiple initiatives. In other words, general EA artifacts contain elements of many potentially unrelated architectural solutions developed for different transformation initiatives.

This common reliance of different digitalization initiatives on the same general EA artifacts for capturing their architectural solutions creates a certain *interdependence* between these initiatives, where decisions made within any one of the initiatives can potentially influence the others, even if they are logically separate and reside at the same level of the initiative hierarchy. Put it simply, the use of general plans artifacts results in mutual interference among all initiatives running in the organization.

For example, technologies included in Technology Reference Models and additional Principles formulated to guide the execution of one transformation strategy can also unintendedly affect the execution of another, entirely independent strategy. Or, changes in Logical Data Models and new Patterns introduced to shape derivative projects in one program can also impact the structure of projects from another "perpendicular" program. Being reflected in common EA artifacts, architectural solutions for different initiatives influence each other, though sometimes similar effects can be exerted even through initiative-specific artifacts. The mechanism of mutual influence and inter-initiative interference via general plans EA artifacts described above is shown schematically in Figure 9.4.

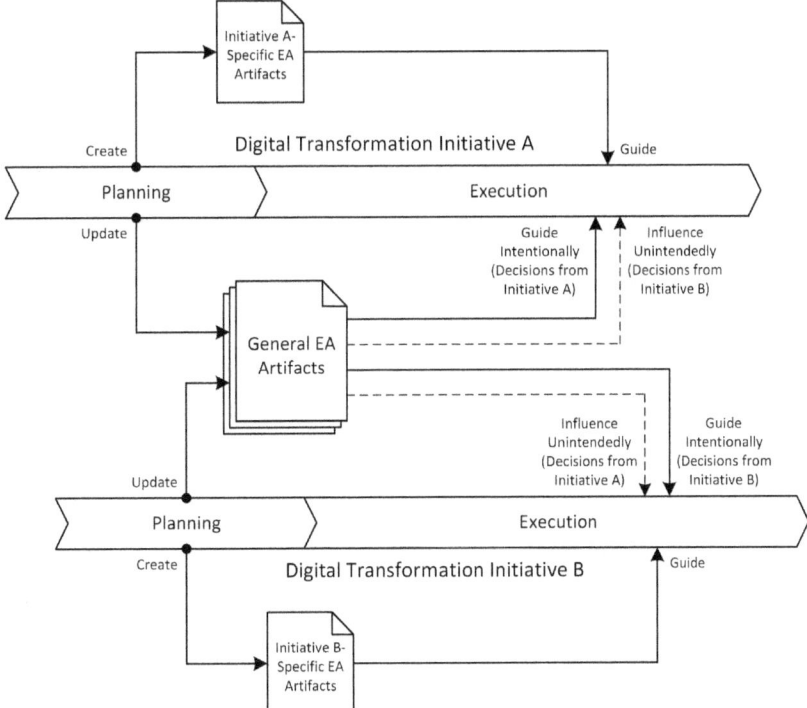

Figure 9.4. Mutual influence between initiatives via general plans EA artifacts

While initiative-specific EA artifacts are obviously needed to capture certain architectural decisions defining the meaning of the respective digitalization initiatives, general artifacts are necessary for maintaining overall organizational coherence, controlling landscape complexity and avoiding spatial, temporal and logical collisions between different initiatives. As all transformation initiatives in the organization coexist in the common "ecosystem", they share the same resources and are bound by the same constraints. In this situation, seeking synergy and ensuring cross-initiative consistency in terms of utilized technologies, adopted approaches, data structures and asset reuse prospects is crucial for the organization as a whole. A systematic reflection of the entire business and IT landscape is also necessary for coordinating the timing of change, so that different transformation initiatives do not intend to modify the same landscape areas at the same time. Besides that, many general EA artifacts actually serve for both capturing architectural solutions and documenting the existing situation and, consequently, must focus on the corporate landscape to be able to fulfill their function of preserving knowledge about the current environment.

Choosing Suitable EA Artifacts for Capturing Architectural Solutions

Among the array of EA artifacts from the collection of enterprise architects, the primary candidates for capturing architectural solutions for digitalization initiatives are plans artifacts perfectly suitable for this purpose by virtue of their orientation to the future. These artifacts, however, differ in their initiative affiliation and, thus, in their capacity for capturing elements of architectural solutions. For instance, some subtypes of plans EA artifacts are always initiative-specific and capable of capturing complete technical and organizational solutions for initiatives, e.g. Solution Designs and Solution Overviews. Other subtypes are always general and capture mostly separate planning decisions constituting architectural solutions, e.g. Technology Reference Models and Business Capability Models. Furthermore, certain plans EA artifacts can be either initiative-specific or general in their initiative affiliation, e.g. IT Roadmaps and Roadmaps. In addition to plans, most actualities EA artifacts, notwithstanding their concentration on the present, can also serve for capturing architectural solutions by recording individual planning decisions.

As discussed earlier, the variety of all possible architectural decisions can be represented as a continuous two-dimensional space of architectural solutions, where all their elements can be placed based on their relevance to different solution components and levels (see Figure 7.3). At the same time, all EA artifacts can be separated into solutions, structures and rules, and this separation highly correlates with their appropriateness for projects, programs and strategies (see Figure 7.9). All artifacts can also be roughly divided into IT-focused and business-focused ones, which corresponds to their suitability for capturing technical and organizational elements of architectural solutions respectively (see Figure 7.10). This linkage of EA artifacts and solution elements allows mapping specific artifacts described previously to the space of architectural solutions, so that their approximate positions on this "map" indicate their fitness for capturing technical and organizational solution components at different levels. The resulting mapping of popular EA artifacts to the space of architectural solutions with their temporal orientation, initiative affiliation and the most typical planning decisions reflected in them is depicted in Figure 9.5[2] (their complementary mapping to the six organizational domains is shown in Figure 8.17).

Chapter 9: Using Enterprise Architecture Artifacts

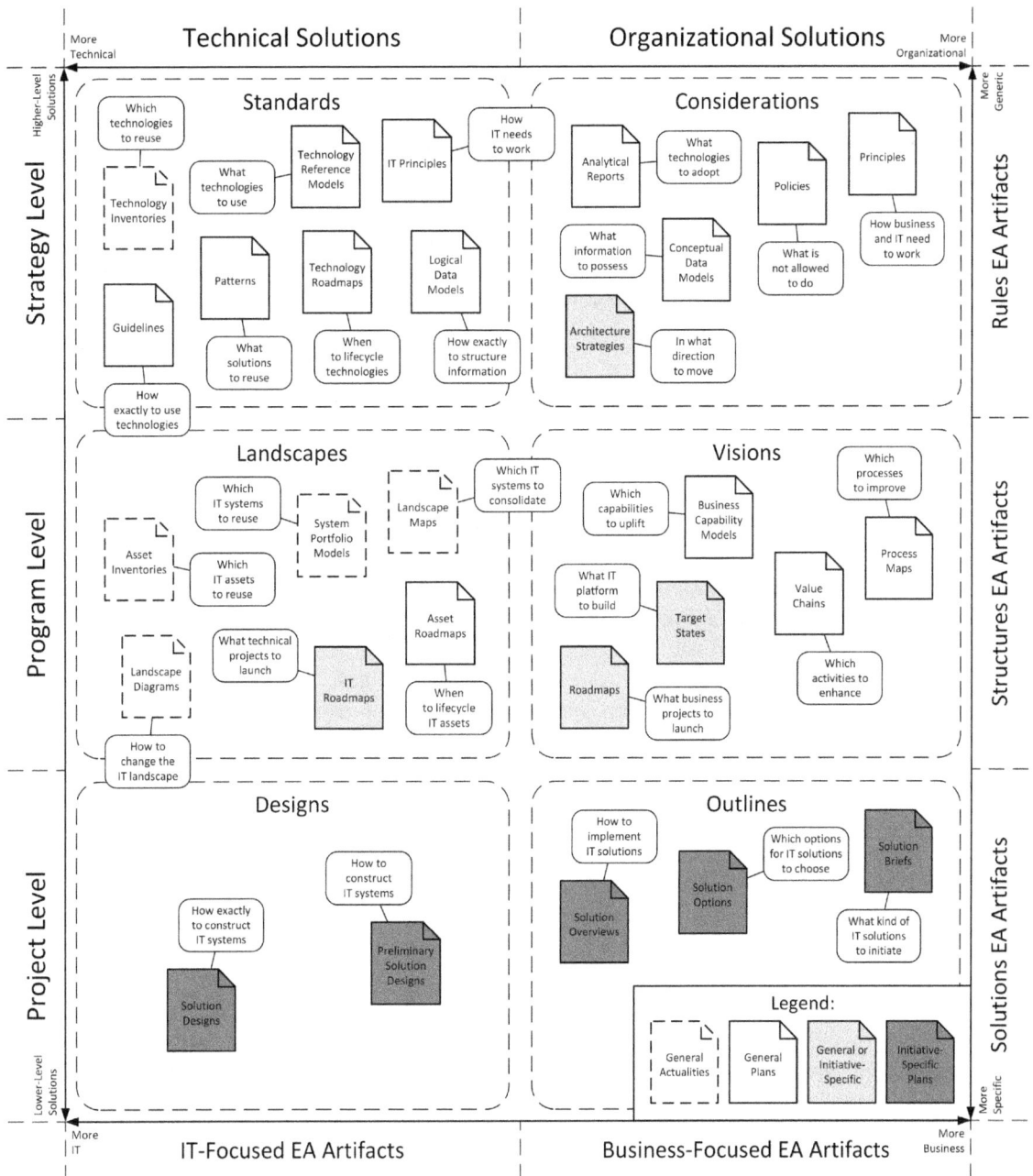

Figure 9.5. Mapping of EA artifacts to the space of architectural solutions

The map of EA artifacts presented in Figure 9.5 helps choose the most suitable instruments for capturing architectural solutions based on target solution elements. Taking into account their relative popularity and prominence in the work of enterprise architects, Architecture Strategies can be fairly regarded as key initiative-specific EA artifacts at the strategy level, Target States and Roadmaps — at the program level, and Solution Designs and Solution Overviews — at the project level.

Importantly, the mapping of EA artifacts to the space of architectural solutions is admittedly rather loose, somewhat subjective and certainly allows various deviations or exceptions from its underlying logic. For example, a digitalization project that pioneers the use of a new promising technology suitable for further, more widescale deployment in the organization may involve adding new Guidelines to regulate its utilization and updating the Technology Reference Model to reflect the respective changes in the corporate technology portfolio, even though both these artifacts are generally more appropriate for capturing architectural solutions for larger initiatives, especially strategies. Or, a local transformation program with a relatively clear scope may develop a program-specific variation of Solution Overview to describe in fair detail what needs to be done and why, even though this artifact is most typically produced for smaller projects. Nevertheless, in spite of all its imperfections, this map offers an intuitive visualization of the potential fitness of different EA artifacts for reflecting diverse technical and organizational elements of architectural solutions for projects, programs and strategies (see Figure 3.6).

Examples of Using EA Artifacts for Capturing Architectural Solutions

The discussion of EA artifacts provided above elucidated their role in capturing architectural solutions for digital transformation initiatives (see Figure 9.2), described the specifics of their use for hierarchical initiatives (see Figure 9.3), explained the mechanism of cross-initiative influence (see Figure 9.4) and assessed the relevance of different artifacts to technical and organizational solutions for initiatives at different levels (see Figure 9.5). These and some other points can be further expounded and illustrated with specific examples of using EA artifacts for capturing architectural solutions for digitalization strategies, programs and projects.

Digital Channels Strategy

For example, a company wants to refocus its sales and marketing activities on digital channels and adopt a mobile-first attitude to providing its services to customers. To accomplish this transition, the company has launched a new strategic initiative, Digital Channels Strategy. This transformation strategy implies profound changes in the way of doing business and involves numerous difficult technical and organizational decisions. The architectural solution for this strategy with its technical and organizational components can be captured in a number of EA artifacts. First, on the organizational side, a new Architecture Strategy can be created to describe the very idea of the respective transformation, outline the substance of desired changes, define their scope, mark major milestones on the way to strategy realization and indicate their possible timelines. Second, Principles can be updated with new imperatives such as "All our services should support omnichannel customer experience" and "No physical documents should be requested from customers" to embrace the new philosophy of interacting with clients. Third, Policies can also be updated to specify the requirements for storing business-sensitive information on customers' devices and limit its inadvertent sharing with mobile network operators. Fourth, on the technical side, new technologies necessary for developing and supporting mobile apps (e.g. Kotlin and React Native) can be added to the company's Technology Reference Model, while some technologies that are not fit for this strategic intent can be marked there as obsolescent. And lastly, integration Patterns can be updated to cover typical interaction scenarios between frontend apps and backend systems. In this way, disparate technical and organizational decisions united by the common strategy are captured in different EA artifacts reflecting its technical and organizational elements.

As part of its Digital Channels Strategy, the company has initiated a number of projects and programs the most important of which, Mobile Platform Program, purports to build a brand-new mobile app with powerful capabilities replacing its older malfunctioning predecessor as well as a new API-based, modular and resilient backend platform. The architectural solution for this program with its technical and organizational components can be captured in several EA artifacts. First, on the organizational side, a Target State can be developed to depict approximately how the new app and platform will work together and please customers. Second, a program-specific Roadmap can be created to show the steps that should be taken to construct the app and the platform and migrate all the affected business operations. Third, on the technical side, IT Principles can be updated with new suggestions aligned with the concept of the platform, e.g. "All services of the backend platform are accessible via open protocols" and "All platform components are designed for high availability and have no single points of failure". And lastly, relevant information systems in the company's System Portfolio Model can be color-coded to indicate whether they should be incorporated into the platform as is, rewritten from scratch as part of the platform, left untouched or removed from the landscape as inappropriate. Thereby, diverse technical and organizational decisions logically related to the same program are captured in different EA artifacts describing its technical and organizational solutions.

Finally, to execute its Mobile Platform Program, the company has launched a series of projects one of which, Identity Validation Project, is intended to enable a fully automatic verification of customers' identity based on the provided electronic copies of identity documents. The architectural solution for this project with its technical and organizational components can be captured in a few EA artifacts. First, on the organizational side, Solution Options can be prepared to present possible solution implementation scenarios, analyze their business advantages and disadvantages and substantiate a particular choice of the solution. Next, a Solution Overview can be created to describe the solution in terms of its conceptual structure, business process impact, timelines, costs and risks. Then, on the technical side, a Solution Design can be developed to specify exactly how the solution should be implemented. In this way, technical and organizational decisions pertaining to the project are captured in different EA artifacts describing its architectural solution from both the technical and organizational sides.

Data Analytics Strategy
Besides moving towards digital channels, this company wants to boost its analytical capabilities by leveraging cutting-edge techniques enabled by machine learning (ML) based on big data. To pursue this aspiration, the company has launched another strategic initiative, Data Analytics Strategy. This transformation strategy also has certain far-reaching implications for the business and IT landscape of the company and comprises multifarious technical and organizational choices. The architectural solution for this strategy with its technical and organizational components can be captured in a number of EA artifacts. First, on the organizational side, a new Architecture Strategy can be created to describe the general concept of the desired transformation, explain what benefits should be realized and the means of their realization, present the overall approach to introducing analytics into the organizational system and impose

some time constraints for completing the effort. Second, the existing Conceptual Data Model can be updated to clarify what pieces of information are particularly important for analysis and need to be accumulated for processing. Third, the company's Business Capability Model can be color-coded to indicate which business capabilities should become the primary and secondary focus of analytical enablement. Fourth, on the technical side, special technologies for implementing analytical applications and handling big data (e.g. Apache Spark and Hadoop) can be included in the Technology Reference Model and some irrelevant ones can be tagged as redundant. And lastly, the Logical Data Model can be updated to specify exactly what data entities and their fields should be collected by information systems and in what form in order to support high-quality analytics.

As part of its Data Analytics Strategy, the company has initiated a number of projects and programs one of which, Data Lake Program, intends to establish a centralized organization-wide repository for stockpiling heterogeneous types of data suitable for analytical purposes. The architectural solution for this program with its technical and organizational components can be captured in several EA artifacts. First, on the organizational side, a Target State can be developed to show the high-level structure of the data lake, its integration into the business context and its contribution to the efficiency of operations. Second, a new Roadmap can be created for this program to display major activities that should be accomplished to build the data lake and take advantage of it in various business applications. Third, on the technical side, the existing IT Roadmap for hardware infrastructure can be updated to include necessary enhancements in storage equipment required to enable the scalability of the data lake in terms of its maximum capacity. And lastly, Guidelines can be updated with new instructions on the proper use of the newly introduced specialized technologies for manipulating data.

Finally, to execute its Data Lake Program, the company has launched a series of projects one of which, Data Extractor Project, purports to extract and preprocess pertinent information from social media for its further placement in the data lake. The architectural solution for this project with its technical and organizational components can be captured in a few EA artifacts. First, on the organizational side, a Solution Overview can be created to explain the business meaning of the solution, present its positive consequences and resulting opportunities for service improvement, roughly assess its costs and timelines. Next, on the technical side, a Preliminary Solution Design can be created to dive deeper into the solution structure, cover its high-level implementation details and produce more precise estimates of time and cost. Then, a Solution Design can be developed with the full technical details of solution construction.

Intra-Initiative Guidance and Inter-Initiative Influence

The hypothetical examples of digital transformation initiatives provided above illustrate the usage of EA artifacts for capturing architectural solutions at different levels with their diverse technical and organizational elements. In these examples, architectural solutions for derivative initiatives are shaped by the solutions developed for their parent initiatives and reflected in the respective artifacts. For instance, the architectural solution for the Mobile Platform Program is guided by the planning decisions captured in EA artifacts associated with the Digital Channels Strategy, i.e. follows from the Architecture Strategy, aligns with the Principles, complies with the Policies, uses the Patterns and technologies from the Technology Reference Model. In a similar vein, the architectural solution for the Data Extractor Project is guided by the decisions reflected in EA artifacts associated with the Data Lake Program, i.e. comes from the Roadmap, builds the Target State and adheres to the Guidelines. It is this mechanism that embodies linked architectural planning of hierarchical transformation initiatives, where higher-level architectural solutions guide decisions within lower-level solutions (see Figure 3.7).

At the same time, because many EA artifacts in these examples are general ones common to all initiatives in the company and both the strategies even update the same Technology Reference Model, cross-initiative influence is also probable (see Figure 9.4). For instance, the structures of core data entities, like customers and orders, described at a high level in the Conceptual Data Model and in great detail in the Logical Data Model for the Data Analytics Strategy are very likely to affect the data aspects of the logically unrelated Mobile Platform Program. Or, various decisions on the status of information systems reflected in the System Portfolio Model for the Mobile Platform Program are likely to influence some of the projects launched under the umbrella of the Data Analytics Strategy. Sample EA artifacts capturing architectural solutions for the two digital transformation strategies and their descendants as well as the mechanisms of intra-initiative guidance and inter-initiative influence described above are shown in Figure 9.6.

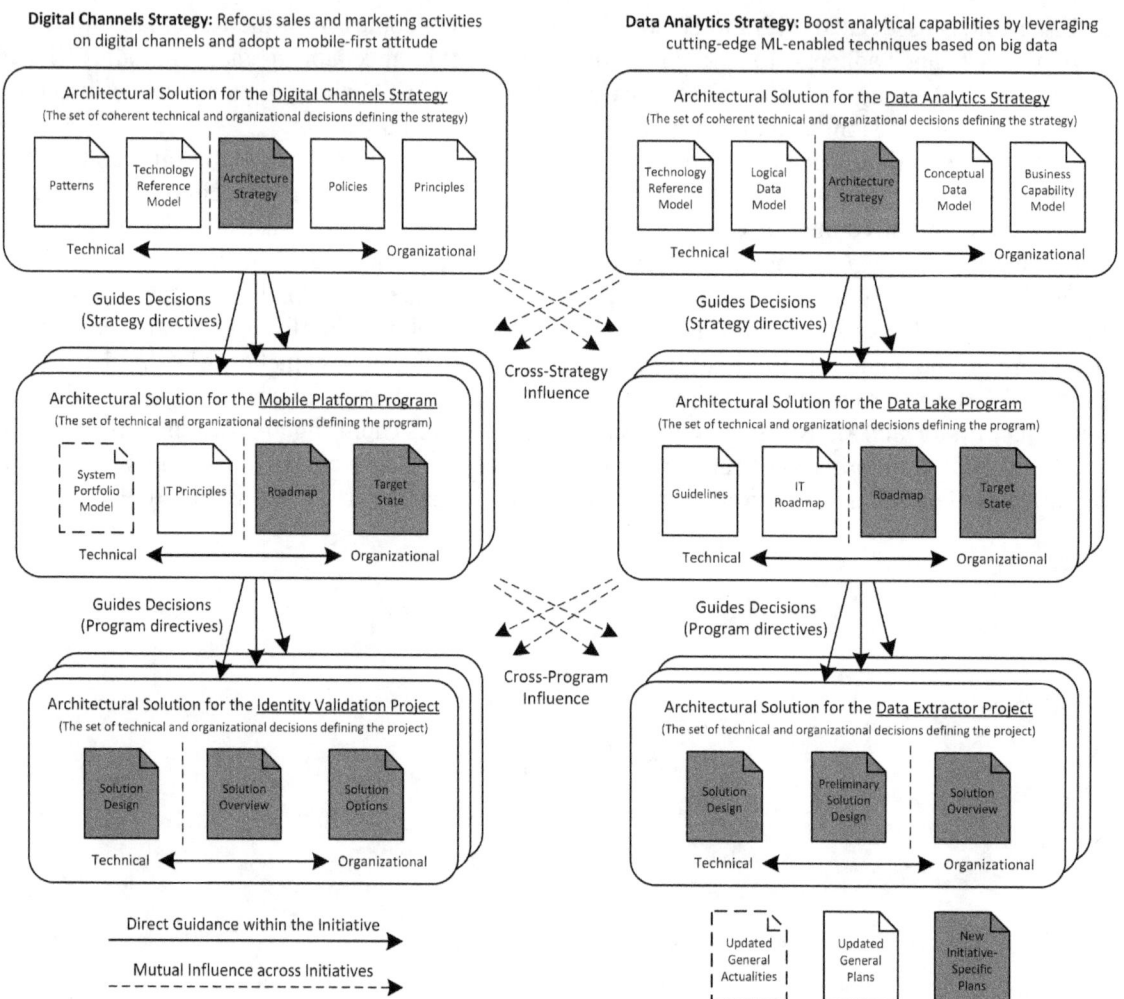

Figure 9.6. Sample EA artifacts capturing architectural solutions for different initiatives

An illustrative situation presented in Figure 9.6 exemplifies the practical usage of various EA artifacts for capturing architectural solutions at different levels and also explains how derivative solutions are shaped within and across different transformation initiatives.

Architectural Context Formed by Architectural Decisions

As it becomes evident from the general mechanisms of influence within and across the hierarchy of initiatives enabled by different types of EA artifacts (see Figure 9.3 and Figure 9.4 respectively), as well as from the specific examples of initiatives and associated artifacts summarized in Figure 9.6, digital transformation initiatives unfold in a truly complex decisional context, where they experience both vertical and horizontal "pressure" of other initiatives. The structure of their architectural solutions is shaped by virtually countless choices, suggestions and concerns dictated not only by their parent initiatives, but also, to varying degrees, by all other initiatives running in the organization. Most notably, Principles, Policies and all sorts of technical Standards, on the one hand, are updated collectively by all initiatives and, on the other hand, affect every single initiative, causing considerable interdependence between initiatives.

Moreover, since general EA artifacts continue their existence even after the completion of initiatives, they tend to accumulate and "remember" all the various planning decisions made as part of numerous initiatives implemented in the past, possibly many years ago. From this point of view, current transformation initiatives are definitely path-dependent and influenced by all the previous initiatives as well. For example, technologies selected for one now-finished change initiative a couple of years ago and added to the Technology Reference Model are likely to be reused in a new initiative with similar needs and influence its architectural solution, even though these two initiatives are unrelated logically and separated temporally.

Conceptually, all plans EA artifacts created in the organization and all architectural decisions reflected in them, taken together, form a global **architectural context** within which all the subsequent decision-making takes place. This context is "woven" from all transformation initiatives running at different levels and partly remnants of earlier initiatives, represents the entirety of all their architectural solutions and plans, and is filled with the respective artifacts. The mapping of popular EA artifacts depicted in Figure 9.5 provides reasonably clear suggestions as to which artifacts populating the context can capture different kinds of decisions that mold it. Because it is formed by the decisions of not only active initiatives, but also completed and even abandoned ones, the architectural context can be viewed, in some sense, as a "graveyard" of initiatives.

Each new digitalization initiative in the organization links to the surrounding architectural context and gets shaped by other initiatives constituting it via strong parent–child guidance (see Figure 9.3), weaker cross-initiative influence (see Figure 9.4) or both these mechanisms in conjunction (see Figure 9.6). At the same time, each new initiative also contributes its own architectural plans in the form of concrete EA artifacts to the context, thereby enriching it with new planning decisions and concerns to be taken into account in all future initiatives. In other words, transformation initiatives create new initiative-specific artifacts and update general artifacts in the architectural context and, in turn, are guided by the decisions of their parent initiatives and influenced by the decisions of parallel initiatives documented in the existing EA artifacts from this context. Because all high-level architectural plans from which derivative initiatives are spawned belong to the architectural context, essentially all derivative initiatives are spawned indirectly *by* the architectural context.

In short, all architectural solutions for digitalization initiatives are developed within the broader architectural context and then organically merge into it, becoming its integral elements. However, higher-level initiatives with a major impact on the organization more often capture their architectural solutions in general EA artifacts that shape the overall context, while lower-level initiatives with a narrow scope and initiative-specific artifacts are usually shaped by it (see Figure 9.5). The architectural context of the organization composed of the extant plans EA artifacts and its relationship to individual transformation initiatives of different sizes are illustrated in Figure 9.7.

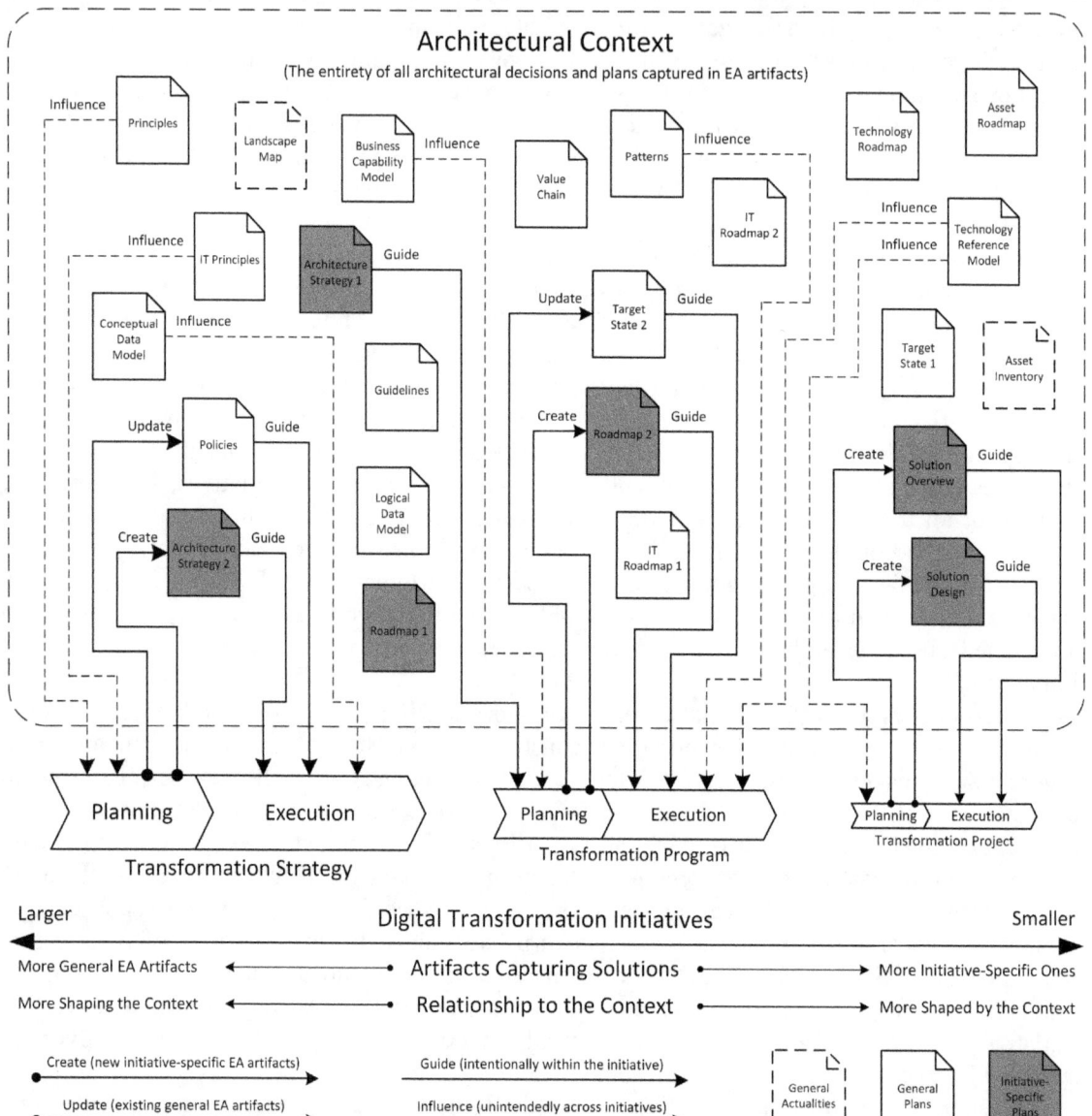

Figure 9.7. Architectural context and its relationship to change initiatives of different sizes

As demonstrated in Figure 9.7, digital transformation initiatives of any scale in the organization cannot exist in isolation from its architectural context. Each and every change initiative has to align with its suggestions.

Overarching Transformational Context

In matters of architectural decision-making, the architectural context aggregating all made planning decisions complements the motivational context aggregating all present transformation drivers (see Figure 1.3). Both the motivational and architectural contexts provide a general background and specific premises for taking decisions relevant to digitalization endeavors. However, these two contexts have disparate origins and their properties are quite different.

While the motivational context evolves naturally being formed by various conditions of the organizational environment exogenous to enterprise architects and often to other organizational actors, the architectural context is endogenous and created artificially by architects and other stakeholders of architectural planning. The motivational context exists primarily in the minds of people eager to transform the organization (i.e. driver proponents) and reflects their current understanding of the situation, whereas the architectural context is recorded in material documents (i.e. EA artifacts) and captures both today's and historical planning decisions.

From the standpoint of digital transformation efforts, the motivational context with its drivers mainly induces new autonomous initiatives and defines their goals (see Figure 2.5). The role of the architectural context, however, is more complex and dual. First, by embracing the architectural plans of high-level initiatives, it spawns lower-level derivative initiatives. Second, by containing multiple authorized planning decisions that have to be respected, the architectural context also shapes the architectural solutions of all change initiatives, autonomous and derivative ones.

The motivational and architectural contexts are the essential constituents of the organizational environment in which digital transformation initiatives get launched and implemented. Both of them play very important roles in the work of enterprise architects. For conceptual convenience, these two contexts can be joined into a single **transformational context** that aggregates all factors influencing architectural decision-making in the organization. The overarching transformational context with its two sub-contexts, their key properties and relationship to autonomous and derivative transformation initiatives is shown in Figure 9.8.

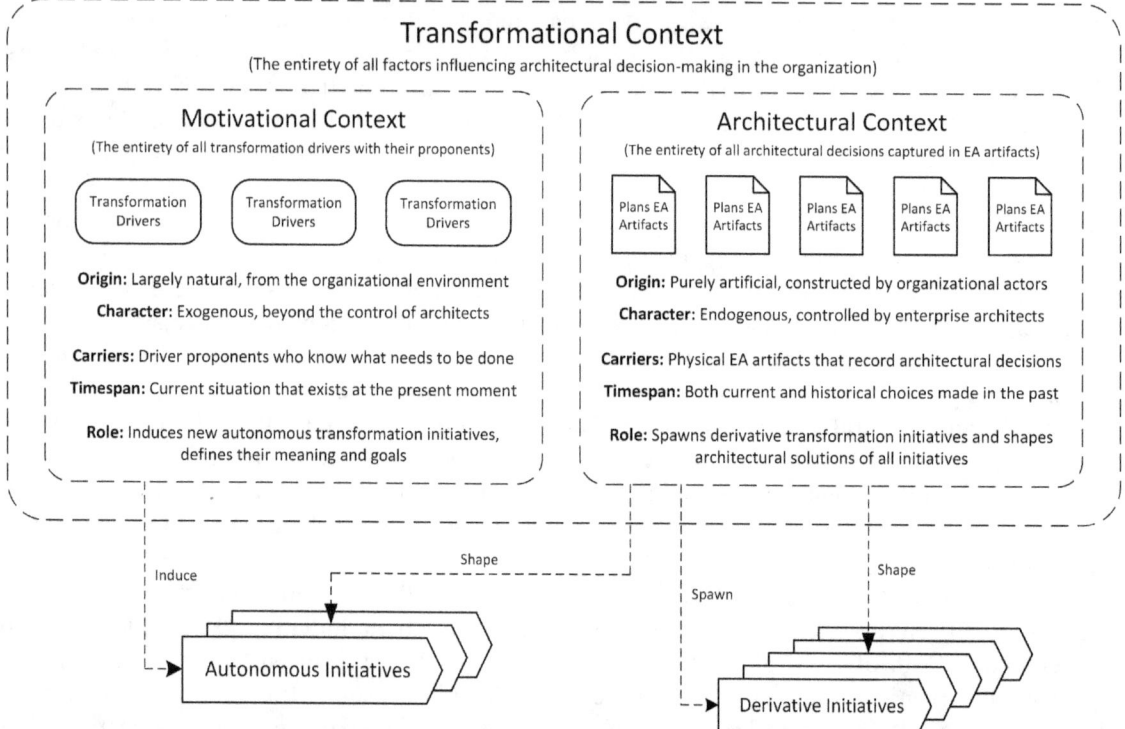

Figure 9.8. Transformational context and its relationship to different types of initiatives

The transformational context of the organization encompassing a multitude of change drivers and architectural decisions provides numerous concerns to be taken into account by enterprise architects when ideating new initiatives and leading their planning.

Digitalization Initiatives in the Transformational Context

The transformational context is relevant, in one way or another, to all digitalization initiatives in the organization. However, because transformation initiatives at different levels of the initiative hierarchy vary substantially from the perspective of their autonomous versus derivative nature (see Figure 2.6), these initiatives relate somewhat differently to its motivational and architectural components (see Figure 9.8).

At the bottom of the initiative hierarchy, projects represent mostly derivative pieces of work subordinate to some higher-order initiatives. They are more often spawned by parent initiatives based on the existing intentions reflected in their architectural plans. For this reason, on average, projects weakly link to the primary motivational context, but at the same time strongly depend on the architectural context from which they originate.

In the middle of the initiative hierarchy, programs can be both autonomous, stemming immediately from some transformation drivers, and derivative, descending from the enacted higher-level architectural plans. Therefore, programs are generally characterized by moderate dependence on both the motivational context and the architectural context.

At the top of the initiative hierarchy, strategies normally represent autonomous change efforts launched independently of other initiatives. They are typically induced directly by specific transformation drivers based on the new ideas generated in the process of initial ideation. For this reason, strategies strongly depend on the motivational context that inspires them, but are only weakly tied to the architectural context.

Importantly, despite their varying contextual dependence, neither of the two components of the transformational context can be completely ignored or neglected by any types of initiatives; both the motivational and architectural contexts should always be taken into account. For instance, some projects can be autonomous and initiated in response to particular transformation drivers, whereas even the largest strategies cannot afford to sweep away all the existing architectural plans.

Hence, for change initiatives at different hierarchical levels, one component of the transformational context tends to come to the fore, while the other fades into the background, though never disappearing entirely. The dependence of digitalization initiatives at different levels on the motivational and architectural components of the transformational context is illustrated schematically in Figure 9.9.

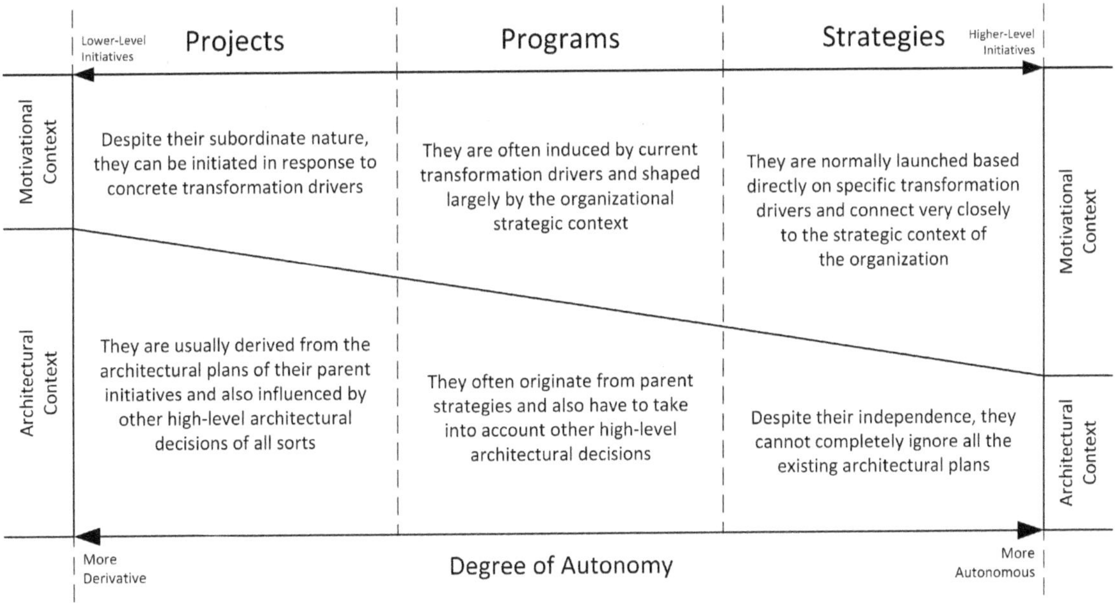

	Projects	Programs	Strategies
Motivational Context	Despite their subordinate nature, they can be initiated in response to concrete transformation drivers	They are often induced by current transformation drivers and shaped largely by the organizational strategic context	They are normally launched based directly on specific transformation drivers and connect very closely to the strategic context of the organization
Architectural Context	They are usually derived from the architectural plans of their parent initiatives and also influenced by other high-level architectural decisions of all sorts	They often originate from parent strategies and also have to take into account other high-level architectural decisions	Despite their independence, they cannot completely ignore all the existing architectural plans

Lower-Level Initiatives ← → Higher-Level Initiatives

More Derivative ← Degree of Autonomy → More Autonomous

Figure 9.9. Transformational context for digitalization initiatives at different levels

As demonstrated in Figure 9.9, on the way down the initiative hierarchy, the relative importance of the motivational context diminishes, but the importance of the architectural context, on the contrary, grows, as initiatives get more "distant" from original transformation drivers and backed more by developed architectural plans.

Chapter Summary

This chapter explained the use and selection of EA artifacts by enterprise architects for the purposes of documenting the existing situation and capturing architectural solutions, provided concrete examples of using EA for capturing architectural solutions for digitalization initiatives at different levels and introduced the architectural and transformational contexts. The key message of this chapter can be summarized in the following essential points:

- For the purposes of documenting the existing situation, EA artifacts can be modified by enterprise architects anytime, by gathering new facts about the landscape and creating new or updating existing artifacts to record these facts
- For documenting the existing situation, enterprise architects use primarily different actualities EA artifacts focusing on the current state, but some plans EA artifacts can also serve this purpose with certain nuances, limitations and caveats
- For the purposes of capturing architectural solutions, EA artifacts can be modified by enterprise architects only as part of the architectural planning of initiatives, by creating new initiative-specific artifacts and updating existing general artifacts
- General EA artifacts capturing architectural solutions often record planning decisions pertaining to different digitalization initiatives, causing unintended mutual influence and interdependence between logically unrelated initiatives
- For capturing architectural solutions, enterprise architects use primarily different plans EA artifacts oriented to the future, but most actualities EA artifacts can also serve this purpose by recording individual planning decisions
- The architectural context of the organization represents the entirety of all architectural decisions captured in EA artifacts, where higher-level initiatives more shape this context and lower-level initiatives are more shaped by it
- The transformational context of the organization unites its motivational and architectural contexts, aggregates all factors influencing architectural decision-making and relates in different ways to autonomous and derivative initiatives
- Digitalization initiatives at all levels strongly depend on the transformational context, but higher-level initiatives depend more on its motivational component and lower-level initiatives depend more on its architectural component

Chapter 10: Basic Activities of Enterprise Architects

Previously, Chapter 4 provided a high-level overview of the work of enterprise architects in organizations. This chapter begins a detailed discussion of the activities of enterprise architects and thoroughly covers their three basic activities. In particular, this chapter starts with introducing two different contexts of activities of enterprise architects and explaining the differences between them. Next, this chapter introduces the five key activities performed by enterprise architects within these contexts and explains their contextuality. Lastly, this chapter describes in great detail the three basic activities of enterprise architects: analyzing the external environment, studying the internal environment and providing advisory services.

Activities Performed by Enterprise Architects

The two hats of Technology Experts and Change Agents worn by enterprise architects provide an expressive, explanatory and powerful conceptualization of their occupation in terms of its overall spirit (see Figure 4.9). This conceptualization, however, barely explains what architects actually do on a day-to-day basis to drive architectural planning and digital transformation in organizations. In short, the two hats of architects convey only the general meaning of their profession, but do not reveal the contents of their job in actionable terms.

At the same time, the typical pattern of the involvement of enterprise architects in the ideation and different lifecycle phases of digitalization initiatives (see Figure 4.5 to Figure 4.8) clarifies only the logical flow of their work, but also at a very high level, without specifying their concrete everyday activities. Basically, the two hats of architects and their roles at different stages of transformation initiatives offer helpful overarching abstractions of their "business" in organizations that lack physical operationalization. To understand the work of architects in a practical sense, as a material embodiment of wearing these hats and fulfilling these roles, it has to be viewed closer from the standpoint of their hands-on activities.

Activities of enterprise architects represent their daily tasks and routines constituting their job in organizations and necessary for leading architectural planning by wearing the hats of Technology Experts and Change Agents. These activities are extremely diverse and specific actions that they can take during their workdays are nearly impossible to enumerate[1]. Moreover, different activities of architects are intertwined in complex ways and the interplay of these activities that composes their work in organizations is very sophisticated. There are arguably no simple ways to explain their activities with acceptable accuracy.

Importantly, even though driving architectural planning efforts is the core responsibility of enterprise architects in organizations (see Figure 4.1), far from all activities of architects relate immediately to architectural planning; many of their activities are relevant to it only indirectly. In other words, leading architectural planning represents the bulk and the most prominent part of the work of architects, but not all of their work, which is much broader and richer than literally "planning". Before proceeding to the detailed discussion of architects' activities, it is first necessary to introduce different contexts in which these activities are carried out.

Two Contexts of Activities

Generally, enterprise architects perform their activities in two different contexts: organizational and initiative. The **organizational context of activities** is a context in which all relevant elements of the organization are taken into account. The organizational context is single, global and embraces the entire organization. This context encompasses all landscape areas and comprises all organizational decision-making processes. It is directed by top-level business strategy and the lower-level motivational context with all its transformation drivers. As organizations are stable but slowly evolving entities, the organizational context has a permanent character and implies a very long, potentially infinite, horizon of concerns. This context involves various organizational actors with diverse interests from all functional units and administrative levels. It also includes all architectural plans constituting the architectural context of the organization and all EA artifacts materializing them (see Figure 9.7). The activities of enterprise architects carried out within the organizational context refer to the organization as a whole and are not connected to any particular transformation initiatives.

By contrast, the **initiative context of activities** is a context in which only those elements that directly relate to specific digitalization initiatives are taken into account. There exist multiple initiative contexts in the organization; each initiative has its own unique context. This context covers only the organizational areas affected by the initiative and contains the three typical phases of its end-to-end implementation lifecycle, from conception to execution (see Figure 2.2). It is guided by the subset of transformation drivers that initially motivated the initiative and concrete initiative goals ensuing from these drivers. As all change initiatives are transient undertakings that periodically come and go, the initiative context is always temporary in nature, so that the horizon of concerns inside it is strictly bounded by the initiative lifetime. This context involves a limited circle of stakeholders pursuing their interests in the initiative implementation (see Figure 2.3). It also includes the architectural plans of the initiative in the form of initiative-specific EA artifacts created for it and possibly some general artifacts updated to reflect its planning decisions (see Figure 9.2). The activities of enterprise architects carried out within the initiative context are confined to the boundaries of a single transformation initiative.

As all digitalization initiatives run inside the broader organizational environment, the initiative context actually represents a *sub-context* of the organizational context and can be viewed as its initiative-specific localization. For this reason, any activities performed by enterprise architects in the organizational context can always be performed on a limited scope but with a more pointed focus in the initiative context as well. The opposite statement, however, is untrue as some activities make sense only within the initiative context and cannot be upscaled to the organizational scope or fulfilled apart from concrete initiatives, though with some clarifications introduced later in Chapter 15 (The Archetype of Enterprise Architects). The same logic of context nesting also applies to the initiative contexts of hierarchical transformation initiatives (see Figure 2.5), where the project context can be a sub-context of the broader program context which, in turn, can be a sub-context of its parent strategy context. The properties of the organizational and initiative contexts of the activities of enterprise architects described above are summarized in Figure 10.1.

Organizational Context of Activities
(All relevant elements of the organization are taken into account)

Scope: Entire organization with its various areas
Quantity: Single, overarching for the organization
Content: All organizational decision-making processes
Nature: Permanent, evolves with the organization

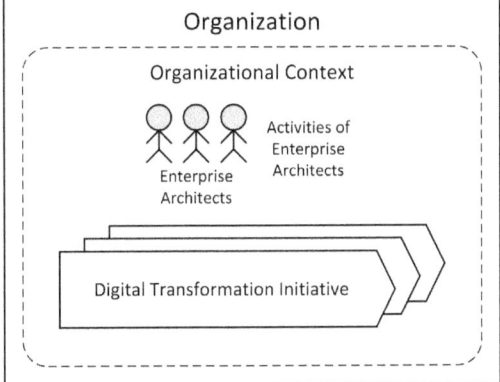

Goals: Global strategic goals of the organization
Drivers: Motivational context with all active drivers
Horizon: Very long, unbounded, potentially infinite

People: All organizational actors from different areas
Plans: Architectural context with all the enacted plans
Artifacts: All EA artifacts existing in the organization

Activities: Refer largely to the organization as a whole
Focus: Broad, widely dispersed across the organization

Initiative Context of Activities
(Only elements related to specific initiatives are taken into account)

Scope: One digital transformation initiative
Quantity: Multiple, unique for each initiative
Content: Three phases of the initiative lifecycle
Nature: Temporary, emerges and then vanishes

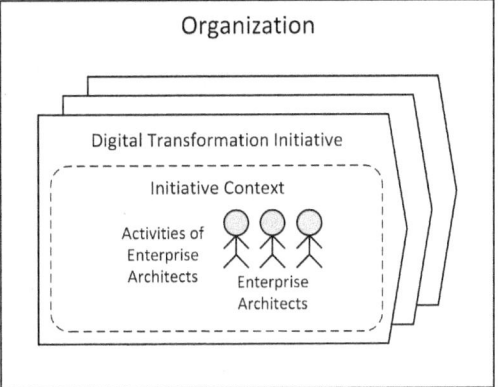

Goals: Goals of the specific transformation initiative
Drivers: Concrete drivers behind the change initiative
Horizon: Strictly bounded by the initiative lifetime

People: Limited audience of initiative stakeholders
Plans: Architectural plans of the transformation initiative
Artifacts: All initiative-specific and some general artifacts

Activities: Confined to the boundaries of the initiative
Focus: Narrow, concentrated on the pertinent details

Figure 10.1. Organizational and initiative contexts of the activities of enterprise architects

In their job, enterprise architects operate in both the organizational and initiative contexts presented in Figure 10.1. These two contexts characterize different settings in which architects work and provide the necessary basis for further discussion of their activities in organizations.

Five Activities of Enterprise Architects

Notwithstanding the wide diversity of their practical tasks and actions, the work of enterprise architects in organizations can be meaningfully analyzed by decomposing it into five different high-level activities that they routinely perform:

- **Analyzing the external environment** — searching, collecting and thinking over new information about the outer technology and market environment

- **Studying the internal environment** — seeking, obtaining and accumulating information on the inner business and IT environment
- **Providing advisory services** — consulting other organizational actors on various IT-related questions and supporting them with sound IT expertise
- **Leading the development of plans** — organizing, orchestrating and facilitating the cooperative processes of architectural planning
- **Ensuring adherence to plans** — following up, tracking and enforcing compliance with the existing architectural plans

These five activities are very different in their substance, aims and modes of working, but each one of them is necessary for the successful performance of enterprise architects. Furthermore, they are also linked with certain logical and partly sequential relationships. Some of these activities belong more to the repertoire of Technology Experts and others — to that of Change Agents.

Interestingly, of the five activities of enterprise architects, only leading the development of plans relates directly to architectural planning, while all the other activities are peripheral to it. For instance, providing advisory services accompanies architectural planning, but does not imply creating any architectural plans. Ensuring adherence to plans follows up architectural planning and guarantees that the produced plans are not neglected. Lastly, analyzing the external environment and studying the internal environment inform architectural planning, but do not contribute to it in any other ways.

Activities in Different Contexts

The five activities of enterprise architects are carried out in different contexts (see Figure 10.1). Namely, analyzing the external environment, studying the internal environment and providing advisory services can be performed in both the organizational and initiative contexts, whereas leading the development of plans and ensuring adherence to plans — only in the initiative context. Because they are conceptually simple, context-neutral and universal but at the same time foundational for the work of architects in organizations, the former three activities can be regarded as their **basic activities**.

Accordingly, in the organizational context, the primary and only activities of enterprise architects are their three basic activities: analyzing the external environment, studying the internal environment and providing advisory services. In the initiative context of activities, the situation is somewhat more complex. As this context is nested in the organizational one, the three basic activities stay in place, but recede into the background and become purely supporting, while the two other activities native to this context — leading the development of plans and ensuring adherence to plans — come to the fore as the primary activities. The relationship between the five activities of enterprise architects and the two contexts of their activities is depicted in Figure 10.2.

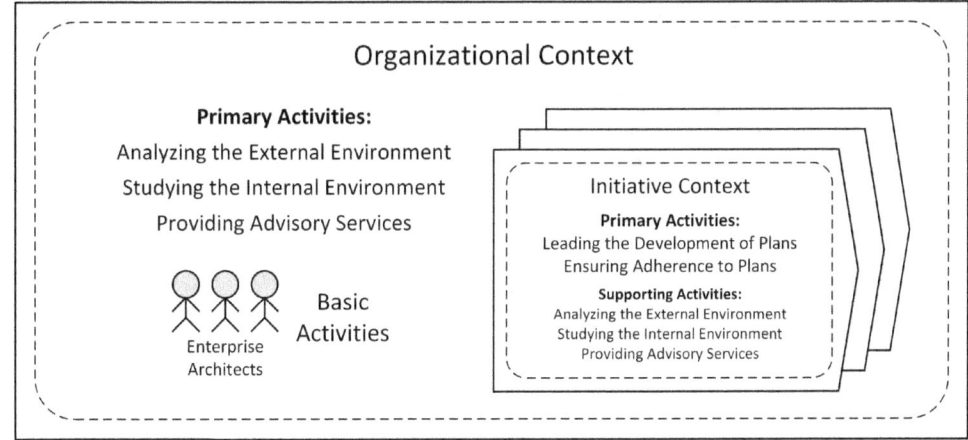

Figure 10.2. Five activities of architects in the organizational and initiative contexts

Each of the five activities of enterprise architects has its own meaning, goals and means of their achievement. Each of these activities is also integrated in its own way into the surrounding context and strongly associated with specific types of regular and auxiliary EA artifacts. For this reason, each activity deserves a separate comprehensive discussion covering all its various aspects. The three basic activities of architects are addressed in the following sections of this chapter and the two remaining activities — in the two subsequent chapters respectively.

Analyzing the External Environment

The first essential activity of enterprise architects is exploring and studying the external environment from the perspective of IT and associated business implications. Analyzing the external environment implies deliberately searching, collecting and thinking over some or the other new information about the outer technology and market environment, thereby expanding general and industry-specific knowledge (see Figure 6.1). This activity is, for the most part, solitary, mental and "inbound" as it involves only the consumption of information by architects with no visible manifestations for others and no tangible outputs for the organization as a whole. Analyzing the external environment is equally important for enterprise architects wearing the hats of both Technology Experts and Change Agents.

Meaning and Goals

The analysis of the external environment purports to scan the market for all sorts of IT-related changes and innovations deemed relevant to the organization and to study in detail their features and properties. It can focus, for example, on entirely new technologies and their possible business applicability, upgrades of existing technologies and specific vendors supplying them, concrete product offerings and differences between them in terms of their characteristics. The general meaning of the environmental analysis carried out by enterprise architects can be best exemplified by the following and similar questions:

- What technologies, vendors and offerings are available on the market?
- What are their capabilities and features, advantages and drawbacks?

- How do these technologies, products and offerings evolve over time?
- What novel technical functions and commercial opportunities do they provide?
- What fundamentally new technologies and business practices are emerging?
- Do these innovations have a disruptive potential for our business?
- How can our organization benefit from their adoption and utilization?
- Are they mature and proven enough to be invested in right now?

To keep up with the rapid technological progress, enterprise architects have to be avid learners and consume vast amounts of information about the external environment[2]. Depending on the position-specific responsibilities of architects, the circle of their interests can range from very narrow classes of niche solutions and technologies to the full gamut of IT-related innovations with special attention to game-changing technologies. Their environmental analysis can also lean towards either covering recent trends in familiar areas of business and IT, or opening a previously uncharted "territory" of knowledge. For instance, it can focus on updates introduced in the latest versions of concrete products and technologies already used in the organization, new offerings from well-known vendors, available IT solutions for specific business sectors, pioneering types of technology or disruptive shifts in the industry at large.

Besides learning new knowledge, analyzing the external environment also implies *unlearning* old knowledge that is no longer valid. As technologies rapidly move forward, knowledge often becomes obsolete, sometimes pulling enterprise architects back in their decision-making. Most notably, with the advent of software-defined infrastructure, the former conceptions, beliefs and precepts about IT infrastructure from the previous age of hardware all turned inadequate, demanding radically different frameworks for thinking[3]. For this reason, in some cases, promptly discarding the detrimental baggage of outdated notions can be equally important for architects[4].

The goals of analyzing the external environment by enterprise architects roughly correspond to the most dynamic fields of general and industry-specific knowledge that require constant renewal, e.g. technology market, industry innovations and competitive environment. Specifically, the purpose of this activity can be largely reduced to three somewhat different goals:

- Learn the details of technologies already or to be adopted by the organization
- Understand how technologies are evolving and what capabilities they provide
- Realize what opportunities and risks new technologies bring to the organization

By continually analyzing the external environment, enterprise architects keep abreast of the cutting-edge advances in business and IT. A broad comprehension of the external business and technology landscape ensuing from this analysis helps architects determine what kind of solutions, technologies and approaches can work best in different situations or are typical for the industry. Being aware of the latest IT developments also allows architects to look into the future, see in what direction the world is going and predict probable consequences of various choices and planning decisions for the organization in the long run[5].

Context of Fulfillment

Being among the basic activities of enterprise architects, analyzing the external environment is performed in the organizational context as one of the primary activities and in the initiative context as a supporting activity (see Figure 10.2). In the organizational context, analyzing the external environment represents largely a continuous, persistent activity of architects. As champions of IT-driven business innovations, architects are expected to demonstrate a zeal for identifying promising opportunities for leveraging IT in their organizations. For this reason, they constantly analyze the external environment for the purposes of general exploration, self-education and awareness. For example, in their spare time, architects periodically review new technologies, emerging solutions and novel ideas for their potential use in the future. This analysis is carried out proactively to stay informed of the latest developments in IT and their possible applications in business. However, because of its broad coverage, shallow depth and lack of a specific focus, general environmental analysis cannot meet all the information needs of architects, particularly when they work on concrete transformation initiatives, where more detailed knowledge is required.

In the initiative context, the analysis of the external environment is triggered reactively, whenever it becomes necessary for specific purposes or tasks related to particular change initiatives. During the initiative implementation process, the environmental analysis is most often performed by enterprise architects specifically within the planning phase, in concert with architectural planning (see Figure 4.7). In this case, it is typically initiated when suitable technologies, solutions and approaches for initiatives are selected. For example, being involved in the architectural planning of a digitalization initiative, an architect will probably search the market for the most appropriate vendors or products based on their match with the stipulated requirements for the envisioned transformation and thoroughly study their details to make the right choice. Likewise, the analysis of the external environment can be initiated by architects during the conception phase to generate possible options for using IT and assess their feasibility. Normally, enterprise architects conduct both the general and initiative-specific types of environmental analysis in different variations and proportions.

Means of Fulfillment

Analyzing the external environment requires gathering vast amounts of relevant information on IT and its business implications. This information can be obtained by various means from rather diverse sources. Specifically, the means of environmental analysis available to enterprise architects include, among others, the following approaches:

- Searching the Internet — Googling for information on pertinent subjects, browsing topical pages, portals and blogs, reading official documentation, whitepapers and press releases, watching videos, speeches and presentations
- Following the news — tracking the news on technology published by specialized websites and online magazines (e.g. CIO, Computerworld and Wired), as well as the mainstream business press (e.g. the Wall Street Journal, BBC and CNN)
- Subscribing to feeds — following the relevant newsmakers and hashtags on X (former Twitter), joining special interest groups and networks on LinkedIn, subscribing to mailing lists from vendors, consultancies and universities
- Reading the literature — studying professional books and articles published in business and technology outlets, like MIT Sloan Management Review, Harvard Business Review and California Management Review

- Studying analytics — reading analytical reports and other materials issued by market research, consulting and advisory firms, e.g. Thoughtworks Technology Radars, Gartner Magic Quadrants, Forrester Waves and IDC MarketScapes
- Networking with colleagues — interacting with peers and fellow architects, including those from other companies and industries, exchanging news and opinions regarding business and IT innovations, discussing specific technologies and sharing experiences of their practical application
- Taking courses — attending formal education classes ranging from free remote one-day trainings from product vendors to week-long certifications from training centers to one-semester massive open online courses (MOOCs) from different providers to full-fledged postgraduate diploma programs from universities
- Visiting events — participating in industry conferences, forums and meetings, listening to presentations on the latest technologies and approaches, talking with acknowledged experts and taking advantage of networking opportunities

All these means can be employed by enterprise architects, alone or in combination, for exploring different aspects of the external environment[6]. Some of them are more appropriate for expanding the horizon of knowledge, while others — for meticulous in-depth research of narrow areas.

Relevant Enterprise Architecture Artifacts

Basically, analyzing the external environment represents a mental exercise that does not require developing or using any special physical artifacts. Adequate environmental analysis can be performed merely by browsing the Internet and speaking with experts. However, in some cases, enterprise architects can benefit from creating certain auxiliary material artifacts to facilitate their analysis and formally document its conclusions, which can be viewed as ad hoc papers (see Table 7.1).

For example, one of the most popular visual techniques for analyzing the external environment in terms of general technology awareness is technology radars. **Technology radars** capture all technologies and concepts considered relevant, classify them into a number of categories based on their perceived importance and readiness for adoption (e.g. hold, assess, trial and adopt) and position them inside concentric circles around the center so that their relative proximity to the core indicates the willingness to start using them. Often, they also color-code these technologies and concepts according to their status (e.g. newly identified, became closer to adoption or unchanged) to reflect the evolution of the situation over time. Technology radars help architects trace potentially applicable technologies and approaches and choose opportune moments for their introduction into the organization. Arguably the most famous industry example of technology radars is Thoughtworks Technology Radar which analyzes the landscape of tools, techniques, platforms, languages and frameworks for software development[7].

Or, another well-known technique more suitable for comparing and selecting technologies or products for specific purposes is analytical quadrants. **Analytical quadrants** position all relevant technologies and products in a two-dimensional space, where their positions along the dimensions quantify some of their important properties, thereby classifying them into four quadrants representing the clusters of items with similar characteristics. These items can also be color, size and shape-coded to indicate some of their less important, secondary properties.

Different variations of analytical quadrants can help architects evaluate candidate technologies, vendors and products for their possible usage in concrete transformation initiatives. Probably the most prominent industry examples of analytical quadrants for analyzing vendors and their products are Gartner Magic Quadrant (ability to execute versus completeness of vision)[8] and Forrester Wave (current offering versus strategy)[9]. The schematic graphical representations of technology radars and analytical quadrants are exhibited in Figure 10.3.

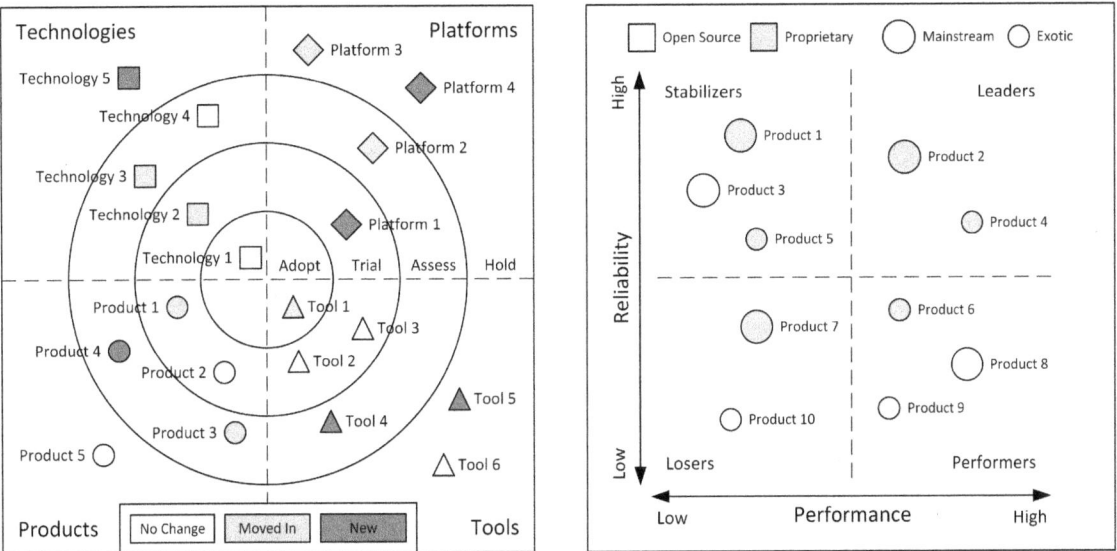

Figure 10.3. Technology radars and analytical quadrants

Technology radars and analytical quadrants illustrated in Figure 10.3, as well as some other, less popular instruments of a similar kind, can all be used by enterprise architects to support their analysis of the external environment. The application of these instruments may result in the creation of the respective physical artifacts, though these techniques and artifacts are really optional.

Additional Concerns

The analysis of the external environment, and especially analysis carried out for the purposes of identifying promising technologies, requires enterprise architects to be visionary, imaginative and somewhat idealistic — able to envision what courses of action can open for the organization in the future. This activity, therefore, is highly speculative and embraces mostly what might be "theoretically".

At the same time, the external technological environment is very ambiguous, inconsistent and volatile. It is replete with irresponsible marketing statements, misleading claims, bizarre opinions, overinflated expectations and incessant hype around virtually every new buzzword. If analyzed naively, this "hostile" environment can easily befool architects, e.g. make them select an unproven, immature technology or approach whose declared efficiency is demonstratable only under perfect, special or otherwise unrealistic conditions.

For this reason, it is crucial for enterprise architects to learn to *interpret* the external environment and various contradictory signals incoming from it properly. To avoid getting disoriented and lost in the immense sea of questionable information about technologies and their prospects, architects should be capable of distinguishing objective reality from artificial rhetoric, substantiated facts from empty promises, true innovations from superficial decorations, tectonic shifts from fleeting fads and fashions[10].

One of the frameworks for thinking that can help enterprise architects interpret the news from the external environment is the concept of hype cycle initially proposed by Gartner[11]. The **hype cycle for technologies** distinguishes five phases through which any technology tends to pass during its maturation, on the way from its inception to widespread industry adoption: technology trigger, peak of inflated expectations, trough of disillusionment, slope of enlightenment and plateau of productivity. First of all, the technology trigger phase marks the emergence of a new technology on the market and the initial interest in it in the mainstream media. Then, the peak of inflated expectations phase represents the apex of enthusiasm and excitement around the technology, when it is widely believed to be a breakthrough, or "panacea", with the potential to solve all organizational problems, dramatically boost productivity or even transform the entire industry. Next, the trough of disillusionment phase signifies the severe "hangover" of the overall disappointment with the technology due to its inability to meet previous, often unrealistic expectations. After that, the slope of enlightenment phase is characterized by the recognition of modest but helpful practical applications of the new technology and the prevalence of a more realistic view of its actual capabilities. And finally, the plateau of productivity phase ends the adoption cycle with a general appreciation of the genuine capabilities, limitations, applicability and usage scenarios of the technology that enables its productive utilization across the industry. The hype cycle for technologies with its five phases described above is illustrated graphically in Figure 10.4.

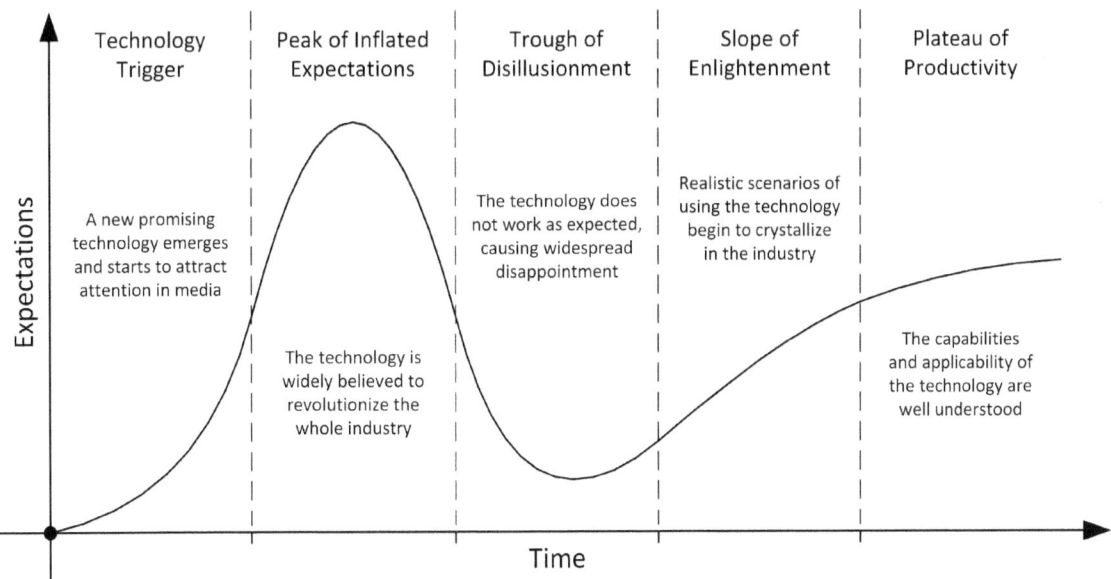

Figure 10.4. The hype cycle for technologies

Understanding the evolution patterns of a typical technology hype cycle can help enterprise architects correctly assess the current status of different technologies, determine their maturity stages and monitor their progression over time, distinguishing the signal from the noise. Also, as explained earlier, practical experience, as one of the key resources of architects (see Figure 6.3), plays an important role in raising the level of realism in architects' judgments. Experience is generally conducive to the skeptical evaluation of available information and enables a more sober analysis of the external environment.

Studying the Internal Environment

The second essential activity of enterprise architects is exploring and scrutinizing the internal environment of the organization with all its details, features and peculiarities. Studying the internal environment implies intentionally seeking, obtaining and accumulating some or the other information on the inner business and IT environment, thereby expanding organization-specific knowledge (see Figure 6.1). Similarly to analyzing the external environment, this activity is mostly solitary, inward and passive as it includes only gathering information by architects, but delivers no apparent outcomes to the organization, except for growing its documented knowledge base. Studying the internal environment is also equally necessary for enterprise architects as both Technology Experts and Change Agents.

Meaning and Goals

Studies of the internal environment intend to explore all aspects of the relationship between business and IT in the organization relevant to architectural planning, the bulk of which represents the current landscape structure and the rest — a number of less material concerns. They can focus, for example, on the specifics of business processes, the composition of the existing IT platform, the decision-making authority of senior managers, long-term corporate plans and presently running digitalization initiatives. The general meaning of the environmental studies performed by enterprise architects can be best illustrated by the following and similar questions:

- What is the business model of our company and how do we make money?
- What IT assets constitute our landscape and what is their purpose and status?
- How do different IT assets relate to each other and to our business operations?
- What are the capabilities of these assets and are they adequate for our needs?
- Who wields power in our organization to make important planning decisions?
- What are the objectives of our organization and its individual business units?
- What worries, problems and issues keep our business leaders up at night?
- What transformation initiatives are active and what are their architectural plans?

To understand the corporate business and IT environment in sufficient detail and keep up with its constant evolution, enterprise architects have to be persistent in seeking germane information on its various properties. Depending on their specific duties, architects can be interested in different scopes and facets of the organization and its IT landscape, ranging from separate business units with their IT systems to the company as a whole with all its IT estate. For instance, they can focus on local business activities and applications, global strategies and enterprise systems, organization-wide hardware infrastructure or technology portfolio.

Besides merely studying the current environment, this activity also involves documenting it in those aspects in which it is practical, mostly in the aspect of landscape structure, so that the respective knowledge becomes explicit, readily available to other actors and can be easily spread across the organization. For example, after exploring a little-studied area of the IT landscape, enterprise architects should better document this area to pass the collected information to others and relieve them of the need to repeat the exploration, making the landscape more transparent. Or, when architects detect inaccuracies in the existing documentation, they can update it and correct these inaccuracies to benefit others, and possibly themselves in the future. For these reasons, this activity actually implies *relaying* knowledge in the organization by acquiring it, materializing it and making it widely accessible.

The goals of studying the internal environment by enterprise architects largely correspond to the elements of organization-specific knowledge, especially those that are not static and change over time, e.g. landscape structure, transformation drivers and launched initiatives. Specifically, the purpose of this activity can be summarized into four major goals:

- Comprehend the constitution of the existing business and IT landscape
- Figure out key decision-makers and the rest of the stakeholder context
- Understand business strategy and the full motivational context (see Figure 1.3)
- Understand current initiatives and the entire architectural context (see Figure 9.7)

By persistently studying the internal environment, enterprise architects gain awareness of the organizational motives and aspirations, capabilities and constraints. A solid understanding of the corporate business and technology landscape in its full complexity ensuing from these efforts facilitates pragmatic, down-to-earth thinking. It helps architects realize what their company can and cannot do, as well as what changes in the company can and cannot be accomplished easily with the available resources. The greater the depth of understanding, the more effective architectural decisions they can promote.

Context of Fulfillment

Similarly to analyzing the external environment, studying the internal environment is conducted as one of the primary activities in the organizational context and as a supporting activity in the initiative context (see Figure 10.2). In the organizational context, for enterprise architects, studying the internal environment represents a continuous activity, which, however, peaks in its intensity at the beginning of their employment in the organization, or their tenure in the role, and then gradually declines down to a certain residual level[12].

Cursory studies of the internal environment are performed by enterprise architects for gaining general awareness of their organization and the settings in which architectural planning is about to take place. These studies are usually rather high-level and cover only core business capabilities and IT systems, mainstream information flows, key constituents of the technology portfolio, senior decision-makers, top-tier strategic goals and major transformations that the organization undergoes, resulting in a basic comprehension of the overall organizational context. Accomplishing basic, general-purpose studies of the internal environment, at least to a certain extent, is a must for all newly hired architects who have just joined the company in order to understand what is going on inside. Often, these studies for newcomers are organized in the form of walkthroughs included in standard introductory procedures for architects, when their colleagues familiarize them with the structure of the organization and the existing IT landscape, introduce them to principal managers and explain to them other important contextual factors.

After the initial strenuous efforts to grasp the internal environment, the intensity of this activity for enterprise architects significantly decreases, but not to zero. As organizations constantly evolve, architects never stop studying them to keep up with the ongoing changes that happen, for example, in their leadership teams and departmental structures, business activities and IT landscapes, future intentions and architectural plans. However, due to their broad scope and focus on the situation as a whole, general studies do not provide architects with a detailed knowledge of specific organizational areas necessary for handling concrete transformation initiatives.

In the initiative context, studies of the internal environment are initiated by enterprise architects reactively on an as-necessary basis, for instance, when a particular fragment of the business and IT landscape needs to be modified, or might need to be modified, by a change initiative. Analogously to the initiative-centric analysis of the external environment, these studies are most often carried out by architects in accompaniment to architectural planning within the planning phase of the initiative implementation process, less often during its conception phase.

Initiative-specific studies of the internal environment tend to be rather thorough and purport to inspect relatively small segments of the organization and its IT infrastructure at a granular level. They go deep and concentrate on concrete details relevant to the task at hand, e.g. separate steps of business processes and the underlying IT components that will be affected. Detailed studies are necessary for acquiring a sufficient understanding of the internals of the current landscape and of the intricacies of the architectural context to be able to conceive and introduce proper changes in the proper way. Normally, enterprise architects perform both general and initiative-specific studies of the internal environment at different periods.

Means of Fulfillment

Like analyzing the external environment, studying the internal environment also requires collecting and processing considerable volumes of information. However, the means of studying this environment are very different from those that can be used for external environmental analysis. These means include, but are not limited to, the following approaches:

- Communicating with architects — eliciting any required information from other architects working in the organization, preferably for a long period of time, and responsible for planning the relevant parts of the landscape
- Speaking with decision-makers — asking senior managers of different organizational areas about their business activities, pain points, immediate priorities, mid-term objectives and long-range visions for the future
- Talking with specialists — finding and questioning subject-matter experts or asset owners from the business and IT sides, e.g. process owners of business processes, business users of IT systems or operations teams supporting these systems
- Analyzing extant documentation — studying available documents, including various EA artifacts, describing the environment from the necessary viewpoints and angles, e.g. organization charts, strategy papers and IT landscape models
- Searching corporate datastores — looking for pertinent information in enterprise portals, web-based corporate wikis, file storages, content management databases and other knowledge management systems
- Examining specialized systems — navigating existing tool-based EA repositories, configuration management databases (CMDBs), project-, license- and asset-tracking systems and extracting information in convenient formats
- Using discovery tools — scanning the IT landscape with automated software tools for asset discovery and monitoring, especially in the realms of IT infrastructure and cloud-sourced business applications, e.g. Zabbix, Zluri and Hava
- Observing the surroundings — watching what is going on in the organization, "sensing" its internal environment, noticing who advocates what interests, expresses what concerns and makes what decisions

All these means can be employed by enterprise architects for studying different elements of the internal environment[13]. As this environment seldom has any "definitive" sources of reliable facts, relevant information about it often needs to be aggregated piece by piece from several disparate but complementary sources, such as people, documents and systems, and collated to reconstruct a complete and consistent picture of the situation[14].

Relevant Enterprise Architecture Artifacts

As listed above, the means of studying the internal environment available to enterprise architects include analyzing the extant documentation of different aspects of this environment. Most of the respective documents are EA artifacts, though some non-architectural business documents can also be valuable as environmental descriptions.

Different goals of the environmental studies pursued by enterprise architects — to understand the current landscape, stakeholder context, motivational context and architectural context — have different connections to EA artifacts. First, the current structure of the business and IT landscape can be, to a large extent, described in EA artifacts. Second, the stakeholder context and associated power arrangements are unlikely to be adequately captured in any artifacts. Third, the motivational context and various transformation drivers can be reflected in EA artifacts, at best, only partly and unreliably. And finally, the architectural context and active digitalization initiatives, ideally, are fully recorded in EA artifacts. In total, of the four major goals of this activity, two — understanding the current landscape and architectural context — can be achieved by architects largely by studying available EA artifacts.

On the one hand, a decent comprehension of the present landscape structure can be gained by studying EA artifacts documenting the existing situation, mostly actualities artifacts concentrating specifically on the current state of the business and IT landscape. Of the six general types of EA artifacts, only most Landscapes and some Standards represent actualities in their temporal orientation and deliberately accumulate precise current-state information (see Figure 7.11). Accordingly, Landscapes and Standards provide major sources of factual knowledge about the organizational landscape, where information on the following subjects can be found:

- Technology portfolio — high-level information on the corporate technology portfolio is captured in Technology Reference Models and more detailed information is contained in Technology Inventories and Technology Roadmaps
- Landscape composition — aggregate information on the composition of the business and IT landscape is reflected in System Portfolio Models and Landscape Maps, more granular technical information can be learned from Asset Inventories and Asset Roadmaps
- Landscape structure — the logical structure of the landscape in terms of connections between its different elements and components is documented in Landscape Diagrams of varying scopes and abstraction levels
- Linkage of business and IT — the overall relationship between business and IT is reflected in System Portfolio Models and Landscape Maps, while more detailed links at the level of specific processes and applications can be found in some forms of Landscape Diagrams

Most Landscapes and Standards describing the corporate landscape as-is can be freely looked up, analyzed and updated by enterprise architects whenever it is necessary. Technically, these EA artifacts can be maintained by architects either as standalone documents created with standard office tools (e.g. MS Visio and Excel), or using EA-specific tools with built-in architectural repositories storing all landscape data (e.g. MEGA HOPEX or Orbus iServer). In the latter case, artifacts can exist only virtually, as generated views or extractions from repositories, and be boosted by the powerful analytical capabilities of the respective tools.

Besides Landscapes and Standards representing the primary sources of knowledge on the current landscape structure, some other EA artifacts intended for different purposes can nevertheless also offer certain valuable information on the subject and, on this basis, be regarded as secondary knowledge sources for enterprise architects. The information for architects contained in these artifacts includes, but is not limited to:

- Business structure — high-level information on the structure of the business and its key activities can be learned from Business Capability Models, Process Maps

and Value Chains, though this information is very abstract, ambiguous and lacks concrete substance
- Data structure — a broad and granular understanding of the data operated by the business can be obtained from Conceptual Data Models and Logical Data Models respectively, though it is not always clear how these idealized models correlate with the actual data stored in databases
- System structure — detailed technical information on the architecture of individual IT systems can be sought in their archived Solution Designs and Preliminary Solution Designs, though these specifications can be outdated, unreliable and require double-checking

Hence, heaps of diverse and helpful information about the current landscape can be extracted by enterprise architects from various EA artifacts, primarily those representing actualities. Each of these artifacts, however, has its own unique viewpoint, features and specifics that determine its possible usage scenarios and limitations in the context of environmental studies. The mapping of EA artifacts to the space of descriptive representations provides a comprehensive summary of the current-state information that can be found by architects in these artifacts with the associated caveats (see Figure 9.1).

On the other hand, an understanding of the architectural context and running transformations can be gained by studying EA artifacts capturing architectural solutions, mostly plans artifacts focusing specifically on the future direction of the business and IT landscape. Of the six general types of EA artifacts, all the types either represent plans in their temporal orientation, or represent actualities but are also capable of reflecting certain planning decisions. Basically, except for some Landscapes embodying pure actualities, all existing EA artifacts form the architectural context of the organization. For this reason, all these artifacts are potentially relevant to enterprise architects for the purposes of comprehending the architectural context, though Outlines and Designs developed for small projects influence this context rather weakly (see Figure 9.7). The mapping of EA artifacts to the space of architectural solutions provides a comprehensive summary of the planning decisions that can be learned by architects from these artifacts, initiative-specific or general (see Figure 9.5). Recording different planning decisions in EA artifacts as part of architectural planning is discussed in great detail later in Chapter 11 (Leading the Development of Plans).

Importantly, when studying the internal environment, enterprise architects not only use the existing EA artifacts, but also update them and even create new ones to capture the results of their studies. For example, if architects find the information in some artifacts to be outdated or incomplete, then they update their descriptions to make them accurate. Or, when they explore undocumented landscape areas, they create new actualities artifacts to document these areas.

On the whole, the practical role of EA artifacts for studying the internal environment, as well as for managing knowledge in organizations, is rather multifaceted and not limited to merely holding information. First, artifacts serve as frameworks for *organizing* knowledge, helping enterprise architects put together and make sense out of multifarious facts on the internal environment. When uncovering new facts about the organization and its IT landscape (e.g. via speaking with asset owners), architects can connect and structure these facts in a meaningful way by updating or creating artifacts. Second, artifacts work as devices for *analyzing* knowledge, helping architects process the available facts on the internal environment. After being formalized in systematic artifacts, these facts become suitable for formal analysis with various quantitative metrics (e.g. landscape size, diversity and complexity) and analytical techniques mentioned earlier. Third, artifacts provide instruments for *preserving* knowledge, helping organizations "memorize" countless facts on their internal environment. Once captured in material artifacts, knowledge is congealed and stored in a durable form that overcomes human forgetfulness, survives personnel rotation and allows its future retrieval. Finally, artifacts represent tools for *sharing* knowledge, helping organizations disseminate the known facts on their internal environment among their members. After being externalized in physical artifacts, knowledge becomes explicit, public and readily accessible to all organizational actors, including architects who leverage it in their environmental studies.

Consequently, producing EA artifacts when studying the internal environment benefits both individual enterprise architects and their organizations. To architects, it helps better understand the situation for their own purposes. To organizations, it creates valuable sources of information diffusing knowledge to other architects studying the environment. For this reason, organizations benefit from establishing and maintaining centralized architectural depositories with various artifacts documenting the existing situation that can be used by all their architects *collectively* for managing knowledge.

Additional Concerns

As opposed to analyzing the external environment, studying the internal environment is an inward-oriented activity that focuses mostly on what is now, rather than what can be. This activity requires enterprise architects to descend from the clouds to the steady ground and face the realities of the existing situation, which is usually far from perfect, but cannot be ignored, neglected or discarded and must be dealt with.

Unlike the external one, the internal environment is pretty constant, stable and tends to change relatively slowly. It is also more concrete, palpable and "objective". Unsurprisingly, studying and understanding this environment is, in some sense, much easier as it does not require special interpretation and critical attitude towards incoming information, e.g. distinguishing waves of hype from genuine trends (see Figure 10.4). However, the internal environment is also more intricate and entangled, especially in matters of landscape structure. Its various business and IT elements constitute a complicated, interwoven network of relationships, where changing any element is likely to affect many other elements. Because of these complexities, modifying the organizational business and IT landscape in a non-trivial way can be extremely problematic.

For this reason, it is critically important for enterprise architects to avoid superficial judgments about the corporate landscape, never underrate its actual complexity and be able to appreciate its structure in its full worth and with sufficient depth. Failure to take into account all the intricacies of business and IT landscapes can routinely lead, for example, to gross underestimations of required efforts for digitalization initiatives, stumbles and delays in their implementation or painful disruptions in business operations, if not spectacular disasters for organizations.

All in all, architects should not think frivolously that changing the current situation is easy as its deceptive oversimplification can ruin an entire transformation effort. Disciplined thinking, as one of the core skills of enterprise architects (see Figure 6.2), stands particularly prominent in this context. It is their mature culture of disciplined thinking that allows architects to see the connections between different entities of the business and IT landscape, grasp its overall composition and achieve the necessary degree of comprehension of its complexity.

Another significant concern related to studying the internal environment is keeping the respective documentation relevant, accurate and up to date. Since obsolete information cannot be trustworthy, actualities EA artifacts quickly lose their value as a source of knowledge on the landscape structure and, eventually, turn into a "wastepaper" unless they are periodically updated to stay current.

For this reason, it is important for enterprise architects to pay attention to all EA artifacts describing the present state of affairs in the organization and ensure their currency. For instance, when new architecturally significant details of the organizational IT environment come to light, architects should create new or update existing actualities artifacts to accurately reflect these details. By doing so, they keep up a comprehensive base of reference materials on the corporate landscape. As these materials are accessible to everyone, the collective efforts of the community of architects to maintain their currency are associated with substantial "economies of scale" and pronounced synergistic effects. In many respects, enterprise architects are the chief owners of the landscape structure and the principal custodians of the corresponding knowledge.

Providing Advisory Services

The third essential activity of enterprise architects is advising regarding technology and its use for the purposes of doing business. Providing advisory services implies consulting other organizational actors on various IT-related questions or otherwise helping them with sound IT expertise and judgment. Whereas organizationally the very occupation of architects can be viewed largely as internal consultancy (see Figure 4.4), this activity embodies consulting in a narrower sense, ranging from brief one-time transactional question–answer interactions with others around concrete issues to continuous long-lasting partnership relations around broader themes. While the two previous activities of architects are idle, purely analytical and mostly invisible to outsiders, the provision of advisory services is an active exercise aimed at assisting others that exposes architects to the surrounding corporate world. Although the sphere of their competence is rather extensive and diversified and they can certainly put forward valuable business ideas, providing advisory services is more associated with enterprise architects wearing the hat of Technology Experts.

Meaning and Goals

The provision of advisory services purports to inform others on different aspects of IT and its connection to the business and, thereby, raise the quality of IT-related decision-making in the organization. It can focus, for example, on the availability of requisite IT capabilities for enabling certain competitive moves, the business functionality of specific classes of information systems and the proper ways of allocating IP addresses and assigning port numbers. The general meaning of the advisory services provided by enterprise architects can be best exemplified by the following and similar questions:

- How can we address a particular business problem, need or desire with IT?
- Is it a good idea to purchase a specific technology, product or cloud application?

- How well does our IT landscape support the intended business course of action?
- How many legacy systems do we have, what is their cost of ownership and what might be the business consequences if we do not migrate to newer systems?
- Which system implementation approaches, methods or patterns are better for us?
- Is a proposed IT solution feasible technically and how much is it likely to cost?
- How risky is the solution from the perspective of operational failures, information security and regulatory compliance?
- Can we easily integrate the IT infrastructure of an acquired company into ours or should we leave it separate?

To market their services as valuable advisors across the organization, enterprise architects have to be very knowledgeable and invariably cultivate their reputation as competent and trustworthy subject-matter experts in complex IT-related issues. Depending on their specialization, architects can be consulted with on various topics, ranging from purely technical questions to technology-related strategic business matters. For instance, they can offer to the rest of the organization their proficiency in digital operating models, industry-specific business applications, big data storage and analytics or cloud hosting infrastructure.

The central goal of providing advisory services by enterprise architects can be formulated as follows: assist individual decision-makers, and indirectly the organization as a whole, in making well-informed, substantiated decisions and choices relevant to IT based on the best available expertise on the subject. Eventually, this activity intends to increase the overall level of IT-savviness in organizational decision-making processes.

By freely providing their advisory services, enterprise architects not only help the organization be more effective, but also elevate their own standing in managerial circles. Interestingly, the "fame" of architects and organizational demand for their consultations form a self-reinforcing mechanism, where their better reputation leads to more consulting engagements which, in turn, allows them to further advertise their expertise and strengthen their reputation as trusted partners in the eyes of other parties. In this way, architects "weave" and extend their communication network with management throughout the organization.

Context of Fulfillment

As one of the basic activities of enterprise architects, providing advisory services is among their primary activities in the organizational context, but represents only a supporting activity in the initiative context (see Figure 10.2). In the organizational context, their advisory services can take two different forms that determine the ways and means of their provisioning: official and unofficial. Official advisory services are stipulated by organizational arrangements constituting an EA practice, while unofficial ones are induced by individual demands for consultations with architects.

Official advisory services are provided by enterprise architects through the existing system of architecture governance bodies established in organizations as part of their EA practices (see Figure 4.3), when these services are required by institutionalized decision procedures. Namely, if architects are included in governance committees by senior management, then they are procedurally obligated to render their advisory services in a formal fashion, by voting, vetoing or simply raising their objections at various governance meetings where some or the other significant decisions are presented, debated and then authorized or rejected. In these meetings, the votes of architects for or against particular decisions, along with the votes of other committee members, have legitimate decision-making power.

For example, organizational governance mechanisms often oblige to endorse an acquisition of every new technology at a formal governance meeting. In this case, as acknowledged experts whose knowledge is highly relevant to the subject, enterprise architects may preside in the respective meetings and participate in technology approval procedures with their voices, which are counted towards ultimate acquisition decisions, turning them into actual decision-makers. Or, governance arrangements can officially assign them to inspect and certify all architectural plans developed by others falling within the area of their mastery (e.g. integration or security) to verify their technical rationality through peer review. In this way, with their official advisory services, architects contribute their deep IT expertise to the organizational decision-making machine, improving its overall quality.

By contrast, **unofficial advisory services** are normally delivered by enterprise architects on request, via informal personal communication with their recipients, whenever these services are needed and solicited by some business or IT "customers". The circle of potential consumers who may benefit from their competent advice, consultation or mentorship is very wide and ranges from project teams and their members to senior business leaders and IT executives. As advisors, architects get contacted for help and called to resolve specific issues by those who require their expertise. When acting in this fashion, they behave literally as traditional management consultants invited for short-term engagements around difficult problems, situations or choices.

Generally, unofficial advisory services can be offered by enterprise architects in virtually all imaginable circumstances where sound IT-related judgment might be found desirable. For example, their presence and expert view can be sought after during strategic planning, investment prioritization and budgeting sessions, task force and problem-solving meetings, business and technical workshops, due diligence procedures and negotiations of procurement contracts with external vendors. In all these situations, architects apply their unique knowledge of IT to ensure the adequacy of resulting decisions. However, because of the unofficial character of these consultations, their advice has no real power and always remains in the status of a personal opinion or "friendly" recommendation that can be ignored by decision-makers.

Due to an infinite variety of possible scenarios of when, how and why the unofficial advisory services of enterprise architects can be provided in the organizational context, their content, meaning and purpose can be largely arbitrary and ad hoc. Nonetheless, several typical consulting scenarios can be loosely distinguished:

- Providing information — informing customers on particular issues (e.g. the structure, composition and capabilities of the current IT landscape), answering their questions and clarifying uncertainties
- Assessing feasibility — evaluating specific business ideas, proposals and plans for their practicability or viability from the standpoint of IT, identifying likely problems on the way to their realization and their workarounds
- Listing options — generating possible options for addressing specified business needs with IT, analyzing their advantages and shortcomings for the organization and recommending the best option

- Making estimations — producing substantiated estimates of concrete pieces of work in terms of their complexity, timelines, costs, resources, risks and future ramifications for the business and IT landscape
- Presenting opportunities — expounding the budding possibilities of leveraging IT for transforming the business, different paths to go forward with technology and their consequences for the organization
- Sharing concerns — expressing doubts and concerns about specific ideas, criticizing them, diagnosing potential risks, explaining what can go wrong during their implementation and illustrating worst-case scenarios
- Coaching juniors — educating ordinary IT specialists in terms of their technical and related knowledge and mentoring less experienced colleagues in terms of their behavioral and practical skills (see Figure 6.3)

Via providing their unofficial advisory services in the organizational context, among other contributions to decision-making, enterprise architects contribute to the ideation of new change initiatives by consulting senior managers as to which transformation drivers can be best tackled with IT and what ideas for digitalization look the most promising to be turned into initiatives (see Figure 4.5). The place of providing official and unofficial advisory services by enterprise architects in the organizational context is shown in Figure 10.5.

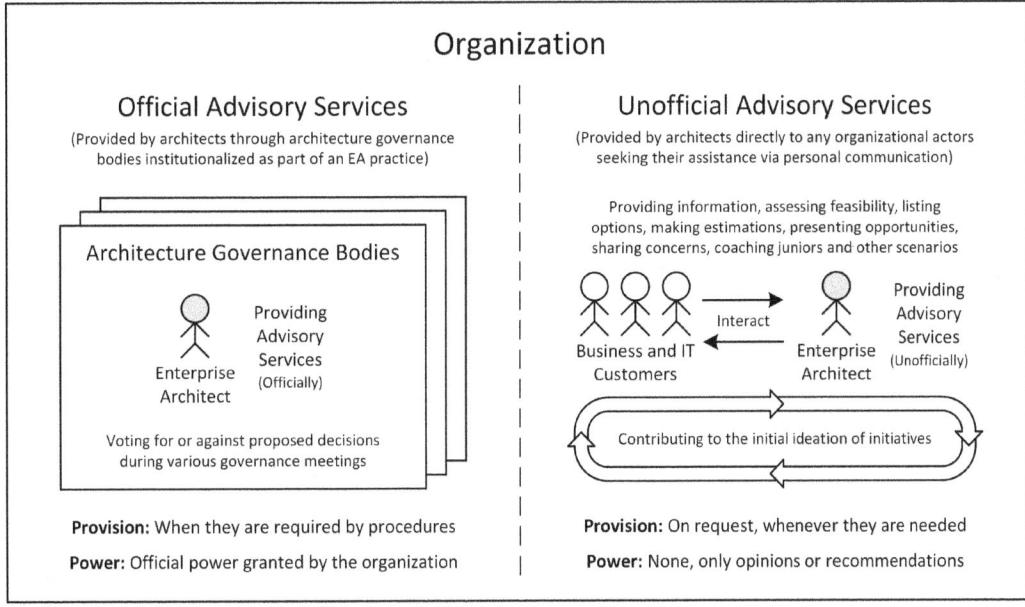

Figure 10.5. Providing advisory services by architects in the organizational context

Because the advisory services of enterprise architects and the forms of their provisioning in the organizational context can be extremely diverse, as demonstrated in Figure 10.5, their place, timing and ways of integration with other organizational processes are nearly impossible to define. Simply put, this activity is very versatile and can happen almost anywhere and anytime.

However, one notable occasion when qualified advisory services are especially important is the formation of new digitalization initiatives.

In the initiative context, unofficial advisory services are actively provided by enterprise architects specifically within the conception phase of the initiative implementation process, when the existing ideas for initiatives are thoroughly examined, evaluated and refined. In these settings, high demand for their advice is generated by initiative sponsors who seek architects' professional opinion on what they are thinking of doing, often at the beginning of the budgeting period, when money is being allocated. To these sponsors, architects offer basically the same "menu" of unofficial advisory services (see Figure 10.5), but the most relevant services in this situation are usually assessing feasibility, listing options and making estimations.

Typically, during the conception phase, prospective sponsors come to architects either with general needs for some IT-related changes, or with more concrete proposals for new initiatives. In the former case, sponsors expect to hear about the possible ways of addressing their needs with technology with their pros and cons, risks and expenses. In the latter case, they expect to receive some feedback from architects on their proposals in terms of their feasibility, potential pitfalls, approximate costs and maybe some alternatives for achieving the same goals by better means.

On the one hand, the primary sponsors of autonomous initiatives are the proponents of some transformation drivers, who discuss with enterprise architects the respective motives that force the organization to change and their ideas on how these motives can be reacted to from the IT side. In other words, their dialog is rooted in the current motivational context with its various drivers. On the other hand, the sponsors of derivative programs and projects are mainly the executors of their parents, who discuss with architects the goals and intentions of their higher-level initiatives and how those can be best achieved via lower-level, more local changes. Because the goals and intentions of parent initiatives are captured in the corresponding EA artifacts, their conversations essentially stem from the architectural context. Generally, coalitions of different actors comprising both driver proponents and parent initiatives' executors can come as initiative sponsors, positioning their ideas in the overarching transformational context and taking into account both its motivational and architectural components (see Figure 9.8).

When assessing the needs and proposals for new initiatives incoming from initiative sponsors, enterprise architects greatly benefit from their awareness of the current IT environment and the architectural context with enacted plans for its future development. This awareness often suggests what kind of initiatives may be appropriate or inappropriate for the organization in light of its existing IT assets and architectural plans. For example, certain functionality that sponsors are asking for may, in fact, be already implemented somewhere in the IT landscape and ready to use. Or, the requested capabilities may actually be included in the plans of one active program to be delivered in several months' time.

Via providing their unofficial advisory services in the initiative context, enterprise architects accomplish architectural pre-planning by confirming the likely existence of acceptable architectural solutions for the respective initiatives (see Figure 4.6). Because conceiving digitalization initiatives necessitates thinking of available technical means for the stated organizational aims, it somewhat resembles rough, tentative architectural planning. Although this process does not produce any material architectural plans, it often results in the fundamental understanding of what, how and why that sets the framework for future architectural solutions and eventually shapes all explicit architectural planning efforts.

In case of the positive evaluation of the prospects of ideas for initiatives on the part of initiative sponsors and architects, these ideas can be elaborated into mature initiative concepts with specific goals and then converted into full-fledged change initiatives. The unofficial advisory services of architects, thus, can lead to the launching of new transformation initiatives. The place of providing advisory services, as one of the activities of enterprise architects, in the context of digital transformation initiatives is illustrated in Figure 10.6.

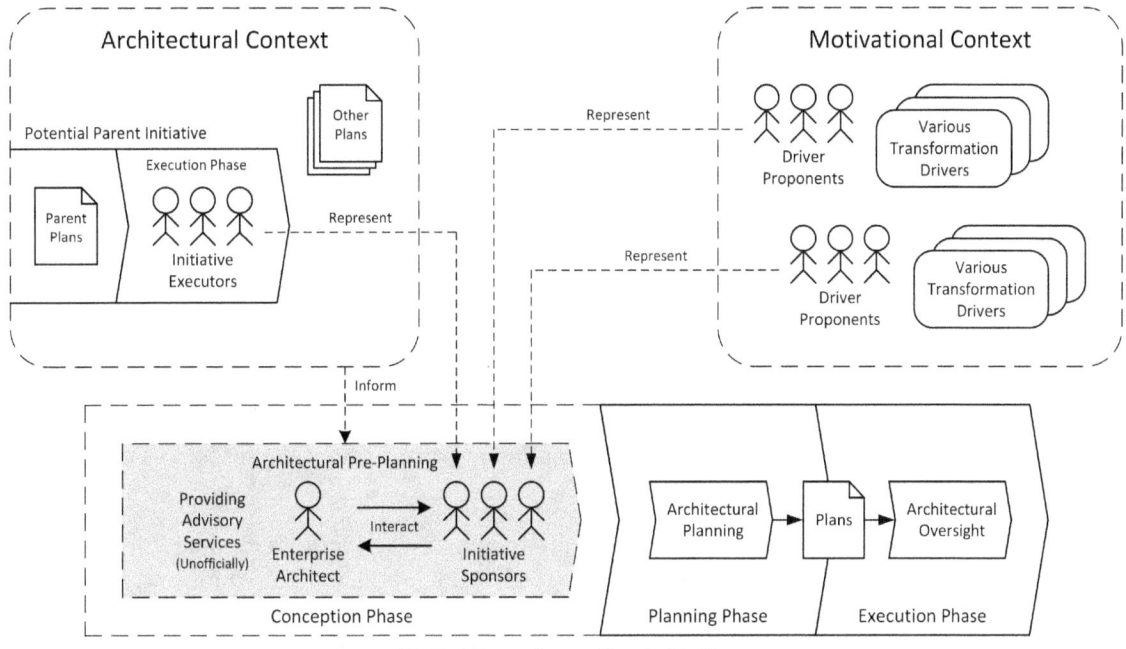

Figure 10.6. Providing advisory services by architects in the initiative context

The provision of unofficial advisory services by enterprise architects during the conception phase of what can then become transformation initiatives is very important for filtering out unpromising ideas for change at their early stages and ensuring that the right initiatives get launched in the right way.

Means of Fulfillment

The means of providing advisory services by enterprise architects depend, first of all, on the form of these services, unofficial or official (see Figure 10.5). As discussed earlier, official advisory services are almost always provisioned by architects in one way: through their membership as subject-matter experts in architecture governance bodies, via participating in their decision-making meetings and voting for decisions.

By contrast, their unofficial advisory services can be delivered in many different ways varying in their duration, richness, formality and degree of involvement. These ways range from brief texting and passing conversations to the preparation of detailed written reports. Specifically, the means of providing unofficial advisory services by architects include, among others, the following approaches:

- Email correspondence — replying to incoming email messages with inquiries from various customers seeking an educated view of enterprise architects on certain issues in textual form
- Phone conversations — answering phone calls with questions from various organizational actors asking for a piece of competent advice from architects in their field of expertise
- Personal meetings — either informal one-on-one talks in the corridor or over a cup of coffee in a nearby cafe, or more formal scheduled appointments in the office or specialized meeting rooms
- Group discussions — participation in group meetings, sessions and forums with multiple parties, where the presence of architects is welcome because of their unique knowledge
- Formal reports — preparing comprehensive written reports addressing a particular subject or analyzing the situation that can be distributed among a wide circle of people for their information and referred to in the future

All these means can be employed by enterprise architects for providing their unofficial advisory and consulting services within the organization. The choice of the most suitable approach depends mostly on the nature, sophistication and criticality of the respective questions.

Relevant Enterprise Architecture Artifacts

As described above, most of the means of providing advisory services are oral and do not imply creating any material products. More often, advisory services are delivered via mere conversations between enterprise architects and their customers. However, during these conversations, architects can choose to use whatever existing EA artifacts they deem necessary to clearly communicate their message to the intended audience.

For example, such EA artifacts as Business Capability Models, Process Maps and Value Chains, as well as their separate fragments, can be very helpful for illustrating the business impact of some or the other choices with color-coding, e.g. anticipated improvements in business capabilities, processes or activities from alternative types of IT solutions. Or, artifacts like System Portfolio Models and Landscape Maps can assist architects in explaining various system-related issues, e.g. what operational risks will ensue from not upgrading or replacing aging IT systems in a timely manner. Besides using regular EA artifacts, architects can opt to create disposable, task-specific diagrams or visualizations to facilitate their conversations with customers, which can be classified as auxiliary communication materials (see Table 7.1).

And yet, some advisory services offered by enterprise architects, mostly unofficial ones, may require preparing formalized written reports that can be regarded as full-fledged auxiliary artifacts, namely as ad hoc papers. Because of the variety of possible situations and contexts in which their advisory services can be provided, the structures, contents and messages of the resulting artifacts can also be very diverse. Unsurprisingly, these artifacts do not have any consistent, commonly accepted titles across the industry. For the sake of example, many of them can be loosely classified into assessment reports and position papers.

On the one hand, **assessment reports** communicate the results of some assessments or evaluations performed by enterprise architects for their customers, often of their proposals for new initiatives during their conception phase (see Figure 10.6), e.g. idea feasibility, business implications, technical difficulties, change impact or implementation cost. These reports tend to describe exactly what is being assessed and then present key conclusions of the conducted assessment in terms of relevant parameters, e.g. dollars, timelines, available routes, required efforts or the magnitude of changes. In their approach and presentation, they can also use some analysis and visualization techniques well suited for the task at hand, e.g. analytical quadrants (see Figure 10.3). Assessment reports are purely informative, analytical and do not put forward any advice or imperatives for action.

On the other hand, **position papers** communicate some affirmative proposals, recommendations or decisions made by enterprise architects for their customers, e.g. choose a specific approach, adopt a particular technology or select one option out of multiple possibilities. They tend to describe the current situation, outline the most desirable way forward for the organization and explain the underlying reasoning. Position papers are more assertive than assessment reports and offer certain suggestions as to what should be done or which solution should be preferred. In short, assessment reports only inform decision-makers, whereas position papers recommend decisions to them.

Both these artifacts typically consist of textual descriptions and simple graphical illustrations organized according to their purposes. As they are developed on demand for concrete customers, their language, terminology and formats can be adapted specifically to the needs of the target audience. The schematic graphical representations of assessment reports and position papers are exhibited in Figure 10.7.

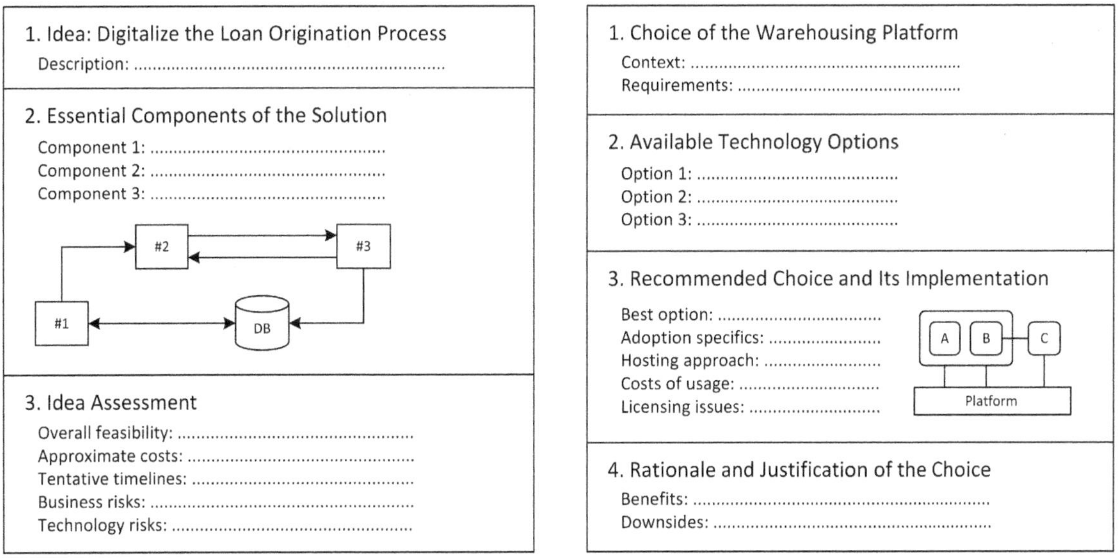

Figure 10.7. Assessment reports and position papers

Assessment reports and position papers presented in Figure 10.7, as well as many other similar auxiliary artifacts, can all be created by enterprise architects as a result of their "consulting engagements" when some formal deliverables are requested by their customers. These artifacts can then be referred to in the future and used to substantiate subsequent decisions and actions.

Additional Concerns

The ability of enterprise architects to offer competent advice to their customers directly depends on the time they invested in the two previous activities — studies of the external and internal environments. It is this very knowledge gained from a deep immersion into these activities that makes architects authoritative advisors, who possess unique expertise missing in everyone else's heads. On the one hand, an intimate understanding of the internal environment with all its intricacies and limitations gives architects a pragmatic, practical outlook on the problem. On the other hand, a broad grasp of the external environment with all its trends and opportunities affords architects to think more holistically and have a wiser view. The sense of a "big picture" allows architects to find the right balance between theoretically desirable and practically achievable outcomes, e.g. propose future-proof solutions that take into account today's realities, demands and resources.

However, in their consulting and advisory services, it is critically important for enterprise architects to "feel" the demands of their customers in terms of the kind, volume, richness and timeliness of information and provide *relevant* advice matching their expectations. In different situations and consulting scenarios, it may mean, for example, avoiding excessive philosophizing and concentrating exclusively on practical matters, enumerating only a few most promising alternatives rather than all imaginable options, presenting a "quick and dirty" analysis instead of a thorough but time-consuming one, or vice versa.

Interestingly, even though enterprise architects generally act as mere consultants to real managers taking decisions (see Figure 4.4), sometimes managers are unable, unwilling or hesitant to make decisions themselves and prefer to rely on the judgment of architects and simply follow their recommendations, essentially delegating to them their decision-making power. For this reason, the expectations of managers regarding the requested advisory services highly depend on their decisiveness. On the one extreme, managers can be very decisive, do not appreciate any suggestions and expect architects only to present them with exhaustive, accurate and value-neutral analytical data to inform their decision-making, e.g. expound possibilities without expressing any opinions, as in assessment reports. On the opposite extreme, managers can be very indecisive, do not seek any factual information and expect architects only to present them with concrete recommendations that can be accepted and acted upon immediately, e.g. propose a specific way forward deemed optimal, as in position papers (see Figure 10.7)[15]. These contrasting extremes represent two different modes of working for architects providing advisory services, though they are certainly not incompatible as their consultations usually combine both descriptive and prescriptive features.

Realizing the expectations of the target audience and picking the right posture is necessary for architects to attain a high degree of satisfaction among their customers with the received advice. The spectrum of possible modes of providing advisory services by enterprise architects depending on the decisiveness of managers is shown in Figure 10.8.

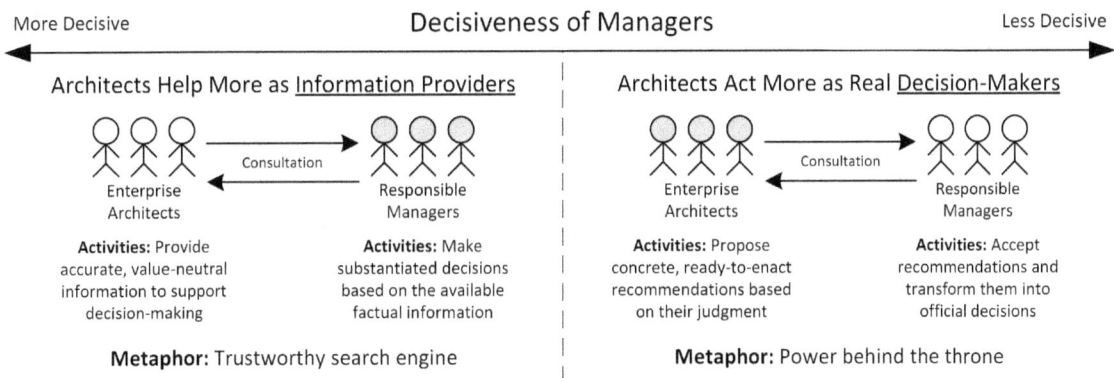

Figure 10.8. Two modes of providing advisory services by enterprise architects

Knowledge, as one of the resources of enterprise architects, definitely represents the key enabler of the provision of high-quality advisory services around various IT-related questions. It is extensive technical (but not only) knowledge that turns architects into competent and sought-after consultants on a wide range of issues. Without the appropriate knowledge horizon, no advisory services can be offered. Moreover, to infuse the organization with novelty and propel its digital transformation, architects' advice has to disseminate pioneering thoughts and ideas about using IT within the management community. For this reason, an innovative mindset, as one of the characteristic traits of enterprise architects (see Figure 6.2), is also particularly important for providing valuable advisory services.

Chapter Summary

This chapter introduced the two different contexts of activities of enterprise architects, described their five high-level activities, explained their relationship to the organizational and initiative contexts and then discussed in great detail the three basic activities: analyzing the external environment, studying the internal environment and providing advisory services. The core message of this chapter can be summarized in the following major points:

- Enterprise architects operate in the organizational context, where all relevant elements of the organization are taken into account, and in the initiative context, where only elements related to specific change initiatives are taken into account
- Enterprise architects perform five activities: analyzing the external environment, studying the internal environment, providing advisory services (the three basic activities), leading the development of plans and ensuring adherence to plans
- The three basic activities are primary in the organizational context but supporting in the initiative context, whereas leading the development of plans and ensuring adherence to plans are performed only in the initiative context as primary
- Analyzing the external environment implies collecting new information about the outer technology and market environment by means of browsing the Internet, reading the literature and talking with people, possibly using some auxiliary artifacts, such as technology radars and analytical quadrants

- Studying the internal environment implies accumulating information on the inner business and IT environment by means of speaking with people, searching repositories and analyzing existing documentation, including various EA artifacts
- Providing advisory services implies consulting others on various IT-related questions by means of emails, phone calls, personal and group meetings, possibly producing some auxiliary artifacts, such as assessment reports and position papers
- Official advisory services are provided by enterprise architects through their membership in architecture governance bodies when these services are required by institutionalized decision-making procedures
- Unofficial advisory services are provided by enterprise architects through their informal personal communication with their recipients whenever these services are requested by any organizational actors

Chapter 11: Leading the Development of Plans

The previous chapter introduced the five activities performed by enterprise architects and thoroughly discussed their three basic activities. This chapter continues the discussion of the activities of enterprise architects and describes in great detail leading the development of plans as their central activity. In particular, this chapter begins with explaining the specifics of leading the development of plans as a distinct activity of enterprise architects. Then, this chapter describes the meaning of leading the development of plans, the primary goals of this activity, the context and means of its fulfillment. Finally, this chapter discusses various regular and auxiliary EA artifacts relevant to leading the development of plans, including artifact templates, presentation packs and decision papers, as well as additional concerns related to this activity.

Leading the Development of Plans as a Distinct Activity

The principal duty of enterprise architects in organizations is leading architectural planning (see Figure 4.1), where they participate as the key actors of the respective processes. Accordingly, the fourth essential activity of architects, and arguably the most prominent of all their activities, is driving the planning of future courses of action in terms of the relationship and synergy of business and IT. Leading the development of plans implies organizing, orchestrating and facilitating the cooperative processes of architectural planning, i.e. the processes of producing optimal architectural solutions and plans for digital transformation initiatives. From an organizational point of view, this activity of architects is identical to leading architectural planning (see Figure 4.7)[1].

As discussed earlier, architectural planning is a complex and multifaceted organizational undertaking that includes multiple actors, activities and documents, and results in architectural solutions and plans for digital transformation initiatives (see Figure 3.1). In this context, leading the development of plans is a concrete activity of enterprise architects that aims to coordinate and steer the collaborative exercise of architectural planning that, besides architects themselves, also involves many other organizational actors — various stakeholders of the corresponding initiatives (see Figure 3.2) — who communicate with each other to discuss planning decisions. For this reason, any actions of architects as individuals *cannot* be equated with architectural planning as a group effort.

Conceptually, this activity constitutes enterprise architects' separate "slice" of a larger architectural planning "pie", or their personal contribution to architectural planning in the form of their actions related specifically to putting together optimal architectural plans. In short, architectural planning is what organizations do, while leading the development of plans is what individual architects do as part of architectural planning.

Of all five activities of enterprise architects, only leading the development of plans constitutes architectural planning and, in fact, represents its pivotal element that integrates all the other elements into a coherent collective action. Metaphorically, the three basic activities of architects (see Figure 10.2), and especially providing advisory services for initiative ideation and conception (see Figure 10.5 and Figure 10.6 respectively), can be viewed as a "prequel" to leading the development of plans, whereas ensuring adherence to plans described in the next chapter — as a "sequel" to it. The relationship between the activities of enterprise architects, leading the development of plans as their core activity and architectural planning as an organizational activity is illustrated in Figure 11.1.

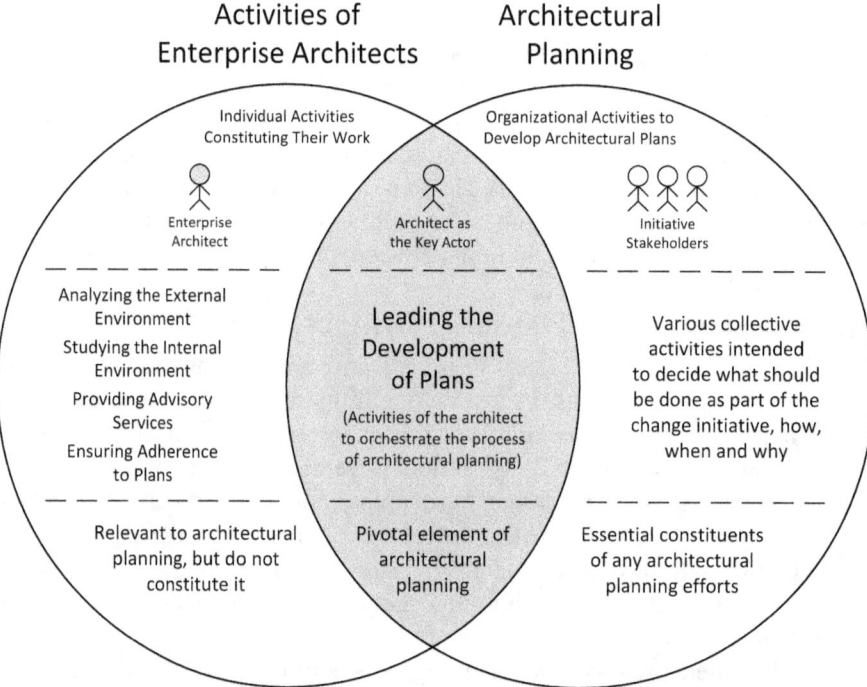

Figure 11.1. Leading the development of plans, other activities and architectural planning

Leading the development of plans is the central activity of enterprise architects and, at the same time, also the most sophisticated of all their activities. While their studies of the external and internal environments are passive and inconspicuous activities that let them stay behind the scenes, this activity puts architects right on the stage, in the "limelight", as the main characters of the digitalization performance. Whereas the provision of advisory services is largely a reactive activity that implies predominantly responding to incoming requests, leading the development of plans is more proactive and requires taking initiative from architects themselves. Unlike the three basic activities performed by architects alone or with only minimal involvement of others as informants or customers, the development of architectural plans for transformation initiatives requires truly *collective* decision-making and, thus, necessitates establishing certain engagement processes, finding effective communication approaches and choosing appropriate language.

In order to lead the development of plans, enterprise architects must wear the hats of Technology Experts and Change Agents to be capable of working on the technical and organizational sides of architectural planning respectively (see Figure 4.9). Furthermore, both hats must be put on *together* as any single conversation with initiative stakeholders may require demonstrating engineering and political abilities on the part of an architect simultaneously. As noted earlier, it is this distinctive combination of competencies and skills that makes architects who they are — special personalities standing out from mere techies and change activists (see Figure 4.10).

Meaning and Goals

Leadership over the development of plans intends to facilitate the production of rational architectural plans reflecting joint future directions for business and IT under the rubric of digital transformation. These plans can address, for example, an overarching enterprise-wide stance towards IT, strategic IT-enabled improvements of business capabilities, reuse of available IT assets and technologies in future solutions, more detailed priorities for prospective IT investments and high-level structures of separate information systems. The general meaning of the development of architectural plans led by enterprise architects can be best illustrated by the following and similar questions:

- What fundamental imperatives should guide our digitalization aspirations?
- What is our desired future in terms of the relationship between business and IT?
- Which of our business activities should be digitalized and to what extent?
- What change projects should be initiated by our organization and when?
- What logical components should a specific IT solution consist of?
- How exactly should a new application be structured and constructed?
- What technologies should be used for creating IT systems in our company?
- Which of our existing IT assets should be leveraged in the future or removed?

To be regarded as masters of architectural planning, enterprise architects have to demonstrate their enthusiasm and eagerness to spearhead organizational transformations. Depending on their profile, architects can be assigned to a variety of initiatives, ranging from those related directly to the IT enablement of business operations to purely infrastructural ones largely invisible to the business. For instance, they can lead the development of plans dealing with frontend mobile applications, backend ERP platforms, enterprise data warehouses or corporate private clouds.

The primary goal of leading the development of plans by enterprise architects can be formulated as follows: produce optimal architectural plans for transformation efforts that satisfy the interests and concerns of all their stakeholders (see Figure 3.2). Importantly, as discussed earlier, the optimality of the resulting plans in organizational settings cannot be evaluated by any objective measures and, except for the cases of sheer inadequacy, is determined subjectively — solely by the extent to which their stakeholders consider them to be optimal.

By proactively leading the development of plans, enterprise architects achieve convergence of the opinions of various business and IT representatives as to what needs to be done in the organization and how. A consensus view of what should be accomplished, in turn, enables resolute collective action towards the desired destination.

Context of Fulfillment

Unlike the three basic activities of enterprise architects that can be performed in both the organizational and initiative contexts, leading the development of plans exists only in the initiative context and makes no sense outside of specific digital transformation initiatives (see Figure 10.2). As a sub-activity of organizational architectural planning (see Figure 11.1), this activity always takes place within the planning phase of the initiative implementation process. As discussed earlier, change initiatives can be conceived and sponsored by any parties capable of generating fruitful ideas for improvement and pushing these ideas for serious consideration, normally after consulting informally with architects (see Figure 10.6). Once initiatives are launched, whether autonomous or derivative ones, if their sponsors invite them as planners, architects start leading the development of their architectural plans by organizing discussions with and among all their stakeholders, where numerous planning decisions are formulated.

Because transformation initiatives "grow" in the overall organizational environment, their architectural decisions cannot be made in isolation from it and are always shaped by the broader architectural context composed of the entirety of all initiatives running in the organization and their plans reflected in EA artifacts (see Figure 9.7). As derivative programs and projects originate straight from higher-level parent initiatives, their planning decisions are strongly guided, or even determined, by the architectural plans of their parents (see Figure 3.7 and Figure 9.3). Planning decisions for every initiative may also be affected by earlier decisions pertaining to other initiatives through the mechanism of cross-initiative influence enabled mainly by general plans EA artifacts (see Figure 9.4).

Besides that, all architectural plans and artifacts produced for new initiatives, in turn, *join* the common architectural context. Hence, when leading the development of plans, architects constantly interact with the architectural context by taking some EA artifacts out of it and putting other artifacts into it. The place of leading the development of plans, as the core activity of enterprise architects, in the context of digital transformation initiatives is illustrated in Figure 11.2.

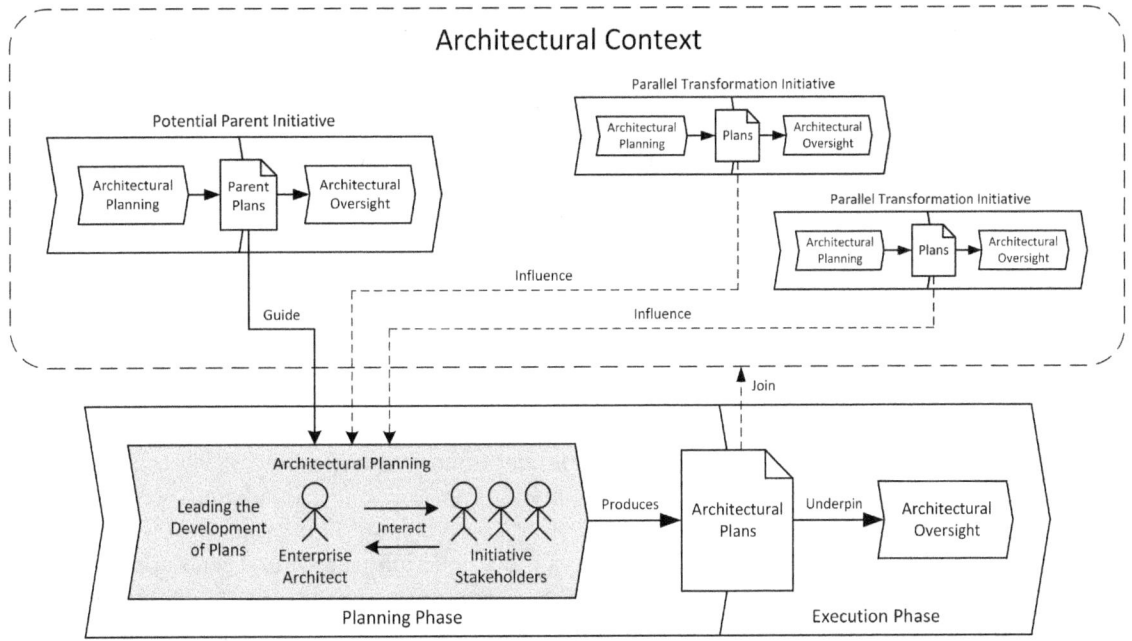

Figure 11.2. Leading the development of plans by architects in the initiative context

As shown in Figure 11.2, leading the development of plans tends to occur within the rich architectural context, under direct "vertical" guidance of parent initiatives (if any) as well as unintended "horizontal" influence of parallel initiatives. For this reason, an adequate comprehension of the full architectural context of the organization is crucial for enterprise architects and represents one of the major goals of studying the internal environment, as discussed earlier.

Means of Fulfillment

Leading the development of plans for digital transformation initiatives requires both technical means of organizing productive communication with initiative stakeholders and logical means of channeling this communication in the right direction, towards the completion of architectural plans. Accordingly, in terms of the means of its fulfillment, this activity relies technically on various planning meetings and logically on a coherent planning process.

Planning Meetings as Technical Means

Technically, enterprise architects lead the development of plans for digitalization initiatives by organizing their architectural planning with the involvement of pertinent stakeholders and orchestrating cooperative planning efforts. As they practice "planning by talking", architects perform this activity by appointing and visiting series of meetings with initiative stakeholders where different conversations take place and different decisions get made. These meetings can happen either in person or, less preferably, over electronic media, e.g. Zoom, MS Teams or

Google Meet[2]. They can also be very diverse in their format, length and intent and range from spontaneous one-on-one meetings to organized planning sessions.

On the one hand, **one-on-one meetings** are informal, personal meetings of enterprise architects with individual initiative stakeholders, or small groups of stakeholders from one area. These meetings imply open, free-flowing conversation between their participants, do not require any presentable materials and often take the form of brief periodic catchups. They can occur largely arbitrarily, at any convenient place in an ad hoc fashion as they are needed, even without a preliminary appointment. For example, an architect can invite a business manager for a coffee, come to the manager's desk, book a separate meeting room or call for a talk remotely. One-on-one meetings are intended mostly to garner some information, clarify specific questions, discuss certain ideas or merely exchange news and opinions, rather than to make any planning decisions, let alone final decisions.

On the other hand, **planning sessions** are structured, formal meetings between enterprise architects and large groups of initiative stakeholders, often involving the full stakeholder circle that may comprise up to tens of people. These meetings are scheduled in advance, tend to have a specific agenda and, in most cases, imply presenting some prepared materials for their collective discussion. Usually, they are held in specially equipped meeting rooms, or even halls, with large screens, projectors and other presentation devices, sometimes via videoconferencing. Planning sessions are those meetings where various planning decisions relevant to architectural solutions for transformation initiatives are debated, made and approved for further action. To achieve better decision traceability, these meetings can be minuted or recorded for future reference. Although all of them embody some forms of organizational decision-making, their formality, intensity, duration, stakeholder representation and purpose can vary greatly. For this reason, planning sessions can hardly be classified strictly into different clear-cut categories, but their loose classification may include, for example, the following types of meetings:

- Discussions — group meetings with a wide presence of stakeholders where significant planning decisions are put forward for consideration, discussed, dismissed or agreed upon
- Workshops — lengthy and intensive working sessions with joint stakeholder participation dedicated to addressing a particular issue or completing a concrete task that requires the maximum concentration of attention and effort
- Presentations — meetings with the broad stakeholder audience where some formalized architectural plans are demonstrated by architects for their discussion, evaluation and feedback collection
- Approvals — assemblies with the full stakeholder audience where finalized architectural plans are presented by architects for their ultimate approval and endorsement

Both one-on-one meetings and group planning sessions are necessary for creating concerted architectural plans for digital transformational initiatives. When leading the development of plans, enterprise architects actively organize, conduct and attend all these types of meetings. However, the choice of appropriate communication approaches wholly depends on the stage of the planning process, questions that need to be talked over and desired stakeholder involvement.

The main differences between one-on-one meetings and planning sessions described above are summarized in Table 11.1.

Meetings	One-on-one meetings	Planning sessions
Formality	Unstructured, mostly informal	Structured, formal to very formal
Participants	Individual stakeholders or small groups	Large groups of stakeholders
Schedule	Ad hoc, as needed, often without appointment	Always scheduled in advance
Venue	Any place convenient for participants	Meeting rooms with presentation equipment
Agenda	May not have any specific agenda	Concrete agenda items to be addressed
Materials	Do not require any presentable materials	Imply some prepared materials for discussion
Activities	Gathering information, clarifying specific questions, discussing certain ideas or merely exchanging news and opinions	Debating and approving for action various planning decisions relevant to architectural solutions for transformation initiatives
Recording	Not officially recorded or even registered	Can be minuted or recorded for reference

Table 11.1. One-on-one meetings and planning sessions

In addition to scheduling and attending countless meetings and planning sessions with initiative stakeholders, leading the development of plans also implies doing some "homework" on the part of enterprise architects to prepare the necessary materials to be demonstrated and discussed during these meetings, e.g. topical EA artifacts, presentation packs or decision papers discussed later in this chapter. Even though the development of architectural plans is fundamentally a collective endeavor that cannot be accomplished by architects on their own, it still requires a certain amount of solitary work on their side.

Planning Process as Logical Means

Logically, enterprise architects lead the development of plans for digital transformation initiatives by gradually arriving at the point of mutual agreement between all initiative stakeholders as to what their architectural solutions should be. As mentioned earlier, the very process of architectural planning can be conceptualized as three sequential high-level steps: discussion, elaboration and approval (see Figure 4.7)[3]. All these steps are arranged by architects via guiding and coordinating the actions of their participants. Each step includes somewhat different activities on the part of architects, requires different types of meetings with stakeholders and produces different kinds of material deliverables, though the boundaries between them can be rather blurred.

The initial **discussion step** of developing architectural plans begins with the identification of relevant stakeholders and ends with a basic understanding of what needs to be done. First of all, enterprise architects figure out who should be involved in the planning process and whose interests should be taken into account (see Figure 2.3). While initiative sponsors are usually well known to architects upfront, other stakeholders who might be affected by the forthcoming transformation or contribute to its execution have yet to be identified.

Most, but not all, planning exercises require the participation of some representatives from both the business and IT sides of the organization. As discussed earlier, business leaders and specialists, as their key patrons and beneficiaries, represent primary stakeholders for the vast majority of digitalization initiatives (see Figure 3.2). Because even seasoned architects, being accomplished Technology Experts, cannot be perfectly aware of all the "nooks and crannies" of the broad and rapidly evolving IT domain, the involvement of some IT specialists as secondary stakeholders can also be necessary, at least as consultants, e.g. subject-matter experts in specific areas or project teams as future system implementers.

After the full stakeholder circle is identified, enterprise architects approach each party and invite them to dialog around the initiative. Then, architects build rapport and establish trustful relationships with these stakeholders to lay the foundation for constructive collaboration. Finally, architects communicate with each party to clarify the goals that they pursue, collect their requirements, understand their views, probe their ideas and shape an approximate vision of what outcome is anticipated.

In the discussion step, communication between enterprise architects and initiative stakeholders is rather informal, relies predominantly on one-on-one meetings, where information is shared but no planning decisions are articulated, and consists largely of verbal conversations (see Table 11.1). For this reason, this step generates little or no material artifacts, possibly some memo notes scribbled by architects and whiteboard drawings sketched during their talks with the stakeholders.

The central **elaboration step** of developing architectural plans represents the peak of planning activities where most actual planning decisions get made. It starts with the proposal of incipient material plans for the initiative execution, often in the form of highly informal "straw-man architecture", and finishes as these plans mature and solidify, turning into more formalized documents. This step requires active efforts on both the technical and organizational sides of architectural planning and implies developing both technical and organizational solutions for the transformation initiative (see Figure 3.3).

Structurally, the elaboration step can be viewed largely as an iterative cycle of proposals and their discussions. First, enterprise architects in the hat of Technology Experts, based on the requirements gathered during the previous step, possibly in consultation with other IT specialists, design an initial technical solution for the initiative (e.g. depict how the necessary systems can be implemented) and present it in general terms to other initiative stakeholders for their consideration[4]. Then, the corresponding organizational solution is debated among the stakeholders to decide whether the solution with given properties is desirable for the organization (e.g. whether it provides the right business capabilities and brings sufficient value for its price) and, if not, how it should be modified. In these discussions, architects, now donning the hat of Change Agents, serve as their conductors and moderators by trying to arrange productive dialog between all the parties, settle the disagreements between different viewpoints and negotiate possible trade-offs between various properties of the solution. Moreover, as legitimate representatives of the IT department, they also act as valid initiative stakeholders advocating technical interests in any negotiations, as discussed later in Chapter 13 (The Work of Enterprise Architects).

As a result, a better understanding of what solution is actually needed emerges within the community of stakeholders and the next iteration of the proposal–discussion cycle described above gets launched with a new technical solution designed by architects and presented for consideration[5]. This cycle stops only when the proposed engineering solution is also found acceptable politically by all constituencies[6]. In other words, this step finishes when technical and organizational solutions for the transformation initiative converge into the whole architectural solution, which is both feasible technically *and* desirable organizationally.

For example, during the preliminary discussion step, an enterprise architect ascertained that the paramount goal of the initiative formulated by its senior business sponsors is to digitalize interactions with customers and composed a brief set of requirements for the envisioned solution. Then, to reach the stated goal, the architect proposes to install a powerful CRM platform with components A, B and C meeting all the initial requirements. The business leaders are impressed with the functional capabilities of the presented solution, but many of them, including the CFO, consider it too expensive and ask the architect whether its price tag can be reduced. In response, the architect redesigns the solution based on components B, C and D to be more affordable. The business leaders, in turn, find the cost of the new solution acceptable, but the head of customer experience now raises an objection that its functional capabilities poorly align with what the organization really needs and asks the architect to refocus the solution to provide capabilities X and Y. However, the architect explains that the demanded capabilities X and Y are not only infeasible, but also contradict some higher-order architectural plans existing in the company, and redesigns the CRM solution once again based on components B, D and E to offer alternative, somewhat different capabilities instead. Now, all the business leaders are generally happy with the proposed solution, except for the compliance officer, who voices the concern that the solution seems to violate corporate data protection policies and wants to veto it. The architect, in reply, assures the audience that this concern can be addressed with proper security measures, making the solution fully compliant. After the last doubts are dispelled, all the initiative stakeholders unanimously agree that this solution is worth to be implemented[7].

As this simple scenario demonstrates, as part of the elaboration step, enterprise architects have to act as both proficient engineers capable of designing the requested solutions and politically savvy negotiators capable of "selling" these solutions to their stakeholders. The exemplary scenario of the elaboration step of the architectural planning process described above is illustrated in Figure 11.3.

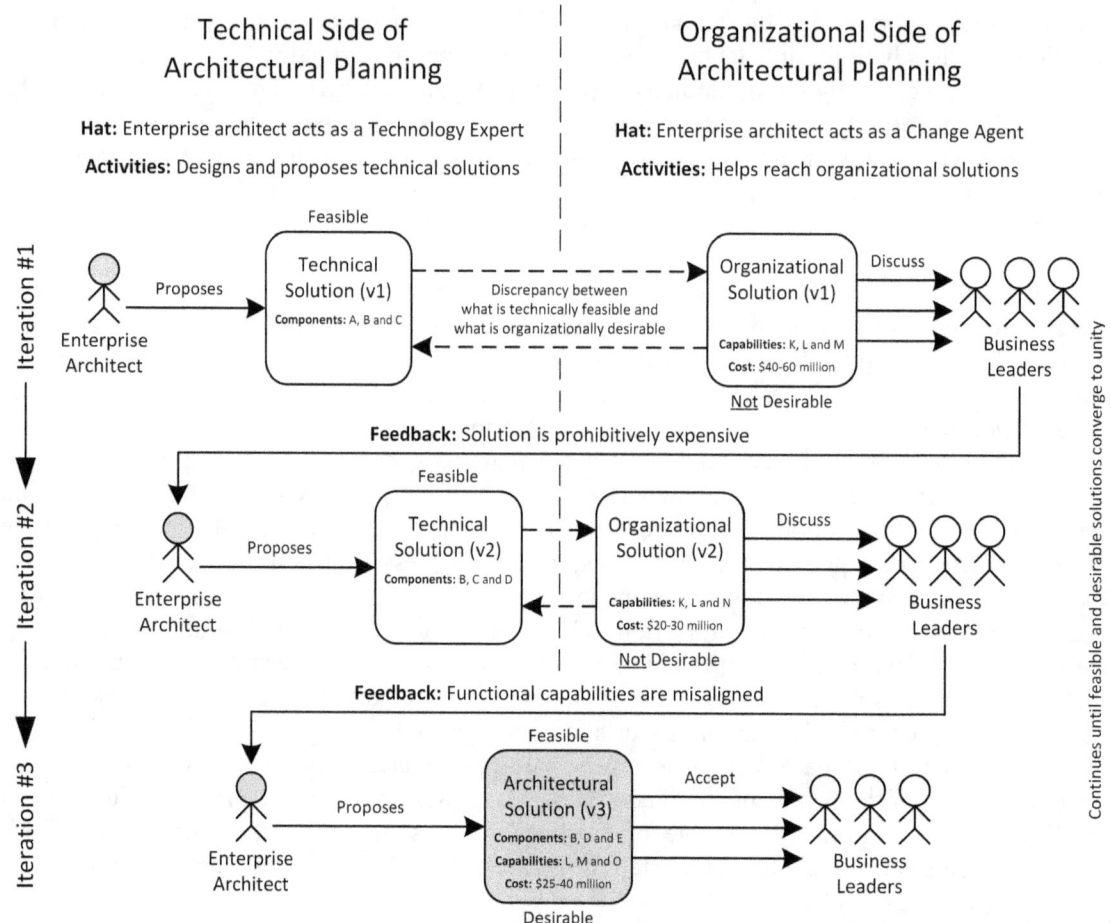

Figure 11.3. An illustrative example of the elaboration step of the planning process

Conceptually, the elaboration step of the planning process can be interpreted as a dialectical refinement of technical and organizational solutions until their convergence to unity. The role of enterprise architects in this step necessitates alternating the hats of Technology Experts and Change Agents to handle the complex interplay of engineering and political activities. Exactly the same logic of dialectical refinement inherent to the elaboration step of the planning process applies to all types of digitalization initiatives, only the level of involved stakeholders and the abstractness of architectural solutions vary (see Figure 3.6).

Because the elaboration step requires an intense *bidirectional* exchange of information between enterprise architects and initiative stakeholders, it includes all forms of individual and group communication — informal one-on-one meetings and formal planning sessions (see Table 11.1), where all conversations similar to those exemplified in Figure 11.3 take place. As output, this step produces semi-completed drafts of EA artifacts that document all the fundamental decisions constituting architectural solutions for transformation initiatives that are not expected to change further in the process.

The concluding **approval step** of developing architectural plans begins with completing the developed architectural plans and ends with issuing an officially sanctioned direction for future actions. First, enterprise architects and stakeholders collectively finalize the plans for the transformation initiative created in the previous step. Although by this moment all the principal planning decisions have already been made, some minor disagreements and details might need to be resolved and clarified. Thereby, the ultimate convergence on the desired future course of action is achieved.

Next, the resulting architectural plans are formally approved by all relevant parties at different organizational levels. First of all, these plans are endorsed by their immediate stakeholders who took part in their development, most importantly, by initiative sponsors. Then, the architectural plans are also likely to require the approvals of some higher-level supervisory authorities. For instance, from the business side, they may need to be approved by senior business leadership for their overall expediency and alignment with business strategy, goals and drivers. Depending on their significance for the organization as a whole, these plans can also be escalated straight to the top-level decision-makers, such as the CEO, executive committee or even the board of directors, for their notification and authorization. From an architectural point of view, the resulting plans are normally reviewed and approved by one or more specialized architecture governance bodies (e.g. technology committees and design committees discussed in the next chapter) that ensure their general adequacy and alignment with higher-order architectural plans, possibly those of the parent initiative. All these stages of approval may include more or less formalized sign-off procedures.

Unlike the two previous steps, the approval step relies, for the most part, on formal communication between enterprise architects and initiative stakeholders within structured planning sessions (see Table 11.1), where the developed architectural plans are ratified by the latter. As an outcome, this step delivers finished EA artifacts capturing completed architectural solutions for digitalization initiatives. After being agreed upon, approved by all direct and indirect stakeholders and possibly sanctioned from the top, the produced architectural plans for the initiative obtain the status of official documents that oblige all the parties to act accordingly and take the respective decisions into account in subsequent planning and decision-making procedures.

The three steps thoroughly described above are loosely followed by enterprise architects leading the development of plans and also shape the organizational process of architectural planning. The three-step process of developing architectural plans for digital transformation initiatives led by architects is shown schematically in Figure 11.4.

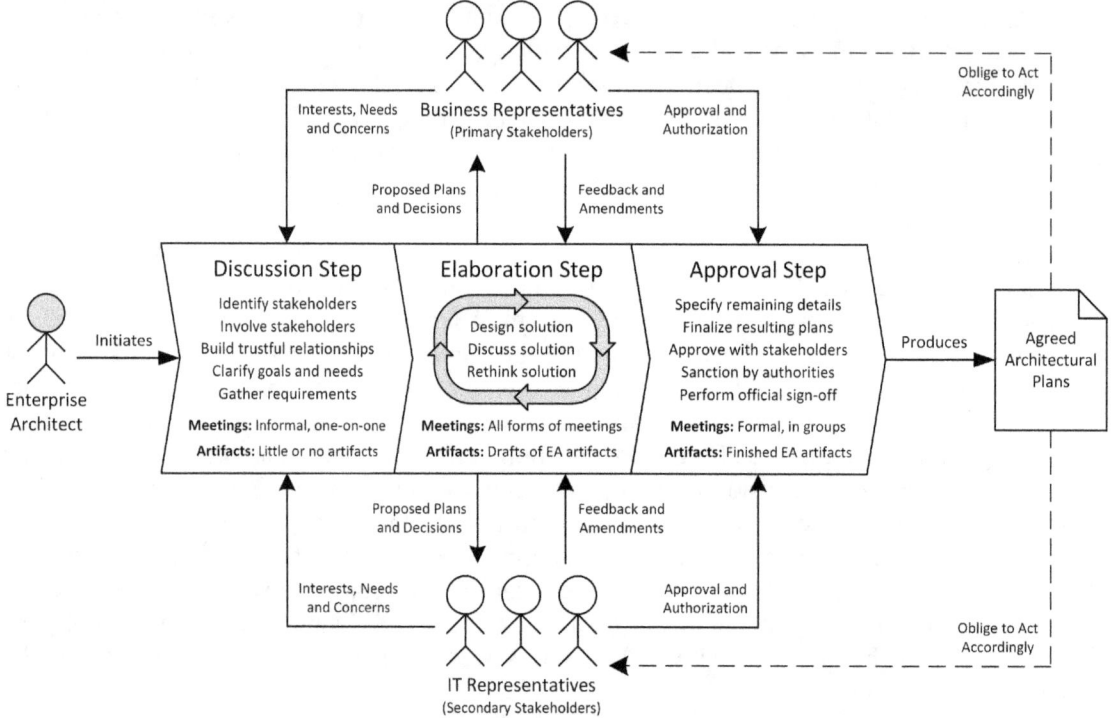

Figure 11.4. The process of developing architectural plans led by enterprise architects

As architectural planning applies to all types of transformation initiatives, leading the development of plans on the part of enterprise architects also does not differ in principle for short-term projects, mid-term programs and long-term strategies. Except for the seniority of participating stakeholders and the granularity of resulting plans, the three-step planning process illustrated in Figure 11.4 tends to be generic, universal and relevant to all sorts of digitalization efforts. Besides that, largely the same process of architectural planning applies to major revisions of the existing plans as well.

Importantly, all transformation initiatives in the organization are bound to its global architectural context and their planning processes should somehow align with it. However, because different types of initiatives relate to this context differently, either shaping it or being shaped by it (see Figure 9.7), planning decisions for smaller initiatives, and especially for derivative ones, tend to be more constrained and experience stronger contextual influence than those for large and autonomous initiatives.

Relevant Enterprise Architecture Artifacts

Capturing architectural solutions for digital transformation initiatives represents the most important practical function of EA artifacts in the work of enterprise architects. Except for pure actualities that provide no suggestions for the future whatsoever, all other EA artifacts contain some planning decisions reflecting various elements of architectural solutions. Namely, plans artifacts explicitly focus on the future, while most actualities artifacts can also highlight some planned changes in the current situation, even though it is not their primary purpose (see Figure 7.7). Both these classes of EA artifacts are immediately relevant to leading the development of architectural plans and actively employed by architects as part of this activity.

When leading the development of plans, enterprise architects both "consume" the existing EA artifacts from the architectural context and produce new artifacts that then join the context (see Figure 11.2). On the input side, of the existing artifacts, any artifacts that constitute the architectural plans of parent initiatives, as well as those of parallel initiatives, can provide important decision premises for this activity. As parent and influential parallel initiatives tend to be high-level strategies and programs, the respective EA artifacts usually relate to rules and structures (see Figure 7.9). On the output side, architects can use any artifacts considered necessary for capturing architectural solutions for particular digitalization initiatives to represent their plans. As discussed earlier, architectural plans can be composed of both newly created initiative-specific artifacts and updated existing general artifacts (see Figure 9.2), where initiative-specific ones are capable of covering complete solution components, while general ones — mostly separate planning decisions (see Figure 7.8).

Because different EA artifacts are "commensurate" with different types of transformation initiatives, the choice of specific artifacts to be utilized for capturing architectural solutions naturally depends, first of all, on the magnitude of the initiative. For instance, Designs and Outlines can be more suitable for smaller initiatives, Landscapes and Visions — for medium-sized initiatives, and Standards and Considerations — for larger-scale initiatives (see Figure 7.11). As EA artifacts can be separated into IT-focused ones concentrating more on technical solutions and business-focused ones covering more organizational solutions, the selection of artifacts also depends on what elements of architectural solutions should be reflected. Besides that, the choice of artifacts is largely determined by the *character* of planning decisions that need to be captured, e.g. data-related aspects of high-level architectural solutions can be best described in Logical Data Models and Conceptual Data Models. The mapping of popular EA artifacts to the space of architectural solutions with an indication of the typical decisions associated with them offers clear suggestions as to what artifacts can be used by enterprise architects to reflect what elements of architectural solutions for different transformation initiatives, though this mapping is certainly rather loose (see Figure 9.5). Concrete examples and scenarios of using various EA artifacts for documenting architectural solutions for projects, programs and strategies have also been provided earlier (see Figure 9.6).

Therefore, leading the development of plans can involve a wide array of EA artifacts, essentially any artifacts deemed appropriate by enterprise architects for capturing architectural solutions for specific transformation initiatives. Their property of duality, in an explicit or implicit form (see Figure 7.5 and Figure 7.6), makes EA artifacts helpful communication devices for heterogeneous business and IT communities, where the representatives of different groups of interest can find answers to their questions to ensure that their concerns are taken into account in proposed solutions. For this reason, the duality of artifacts is conducive to finding mutually acceptable planning decisions for initiative stakeholders from the business and IT sides of the organization and reaching agreements on the resulting architectural solutions. However, some non-dual EA artifacts with purely technical decisions needed to fully reflect architectural solutions (e.g. server deployment Guidelines) are normally interesting solely to IT specialists, whereas non-dual business documents having no technical elements (e.g. business cases), on the contrary, can be interesting mostly to business managers (see Figure 7.10), making them relevant only within these communities, but not for intercommunity collaboration.

As materializations or physical representations of different aspects of architectural solutions for digitalization initiatives, EA artifacts can be demonstrated to the audience, shared with others, studied by all parties, discussed among people and modified as a result of these discussions. Owing to these qualities, artifacts can be viewed as prime material objects that enterprise architects bring to their meetings and planning sessions with initiative stakeholders to negotiate the respective architectural solutions, gather feedback and react to it (see Figure 11.3). By virtue of their duality and ensuing value for communication, EA artifacts are actively used by architects in the course of the process of architectural planning, most importantly, during the elaboration step for discussing preliminary plans and during the approval step for endorsing finalized plans (see Figure 11.4).

The usage of EA artifacts by enterprise architects in different steps of the planning process, however, has certain specifics and is supported by different types of auxiliary artifacts. Specifically, along the successive stages of architectural planning, architects can benefit from using, first, artifact templates, then presentation packs and finally decision papers.

Artifact Templates

During the early discussion and elaboration steps of the planning process, there can be considerable uncertainty as to what EA artifacts should be delivered, what they should look like and what information they should contain. In other words, at the very beginning of architectural planning, it can be rather unclear exactly what planning decisions should constitute architectural solutions for particular digitalization initiatives and be captured in EA artifacts, or what technical and organizational elements of architectural solutions should be covered.

In these situations, enterprise architects can use, or even be organizationally obliged to use, standardized **artifact templates** — empty skeletons of EA artifacts that need to be filled with the actual "meat" of architectural decisions, which belong to auxiliary meta-EA artifacts (see Table 7.1). They map out a fixed section structure that suggests what information should be gathered, what questions should be answered, what decisions should be made and how they should be recorded to produce completed artifacts. In short, artifact templates define the informational contents of resulting EA artifacts.

In EA practices, artifact templates are developed mostly for initiative-specific EA artifacts of which multiple instances are created, especially for solutions artifacts intended for projects, as the most numerous change initiatives. However, some general artifacts, such as Target States and Roadmaps for different business areas, can also be templated. For these EA artifacts, their standardized templates provide certain reliable default patterns of content that guide enterprise architects in producing separate instances of artifacts for concrete transformation initiatives and situations. In each case, templates can be flexibly adapted by architects to the task at hand, for example, by deleting redundant sections from their structure and adding custom sections with the necessary information. The schematic graphical representations of artifact templates for general Roadmaps and Solution Designs are exhibited in Figure 11.5.

Chapter 11: Leading the Development of Plans

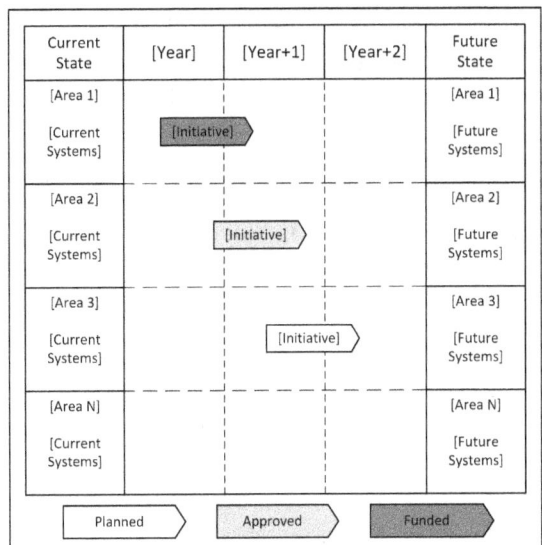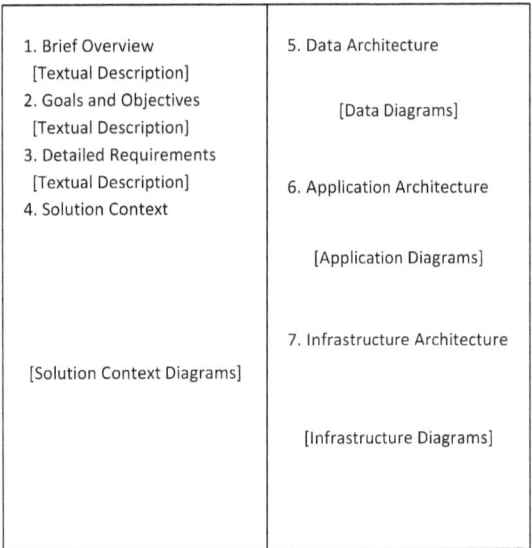

Figure 11.5. Artifact templates for Roadmaps and Solution Designs

The use of artifact templates offers a number of valuable benefits to individual enterprise architects as well as to the organization as a whole. First, they give architects some foundation to start architectural planning, reducing the initial level of uncertainty and accelerating the planning process. Second, they help architects achieve the consistently high quality of the developed EA artifacts and guarantee that no critical information is missing and no important concerns are overlooked in the resulting architectural plans. Organizationally, artifact templates facilitate the accumulation and reuse of best practices, enable the repeatability of planning approaches and ensure the predictability of stakeholder experience.

Presentation Packs

During both the elaboration and approval steps of the planning process, in many cases, bringing original EA artifacts to planning sessions can be inconvenient, impractical or otherwise undesirable. For example, artifacts can comprise too many sections irrelevant to the current meeting agenda or incomprehensible to the target audience, being included there for the mechanism of explicit duality (see Figure 7.5). They can also provide the wrong level of abstraction, e.g. contain extensive details inappropriate for senior decision-makers interested only in fundamental questions and decisions. Or, original EA artifacts can tell the public only fragmented snippets of the story behind the initiative, but not the whole story end-to-end.

In these situations, enterprise architects normally produce custom **presentation packs** — presentations summarizing the most important aspects of architectural solutions for digital transformation initiatives relevant to the intended audience in the current context[8]. Presentation packs usually contain some "slices" of original EA artifacts, or their adapted simplifications, complemented with additional textual explanations to ensure a logical flow of the presentation. Often, they include excerpts from multiple artifacts (e.g. Target States and Roadmaps) combined into a coherent story around the transformation initiative. Conceptually, presentation packs represent *derivatives* from original EA artifacts, where these artifacts provide the "master data" which is then extracted, transformed, enriched and recomposed into a new form better suited to the specific information needs of a particular audience. Like most EA artifacts, presentation packs aimed at mixed business and IT audiences are also dual and satisfy the information demands of both business and IT representatives.

Presentation packs prepared by enterprise architects for planning sessions can be fairly regarded as special auxiliary artifacts, specifically as disposable communication materials (see Table 7.1). Unlike "real" durable EA artifacts, presentation packs are meeting-specific and lose their relevance when these meetings are over. As one-off products, they are created to convey a certain message to initiative stakeholders and support subsequent discussions, questions and answers in concrete planning sessions, but can then be archived, reworked for follow-up sessions or discarded largely as waste.

The use of presentation packs for communicating with initiative stakeholders can be illustrated based on the earlier examples of EA artifacts developed for two hypothetical transformation initiatives — Data Analytics Strategy and Mobile Platform Program (see Figure 9.6). Both these initiatives are complex, multifaceted and their architectural solutions are captured in several EA artifacts. However, each of these artifacts provides only a partial, one-sided view of some aspects of these initiatives; none of them tells the full story about the initiatives in all their aspects. For this reason, to discuss these initiatives with their stakeholders, enterprise architects can prepare presentation packs with select excerpts from the respective EA artifacts joined into logical storylines.

For example, the whole architectural solution for the Data Analytics Strategy is reflected in five different EA artifacts: Technology Reference Model, Logical Data Model, Architecture Strategy, Conceptual Data Model and Business Capability Model (see Figure 9.6). Accordingly, the architect can extract specific views, diagrams and other pertinent pieces of information from these artifacts, adapt them to the audience's needs and compose a presentation pack with a balanced, holistic but concise description of the Data Analytics Strategy covering all its important aspects. In this case, the presentation pack can include, besides the title and a brief introduction, the anticipated benefits for the company and the overall strategy realization approach (taken from the Architecture Strategy developed for the initiative), target business capabilities to be uplifted with analytics (extracted from the Business Capability Model), the main sources of information and the basic principles of their analysis (adapted from the Conceptual Data Model and the Logical Data Model respectively), the underlying technologies enabling the analytics (extracted from the Technology Reference Model), major milestones on the way to strategy execution and their approximate timelines (also taken from the Architecture Strategy). Thus, the resulting presentation pack comprehensively describes the Data Analytics Strategy by integrating diverse information "scattered" in the original EA artifacts.

Similarly, the architectural solution for the Mobile Platform Program is captured in four different EA artifacts: System Portfolio Model, IT Principles, Roadmap and Target State (see Figure 9.6). The key information contained in these artifacts can be put together by the architect to form a presentation pack that includes, for instance, the goals of the transformation program (adapted from the Target State developed for the initiative), technical principles guiding the program (summarized from the respective IT Principles), available IT assets to be leveraged for transformation (extracted from the System Portfolio Model), depictions of the current state and the desired future state (also extracted from the Target State), step-by-step implementation plans for each program component and the associated investment demands (extracted directly and derived from the Roadmap respectively). The resulting presentation pack provides an end-to-end overview of the Mobile Platform Program based on the fragmented information from the original EA artifacts.

For both the Data Analytics Strategy and Mobile Platform Program, their original EA artifacts capture different kinds of planning decisions essential to their architectural solutions, but none of these artifacts presents the entire story of them, which necessitates the creation of presentation packs. The schematic graphical representations of the presentation packs for the digital transformation strategy and program described above with an indication of source EA artifacts are exhibited in Figure 11.6.

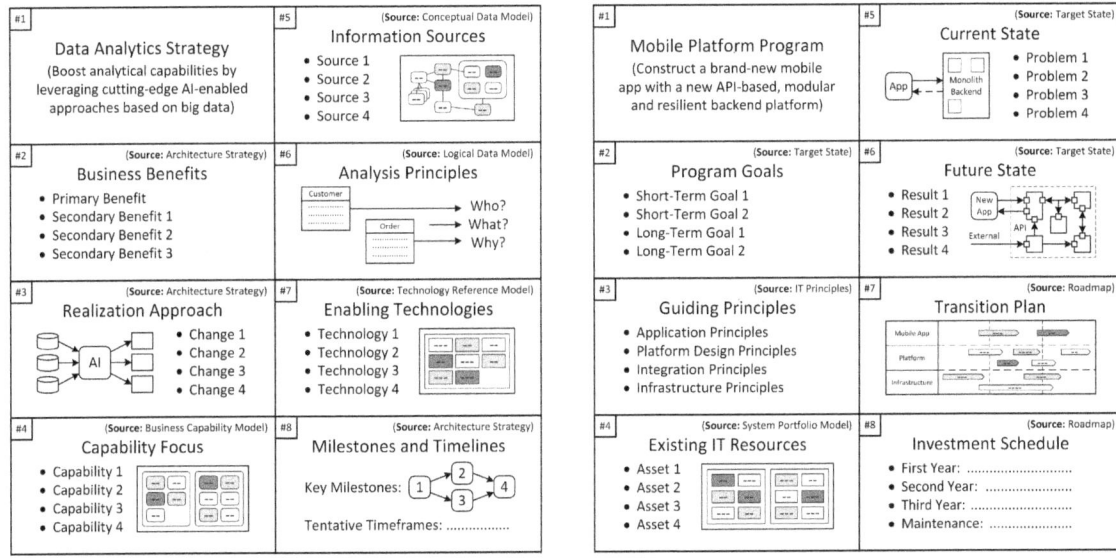

Figure 11.6. Presentation packs for digital transformation strategies and programs

Importantly, presentation packs complement real EA artifacts in communication-related matters, but never substitute for them. They can be either demonstrated to initiative stakeholders instead of original artifacts, or presented together with them. For example, architects often distribute source EA artifacts among the stakeholders aforehand, before the scheduled planning sessions, to allow their thorough study to those who seek detailed information. Or, they can also send out the originals to the interested parties on request after their meetings.

Decision Papers

During the closing approval step of the planning process, when finalized architectural plans for digitalization initiatives are submitted to higher-level supervisory authorities for their official ratification (see Figure 11.4), comprehensive presentation packs similar to those shown in Figure 11.6 can be excessive and not always practical. As senior executives and members of various governance committees are interested only in the summary of planning decisions, but not in their details, regular presentation packs prepared for direct initiative stakeholders are often found too granular, "heavyweight" and full of irrelevant information.

In these situations, enterprise architects can create compact **architecture decision papers** — special mini presentation packs intended solely for the purposes of introducing major planning decisions to supervisory authorities in a brief, very compressed form, which can also be regarded as auxiliary communication materials. These papers can describe any architecturally significant decisions for transformation initiatives that need to be sanctioned from above, typically extracted from their original EA artifacts. They normally focus on either individual planning decisions or small sets of linked decisions. For example, architecture decision papers can introduce the fundamental decision to change the overall philosophy of production automation captured in the Target State or a bundle of related decisions on the adoption of new technologies taken from the Technology Reference Model. Or, new Principles and IT Principles can be presented for ratification one by one, each as a separate decision paper.

Because projects represent the vast majority of initiatives launched in organizations with the most detailed architectural plans, the approval of their full-fledged EA artifacts, and particularly of their voluminous technical Designs, by architecture governance bodies is especially burdensome. For this reason, project governance procedures often hinge on **key design decisions (KDDs)** — a distinct variation of architecture decision papers associated specifically with Designs. Key design decisions are created by enterprise architects for projects to summarize the most critical planning decisions and choices made in their Designs and presented to governance committees for endorsement instead of the original artifacts. By spotlighting the pivotal aspects of proposed architectural solutions, they eliminate the necessity to study original Designs abundant with details not-so-relevant for governance purposes.

General architecture decision papers and key design decisions, as their narrow subtype, are very similar artifacts that purport to facilitate governance processes around transformation initiatives by clearly formulating architectural decisions that require official authorization in a simple, succinct and presentable format. The schematic graphical representations of architecture decision papers and key design decisions are exhibited in Figure 11.7.

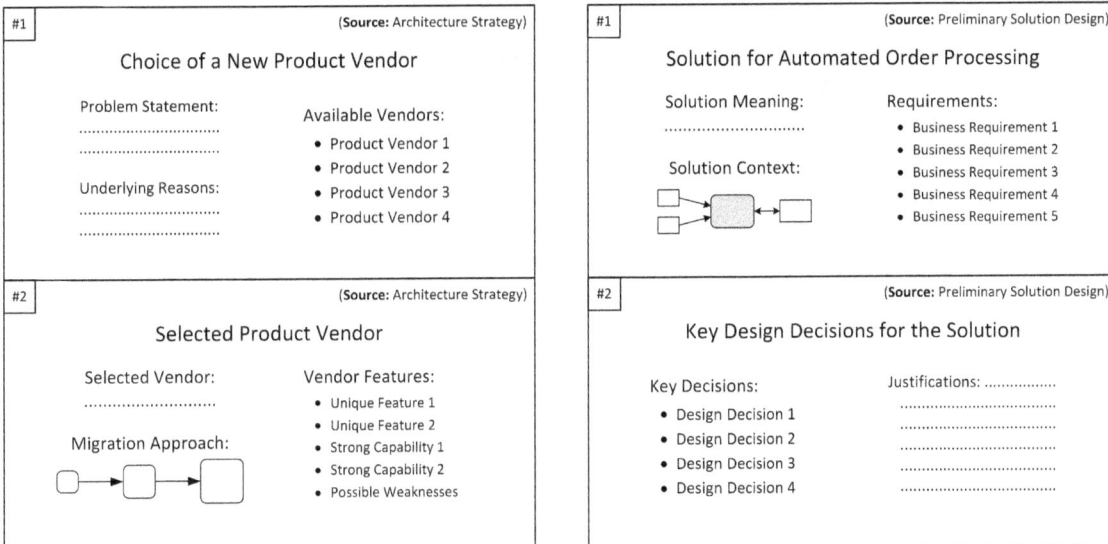

Figure 11.7. Architecture decision papers and key design decisions

On a general note, due to their ability to facilitate collaboration, EA artifacts, being either used directly or "wrapped" in presentation packs, are indispensable for enterprise architects while leading the development of plans. In fact, utilizing some or the other EA artifacts is essential for the successful fulfillment of this activity as it is artifacts that formalize the agreements reached between initiative stakeholders and capture the developed architectural solutions for future reference during the execution phase of digital transformation initiatives.

Additional Concerns

With regard to this activity, it is important to emphasize once again that enterprise architects never develop or update any architectural plans alone, but only organize and lead their development with the involvement of all stakeholders of these plans. To do that, architects invite relevant parties to dialog, bring their unique IT expertise to the table, discuss possible IT-backed responses to pressing business demands and then decide collectively what should be done.

Nevertheless, the actual role of enterprise architects in architectural planning can vary significantly from case to case, depending on how actively their stakeholders are engaged in the process. On the one extreme, when the stakeholders are very reactive, architects have to act largely as sole planners wearing mostly the hat of Technology Experts. In this situation, they gather stakeholder requirements, propose architectural solutions and then get them approved. On the opposite extreme, when the stakeholders are very proactive, architects can serve as mere stewards of the collaborative planning process wearing predominantly the hat of Change Agents. In this situation, they bring initiative stakeholders together, arrange their dialog and let *them* produce architectural plans. These contrasting extremes represent two different modes of working for architects leading the development of plans[9], though they obviously cannot be viewed as "black and white" and most real-life planning scenarios tend to lie somewhere in between.

In any case, deliberate and timely participation of all initiative stakeholders in the development of architectural plans is vital for a number of reasons. First, no single actor in an organization possesses enough knowledge to decide competently what the best decision is for the organization as a whole; only the collective knowledge of multiple actors can ensure that. Second, strong organizational commitment to the made decisions can be achieved only when these decisions are understood and supported by their stakeholders. Lastly, the involvement of stakeholders in the planning process brings an important symbolic value, e.g. treating stakeholders duly, accentuating their status and demonstrating respect for their interests.

Ultimately, it is this involvement of proper stakeholders that guarantees the high quality of the resulting architectural plans and maximizes the likelihood of their future adherence. During their cooperative development processes, these plans get optimized by discussing them among their stakeholders, addressing their concerns, resolving conflicting interests and reaching mutual agreements on the desired future course of action.

To summarize, the more active the stakeholder participation in the planning exercise, the better the quality of the produced architectural plans and the greater the chance that these plans will be treated seriously in the organization, and vice versa. This fact largely explains why pure techies incapable of dealing with stakeholders cannot become effectual agents of digital transformation in organizations. The spectrum of possible modes of leading the development of plans by enterprise architects depending on the stakeholder activity with their features and likely outcomes is shown in Figure 11.8.

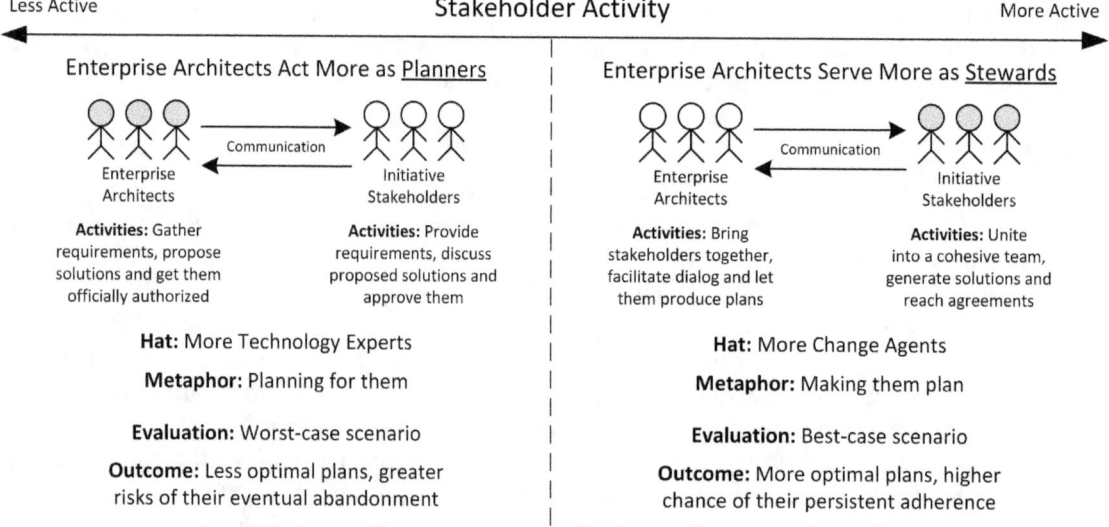

Figure 11.8. Two modes of leading the development of plans by enterprise architects

Leading the development of plans activates multiple resources of enterprise architects (see Figure 6.3). Of all their numerous skills and abilities, communication skills, collaborative attitude and innovative mindset seem to be the most relevant to orchestrating architectural planning. Namely, effective communication skills are of critical importance and indispensable for interacting with multifarious stakeholders of transformation initiatives as part of the planning process. A collaborative attitude is required for negotiating trade-offs and finding the best mutually acceptable architectural decisions reflecting diverse stakeholder interests. An innovative mindset is a must for devising truly novel IT-driven solutions for digitalization efforts. In addition to well-developed skills, sound knowledge and understanding of both the external and internal environments are also necessary for leading the development of plans.

Chapter Summary

This chapter discussed leading the development of plans as a distinct activity of enterprise architects with its meaning and goals, explained the context of its fulfillment, described planning meetings and the planning process as technical and logical means of its fulfillment, discussed regular and auxiliary EA artifacts relevant to this activity and introduced additional concerns related to its fulfillment. The key message of this chapter can be summarized in the following essential points:

- Leading the development of plans implies organizing, orchestrating and facilitating the cooperative processes of architectural planning to develop architectural solutions for digital transformation initiatives
- The primary goal of leading the development of plans by enterprise architects is producing optimal architectural plans for digitalization initiatives that satisfy the interests and concerns of all their stakeholders
- Leading the development of plans is performed within the planning phase of the initiative implementation process, under the strong (possible) guidance of the parent architectural plans and influence of the broader architectural context
- Technically, leading the development of plans is performed by enterprise architects via communicating with initiative stakeholders in different formats, ranging from informal one-on-one meetings to structured planning sessions
- Logically, leading the development of plans is performed by gradually arriving at the point of agreement between all stakeholders regarding architectural solutions via following the three-step process: discussion, elaboration and approval
- Leading the development of plans involves using any EA artifacts appropriate for capturing architectural solutions for particular initiatives and various auxiliary artifacts, including artifact templates, presentation packs and decision papers
- Depending on the stakeholder activity, the role of enterprise architects in leading the development of plans can vary from planners, who push architectural solutions, to stewards, who let stakeholders develop architectural solutions

Chapter 12: Ensuring Adherence to Plans

The two previous chapters discussed the activities performed by enterprise architects and thoroughly addressed four of their five activities. This chapter concludes the discussion of the activities of enterprise architects and describes in great detail ensuring adherence to plans as their last activity. In particular, this chapter starts with explaining the difficulties of achieving adherence to plans for enterprise architects and the role of architecture governance bodies in this activity. Next, this chapter describes the meaning of ensuring adherence to plans, the primary goals of this activity, the context and means of its fulfillment. Finally, this chapter discusses various regular and auxiliary EA artifacts relevant to ensuring adherence to plans, including compliance checklists, exception forms and amendment forms, as well as additional concerns related to this activity.

Ensuring Adherence to Plans as a Distinct Activity

Developing any architectural plans in organizations is a futile exercise unless adherence to these plans is achieved by applying architectural oversight, where one of the leading roles belongs to enterprise architects. Accordingly, the last essential activity of architects is ensuring the proper implementation of plans developed earlier as a result of previous architectural planning efforts. Ensuring adherence to plans implies following up, tracking and enforcing compliance with the agreed architectural plans for digital transformation initiatives by all organizational actors involved in their execution as part of architectural oversight. Organizationally, this activity of architects is identical to exercising architectural oversight (see Figure 4.8)[1].

As mentioned earlier, architectural oversight is a complex set of organizational measures that includes various actors, committees and procedures, and assures that the developed architectural plans for digitalization initiatives are actually followed. In this context, ensuring adherence to plans represents a concrete activity of enterprise architects that intends to drive and operate the administrative system of architectural oversight that, besides architects themselves, also involves other decision-makers controlling the realization of plans. For this reason, any actions of architects as individuals cannot be equated with architectural oversight as an organizational mechanism.

In the same sense in which leading the development of plans constitutes enterprise architects' personal contribution to architectural planning (see Figure 11.1), ensuring adherence to plans constitutes their personal contribution to architectural oversight in the form of their actions related specifically to monitoring the execution of architectural plans. In short, architectural oversight is what organizations do, while ensuring adherence to plans is what individual architects do as part of architectural oversight.

While the development of plans generates new courses of action for the organization, the control of adherence to plans merely assures that these courses are actually pursued and not deviated from. Even though a decent understanding of technology is necessary for supervising the execution of any IT-related plans, ensuring adherence to plans is arguably more characteristic for the repertoire of enterprise architects wearing the hat of Change Agents.

Difficulties of Achieving Adherence Without Managerial Authority

Ensuring adherence to plans for any transformation initiative implies influencing the decisions and actions of its executors. However, being largely in a position of invited consultants (see Figure 4.4), enterprise architects possess no official management authority to be able to simply order initiative executors to follow the plans or enforce their compliance with specific agreements by applying punitive sanctions for disobedience. For this reason, architects generally *cannot* achieve adherence to the existing plans in a straightforward manner[2].

Instead, enterprise architects have to seek adherence to architectural plans somewhat indirectly, in a more delicate fashion, through using a combination of their informal power by persuasion and some limited formal power granted to them by administrative arrangements, which may require great political sagacity on their part. Their informal power can be exerted, for example, by reminding initiative executors why certain decisions were made, why these decisions are optimal, whose interests they reflect, what powerful actors stand behind them or even by inviting the interested managers in person to enforce compliance[3]. The formal power of architects is manifested mainly in their voice, decision and veto rights ensuing from their membership in official decision-making committees exercising architectural oversight, most notably, architecture governance bodies.

Leveraging Architecture Governance Bodies for Achieving Adherence

The core element of administrative arrangements enabling formalized architectural oversight are architecture governance bodies institutionalized in organizations as part of their EA practices (see Figure 4.3). Governance committees involve many senior members of both business and IT communities, including enterprise architects, and are endowed with the power to authorize important planning decisions on behalf of the organization. Among other duties, these committees supervise, validate and sanction architectural solutions for new transformation initiatives, or separate components of these solutions falling within their zone of authority. They meet regularly, typically on a scheduled basis (e.g. fortnightly or monthly), to verify the adequacy of proposed architectural solutions and ensure their alignment with the overarching transformational context in both its motivational and architectural aspects (see Figure 9.8).

The structure of architecture governance bodies is always organization-specific and highly contingent on the size, structure, complexity and other features of the organization. More often, organizations establish a hierarchy of governance bodies empowered with different mandates and having different scopes, duties and decision powers. These bodies range from global strategy-level assemblies to technical project-level panels and can bear somewhat peculiar titles, e.g. enterprise architecture councils, technology steering committees, investment portfolio forums, architecture review boards and design authorities. However, all governance bodies can be loosely classified, based on their seniority and on the components of architectural solutions that they verify, into four broad categories: strategy committees, technology committees, investment committees and design committees.

Specifically, **strategy committees** endorse organizational solutions for large transformation initiatives, like strategies and programs (e.g. whether the proposed course of action is desirable for the organization as a whole), and include mostly business leaders and senior enterprise architects. **Technology committees** also endorse architectural solutions for large initiatives, but from their technical side (e.g. whether the proposed direction is acceptable for the corporate IT landscape) and involve mostly IT leaders and senior architects. **Investment committees** endorse organizational solutions for small transformation initiatives, mainly for projects (e.g. whether the proposed solution is worth to be implemented), and include mostly business managers and architects. And finally, **design committees** also endorse architectural solutions for small initiatives, but only their technical component (e.g. whether the proposed solution is technically correct) and involve mostly IT managers, subject-matter experts and architects. Because these governance bodies focus on different elements of architectural solutions, architectural plans for a single initiative are often reviewed independently by two, or sometimes more, committees from technical and organizational standpoints.

Analogously to EA artifacts, architecture governance bodies can be roughly mapped to the space of architectural solutions to delineate their zones of authority over different solution components and levels, which also indicates what general types of artifacts are more relevant to them (see Figure 9.5). The resulting mapping of the four categories of architecture governance bodies described above to the space of architectural solutions is depicted in Figure 12.1.

Figure 12.1. Mapping of governance bodies to the space of architectural solutions

In addition to the four types of architecture governance bodies shown in Figure 12.1 that can be established in organizations on a permanent basis, temporary initiative-specific governance bodies can also be created for large-scale change initiatives that require separate oversight. For example, major transformation programs often organize dedicated program steering committees consisting of their senior stakeholders, including architects, to authorize key planning decisions pertaining to these programs.

Regardless of the specific governance structure existing in the organization, the community of enterprise architects plays a crucial role in operating all kinds of permanent and initiative-specific architecture governance bodies, which allows its representatives to leverage their official authority for ensuring adherence to plans. Namely, by validating and endorsing architectural solutions for derivative initiatives at governance meetings, architects can enforce their compliance with the plans of the parent initiatives that they are driving. For example, an architect who led the development of architectural plans for a digitalization program then ensures adherence to these plans by approving its subordinate projects. In fact, their seat in governance committees provides essentially the only way for architects to exert some formal decision-making power over the execution of plans otherwise unavailable to them. Although architects do not possess any individual power, they are involved in *collegial* power exercised collectively via special administrative procedures.

All in all, in their work, enterprise architects take advantage of the authority of architecture governance bodies in two different scenarios: when ensuring adherence to their own plans, as described above, and when providing official advisory services concerning other decisions, as discussed earlier (see Figure 10.5). In the first scenario, they sign off lower-level architectural solutions based on their alignment with the higher-level plans they developed and the execution of which they are currently supervising. In the second scenario, architects verify architectural deliverables produced by other architects for parallel initiatives as a form of peer review or ratify some other, more general decisions possibly unrelated to any particular initiatives.

Meaning and Goals

The control of adherence to plans intends to ensure that all sorts and varieties of architectural plans produced previously are taken into account during the subsequent decision-making and guide the succeeding choices and actions in the organization. It equally relates, for example, to the execution of global digitalization strategies, local transformation programs, smaller change projects and even separate information systems. The general meaning of the adherence to plans ensured by enterprise architects can be best exemplified by the following and similar questions:

- Do our everyday decisions align with our strategic decisions on the use of IT?
- Do our digitalization efforts really concentrate on those business areas that we previously identified as critical for our prosperity?
- Are we really moving towards our desired long-term future state?
- Are our yearly IT spendings consistent with the agreed investment strategy?
- Is this IT solution being implemented in the way that we envisioned it earlier?
- Is this information system being constructed exactly as it was designed?
- Are we sticking in our IT solutions to the technologies we decided to employ?
- Are we reusing the IT assets that we consider strategic and not reusing those that we classify as legacy?

As discussed earlier, different types of digital transformation initiatives are disparate from the standpoint of their execution and require taking quite different actions (see Figure 2.6). On the one hand, strategies and programs are executed by launching and planning the proper derivative initiatives. In this case, higher-level initiatives merely engender a number of lower-level initiatives, but do not introduce any actual modifications in the landscape structure. For strategies and programs, their execution is carried out essentially by architects of their subordinate initiatives, who lead their architectural planning through the three steps thoroughly described earlier: discussion, elaboration and approval (see Figure 11.4).

On the other hand, projects are usually executed by constructing new information systems and changing business processes to benefit from their capabilities. Unlike strategies and programs, they introduce tangible modifications in the business and IT landscape, resulting in certain improvements in business operations. For projects, their execution is carried out by dedicated project teams, who accomplish all the necessary activities that constitute the project delivery process and include, in some form or the other, building, testing and deployment (see Figure 2.7). Depending on the nature of the executed project, these activities can be performed using either a more linear waterfall methodology, or a more iterative agile methodology (see Figure 2.8).

With this in mind, ensuring adherence to plans, as an activity of enterprise architects, equally relates to architectural plans for strategies, programs and projects, irrespective of the fundamental differences in their execution described above. In other words, this activity implies ensuring both that the right derivative initiatives are being planned by their architects and that the right information systems are being constructed by their project teams.

To be able to achieve adherence to architectural plans, enterprise architects have to understand these plans with their nuances as well as the underlying reasoning behind them. Depending on their profile, architects can supervise different kinds of plans, ranging from those dealing directly with business information systems to purely technical ones largely irrelevant to the business. For instance, they can control the execution of general transformation plans, plans regarding the utilization of technologies or only plans related to security.

Besides literally ensuring adherence to plans, this activity also involves dealing with various contingencies during their execution, coping with unanticipated difficulties and taking appropriate measures whenever something goes awry. For example, if a straightforward execution of the existing architectural plans turns out impractical, then tactical detours and temporary deviations from these plans may be necessary. Or, in some cases, even the plans themselves can prove inadequate and require considerable modifications. For these reasons, this activity, in fact, implies *balancing* the benefits of strict compliance with plans against the benefits of departing from plans.

The primary goal of ensuring adherence to plans by enterprise architects can be formulated as follows: guarantee that the approved architectural plans for digitalization initiatives are not shelved, but get executed and converted into material organizational improvements. Simply put, this activity ensures that digital transformation plans actually result in intended business transformations.

By being somewhere "near" the execution of architectural plans, enterprise architects can oversee the respective efforts, ensure adherence to these plans and secure their proper interpretation by their implementers. The proximity to the execution also allows architects to promptly resolve various issues arising in the course of this process, discuss possible deviations from the plans and initiate their revisions.

Context of Fulfillment

Like leading the development of plans, ensuring adherence to plans is also relevant only in the initiative context and makes no sense without concrete digitalization initiatives (see Figure 10.2). As a constituent of organizational architectural oversight, the control of adherence to plans is always exercised by enterprise architects in the course of the execution phase of the initiative implementation process. In this activity, existing architectural plans for initiatives agreed upon and signed off by their stakeholders at the conclusion of their development processes provide authoritative reference materials against which all the subsequent decisions and actions of initiative executors can be compared and validated. Interestingly, because architects continue to serve transformation initiatives during their execution, they can also be fairly viewed as initiative executors and, as the executors of high-level initiatives, can even be among the sponsors of their descendants.

As the development of plans normally takes much less time than their practical realization, ensuring adherence to some or the other architectural plans often becomes a continuous but not particularly time-consuming "background" task for enterprise architects. For instance, architects can periodically engage in the respective activities for various initiatives, for which they led the development of plans in the past, by interacting with their executors. For every initiative, these activities finish either when the initiative is implemented and its architectural plans get completely materialized, or when its execution is, for any reason, canceled.

Importantly, ensuring adherence to plans during the implementation of a specific transformation initiative refers not only to architectural plans produced specifically for this initiative, but rather to *all applicable plans* from the entire architectural context of the organization (see Figure 9.7). For example, the execution of a digitalization program manifested in the initiation of its derivative projects, besides being guided by its own architectural plans captured, say, in a Target State and Roadmap, can also be impacted by the architectural plans of some other programs or strategies in the form of global Principles and Policies. Or, delivery-level efforts for a change project that include writing software code, besides being shaped by its own Solution Overview and Solution Design, can also be influenced by Guidelines for interface naming, protocol selection and microservice deployment developed for another, unrelated transformation program. In other words, architectural oversight for a particular initiative is definitely underpinned by its own architectural plans and *potentially* underpinned by the plans of all other initiatives as well.

Basically, all architectural plans in the organization can provide certain input to this activity. For this reason, when ensuring adherence to plans, architects take into account the full architectural context, rather than only "local" architectural plans for the respective initiative. The place of ensuring adherence to plans, as one of the activities of enterprise architects, in the context of digital transformation initiatives is illustrated in Figure 12.2.

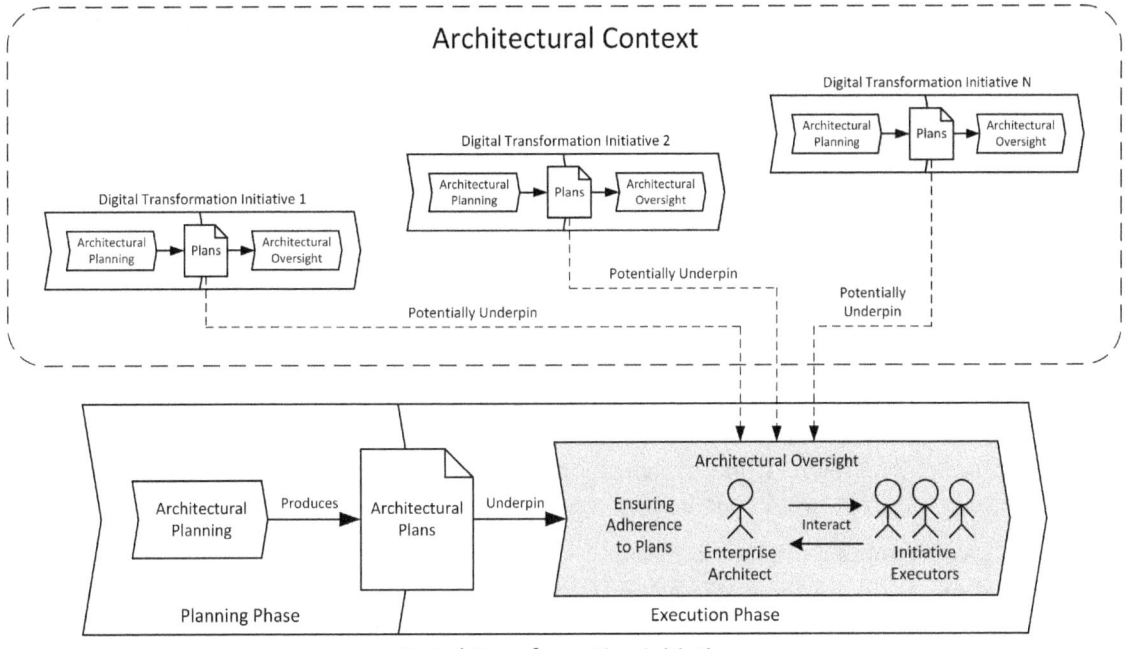

Figure 12.2. Ensuring adherence to plans by architects in the initiative context

Since the execution of higher-level initiatives is manifested in the planning of their lower-level descendants, the place of ensuring adherence to plans within the execution phase, as demonstrated in Figure 12.2, and the place of leading the development of plans within the planning phase, as shown earlier in Figure 11.2, are, in fact, *reciprocal* in the architectural context. This reciprocity is unsurprising and natural as the architectural planning of derivative initiatives always happens under the architectural oversight of their parent initiatives and both these activities are equally informed by the surrounding architectural context.

Specifically, the execution of a parent initiative is underpinned, first, by its own architectural plans and, second, by the additional relevant plans of other initiatives (see Figure 12.2), while the planning of its derivative initiatives is also guided, first, by their parent's architectural plans and, second, by the same additional plans from the architectural context (see Figure 11.2). Consequently, both activities are guided by precisely the same collection of architectural plans. Moreover, in many respects, these two activities represent merely the opposite sides of exactly the same process, where architectural oversight offers a top-down point of view and architectural planning — a bottom-up point of view.

This distinction in viewpoints, however, is very important and cannot be neglected because parent and derivative initiatives are often handled by *different* enterprise architects, so that the architect exercising architectural oversight for the parent initiative supervises other architects leading architectural planning for its derivative initiatives. In these situations, lower-level planners take the architectural context into account in their planning decisions, whereas their higher-level supervisors check that this context has actually been taken into account, both referring to the same context.

In summary, enterprise architects are informed by the overall architectural context when they lead the development of plans as well as when they ensure adherence to plans in order to guarantee the best possible alignment of the resulting transformations with the context. This is why an understanding of current transformation initiatives and their architectural plans constituting this context is so important for architects and represents one of the main goals of studying the internal environment, as discussed earlier.

Means of Fulfillment

Ensuring adherence to plans during the execution of digital transformation initiatives can be fulfilled by enterprise architects via different means, both personally and organizationally. Personal means of achieving adherence include various individual approaches that can be applied by architects on their own, while organizational means rest predominantly upon governance procedures administered by architecture governance bodies.

Individual Approaches as Personal Means

As personal means of fulfilling this activity, **individual approaches** to ensuring adherence to plans rely primarily on various forms of *personal* communication between enterprise architects and initiative executors, i.e. organizational actors involved in the initiative execution whose decisions or actions are affected by the plans (see Figure 2.3). These approaches are simple, flexible and do not require any sophisticated organizational arrangements. Individual approaches to achieving adherence actively used by the majority of architects include five basic methods: product inspection, documentation review, passive observation, active participation and keeping in touch. Each of these approaches has its own advantages, disadvantages and limitations to its practical applicability.

First, **product inspection** implies the examination and verification of the very outputs of initiative execution in the form of resulting tangible deliverables by enterprise architects to guarantee that the actual outcomes of initiatives match with those described in their architectural plans. For projects, product inspection naturally targets various physical IT artifacts created by project teams to construct information systems, e.g. program source code, database table schemas, infrastructure-as-code definition files, build and deployment scripts, cloud environment configurations, running operating system processes or even mounted hardware devices and networking cables. For example, an architect can be granted access to an internal version control system (e.g. Subversion or Perforce) or an external code repository (e.g. GitHub or Bitbucket) where all source files are kept to be able to explore them and validate their compliance, possibly using automated code sniffers. Or, an architect can be given credentials to log into servers and databases in the testing or production environment and check what their configuration is, what software packages are installed, what data is stored, what network connections are active, where the traffic flows and what is being written into logs to ensure that the system is set up properly and behaves as expected in "live" settings. Product inspection offers architects the opportunity to exercise stringent control over the execution of projects, but demands considerable effort and a keen attention to detail. As for programs and strategies, because their execution is manifested in the planning of their derivative projects and produces mostly EA artifacts (i.e. their products are documents), product inspection for these types of initiatives is largely equivalent to documentation review discussed next.

Second, **documentation review** implies the perusal and validation of some or the other "downstream" planning documents by enterprise architects to certify their conformance to the agreed architectural plans for transformation initiatives as well as to all other relevant plans from the broader architectural context. For strategies and programs, these documents represent lower-level architectural plans developed for derivative initiatives by their architects, while for projects — more detailed design documents produced by their project teams as part of delivery efforts (see Figure 2.7). For example, an architect can request and study the EA artifacts created during the architectural planning of a descending initiative to ensure their alignment with the higher-order plans and intervene in the process in case of deviations. Alternatively, all documents produced in the course of the execution phase of a transformation initiative can be automatically sent to the corresponding architect for approval. Documentation review is rather effective in terms of the strictness of control and time consumption, but it can be applied only to initiatives whose execution involves preparing some mandatory documents that can be validated. For this reason, this approach to achieving adherence is generally unhelpful for projects following paperwork-free agile methodologies.

Third, **passive observation** implies periodic visits to initiative execution sites by enterprise architects as mere observers to see what happens there, communicate with the involved actors and check whether the existing architectural plans are taken into account and complied with. For strategies and programs, passive observation often requires the presence of architects as inert stakeholders at various planning sessions for derivative initiatives, where important decisions are debated. For projects, it usually means visiting project delivery shops, where the progress in their implementation is discussed. For example, an architect can be invited to each meeting where major decisions regarding a subordinate initiative are ratified. Likewise, every Monday morning, an architect can come to the stand-up area of the project team to listen to the status reports of its members and chat with the project manager. Passive observation is a relatively effective, undemanding and universal approach that can be applied to most transformation initiatives, but incurs noticeable time expenses on the part of architects.

Fourth, **active participation** implies the immediate, hands-on partaking of enterprise architects in the activities necessary for initiative execution with a deep immersion in their details as regular members of the respective teams and ensuring adherence to architectural plans with their own decisions and actions. For projects, active participation can include writing software code, creating database tables, configuring operating systems or installing hardware infrastructure, while for higher-level initiatives — being involved in the architectural planning of their descendants as either their lead planners or energetic stakeholders advocating their alignment with the architectural context. For example, an architect can implement with their own hands the most critical system components, backbones or interfaces. Or, an architect can help launch derivative initiatives, co-lead their architectural planning and assist in developing key plans EA artifacts. Active participation allows architects to exert a maximum degree of control over the execution of transformation initiatives, but necessitates serious dedication and expends a huge portion of their productive time. Furthermore, this approach can be applied only if architects are very knowledgeable in the utilized technologies, which is not always the case.

Lastly, **keeping in touch** implies that enterprise architects become accessible for contact, open to questions and receptive to feedback from initiative executors to be capable of facilitating adherence to architectural plans by removing potential roadblocks, resolving emerging difficulties and serving as the point of escalation for the associated problems. For strategies and programs, keeping in touch means establishing direct communication channels with the architects and possibly other stakeholders of derivative initiatives, for projects — with their project teams. For example, an architect can share his "coordinates" in instant messengers, like WhatsApp or Telegram, with some participants of a subordinate initiative for their requests. Similarly, an architect can give her personal phone number to the team lead to enable immediate communication. Keeping in touch is a very simple, time-efficient and universal approach applicable to nearly all transformation initiatives, but it is mostly reactive and provides rather weak guarantees that their architectural plans are properly followed. The five individual approaches to ensuring adherence to plans described above with their advantages and shortcomings are summarized in Table 12.1.

Approach	Meaning	Advantages	Shortcomings
Product inspection	Verifying the very outputs of initiatives against their architectural plans	Allows architects to exercise stringent control over the execution of initiatives	Applicable only to projects, demands considerable effort and attention to details
Documentation review	Validating downstream planning documents against the agreed architectural plans	Effective in terms of the strictness of control and the consumption of time	Unsuitable for initiatives that do not produce documents, e.g. agile projects
Passive observation	Visiting initiative execution sites to check whether their plans are taken into account	Relatively effective, practical, universal and widely applicable approach	Requires noticeable time expenditures on the part of architects
Active participation	Executing initiatives with own hands according to their architectural plans	Allows architects to exert a maximum degree of control over the initiative execution	Requires dedication, huge time expenses and a working knowledge of technology
Keeping in touch	Staying in contact with initiative executors to help them comply with the plans	Very simple, time-efficient and universally applicable approach	Reactive, provides weak guarantees that plans are properly followed

Table 12.1. Individual approaches as personal means of ensuring adherence to plans

Individual approaches to ensuring adherence to plans available to enterprise architects are rather straightforward, adaptable and can be employed at their own discretion, whenever they seem applicable and efficacious. However, due to the lack of managerial authority and power on the part of architects, individual approaches on their own are typically insufficient to guarantee that the agreed architectural plans are duly respected; formal organizational oversight is needed.

Governance Procedures as Organizational Means

In contrast to the personal means described above that can be used by enterprise architects on their own, organizational means of ensuring adherence to plans are *administrative* in nature and require establishing architecture governance bodies as special institutional arrangements for exercising architectural oversight (see Figure 12.1). These means are much stricter and more authoritative, but also clumsier and more bureaucratic. Organizational means of achieving adherence are embodied, for the most part, in standard **governance procedures** carried out by governance committees, where enterprise architects participate as influential members with voting rights.

Governance procedures imply examining proposed architectural plans for their appropriateness for the organization with its transformational context and then endorsing or rejecting them. In case of their endorsement and sign-off, these plans turn into official policy documents guiding the execution of the respective initiatives. In the opposite case, these plans are either returned for rework to their creators, or even the very initiatives can be canceled. By taking part in governance procedures and influencing their resolutions, enterprise architects can ensure that lower-level architectural decisions comply with the existing plans for change initiatives that they drive. For example, an architect who led the development of plans for a transformation program, through governance mechanisms, can achieve the adherence of derivative project-level plans to these program plans.

Technically, governance procedures are implemented as group meetings, in their format, highly resembling formal planning sessions (see Table 11.1). Because of their great decision power and concomitant responsibility, these meetings, especially at the senior level, are often recorded or minuted to enable future auditability. Analogously to architecture governance bodies, concrete decision-making procedures that they fulfill are always organization-specific in their titles, routines and other details. Nevertheless, all governance procedures in which enterprise architects participate can be loosely classified, based on what is being scrutinized and approved, into three different types: decision approvals, artifact approvals and plan approvals.

First, decision approval procedures, or simply **decision approvals**, represent a separate class of governance procedures with the narrowest coverage, where only individual planning decisions constituting architectural solutions for transformation initiatives are authorized. Decisions that can be subjected to these procedures may include, but are not limited to, selecting a particular implementation approach for an initiative, limiting its scope to specific capabilities and using a concrete technology to meet its requirements. During decision approval procedures, these and similar planning decisions can be explained to an architecture governance committee for their discussion and ratification.

Next, artifact approval procedures, or simply **artifact approvals**, represent the set of governance procedures with medium coverage, where separate EA artifacts reflecting only certain aspects of architectural solutions for transformation initiatives are endorsed. Artifacts that can go through these procedures may include, among others, updated general Conceptual Data Models, recomposed initiative-specific Roadmaps and newly created Solution Designs produced for strategies, programs and projects respectively. As part of artifact approvals, these and similar EA artifacts can be presented to an architecture governance committee for their analysis and validation.

Finally, plan approval procedures, or simply **plan approvals**, represent a separate class of governance procedures with the widest coverage, where full plans capturing architectural solutions for transformation initiatives in their entirety are sanctioned. Plans that can undergo these procedures may include, for example, abstract outlines for the cloud migration strategy, high-level blueprints for the production automation program and fairly detailed designs for the sales analytics project. In plan approval procedures, these and similar architectural plans can be introduced to an architecture governance committee for their consideration and sign-off. The three types of governance procedures implemented by architecture governance bodies described are shown schematically in Figure 12.3.

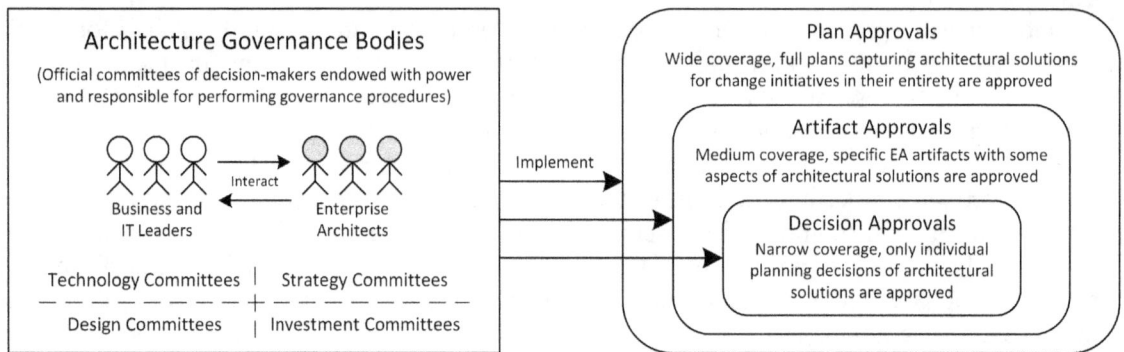

Figure 12.3. Governance procedures as organizational means of ensuring adherence to plans

Official governance procedures are somewhat sluggish, rather inflexible and involve an extra burden of group assemblies and associated paperwork. However, they add the missing authority to enterprise architects in terms of their ability to enforce the execution of developed architectural plans.

Combining Different Means of Achieving Adherence

As it is evident from the descriptions of the different personal and organizational means of ensuring adherence provided above, these approaches are not mutually exclusive, but rather complementary and can be applied in conjunction. In fact, owing to their synergy, enterprise architects normally use a combination of multiple approaches simultaneously to achieve better adherence to plans with fewer resources. Most importantly, mixing these approaches allows architects to benefit from both the flexibility of "lightweight" individual approaches (see Table 12.1) and the authority of formal governance procedures (see Figure 12.3). For example, an architect assigned to a transformation program, during its execution phase, can get acquainted with the architects of subordinate projects (i.e. encourage keeping in touch), occasionally attend various planning sessions where the architectural plans for these projects are discussed (i.e. engage in passive observation), subscribe to emails with the invitations to review the resulting artifacts and requests for their approval (i.e. perform documentation review), and then also preside at governance committee meetings where the finalized plans for these projects are approbated (i.e. grant plan approvals).

At the same time, none of the approaches to ensuring adherence to plans is universal and suitable for all transformation initiatives in all circumstances. Instead, each approach has its own unique specifics that determine its practical applicability in different situations. First, these approaches have different suitability for following up architectural plans for strategies, programs and projects. Second, these approaches have different relevance at different stages of the initiative execution. Lastly, their applicability can also depend on many other personal, initiative-specific and organizational factors and conditions, e.g. time availability, physical proximity, the desired degree of control, relationships with stakeholders, access to documentation and source code, support from the CIO, existence of architecture governance bodies and institutionalized approval procedures. For this reason, enterprise architects should always pick the most appropriate approaches to achieving adherence based on their fitness for concrete transformation initiatives in given circumstances.

Nevertheless, two general patterns of applicability of different approaches to ensuring adherence to plans can still be articulated. First, architecture governance procedures tend to be less suitable for enforcing compliance with architectural plans for smaller initiatives, particularly projects. Because the execution of projects implies making actual changes in the landscape structure, rather than producing more detailed architectural plans that can be formally verified, the respective delivery-level activities stay largely invisible to documentation-centric governance bodies, especially when they stick to "paperless" agile methodologies. Monitoring adherence to architectural plans for projects by their project teams, thus, typically remains out of reach for any "large-caliber" governance mechanisms and can be achieved by architects only via using their "fine-grained" personal means, including direct product inspection.

Second, even for larger initiatives, like programs and strategies, governance procedures can be applied only at certain, quite special moments of their execution, predominantly during the approval steps of the planning processes of their derivative initiatives, after their more or less mature architectural plans have been put together for examination (see Figure 11.4). As the opening steps of the planning phase of transformation initiatives include mostly oral conversations and verbal agreements, they produce no documented substance that can be subjected to formal governance. Hence, only individual approaches can be used by architects to ensure adherence to plans at the early stages of their subordinate initiatives' implementation.

Although the two patterns described above are rather loose, somewhat simplistic and allow numerous exceptions, they help better understand the overall context in which various personal and organizational means of achieving adherence can be employed. The applicability of different approaches to ensuring adherence to plans in different situations is illustrated in Figure 12.4.

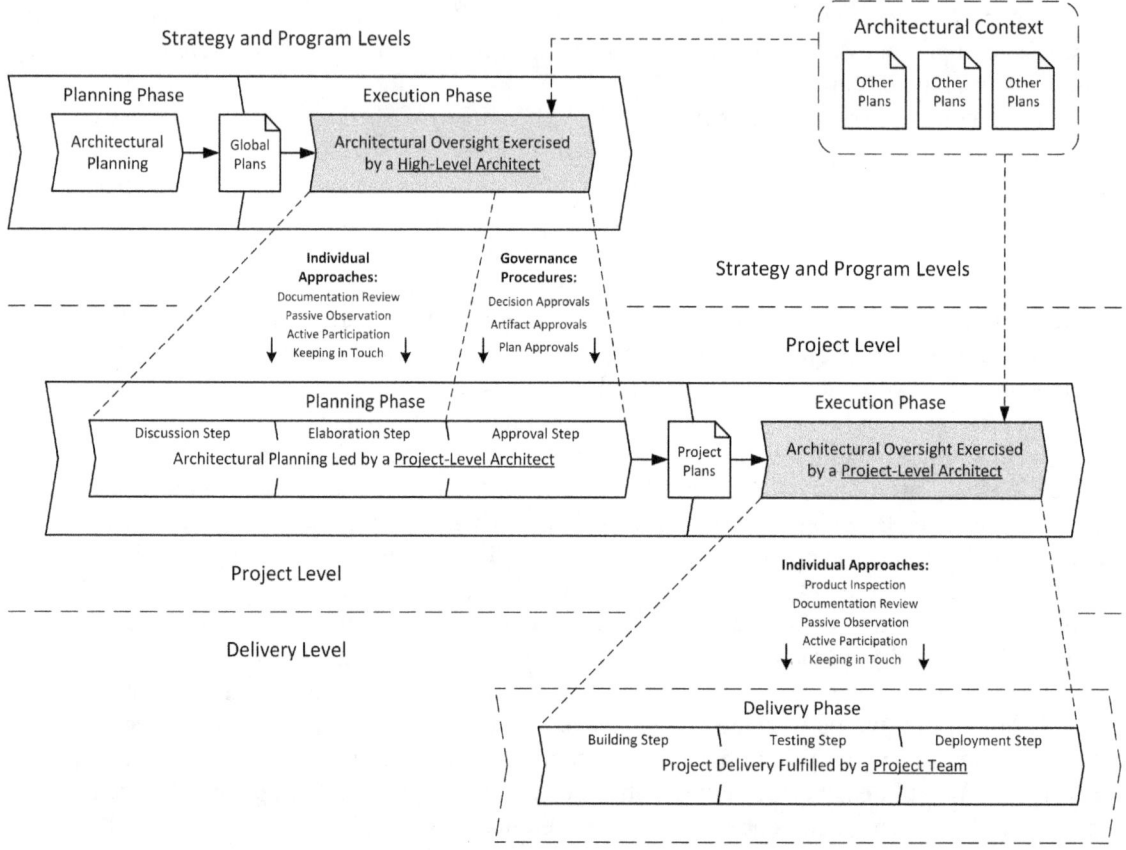

Figure 12.4. Applicability of different means of ensuring adherence in different situations

Because of the complementarity of personal and organizational means of ensuring adherence to plans, both these classes of approaches are actively used by enterprise architects depending on the situation, as shown in Figure 12.4. However, in any case, to monitor the fate of the existing architectural plans and facilitate their materialization, architects have to seek opportunities for involvement in the subsequent decision-making and implementation efforts that build upon these plans.

Relevant Enterprise Architecture Artifacts

When ensuring adherence to plans, enterprise architects do not produce any new EA artifacts themselves, but work with the already existing artifacts and possibly with new artifacts produced by others. On the one hand, since architectural oversight for transformation initiatives is underpinned by their own architectural plans and potentially also by other plans from the architectural context (see Figure 12.2), all EA artifacts representing these plans are obviously relevant to ensuring adherence to plans. Namely, various artifacts capturing the developed architectural solutions for digitalization initiatives provide the necessary foundation for this activity as it is the planning decisions recorded in these artifacts that should be adhered to during their execution phase. The mapping of popular EA artifacts to the space of architectural solutions explains what specific types of decisions can be reflected in different artifacts (see Figure 9.5). For ensuring adherence to plans, architects use existing EA artifacts as veracious reference materials against which all the implementation activities are compared and validated.

On the other hand, the execution of high-level transformation initiatives, like strategies and programs, also implies producing EA artifacts as part of the architectural planning of their derivative initiatives and many approaches employed by enterprise architects for ensuring adherence to plans rely on examining these artifacts. In particular, individual documentation reviews and all forms of governance procedures require studying EA artifacts created at different stages of the planning processes of subordinate initiatives to verify their quality and linkage to the architectural plans of their parents (see Figure 12.4). Consequently, as part of this activity, besides using EA artifacts belonging to the initiative being executed, architects often also work with the artifacts of its descendants as their chief inspectors.

For instance, documentation reviews performed by enterprise architects individually can cover any EA artifacts of derivative initiatives, including their preliminary versions and even early sketches. Artifact approval procedures administered by architecture governance bodies (see Figure 12.3), in most cases, consider only finalized EA artifacts. Plan approval procedures typically process either collections of original EA artifacts constituting the proposed plans, or presentation packs containing excerpts from these artifacts and summarizing their most important points (see Figure 11.6). Lastly, decision approval procedures usually endorse architecture decision papers or key design decisions all of which put forward and explicate certain architectural decisions (see Figure 11.7).

However, besides dealing with EA artifacts embodying architectural plans themselves, whether those for initiatives being executed that need to be enforced or those for derivative initiatives that need to be verified, enterprise architects can also utilize specialized auxiliary meta-EA artifacts (see Table 7.1) specifically to facilitate *alignment* with the existing plans. Most often, architects use compliance checklists to promote adherence to plans, exception forms to handle deviations from plans and amendment forms to make adjustments to plans.

Compliance Checklists

To stimulate compliance with architectural plans, enterprise architects disseminate various **compliance checklists** intended to evaluate whether, or to what extent, the enacted high-level plans are followed in new change initiatives at lower levels and, at the same time, give a hint as to how conformity can be achieved. These checklists can be aimed from different angles at initiatives of different scales. For example, two of the multitude of possible checklists that can be employed by architects to assess and facilitate the adherence of initiatives to higher-order architectural plans are project evaluation worksheets and standards conformance checklists.

Project evaluation worksheets consider digitalization projects, and especially organizational components of their architectural solutions, as a whole and "measure" their overall fitness in the architectural context from a strategic point of view, i.e. whether a project is generally appropriate for the organization with its long-range architectural plans or not. These sheets may include multiple criteria for assessing projects addressing, for instance, their alignment with Architecture Strategies, their contribution to Target States and their congruence with Roadmaps. Project evaluation worksheets are used by enterprise architects to ensure the adherence of transformation projects to the suggestions of current programs and strategies.

Standards conformance checklists inspect digitalization projects, particularly technical components of their architectural solutions, "under the hood" and verify their compliance with the architectural context in matters of technical correctness, i.e. whether a project sticks to the adopted system implementation approaches, normative rules and best practices. These lists tend to include numerous checkboxes grouped into coherent sections that represent various prescriptions to be followed in all IT solutions derived from the existing Guidelines, Patterns and IT Principles. Standards conformance checklists are used by enterprise architects to ensure the adherence of transformation projects to the established body of Standards. The schematic graphical representations of project evaluation worksheets and standards conformance checklists are exhibited in Figure 12.5.

Investment Evaluation Sheet for Project <u>Alpha</u>			
Fitness Criteria	Assessment of the Initiative		
Conformity to Architecture Principles	Not Conformant	Partial Conformity	Full Conformity
	Comments:		
Contribution to Strategic Target State	Obstructs Realization	Neutral Impact	Contributes Substantially
	Comments:		
Consistency with Investment Roadmaps	Included in Roadmaps	Compelling Business Case	Externally Imposed
	Comments:		
Alignment with Technology Portfolio	Major Deviations	Minor Deviations	Perfect Alignment
	Comments:		
All IT investments deviating from the long-term architecture strategy must be escalated to the architecture governance council for their explicit approval			

Standards Conformance List for Solution <u>Beta</u>	
Exposure through web interfaces? <u>Yes</u> / No	
All web pages are accessible only via HTTPS	v
Session ID is always passed in cookies	x
IP addresses and timestamps of all requests are logged	v
Operations with sensitive data? Yes / <u>No</u>	
~~All sensitive data is stored in an encrypted form~~	N/A
~~All encryption keys are periodically rotated~~	N/A
~~Data objects are exposed externally only via proxy ID~~	N/A
Interactions with other systems? <u>Yes</u> / No	
All interactions with external systems are done via ESB	x
All data is passed in standard open formats, e.g. XML	v
In case of any nonconformance, please contact the architecture team	

Figure 12.5. Project evaluation worksheets and standards conformance checklists

Project evaluation worksheets and standards conformance checklists illustrated in Figure 12.5, as well as many other analogous artifacts, can all be employed by enterprise architects to promote adherence to the agreed architectural plans by lower-level change initiatives. On the one hand, the architects of higher-order initiatives can distribute appropriate checklists among the architects of descending initiatives and monitor their compliance. On the other hand, the latter can use these checklists as a convenient self-service guide to achieving adherence, greatly simplifying the organizational mechanism of architectural oversight.

Exception Forms

To allow justified exceptions and reasonable deviations from architectural plans in lower-level transformation initiatives, enterprise architects provide special **exception forms** intended to capture the proposed divergences, evaluate their criticality and validity. These forms can address different facets of initiatives at different levels of their hierarchy. For example, two of many possible forms that can be utilized by architects to assess and control the deviations of initiatives from higher-order architectural plans are project dispensation cards and solution exemption forms.

Project dispensation cards present digital transformation projects in view of their departure from global architectural plans, i.e. explain why a project is necessary for the organization despite its incompatibility with the declared strategic intentions. These cards usually highlight various aspects of projects important for understanding the value and positive outcomes of their implementation, as well as the risks and negative consequences of their cancellation. Project dispensation cards are used by enterprise architects to knowingly permit or deny the launch of new projects conflicting with the agreed plans, e.g. major changes contradicting the general course set by Architecture Strategies, Target States and Roadmaps.

Solution exemption forms present digital transformation projects in light of their departure from the adopted technical Standards, i.e. justify why an IT solution should be constructed with unusual methods, technologies and building blocks. These forms typically explain what exotic approaches are applied in the solution, what potential problems they introduce, what rationale stands behind them and why the analogous results cannot be attained by regular means. Solution exemption forms are used by enterprise architects to consciously sanction or reject the implementation of technically deviant projects, e.g. information systems based on nonstandard equipment, products or patterns. The schematic graphical representations of project dispensation cards and solution exemption forms are exhibited in Figure 12.6.

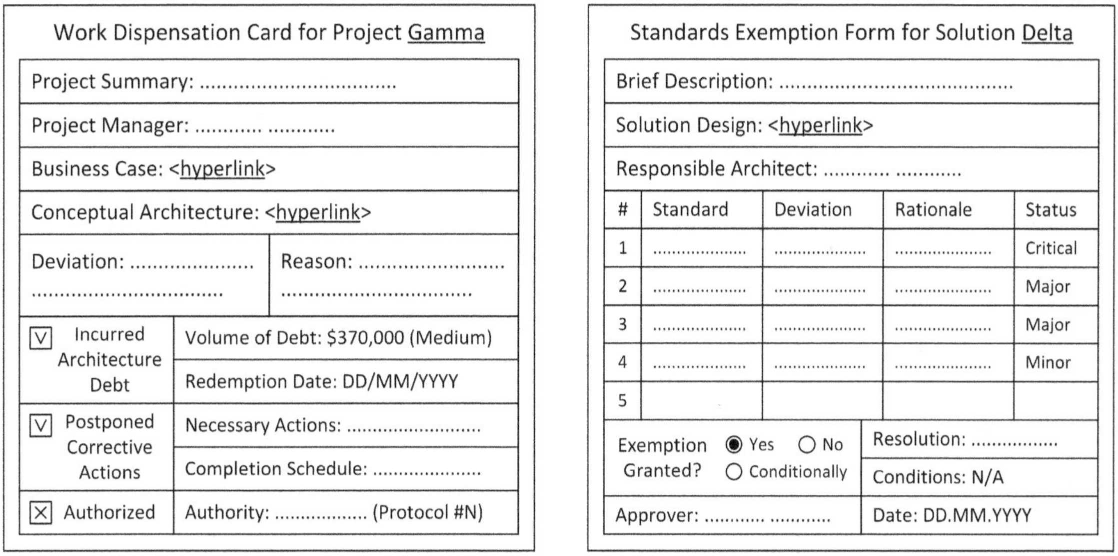

Figure 12.6. Project dispensation cards and solution exemption forms

Project dispensation cards and solution exemption forms illustrated in Figure 12.6, as well as other analogous artifacts, can all be employed by enterprise architects to handle the deviations of lower-level initiatives from the architectural plans they developed. Specifically, whenever it is necessary, the architects of descending initiatives can fill out requisite forms and submit them to appropriate architecture governance bodies for their consideration and approval. By approving the incoming exception forms, governance committees officially give these architects "carte blanche" to launch the initiatives or use the approaches they advocate. In this way, through established governance arrangements, the architects of higher-order transformation initiatives supervise follow-up architectural decisions by authorizing or refusing their effectuation.

Amendment Forms

To enable desired amendments and forced adjustments of architectural plans during the execution of the respective initiatives, enterprise architects complete special **amendment forms** intended to record the suggested corrections, evaluate their significance and meaning. These forms can equally relate to all types of transformation initiatives and their plans. For example, two of many possible forms that can be utilized by architects to introduce necessary modifications into the architectural plans of running initiatives are architecture change requests and design alteration forms.

Architecture change requests address high-level architectural plans, deal with major architectural decisions and propose far-reaching shifts in future scenarios, e.g. adjustments in Architecture Strategies, Target States or technical Standards. These requests explain why the change of overall direction is needed in the face of current circumstances, present a new way forward and justify its benefits over the available alternatives. Architecture change requests are used by enterprise architects to initiate urgent amendments to the enacted architectural plans for strategies and programs in the course of their execution, often necessitated by environmental turbulence and accompanying changes in the motivational context of the organization.

Design alteration forms address project-level architectural plans, typically Solution Designs, and deal with relatively minor but still architecturally noticeable decisions the impact of which is likely to transcend the boundaries of individual projects. These forms explain the reasons for demanding modifications to the approved plans and propose redesigned IT solutions, or their separate components, with their rationales. Design alteration forms are used by enterprise architects to request amendments to the existing architectural plans for projects in the middle of their delivery, often dictated by "unhappy surprises" associated with unexpected dependencies, unproven technologies or other difficulties encountered during the system construction. The schematic graphical representations of architecture change requests and design alteration forms are exhibited in Figure 12.7.

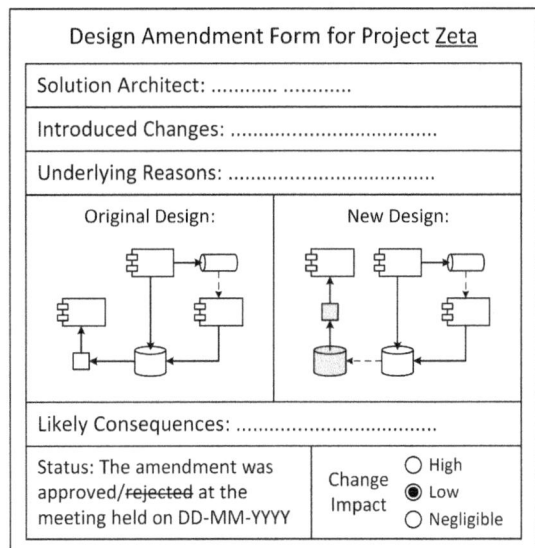

Figure 12.7. Architecture change requests and design alteration forms

Architecture change requests and design alteration forms illustrated in Figure 12.7, as well as other analogous artifacts, can all be employed by enterprise architects to amend architectural plans for digital transformation initiatives "on the run", right during their execution. Specifically, whenever it is necessary, the architects of initiatives requiring modifications can fill out requisite forms and submit them to appropriate architecture governance bodies for their review and authorization. By authorizing the incoming amendment forms, governance committees officially sanction the changes in plans proposed by these architects as well as the continuation of initiative execution based on the updated plans. In this way, through established governance procedures, architects get the opportunity to adjust their architectural plans in a disciplined manner.

Various compliance checklists, exception forms, amendment forms and some other related meta-EA artifacts are important elements of the organizational system of architectural oversight that controls the execution of plans. Normally, compliance checklists and exception forms are used as part of institutionalized governance procedures that derivative initiatives undergo during their approval step (see Figure 12.4). Similarly to governance mechanisms, these artifacts are relevant predominantly to the execution of high-level initiatives that imply launching subordinate initiatives amenable to formal analysis, i.e. to strategies and programs, but not to projects. By contrast, amendment forms are relevant to all kinds of transformation initiatives and can be used at any moment along their execution.

Additional Concerns

Ensuring adherence to architectural plans by enterprise architects is associated with a number of difficult concerns that require balancing, in one sense or another, the perseverance of sticking to the developed plans versus the benefits of not doing so. In particular, architects have to deal with the revisions of plans, deviations from plans and explorations beyond plans.

Revising the Existing Plans

As the famous military adage says, "No plan survives contact with the enemy"[4]. The same wisdom also holds true in the universe of enterprise architecture: no architectural plan can be executed exactly as intended, at least in every detail. Information systems are very complex entities whose structure cannot be planned precisely at a detailed level. The future of the business environment is too uncertain to be anticipated in advance, even in essential aspects. Technology does not always work as expected or described in the documentation, let alone as promised by vendors. For all these and other reasons, any architectural plans can accurately reflect, at best, only a *current* understanding of the situation, but they have to be amended or adapted when new pertinent information comes to light. This information can be of both internal origin (e.g. new complications in the corporate IT landscape were uncovered) and external origin (e.g. competitors changed their behavior and released new products).

In these circumstances, any breaking news may trigger the necessity to reconsider the existing architectural plans by returning back to the planning process and redeveloping them. Administratively, this opportunity is usually supported by special governance procedures for authorizing corrections in plans and backed by various amendment forms filled in by the architects of initiatives that need to change their course, as discussed earlier (see Figure 12.7). Moreover, architectural plans for all long-running transformation initiatives, such as multiyear programs and strategies, are periodically reviewed and revised by their architects and stakeholders, as discussed later in Chapter 15 (The Archetype of Enterprise Architects). In any case, enterprise architects should not regard the present plans as something constant or immutable, but merely as a product of the best available information at the moment of their creation, and be ready to update these plans whenever it becomes necessary.

Deviating from Plans

Interestingly, in many situations, strict adherence to the existing architectural plans can be deemed infeasible or undesirable, though without causing the need to modify the plans themselves. For example, every organization launches urgent, unplanned but compelling projects missing in their current transformation programs and official investment Roadmaps. Likewise, not all IT systems can be constructed rationally in full accordance with the accepted technical Standards, e.g. structured exactly as prescribed by the established Patterns. At the same time, superfluous standardization and stubborn demand for conformity on the part of enterprise architects can make their presence unwelcome and eventually lead to the proliferation of so-called shadow IT not sanctioned by the organization[5], as discussed later in Chapter 18 (Challenges of Enterprise Architects).

For these reasons, some "legal" ways to depart from the agreed architectural plans should be provided. Administratively, they are typically implemented via special governance procedures for approving deviations and backed by various exception forms filled in by the architects of deviating initiatives, as discussed earlier (see Figure 12.6). In a personal capacity, enterprise architects exercising architectural oversight should, if necessary, assist initiative executors in diverging from the plans with *minimal harm* to the organization, e.g. help the architects of subordinate projects select the least inconsistent technologies for their IT solutions or help project teams break security Guidelines in the most secure fashion[6].

Because some deviations from architectural plans can be advantageous or even necessary for the normal functioning of the organization, a certain degree of improvisation in interpreting and following these plans is required. Whereas absolute compliance with plans results in stifling bureaucracy and the inability to react to emerging needs, their total neglect leads to anarchy and disorder in decision-making. Therefore, when ensuring adherence to plans, it is important for enterprise architects to determine a healthy balance between the desired levels of conformance and flexibility, which is likely to benefit the organization as a whole.

Exploring Beyond Plans

In addition to the fact that following Standards to the letter is often impractical, some experimentation with technologies and system implementation approaches on the technical side of architectural planning is necessary from the standpoint of organizational learning. While the persistent use of the same technologies and approaches allows organizations to grow their competencies in using them and reap the associated benefits manifested, among other things, in faster speed and reduced risks of project delivery, this persistence also prevents organizations from trying and adopting new, potentially better technologies and approaches that, if mastered, can lead to higher performance in the long run. For example, building IT systems exclusively on the proven platforms permitted by the Technology Reference Model accelerates system construction and further accumulates organizational experience with these platforms, but at the same time leaves the organization with an obsolescent technology base jeopardizing its future prosperity.

These and similar situations represent a common industry phenomenon widely known as a "competency trap"[7]. To avoid falling into dangerous competency traps, enterprise architects have to find a difficult trade-off between, on the one hand, the exploitation of existing organizational competencies in technologies and approaches and, on the other hand, the exploration of new technologies and approaches that may eventually prove superior[8]. In other words, architects should decide when to use old but reliable ways of doing things and when to try new but uncertain ways.

Finding the Right Balance

On the whole, adherence to plans renders complex effects on organizations with positive and negative features. Both strengthening and weakening the strictness of control have significant implications in terms of flexibility, adaptiveness and organizational learning. The analysis of the influence of the exerted strictness of adherence to architectural plans on the likely outcomes for organizations provided above is summarized in Figure 12.8.

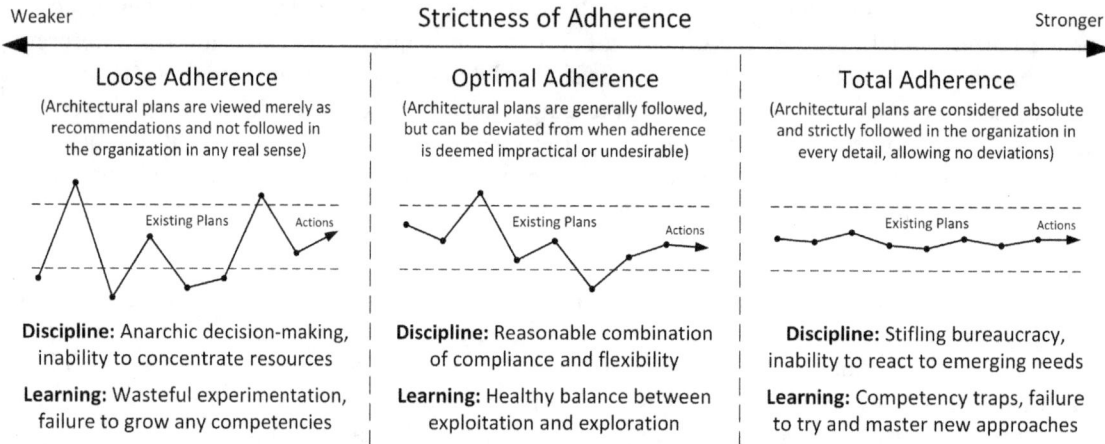

Figure 12.8. Varying strictness of ensuring adherence to plans by enterprise architects

In light of the analysis presented in Figure 12.8, ensuring adherence to plans certainly refers to the *optimal* degree of adherence, which tolerates justified selective deviations, rather than to complete adherence in every aspect. Unsurprisingly, in practice, architectural plans are followed somewhat loosely, by constantly weighing the benefits of temporary detours against the benefits of staying on course.

Of all the resources of enterprise architects, it is arguably a collaborative attitude that enhances their ability to balance immediate and long-term interests advocated by different parties (see Figure 6.2). The eternal trade-off between the future-oriented mindset that favors adherence to plans and here-and-now thinking that chases current opportunities poses a major challenge for organizations and their architects.

Chapter Summary

This chapter discussed ensuring adherence to plans as a distinct activity of enterprise architects with its difficulties, meaning and goals, explained the context of its fulfillment, described individual approaches and governance procedures as personal and organizational means of its fulfillment, discussed regular and auxiliary EA artifacts relevant to this activity and introduced a number of additional concerns related to its fulfillment. The core message of this chapter can be summarized in the following major points:

- Ensuring adherence to plans implies following up, tracking and enforcing compliance with the agreed architectural plans for digital transformation initiatives by all organizational actors involved in their execution
- Because enterprise architects have no managerial authority to control initiative executors, ensuring adherence to plans requires combining their informal power by persuasion and limited formal power granted to them administratively
- The primary goal of ensuring adherence to plans by enterprise architects is guaranteeing that the approved architectural plans for digitalization initiatives are converted into material organizational improvements

- Ensuring adherence to plans is performed within the execution phase of the initiative implementation process, being underpinned by the agreed architectural plans of the initiative and potentially also by the broader architectural context
- Individual approaches to ensuring adherence to plans rely on personal communication between enterprise architects and initiative executors and include product inspection, documentation review, passive observation, active participation and keeping in touch
- Governance procedures ensuring adherence to plans are carried out by architecture governance committees with the participation of enterprise architects and include decision approvals, artifact approvals and plan approvals
- Ensuring adherence to plans involves using all EA artifacts representing the architectural plans of the initiative with the broader context and various auxiliary artifacts, including compliance checklists, exception and amendment forms
- Ensuring adherence to plans requires finding the right balance between compliance and flexibility that results in optimal outcomes for organizations in terms of persistence, adaptiveness and organizational learning

Chapter 13: The Work of Enterprise Architects

The three previous chapters discussed separately the five key activities performed by enterprise architects in different contexts. This chapter entwines these activities into a single storyline and provides an integrated, end-to-end view of the work of enterprise architects in organizations. In particular, this chapter begins with describing the occupation of enterprise architects as a dynamic mixture of their five activities interlinked by complex logical and sequential relationships and presenting the value stream of activities. Then, this chapter describes the work of enterprise architects through their five activities in the organizational context, in the initiative context and holistically in its entirety, and analyzes their working schedule with its peculiarities. Finally, this chapter discusses enterprise architects as the advocates of technical interests, including their role as initiative stakeholders and driver proponents, and introduces technical rationalization initiatives as a special type of organizational change initiatives.

The Occupation of Enterprise Architects as the Unity of Five Activities

The job of enterprise architects generally involves five high-level activities performed in different contexts: analyzing the external environment, studying the internal environment, providing advisory services, leading the development of plans and ensuring adherence to plans (see Figure 10.2). Each of these activities is unique in its meaning, goals and means of their achievement, relevant EA artifacts and associated concerns.

Earlier, the five essential activities of enterprise architects were described in great detail but separately, as if they are unrelated to each other and carried out by architects independently. In reality, however, all their activities are practically inseparable, closely intertwined with each other and bound with various logical and sequential relationships. It is their complex dynamic interplay interwoven into the surrounding context that constitutes the occupation of architects in organizations.

Logical Relationships Between Different Activities

Logical relationships between the different activities of enterprise architects rest mainly upon specific *resources* that are being produced, exchanged and transferred between them. These resources include mostly intangible assets (e.g. valuable information), but also some tangible materials (e.g. EA artifacts).

For instance, analyzing the external environment and studying the internal environment are self-sufficient activities that do not depend on other activities of enterprise architects and do not "consume" any external resources produced by them. However, both these activities are vital for the performance of architects because they supply them with the two distinct but mutually complementary kinds of knowledge needed for their work (see Figure 6.1). Namely, analyzing the external environment sharpens, extends and refreshes their knowledge of the business capabilities of technology, while studying the internal environment accumulates and refines their knowledge of the organization, its landscape and motives. These invisible knowledge resources embody a massive "underwater part of the iceberg" as they actually underpin all the other activities of architects and enable various practical aspects of their job. Put it simply, analyzing the external environment and studying the internal environment, in conjunction, inform all the "real" activities of architects — providing advisory services, leading the development of plans and ensuring adherence to plans.

Providing advisory services evidently relies on the availability of knowledge resources of enterprise architects. For this reason, the very fulfillment of this activity is unimaginable without prior in-depth studies of the external and internal environments. The successful provision of advisory services, in turn, generates certain "reputational capital" — a critically important intangible resource that elevates the status of architects in the eyes of other organizational actors. For architects as mere consultants deprived of any managerial power (see Figure 4.4), attaining reputation-based authority represents nearly the only available way to gain political weight to be able to influence planning decisions. Basically, their reputation as valued partners is the sole reason why business managers seek their help, listen to their opinions and involve them in digital transformation initiatives. It is this reputation that endows architects with the necessary credit to be entrusted, among other assignments, with the task of leading the development of plans[1]. The role of reputation as a special resource enabling the work of architects in organizations is discussed in detail later in Chapter 18 (Challenges of Enterprise Architects).

Leading the development of plans leverages both the knowledge resources of enterprise architects, acquired in their environmental studies, and their reputation as trustworthy experts, deserved as a result of providing advisory services, to be in a position to put together a credible common way forward for business and IT. As output, this activity produces a conspicuous tangible resource: architectural plans for digitalization initiatives in the form of physical EA artifacts capturing different elements of their architectural solutions, which are then used for ensuring adherence to plans.

Finally, ensuring adherence to plans, besides depending on the basic knowledge and partly reputational resources, obviously makes no sense and cannot be carried out unless the respective architectural plans have been developed and provided as input to underpin it. This activity does not produce any material or immaterial resources for other activities, but only imbues leading the development of plans with meaning by guaranteeing their execution.

Sequential Relationships Between Different Activities

Sequential relationships between the different activities of enterprise architects are manifested primarily in the initiative context (see Figure 10.1), namely in sequential engagement in these activities during the implementation of digital transformation initiatives. As discussed earlier, providing advisory services, leading the development of plans and ensuring adherence to plans loosely correspond to the three successive phases of the initiative implementation process: conception, planning and execution (see Figure 10.6, Figure 11.2 and Figure 12.2 respectively).

First, digitalization initiatives in organizations often start their existence as such after some or the other advisory services have been provided to their sponsors by enterprise architects. For example, after consulting with an architect about the feasibly of a certain idea and receiving rough estimations of its possible realization cost, business managers can finance this idea to turn it into a full-fledged transformation initiative and begin its architectural planning, so that the initiative proceeds from its conception phase to the next planning phase. Hence, initiatives can flow out of architects' consultations. In these cases, leading the development of plans can be viewed largely as a follow-up activity succeeding the provision of advisory services.

Next, ensuring adherence to plans clearly represents a follow-up activity in relation to leading the development of plans. After finalized architectural plans are produced, transformation initiatives progress from the planning phase to the execution phase to materialize these plans. At this point, enterprise architects, who led the development of plans, switch their focus to ensuring adherence to them. Normally, architects supervise the execution of plans whose development processes they conducted.

In addition to the straightforward linkage of activities to the implementation lifecycle of digitalization initiatives described above, some other "nonlinear" sequential relationships between the activities of enterprise architects can also be articulated. For instance, as noted earlier, when the existing architectural plans prove inadequate during their execution, these plans may need to be revised or redeveloped. In these situations, ensuring adherence to plans can roll the process back to leading the development of plans on the part of architects. Or, knowledge gaps that are often revealed when providing advisory services or leading the development of plans can cause the need for more information. As a result, these activities can trigger both external and internal environmental studies.

Dynamic Interplay Between Different Activities

The logical and sequential relationships between the different activities of enterprise architects described above unite all these activities into a single web of interdependencies, where each activity somehow interacts with the other activities. These interactions form a rich and energetic interplay of activities that constitutes the occupation of architects in organizations. The dynamic cooperation between the five activities of enterprise architects ensuing from their logical and sequential relationships is demonstrated graphically in Figure 13.1.

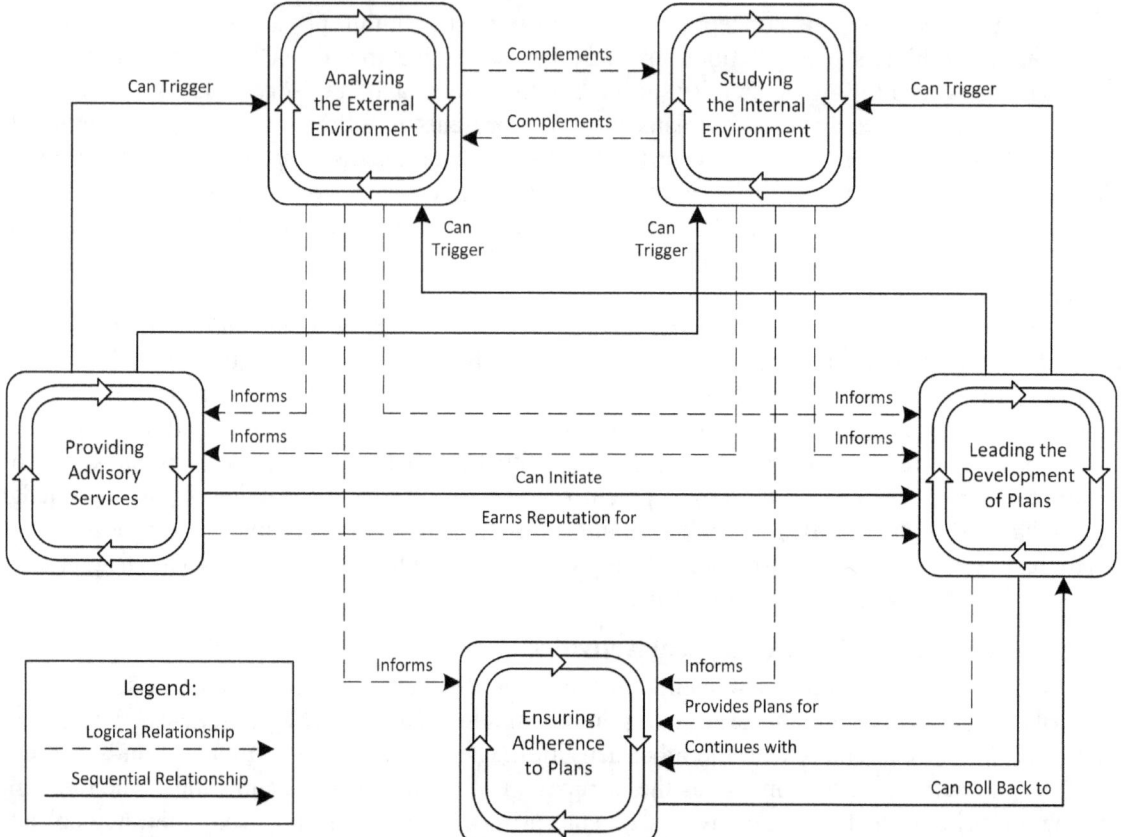

Figure 13.1. Dynamic interplay between the five activities of enterprise architects

As it becomes apparent from the depiction of the relationships between the different activities of enterprise architects provided in Figure 13.1, their job represents a truly complex plexus of diverse but interconnected actions that can follow up and trigger each other. However, for many reasons, it cannot be reduced to a deterministic automaton, or a state machine, with strictly defined transitions between its different states.

Activities of Enterprise Architects in Different Lifecycle Phases of Initiatives

The place of the five activities of enterprise architects in their occupation can also be better understood if these activities are explicitly mapped to the three lifecycle phases of digital transformation initiatives: conception, planning and execution (see Figure 2.2). As discussed earlier, even though the principal duty of architects in organizations is leading the architectural planning of digitalization initiatives, far from all their practical activities relate to architectural planning (see Figure 11.1), and even to specific change initiatives. Instead, their activities are spread across the different lifecycle phases of transformation initiatives and also happen "around" initiatives.

Namely, the studies of both the external and internal environments can be carried out by enterprise architects either for general education and awareness (e.g. understanding the technology market and the overall landscape structure, respectively), or for concrete digitalization initiatives, mostly during their planning phase (e.g. searching for suitable vendor products and scrutinizing the affected landscape areas, respectively). Providing advisory services is a rather universal activity that can be performed in a variety of situations, but most typically either outside of any transformation initiatives (e.g. evaluating the strategic fitness of the current IT landscape) or inside initiatives specifically during their conception phase (e.g. assessing the technical feasibility of business ideas). Leading the development of plans represents the pivotal activity of architects that drives the entire process of architectural planning, which is confined exclusively to the planning phase of transformation initiatives. Likewise, ensuring adherence to plans makes no sense outside of initiatives and naturally occurs only within their execution phase. The mapping of the five activities of enterprise architects to the three lifecycle phases of digital transformation initiatives described above is illustrated in Figure 13.2.

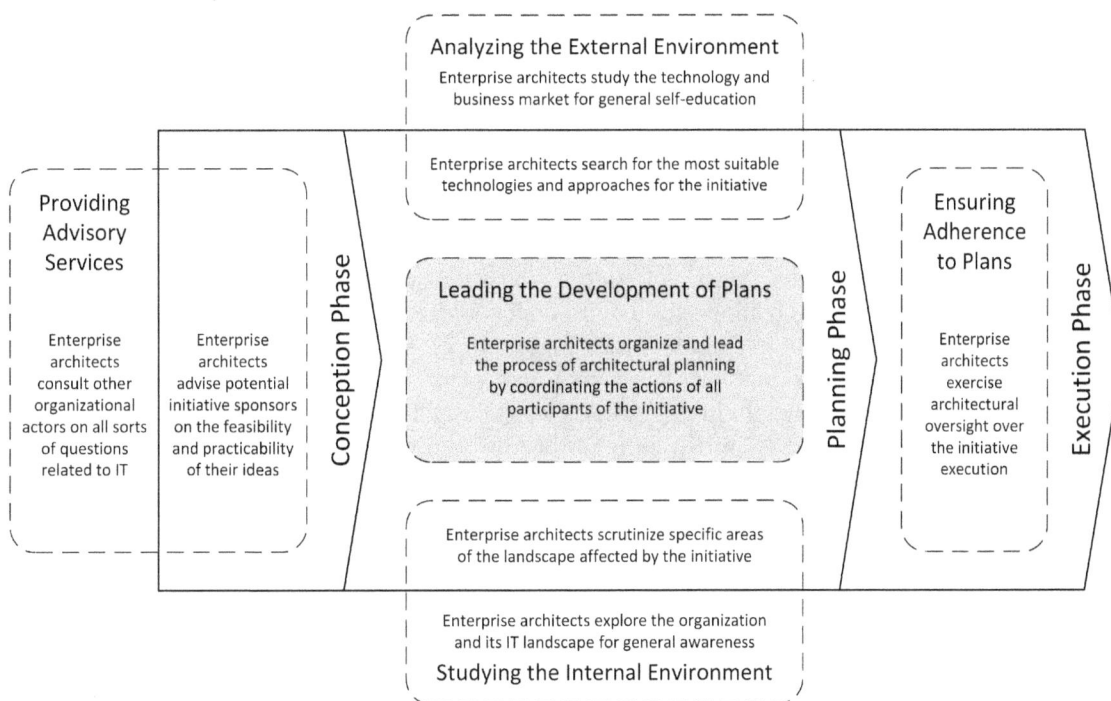

Figure 13.2. Activities of enterprise architects in different lifecycle phases of initiatives

As Figure 13.2 clearly demonstrates, the relationship between the activities of enterprise architects and digital transformation initiatives is, in fact, rather complex. On the one hand, although architects occupy the niche of chief initiative planners, many of their activities actually lie outside of specific initiatives and their architectural planning. On the other hand, the architectural planning effort may require, besides leading the development of plans, engaging in other activities on the part of architects as well. Furthermore, these activities are often intricately intertwined and can hardly be disentangled from one another.

The Value Stream of the Activities of Enterprise Architects

The five essential activities of enterprise architects can be conveniently summarized and presented in the form of a **value stream of activities** with four successive "stages", where more basic activities are placed on the left and more advanced ones on the right, so that its structure takes into account and loosely reflects the flow of resources between different activities (see Figure 13.1), as well as the sequential aspects of their mapping to the implementation lifecycle of digital transformation initiatives (see Figure 13.2). With this structure, fulfilling any activity is inconceivable without fulfilling all the activities from the previous stages. In other words, performing advanced activities requires performing all the more basic ones.

In this value stream, analyzing the external environment and studying the internal environment together constitute its most basic, leftmost stage as no other activities of architects seem possible if they do not possess relevant information and do not adequately understand the surrounding environment. Providing advisory services is the next stage of the value stream because earning a strong positive reputation as trusted partners is prerequisite for succeeding with more advanced activities. Leading the development of plans represents the third, more advanced stage that, in turn, produces the necessary input for the last activity of architects in the form of agreed architectural plans to be executed. And finally, ensuring adherence to plans is the most advanced, rightmost stage of the value stream, which is made possible by all the previous stages and can hardly be performed if any of the preceding activities are neglected. In this way, more basic activities of architects enable their more advanced activities.

The three basic activities on the left side of the value stream are carried out by enterprise architects in both the organizational and initiative contexts, but the two advanced right-side activities — only in the initiative context (see Figure 10.2). In addition, the overall logic of this value stream also indicates that the basic activities of architects tend to be unassertive and private, while their advanced activities — more proactive and collective. Consequently, this logic suggests that architects have to fulfill certain "boring" activities in the background across the organization to establish their standing before being in a position to come to the fore and spearhead any concrete digitalization initiatives. The resulting value stream of the activities of enterprise architects is shown in Figure 13.3.

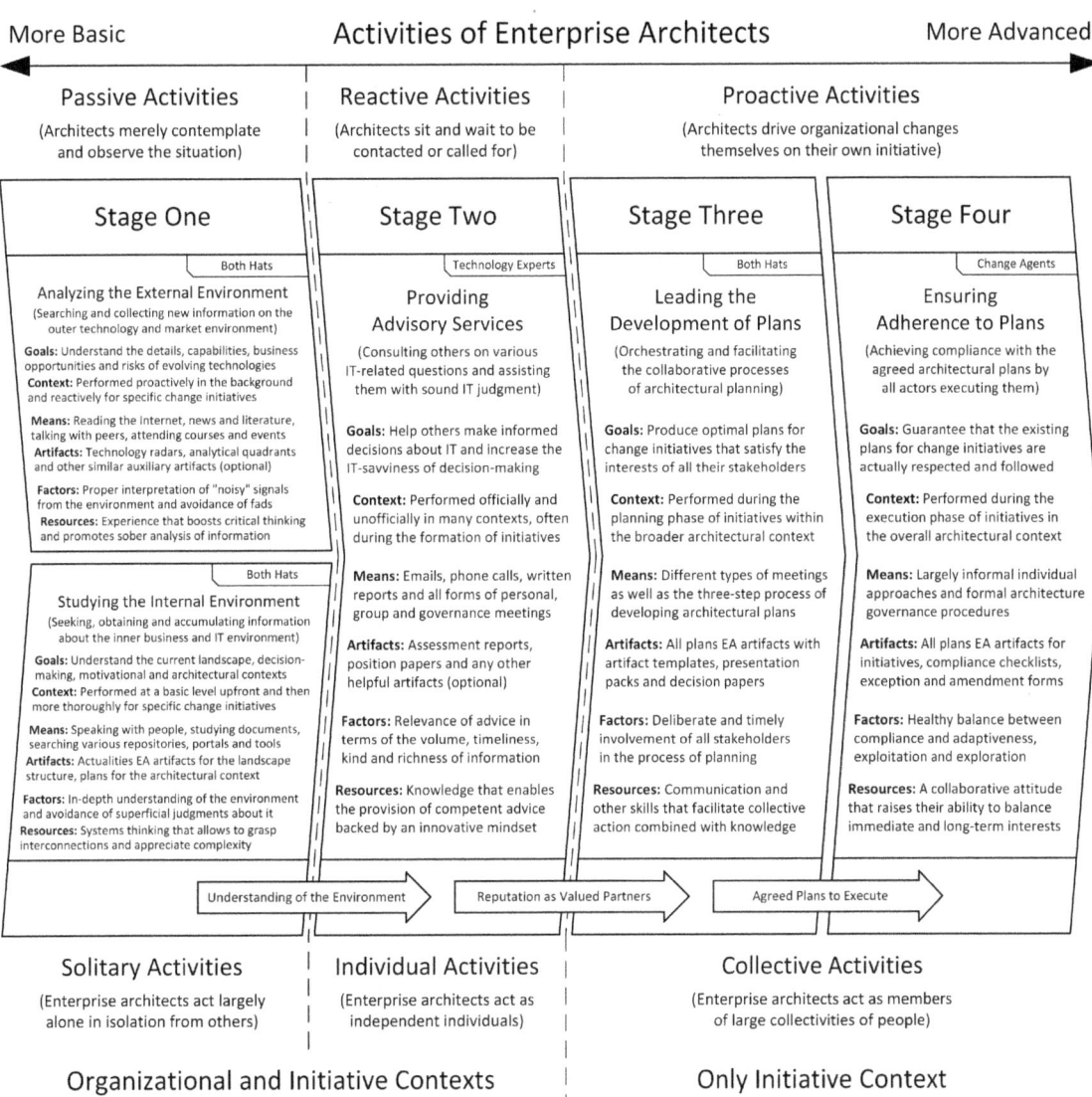

Figure 13.3. The value stream of the activities of enterprise architects

The value stream depicted in Figure 13.3 presents the activities of enterprise architects as a neat, linear sequence of distinct stages. This sequence is, however, purely logical, not causal or temporal. In reality, all their activities are carried out in parallel, being interlaced in time, as discussed later in this chapter. Moreover, in many cases, boundaries between different activities of architects cannot be precisely delineated. For example, it is not always clear where exactly providing advisory services finishes (i.e. mere discussions of ideas for initiatives) and leading the development of plans begins (i.e. more formalized architectural planning of initiatives).

More interestingly, as the execution of higher-level initiatives is manifested in the proper planning of their lower-level descendants, the respective activities of enterprise architects can effectively merge into one. Specifically, when both parent and derivative initiatives are handled by the same architect, this architect simultaneously leads the development of architectural plans for the derivative initiative *and* ensures adherence to plans for the parent initiative by means of active participation (see Table 12.1), i.e. ensures adherence to higher-level plans *by* leading the development of lower-level plans (see Figure 12.4). For example, for an architect assigned to a transformation program with all its subordinate projects, ensuring adherence to program plans and leading the development of project plans practically overlap, which is frequently observed in small organizations, as discussed later in Chapter 17 (Architecture Positions in Organizations). In this and similar scenarios, these two activities of architects become largely identical to each other.

The Work of Enterprise Architects in Organizations

The five activities of enterprise architects are the integral constituents of their occupation and the elementary "ingredients" of which their work in organizations is composed. The value stream of the activities of architects provides a convenient summary of these activities that explains their salient properties and key logical relationships between them (see Figure 13.3). However, by accentuating separate activities, this value stream fails to present a holistic picture of architects at work that unifies all their activities into a cohesive whole. In other words, it does not tell a vivid, dynamic and live story of how architects actually work in organizations through the lens of their five activities.

As discussed earlier, when working in organizations, enterprise architects operate and carry out their activities in both the organizational and initiative contexts (see Figure 10.1). Due to the disparate nature of these contexts, as well as of the work performed by architects within them, the overall meaning of their work can be best understood if their activities in the organizational and initiative contexts are first discussed separately.

The Work of Enterprise Architects in the Organizational Context

In the organizational context, the work of enterprise architects is embodied in the continuous fulfillment of their three basic activities: analyzing the external environment, studying the internal environment and providing advisory services. As part of their analysis of the external environment, architects browse the Internet and use other available means to keep an eye on new technology capabilities, their possible business applications and other relevant trends in business and IT. As part of their studies of the internal environment, they explore pertinent documentation and communicate with various organizational actors to keep track of what is going on in the organization, what transformation drivers come to light and what business leaders plan for the future. Lastly, during the provision of their advisory services, architects sit as officially appointed experts in governance committees supporting organizational decision-making, unofficially consult numerous "customers" across the organization on omnifarious IT-related questions (see Figure 10.5) and, thereby, deepen their understanding of what people are actually doing and thinking about.

By continually performing their basic activities in the organizational context, enterprise architects keep their fingers on the pulse of the organization, gain awareness of what ideas are circulating in the minds of its managers and assist them with sound IT judgment. Most importantly, through these activities, architects get involved in the initial ideation of digitalization initiatives, where they contribute their knowledge, expertise and insights to the generation of promising ideas for change and the formation of reasonable initiatives appropriate for the current motivational context (see Figure 4.5)[2]. Besides that, carrying out their basic activities also allows architects to expand their communication networks, build lasting relationships with business leaders, improve their reputation as valuable partners and increase their informal authority in business circles[3].

The Work of Enterprise Architects in the Initiative Context

The work of enterprise architects in the initiative context is embodied in serving digital transformation initiatives end-to-end, through all phases of their implementation lifecycle, from conception to execution. This work on the whole, as well as specific activities constituting it during different phases of the initiative implementation process, were thoroughly described earlier. To recapitulate, the role of architects in the course of the initiative implementation switches from competent advisors helping shape the right initiatives to lead planners conducting their architectural planning and, eventually, to chief supervisors exercising architectural oversight over their execution (see Figure 4.6 to Figure 4.8).

From the standpoint of their activities and stakeholders along the initiative implementation process, first, enterprise architects provide their unofficial advisory services to initiative sponsors and accomplish architectural pre-planning (see Figure 10.6). Then, they lead the development of plans with the involvement of all initiative stakeholders by following the three-step planning process (see Figure 11.2 and Figure 11.4). Finally, architects ensure adherence to plans by initiative executors by combining various personal and organizational means (see Figure 12.2 and Figure 12.4). This progression was illustrated previously in the mapping of their activities to the three phases of the initiative implementation lifecycle (see Figure 13.2).

By accomplishing their activities in the initiative context, enterprise architects structure digitalization efforts, optimize the utilization of organizational resources and bring specific transformation initiatives to completion. Besides that, succeeding with these activities also allows them to prove their value to the organization, strengthen their partnership ties with business leaders, further elevate their reputation as trustworthy experts and reach a higher status in terms of their informal influence on decision-making.

The Work of Enterprise Architects in Its Entirety

The descriptions of the activities of enterprise architects within the organizational and initiative contexts provided above presented them as two separate sets of activities detached from each other, as if they are unrelated. However, because all transformation initiatives emerge in the surrounding organizational environment, these two contexts and the corresponding activities of architects are obviously strongly linked, so that their work actually spans from the very origination of ideas for initiatives to their complete physical materialization.

Namely, at some point in the process of initial ideation, the ideas of initiative sponsors, after being discussed with enterprise architects providing their advisory services in the organizational context, turn into distinct digitalization initiatives and start off their regular implementation lifecycle with their conception, where these early ideas are elaborated into more mature concepts to be planned and then executed, also with the involvement of architects. In other words, at some moment, abstract talks about what the organization needs to achieve come down to more focused talks about specific proposals for action. In this particular moment, which is extremely difficult to pinpoint precisely, it begins to make sense to speak of initiatives as such, the initiative context is set and the work of architects moves from the broader organizational context into the newly created initiative one, so that the context of their activities becomes narrowed down and fixed. In this way, architects' activities in the organizational context result in launching new autonomous initiatives and generating the respective sub-contexts.

Basically, concrete digitalization initiatives in organizations, be it small projects, larger programs or global strategies, tend to originate from more general conversations of business leaders, as potential initiative sponsors, and enterprise architects about what can or should be done to improve the situation. These initiatives "flow out" of the space of ideas on how various transformation drivers can be responded to with IT. Metaphorically, the ideas of managers and architects can be compared to seeds that germinate into initiatives.

In the "birth" of autonomous initiatives, the conception phase of the initiative implementation process represents a vital "umbilical cord" that connects the organizational and initiative contexts by converting loose ideas wandering in the organization into formed change initiatives. As for derivative initiatives, they are launched later based on the goals and intentions of their parents as part of their hierarchical execution and their initiative contexts, in turn, represent nested sub-contexts of their parent initiatives, as mentioned earlier. The relationship between the work of enterprise architects in the organizational and initiative contexts via the processes of the formation of specific initiatives from general ideas described above is demonstrated schematically in Figure 13.4.

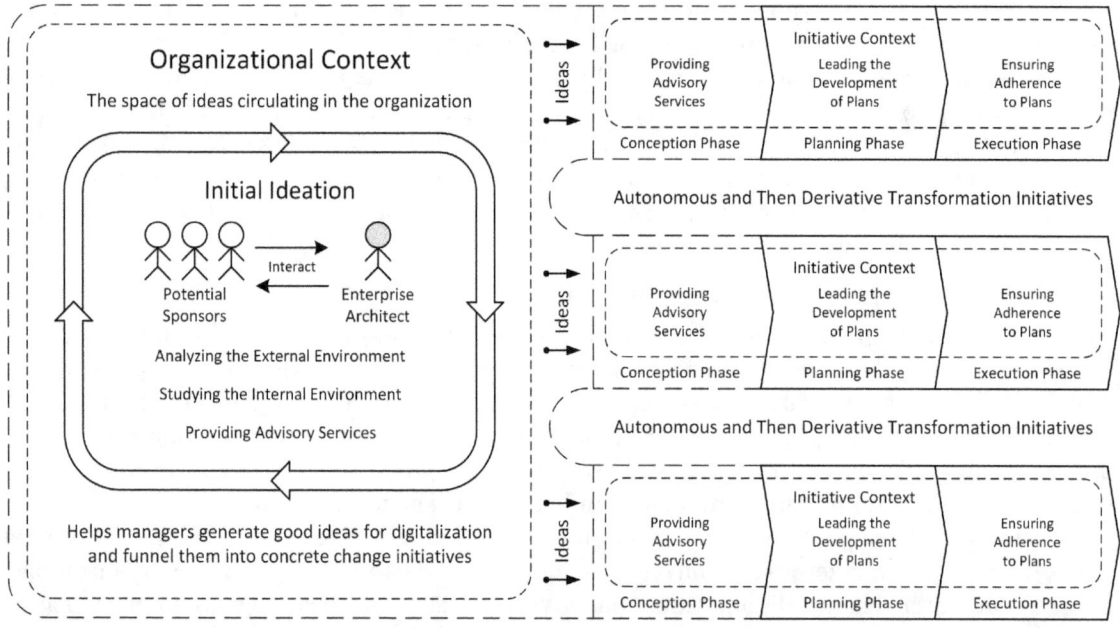

Figure 13.4. The work of enterprise architects in its entirety across the two contexts

The linkage of the organizational and initiative contexts shown in Figure 13.4 explains where new digitalization initiatives come from, what role enterprise architects play in their generation and when the context of their activities switches from organizational to initiative. This figure also captures the work of architects as a whole, integrating their activities in both contexts into a coherent story, where they consult potential initiative sponsors by operating in the organizational context, identify nascent initiatives across the organization and then bring them to completion by operating in the initiative context.

The Schedule of Enterprise Architects

All the discussions of the activities of enterprise architects provided earlier distinguished and revolved around five high-level activities, which jointly cover everything that they do in organizations. These activities are interconnected with various logical and sequential relationships (see Figure 13.1), partly linked to the initiative implementation lifecycle (see Figure 13.2) and can be represented as a four-stage value stream (see Figure 13.3). These activities also compose the work of architects in organizations, within both the organizational and initiative contexts (see Figure 13.4).

It is, however, important to realize that the division of architects' occupation into the five activities, as well as the different ways of their structuring, are purely conceptual, but in no case temporal (or temporal only in the context of a single transformation initiative in the sense that these activities align with its lifecycle phases, as shown in Figure 13.2). These activities and their relationships reflect only the meaning of what architects do as part of their job, but give no clue as to what their hourly schedule is or how their working days might be organized.

The Daily Timetable of Enterprise Architects

From a temporal perspective, all five activities of enterprise architects are usually intermeshed in time. They are performed by architects simultaneously in the sense that any single day of their work can include many or even all of them in varying proportions. Moreover, those of their activities that are carried out in the initiative context (i.e. most activities except for general self-education and advisory services) can belong to different transformation initiatives.

For example, for one transformation program, within a single working day, an enterprise architect can search the Internet for the appropriate hardware (i.e. analyze the external environment), speak with asset owners to better understand the current situation in the affected fragment of the IT landscape (i.e. study the internal environment) and attend two planning sessions with program stakeholders (i.e. lead the development of plans). During the same day, this architect can also visit a morning stand-up meeting for another project to check its delivery progress (i.e. ensure adherence to plans) and consult the IT leadership team about possible obstacles to implementing yet another digitalization strategy (i.e. provide advisory services). In addition to these initiative-related activities, in the organizational context, the architect can read some industry news on technology (i.e. analyze the external environment) and have a chat with three business managers about their current needs and visions for the future (i.e. provide advisory services), assisting in the initial ideation of initiatives. Besides that, like all other employees, architects are periodically distracted by common organizational routines having little or no direct relationship to the substance of their job, e.g. responding to internal surveys, filling necessary forms and sitting at general corporate meetings[4].

Because enterprise architects widely promote their advisory services and practice "planning by talking", communicating with others is the central element of their work. Communication generally takes the lion's share of architects' time as they tend to spend most of their business hours in some or the other conversations[5]. Their communication with other actors is normally organized in meetings, scheduled or unscheduled, formal or informal, one-on-one or in groups (see Table 11.1 for variations of planning meetings). The weekly calendar of architects, as active communicators, is usually packed with various meetings. They can routinely visit several meetings in a day and some of their days can be fully occupied with meetings.

Most meetings with others attended by enterprise architects, especially formal planning sessions, are scheduled meetings. **Scheduled meetings**, or booked meetings, are special meetings that are always appointed in advance and held exactly at the specified date, time and location. These meetings can embody all sorts of information inquiries, consultations, presentations, workshops and other discussions. Scheduled meetings are collective efforts that require finding and booking available timeslots convenient for all their participants, potentially very busy people. Once agreed upon and accepted by all parties, these timeslots may be difficult to renegotiate. For this reason, scheduled meetings essentially represent certain immovable blocks in the timetable of architects that shape the stiff "skeleton" of their working days.

In these circumstances, the remaining time of enterprise architects, which is not booked for any meetings, can be regarded as their "free" time, i.e. the time they can expend at their own discretion without being bound by obligations to others. Architects typically use this time for accomplishing their solitary tasks that do not imply anyone else's involvement. These tasks include, for example, reading news, studying specifications, drawing diagrams, creating EA artifacts, preparing presentation packs for upcoming planning sessions and appointing these sessions. As solitary tasks do not depend on other actors and their availability, they can be easily split, moved or canceled to accommodate other demands. Due to the flexibility of their timing, the solitary tasks of architects can be viewed as the soft "stuffing" of their workdays.

The combination of scheduled meetings, the timing of which is often dictated by external conditions arbitrary for architects, and their free time devoted to solitary tasks yields a rather peculiar and very fragmented work schedule consisting of multiple intermittent activities jumbled in time. As a result, in practice, any particular activity of architects seldom lasts for longer than 1–2 hours in an uninterrupted fashion[6]. An illustrative sample of the timetable of an enterprise architect for two consecutive working days with exemplary tasks and their classification into different activity types and different contexts of their fulfillment, either organizational or initiative-specific, is provided in Figure 13.5[7].

Chapter 13: The Work of Enterprise Architects

Tuesday, February 18, 2025

Time	Brief description of the task	Activity	Context
9:00	Reading the news on disruptive technologies for self-education	Analyzing the External Environment	Organizational Context
	Visiting the daily stand-up for the web UI project to check its progress	Ensuring Adherence to Plans	Initiative #3
10:00	Talking with the support team to find out what systems are in use	Studying the Internal Environment	Initiative #4
	Drinking coffee and thinking	Other	—
11:00	Attending the quarterly budgeting session to promote the alignment of IT investments with the enacted cloud migration strategy	Ensuring Adherence to Plans	Initiative #1
12:00	Filling in the yearly employee satisfaction survey from HR	Other	—
13:00	Lunching with two senior managers from the logistics department to discuss their ideas for optimizing delivery routes	Providing Advisory Services	Initiative #7 (Potential)
	Replying to emails with various technical questions and inquiries	Providing Advisory Services	Organizational Context
14:00	Navigating the architectural repository to understand how the current IT landscape is structured	Studying the Internal Environment	
15:00	Calling other architect to clarify some details of the IT landscape		
	Preparing PowerPoint materials for the forthcoming strategy workshop		Initiative #4
16:00	Organizing the workshop with the executives of the retail line of business to finalize their long-term digitalization strategy	Leading the Development of Plans	
17:00	Sending calendar invitations to appoint some follow-up meetings		

Wednesday, February 19, 2025

Time	Brief description of the task	Activity	Context
9:00	Attending the planning meeting with business and IT managers to discuss the prospects for a new production automation program	Leading the Development of Plans	Initiative #6
10:00	Studying and comparing alternative technologies that can be utilized for automating production processes	Analyzing the External Environment	
11:00	Leading the roadmapping session with business leaders for the ongoing ERP replacement program	Leading the Development of Plans	Initiative #5
12:00	Lunching alone and ruminating	Other	—
13:00	Searching for the documentation from previous ERP-related projects	Studying the Internal Environment	Initiative #5
	Responding to the call from a team lead about security requirements	Providing Advisory Services	Organizational Context
14:00	Participating in the research interview on enterprise architects' work with Dr. Svyatoslav Kotusev	Other	—
15:00	Having a coffee break with the VP of global customer experience	Providing Advisory Services	Initial Ideation
	Examining the proposed designs of two projects from the AI program	Ensuring Adherence to Plans	Initiative #2
16:00	Attending the regular fortnightly architecture review board meeting to endorse the designs of the projects from the AI program		
17:00	Exploring vendors of IT solutions for the retail sector and their products	Analyzing the External Environment	Initiative #4
	Scrolling the news about business and society for general awareness	Analyzing the External Environment	Organizational Context

[Free Time] [Scheduled Meetings]

Figure 13.5. An illustrative sample of the timetable of an enterprise architect for two days

As it is evident from the exemplary timetable presented in Figure 13.5, the job of enterprise architects is, in fact, rather hectic, loosely structured and somewhat chaotic, where business-related interactions can occur even during lunchtime. Each day of their work often comprises an array of very diverse activities virtually unrelated to each other. Moreover, little or no correlation in terms of their content can be observed even between two adjacent days. Basically, all workdays of architects are unique; no day is like the other.

In this light, the five key activities of enterprise architects discussed earlier should be considered mainly as conceptual building blocks from which their actual working days are composed, and each day can combine them in every possible way. Nevertheless, taken together, these activities tend to encompass and describe everything that architects do as part of their job in organizations. Except for occasional distractions, they occupy all eight hours of their typical workday.

Although the precise proportions of time allocated by enterprise architects to each activity undoubtedly depend on innumerable factors, such as position specifics, formal duties, current tasks and tenure in the company, these proportions on average can be *very roughly* assessed as follows: analyzing the external environment — 5–10%, studying the internal environment — 5–10%, providing advisory services — 15–25%, leading the development of plans — 30–60%, and ensuring adherence to plans — 15–25%. These proportions can also vary heavily across different periods, e.g. days of the week, weeks of the quarter or months of the year. For example, at the beginning of each year, more planning sessions usually take place, where architects lead the development of plans, while the rest of the year is dedicated more to their execution, where ensuring adherence to plans becomes more prevalent.

The Schedule of Enterprise Architects and the Pipeline of Initiatives

As discussed earlier, digital transformation initiatives in organizations normally progress linearly, from conception to execution, and the five activities of enterprise architects align with the respective phases of their implementation lifecycle. However, one of the noteworthy features of the schedule of architects is that they tend to be involved in *more than one* transformation initiative at the same time (see Figure 13.5). These initiatives can be at different stages of their implementation — conception, planning or execution — and architects with their daily activities gradually advance each of them forward. By contributing their attention and energy to multiple initiatives concurrently, architects make them all progress steadily, little by little towards completion.

Essentially, enterprise architects usually deal with a small *portfolio* of digitalization initiatives of different sizes, impact and criticality. In their day-to-day work, they allocate their time in necessary portions and apply their efforts in suitable ways to every initiative in their portfolio, depending on their priority and lifecycle phase. Only relatively rarely can architects fully concentrate on serving a single change initiative.

Using the metaphorical analogy from manufacturing, the initiative portfolio handled by enterprise architects can be more accurately described as the **pipeline of initiatives**, where different initiatives are processed in parallel, some initiatives enter the pipeline at their ideation, whereas others leave the pipeline at their completion. The relationship between the daily activities of enterprise architects and the implementation of digital transformation initiatives from their pipeline corresponding to the sample timetable from Figure 13.5 is shown in Figure 13.6.

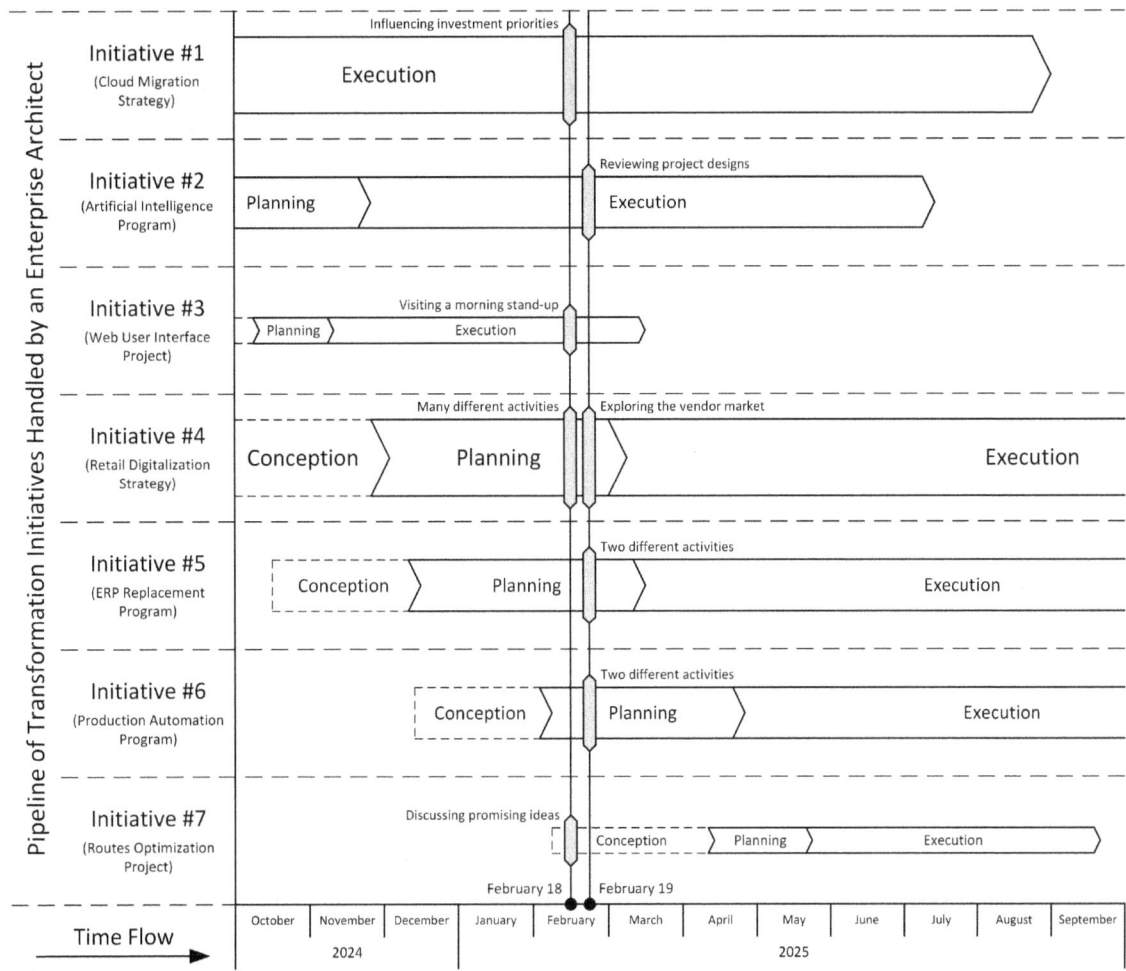

Figure 13.6. Daily activities of enterprise architects and the pipeline of initiatives

As Figure 13.6 clarifies, digitalization initiatives served by enterprise architects form a continuous stream, where some initiatives periodically finish by completing their execution phase while others occasionally emerge from their conception phase. Importantly, this figure demonstrates a rather extreme, but plausible case when an architect embraces the full spectrum of initiatives and works at all levels of transformation, i.e. drives projects, programs and strategies. For architects with a more narrowly defined sphere of responsibilities, their activities can be somewhat less diversified.

Enterprise Architects as the Advocates of Technical Interests

Although propelling digital transformation represents the most prominent and "glorious" part of the occupation of enterprise architects, for which they are celebrated in the industry press and around which all their responsibilities were previously framed, their work in organizations cannot be described solely in this light. In reality, their job is somewhat more diverse and also involves other important, but more prosaic duties unrelated to business transformation the bulk of which imply advocating technical interests in the face of pressing business demands.

As discussed earlier, business managers of different functional areas in organizations assert different interests aligned with these areas, and IT, as a major functional area, is also associated with certain technical interests that need to be asserted (see Figure 1.4). Some of the most ardent advocates of these technical interests in organizations are enterprise architects. It is architects who, along with senior IT managers, promote the ideas of ubiquitous technology optimization and rationality across the organization and are accountable for "keeping the lights on" in an operational sense[8].

Technical interests reflect the specifics of IT as a complicated subject area and address different aspects of *efficiency* in IT-related matters that do not necessarily affect any business processes, at least directly. Typically, these interests revolve around such issues as the costs of operating the IT landscape, maintainability of the existing systems, complexity of the landscape structure, obsolescence of infrastructure, proliferation of assets and technologies, operational risks and cybersecurity, as well as the technically correct construction of new IT solutions. It is these issues that, in the field of systems engineering, are closely associated with *non-functional* requirements. The general meaning of the technical interests advocated by enterprise architects can be best illustrated by the following and similar questions:

- Can we make our corporate IT landscape more cost-effective and less wasteful?
- How can we reduce our efforts on system support, upgrade and maintenance?
- Is our IT environment unduly complex, overly fragile and resistive to change?
- What needs to be done to remove, replace or modernize our aging equipment?
- Can we deduplicate and consolidate our application and technology portfolio?
- How can we mitigate our risks in terms of reliability and availability?
- Can we better protect ourselves from malicious activities and security threats?
- Does this IT solution apply the proper technical approaches and best practices?

Technical interests are clearly disparate from typical business interests. Furthermore, their differences lie in at least three orthogonal dimensions. First, these interests are dissimilar from the standpoint of their *core values*. While business interests reflect such *commercial* values as operating income, competitive advantage and customer experience, technical interests center around a completely different set of *engineering* values: simplicity, consistency, modularity, decoupling, reusability, deduplication, correctness, elegance and "beauty". Second, technical interests and business interests differ in their *organizational scopes*. Business interests are usually more localized organizationally and often confined to the boundaries of specific business units or areas that the interested parties represent, whereas technical interests tend to be more global and often transcend the boundaries of individual units and areas, affecting the whole landscape. Third, technical interests and business interests also differ in their *time horizons*. Business interests are usually more myopic, short-term oriented and can be limited only to the next year's profits or other performance indicators, but technical interests are more forward-thinking, reflective of timeframes commensurate with the lifecycles of information systems and concerned with the sustainability of the organizational IT estate in the long run.

In total, business interests can be characterized metaphorically as more tactical, "domestic" and "egoistic", while technical interests — as more strategic, "exterritorial" and "altruistic". The main differences between business interests and technical interests described above are summarized in Table 13.1.

Interests	Business interests	Technical interests
Advocates	Business leaders of different units and areas	Enterprise architects and IT leaders
Core values	Commercial values, e.g. operating income, inventory turnover, competitive advantage, process efficiency and customer experience	Engineering values, e.g. simplicity, consistency, modularity, decoupling, reuse, deduplication, correctness and elegance
Organizational scope	More local, often confined to the boundaries of specific business units or areas	More global, often transcend the boundaries of units and affect the whole landscape
Time horizon	More short-term, often limited only to the next year's performance indicators	More long-term, often commensurate with the lifecycles of information systems
Character	More tactical, domestic and egoistic	More strategic, exterritorial and altruistic

Table 13.1. Business interests and technical interests

Advocating technical interests cannot be regarded as a separate activity of enterprise architects complementary to their five core activities as it does not alter the overall pattern of their work in organizations (see Figure 13.4) and is not reflected explicitly in their working schedule (see Figure 13.5). Instead, the advocacy of technical interests represents a *constant concern* of architects that implicitly permeates all their activities, most notably providing advisory services and leading the development of plans, and adds an additional dimension to their occupation. In practical terms, this advocacy is manifested through the daily decisions and actions of architects in various situations and circumstances, influencing their work in the context of specific digitalization initiatives as well as in the broader organizational context.

Enterprise Architects as Initiative Stakeholders

Previously, within the architectural planning of digital transformation initiatives, enterprise architects were portrayed as actors having no interests of their own and completely subservient to the interests of others. Namely, they were described as lead planners responsible for finding mutually acceptable planning decisions meeting the heterogeneous interests of diverse stakeholder groups (see Figure 11.4), especially those of business representatives as the primary initiative stakeholders. Only for derivative initiatives, where they ensure adherence to plans through passive observation or active participation (see Table 12.1), were architects presented as special stakeholders advocating their alignment with higher-level architectural decisions.

This description of their role in the process of architectural planning is, however, not perfectly accurate as it omits the fact that enterprise architects are *not* "innocent" servants of initiative sponsors, but pursue certain objectives in the planning effort and also have their own stake in the resulting decisions. In particular, as legitimate representatives of the IT department, they defend the technical interests of engineering simplicity, correctness and rationality, joining the circle of actual initiative stakeholders.

In the context of architectural planning, the technical interests advocated by enterprise architects aggregate all sorts of important IT-specific considerations that cannot be fully appreciated by business stakeholders and balanced adequately against their other interests, e.g. poor system extensibility, future integration difficulties and dangerous vendor dependence. Along with regular business interests, these technical interests shape organizational solutions for digitalization initiatives (see Figure 3.3).

One notable concern of enterprise architects associated specifically with technical interests is achieving better alignment of architectural solutions for transformation initiatives with the architectural context from the technical side (see Figure 9.7). Sticking to already accepted technical decisions is highly desirable from an IT point of view as it helps stay in an established rut, avoid multiplying diversity and ensure greater consistency in the reuse of assets, technologies and best practices. Most importantly, Standards provide the principal source of technical decisions on the adopted implementation approaches that should be adhered to in new architectural solutions. Promoting compliance with the existing Standards for the sake of technical efficiency, therefore, represents a major task for architects during architectural planning.

When leading the development of plans for change initiatives, enterprise architects protect technical interests in political negotiations with other initiative stakeholders (see Figure 11.3), where these interests can collide with business interests along all three dimensions of their discrepancy: values, scope and time (see Table 13.1). First, business imperatives can conflict with technical ideals, e.g. perverse IT solutions enabling quick time-to-market. Second, local optima for separate units can conflict with global optimization, e.g. highly specialized, though not reusable solutions. Third, short-term benefits can conflict with long-range goals, e.g. solutions boosting quarterly performance, but not sustainable growth. Respecting technical interests, thus, often requires some trade-offs with business interests.

However, because enterprise architects have no official management authority, usually they cannot simply claim their interests against business interests in an upfront manner. Instead, to protect technical interests, architects can only resort to different *indirect* measures and rhetorical devices, ranging from very democratic to covert and manipulative ones. These measures include, in order of increasing assertiveness, the following approaches:

- Presenting honest information on the technical advantages and drawbacks of the available options in simple terms to business stakeholders and letting them make the final choice based on all the objective facts and best available evidence
- Presenting biased information exaggerating the pros and cons of the available options according to the architect's subjective preferences, but letting business stakeholders make the final choice, as if this choice is free and unbiased
- Presenting information on all available options with the architect's strong recommendation on the right way to go and pushing business stakeholders towards accepting the advice, though also allowing them to reject it
- Presenting to business stakeholders exclusively the options considered technically optimal by the architect and letting them make the final choice from the set of preselected scenarios, as if these scenarios are the only possible

Using these and other methods of persuasion helps enterprise architects guarantee that the developed architectural solutions for transformation initiatives satisfy not only the business interests of their sponsors, but also the best technical interests dictated by the needs of IT and are reasonable from an engineering point of view. Excessive insistence on technical interests on the part of architects, however, can alienate them from business stakeholders and undermine their productive cooperation, as discussed later in Chapter 18 (Challenges of Enterprise Architects).

Enterprise Architects as Driver Proponents

Besides acting as IT stakeholders advocating technical interests during the architectural planning of particular digitalization initiatives, enterprise architects also act as the proponents of IT-side transformation drivers and motivate new change efforts. Namely, architects are vocal proponents of technical concerns as various IT-specific factors that necessitate modifications in organizations (see Figure 1.2). For instance, they would be among the first to notice existing bottlenecks, unwanted redundancies, security holes and impending problems in the corporate IT landscape and argue for their elimination.

Moreover, as active driver proponents, enterprise architects often come as the sponsors of new autonomous change initiatives (see Figure 2.3). Their sponsorship of initiatives, though, can only be of ideological, rather than material character. Again, as architects possess no managerial power and control no budgets to be able to launch initiatives at their personal will, they can only convince real managers and decision-makers of their necessity to get them launched. For example, architects can prove the need for certain technical optimizations to the CIO to secure initiative funding. Or, less likely, they can persuade business leaders of the necessity to invest in the renovation of old IT infrastructure and win support in their circles.

Technical Rationalization Initiatives

Previously in this book, all IT-related change initiatives were presented specifically as digital transformation initiatives — initiatives transforming the business of organizations with the use of IT by introducing some information systems that enhance their business activities, e.g. automate manual processes, improve customer experience or offer new digital products. However, in addition to regular digitalization initiatives thoroughly discussed earlier, another type of change initiatives concerned exclusively with technical interests and aimed to rationalize the existing landscape structure also run in organizations.

Technical rationalization initiatives, or architectural initiatives, are special change initiatives intended primarily to improve the technical quality of the organizational IT landscape in terms of cost-effectiveness, flexibility, manageability, interoperability, risk exposure or other valuable properties. These initiatives can vary greatly in their scale and include, for example, a project to remove an unused business application from the landscape, a program to upgrade all the outdated security equipment and a strategy to migrate core information systems to the cloud hosting environment.

In contrast to "honorable" digital transformation initiatives, technical rationalization initiatives are less conspicuous organizationally, may not impact any business operations and involve more "dirty work". And yet, these initiatives are necessary for ensuring the sustainability of organizations as viable business entities in the long run. Unsurprisingly, various rationalization initiatives are periodically launched in every organization as the respective needs arise.

From the standpoint of their implementation, technical rationalization initiatives do not differ substantially from ordinary digitalization initiatives. For instance, they go through exactly the same phases of the initiative implementation lifecycle (see Figure 2.2), imply the same three-step process of architectural planning and generally require the same kind of activities on the part of enterprise architects during their different lifecycle phases (see Figure 13.2).

The motivation, stakeholders and domain affiliation of technical rationalization initiatives, however, are quite different from those of digital transformation initiatives. Whereas digitalization initiatives are induced by some business-side transformation drivers from the motivational context, rationalization initiatives are driven by IT-side technical concerns. The former usually have more or less articulate business cases for the changes they suggest, but the latter may have no meaningful business cases, except for possible cost-cutting opportunities. For digital transformation initiatives, their primary sponsors and beneficiaries are business representatives, while technical rationalization initiatives are typically backed by IT leaders, often under the influence of enterprise architects.

Because technical rationalization initiatives do not seek any perceptible business improvements, but only certain purely technical optimizations, their architectural solutions, particularly their organizational components, normally shift their focus in terms of domain coverage (see Figure 3.5), switching from functional to non-functional domains (see Table 3.2). Accordingly, the circle of stakeholders involved in their development may not include any business managers and consist only of various IT representatives (see Figure 3.2), which, thanks to their common background, makes these initiatives somewhat easier for architects to deal with. For this reason, digital transformation initiatives and technical rationalization initiatives have important distinctions in their architectural planning.

Of course, the features of these two archetypes of initiatives are *not* incompatible or mutually exclusive as every initiative can combine some elements of both business transformation and technology rationalization, though in different proportions. For example, a single initiative can introduce a new application to radically reshape some business processes (i.e. perform digital transformation) and, at the same time, also decommission a number of legacy applications that are no longer used or whose functionality is replaced by the new application, along with the underlying IT infrastructure (i.e. achieve technical rationalization). For this reason, depending on their content, all change initiatives can be placed somewhere on a continuous spectrum between the two opposite extremes of pure transformation and pure rationalization. The differences between digital transformation and technical rationalization initiatives, as well as the spectrum of possible change initiatives, are summarized in Figure 13.7.

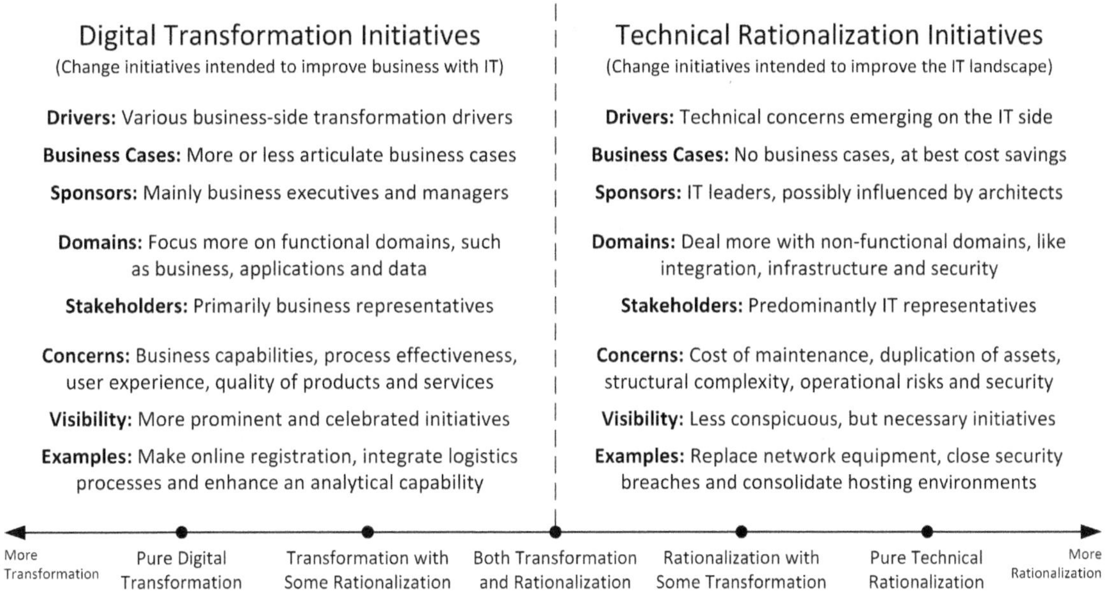

Digital Transformation Initiatives
(Change initiatives intended to improve business with IT)

Drivers: Various business-side transformation drivers
Business Cases: More or less articulate business cases
Sponsors: Mainly business executives and managers
Domains: Focus more on functional domains, such as business, applications and data
Stakeholders: Primarily business representatives
Concerns: Business capabilities, process effectiveness, user experience, quality of products and services
Visibility: More prominent and celebrated initiatives
Examples: Make online registration, integrate logistics processes and enhance an analytical capability

Technical Rationalization Initiatives
(Change initiatives intended to improve the IT landscape)

Drivers: Technical concerns emerging on the IT side
Business Cases: No business cases, at best cost savings
Sponsors: IT leaders, possibly influenced by architects
Domains: Deal more with non-functional domains, like integration, infrastructure and security
Stakeholders: Predominantly IT representatives
Concerns: Cost of maintenance, duplication of assets, structural complexity, operational risks and security
Visibility: Less conspicuous, but necessary initiatives
Examples: Replace network equipment, close security breaches and consolidate hosting environments

◄──►
More Transformation | Pure Digital Transformation | Transformation with Some Rationalization | Both Transformation and Rationalization | Rationalization with Some Transformation | Pure Technical Rationalization | More Rationalization

Figure 13.7. Digital transformation and technical rationalization initiatives

As prominent advocates of technical interests and influential proponents of technical concerns as transformation drivers, enterprise architects can be regarded largely as ideological owners of technical rationalization initiatives in organizations. Although addressing various IT-specific interests and concerns and leading the respective change efforts represent a less prestigious and "noble" side of their work than promoting digitalization, these responsibilities are essential to their occupation.

All in all, the work of enterprise architects in organizations is richer than only facilitating their digital transformation endeavors, involves a somewhat broader set of duties and can even be viewed as consisting of two relatively independent components. First, their work implies responding to business interests, serving digitalization initiatives and improving business and IT alignment. Second, it implies advocating technical interests, driving rationalization initiatives and increasing internal IT efficiency.

Chapter Summary

This chapter discussed the occupation of enterprise architects as the unity of their five activities, described their work separately in different contexts and in its entirety, discussed the daily schedule of enterprise architects and its relationship to the pipeline of initiatives and explained their role as the advocates of technical interests in organizations. The key message of this chapter can be summarized in the following essential points:

- The five activities of enterprise architects constituting their occupation are inseparable and interconnected with various logical and sequential relationships, forming a dynamic interplay interwoven into the surrounding context

- The five activities of enterprise architects can be presented as a four-stage value stream, progressing from more basic activities to more advanced ones, loosely reflecting the flow of resources between different activities
- The work of enterprise architects in the organizational context involves analyzing the external environment, studying the internal environment and providing advisory services to understand the organization, assist managers with sound IT judgment and contribute to the initial ideation of digitalization initiatives
- The work of enterprise architects in the initiative context covers the initiative implementation process end-to-end and involves providing advisory services during the conception phase, leading the development of plans during the planning phase and ensuring adherence to plans during the execution phase
- The work of enterprise architects in its entirety spans both the organizational and initiative contexts and embraces both the initial ideation of new digitalization initiatives and their subsequent implementation through different phases
- The timetable of enterprise architects is very fragmented, includes many intermittent activities jumbled in time and consists of scheduled meetings with others and intervals of free time spent on various solitary tasks
- In their work, enterprise architects are usually involved in multiple initiatives at different stages of their implementation, where they invest their energy in all initiatives concurrently, making each of them progress towards completion
- The work of enterprise architects also implies advocating technical interests and serving as active stakeholders of digital transformation initiatives, as proponents of technical concerns and as sponsors of technical rationalization initiatives

Chapter 14: The Profession of Enterprise Architects

The previous chapters provided an exhaustive, in-depth coverage of the resources, instruments, activities and work of enterprise architects. This chapter presents a more abstract discussion of the profession of enterprise architects with its specifics in the broader context. In particular, this chapter starts with framing the job of enterprise architects as a separate profession, introducing the integrative framework of their profession and analyzing their profession as a motley blend of art, craft and science. Next, this chapter describes the long historical evolution of enterprise architects in the industry, including their little-known past, glorious present and possible future. Lastly, this chapter discusses terminological ambiguity around enterprise architects and their different understandings as a profession, archetype and position, as well as some other less valid meanings.

The Job of Enterprise Architects as a Separate Profession

Enterprise architects are specialized industry professionals dedicated to driving architectural planning in organizations to enable their digital transformation (see Figure 4.1). The general meaning of their peculiar occupation is represented by the two disparate hats that they wear: Technology Experts and Change Agents (see Figure 4.9). Due to an unusual combination of qualities necessary for wearing these hats, their resources are quite unique and barely resemble those of any other organizational actors. The same conclusion is equally valid for their instruments and activities as well. Because largely the same set of resources, instruments and activities is typical for all individuals occupying the positions of enterprise architects, their job can be considered as a separate profession, though not nearly as well-defined as most classic professions.

Is the Job of Enterprise Architects a Profession?

Professions are characterized by certain standards of conduct, bodies of knowledge and best practices adopted by their members. For traditional professions, these elements are largely context-neutral and can be *codified* to ensure the consistent application of methods, approaches and techniques that proved their effectiveness by all representatives of the profession. Exemplary professionals, such as doctors, lawyers and engineers, are formally educated according to their codes and often *certified* or even licensed based on their conformity to professional norms and requirements.

By contrast, among other jobs, the job of general managers is incredibly versatile, extremely context-specific and practically impossible to codify. Due to its inherent diversity and intractability to codification, their occupation cannot be viewed as a profession similar to medicine, law and engineering, but rather as a somewhat ad hoc and unsystematic practice. For this reason, managers require quite different forms of training and can hardly be certified, let alone licensed[1].

In this spectrum, the job of enterprise architects can be positioned somewhere between the fully codifiable professions of various specialists and the non-codifiable practice of general managers. On the one hand, as with professionals, the core categories of activities, instruments and resources of architects are rather stable and common to all denominations of architects, which makes it possible to gather a coherent corpus of knowledge on various aspects of their work. On the other hand, as with managers, the details of their activities and other attributes are always determined by unique organizational circumstances, which makes it impossible to offer any specific recipes, straightforward prescriptions and even algorithmic instructions to guide their actions. Consequently, their job is highly context-dependent, but still amenable to partial codification — an ambitious task attempted in this book.

On this basis, the job of enterprise architects can arguably be regarded as a *loose profession* with numerous distinctive features, but without a precisely defined knowledge base and strict standards of behavior. For this reason, architects cannot be licensable, but some forms of their professional certification can be helpful, as discussed later in Chapter 19 (Other Aspects of Enterprise Architects)[2]. The place of the job of enterprise architects as a partly codifiable, loose profession in the context of other jobs is shown in Figure 14.1.

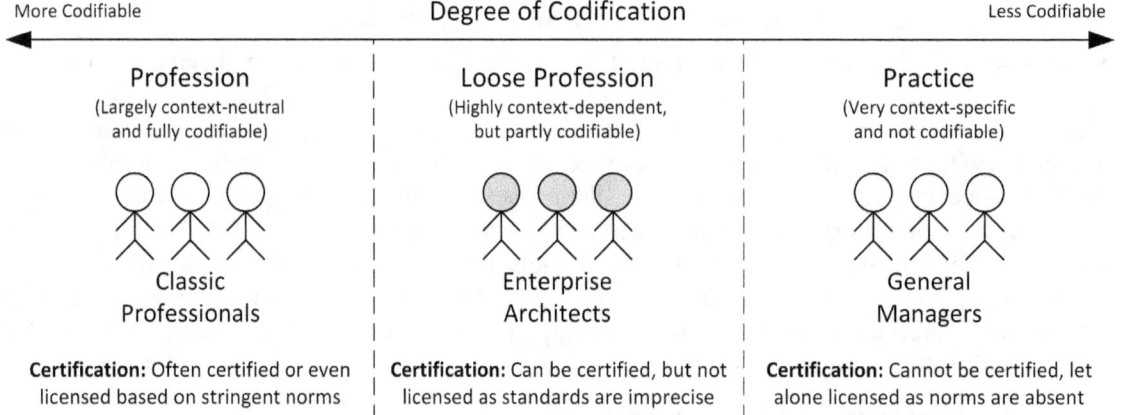

Figure 14.1. The job of enterprise architects as a partly codifiable, loose profession

However, it is not only the possibility of partially codifying the job of enterprise architects that allows calling it a profession. For instance, their occupation is clearly distinct from all other existing professions and differs from them in many aspects, securing architects a separate niche in the organizational ecosystem (see Figure 5.2). Their occupation is also characterized by its own rich terminology, professional jargon, educational credentials, industry associations and practitioner networks. Moreover, it has even created a developed and diversified market of various services intended specifically for architects, as discussed later in this chapter. All these and some other signs definitely allow speaking of enterprise architects as representatives of an established professional community[3].

The Integrative Framework of the Profession of Enterprise Architects

To do their job, enterprise architects possess three major classes of resources: knowledge, skills and experience (see Figure 6.3). As their working instruments, they employ mainly six general types of EA artifacts: Considerations, Standards, Visions, Landscapes, Outlines and Designs (see Figure 7.11). Being empowered by these resources and equipped with these instruments, architects perform five essential activities: analyzing the external environment, studying the internal environment, providing advisory services, leading the development of plans and ensuring adherence to plans (see Figure 13.3), which compose their work in organizations (see Figure 13.4). All these attributes of architects can be integrated into a comprehensive framework outlining the key elements of their loose profession and the relationships between them. Specifically, this framework can be constructed by clarifying the conceptual relationships between their resources, instruments and activities.

First, the resources of enterprise architects enable their activities since they cannot be performed by unqualified persons without special background. For example, carrying out successfully such activities as providing advisory services and leading the development of plans seems improbable without considerable knowledge of business and IT, excellent communication and teamwork skills, as well as extensive experience with technology. Conversely, the fulfillment of these activities by architects leads to the further accumulation of their resources through the mechanisms of personal learning. For instance, analyzing the external environment and studying the internal environment obviously augment architects' knowledge, while their skills and experience are "automatically" honed and accumulated along the way as they perform all other, more practical activities. In short, learning adds to knowledge, doing contributes to skills and working — to experience.

Second, the instruments of enterprise architects support their activities as they cannot be performed without material substance. At the same time, many activities of architects, in turn, produce some or the other instruments in the form of physical EA artifacts. Most notably, leading the development of plans, on the one hand, uses the existing EA artifacts from the architectural context to align the respective initiatives with higher-order plans and, on the other hand, generates new artifacts to capture the resulting architectural plans for those initiatives (see Figure 11.2). Likewise, when studying the internal environment, architects analyze the available actualities EA artifacts to understand the current situation and also update these artifacts, or even create new ones, if their descriptions turn out inaccurate or incomplete.

These relationships allow connecting the resources (represented by their pyramid from Figure 6.3), instruments (represented by the CSVLOD taxonomy for EA artifacts from Figure 7.11) and activities (represented by their value stream from Figure 13.3) together to form a holistic framework defining all aspects of the profession of enterprise architects. All elements of this framework can also be tagged to indicate whether they pertain to architects wearing the hat of Technology Experts, the hat of Change Agents or both hats. The resulting integrative framework of the profession of enterprise architects with their resources, instruments and activities is depicted schematically in Figure 14.2.

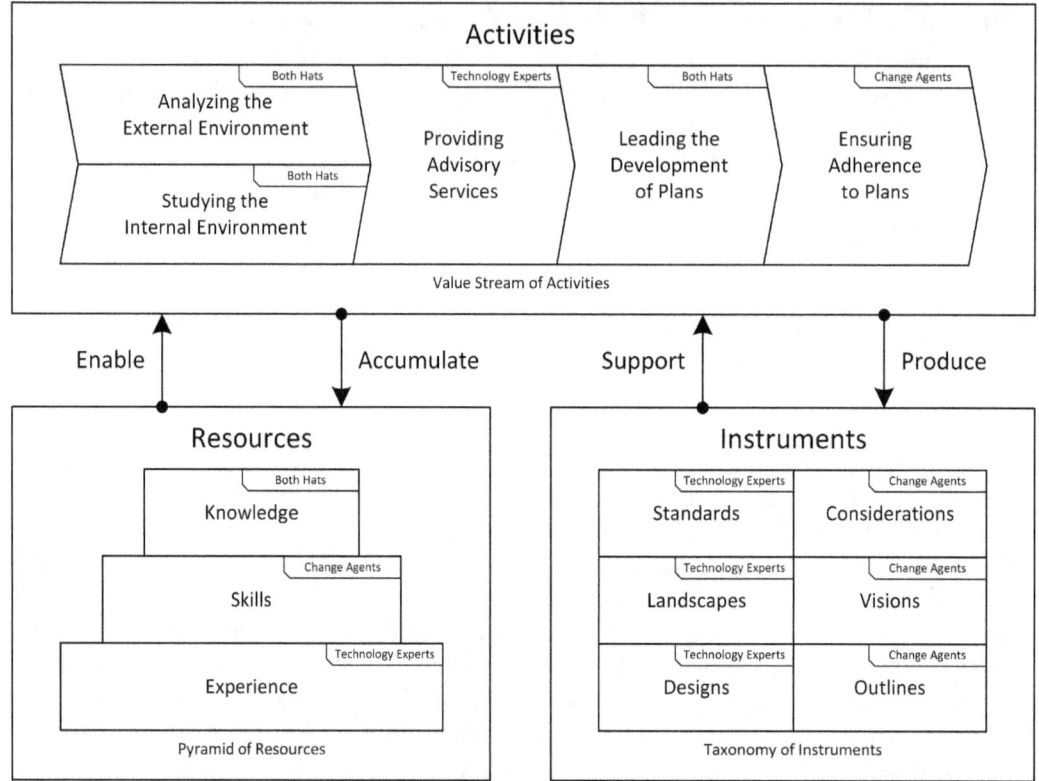

Figure 14.2. The integrative framework of the profession of enterprise architects

The conceptual framework presented in Figure 14.2 delineates the profession of enterprise architects as a whole. All elements of this framework are generic and valid for all varieties of architects, regardless of their specializations. The framework also demystifies their profession by answering the most basic questions about it, e.g. who enterprise architects are, what they do, what they own and what they use.

Art, Craft and Science in the Profession of Enterprise Architects
The profession of enterprise architects is very complex, multifaceted and rich with diversity. It embraces many heterogeneous aspects and "stretches" from dealing with implementation-level technicalities to discussing business transformations with executives to generating innovative ideas for the use of IT. Should this profession be viewed more as an art, craft or science?[4]

In fact, the analysis of the resources, instruments and activities of enterprise architects (see Figure 14.2) suggests that their profession actually involves distinct elements of each of these three realms of human activity. Some aspects of their occupation gravitate towards science, some aspects certainly represent craft, while others can be clearly regarded as a form of art.

First, many aspects of the work of enterprise architects in organizations undoubtedly border with **science** and leverage its rigorous methods. Those are the aspects of their occupation that rely on formal logic, theoretical constructs, precise calculations, rational analysis and systematic evidence. They include various tasks dealing with the following, but not only, issues:

- Algorithm design — the development of computationally efficient algorithms and optimal data structures is deeply rooted in computer science and can even be viewed as a major part of it
- Software design — designing software components of information systems with the properties of reliability, scalability, extendibility, maintainability, recoverability and security has pronounced scientific features
- Hardware design — designing cost-effective hardware and cloud infrastructure with the necessary processing power, transaction throughput, storage capacity and all sorts of "-ilities" is also strongly associated with science

These and similar elements of the profession of enterprise architects have a dominating scientific component. They "enarm" architects with analytical thinking and classic engineering approaches to problem solving. For the most part, these elements are introduced to the profession via formal classroom training and conventional theoretical education. However, all tasks that require scientifically substantiated techniques belong predominantly to the repertoire of architects in the hat of Technology Experts. From the standpoint of architects' resources, the realm of science is represented chiefly in their knowledge.

Second, many practical aspects of the work of enterprise architects essentially constitute a rather sophisticated **craft** and, in many respects, resemble traditional managerial competencies. Those are the aspects of their occupation that are based primarily on behavioral habits, "muscle memory", learning through experience and practice. They include, but are not limited to, the following routine tasks filling the workdays of architects:

- Dealing with an audience — communicating with different audiences, giving presentations, expressing ideas, listening to opinions, collecting feedback and reacting to it
- Orchestrating processes — involving necessary stakeholders, organizing collective decision-making sessions, capturing their outcomes and pushing the processes forward towards completion
- Coping with conflicts — resolving conflicts of interests between different parties, finding the "common ground" between diverging viewpoints, proposing mutually acceptable compromises and choices

These and many other elements in the profession of enterprise architects can be clearly classified as craftsmanship, not science. They provide architects with the necessary abilities to work with people and exhibit proper behavior in difficult situations. These elements can hardly be brought to the profession by means of formal classroom education, but require prolonged hands-on practice to master. The majority of these elements, though, relate specifically to architects wearing the hat of Change Agents. Of all their resources, craft is reflected mostly in their skills and experience.

Finally, some aspects of the work of enterprise architects fully deserve to be credited as a special form of **art** and make their job far from formulaic, repetitive and boring. Those are the aspects of their occupation that are associated with unique vision, ingenuity, originality, intuition, imagination and creative insights. They permeate, to varying degrees, virtually all their tasks and include, among others, the following manifestations of creativity on the part of architects:

- Impressive visualizations — drawing easily understandable, highly intuitive or particularly persuasive graphical diagrams of the complex organizational reality that effectively appeal to different audiences
- Ingenious solutions — designing unexpected IT solutions that address the stated business problems and needs with especial elegance, surprising simplicity or unprecedented efficacy
- Innovative approaches — inventing new, possibly revolutionary ways of utilizing IT for doing business, providing digital services or automating business operations unheard of in the industry

These and similar constituents of the profession of enterprise architects represent more art, than craft or science. They endow architects with a creative drive and capacity to transform the surrounding reality and even their own work for the better. These elements, probably, lean largely on idiosyncratic personal gifts and talents that are difficult to acquire. Various elements of art can definitely be identified in the actions of architects as both Technology Experts and Change Agents. In terms of their resources, the realm of art arguably does not relate directly to any of them.

All the elements of art, craft and science described above are immediately relevant to the profession of enterprise architects. Each of these realms contributes to the profession its own unique potential and enriches it with respective capabilities, though their elements are incorporated there in different ways and pertain to different hats worn by architects. The profession of enterprise architects, as an intricate overlapping of the realms of art, craft and science, is shown in Figure 14.3.

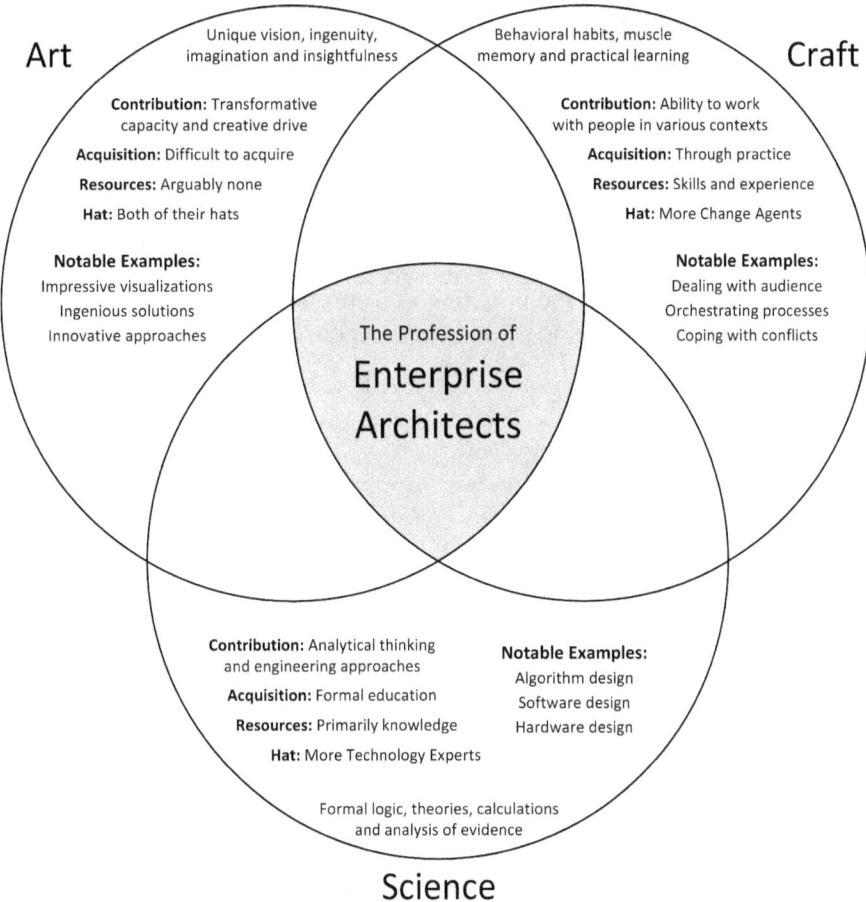

Figure 14.3. The profession of enterprise architects as a medley of art, craft and science

As demonstrated in Figure 14.3, the profession of enterprise architects cannot be regarded exclusively, or even mostly, as an art, craft or science, but rather represents a harmonious composition of these three disparate realms, borrowing some valuable elements from each of them[5]. The truly distinctive melange of competencies, abilities and talents required to fulfill their job in organizations explains the segregation of specialized architects from the broader IT community many decades ago, which eventually gave birth to this entirely new profession.

The Historical Evolution of Enterprise Architects

Enterprise architects, as an industry phenomenon, did not emerge yesterday out of the blue, but went through a decades-long evolutionary path. Starting their initial existence as exotic and singular information systems planners endemic to only the few largest companies, they have later expanded their "habitat", spread widely across the industry and permeated, in some form, into most organizations of non-trivial size.

The Past of Enterprise Architects

In May 1949, J. Lyons & Co. in the United Kingdom commenced the pioneering work on an innovative business-oriented computer called the Lyons Electronic Office (LEO). In November 1951, the first regular computational job was run on LEO and, by the end of 1953, the machine was finished. LEO is generally considered to be the world's first commercial information system that gave rise to the new field of business computing[6].

The LEO project was envisaged and headed by a mathematician named John Simmons passionate about streamlining routine clerical operations with advanced office machinery. Simmons played the starring role in the initiative as a "maestro of technology", who orchestrated and coordinated the respective planning efforts from the business and IT sides:

> *"Simmons was a quintessential "maestro of technology". [A maestro] is positioned between the top executives and the board on one side, and a strong technical team on the other. He [...] communicates well with each side, translating differing languages and view points between the two parties. Importantly, a maestro understands deeply how the technology can be aligned with the business' needs and goals. He plans and implements new technological infrastructures; [...] and insures that organizational processes are changed to take full advantage of the technology's potential"* (Mason, 2004, pp. 191-192)

The job of the maestro John Simmons in the LEO project was described as that of balancing the interests of different business and IT constituencies and reaching a consensus view of what solution is needed by the organization:

> *"The maestro negotiates among the interests of senior management, business operating personal representing various units, information specialists, and technologists and leads them to a common solution, one aimed at achieving the organization's overall goals"* (Mason, 2004, pp. 194-195)

Eventually, after the initial success with LEO, John Simmons developed a comprehensive "master plan" for the future use of the computer across the whole company, which defined the ideal long-term target state in terms of the key computing jobs and information flows between them linked to the structure of management and business units[7]. Furthermore, much earlier, he also realized that a specialized organizational function was necessary for bridging the widening gap between business and IT people in the organization and marrying its business needs with suitable technologies[8]:

> *"Simmons and his colleagues recognized that a deep chasm might emerge between the company's operating managers and its technologists and information systems specialists unless some mediating organization was created. [...] At Lyons, Systems Research [department established by Simmons] undertook this crucial mediating task"* (Mason, 2004, p. 194)

Therefore, the available historical evidence clearly suggests that what was done at the dawn of business computing during the 1940s–1950s at J. Lyons & Co. from the standpoint of systems planning actually closely resembles what enterprise architects do in organizations today. On this basis, it can be stated with a certain level of confidence, surprisingly, that the profession of enterprise architects is as old as information systems themselves and that John Simmons from J. Lyons & Co. was the primordial representative of this profession. Although never explicitly titled as such (and despite his managerial duties), Simmons can arguably be honored as the world's first enterprise architect.

Then, along with the subsequent spreading of business computers in large, progressive organizations over the 1960s–1970s, full-time information systems planners and dedicated planning functions analogous to modern enterprise architects and architecture functions[9], in some form or the other, became the norm among the early IT adopters[10]. For example, during this period, many U.S. industry giants from different sectors, such as Mobil Oil, Xerox, Consumers Power, IBM and Trans World Airlines, established permanent systems planning groups responsible for leading the introduction of IT and automating their operations[11].

Later, with the further proliferation of IT in the 1980s, driven by the pressing demand for improving its alignment with business needs[12], specialized information systems planners, separate planning functions and systematic planning practices became more prevalent and emerged in a noticeable but still rather small fraction of organizations across the industry[13]. In the 1990s, their numbers continued to grow rapidly and already reached a considerable share, though not yet the majority, of all organizations[14].

Lastly, during the 1990s, manifold variations of information systems planners, also known in different organizations and time periods as long-range systems planners, strategic information planners, IT planners, systems designers and information engineers[15], gradually converged and propagated further under a common umbrella title by which they are ubiquitously known in the industry today — enterprise architects[16]. Somewhere around the turn of the century, a loose professional community of systems planners finally consolidated into a distinct profession of enterprise architects.

Hence, even though the term "enterprise architect" itself originated only in the 1990s and gained widespread popularity somewhat later in the 2000s[17], the very occupation of architects is certainly much older, has existed in some form for decades and, in fact, can be traced back to the earliest days of business computing, as expounded above. Although rhetorically the profession of architects was "discarded" and "rediscovered" by the industry a few times in different periods under different labels, like successive waves of fashion, in reality their profession underwent a slow continuous evolution through the ages, co-evolving in tandem with IT (see Figure 1.1)[18]. Ironically, enterprise architects drove digital transformation in organizations long before they were called enterprise architects and the innovative use of IT was called digital transformation.

The Present of Enterprise Architects

By the present moment, enterprise architects have long achieved universal recognition in the industry, while their occupation has turned into a respectable profession with its own catchy label, clear career paths and requisite credentials. Nowadays, dedicated architecture functions with permanent positions for architects exist in the majority of large and medium-sized organizations in industrialized countries across the globe[19].

Besides that, the establishment of enterprise architects as a full-fledged profession with its own paraphernalia has engendered a remarkably rich market of information, education, certification and other services for architects with numerous commercial and not-for-profit, international and local, institutional and individual players. Many of these players are active today, while others are no longer "alive" but, owing to their prominence in the recent past, their "post-mortem" influence is still noticeable and their echoes still haunt the industry. Therefore, this market is very diverse and includes the following categories of players:

- Professional associations aiming to cultivate, advance and consolidate the profession of enterprise architects, e.g. the Association of Enterprise Architects (AEA)[20], the Architectural Thinking Association[21] and the no longer functioning Federation of Enterprise Architecture Professional Organizations (FEAPO)[22]
- Advisory companies issuing analytical reports, white papers and practical recommendations for architects, e.g. Gartner[23], Forrester[24] and Cutter Consortium[25]
- Genuine and self-appointed thought leaders and gurus spreading their ideas in the community and shaping the worldviews of enterprise architects
- Industry consortia and standards bodies creating and promoting what they position as standards relevant to enterprise architects, e.g. The Open Group[26] and the Object Management Group (OMG)[27]
- Accredited training and certification providers aligned with the popular EA-related standards, e.g. TOGAF, ArchiMate, UML and BPMN
- Independent EA training and certification centers with their own proprietary, multilevel systems of credentials, e.g. the Federal Enterprise Architecture Certification (FEAC) Institute[28] and the Enterprise Architecture Center of Excellence (EACOE)[29]
- Classic universities, including some with reputable, world-famous names, granting bachelor's and master's degrees to prospective enterprise architects[30]
- Research centers affiliated with universities and conducting EA-related studies, e.g. the Center for Information Systems Research (CISR) at the Massachusetts Institute of Technology (MIT)[31] and Software Engineering for Business Information Systems (SEBIS) at the Technical University of Munich (TUM)[32]
- Other self-proclaimed "institutes" that rose on the wave of hype around enterprise architecture and apparently never conducted any serious studies or research, e.g. the Institute for Enterprise Architecture Developments (IFEAD)[33] and the Zachman Institute for Framework Advancement (ZIFA)[34], both now defunct
- Specialized journals and magazines intended for enterprise architects, e.g. the Journal of Enterprise Architecture (JEA)[35], Enterprise Architecture Professional Journal (EAPJ)[36] and Architecture & Governance Magazine[37]
- Major vendors of software tools for enterprise architecture promoting their products and associated practices, e.g. Bizzdesign[38] and LeanIX[39]
- Local practitioner communities, discussion forums and specialist interest groups for enterprise architects, e.g. the British Computer Society (BCS) Enterprise Architecture Specialist Group (EASG)[40] and the discontinued Netherlands Architecture Forum (NAF)[41]
- Online professional groups for enterprise architects on LinkedIn, e.g. The Enterprise Architecture Network[42], Enterprise Architecture Forum[43] and Australasian Architecture Network[44]

- Similar organizations and associations in the adjacent disciplines and fields of knowledge, e.g. Iasa Global (the former International Association of Software Architects, IASA)[45], DAMA (Data Management Association) International[46], and the Business Architecture Guild[47]

Because the landscape of EA-oriented information suppliers is very dense, contemporary enterprise architects live in an informationally oversaturated environment and are overwhelmed with various suggestions and prescriptions as to what they should do or how they are expected to behave incoming from all parties[48]. However, as this market is rather lucrative and its entry barriers are relatively low, many of its players evidently pursue their own pecuniary interests at the expense of architects by "peddling" information of dubious quality. Unsurprisingly, much of the available advice for architects is contradictory, shallow and unrealistic. Far from everything advertised by someone as "best practice" (e.g. TOGAF and most other EA frameworks) represents such practice. Interestingly, despite the sheer abundance of information for architects, *trustworthy* information remains very scarce and difficult to find.

The Future of Enterprise Architects

Foretelling the future admittedly represents an easy but futile exercise as in our infinitely complex world most predictions tend to fail, and even those of them that come true can be attributed more to happenstance than to the brilliant analytical capabilities of their authors[49]. Nevertheless, some timid and discreet suppositions about the future of enterprise architects, based predominantly on historical observations and extrapolation of the existing trends, can still be attempted.

First, from a conceptual perspective, because IT will inevitably continue to progress further, as it has done steadily for all the previous decades, digital transformation will only intensify and the need for the services of qualified enterprise architects will increase accordingly[50]. The overall industry demand for competent architects, as well as the standing of architects in organizations, thus are likely to rise in the future[51].

Second, from a quantitative perspective, every year companies invest more and more dollars in technology and their IT budgets are growing respectively by 3–4% annually[52]. As organizations employ more IT personnel and deploy more information systems, the number of positions for enterprise architects will increase proportionally (see Figure 5.1). Moreover, historically, the very *proportion* of architects among IT staff has also been slowly rising, seemingly increasing roughly twofold over the last couple of decades[53]. For these reasons, the total quantity of architects in organizations, as well as throughout the industry on the whole, is likely to grow in the future.

Third, from a work perspective, since the role and place of IT in organizations are going to strengthen, the occupation of enterprise architects will undoubtedly continue its further evolution and enrichment in terms of practical content. However, except for the apparent shift in their technology focus[54], it would be naive and absolutely pointless to speculate about how exactly their behavior, activities and approaches to planning may change in the future as their current practices have not really been predicted by anyone in the past[55]. Only the passing of time can reveal their future practices.

Interestingly, in the future, the profession of enterprise architects might be renamed[56], in the same way as it has already happened a few times in the past, as discussed earlier. Mere rebranding, though, cannot alter the substance of their job, nor can it eliminate their niche in the organizational ecosystem or fill this niche with someone else.

To summarize, in the future, the profession of enterprise architects is likely to become more prestigious and prevalent in the industry and will somehow evolve to accommodate the alterations in the organizational reality[57]. As the challenges of digital transformation are not going to disappear, no fundamental factors suggest that enterprise architects can turn out unnecessary and go extinct, unless all human beings will be someday replaced with robots.

Different Understandings of Enterprise Architects

Previously, the organizational actors discussed in this book were called simply "enterprise architects" and the book's narrative was centered around this notion. However, the very term "enterprise architect" is rather ambiguous, has no commonly accepted meaning across the industry and is often used inconsistently in different contexts[58]. For this reason, it can be a subject of multiple divergent interpretations in the professional discourse.

Specifically, depending on what exactly is meant to fall within its purview in terms of organizational domains, business areas and abstraction levels, the term "enterprise architect" can be understood in significantly different senses. In particular, based on the implied scope of concern, this term has at least three equally valid meanings: a general profession, a prevalent archetype and a specific position, not to mention some other, not-so-valid meanings. Realizing the distinctions and relationship between these meanings is essential for comprehending the coverage, structure and further exposition of this book.

Enterprise Architects as a Profession

First, in the broadest sense, enterprise architects can be understood as a *general overarching profession* that unites all architects concerned with the structure of business and IT landscapes in organizations, irrespective of the scope of their particular responsibilities. In this meaning, enterprise architects are usually referred to in the industry as unclassified "architects" and include all of the following, and not only, categories of architects:

- Architects concentrating on concrete IT solutions in the broader context of the organizational business and IT landscape
- Architects focusing on all business applications supporting a specific business geography constituting a fairly large landscape segment
- Architects in charge of the entire business and IT landscape of the organization across all its layers

As a profession, enterprise architects embrace architects of all sorts, profiles and denominations, basically everyone who can be reasonably labeled as an "architect". In this interpretation, they represent more an umbrella term for all information systems planners than any definite roles.

Enterprise Architects as an Archetype

Second, in a narrower sense, enterprise architects can be understood as a *prevalent generic archetype* of architects within the profession that involves planning substantial parts of the organizational business and IT landscape at a high abstraction level. In this meaning, enterprise

architects are most often referred to in the industry exactly as "enterprise architects" and include all of the following categories of architects:
- Architects responsible for the end-to-end IT enablement of a single business function of the organization
- Architects developing the corporate data analytics capability shared across multiple independent lines of business
- Architects focusing on enterprise-wide networking infrastructure provided to all business units of the organization

However, enterprise architects in this interpretation exclude, for instance, solution architects as a distinct archetype of architects concentrating only on individual IT solutions with a limited scope[59]. Put it simply, as an archetype, enterprise architects encompass all architects dealing with any landscape slices wider than separate IT solutions.

Enterprise Architects as a Position

Third, in the narrowest sense, enterprise architects can be understood as a *specific organizational position* of architects within the archetype that implies dealing precisely with the whole business and IT landscape in all its aspects at the highest level of abstraction. In this meaning, enterprise architects are sometimes referred to in the industry as "chief architects" and *exclude* all of the following categories of architects:
- Domain architects as a distinct position of architects responsible exclusively for specific organizational domains (see Figure 3.4)
- Business area architects as a distinct position of architects assigned to serve particular areas of the business
- Any other architects with limited or partial coverage of the organizational business and IT landscape

As a position, enterprise architects include only those architects who are literally "enterprise" architects covering all domains and business areas of organizations[60]. In this interpretation, they represent a relatively strictly defined role with set boundaries and a rather clear circle of duties.

Other Understandings of Enterprise Architects

In addition to the three valid meanings of enterprise architects explained above, each having a certain practical sense, the term "enterprise architects" can also occasionally be used in some sources in two other meanings that determine their scopes of concern: a figurative metaphor and a mythical fiction. As a metaphor, enterprise architects represent powerful actors who actually shape organizations by their decisions and actions, usually their CEOs or other influential executives, e.g. "CEOs as genuine architects of enterprises"[61]. As a fiction, enterprise architects allegedly represent universal, not IT-centric architects capable of designing any strategy-driven enterprise transformations in *all* their facets (e.g. business models, product lines, supply chains and marketing), possibly but not necessarily also involving IT as one of the facets[62]. These all-purpose architects, however, do not exist in reality because of truly superhuman intellectual demands imposed on such individuals.

Unlike the previous meanings, these meanings of enterprise architects have no practical sense or embodiment, can be considered misguiding and, to avoid confusion, should be clearly distinguished from the valid meanings of this term. As for the literal meaning of enterprise architects as the architects of enterprises, they also do not exist in the real world since organizations cannot be designed and then constructed in a way similar to buildings, as discussed earlier.

Different Understandings of Enterprise Architects and the Structure of This Book

All the meanings of the term "enterprise architect" introduced above, and possibly some other bizarre meanings, can be encountered in the industry discourse and professional literature. This book, however, covers and expounds only the three valid meanings of this term — as a profession, archetype and position.

In particular, enterprise architects as a profession give the title to this book and represent its focal subject. All the discussions of various attributes of architects provided up to this point and summarized at the highest level in Figure 14.2 and Figure 14.3 relate to their profession in general. Enterprise architects as an archetype within this profession are discussed in detail specifically in Chapter 15 (The Archetype of Enterprise Architects), while the complementary archetype of solution architects is thoroughly addressed in Chapter 16 (The Archetype of Solution Architects). Finally, enterprise architects as a position within the archetype, as well as the adjacent positions of domain architects and business area architects, are discussed in Chapter 17 (Architecture Positions in Organizations).

These three understandings of enterprise architects form a nested set, where broader understandings comprise narrower ones. The schematic relationship between the different meanings of enterprise architects and the structure of this book described above is depicted in Figure 14.4.

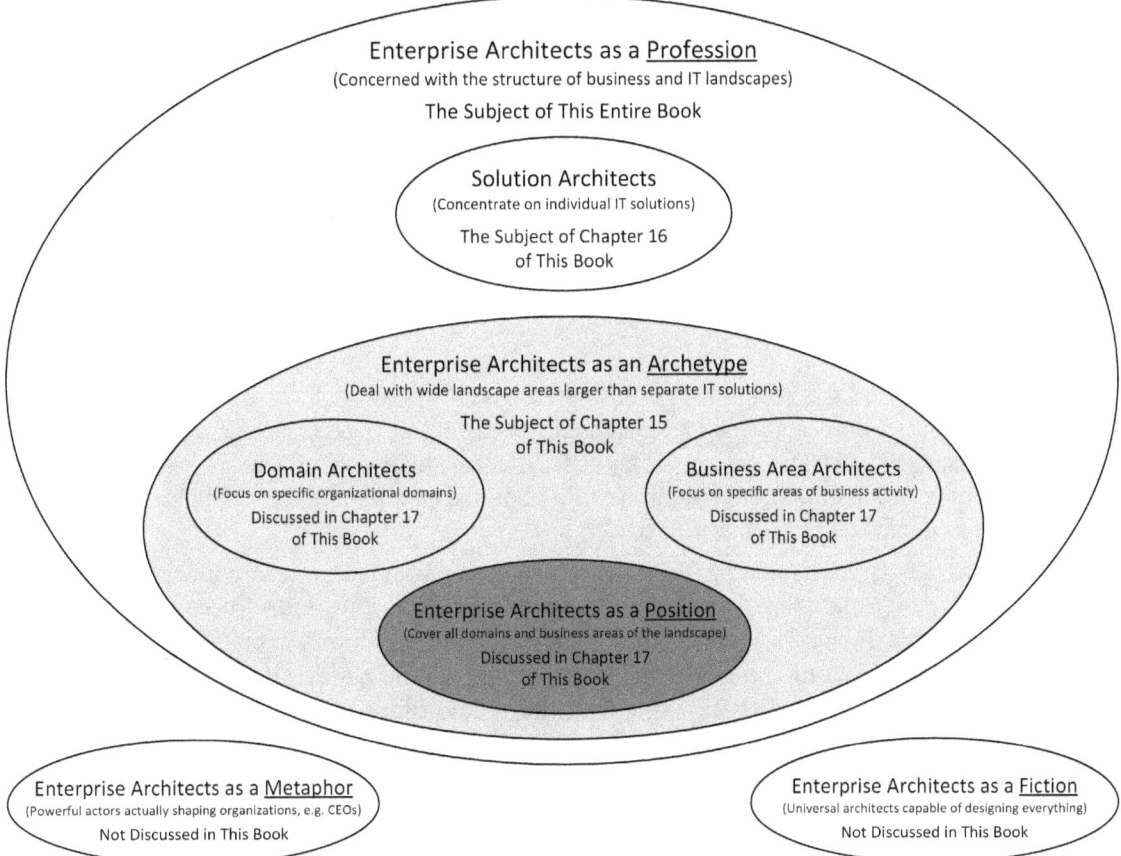

Figure 14.4. Different understandings of enterprise architects and the structure of this book

As showcased in Figure 14.4, the profession of enterprise architects encircles under its umbrella a number of rather diverse archetypes and positions. Although it is debatable whether, or to what extent, some of them, and especially solution architects, belong to this profession, all these archetypes and positions arguably have more similarities than differences and, on this basis, can be related to the common profession of enterprise architects.

First, all of them possess largely the same resources, employ identical instruments and perform analogous activities, albeit with different specifics, fitting into the same high-level framework (see Figure 14.2). Second, in the organizational ecosystem, all of them typically work as a cohesive architecture team, closely cooperate with each other and socialize within the same occupational community. Third, boundaries between huge IT solutions, domain-wide changes and enterprise-scale transformations are naturally blurred and cannot be strictly delineated. And lastly, specific positions for architects established in organizations can imply virtually arbitrary duties often combining the responsibilities of different archetypes of architects, e.g. require acting as both enterprise and solution architects at the same time. For all these reasons, various archetypes and positions for architects can hardly be clearly separated and analyzed in isolation, but should be best viewed as different *specializations*, or instantiations, of a single all-embracing profession — enterprise architects[63].

Different understandings of enterprise architects summed up in Figure 14.4 offer an overall conceptual framework for organizing this book. Namely, Parts I and II introduced and described the profession of enterprise architects as a whole in the most general strokes, thereby providing a common foundation for all the subsequent discussions. Next, in Part III (Enterprise Architects in Organizations), Chapters 15 and 16 will discuss specifically the archetypes of Enterprise Architects and Solution Architects respectively as the two main specializations of this profession, while Chapter 17 — concrete organizational positions belonging to the former archetype.

Chapter Summary

This chapter discussed the profession of enterprise architects as such, its integrative framework and elements of art, craft and science, analyzed the historical evolution of enterprise architects through the past, present and future, discussed different meanings of enterprise architects and explained their relationship to the structure of this book. The core message of this chapter can be summarized in the following major points:

- Due to its high context dependence, the job of enterprise architects can be regarded as a loose profession without a precise knowledge base and strict standards of behavior, which can be subjected to some forms of certification
- The profession of enterprise architects can be summarized at the highest level in the integrative framework explaining the relationships between their pyramid of resources, taxonomy of instruments and value stream of activities
- The profession of enterprise architects is remarkably rich with diversity and represents a harmonic composition of heterogeneous elements pertaining to the disparate realms of art, craft and science
- The past of enterprise architects can be clearly traced through decades back to the very first business computer, LEO, built in the United Kingdom around 1950, where John Simmons was a prototypical architect marrying business and IT
- The present of enterprise architects is pretty sunny as they are widespread across the industry, their importance is universally recognized, their occupation is viewed as a respectable profession and surrounded by a rich market of services
- The future of enterprise architects can only be speculated about, but the current trends suggest that the overall demand for their services in the industry, as well as their standing and numbers in organizations, are all likely to rise in the future
- The term "enterprise architects" has at least three valid meanings: a profession that unites all architects concerned with the landscape structure, an archetype of architects that involves planning substantial parts of the landscape and a specific position of architects that implies dealing with the whole landscape in all aspects
- This book describes the profession of enterprise architects, the archetypes of Enterprise Architects and Solution Architects are covered in Chapters 15 and 16 respectively and the position of enterprise architects is discussed in Chapter 17

PART III: Enterprise Architects in Organizations

Part III of this book covers various aspects of enterprise architects related to their work in organizations. This part discusses the specialization of enterprise architects in architecture functions in terms of their general archetypes and specific architecture positions, the challenges of their engagement with business leadership, their professional careers and many other questions of immediate relevance to their occupation.

Part III consists of five consecutive chapters. Chapter 15 describes Enterprise Architects as a major archetype of architects driving high-level digitalization efforts with the specifics of their resources, instruments, activities and work in different contexts. Chapter 16 describes Solution Architects as another major archetype of architects serving separate digitalization projects with the specifics of their resources, instruments, activities and work in different contexts. Chapter 17 discusses concrete positions in architecture functions through the lens of the archetypes of Enterprise Architects and Solution Architects with their dependence on the size and structure of organizations. Chapter 18 analyzes the problem of achieving effective engagement between enterprise architects and business leaders with the ensuing individual and organizational challenges faced by architects. Finally, Chapter 19 discusses the career paths of enterprise architects with the associated difficulties, the role of modeling languages, software tools, EA frameworks and professional certifications in their job, as well as the central conundrums of architects.

Chapter 15: The Archetype of Enterprise Architects

Previously, Chapter 14 introduced Enterprise Architects as a prominent archetype within the overarching profession of architects. This chapter provides a detailed discussion of the archetype of Enterprise Architects, as a well-defined specialization of architects, with all its distinctive attributes, features and properties. In particular, this chapter begins with describing the specifics of the place, resources and instruments of Enterprise Architects as compared to the profession in general. Then, this chapter thoroughly describes the activities of Enterprise Architects in the organizational and initiative contexts, discusses their work across the two contexts and also introduces an alternative, organization-centric view of their work. Finally, this chapter discusses the domain specialization of Enterprise Architects, clarifies its influence on different aspects of their work in organizations and presents the integrative framework of their archetype.

Enterprise Architects as a Distinct Archetype of Architects

The profession of enterprise architects is very broad and encompasses two generic archetypes of architects and multiple specific positions for architects in organizations (see Figure 14.4). The first consistent archetype of architects within this profession is Enterprise Architects dealing with vast areas of the organizational business and IT landscape.

Enterprise Architects (capitalized to distinguish from the profession as a whole) is a special archetype of architects responsible for leading the architectural planning of large-scale digitalization efforts *higher-level than separate projects*, such as programs and strategies of *enterprise-wide* significance, which gives this archetype its popular title prevalent in the industry today. The respective initiatives reside at the higher end of the size spectrum and are characterized by extensive scopes, long timeframes, vague boundaries, abstract constructs and order-of-magnitude estimations (see Figure 2.4). Although transformation efforts driven by Enterprise Architects can vary in their importance, impact and business consequences, generally their work can be fairly regarded as strategic for the organization.

As high-level digitalization initiatives are usually autonomous and, except for programs derived from strategies, based on entirely new ideas, Enterprise Architects actively participate in the process of their initial ideation. At the same time, because all these initiatives eventually materialize through derivative projects, which are out of the scope of Enterprise Architects' duties, for their materialization they rely on lower-level Solution Architects discussed in the next chapter. In short, Enterprise Architects help generate ideas for improving the organization with IT and drive the ensuing initiatives at the strategy and program levels, whereas Solution Architects complete their execution at the project level.

Since high-level digitalization initiatives are usually induced squarely by concrete transformation drivers and weakly influenced by the existing architectural plans (see Figure 9.9), the motivational context is more relevant to these initiatives than the architectural one. For this reason, when serving programs and especially strategies within the overarching transformational context (see Figure 9.8), Enterprise Architects in their decision-making refer more to its motivational part than to the architectural one.

The place of Enterprise Architects in the initiative hierarchy and their relationship to the transformational context outlined above largely predetermine their typical communication network in organizations. On the one hand, because high-level initiatives embody standalone, strategic transformative undertakings, key stakeholders of Enterprise Architects are various business leaders who define long-term future directions by advocating some or the other transformation drivers. These business leaders include both top-tier executives making global planning decisions for the whole company and middle managers deciding on the behalf of their individual business units. Interestingly, except for small organizations, C-level executives and the like are typically not knowledgeable in business details well enough to participate in architectural planning in any capacity other than supervisory, whereas actual driver proponents and decision-makers constituting the core stakeholder audience of Enterprise Architects are lower-rank managers, who better understand the situation "on the ground", e.g. heads of business departments and their deputies (see Figure 1.3)[1].

On the other hand, as strategies and programs are executed by means of launching and guiding their subordinate projects, Enterprise Architects closely collaborate with Solution Architects serving these projects, providing them with the necessary details of the architectural context while controlling their activities and products for their alignment with this context. Staying distant from down-to-earth project design and delivery efforts, Enterprise Architects seldom communicate with ordinary business specialists and project teams. Also, except for the cases when program-level architects are supervised by strategy-level ones, Enterprise Architects normally work without any higher-level supervision in matters of architectural planning.

Since implementing higher-order digitalization initiatives does not involve constructing any information systems in a physical sense, Enterprise Architects can be, to a certain degree, abstracted from concrete technologies and their nuances. At the same time, because of their multifarious stakeholders with very different, possibly inconsistent and sometimes even antagonistic views and objectives, their planning requires reconciling difficult conflicts of interests between different parties. Accordingly, challenges associated with programs and strategies are determined primarily by the factor of stakeholder diversity and are more organizational than technical in character (see Figure 2.9). To cope with these challenges, Enterprise Architects have to wear more the hat of Change Agents than that of Technology Experts and, in their behavior, lean somewhat closer towards visionary leaders.

Because strategies and even programs in organizations are often not formalized administratively (see Figure 2.6), interactions between business leaders and Enterprise Architects during their implementation can rarely occur in a mandatory fashion being imposed by any administrative mechanisms. For high-level initiatives, Enterprise Architects can be involved in the respective decision-making processes mainly if they are invited to participate voluntarily by business representatives (see Figure 4.4). Financially, as strategies and programs usually do not have their own allocated budgets, the work of Enterprise Architects relates mostly to operating expenses (OPEX) and is funded predominantly on a business-as-usual basis. The position of Enterprise Architects with their responsibilities and interactions in the overall organizational ecosystem is shown in Figure 15.1.

Chapter 15: The Archetype of Enterprise Architects

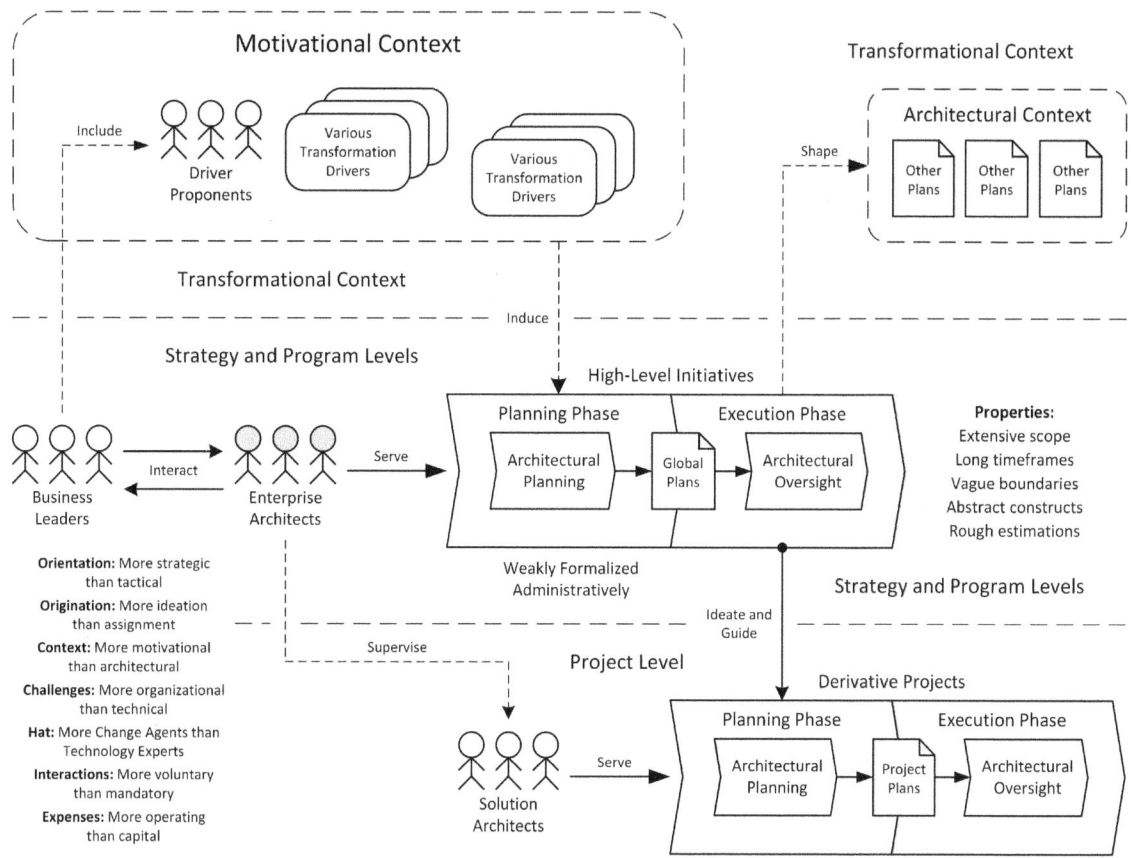

Figure 15.1. The position of Enterprise Architects in the organizational ecosystem

Although all the resources, instruments and activities of Enterprise Architects correspond to the general framework of the profession of architects, they have many notable features attributed to the specifics of high-level digitalization efforts illustrated in Figure 15.1. In other words, Enterprise Architects can be viewed as a consistent *specialization* of architects adjusted to the realities of transformation strategies and programs. Typical properties of these initiatives define the peculiarities of their job in organizations and allow recognizing them as a separate, clear-cut and stable archetype of architects widespread across the industry.

Resources of Enterprise Architects

Even though the resources of Enterprise Architects do not differ fundamentally from those possessed by all architects, their knowledge, skills and experience have certain distinctive characteristics aligned with their focus on higher-order transformation efforts. Specifically, their resources lean towards a broader outlook, greater political mastery and more extensive experience.

Knowledge

Because programs and especially strategies affect large parts of the organization and its IT landscape but are rather distant from their details, knowledge of Enterprise Architects tends to be broad but relatively shallow in both business and IT aspects, except for pretty narrow areas in which they previously had personal first-hand practical experience. Their external business-related knowledge can either be largely industry-agnostic and cover business in general, or accentuate specific industry sectors in which they specialize, e.g. insurance, healthcare or natural resources. Their external IT-related knowledge is usually uneven, or V-shaped[2], across different domains of technology according to their technical background, e.g. stronger in applications and integration, but weaker in infrastructure and security[3]. Their internal business-related knowledge covers ideally all business activities of the organization, its business strategy, all principal decision-makers, their transformation drivers and the rest of the motivational context. Their internal IT-related knowledge also aims at the "big picture" and embraces preferably the entire organizational IT landscape, all active change initiatives and the full architectural context.

For example, an Enterprise Architect can specialize in the utilities sector, understand well the legislation, best practices, current trends and business models prevalent in this sector, be aware of potentially disruptive technologies relevant to utilities and know major niche vendors supplying software platforms in this area with their capabilities. Internally, this architect can realize the situation in the organization relative to the industry as a whole, be acquainted with influential business leaders accountable for defining its strategy, understand their long-term vision with the most pressing drivers and know all the core IT systems supporting the business as well as the existing plans for their future improvement. However, the specialization of Enterprise Architects can also be more technical, industry-neutral and largely unrelated to any particular kind of business.

Skills

The biggest challenges associated with large-scale transformations in organizations are political in nature, where the most acute and insidious difficulties ensue specifically from the conflicts of interests between different constituencies trying to reach an agreement on what needs to be done and what course of action should be followed (see Figure 2.9). In this light, the importance of various behavioral skills relevant to consensus building that enable collaborative decision-making is paramount for Enterprise Architects.

First, superb communicative abilities are a must for interacting with diverse stakeholder audiences — representatives of disparate functional areas at senior and middle administrative levels — to understand their talks, appreciate their concerns and explain how these concerns can be addressed. Second, excellent negotiation and conflict resolution skills complemented with political perspicacity are required to deal with different coalitions of interests, bring their positions together and find a common ground for collective action. Moreover, as large transformation initiatives normally last for a long period of time and their circle of decision-makers is relatively constant, a developed capacity for building trustful, long-term partner relationships with stakeholders is necessary for Enterprise Architects.

Experience

The practical experience accumulated by Enterprise Architects is very diversified, multifaceted and extensive. Qualitatively, it normally stems from working with technology and includes dealing, as technical specialists of different profiles and Solution Architects, with numerous IT solutions in different settings, circumstances and organizations, possibly within their areas of specialization. Quantitatively, their experience usually encompasses, in total, at least 16–24 years of full-time employment in the industry with the last 8–12 years typically spent specifically as Solution Architects. Possible career paths of architects are discussed in detail later in Chapter 19 (Other Aspects of Enterprise Architects).

Instruments of Enterprise Architects

As their working instruments, Enterprise Architects employ exactly the same general types of EA artifacts as all architects. However, because they concentrate on large-scale transformation efforts, their usage patterns of EA artifacts are very different, on the one hand, for rules and structures artifacts covering broad organizational scopes and, on the other hand, for solutions artifacts covering narrow organizational scopes.

Considerations, Standards, Visions and Landscapes

As the level of detail and organizational scope covered by Considerations, Standards, Visions and Landscapes (rules and structures artifacts) perfectly match the extent of transformations that Enterprise Architects drive, these general types of EA artifacts are immediately relevant to their occupation. Specifically, Enterprise Architects use all these artifacts on a daily basis for the purposes of both documenting the existing situation and capturing architectural solutions.

As for documenting the existing situation, Enterprise Architects routinely maintain and study various actualities EA artifacts, mainly Landscapes and some Standards, to accumulate valuable current-state knowledge on the corporate landscape. However, in search of necessary information, they can also resort to studying some plans artifacts, like Visions and Considerations. Because different EA artifacts contain different information with different caveats, architects have to refer to different sources of knowledge, depending on their needs (see Figure 9.1).

As for capturing architectural solutions, Enterprise Architects actively create and update various plans EA artifacts, mostly Visions, Considerations and Standards, during the architectural planning of transformation initiatives to record made planning decisions and represent their architectural plans. However, some architectural decisions can also be reflected in actualities artifacts, primarily in Landscapes. Because different EA artifacts capture different kinds of planning decisions pertaining to different components of architectural solutions, architects have to pick the most appropriate artifacts from their toolkits suitable for particular change initiatives.

Although the arsenal of EA artifacts available to Enterprise Architects is very rich and diverse, Roadmaps (see Figure 8.8) can arguably be regarded as the single most important artifacts that they use in practice for capturing architectural solutions[4]. It is these artifacts that document the character and sequence of derivative projects that should be initiated to execute the respective programs and strategies. Unsurprisingly, almost every high-level transformation initiative is eventually translated into one or more, general or initiative-specific Roadmaps.

Outlines and Designs

As Outlines and Designs (solutions artifacts) are too granular and their scope is too narrow for the large-scale transformations they lead, Enterprise Architects typically do *not* use these general types of EA artifacts for their own needs, either for documenting the existing situation or for capturing architectural solutions. Nonetheless, Outlines and Designs are still relevant to their job, though rather indirectly, as "gears" in the mechanism of architectural oversight as part of which they passively review these artifacts to control the compliance of projects with higher-order architectural plans.

Namely, when ensuring adherence to plans, Enterprise Architects verify Outlines and Designs produced by Solution Architects at different stages of the project implementation process for their conformity to high-level architectural plans that they developed and other plans from the architectural context. For example, as part of the established governance procedures (see Figure 12.3), they can examine Solution Overviews to ensure that the respective projects actually align with the Roadmaps of their parent programs and improve the strategic capabilities highlighted in Business Capability Models. Or, they can inspect Solution Designs to check that the proposed information systems are built with the proper technologies from Technology Inventories and stick to the right Patterns. Additionally, inchoate sketches of these EA artifacts can also be reviewed by Enterprise Architects in a personal capacity for the same purposes and pre-approved informally at their earlier stages, before their presentation to architecture governance committees. In this way, architectural oversight is exercised by means of, first, individual documentation reviews and then official approval procedures.

Activities of Enterprise Architects in the Organizational Context

As discussed earlier, the activities of architects fulfilled in the organizational context relate to the organization as a whole and take all pertinent organizational elements into account (see Figure 10.1). Generally speaking, in the organizational context, Enterprise Architects perform the same basic activities as all architects: analyzing the external environment, studying the internal environment and providing advisory services (see Figure 10.2). However, because of their concentration on high-level transformation efforts, each of these activities is "colored" by the specifics of their job that allow refining the general patterns.

Analyzing the External Environment

In their analysis of the external environment, Enterprise Architects pay comparatively less attention to the details of particular technologies, products and vendor offerings. Instead, they are more interested in knowing, for example, what happens in the industry at large, what kind of IT-related innovations emerge on the market, how these innovations reshape the competitive landscape, how they disrupt the existing businesses, what digital products they enable, what business models they engender and what their relevance is specifically to the business of their organization.

As a result, the focus of Enterprise Architects in terms of their top information sources partly switches from vendor websites with technical or semi-technical materials towards more general business and technology media with the industry news they publish. In a similar vein, quite infrequently do they visit technology-specific industry events and hands-on technical trainings, but seek broader market and innovation analytics.

Studying the Internal Environment

In their studies of the internal environment, Enterprise Architects are also more interested in "big things" than minutiae. Rather than thinking about separate business units, their objectives, processes and IT systems, they concentrate more on such global issues as the business economics of their company, the sources of its competitive edge, its long-term strategy and goals, the connection between its business and IT capabilities and the overall composition of its IT landscape.

Because much of this information is not factual but highly conceptual and intractable to explicit documentation, to gather it, Enterprise Architects mainly contact a wide circle of managers across the organization representing different areas of business and IT. Of EA artifacts, as another major source of knowledge on the internal environment, they benefit more from those that help grasp the situation as a whole, e.g. Business Capability Models and Process Maps on the business side and System Portfolio Models and Landscape Maps on the IT side.

Providing Advisory Services

The advisory services of Enterprise Architects more often deal with the questions of conceptual relationship between business and IT. These services usually leverage their good understanding of the high-level structure of the organization with its IT landscape to answer pretty abstract queries about their possible coevolution.

Like all architects, Enterprise Architects provide their advisory services to the rest of the organization in both official and unofficial formats (see Figure 10.5). Officially, Enterprise Architects are included in architecture governance bodies as acknowledged mavens of the business and IT landscape. Owing to their vast competence, they are often demanded in all four types of governance committees (see Figure 12.1). In strategy committees, they contribute their expert knowledge of business and IT to assess the strategic fitness of various technology-related planning decisions for the entire organization. In technology committees, they apply their professional judgment and practical wisdom to decisions on the selection of technologies and approaches based on their suitability for business plans and needs. In investment committees, they analyze Solution Overviews and other documents for proposed projects to evaluate their general adequacy and alignment with the plans of their parent initiatives, if any, as well as with the surrounding architectural context. And lastly, in design committees, they study Solution Designs and associated documentation to check their technical adequacy, though often without diving into deep technicalities, leaving this task to Solution Architects more knowledgeable in the respective technologies. The status of regular members of architecture governance bodies gives Enterprise Architects more opportunities to use their unusually extensive expertise to improve the quality of IT-related decision-making in the organization.

Unofficially, Enterprise Architects offer their advisory services on demand to other organizational actors, often high-ranking ones, willing to benefit from their broad understanding of the situation. For example, they can consult business executives on the possibilities for adopting some elements of digital business models, the viability of certain IT-driven business strategies and the availability of necessary IT capabilities for supporting specific competitive moves. Or, they can provide their advice to IT leaders on the better ways of merging the existing system landscape with the landscape of a newly acquired company, reducing detrimental dependencies on particular vendors and moving some landscape fragments to the cloud. They can also educate Solution Architects on the global future business and IT directions that should be reflected in project-level architectural decision-making.

Involvement in the Initial Ideation of Digital Transformation Initiatives

By exploring the organizational environment and providing their advisory services to senior decision-makers, architects facilitate the process of initial ideation and help managers structure their thoughts and ideas into effective digitalization initiatives (see Figure 13.4). As programs and strategies tend to be autonomous initiatives induced directly by some transformation drivers, Enterprise Architects are heavily involved in their generation.

In fact, Enterprise Architects work at the forefront of initiative ideation and spend a lot of their time in rather abstractive conversations with business leaders about where the company is going and what kind of changes in its operations might be desirable in the future. By interacting personally with management and understanding their strategy and drivers, Enterprise Architects stay in a position to identify promising opportunities for using IT that resonate with business motives and propose fruitful innovative ideas for digitalization, which then materialize through concrete change initiatives. Furthermore, if they are particularly business-savvy, architects can suggest new business-side transformation drivers (e.g. see novel commercial applications of IT demanded by the market) and, if they reach high enough, can theoretically even contribute to top-level business strategy[5]. In short, Enterprise Architects closely communicate with business leaders to comprehend in full, and possibly influence, the motivational context of the organization and inspire its digitalization endeavors.

Interestingly, generating good ideas for digital transformation by Enterprise Architects implies a *two-way* matching of existing business ends and available IT means. On the one hand, newly identified business needs can often be effectively addressed with old technologies. On the other hand, newly developed technologies can often provide effective solutions for old business needs. The greater awareness of *both* organizational needs and technology innovations on the part of architects, therefore, increases the chances of finding good matches between them and producing brilliant ideas for change. For this reason, constantly studying the internal environment and analyzing the external environment for the awareness of present business ends and IT means respectively are equally critical for the successful performance of Enterprise Architects in the initial ideation of digitalization initiatives.

Activities of Enterprise Architects in the Initiative Context

All activities of architects performed in the initiative context belong to specific digital transformation initiatives and consider only those elements that are relevant to these initiatives. Conceptually, the activities of Enterprise Architects within different phases of the initiative implementation lifecycle are identical to those constituting the repertoire of all architects. At a more granular level, however, their activities have a number of pronounced attributes ensuing from the specifics of high-level digitalization initiatives that they drive. To better understand the activities of Enterprise Architects in the initiative context, it is first necessary to discuss this context for programs and strategies in greater detail. In particular, the implementation process of high-level transformation initiatives whose planning they lead and whose execution they supervise needs further elucidation.

The Implementation Process of High-Level Transformation Initiatives

Even though the implementation process of high-level transformation initiatives fits well into the frames of the generic three-phase initiative implementation lifecycle (see Figure 2.2), these initiatives have two unique features that affect the activities of Enterprise Architects carried out in the course of their implementation. First, as opposed to projects, programs and especially strategies represent much less cohesive transformation efforts. While projects are characterized by clear scope, stakeholder circle, shape, impact, timelines and funding needs, higher-order initiatives are not endowed with any of these characteristics. Unlike projects, programs and strategies do not have a solid structure as their logical, spatial, temporal and financial boundaries are blurred and can even be largely open-ended. For this reason, these initiatives often look more like bundles of loosely coupled planning decisions on the future than articulate courses of action. In extreme cases, more or less meaningful transformation programs and strategies may be running in organizations without being explicitly labeled as programs and strategies, or even without being regarded as distinct change initiatives. Metaphorically, projects can be compared to a congealed matter, whereas their higher-level counterparts — to more liquid, amorphous substances. These properties of programs and strategies demand special treatment on the part of Enterprise Architects.

Second, because programs and especially strategies represent long-lasting, often multiyear transformation initiatives, they generally cannot be planned upfront for their entire duration with any reasonable, acceptable degree of accuracy. On the one hand, the external environment is continuously evolving and its future can be predicted, at best, in probabilistic terms. On the other hand, even those aspects of the environment that stay constant cannot be perfectly foreseen in advance in all their implications due to the limited mental capacity of humans. For these reasons, details relevant to high-level transformation initiatives normally unfold with time, along with the progress in their implementation. This fact is key for the lifecycle of these initiatives and necessitates periodic updates of their plans as new information becomes available. In other words, architectural plans for programs and strategies have to be continually refined, adjusted or even radically modified to accommodate changing circumstances. In some cases, the very initiatives may be canceled if they no longer seem advantageous to the organization, notwithstanding their sunk costs.

To dynamically adapt to the new understanding of the environment emerging along the way, the implementation process of high-level transformation initiatives usually includes *multiple* episodes of architectural planning: the initial one and a series of follow-ups. First, the initial upfront episode takes place within the planning phase of the initiative implementation process. It starts from the underlying concepts of initiatives that ripened during the previous conception phase, goes through the full three-step process of architectural planning and produces original architectural plans that begin to guide the initiative execution. This episode is based on the best available information on the environment at the time of the initiative formation and reflects this information in the resulting plans.

Then, the follow-up episodes of architectural planning occur amidst the initiative execution. They start from the existing architectural plans for the initiative, go through the *shortened* process of architectural planning, skipping the discussion step, and result in updated plans that continue to guide the initiative execution. These episodes take into account the latest available information on the environment, as well as the work that has already been accomplished as part of the initiative, to revise its architectural plans based on the current view of the situation. Follow-up episodes of architectural planning tend to repeat periodically until the completion of the initiative, either on a regular quarterly, semiannual or annual basis, or in an unscheduled manner, being caused by some events or disruptions in the business environment.

From the standpoint of the initiative implementation lifecycle, these follow-up episodes of architectural planning can be best viewed as an additional intermediate **revision phase**. Logically, the revision phase is "scattered" across the execution phase of transformation initiatives and includes only the temporary bursts of successive architectural planning efforts intended to update their architectural plans in light of new circumstances. In other words, there can be many instances of the revision phase inserted at different moments along the initiative execution. It is this phase that allows stakeholders to steer the long-running initiative implementation process and adapt to new conditions while staying on course.

For high-level transformation initiatives, their architectural plans are sanctioned by senior architecture governance bodies, namely by the technology and strategy committees that authorize technical and organizational components of their architectural solutions respectively (see Figure 12.1). Because programs and strategies are not-so-cohesive change efforts and different elements of their architectural solutions are often diffused across many diverse EA artifacts, their approval procedures can be organized differently, either piece by piece or in one shot, e.g. decision by decision, artifact by artifact or all plans at once. For example, individual planning decisions constituting their architectural solutions can be presented to the appropriate committees one by one in the form of separate architecture decision papers (see Figure 11.7). Or, various EA artifacts capturing different aspects of their architectural solutions can be ratified by the committees one after another. Alternatively, comprehensive plans for initiatives summarized in presentation packs can be endorsed all together (see Figure 11.6). In some cases, initiative-specific EA artifacts suitable for programs and strategies can be based on standardized artifact templates (see Figure 11.5).

Although the implementation process of high-level transformation initiatives is weakly formalized from an administrative point of view and often does not include any explicit, clearly defined and firmly institutionalized control gates, where their status is assessed and further support is assured, all the various governance procedures exercised on the way to their execution can be loosely grouped into the virtual **initiative approval gate**. This gate aggregates a series of formal approvals *dispersed in time* that are necessary to consider initiatives as sanctioned for execution.

The description of architecture governance procedures provided above equally relates to both the initial episode of architectural planning performed during the planning phase and its follow-up episodes carried out as part of the revision phase. Simply put, both original and updated architectural plans require some form of official sign-off. However, at the end of the planning phase, the very initiative is approved for execution, while within the revision phase — only its specific updates. Analogously to the initiative approval gate introduced previously for the planning phase, all the time-dispersed governance procedures necessary to authorize the further execution of updated plans in the revision phase can grouped into the **updates approval gate**.

The execution of high-level transformation initiatives is always fulfilled by launching and guiding their subordinate lower-level initiatives, mostly projects, implied by their architectural plans. These derivative initiatives are launched throughout the whole period of their execution, first based on their original plans developed in the planning phase and then based on their plans updated in the revision phase. The end-to-end initiative implementation process described above with its phases, approval gates and architectural plans is summarized in Figure 15.2.

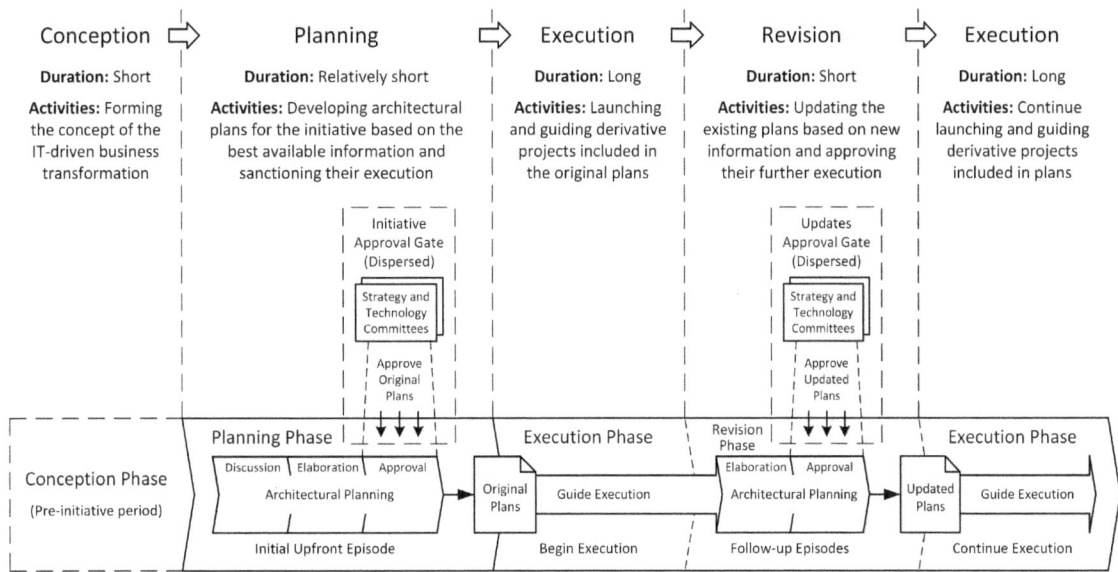

Figure 15.2. The implementation process of high-level transformation initiatives

The detailed view of the implementation process relevant to strategies and programs presented in Figure 15.2 reflects its internal specifics that distinguish it from the project implementation process discussed in the next chapter. This view provides the necessary baseline and context for discussing in more detail the activities of Enterprise Architects in high-level transformation initiatives and some other aspects of their work in organizations.

Activities During the Conception Phase

During the first conception phase of the initiative implementation process (see Figure 15.2), Enterprise Architects discuss with business leaders the seminal ideas for digital transformation and the opportunities for converting these ideas into concrete digitalization initiatives. As the majority of high-level transformation initiatives originate straight from the motivational context of the organization being induced by some of the existing drivers, the core audience of Enterprise Architects in this phase is the proponents of transformation drivers searching for effective ways of responding to these drivers with IT and ready to sponsor the respective change efforts. Because large initiatives are typically motivated by many different drivers (see Figure 2.4), architects often have to deal with heterogeneous groups of driver proponents with overlapping but different interests, which makes it difficult to build a strong coalition of like-minded supporters to actually launch any transformations. However, for derivative programs ensuing from the intentions of higher-order strategies, Enterprise Architects communicate with the executors of their parents and the situation with their formation can be somewhat simpler.

As programs and strategies represent large-scale transformation efforts aimed at wide landscape areas, the discussions of their initiation within the conception phase focus more on improving the overall way of doing business than on addressing specific business needs. Because of their abstract nature, they are often qualitative in style and revolve around rather elusive high-level notions, like business and IT capabilities, without diving into their details. Accordingly, in these discussions, Enterprise Architects analyze mostly conceptual benefits, consequences and difficulties of the possible realization of some or the other ideas.

Although the participation of Enterprise Architects in the conception phase of the initiative implementation process can take various forms and conceiving high-level initiatives is often indistinguishable from mere "business talks", the intensity of their work during this phase can be roughly classified as moderate, or equivalent to part-time involvement. Generally, the conception phase is driven by the following and similar questions about potential digitalization opportunities:

- What global goals or improvements in the business should be pursued with IT?
- Are the proposed ideas for digital transformation promising and feasible?
- What business areas should be digitalized, how and to what extent?
- Is the current level of our IT capabilities sufficient to fulfill our ambitions?
- Are our ideas for digitalization mature enough to be turned into initiatives?

At this stage, the principal intent of discussions taking place between Enterprise Architects and business leaders is only to evaluate the existing ideas for IT-driven business transformations and assess their viability and strategic impact, rather than to elaborate these ideas into something executable. In particular, Enterprise Architects accomplish only provisional architectural pre-planning to ensure that the requested business capabilities can potentially be enabled by the available capabilities of technology within realistic timeframes and budgeting expectations (see Figure 4.6). For this reason, the conception phase does not imply developing any specific architectural plans. Nevertheless, some auxiliary artifacts can be produced to formalize the outcomes of preliminary analysis, e.g. position papers conveying the recommendations of architects regarding the implementation of certain business ideas (see Figure 10.7).

Even though programs and strategies exert a major influence on the global architectural context and largely shape it (see Figure 9.7), previous planning decisions constituting this context cannot be neglected by Enterprise Architects during the conception of initiatives. Specifically, it is their responsibility to think about how new programs and strategies interrelate with those that are already running in the organization and whether their suggestions are consistent and can coexist harmoniously together. For example, some newly proposed strategies can move the organization in the direction opposite to that proclaimed by current transformation strategies. Or, some programs can require incompatible or mutually exclusive modifications of corporate IT assets, coming into collision. These and similar concerns have to be taken into account by Enterprise Architects when discussing ideas for digitalization.

After the tentative ideas for digital transformation undergo initial scrutiny and grow into more developed concepts that are considered worthwhile and realistic by Enterprise Architects and other stakeholders, these concepts form the basis for full-fledged change initiatives — programs or strategies, depending on their scope and significance. At this point, the initiative implementation process advances to the next planning phase, where these initiatives are elaborated via architectural planning.

Activities During the Planning Phase

In the second planning phase of the initiative implementation process, Enterprise Architects switch to fulfilling their primary purpose in organizations — leading the architectural planning of digital transformation initiatives. During this phase, they begin orchestrating collaborative processes of architectural planning with the involvement of business leaders, where concrete planning decisions regarding the execution of initiatives are made.

For Enterprise Architects, the planning phase of the initiative implementation process represents the peak period of their activity in terms of the intensity of work and the concentration of energy required to conduct architectural planning, preferably on a full-time basis. Generally, this episode of architectural planning is driven by the following and similar questions about the respective digitalization initiative:

- What strategic impact is anticipated from the transformation initiative?
- What changes should happen from the standpoint of business and IT capabilities?
- What conceptual ideas and prescriptions define the meaning of the initiative?
- What underlying technologies will enable the desired business improvements?
- What components constitute the initiative and when should they be implemented?

On the whole, the initial upfront episode of architectural planning carried out within the planning phase follows the standard three-step planning process (see Figure 11.4), where Enterprise Architects cooperate with the relevant stakeholders to reach mutually agreed planning decisions that form the initiative. However, the dispersed and loosely structured character of high-level transformation initiatives affects virtually all aspects of this process, including stakeholders, decisions, EA artifacts and approval procedures, posing a number of special challenges for architects.

First, since large-scale transformation efforts have a broad impact and can cause multiple effects throughout the organization, the exact circle of their stakeholders is often difficult to delineate. Moreover, as the scope of these efforts itself represents a product of decision-making, their stakeholder circle is *flexible* and directly depends on what is considered in scope and what is not. In short, initiative stakeholders decide on the scope of the initiative which, in turn, determines its stakeholders. For example, if at one moment stakeholders collectively realize that a certain business area should also be affected by the transformation, then the heads of this area join the stakeholder community to influence subsequent planning decisions, possibly again reshaping its scope. For this reason, for programs and strategies, the set of stakeholders is not fixed and cannot be clearly identified in advance. Instead, their actual stakeholders need to be *discovered* by Enterprise Architects as part of architectural planning and involved in the process for further iterations of planning. Thereby, their circle of stakeholders is continually refined along with their scope until the planning process settles down. As noted earlier, although this circle potentially includes both senior executives and middle managers, "real" decisions are typically made by managers more knowledgeable in business details, while executives, for the most part, only sanction these decisions from the top.

Second, as high-level transformation initiatives often comprise many diverse but loosely related architectural decisions relevant to different organizational areas, each decision can have its own stakeholder audience that may only partly overlap with the audiences of other decisions belonging to the same initiative. In these situations, the whole group of initiative stakeholders can be divided into multiple narrow sub-groups centered around specific categories of planning decisions. Also, the very process of architectural planning can be split into a number of *parallel sub-processes* where different sorts of decisions are developed, though staying consistent at the initiative-wide level. In other words, for programs and strategies, their architectural planning can often be best accomplished in multiple semi-independent flows of decision-making involving only limited subsets of initiative stakeholders. Essentially, for a single change initiative, Enterprise Architects may need to orchestrate *more than one* process of architectural planning at the same time. This scenario can be especially tricky for multi-driver initiatives as their stakeholders often split into separate factions around different transformation drivers, exacerbating the tension and conflicts of interests between them[6].

Third, because different architectural decisions for high-level transformation initiatives are usually captured in different EA artifacts, their architectural planning often creates and updates many artifacts to reflect the entire set of necessary planning decisions (see Figure 9.5). Furthermore, these artifacts often result from different sub-streams of architectural planning, where they are demonstrated to different audiences, as discussed above. Unlike projects, whose implementation process implies creating basically the same list of EA artifacts in a more or less linear sequence, programs and strategies have neither a fixed set of artifacts that need to be produced, nor a definite sequence in which they should be developed. Instead, different high-level initiatives can require very dissimilar, barely overlapping and ad hoc collections of EA artifacts to capture their architectural solutions (see Figure 9.6). Hence, when driving programs and strategies, Enterprise Architects may need to handle the full array of EA artifacts, picking those that seem most suitable for documenting particular planning decisions.

Finally, the approval of the resulting architectural solutions for high-level transformation initiatives also represents a complex activity distributed in time and space in the sense that different decisions, EA artifacts or other elements of their architectural plans can be approved by different architecture governance bodies independently from each other, i.e. the respective initiative approval gate is "diffused" (see Figure 15.2). Most notably, technical components of architectural solutions captured in Standards and Landscapes can be ratified by the technology committee separately from the endorsement of their organizational components reflected in Considerations and Visions by the strategy committee. The same logic also applies at a more granular level to individual planning decisions that are not explicitly related. For this reason, for a single change initiative, Enterprise Architects may need to organize and participate in multiple approval procedures to make the initiative fully authorized for execution.

While leading architectural planning, Enterprise Architects cannot ignore the presence of the overall architectural context. Namely, all new initiatives, regardless of their magnitude, should harmonize with the current initiatives and other planning decisions made in the organization in the past. For this purpose, architects have to ensure that new programs and strategies do not conflict with the existing Principles, IT Principles, Architecture Strategies, Roadmaps, IT Roadmaps and other EA artifacts forming the architectural context. Besides that, many of these artifacts need to be reviewed and possibly modified to align with, or at least not contradict, the ideas of new change initiatives.

Activities During the Execution Phase

In the next execution phase of the initiative implementation process, Enterprise Architects refocus their activities from leading the development of architectural plans to exercising architectural oversight over their execution. Specifically, they start to follow up on the agreed plans for strategies or programs to ensure that their derivative initiatives, mostly projects served by Solution Architects, align with their conceptual prescriptions and also with other relevant suggestions of the architectural context (see Figure 15.1).

The execution phase of the initiative implementation process represents a rather "lazy" period for Enterprise Architects as it requires only periodic involvement in various activities intended to control adherence to the existing plans. Generally, this phase is driven by the following and similar questions about high-level architectural plans and their descending initiatives:

- Do the initiatives that we launch come from higher-order architectural plans?
- Do these initiatives contribute to the construction of the desired long-term state?
- Do our projects fit into the "big picture" described in global architectural plans?
- Do these projects focus on the strategic capabilities that are critical for us?
- Do these projects reuse the proper IT assets, technologies and approaches?

As discussed earlier, the execution of higher-level initiatives is manifested in the conception and planning of their lower-level descendants (see Figure 2.6). Accordingly, in the course of the execution phase, Enterprise Architects supervise the architectural planning of subordinate initiatives to ensure that their architectural solutions link to the planning decisions of their parents (see Figure 3.7). To do that, architects employ a combination of different means including both informal individual approaches and formal governance procedures (see Figure 12.4).

First, individual approaches are used during the early steps of the architectural planning process of derivative initiatives, when their architectural plans are under development. For example, for subordinate projects, Enterprise Architects can attend some of their planning sessions, stay in contact with their Solution Architects, help them make the right project-level planning decisions and review the preliminary versions of their Outlines and Designs to provide timely feedback. Or, Enterprise Architects can even "roll up their sleeves" and co-develop project plans in their most fundamental aspects at the initial stages of the project implementation process. To facilitate adherence to their high-level plans, Enterprise Architects can also provide appropriate compliance checklists to guide the decision-making of Solution Architects (see Figure 12.5).

Next, governance procedures are used exclusively within the concluding approval step of the architectural planning process of derivative initiatives, when their plans are completed and ready for verification. To apply these procedures, Enterprise Architects take advantage of their membership in various architecture governance bodies that authorize different kinds of architectural plans at all opportune moments and control points. For example, for subordinate projects, they can endorse their Solution Overviews, as members of the investment committee, and then sign off their Solution Designs, as members of the design committee, or authorize both these EA artifacts through an initiative-specific steering committee. As part of these procedures, Enterprise Architects also review and approve all the exception forms filled by Solution Architects when their projects need to deviate (see Figure 12.6). After the official approval of their architectural plans, projects proceed to their execution and delivery under the supervision of their assigned Solution Architects, normally without any further assistance or participation of Enterprise Architects.

The execution phase of transformation strategies and programs continues until all the necessary projects implied by their architectural plans are implemented. If any adjustments in these plans are needed urgently, Enterprise Architects can submit requisite amendment forms, such as architecture change requests (see Figure 12.7), for the consideration of the technology committee or the strategy committee, depending on the implications of the required changes. Otherwise, all architectural plans of high-level initiatives are routinely revised on a periodic basis to be adapted to ever-changing conditions.

Activities During the Revision Phase

In the revision phase of the initiative implementation process, Enterprise Architects return to architectural planning activities in order to revisit the existing plans and adjust them to match new realities. During this phase, they meet with business leaders to discuss the progress in the execution of initiatives and introduce the necessary modifications to their architectural plans by means of follow-up architectural planning.

Although follow-up episodes of architectural planning performed within the revision phase represent rather short-term exercises, they may require significant efforts and nearly full-time involvement on the part of Enterprise Architects and tend to represent periods of highly intensive work, though somewhat less strenuous than in the initial episode during the main planning phase. Generally, these episodes of architectural planning are driven by the following and similar questions about the existing architectural plans:

- What has changed in the business environment since the plans were developed?
- To what extent have the original architectural plans been executed?
- What new factors facilitating or inhibiting their execution came into play?
- What modifications should be introduced to the plans to continue their execution?
- Should the execution of the initiative be canceled in light of new circumstances?

Because follow-up episodes of architectural planning start from the existing plans, they go through a shortened planning process without the initial discussion step. To refresh these plans, Enterprise Architects gather their stakeholders together, collectively decide on what amendments are required, update the respective EA artifacts to document them and finally get these changes approved by the technology and strategy committees at the dispersed updates approval gate (see Figure 15.2). For example, for a three-year transformation program, every quarter the designated architect can meet with its business sponsors to discuss their current priorities, rearrange the program Roadmap to reflect these priorities and then present it to the strategy committee for ratification.

At the same time, all the features of architectural planning associated with the loosely structured nature of high-level digitalization initiatives described earlier in relation to the planning phase are relevant to the revision phase as well and have to be dealt with by Enterprise Architects in follow-up planning episodes. Moreover, because these initiatives are long-running and people occupying managerial positions periodically rotate, when their architectural plans are being revised, some of their original sponsors may no longer be among their stakeholders. For this reason, forming a new coalition of supporters and political realignment of interests might be necessary to proceed with their implementation, posing additional challenges for architects[7].

Except for the cases of their deliberate cancellation as no longer promising, after the update of their architectural plans, transformation initiatives return to the execution phase, where they get back into their regular rut, though until the next revision phase, where their plans are updated again. The revision-execution cycle, thus, continues until initiatives are completed or abandoned.

Activities Along the Initiative Implementation Process

The activities carried out by Enterprise Architects in the course of the implementation process of high-level transformation initiatives described above constitute the bulk of their occupation in organizations. These activities exactly correspond to the general mapping of the activities of architects to the three lifecycle phases of digitalization initiatives (see Figure 13.2), though with an addition of the revision phase typical for programs and strategies. The activities of Enterprise Architects during the different phases of the initiative implementation process are summarized in Figure 15.3.

328 PART III: Enterprise Architects in Organizations

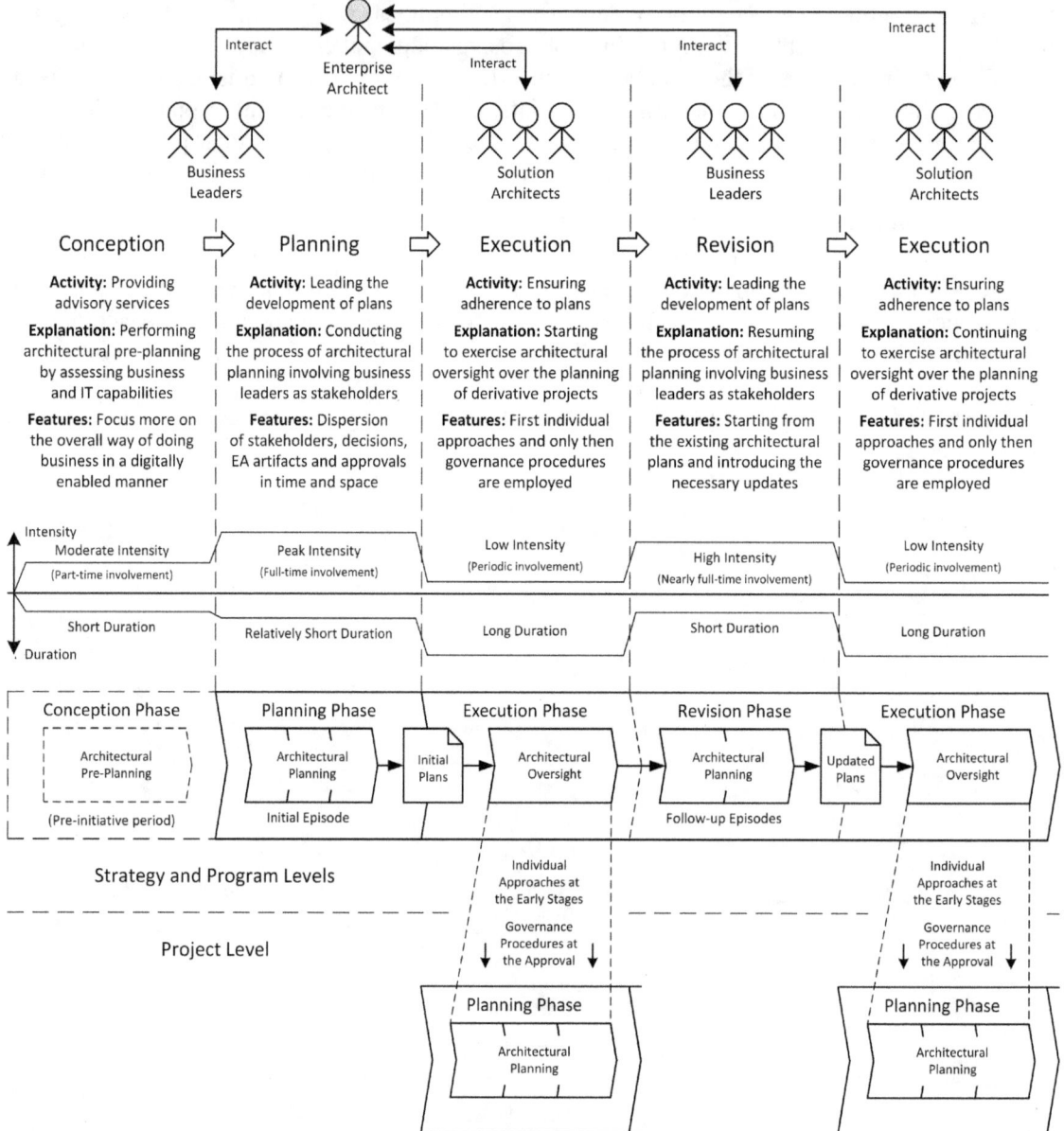

Figure 15.3. Activities of Enterprise Architects along the initiative implementation process

The outlook presented in Figure 15.3 offers a comprehensive view of the successive activities of Enterprise Architects performed in the initiative context, which complement their basic activities in the organizational context. Together, these two disparate sets of activities form the substance of their work in organizations.

The Work of Enterprise Architects

The unity of their activities in the organizational and initiative contexts described above constitutes the work of Enterprise Architects in organizations, where they study the organization with its environment, consult senior managers, assist in the initial ideation of high-level digitalization initiatives and then drive these initiatives to completion through their different lifecycle phases (see Figure 15.3). Besides engaging in these activities, their work also implies protecting the technical interests of global landscape optimization (see Table 13.1), advocating technical concerns as valid IT-side transformation drivers (see Figure 1.2) and promoting technical rationalization initiatives (see Figure 13.7).

Enterprise Architects are actively involved in the ideation processes of autonomous strategies and programs and their subsequent conception and planning, helping business leaders innovate with IT. However, they do not go the "last mile" and delegate the implementation of derivative projects as part of their execution to subordinate Solution Architects specialized in the relevant technologies. The work of Enterprise Architects in its entirety is summarized graphically in Figure 15.4.

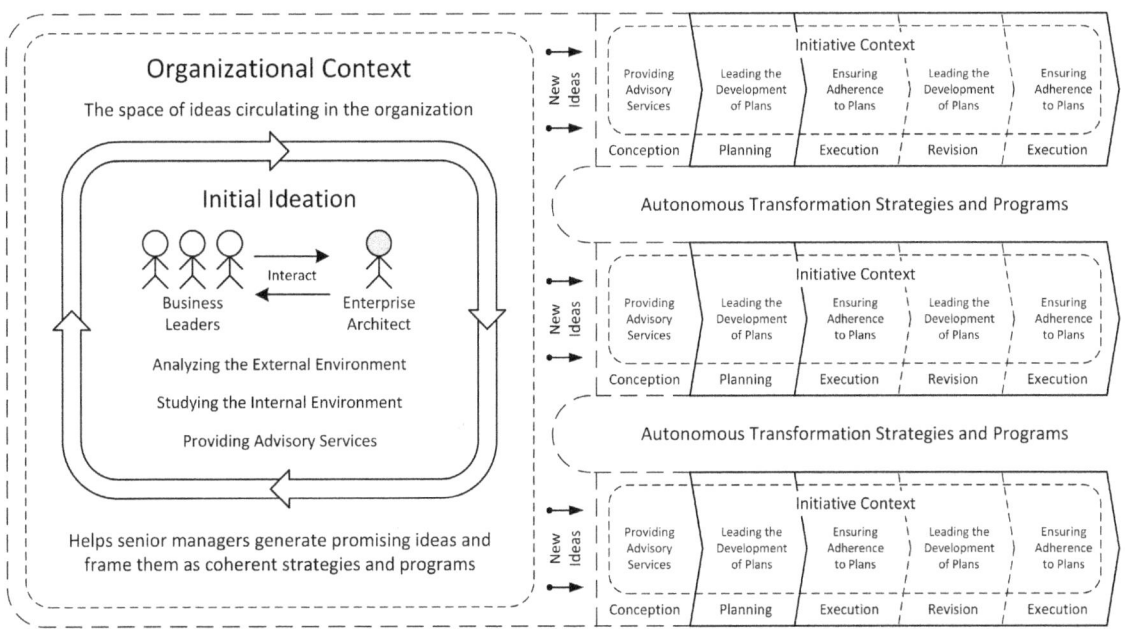

Figure 15.4. The end-to-end work of Enterprise Architects in organizations

Importantly, from a temporal standpoint, all the activities shown in Figure 15.4 are performed by Enterprise Architects during their workdays in parallel, so that they contribute their efforts simultaneously to the ideation of new initiatives as well as to the progress of multiple running initiatives from the pipeline (see Figure 13.6). For instance, Enterprise Architects are often involved concurrently in a number of digitalization strategies and programs at different stages of their implementation and, at the same time, also participate in the discussions of budding ideas for new transformations. This dissipation of attention on their part generates a variegated work schedule consisting of very diverse tasks related to different endeavors (see Figure 13.5), which does not resemble the series of sequential activities outlined in Figure 15.3.

Organization-Centric Work of Enterprise Architects

The description of the work of Enterprise Architects presented above clearly differentiated their activities in the organizational context, where they are involved in the ideation of new transformation initiatives, and in the initiative context, where they serve these initiatives along their lifecycle (see Figure 15.4). This division of activities into the two disparate contexts, however, does not always provide an accurate representation of their work since high-level change initiatives in organizations are often strongly interlaced, not made explicit or even not articulated as such, resulting in partial or complete dissolution of the very initiative context. In this case, the respective activities of Enterprise Architects move into the broader organizational context with numerous practical implications for their work.

Intertwined, Implicit and Inarticulate High-Level Transformation Initiatives

Because programs and strategies are "fluid" but broadly scoped and their boundaries can be very indistinct, these initiatives may greatly *overlap* in the sense that various actors, decisions and activities can relate to more than one change initiative at once. Their overlapping can lie in a number of different dimensions, including affected organizational areas, underlying transformation drivers, involved stakeholder parties, pertinent EA artifacts and even concrete planning sessions.

First, different programs and strategies can certainly target and modify the same business units, capabilities and operations. For example, both the Digital Channels Strategy and Data Analytics Strategy discussed earlier as examples (see Figure 9.6) are likely to transform multiple sales and customer relationship management processes, though in different ways. Second, in terms of their intentions, different high-level digitalization initiatives can be induced by partly the same transformation drivers from the motivational context. For example, the Digital Channels Strategy and Data Analytics Strategy definitely share the motives of increasing profits and getting closer to the customer. Third, different programs and strategies can have the same business leaders among their sponsors and stakeholders. For example, both the Digital Channels Strategy and Data Analytics Strategy, most probably, include at least the team of corporate-level executives and the groups of business leaders responsible for sales and customer relationships as common members of their stakeholder circles. Fourth, because the vast majority of EA artifacts relevant to high-level transformation initiatives are general and shared physically between all initiatives (see Figure 9.5), different programs and strategies are also interconnected materially via largely the same set of artifacts capturing their architectural decisions. For example, the Digital Channels Strategy and Data Analytics Strategy jointly reflect all their technology choices in the Technology Reference Model. Lastly, elements of different programs and strategies can be discussed during the same decision-making meetings. For example, rearrangements of Roadmaps accomplished during one planning session can be conducive to multiple programs whose projects are included in these Roadmaps. Or, the decision to decrease the status of some information systems from strategic to legacy in the System Portfolio Model can be equally necessary for implementing two independent transformation strategies.

Unlike projects, for high-level digitalization initiatives, their linkage to specific organizational areas, transformation drivers, stakeholders, artifacts and decisions can be rather loose. Owing to numerous overlaps in many of their aspects described above, it is often difficult to tell exactly to which initiatives particular activities actually belong. When the overlapping between different high-level initiatives is extreme, all programs and strategies in the organization can be intertwined together so tightly that they can no longer be clearly distinguished from one another as separate storylines or aspirations, fusing into a single composite strategic effort. In this case, the entire pipeline of initiatives can be best viewed as a united, global and continual transformative exercise; speaking of individual change initiatives ceases to make sense.

Besides being closely intertwined, high-level digitalization initiatives can also be *implicit* — exist as coherent initiatives only tacitly in the perception of their stakeholders, without having any explicit manifestations in the form of special labels, official documents or organizational arrangements. In contrast to projects requiring certain administrative treatment as physical units of change, programs and strategies, as more ethereal constructs, can be not formalized administratively, staying largely invisible to the rest of the organization (see Figure 2.6). For instance, business leaders can bear in mind that some projects are conceptually related, unified by a common purpose and should be implemented in a specific sequence, but do not refer to them collectively as a program in any oral or written communication.

In other cases, a determined outlook for the future can be embodied merely in the collection of desired projects planned for implementation, but not structured logically into any higher-order initiatives, even implicitly, so that no programs and strategies exist in the organization at all. For example, business leaders can have a lucid vision for the future in the form of an orderly set of independent pieces of work for the next few years that implies no high-level transformation initiatives. To summarize, in many circumstances, the initiative-centric view of digital transformation efforts, as well as of the work of Enterprise Architects as part of these efforts, presented earlier can be inadequate.

Organization-Centric View of Digital Transformation

Intertwined, implicit or inarticulate high-level transformation initiatives render new realities of digitalization for Enterprise Architects, where the initiative context of activities becomes blurred or even completely disappears. These realities necessitate an alternative, initiative-agnostic look at digital transformation endeavors in organizations suitable for explaining the work of Enterprise Architects in the absence of well-defined strategies and programs.

In situations when strategies and programs are mingled, indistinct or missing altogether, the focus of high-level architectural planning in organizations shifts from individual initiatives to the entire enterprise-wide project portfolio. The **project portfolio** represents a common pool of all projects envisioned in the organization, or all the present intentions for implementing projects. The project portfolio embraces change projects of any origin, including autonomous and independent projects as well as those derived from different implicit or explicit higher-order transformation initiatives.

Architectural planning for the global project portfolio does not differ in principle from that for strategies and programs and also involves conjoining business ends and IT means (see Figure 3.3), but deals mostly with planning decisions regarding the portfolio composition and covers potentially all organizational areas instead of specific transformation initiatives. Conceptually, the architectural planning of the project portfolio is equivalent to the architectural planning of a virtual, all-encompassing, never-ending and loosely structured digitalization strategy for the whole organization, which is being continuously revised and constantly executed. For the corporate project portfolio, its architectural plans aggregate all the agreed strategy- and program-level planning decisions from the overall architectural context of the organization reflected in all the existing EA artifacts.

Redefining the object, process and product of architectural planning as above yields a new conceptual apparatus, or framework, that allows interpreting organizational digitalization efforts in a meaningful fashion even when articulate high-level transformation initiatives are absent. Specifically, with this framework, the flow of digitalization can be interpreted as follows: high-level architectural planning continually produces some plans forming the architectural context of the organization which, in turn, guides its project portfolio in terms of included projects scheduled for implementation[8]. In this interpretation, projects ensue, as usual, from some higher-order architectural plans, though not from concrete programs or strategies. The work of Enterprise Architects switches accordingly from serving particular high-level transformation initiatives to *serving the project portfolio* in its entirety by driving various decision-making processes around its structure, focus and timing.

Because all the entities constituting the new interpretative framework relate to the organization as a whole instead of its individual change initiatives, the resulting view of digitalization can be called organization-centric. The **organization-centric view of digital transformation** describes the respective efforts in organizations without trying to divide them into separate high-level transformation initiatives. Basically, it presents the entire digitalization journey of the organization as one comprehensive transformation strategy. This alternative, somewhat more abstract but universal view can be opposed to the more granular initiative-centric view adopted previously in this book for explicating digitalization endeavors[9].

Importantly, the organization-centric view of digital transformation is by no means incompatible with the initiative-centric one, but rather complements it in those conditions when coherent strategies and programs cannot be discerned. In fact, both views can offer reasonable interpretations of the organizational reality at the same time, but the accuracy of these interpretations, however, depends on the degree of the clarity of high-level digitalization initiatives in the organization. The differences between the initiative-centric and organization-centric views of digital transformation, as well as the spectrum of possible situations with high-level initiatives, are summarized in Figure 15.5.

Chapter 15: The Archetype of Enterprise Architects

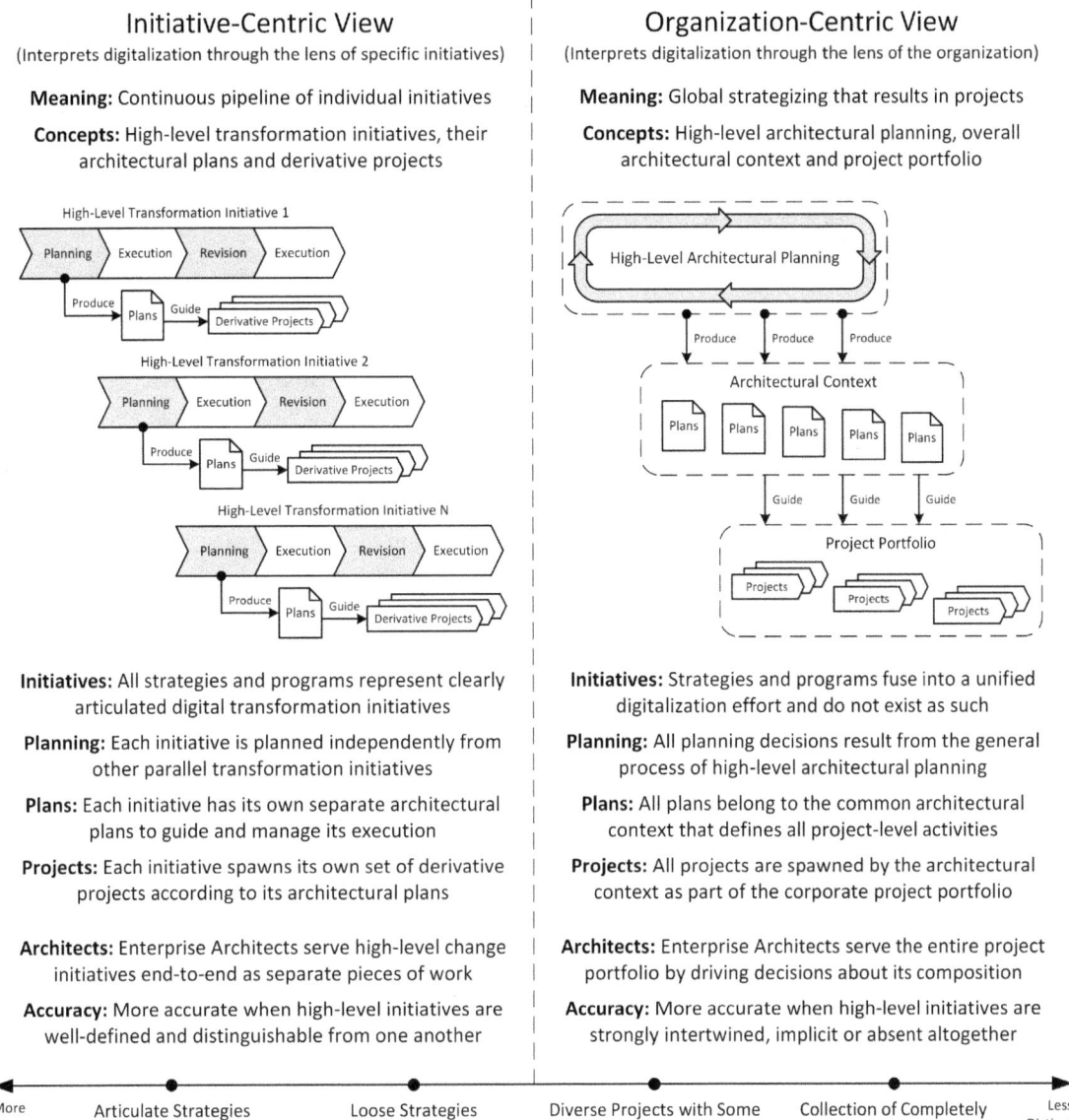

Figure 15.5. The initiative-centric and organization-centric views of digitalization

In many cases and respects, the organization-centric view of digital transformation shown in Figure 15.5 provides a more adequate depiction of the settings in which Enterprise Architects operate. In particular, this view helps understand the place of Enterprise Architects in the organizational ecosystem when no clear-cut high-level digitalization initiatives are present.

Enterprise Architects in the Organization-Centric View

In spite of the radically different framing of digitalization efforts offered by the organization-centric view, the overall position of Enterprise Architects in terms of their standing, duties and communication patterns in this view is *not* different from their typical position in the initiative-centric view. Exactly as in the initiative-centric view, they interact with various business leaders, discuss their transformation drivers, develop high-level architectural plans and supervise lower-level Solution Architects acting according to these plans (see Figure 15.1).

However, because in the organization-centric view of digitalization articulate transformation strategies and programs are missing and all their derivative projects unite into a common project portfolio (see Figure 15.5), Enterprise Architects essentially serve the full project portfolio rather than specific high-level initiatives. Furthermore, in this view, the very strategy and program levels of the initiative hierarchy at which Enterprise Architects normally work lose their meaning and can be merged conceptually into a single **project portfolio level**, which represents a virtual level aggregating all strategy- and program-level planning decisions shaping the project portfolio. Decision-making processes at the project portfolio level are characterized by global scopes, long timeframes, definite boundaries, abstract constructs and ballpark estimates. The position of Enterprise Architects with their responsibilities and interactions in the organization-centric view of digital transformation is shown in Figure 15.6.

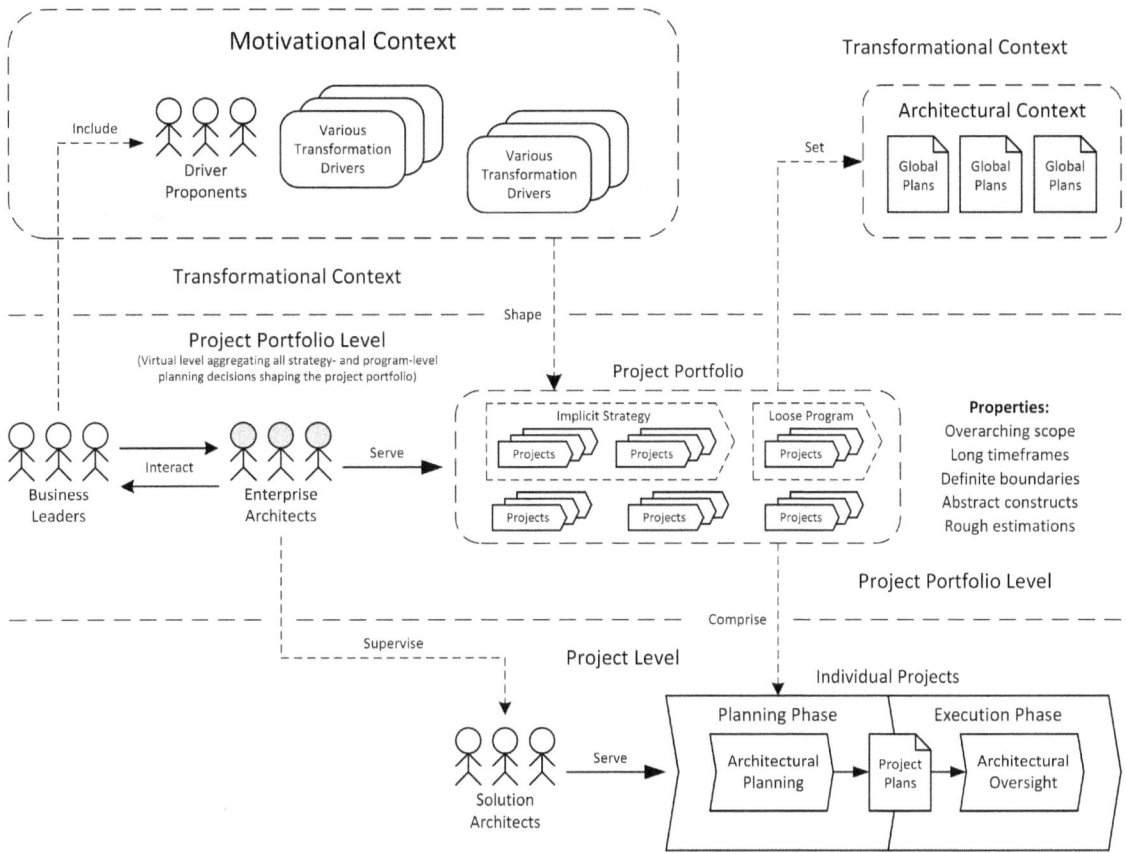

Figure 15.6. The position of Enterprise Architects in the organization-centric view

The place of Enterprise Architects in the organizational ecosystem without clearly defined strategies and programs depicted in Figure 15.6 helps analyze their specific activities in situations when the very initiative context is lacking.

Activities of Enterprise Architects in the Organization-Centric View

Fundamentally, all the key challenges of digital transformation in organizations remain exactly the same, irrespective of the applied interpretative scheme, whether with or without high-level change initiatives (see Figure 15.5). Consequently, in the organization-centric view of digitalization, both the technical and organizational sides of architectural planning necessary for addressing these challenges stay perfectly relevant and the general logic of dialectical refinement of technical and organizational components also holds valid (see Figure 11.3). For these reasons, in the absence of distinct strategies and programs, the activities of Enterprise Architects in organizations remain largely the same, except for two noteworthy "spatial" and "temporal" modifications in their specifics.

Spatially, without high-level transformation initiatives, the initiative context in which they are implemented practically vanishes and all the activities of Enterprise Architects normally performed in this context relocate into the broader organizational context. In short, the initiative context of activities merges into the organizational one. As a result, all germane elements of the initiative context get substituted with their "extended" organizational analogs (see Figure 10.1). Namely, the scope of work changes from a single digitalization initiative to the whole organization, local initiative goals — to the strategic goals of the organization, the underlying drivers of the initiative — to the full motivational context, initiative sponsors — to the community of driver proponents, initiative stakeholders — potentially to all business and IT leaders, the architectural plans of the initiative — to the aggregate architectural context, initiative-specific EA artifacts — to all general plans EA artifacts, derivative projects — to the entire project portfolio.

Temporally, without being confined to the successive phases of particular initiatives, all the organizational activities in which Enterprise Architects participate that are normally performed during these phases become unbounded in time and transform into ongoing processes. In short, discrete and intermittent activities turn into continuous ones. First, all the bursts of architectural pre-planning from the conception phase unite into continuous architectural pre-planning, where various ideas for digitalization are constantly assessed for their feasibility and elaborated into more mature concepts. Second, all the episodes of architectural planning taking place within the planning and revision phases amalgamate into continuous architectural planning, where these concepts are continually converted into the amendments of high-level architectural plans forming the architectural context (see Figure 15.5). Finally, all architectural oversight exertions from the execution phase fuse into continuous architectural oversight, where the alignment of individual projects with higher-order plans from the architectural context is persistently monitored.

Therefore, when articulate high-level transformation initiatives are missing and the organization-centric view of digitalization proves more accurate, all the activities of Enterprise Architects are fulfilled in a continuous manner within the organizational context, but retain their original meaning. Because different activities are carried out in different contexts, their "migration" from the initiative-centric view to the organization-centric one affects them quite differently, so that some activities stay nearly the same, while others alter in certain aspects rather substantially.

On the one hand, of the five activities of architects, their three basic activities, being primary in the organizational context but only supporting in the initiative context, remain virtually unchanged relative to their "canonical" versions in the initiative-centric view thoroughly described earlier. For instance, in the organization-centric view, both analyzing the external environment and studying the internal environment are performed by Enterprise Architects for general education, often contributing to the process of initial ideation, or in any other circumstances when the respective knowledge is needed, exactly as in the initiative-centric view. Likewise, advisory services are provided by Enterprise Architects for many purposes, including the initial origination of ideas for digitalization and their architectural pre-planning, though without their structuring into concrete initiatives as in the initiative-centric view.

On the other hand, the two more advanced activities of architects, leading the development of plans and ensuring adherence to plans, which are native to the initiative context, undergo noticeable changes associated with the switching of the context of their fulfillment to organizational and look somewhat different in the organization-centric view. Most importantly, leading the development of plans by Enterprise Architects mutates notably in terms of the resulting product, involved stakeholders, employed EA artifacts and followed process flows.

First, instead of developing cohesive architectural solutions for specific initiatives, this activity makes various architectural decisions about the composition of the project portfolio guided, for the most part, by the following question: "What projects are both feasible technically and desirable organizationally to be included in our portfolio?" Second, instead of a limited circle of initiative stakeholders, as part of this activity in the organizational context Enterprise Architects deal with the whole management community. Third, as the very notion of initiative-specific EA artifacts in the organizational context ceases to exist, Enterprise Architects use only general artifacts for capturing produced architectural plans, e.g. enterprise-wide Principles and Standards, more local Architecture Strategies and Target States, and eventually Roadmaps and IT Roadmaps for different areas to define the projects themselves that constitute the portfolio. And lastly, as the process of architectural planning in the organizational context becomes continuous, it is manifested in constant updates of the existing architectural plans and their periodic reapproval by architecture governance bodies, i.e. by the technology and strategy committees authorizing all major planning decisions at the project portfolio level. Additionally, the loosely structured character of the project portfolio itself further disperses architectural planning efforts on the part of Enterprise Architects in all their aspects, essentially generating a continuous flow of rather weakly related technical and organizational decisions.

As for ensuring adherence to plans, this activity in the organizational context has no plans for concrete initiatives to underpin architectural oversight, but only the general architectural context instead. These alterations of spatial and temporal nature in the five activities of Enterprise Architects in the organization-centric view of digitalization necessitate a somewhat different conceptualization of their work.

The Work of Enterprise Architects in the Organization-Centric View

Because in the organization-centric view of digitalization all the discrete activities from different initiative lifecycle phases merge into continuous processes, the work of Enterprise Architects changes accordingly from accomplishing sequential activities for specific initiatives to participating in ongoing processes running in the organization. Namely, providing advisory services during the conception phase turns into continuous architectural pre-planning, leading the development of plans during the planning and revision phases — into continuous architectural planning, while ensuring adherence to plans during the execution phase — into continuous architectural oversight. In other words, in the organization-centric view, Enterprise Architects still communicate with business leaders, help them generate ideas for digital transformation, assess the viability of these ideas, convert them into high-level architectural plans and ensure that lower-level projects stick to these plans, but do all that in the form of ongoing organizational processes instead of progressive phases of separate initiatives, as in the initiative-centric view (see Figure 15.4). With similar modifications, they also advocate technical interests and promote technical concerns as transformation drivers, sometimes eventually resulting in concrete technical rationalization projects (see Figure 13.7).

For example, in a relatively small company, an Enterprise Architect can have a constant circle of stakeholders consisting of about 15–20 senior to mid-level managers, mostly the heads of different business units. The architect can visit each of these parties in person, say, on a monthly basis to discuss the current status of their projects, inquire about their most pressing drivers and ask what they are thinking of doing in the future. During these conversations, the architect advises the stakeholders as to what IT could do with regard to their drivers, together they come up with fruitful ideas for digitalization and, by applying more careful thought in subsequent meetings, turn them into sound concepts. After that, the architect can organize a few follow-up planning sessions to produce updated architectural plans reflecting these and maybe some other previously discussed concepts, e.g. amend Policies, modify Target States and add the necessary projects to Roadmaps (in many cases, however, identified business needs can be straightforwardly put on Roadmaps as potential projects, without any serious planning, as on simple to-do lists). Being a permanent member of the investment committee, the architect can continually observe what projects are initiated throughout the year and ensure that these projects align with the existing plans, e.g. comply with the enacted Policies, contribute to the approved Target States and correlate with the agreed Roadmaps.

Or, as the proponent of technical concerns of efficiency, simplicity and security, an Enterprise Architect, after consultations with competent subject-matter experts, can introduce a number of high-level architectural decisions on recommended approaches, patterns and technologies for implementing IT systems and capture these decisions in the appropriate Standards. Then, as the chair of the design committee, the architect can verify that each new project actually conforms to the established code of Standards. Driven by technical concerns, the architect can also initiate a special infrastructure security project to address critical vulnerabilities in the corporate IT landscape and strengthen its protection against malware and associated threats of data leakage.

Thereby, Enterprise Architects serve the organization by supporting its IT-related decision-making processes, all the way from the origination of new ideas for digitalization to their physical materialization through projects. The work of Enterprise Architects in the organization-centric view with the distinctive features of their activities relative to the "classic" initiative-centric view is summarized graphically in Figure 15.7.

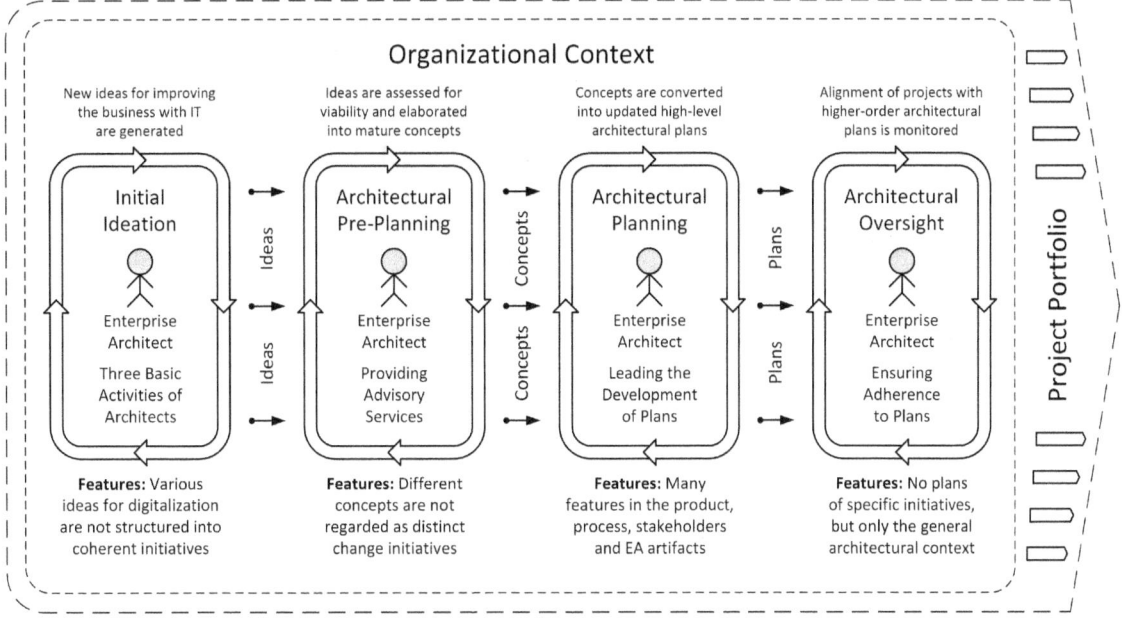

Figure 15.7. The work of Enterprise Architects in the organization-centric view

As it is evident from the above discussions, the work of Enterprise Architects in organizations is extremely versatile and can be framed very differently in different circumstances. Depending on the situation, they can either lead some high-level transformation initiatives (e.g. a CRM consolidation strategy or an ERP replacement program) as per the initiative-centric view (see Figure 15.4), or simply drive the project portfolio for the entire organization or some of its areas as per the organization-centric view (see Figure 15.7)[10]. Moreover, in practice, in many cases, elements of both these duties can be assigned to them, resulting in combined initiative- and organization-centric views of their responsibilities. In fact, relatively rarely can the work of Enterprise Architects be viewed as purely initiative-centric.

Domain Specialization of Enterprise Architects

As mentioned earlier, the expertise of Enterprise Architects is usually unequal across different organizational domains (see Figure 3.4), sometimes manifesting in pronounced *domain specialization* of their job. Because the six major domains cover diverse subjects and differ significantly in their properties, domain specialization affects many aspects of the work of Enterprise Architects in organizations, including their resources, instruments and activities, so that the inherent specifics of their focal domains determine the specifics of their work.

First of all, resources possessed by Enterprise Architects obviously reflect their domain specialization. In particular, their knowledge and experience are more extensive in those organizational domains in which they specialize and less extensive in other domains. For example, an Enterprise Architect specializing in the infrastructure domain is naturally more competent in server, storage and network equipment than in programming languages, database engines and messaging middleware. Besides the respective technology areas, they are more versed in domain-specific frameworks and bodies of knowledge, e.g. SABSA for security and DMBOK for data.

Instruments employed by Enterprise Architects also correlate rather directly with their domain specialization. Because most EA artifacts are associated with some organizational domains more strongly than with the others (see Figure 8.17), their relevance to architects specializing in the corresponding domains varies accordingly. For example, Conceptual Data Models and Logical Data Models are exclusive and definitive for the data domain and, thus, essential for Enterprise Architects with this specialization. Or, Policies and Guidelines, though not domain-specific, are particularly appropriate for specifying mandatory security requirements and very useful to architects specializing in the security domain. By contrast, Landscape Diagrams are completely domain-neutral, suitable for depicting relationships between any kinds of entities and, for this reason, equally useful for Enterprise Architects of all domain specializations.

Finally, and most importantly, activities performed by Enterprise Architects link to their domain specialization as well, but in a more complex way. First, their activities are somewhat different for architects specializing in functional and non-functional domains (see Table 3.2). On the one hand, specialization in functional domains — business, applications and data — requires communicating more with business stakeholders, paying closer attention to various business-side transformation drivers and leading more *digital transformation initiatives* for enhancing the business with IT. On the other hand, specialization in non-functional domains — integration, infrastructure and security — requires interacting more with IT stakeholders, concentrating more on technical concerns as IT-side transformation drivers and leading more *technical rationalization initiatives* for increasing IT efficiency (see Figure 13.7).

Second, their activities can be fairly different for Enterprise Architects specializing in substantive and non-substantive domains (see Table 3.3). On the one hand, specialization in substantive domains — business, applications and infrastructure — involves more *proactive architectural planning* of structural modifications in the corporate landscape to ensure that the right changes are implemented. In other words, this specialization implies more leading the development of new architectural plans for change initiatives represented more by structures EA artifacts and generally performing more initiative-centric work around particular initiatives (see Figure 15.4). For instance, Enterprise Architects specializing in substantive domains more often drive coherent transformation initiatives intended to improve business capabilities with IT systems or prepare the necessary infrastructure for future capability improvements, producing such artifacts as Process Maps, Roadmaps and IT Roadmaps.

On the other hand, specialization in non-substantive domains — data, integration and security — involves more *reactive architectural oversight* over modifications taking place in the corporate landscape to ensure that all changes are implemented in the right way. In other words, this specialization implies more ensuring adherence to existing architectural plans represented more by rules EA artifacts, less initiative-specific ones, and generally performing more organization-centric work unrelated to particular initiatives (see Figure 15.7). For instance, Enterprise Architects specializing in non-substantive domains more often supervise other transformation initiatives to guarantee organization-wide data consistency, proper integration and reliable security, referring to such artifacts as Conceptual Data Models, Patterns and Guidelines.

Hence, domain specialization of Enterprise Architects actually has considerable implications for their job in terms of their resources, instruments and activities, influencing even the most general patterns of their work in organizations. Furthermore, due to their unique specifics, specializing in each organizational domain introduces its own characteristic perceptible "flavor" to their occupation. Distinctive specifics of the six organizational domains and their typical effects on the work of Enterprise Architects specializing in them are summarized in Table 15.1.

Domain	Specifics of the domain	Specifics of the work of Enterprise Architects
Business	Native to business leaders, represents business capabilities, constitutes the landscape substance and causes new change initiatives	Communicate mainly with business leaders, perform more initiative-centric work, more lead architectural planning producing new structures EA artifacts (e.g. Process Maps) for digital transformation initiatives
Applications	Relevant to business leaders, enables business capabilities, constitutes the landscape substance and causes new change initiatives	Communicate more with business leaders, perform more initiative-centric work, more lead architectural planning producing new structures EA artifacts (e.g. Roadmaps) for digital transformation initiatives
Data	Relevant to business leaders, enables business capabilities, does not constitute the landscape substance but ensures proper initiative implementation	Communicate more with business leaders, perform more organization-centric work, more exercise architectural oversight using existing rules EA artifacts (e.g. Conceptual Data Models) but sometimes drive digital transformation initiatives
Integration	Irrelevant to business leaders, does not shape business capabilities, does not constitute the landscape substance but ensures proper initiative implementation	Communicate more with IT stakeholders, perform more organization-centric work, more exercise architectural oversight using existing rules EA artifacts (e.g. Patterns) but sometimes drive technical rationalization initiatives
Infrastructure	Irrelevant to business leaders, does not shape business capabilities, but constitutes the landscape substance and causes new change initiatives	Communicate more with IT stakeholders, perform more initiative-centric work, more lead architectural planning producing new structures EA artifacts (e.g. IT Roadmaps) for technical rationalization initiatives
Security	Irrelevant to business leaders, does not shape business capabilities, does not constitute the landscape substance but ensures proper initiative implementation	Communicate more with IT stakeholders, perform more organization-centric work, more exercise architectural oversight using existing rules EA artifacts (e.g. Guidelines) but sometimes drive technical rationalization initiatives

Table 15.1. Domain specialization of Enterprise Architects

In practice, Enterprise Architects can specialize in any one or a few related organizational domains, usually adjacent in the domain stack (e.g. data and integration), with the ensuing consequences for their work explained in Table 15.1. However, because business activities and underlying IT systems are very tightly coupled, specializations in the business and applications domains are normally coupled as well and are rather untypical for Enterprise Architects as separate specializations[11]. Importantly, as their job demands a broad understanding of business and IT, they should have at least a basic level of competence across all organizational domains, regardless of their domain specialization.

The Integrative Framework of the Archetype of Enterprise Architects

The comprehensive description of the resources, instruments and activities of Enterprise Architects and their overall work in organizations provided above suggests that all these facets of their occupation fit into the integrative framework of the profession of architects (see Figure 14.2), albeit with certain refinements attributed to their exclusive focus on high-level digitalization efforts (see Figure 15.1 and Figure 15.6). In other words, Enterprise Architects generally do what all architects do, but in a manner adapted specifically to the realities of large-scale organizational transformations. The integrative framework of the archetype of Enterprise Architects with their resources, instruments and activities is depicted schematically in Figure 15.8.

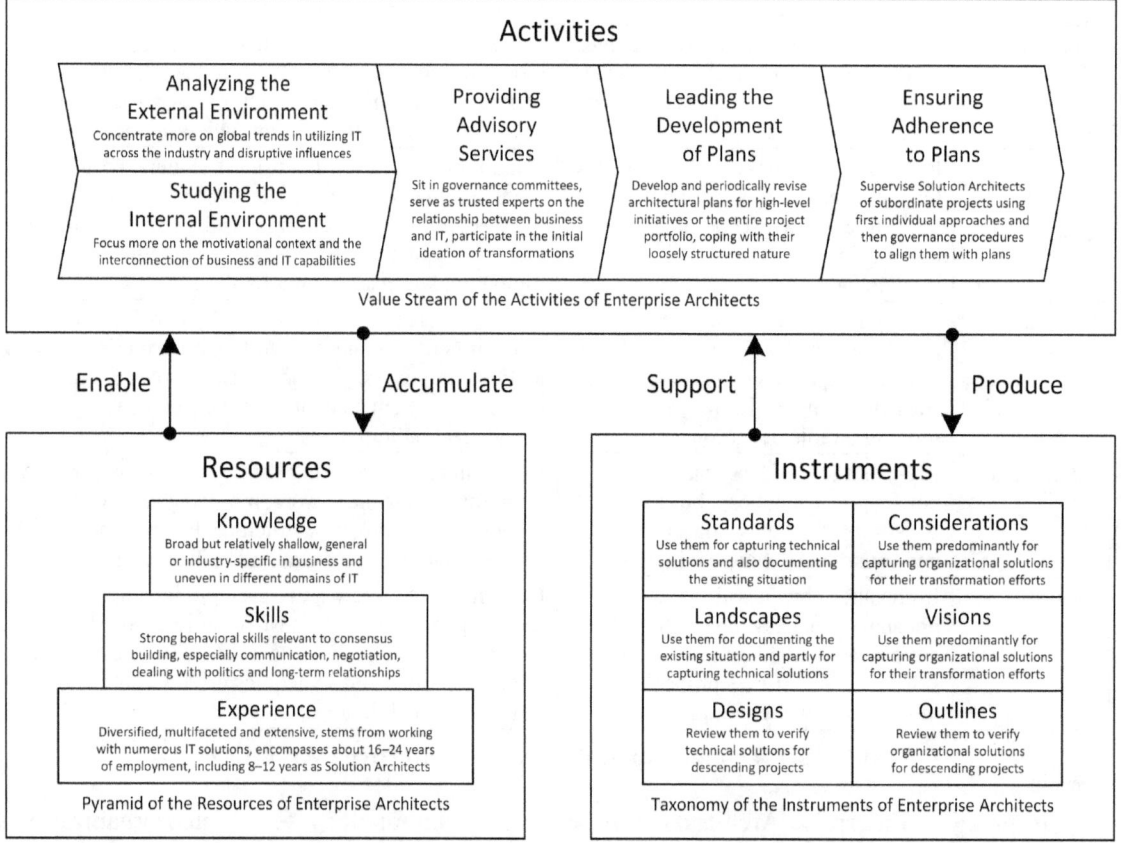

Figure 15.8. The integrative framework of the archetype of Enterprise Architects

The alignment of the properties of Enterprise Architects with the broader conceptual framework of the profession of architects at large allows considering Enterprise Architects as a special archetype of architects concentrating on high-level digitalization efforts.

Chapter Summary

This chapter described the resources, instruments and activities of Enterprise Architects in the organizational and initiative contexts, discussed the work of Enterprise Architects in its entirety across the two contexts, introduced an organization-centric view of digital transformation, explained their activities and work in this view, discussed the domain specialization of Enterprise Architects and presented their integrative framework. The key message of this chapter can be summarized in the following essential points:

- Enterprise Architects is a special archetype of architects responsible for leading the architectural planning of large-scale digitalization efforts higher-level than separate projects, operating only at the program and strategy levels
- Knowledge of Enterprise Architects is broad but relatively shallow, their skills are particularly strong in communication and negotiation, their experience is very diversified and includes 16–24 years of work, the last half as Solution Architects
- Considerations, Standards, Visions and Landscapes are used by Enterprise Architects for documenting the existing situation and capturing architectural solutions, but Outlines and Designs are only reviewed for architectural oversight
- In the organizational context, Enterprise Architects analyze global industry trends and disruptions, study the motivational context and existing capabilities, advise on strategic IT questions and participate in the initial ideation of transformations
- In the initiative context, Enterprise Architects serve high-level digitalization initiatives along their entire lifecycle by providing advisory services during the conception phase, leading the development of plans during the planning and revision phases and ensuring adherence to plans during the execution phase
- In their work, Enterprise Architects cover the initial ideation of autonomous strategies and programs, their conception and planning, but delegate their execution at the project level to Solution Architects specialized in technologies
- When high-level digitalization initiatives are indistinct, an alternative organization-centric view of digital transformation, where high-level architectural planning targets the entire project portfolio, becomes more accurate
- In the organization-centric view of digital transformation, all the activities of Enterprise Architects are performed continuously in the organizational context with the same general meaning, but with the necessary contextual modifications
- Domain specialization of Enterprise Architects determines their stakeholder circle (business or IT), work orientation (initiative- or organization-centric), activities (architectural planning or oversight), EA artifacts (domain-specific structures or rules) and types of initiatives (digital transformation or technical rationalization)

Chapter 16: The Archetype of Solution Architects

Previously, Chapter 14 introduced Solution Architects as a prominent archetype within the overarching profession of architects. This chapter provides a detailed discussion of the archetype of Solution Architects, as a clear-cut specialization of architects, with all its distinctive attributes, features and properties. In particular, this chapter starts with describing the specifics of the place, resources and instruments of Solution Architects in contrast with the profession in general. Next, this chapter thoroughly describes the activities of Solution Architects in the organizational and initiative contexts and discusses their work as a whole across the two contexts. Lastly, this chapter discusses the domain specialization of Solution Architects, clarifies its influence on different aspects of their work in organizations, presents the integrative framework of their archetype and provides their summary-level comparison with Enterprise Architects.

Solution Architects as a Distinct Archetype of Architects

The blanket profession of enterprise architects covers two generic archetypes of architects with multiple specific positions for architects in organizations (see Figure 14.4). The second consistent archetype of architects within this profession is Solution Architects concentrating on narrow areas of the organizational business and IT landscape.

Solution Architects is a special archetype of architects responsible for leading the architectural planning of *individual digitalization projects*, resulting in separate *IT solutions*, which gives this archetype its common title widely accepted in the industry today[1]. Projects reside at the lower end of the size spectrum of transformation initiatives and are characterized by limited scopes, short timeframes, clear boundaries, detailed structures and accurate estimations (see Figure 2.4). Although projects driven by Solution Architects can certainly be business-critical, have profound effects and make a considerable difference for the organization in the long run, generally the orientation of their work is more tactical than strategic.

Because projects often represent derivative initiatives spawned by some higher-order programs or strategies based on the existing intentions or simply belong to prearranged project portfolios (see Figure 15.5), Solution Architects are relatively rarely involved in the initial ideation process. Instead, they tend to follow up on the pre-planned work handed over to them by higher-level Enterprise Architects (see Figure 15.1 and Figure 15.6), being *assigned* to nascent projects. In short, Solution Architects may not generate any novel ideas for digitalization or inspire new initiatives, but continue at the stage where Enterprise Architects leave to finish the respective transformations by materializing their separate pieces[2].

Since digitalization projects, and especially subordinate ones, are heavily shaped by the existing architectural plans but may not be connected directly to concrete transformation drivers (see Figure 9.9), the architectural context is more relevant to these initiatives than the motivational one. For this reason, when serving projects within the overarching transformational context (see Figure 9.8), Solution Architects in their decision-making refer more to its architectural part than to the motivational one.

The place of Solution Architects in the initiative hierarchy and their relationship to the transformational context outlined above largely define their regular patterns of communication in organizations. First, as projects are mostly tactical undertakings, the core stakeholder audience of Solution Architects is *middle* business managers making local decisions, though both higher-level executives and lower-level specialists can be engaged as well. Second, because projects are strongly influenced by the architectural context, especially when they originate from some higher-order digitalization efforts, Solution Architects normally work under the supervision of Enterprise Architects, who ensure that this context is duly taken into account. Lastly, Solution Architects always deal directly with project teams performing project delivery and supervise their activities during the delivery process. These three parties constitute the main public of Solution Architects with which they interact in their occupation. In contrast to Enterprise Architects, they seldom communicate closely with business executives.

Since implementing digital transformation projects includes constructing concrete information systems based on specific technologies, it necessitates a deeper immersion in the "nuts and bolts" of these technologies on the part of Solution Architects. At the same time, due to a fairly narrow and not-so-heterogeneous circle of their stakeholders, their implementation involves relatively little politics, negotiations and compromises. Accordingly, challenges associated with digitalization projects are determined primarily by the factor of technical granularity and are more technical than organizational in nature (see Figure 2.9). To address these challenges, Solution Architects have to wear more the hat of Technology Experts than that of Change Agents and, in their conduct, shift somewhat closer towards traditional engineers.

Because digital transformation projects in organizations are always formalized administratively (see Figure 2.6), interactions between business managers and Solution Architects typically happen not only voluntarily on the initiative of managers, but also in a mandatory fashion (see Figure 4.4). Namely, for projects, mandatory interactions with Solution Architects are usually enforced by the official requirement to produce architectural plans and present these plans for approval at different stages of project implementation, so that their involvement in the process becomes organizationally institutionalized[3]. Financially, as projects are normally administered as investments with their own budgets, the work of Solution Architects relates mostly to capital expenditures (CAPEX) predominantly with project-based funding from the respective sources. The position of Solution Architects with their responsibilities and interactions in the overall organizational ecosystem is shown in Figure 16.1.

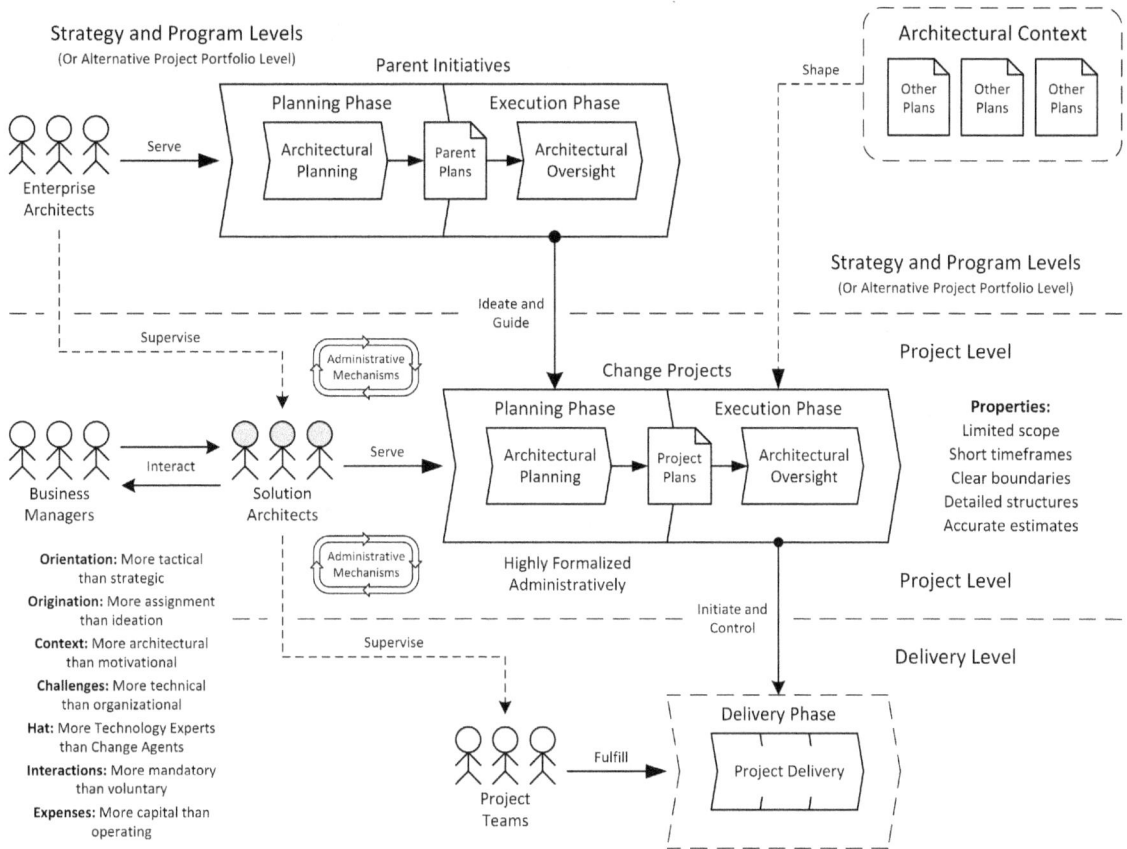

Figure 16.1. The position of Solution Architects in the organizational ecosystem

Although all the resources, instruments and activities of Solution Architects fit into the general framework of the profession of architects, they have many noteworthy features attributed to project specifics illustrated in Figure 16.1. In other words, Solution Architects can be viewed as a consistent *specialization* of architects adapted to the realities of digitalization projects. Unique properties of projects determine the characteristics of their job in organizations and allow distinguishing them as a separate, well-defined and steady archetype of architects prevalent across the industry.

Resources of Solution Architects

Even though the resources of Solution Architects do not differ in principle from those possessed by all architects, their knowledge, skills and experience have certain distinctive traits aligned with their focus on digital transformation projects. Specifically, their resources lean towards deeper expertise, higher engineering proficiency and more specialized experience.

Knowledge

Owing to the need for a detailed understanding of business activities that they intend to change and technologies that can be applied to do it, knowledge of Solution Architects tends to be relatively narrow but deep in both business and IT matters. Their external business-related knowledge often, but not necessarily, targets specific business aspects or capabilities with associated terminology and legislation, e.g. merchandising, production or finance management. Their external IT-related knowledge normally centers around concrete technologies they master, possibly subject area-specific ones, e.g. virtualization infrastructure, CRM solutions or banking platforms. Their internal business-related knowledge concentrates on relevant business activities and processes, their business owners and stakeholders with their particular transformation drivers from the motivational context. Their internal IT-related knowledge is also localized and encompasses mostly their segments of the IT landscape, active initiatives modifying these segments and the subset of the architectural context influencing them.

For example, a Solution Architect can specialize in IT solutions for logistics, understand industry regulations, norms and best practices in this area and know the leading vendors of logistics products with their functionality and future vision. Internally, this architect can understand current logistics processes and systems in the organization, be familiar with their business and IT owners, know the terms and conventions that they use and be aware of their long-range objectives for developing the logistics capability. However, the specialization of Solution Architects can also be more technical, business-agnostic and largely unrelated to any particular functional areas[4].

Skills

The biggest challenges associated with digitalization projects in organizations are engineering in nature as their implementation requires thinking over numerous technical details and organizing them formally into certain logical schemes (see Figure 2.9). Therefore, the most demanded skills for Solution Architects are various mental skills relevant to designing IT solutions that foster disciplined imagination, engineering rigor and order of thought.

Most importantly, a strong engineering mindset is a must for designing robust technical solutions that meet high quality standards and satisfy non-functional requirements in the most efficient way. Also, excellent problem-solving skills are needed to address intricate technical difficulties accompanying any attempts to modify a functioning IT landscape, especially when legacy systems are affected.

On the flip side, because projects generally involve less diverse constituencies and reveal fewer conflicts of interests than large-scale transformation endeavors, Solution Architects can be somewhat less skilled in adapting their language, leading negotiations, reaching consensus decisions and dealing with organizational politics. Furthermore, as projects represent temporary efforts with rather short timeframes, their work can be largely engagement-based and may not require building stable, long-lasting relationships with stakeholders, especially when they are in constant rotation.

Experience

The practical experience of Solution Architects is rich and dense, but concentrated around specific spheres of competence. Qualitatively, it is almost always deeply rooted in IT and covers primarily those technologies, products and solutions that reflect their areas of specialization. Quantitatively, their experience usually comprises at least 8–12 years of full-time employment in the industry as technical specialists of different profiles in software development, databases, infrastructure or security.

Instruments of Solution Architects

Basically, Solution Architects employ exactly the same general types of EA artifacts as their instruments as all architects. However, due to the pronounced project centricity of their work, their usage scenarios of EA artifacts are quite different, on the one hand, for rules and structures artifacts covering broad organizational scopes and, on the other hand, for solutions artifacts covering narrow organizational scopes.

Considerations, Standards, Visions and Landscapes

As Considerations, Standards, Visions and Landscapes (rules and structures artifacts) are too abstract and their scope is too broad for their local change projects, Solution Architects usually do not use these general types of EA artifacts for capturing architectural solutions that they develop. However, all these artifacts are relevant to their job as means of documenting the existing situation and carriers of the architectural context.

First, Solution Architects routinely refer to various actualities EA artifacts, predominantly Landscapes and Standards, as well as plans EA artifacts, mostly Visions and Considerations, to study, or elicit with the inherent limitations, necessary information on the current state of the corporate landscape (see Figure 9.1). Moreover, they can also update actualities EA artifacts to record modifications in the landscape structure that they introduce with their projects, or simply to improve the accuracy of documented knowledge.

Second, because all projects are implemented within the global architectural context of the organization and strongly influenced by it, Solution Architects also explore existing Considerations, Standards, Visions and partly Landscapes that form this context. All these artifacts contain numerous higher-order planning decisions, possibly of their parent initiatives, that should be taken into account during the architectural planning of transformation projects. In this capacity, EA artifacts are used by Solution Architects passively, in a "read-only" mode, largely as reference materials to be studied and aligned with their suggestions.

Outlines and Designs

As the level of detail and organizational scope covered by Outlines and Designs (solutions artifacts) perfectly match the size of projects that Solution Architects serve, these general types of EA artifacts are directly relevant to their occupation. It is these artifacts that represent the primary instruments of Solution Architects which they employ for capturing architectural solutions for their projects.

Unlike other general types of EA artifacts, Outlines and Designs are used by Solution Architects actively, in a "create" mode, i.e. produced during the architectural planning of digitalization projects to record made planning decisions and constitute their architectural plans. Because of their different focus, Designs and Outlines address technical and organizational components of architectural solutions respectively.

In particular, Solution Designs (see Figure 8.16) are arguably the single most important EA artifacts for Solution Architects central to their work. It is these artifacts that provide the most detailed documentation of developed architectural solutions for projects and eventually guide their execution and delivery by project teams, though their volume and granularity can be very project-specific and vary substantially for waterfall- and agile-style projects.

As for documenting the existing situation, Outlines and Designs are normally not maintained up to date after the respective projects are implemented. However, Solution Architects can still refer to archived Outlines and Designs in search of detailed but potentially outdated information on the constructed IT solutions.

Activities of Solution Architects in the Organizational Context

As discussed earlier, the activities of architects carried out in the organizational context relate to the organization in general and take all relevant organizational elements into consideration (see Figure 10.1). By and large, in the organizational context, Solution Architects fulfill the same basic activities as all architects: analyzing the external environment, studying the internal environment and providing advisory services (see Figure 10.2). However, because of their concentration specifically on digital transformation projects, each of these activities has a number of distinctive characteristics.

Analyzing the External Environment

In their analysis of the external environment, Solution Architects pay more attention to the technical side of things reflecting their core specialization. Although Solution Architects continually "sharpen their saw" by following general news on business and technology, due to the tactical rather than strategic orientation of their work, they tend to focus more on the details of specific technologies, products and innovations that they deal with directly than on global industry shifts, disruptive technologies and IT-driven changes in business models.

Accordingly, for Solution Architects, official vendor portals with introductory whitepapers and more thorough technical documentation represent one of the most important sources of information on the external environment. In a similar vein, they are more interested in practical trainings offered by product vendors and specialized literature on technical or semi-technical subjects than in abstract analyses of the technology market.

Studying the Internal Environment

In their studies of the internal environment, Solution Architects also pay more attention to detailed facts on the organization and its IT landscape necessary for project-level architectural planning, rather than to the overall situation less relevant for this purpose. For instance, they can concentrate more on specific business processes, information systems, their owners and local transformation drivers. Additionally, because of its great significance for their work and strong impact on all their decisions, they need to adequately comprehend the surrounding architectural context.

To gather detailed current-state information, besides asking other people, Solution Architects often refer to Landscape Diagrams, Asset Inventories and other actualities EA artifacts providing granular views of the corporate landscape. When an in-depth understanding of concrete IT systems is required, they can try to look up their archived Solution Designs as particularly valuable sources of germane knowledge. In search of precise technical details of the IT environment, they can also access specialized asset-tracking systems, such as CMDBs, or run automated environmental scans enabled by modern asset discovery tools. To grasp the architectural context, Solution Architects mindfully explore various EA artifacts forming this context, and especially Standards as the primary source of technical recommendations influencing their decision-making.

Providing Advisory Services

The advisory services of Solution Architects tend to reflect the main field of their specialization in IT and partly in business. These services usually leverage their deep understanding of particular technologies or broader technology domains to answer pretty narrow questions about their application to various business needs, problems and situations. More often, they address very specific issues on the use of IT in business activities.

Like all architects, Solution Architects offer their advisory services to the rest of the organization via both official and unofficial channels (see Figure 10.5). Officially, Solution Architects participate in the operations of architecture governance bodies as recognized subject-matter experts in technology. As venerable technical "gurus", they are typically included in design committees, technology committees and, less often, investment committees (see Figure 12.1). In design committees, Solution Architects peer review Solution Designs and other technical documentation developed by their fellow architects as part of the project implementation process to ensure their quality and the proper use of specific products, technologies and methods. In technology committees, they contribute their specialized experience to various decisions on technology selection and adoption of standardized system implementation approaches. In investment committees, they also peer review Solution Overviews and associated documents produced by other architects to ensure that proposed architectural solutions are adequate and that sober IT investments are made. However, because the demand for their narrow expertise is not constant, but arises only when the corresponding decisions are debated, Solution Architects are often invited to committee meetings as needed. The position of guest members of architecture governance bodies allows Solution Architects to bring their knowledge to the table and apply their unique competencies to improve the quality of organizational decision-making in IT-related matters.

Unofficially, Solution Architects provide their advisory services on request to any organizational actors seeking their specialized expertise. For example, they can consult business managers on the available ways of automating certain business processes in their subject area with popular COTS products and their pros and cons. Or, they can explain to Enterprise Architects the specifics of particular cloud-based storage technologies that they master. They can also offer their advice to infrastructure engineers as to what network deployment patterns represent industry best practice and how exactly routers should be configured to implement them properly.

Involvement in the Initial Ideation of Digital Transformation Initiatives

By performing their basic activities in the organizational context, architects take part in the initial ideation process and, explicitly or implicitly, contribute to the generation of new ideas for digitalization and their conversion into concrete change initiatives (see Figure 13.4). Hence, the three activities of Solution Architects described above can undoubtedly lead to the genesis of new autonomous initiatives.

However, for Solution Architects, this scenario is comparatively untypical. Due to their concentration on projects, which are often derived from the existing architectural plans of programs and strategies or simply included in pre-planned project portfolios (see Figure 15.5), Solution Architects tend to be less involved in the process of initial ideation, where tentative suggestions for digitalization are discussed. Instead, they communicate more with Enterprise Architects, as the executors of higher-level transformation initiatives or owners of project portfolios, to understand what work is upcoming and are often assigned to already pre-formed projects at their early conception stage to guide them further along their lifecycle. In short, Solution Architects more often pick up existing ideas for projects from some higher-order architectural plans to materialize them.

Activities of Solution Architects in the Initiative Context

All activities of architects carried out in the initiative context pertain to specific digital transformation initiatives and take into account only the elements related to these initiatives. At a high level, the activities of Solution Architects during different phases of the initiative implementation lifecycle do not differ fundamentally from those of all architects. However, their exclusive focus on transformation projects introduces there some notable specifics. To understand the activities of Solution Architects in the project context in more detail, it is first necessary to better understand this context itself. Namely, the implementation process of digitalization projects in which they participate as lead planners has to be further clarified.

The Implementation Process of Digital Transformation Projects

The implementation process of digital transformation projects, or simply the **project implementation process**, represents a more detailed, project-specific specialization of the generic, end-to-end, three-phase initiative implementation process (see Figure 2.2)[5]. As a distinct type of transformation initiatives with a physical component, projects have two unique features that influence their implementation lifecycle and result in important differences relative to the standard lifecycle of higher-level, more conceptual initiatives. First, because projects propose very concrete business improvements and technical means of their achievement, their benefits, timelines and costs can be assessed with reasonable, ever-increasing accuracy at different stages of the progress in their planning, which allows their stakeholders to judge their value early in the process and decide whether their implementation should be continued or abandoned. Second, due to their tangible nature, executing projects requires planning many purely technical details of the respective information systems, which often requires significant time and effort, but does not add much in terms of an understanding of their desirability for the organization by their sponsors.

Because of these features, the process of project implementation typically involves a *multistage* planning phase with a number of successive control gates. These gates represent certain checkpoints that the project passes through on the way to its delivery, where its status is evaluated by stakeholders and supervisory governance bodies. At each gate, based on the current best-available estimates of the project's value and cost, the decision can be made either to invest more efforts and proceed to the next gate, or to discontinue the project if it no longer seems expedient. Since elaborating the technical component of the project's architectural solution brings diminishing returns in terms of refining these estimates (i.e. does not change substantially the properties of its organizational component), the planning of its low-level technicalities is typically postponed and completed at the end of its planning phase, when its commercial desirability for the organization is considered beyond doubt. This approach to project implementation is usually found to be optimal as it allows sponsors to cancel organizationally unpromising projects at their early stages before elaborating their minute technical details, thereby sparing limited resources. As a result, for projects, organizational elements of their architectural solutions are normally developed first and "gory" technical elements — last.

Although the details of the project implementation process in terms of concrete steps, control gates and their titles are always organization-specific[6], this process is always highly formalized administratively and typically includes two key decision-making gates explicitly linked to the official mechanisms of funding and resourcing: investment decision gate and technical design gate. The **investment decision gate** is the first major checkpoint in the planning phase of the project implementation process where the fundamental desire to execute the project is asserted, i.e. an investment decision regarding it is made. The investment decision is based on a comprehensive assessment of the organizational component of its architectural solution through the prism of value, e.g. capabilities, functionality, costs and timelines. This decision also takes into account its alignment with the higher-order architectural plans of the parent initiative or portfolio, if any, as well as its congruence with the broader architectural context.

Of material documents, the investment decision gate most often rests upon Solution Overviews produced for projects by means of architectural planning, which provide high-level business-oriented descriptions of proposed IT solutions and allow their meaningful evaluation. In addition to Solution Overviews, this gate typically also requires presenting formal business cases. **Business cases** are largely IT-agnostic documents prepared for digital transformation projects by their sponsors to justify the respective investments. These documents focus mostly on the financial side of projects and often use sophisticated quantitative valuation techniques to estimate their likely ROI. As part of the investment decision gate, both Solution Overviews and business cases are submitted to the investment committee for their ratification and sign-off (see Figure 12.1). Alternatively to original EA artifacts, this gate can also hinge on more "palatable" presentation packs telling the story behind proposed projects and explaining why their realization will benefit the organization (see Figure 11.6). After the project passes through the investment decision gate, the elaboration of the technical component of its architectural solution begins.

Next, the **technical design gate** is the second major checkpoint in the planning phase of the project implementation process where more peripheral IT-specific details of the project relevant to its execution are certified, i.e. its technical design is approved for construction. The approval procedure involves a scrupulous examination of the technical component of its architectural solution through the prism of quality, e.g. building blocks, connections, technologies and security. This procedure also enforces its alignment with various technical elements of the architectural context, e.g. adherence to adopted recommendations and proven best practices.

Of material documents, the technical design gate almost always relies on Solution Designs produced for projects by means of architectural planning, which provide low-level IT-oriented descriptions of proposed information systems and allow their careful scrutiny. Besides Solution Designs, this gate may also require presenting formal project management plans. **Project management plans** are largely non-technical documents prepared for digital transformation projects by their project managers to plan their delivery. These documents focus mainly on the managerial side of projects and address such areas of concern as scheduling, staffing, budgeting, quality assurance and risk mitigation. As part of the technical design gate, Solution Designs, sometimes bundled with project management plans, are submitted to the design committee for their authorization and endorsement. As a viable alternative to voluminous EA artifacts, this gate can also use more pointful key design decisions summarizing the crucial junctions of proposed IT systems and explaining the rationale behind them (see Figure 11.7). After the project passes through the technical design gate, it proceeds to delivery and its execution is officially kicked off.

These two control gates define the overall logical flow of the project implementation process and represent its key milestones from the standpoint of architectural planning. Specifically, for projects, the planning phase essentially includes *two separate episodes* of architectural planning, where different sides of their architectural solutions are highlighted. The first episode starts from the underlying concepts of projects, goes through the full three-step process of architectural planning, concentrates mostly on the organizational component of their architectural solutions (though always with some basic technical elements necessary to determine its properties, e.g. business impact, value and cost), produces Solution Overviews to capture "half-baked" architectural solutions and ends with the investment decision gate, where these EA artifacts are approved.

The second episode starts from the approved Solution Overviews for projects, goes through the *shortened* process of architectural planning without the initial discussion step, concentrates solely on the technical component of their architectural solutions (as the organizational one has already been developed), produces Solution Designs to capture full architectural solutions and ends with the technical design gate, where these EA artifacts are authorized. On the whole, the planning phase of the project implementation process represents a gradual elaboration of the respective architectural solutions, starting with their organizational elements and ending with purely technical ones. Unsurprisingly, in this process, EA artifacts supporting it are often "released" incrementally, by augmenting or enriching preceding artifacts with more detailed information on the architectural solution. For instance, Solution Designs can be produced simply by adding new technical sections to existing Solution Overviews.

The separation of the planning phase of the project implementation process into two quite different episodes of architectural planning described above allows presenting this process in a somewhat different light with a new, more expressive project-specific terminology by splitting it into two consecutive top-level steps: initiation and realization. The **initiation step** of the project implementation process spans from the beginning of its conception phase to the end of the first, organizational episode of architectural planning, when Solution Overviews are approved at the investment decision gate. The general meaning of this step is to progress from an abstract, often vague, business need or idea for digitalization to a mature, signed-off conceptual view of the required IT solution. In the course of the initiation step, all discussions revolve chiefly around business aspects of the desired IT solution (e.g. what exactly it should do), though always taking into account the capabilities and limitations of technology that can be used to implement it. Accordingly, key stakeholders during this step of the process are various business representatives, mostly business managers acting as project sponsors.

The top-level initiation step can be further divided into two sub-steps: concept and decision. The **concept step** exactly corresponds to the conception phase of the project implementation process. This sub-step involves forming the very concepts of new projects with their goals, purposes and scopes, for derivative projects, from the intentions of their parent initiatives or portfolios or, for autonomous projects, from new ideas for responding to transformation drivers. The concept step is often rather short and takes only a small fraction of the total implementation time, say, 10–15% of it. The **decision step** corresponds to the first episode of architectural planning. This sub-step implies developing a more or less complete organizational solution for the incipient project reflected in its Solution Overview and obtaining official permission to proceed towards delivery. The decision step is also relatively short and can consume roughly around 10–20% of the entire project duration.

The **realization step** of the project implementation process spans from the beginning of the second, technical episode of architectural planning to the end of its execution phase[7]. The general meaning of this step is to progress from a sound conceptual understanding of the required IT solution to a materialized, functioning system deployed in the corporate landscape. During the realization step, all discussions revolve predominantly around technical aspects of the desired IT solution (e.g. how exactly it should be constructed), though always taking into account potential business-related implications of various technical choices. Consequently, in this step of the process, project executors, particularly project team members involved in delivery efforts, become its principal stakeholders instead of business representatives.

The top-level realization step can also be divided into two sub-steps: design and delivery. The **design step** corresponds to the second episode of architectural planning. This sub-step implies developing the remaining technical elements of the architectural solution for the project, thereby converting its high-level Solution Overview into a more detailed Solution Design, and obtaining formal approval to deliver it. The design step is relatively short and often consumes approximately about 10–20% of the total project length. The **delivery step** exactly corresponds to the delivery, or execution, phase of the project implementation process. This sub-step includes delivering the project in a physical sense by project teams via building, testing and deploying the system, or systems, defined in its architectural solution and documented in its Solution Design according to a certain waterfall or agile methodology (see Figure 2.8). The delivery step normally represents the lengthiest part of project implementation and can take up to 70% of its entire duration, sometimes even more.

Interestingly, because of financing considerations, different steps and sub-steps of the project implementation process are often decoupled and dispersed in time into different budgeting periods. For example, the concept and decision steps of the process can be completed by the middle of 2024, but the subsequent design and delivery steps can continue only after several months, in the next budgeting cycle beginning in 2025. Likewise, Solution Designs for a project can be approved this year, but then the project can be put on hold and resumed for the actual delivery only in the following year, when the necessary funding becomes available.

The investment decision gate and the technical design gate are the two most prominent institutionalized checkpoints in the project implementation process that exist, in some form or the other, in the vast majority of organizations. However, their processes can actually be somewhat more sophisticated, e.g. include additional intermediate checkpoints, involve more episodes of architectural planning and leverage other EA artifacts along the way[8]. For example, Solution Briefs can be created at the very beginning of the decision step to secure the seed funding sufficient to continue the project, while Solution Options can be developed later in the process to select the best option for going forward before converging to a concrete investment case. Or, Preliminary Solution Designs can be produced after the investment decision is made to confirm the underlying estimates before finalizing the technical solution. Therefore, a series of various EA artifacts, starting from Outlines and ending with Designs, can be used in the process of project implementation to facilitate the progressive refinement of architectural solutions[9]. In practice, all solutions EA artifacts are typically based on standardized artifact templates prescribing their informational contents (see Figure 11.5).

Besides EA artifacts capturing architectural solutions, business cases and project management plans, the project implementation process may also generate more granular design documentation as a byproduct of project delivery efforts. The respective **detailed design documents** describe very low-level technicalities of IT systems necessary for their construction, but negligible in the broader organizational context, e.g. class diagrams, component interaction models, database table definitions, infrastructure configurations and many other similar specifications. They can be produced internally by project teams during the delivery step of project implementation based on approved Solution Designs to aid further actions, like code writing, database creation and system deployment. Detailed design documents can facilitate teamwork, improve communication between different project participants or otherwise play a significant role in the project delivery process. However, the type, volume and even the very existence of these documents are project-specific as they are more characteristic of projects following waterfall methodologies. Because detailed design documents are confined to the delivery level, they are typically considered non-architectural and are not discussed in detail in this book[10]. The end-to-end project implementation process described above with its steps, sub-steps, control gates, EA artifacts and other relevant documents is summarized in Figure 16.2.

Chapter 16: The Archetype of Solution Architects

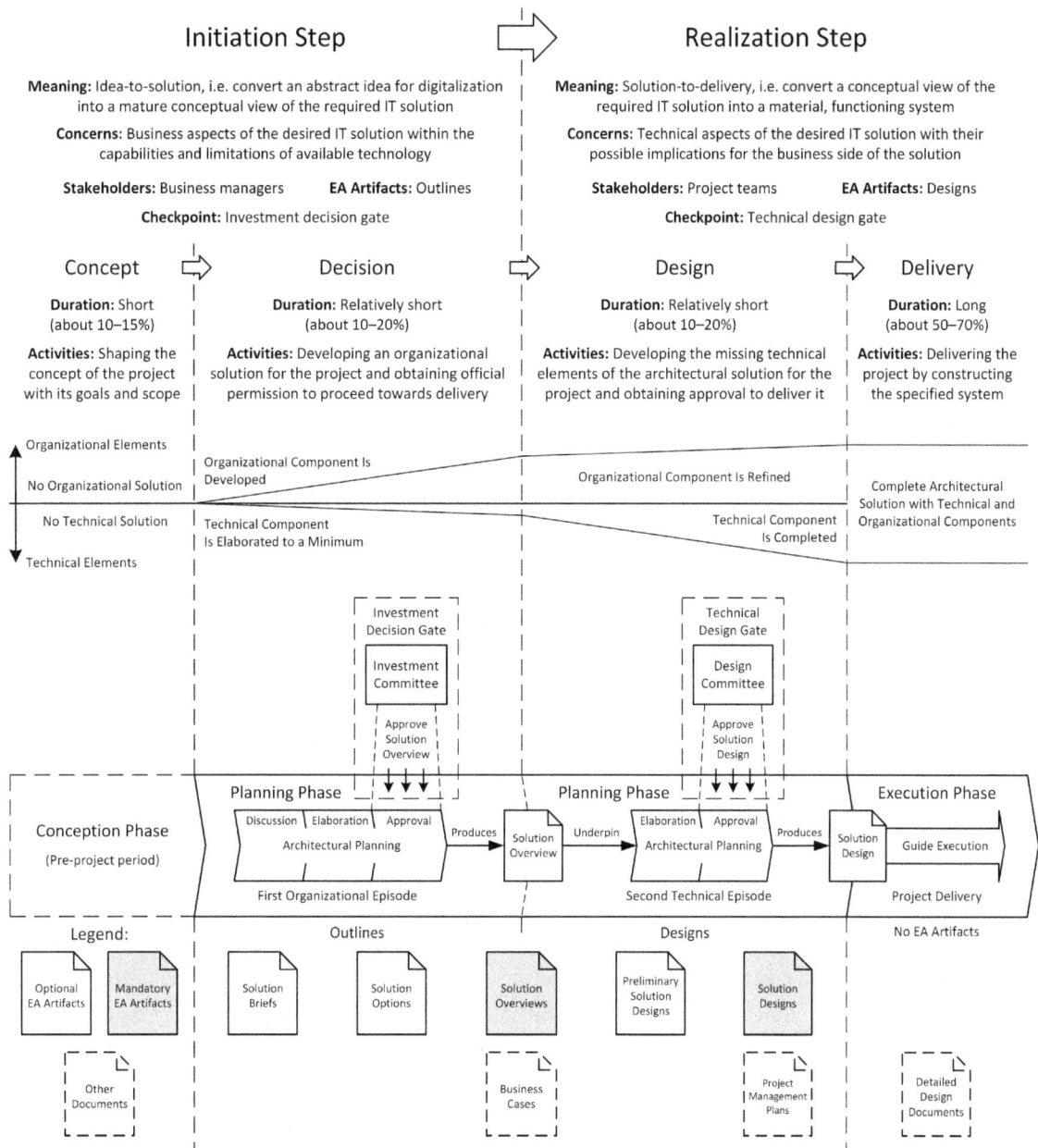

Figure 16.2. The implementation process of digital transformation projects

The detailed view of the project implementation process presented in Figure 16.2 reflects its internal specifics that distinguish it from the implementation processes of programs and strategies (see Figure 15.2). This view provides the necessary foundation and context for discussing in greater detail the activities of Solution Architects in digital transformation projects and some other aspects of their work in organizations.

Activities During the Concept Step

During the first concept step of the project implementation process (see Figure 16.2), Solution Architects discuss the seminal ideas for digital transformation projects and the opportunities for turning them into actual projects with their sponsors as competent advisors. For derivative projects descending from programs or strategies, their sponsors are typically the executors of their parent initiatives, including some of their business stakeholders as well as Enterprise Architects assigned to these initiatives (see Figure 15.1). Likewise, for projects from pre-planned project portfolios, their sponsors are typically the owners of these portfolios, including some business leaders as well as Enterprise Architects serving these portfolios (see Figure 15.6). In these scenarios, Enterprise Architects, Solution Architects and business representatives collectively decide what can be done at the project level to implement the intentions of the parent initiative or portfolio in the most optimal way. By contrast, for autonomous projects that do not belong to any higher-order initiatives or portfolios, their sponsors are the proponents of the underlying transformation drivers from the motivational context, who discuss with Solution Architects their ideas for using IT to respond to these drivers.

Because projects represent small-scale change efforts aimed at narrow areas of the organization, discussions taking place during their concept step usually focus on rather concrete proposals for modifying the corporate landscape or solving specific business needs with IT. Due to their down-to-earth character, they tend to revolve around basic requirements for the desired IT solutions and may operate with numbers. Particularly often, in these discussions, Solution Architects analyze the practical feasibility, possible price and hidden pitfalls of implementing some business ideas.

Although the degree of involvement of Solution Architects in the concept step of the project implementation process can vary, on average, it can be regarded as a work period of moderate intensity, when they can comfortably serve on a part-time basis. Generally, this step is driven by the following and similar questions about ideas for digitalization and potential projects:

- What specific intentions, objectives or demands should be addressed with IT?
- Are the proposed ideas for using IT realistic, reasonable and cost-effective?
- What kind of IT solutions are expected or can be considered satisfactory?
- Can these solutions be implemented with the available IT resources?
- Are these solutions promising enough to launch projects and start their planning?

Importantly, the concept step does not imply any serious planning exercises or substantiated quantitative estimations, but only elementary assessments of the existing ideas about the use of IT by means of an educated guess for their "face validity" to determine whether these ideas should actually be converted into full-fledged transformation projects. At this stage, Solution Architects accomplish only rough architectural pre-planning to ensure that IT systems with the requested functionality can be built with current technologies within the given time and budget constraints (see Figure 4.6). For this reason, this step does not require developing any architectural plans, though some auxiliary artifacts, like feasibility assessment reports (see Figure 10.7), can be produced if necessary.

An essential part of the responsibilities of Solution Architects in the concept step of the project implementation process is assessing ideas for projects from the perspective of their appropriateness in the global architectural context of the organization (see Figure 9.7). For example, some projects can be well aligned with the enacted Architecture Strategies, Target States and Roadmaps, some projects can be neutral to their suggestions, while others can go manifestly against them, accumulating the so-called **architecture debt**[11]. As Solution Architects may not be fully aware of all facets of the architectural context, consultations with more knowledgeable Enterprise Architects may be needed. These concerns, however, relate primarily to autonomous projects initiated independently of larger programs, strategies and portfolios as their derivative counterparts ensue directly from the architectural context and are naturally congruent with it.

When the proposed ideas for projects pass through an initial critical evaluation and Solution Architects with other stakeholders turn them into more thought-out project concepts that they find promising or necessary, these concepts grow into real projects. At this moment, the project implementation process progresses to the next decision step, where these projects are elaborated, planned in an architectural sense and funded.

Activities During the Decision Step

In the second decision step of the project implementation process, Solution Architects begin to lead actual architectural planning efforts to produce some architectural plans for the project and substantiate the decision to invest money in its realization. They start specifically from the organizational side of architectural planning with an intention to develop mostly the organizational component of the necessary architectural solution and formulate what the project will bring to the business (see Figure 3.3), though this component cannot be completed, even partially, without elaborating at least some technical elements of the solution, e.g. what kind of technologies will be used.

For Solution Architects, the decision step of the project implementation process represents a period of very intensive work that demands strong dedication and preferably full-time participation to orchestrate architectural planning. Generally, the first organizational episode of architectural planning is driven by the following and similar questions about the respective IT solution:

- What immediate and long-term business value is expected from the solution?
- How should the solution improve our business operations and processes?
- What major components constitute the solution and how do they work together?
- What information is required for the solution and where can it be retrieved from?
- What products, software and hardware can be utilized to construct the solution?

In this episode, architectural planning follows the standard three-step planning process (see Figure 11.4), where Solution Architects bring all the relevant business representatives together as project stakeholders, initiate dialog regarding what needs to be achieved, gather more detailed requirements, come up with specific options, discuss them with the stakeholders, eventually reach a mutually agreed organizational solution and present this solution to the investment committee for their approval as part of the investment decision gate (see Figure 16.2). In this process, different parties voice their own, often contradicting concerns that determine the contours of the resulting solution. For instance, business leaders usually argue more for greater strategic contribution, while ordinary business specialists — for tangible operational improvements. The ensuing incomplete architectural solutions with rudimentary technical components are most often captured in Solution Overviews. However, other Outlines, such as Solution Briefs and Solution Options, can also be produced earlier in the process to obtain preliminary solution approvals and analyze available options respectively.

As architectural planning is always fulfilled in the broader architectural context and transformation projects are especially context-dependent, partly because of their small size and partly because of their often-subordinate nature, Solution Architects exert significant efforts to align individual architectural solutions for projects with this context, or embed them into it. For derivative projects, their architectural solutions are developed within the framework of higher-order architectural plans of their parent initiatives or portfolios (see Figure 3.7) and under the direct supervision of their Enterprise Architects (see Figure 16.1). For example, if a project represents one of the building blocks of a more global Target State, then many or even most of its architectural decisions can be already predetermined. For autonomous projects, their connection to the architectural context can be weaker, but still cannot be neglected.

In any case, because at this stage architectural solutions are incomplete from their technical side, they are shaped by the architectural context only in "broad strokes", but not in details. For instance, in this episode of architectural planning, particular attention is paid to such high-level issues as agreement with general Principles and Architecture Strategies, alignment with more specific Target States and Roadmaps, as well as the reuse of suitable assets and technologies, leaving many other important technical elements of the context aside until the next episode of architectural planning performed in the subsequent design step. To help them roughly fit architectural solutions into the context, Solution Architects can be provided with relevant compliance checklists, e.g. project evaluation worksheets (see Figure 12.5). If solutions cannot be fitted properly into the context, then architects have to seek deviation approval from the investment committee by filling out appropriate exception forms, e.g. project dispensation cards (see Figure 12.6).

Besides leading the development of plans within the surrounding architectural context, in this step, Solution Architects often participate in the formation of business cases for projects to assist in "selling" the corresponding investments to the investment committee. To help justify digitalization projects financially, they can either co-develop business cases with project sponsors, or merely consult them on various technical questions related to solution economics. If the solution implies buying proprietary vendor products, architects can also aid in negotiating the licensing terms and preparing the procurement contracts.

Activities During the Design Step
In the third design step of the project implementation process, Solution Architects continue to lead architectural planning efforts commenced in the previous step to finish architectural plans for the project and design them to the extent sufficient to begin its physical delivery. In this step, they switch specifically to the technical side of architectural planning with an intention to complete the underdeveloped technical component of the architectural solution and specify exactly how the system will be constructed (see Figure 3.3), though staying within the constraints imposed by its organizational component sanctioned earlier, e.g. anticipated changes in business processes.

For Solution Architects, the design step of the project implementation process represents another peak period, when active daily work, ideally with full-time involvement, is required on

their part to conduct architectural planning. Generally, the second technical episode of architectural planning is driven by the following and similar questions about the respective information system:
- What application components should be developed to constitute the system?
- What data entities should be used and processed in the system?
- How should the system be integrated with other systems and data sources?
- What hardware or cloud infrastructure needs to be provided to host the system?
- What measures should be applied to protect the system from possible attacks?

Because this episode of architectural planning does not start from scratch, it follows a shortened planning process where the initial discussion step is omitted as unnecessary. To proceed with architectural planning, Solution Architects invite various members of the project team as new stakeholders to elaborate the architectural solution technically based on the approved Solution Overview, discuss numerous IT-specific details, reach a mutually acceptable technical solution and present this solution to the design committee for their endorsement as part of the technical design gate (see Figure 16.2). In this process, different stakeholder groups advocate their own, often conflicting interests that ultimately shape the resulting solution. For instance, business specialists typically stand for the fulfillment of certain business requirements, IT specialists — for using practical implementation approaches, and project managers — for realistic deadlines and resource demands. Nevertheless, coming to firm agreements regarding the system structure within the project team is vital for de-risking their future delivery efforts[12]. The ensuing complete architectural solutions for projects are normally captured in Solution Designs. However, other Designs, like Preliminary Solution Designs, can also be produced earlier in the process to formalize and pre-approve tentative technical solutions.

Importantly, some or the other upfront technical Designs are created for all projects, irrespective of their delivery methodologies. As many project-level decisions may have far-reaching consequences for organizations, they cannot be simply left at the discretion of project teams, but should be carefully thought over by Solution Architects in advance. For instance, even the most agile projects require certain architectural decisions, such as those related to technology choices, integration points and security measures, to be made beforehand for the sake of overall landscape consistency[13]. For this reason, during architectural planning in this step, architects have to rely on their own judgment, experience and common sense to determine the necessary subtypes of Designs to be produced for particular projects and their appropriate level of granularity, as well as exactly which decisions should be captured there and which ones can be safely delegated to project teams.

Analogously to the previous episode of architectural planning, in this episode Solution Architects are also responsible for aligning the developed architectural solutions with the broader architectural context. However, unlike the organizational component of architectural solutions, whose connection to the context is more conceptual and pretty loose, their technical component is strongly linked to the context in almost every subdomain of IT. In practice, most technical elements of architectural solutions can be largely dictated by the existing architectural context, rather than chosen independently of it.

For example, all technology choices are usually guided by such EA artifacts as Technology Reference Models, Technology Inventories and Technology Roadmaps, asset reuse decisions —

by System Portfolio Models, Asset Inventories and Asset Roadmaps, data structures — by Conceptual Data Models and Logical Data Models, integration approaches — by integration Patterns and possibly IT Principles, infrastructure choices — among other artifacts, by IT Roadmaps, and security precautions — by security Policies and Guidelines. For each technical domain, there are a number of EA artifacts relevant to it that provide various suggestions influencing the corresponding planning decisions (see Figure 8.17).

Hence, Solution Architects should be aware of their architectural context to be able to properly fit new architectural solutions into it. For this reason, in this episode of architectural planning, they often work under the supervision of more context-savvy Enterprise Architects, or at least in consultation with them. To help them align technical solutions with the context, Solution Architects can be provided with relevant compliance checklists, e.g. standards conformance checklists (see Figure 12.5). If solutions cannot be aligned technically with the context, then architects have to seek deviation approval from the design committee by filling out appropriate exception forms, e.g. solution exemption forms (see Figure 12.6).

Besides leading the development of architectural plans and fitting them into the architectural context, in this step, Solution Architects may also assist project managers in preparing project management plans and justifying them to the design committee. By contributing their knowledge and expertise to project management plans, architects can help improve their quality and increase the accuracy of associated estimates. If the project requires engaging external delivery partners, they can also aid in negotiating the partnership terms and preparing the outsourcing agreements.

Activities During the Delivery Step

In the last delivery step of the project implementation process, Solution Architects finally switch from being the lead developers of architectural plans for the project to chief supervisors exercising architectural oversight over their execution. Specifically, they start to follow up on the agreed plans to ensure that these plans are respected by the members of the project team involved in their delivery (see Figure 16.1).

For Solution Architects, the delivery step of the project implementation process typically represents a period of low, largely background activity, which requires, for the most part, only episodic attendance to delivery-related tasks, often on an as-necessary basis. Generally, this step is driven by the following and similar questions about architectural plans and their execution:

- Do the delivery activities stick to the approved architectural plans for the project?
- Does the written code correspond to the application part of the technical solution?
- Are the databases created in accordance with the schemas defined in the plans?
- Does the provided infrastructure match with the one described in the plans?
- Has the system been secured exactly as prescribed by its architectural plans?

As discussed earlier, project delivery can be viewed roughly as a three-step process performed by project teams: building, testing and deployment (see Figure 2.7). During all these steps, Solution Architects oversee the activities of project teams to ensure their compliance with architectural plans, namely with the Solution Designs for projects authorized by the design committee in the previous step. However, because the most crucial actions are usually taken at the beginning of system construction, their involvement in the delivery efforts tends to decrease along with their progress, e.g. be maximal in the first iterations and minimal in the last iterations.

To ensure adherence to plans, Solution Architects can opt to use any convenient means suitable for projects, i.e. primarily individual approaches including product inspection, documentation review, passive observation, active participation and keeping in touch (see Figure 12.4). While documentation review can be applied mostly to projects that follow waterfall methodologies, which imply producing some detailed design documents that can be verified by architects (see Figure 2.8), all the other methods are quite universal and applicable to virtually any project, though with their inherent limitations and shortcomings mentioned earlier. For example, Solution Architects can visit weekly sprint review meetings, liaise with the team lead, keep an eye on the project wiki with working materials and occasionally fetch the actual source code for its cursory overview and automated checking with a specialized linter for possible security vulnerabilities, quality issues and conformance to coding conventions.

Importantly, not all pertinent suggestions of the architectural context can be incorporated into projects at the stage of their architectural planning and reflected in the resulting architectural plans; some of them can be taken into account only at the stage of their execution. For example, secure coding Guidelines, exact field definitions from Logical Data Models and some other low-level technical prescriptions are impractical, difficult or even impossible to put in Solution Designs to be able to validate the delivery outcomes solely against these artifacts. Furthermore, compliance with these and similar detailed prescriptions can hardly be guaranteed by such mild means as passive observation or keeping in touch, but requires more "invasive" methods like product inspection (e.g. performing code reviews) or active participation (e.g. writing critical code snippets)[14]. For this reason, even during the project delivery, Solution Architects have to bear in mind the existence of other EA artifacts from the architectural context and be ready to resort to the necessary approaches for achieving the adherence of projects to their suggestions.

Interestingly, when supervising project teams, Solution Architects have no formal managerial power over them and, due to the inapplicability of governance procedures at the project level, are not able to take advantage of the official authority of governance bodies to enforce compliance with plans. For this reason, possible disputes and disagreements with various team members around the existing architectural plans can be difficult for architects to resolve and typically necessitate exerting their informal competence-based authority or even escalating the conflicts to the respective managers[15].

The delivery step of transformation projects continues until all the system components described in their architectural plans are deployed. If any adjustments in these plans are needed in the middle of project delivery, Solution Architects can submit requisite amendment forms, such as design alteration forms (see Figure 12.7), for the approval of the design committee or even the investment committee, depending on the impact of required changes. After the completion of projects and their rolling out to production, architects normally update relevant actualities EA artifacts (e.g. Landscape Diagrams and Asset Inventories) to document the structural landscape modifications introduced by these projects. Furthermore, they can also update their Solution Designs to reflect there any intended and unintended deviations from the original plans that might have taken place during their execution. This approach helps improve the accuracy of the archived documentation of the current IT environment, increasing its value for future reference.

Activities Along the Project Implementation Process

The activities carried out by Solution Architects in the course of the implementation process of digital transformation projects described above constitute the core of their occupation in organizations. These activities closely correspond to the general mapping of the activities of architects to the three phases of the initiative implementation lifecycle (see Figure 13.2), but represent its project-specific specialization. The activities of Solution Architects during the different steps and sub-steps of the project implementation process are summarized in Figure 16.3.

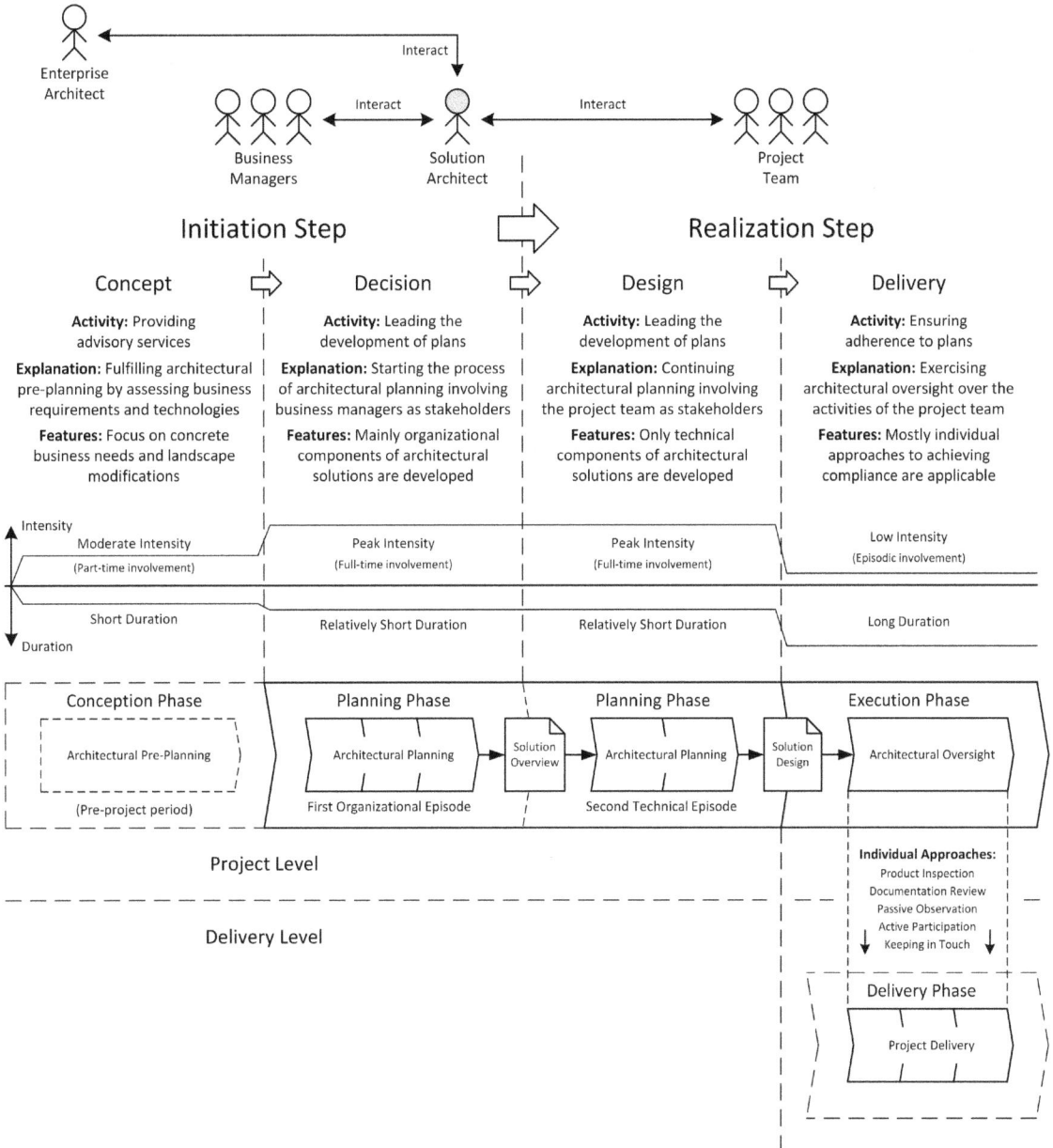

Figure 16.3. Activities of Solution Architects during the project implementation process

The view presented in Figure 16.3 offers a comprehensive summary of the successive activities of Solution Architects performed in the project context, which complement their rather limited basic activities in the organizational context. Together, these two sets of activities compose the content of their work in organizations.

The Work of Solution Architects

The unity of their activities in the organizational and project contexts described above constitutes the work of Solution Architects in organizations, where they study relevant parts of the organization and its environment, consult various actors on the capabilities of specific technologies, get assigned to concrete transformation projects and drive these projects to completion through the different steps of their lifecycle (see Figure 16.3). Besides engaging in these activities, their work also implies advocating the technical interests of engineering correctness, orderliness and elegance (see Table 13.1).

Although Solution Architects can bring their innovative ideas to the table and contribute to the initial ideation of digitalization projects, this forward thinking is more often applied by Enterprise Architects, who appoint them to already existing projects conceived earlier as part of some higher-order initiatives or portfolios. Instead, Solution Architects represent the "last link" in the implementation chain of hierarchical transformation initiatives, gradually materializing strategies and programs via individual projects. The work of Solution Architects in its entirety is summarized graphically in Figure 16.4.

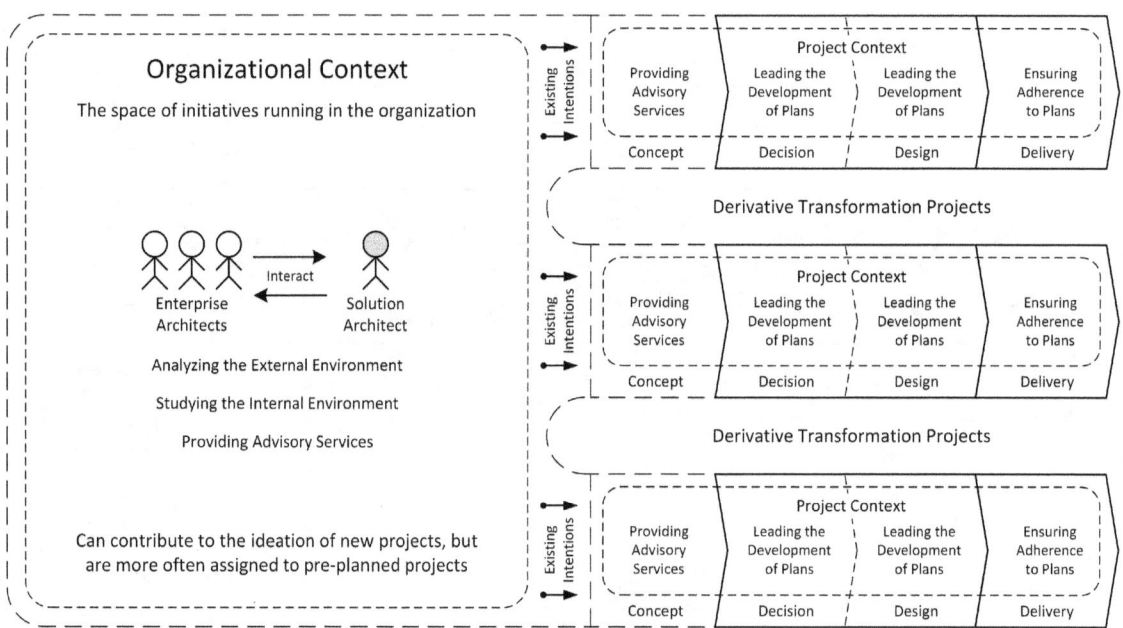

Figure 16.4. The end-to-end work of Solution Architects in organizations

Importantly, from a temporal perspective, all the activities shown in Figure 16.4 are accomplished by Solution Architects during their working days in parallel, so that they "invest" their energy in multiple active projects simultaneously. In fact, Solution Architects are typically involved concurrently in several transformation projects at different stages of their implementation, handling a continuous pipeline of projects (see Figure 13.6).

Because the decision and design steps require serious commitment and intensive work on the part of Solution Architects, they can comfortably serve no more than 2–3 projects in these steps, at least with a due level of quality. At the same time, other lifecycle steps, and especially delivery, are less strenuous and do not demand such a strong concentration of their attention, which allows architects to attend to a much greater number of projects in their concept and delivery steps.

In total, a single Solution Architect can deal with tens of transformation projects per year, depending on their size and the degree of involvement (many of these projects, though, may not progress beyond their concept or decision step and never reach their delivery). This diffusion of architects' efforts results in a fragmented timetable filled with diverse tasks related to different projects (see Figure 13.5), which does not resemble the linear sequence of activities presented in Figure 16.3.

Domain Specialization of Solution Architects

As mentioned earlier, the expertise of Solution Architects normally centers around specific technologies belonging to the respective organizational domains (see Figure 3.4), leading to strong *domain specialization* of their job. As the six major domains represent disparate subjects and differ considerably in their properties, domain specialization influences certain aspects of the work of Solution Architects in organizations, including their resources, partly instruments and activities. Moreover, owing to the inherent differences between the nature of domains, the *prevalence* of Solution Architects with different domain specializations varies greatly across the industry as well.

First, resources possessed by Solution Architects precisely mirror their domain specialization. In particular, their knowledge and experience are deeper in those technologies in which they specialize, less deep in related technologies and can be rather shallow in other technologies. For example, a Solution Architect specializing in web technologies, as a subset of the applications domain, can be very competent in frontend languages and frameworks, less competent in backend platforms and databases and only superficially knowledgeable in such "distant" technologies as data warehouses, integration buses and hypervisors. Besides that, they are also more proficient in domain-specific best practices and more likely to hold professional certifications in their profile technologies, e.g. AWS Certified Solutions Architect and Cisco Certified Architect.

Second, instruments employed by Solution Architects in part depend on their domain specialization. On the one hand, all Solution Architects produce basically the same solutions EA artifacts for their projects, most importantly Solution Overviews and Solution Designs (see Figure 16.2), but the informational contents of these artifacts in terms of included sections and presented viewpoints are highly domain-specific and largely determined by their target landscape layers that they aim to modify, e.g. process models, data diagrams or connectivity schemes. On the other hand, when aligning their solutions to the architectural context, they study primarily those rules and structures EA artifacts that are relevant to their particular domains (see Figure 8.17). For example, a Solution Architect specializing in networks will most probably refer to Technology Reference Models, IT Principles and Patterns, but not to Logical Data Models, Process Maps and Value Chains.

Third, activities performed by Solution Architects are somewhat different for architects specializing in functional and non-functional domains (see Table 3.2). On the one hand, specialization in functional domains — business, applications and data — requires communicating more with business managers and serving more *digital transformation projects* for improving the business with IT. On the other hand, specialization in non-functional domains — integration, infrastructure and security — requires interacting mostly with IT stakeholders and serving more *technical rationalization projects* for improving the IT landscape (see Figure 13.7). For example, a Solution Architect specializing in storage solutions can communicate, for the most part, with IT managers and operations teams and lead change projects intended to decrease the costs of storing big data and increase the efficiency of backup procedures.

Finally, and most importantly, the very prevalence of Solution Architects varies for architects specializing in substantive and non-substantive domains (see Table 3.3). Substantive domains — business, applications and infrastructure — constantly cause new transformation projects to develop the business and IT landscape, whereas non-substantive domains — data, integration and security — cause new projects relatively infrequently. For this reason, the demand for Solution Architects with different domain specializations to drive the respective projects is uneven. Unsurprisingly, most Solution Architects working for organizations specialize specifically in the business and applications domains. Of the remaining architects, the majority specialize in the infrastructure domain and only the rest — in the three non-substantive domains[16].

Therefore, domain specialization of Solution Architects has significant implications not only for their job in terms of their resources, instruments and activities, but even for the demand for their services in organizations. Distinctive specifics of the six organizational domains and their typical effects on the prevalence and work of Solution Architects specializing in them are summarized in Table 16.1.

Domain	Specifics of the domain	Specifics of the work of Solution Architects
Business	Native to business managers, represents business processes, constitutes the landscape substance and causes new change projects	Most prevalent in organizations, communicate mainly with business managers and serve more digital transformation projects by creating solutions EA artifacts full of process models
Applications	Relevant to business managers, supports business processes, constitutes the landscape substance and causes new change projects	Most prevalent in organizations, communicate more with business managers and serve more digital transformation projects by creating solutions EA artifacts full of system viewpoints
Data	Relevant to business managers, supports business processes, does not constitute the landscape substance and seldom causes new projects	Relatively rare in organizations, communicate more with business managers and serve more digital transformation projects by creating solutions EA artifacts full of data diagrams
Integration	Irrelevant to business managers, does not impact business processes, does not constitute the landscape substance and seldom causes new projects	Relatively rare in organizations, communicate more with IT stakeholders and serve more technical rationalization projects by creating solutions EA artifacts full of interaction patterns
Infrastructure	Irrelevant to business managers, does not impact business processes, but constitutes the landscape substance and causes new change projects	Quite prevalent in organizations, communicate more with IT stakeholders and serve more technical rationalization projects by creating solutions EA artifacts full of node schemes
Security	Irrelevant to business managers, does not impact business processes, does not constitute the landscape substance and seldom causes new projects	Relatively rare in organizations, communicate more with IT stakeholders and serve more technical rationalization projects by creating solutions EA artifacts full of security views

Table 16.1. Domain specialization of Solution Architects

In practice, Solution Architects usually specialize in a single organizational domain, or a couple of related domains adjacent in the stack (e.g. infrastructure and security), with the ensuing consequences for their work explained in Table 16.1. However, because they have to master some or the other technologies to be able to design in fair detail technical solutions for their projects, they *cannot* specialize solely in the business domain[17]. For Solution Architects, specialization in the business domain is always complemented with that in some technical domains, most often applications. Conversely, specializing in the applications domain can require also specializing in the business domain if the respective applications are highly specific to the subject area, e.g. accounting, telecom or medical systems.

Additionally, because Solution Architects who fully specialize in non-substantive domains can be "rare birds" in organizations (see Table 16.1), these domains often become a *secondary* specialization for architects specializing in substantive domains. For example, a Solution Architect whose major specialization is applications can also assume the data or integration domain as their complementary, minor specialization.

The Integrative Framework of the Archetype of Solution Architects

The comprehensive description of the resources, instruments and activities of Solution Architects and their overall work in organizations provided above suggests that all these aspects of their occupation fit into the integrative framework of the profession of architects (see Figure 14.2), though with certain refinements ensuing from their exclusive focus on digital transformation projects (see Figure 16.1). Generally speaking, Solution Architects do what all architects do, but in a manner suitable for the realities of limited-scope digitalization projects. The integrative framework of the archetype of Solution Architects with their resources, instruments and activities is depicted schematically in Figure 16.5.

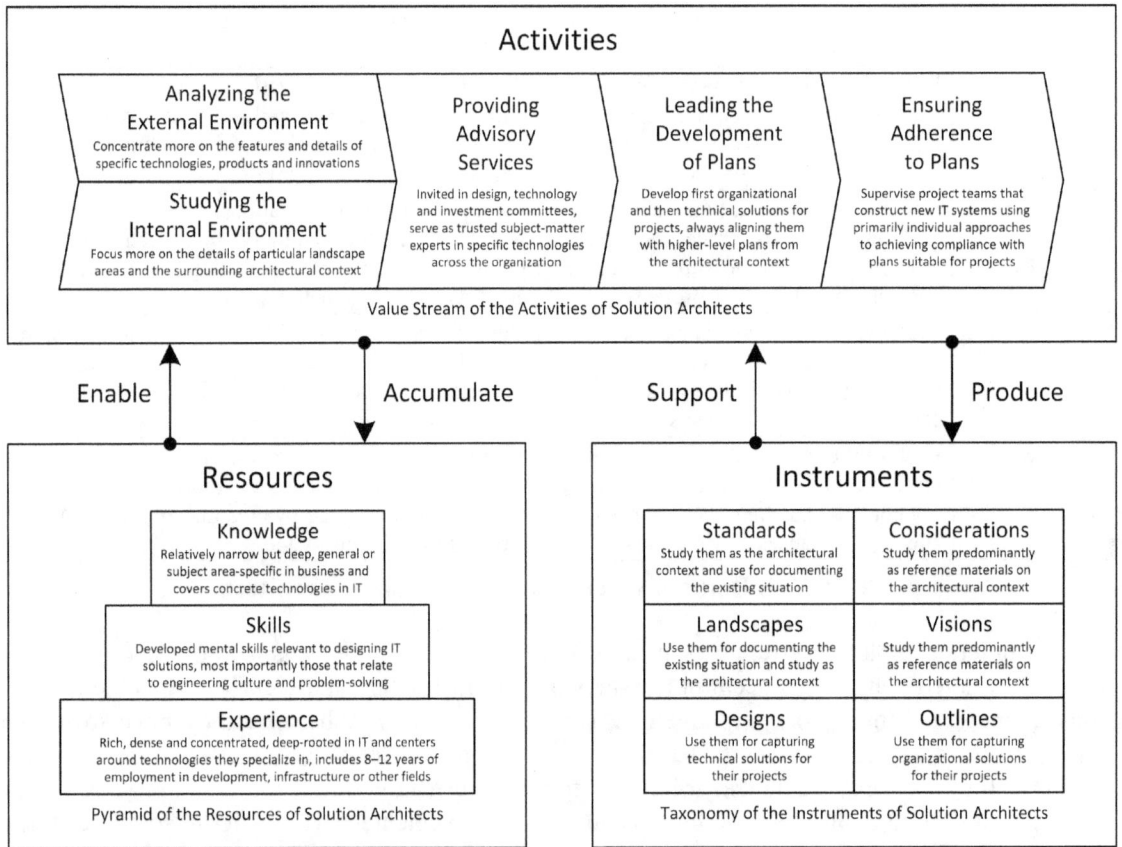

Figure 16.5. The integrative framework of the archetype of Solution Architects

The correspondence of the attributes of Solution Architects to the broader conceptual framework of the profession of architects as a whole allows viewing Solution Architects as a distinct archetype of architects concentrating on digital transformation projects.

Enterprise Architects and Solution Architects

Enterprise Architects and Solution Architects are the two major archetypes of architects that split their profession "vertically" into two halves: those who drive high-level digitalization efforts and those who concentrate on low-level projects. This distinction determines numerous qualities of their personality as well as numerous features of their occupation. For instance, in their character,

Enterprise Architects are more broad-minded generalists and business-oriented entrepreneurs, while Solution Architects are more narrow-focused specialists and technically orientated executors[18]. The work of Solution Architects is more structured around the project lifecycle where they serve the interests of a small group of stakeholders, but the work of Enterprise Architects is more disorderly, has no regular rhythm and requires dealing with diverse constituencies across the organization[19]. Solution Architects have definite milestones when their job can be considered done linked to the completion of projects, whereas the job of Enterprise Architects is largely open-ended and, in some sense, is never done; there is always something else they can do to help their organization[20]. The main differences between Enterprise Architects and Solution Architects ensuing from these and other previous discussions of their roles are summarized in Table 16.2.

Archetype	Enterprise Architects	Solution Architects
Initiatives	Strategies and programs, or project portfolios	Separate projects
Context	The organizational and initiative contexts	Predominantly the project context
Drivers	Many, often mutually incompatible	One, or a few closely related
Stakeholders	High-level business leaders	Mid-level business managers
Supervision	Supervise Solution Architects	Supervise project teams
Job	Largely open-ended, continuous	Mostly project-based, discrete
Milestones	No, moving towards the horizon	Reaching project completion
Resources	Communication and negotiation skills	Technical knowledge and proficiency
Expertise	Broad but shallow	Narrow but deep
Metaphor	Politicians and entrepreneurs	Engineers and executors

Table 16.2. The archetypes of Enterprise Architects and Solution Architects

Thinking about the two archetypes of Enterprise Architects and Solution Architects is helpful for understanding the complex profession of architects in its entirety as well as their specific activities in different situations. Concrete positions for architects in real architecture functions, however, relatively rarely exactly correspond to these archetypes in their pure forms. More often, organizations either combine or further specialize them to define their architecture positions.

Chapter Summary

This chapter described the resources, instruments and activities of Solution Architects in the organizational and initiative contexts, discussed the work of Solution Architects in its entirety across the two contexts, discussed the domain specialization of Solution Architects, presented their integrative framework and compared them with Enterprise Architects. The core message of this chapter can be summarized in the following major points:
- Solution Architects is a special archetype of architects responsible for leading the architectural planning of individual digitalization projects, operating exclusively at the project level

- Knowledge of Solution Architects is relatively narrow but deep, their skills are particularly strong in engineering and problem solving, their experience is very dense and includes 8–12 years of practice as IT specialists of different profiles
- Outlines and Designs are used by Solution Architects for capturing architectural solutions, but Considerations, Standards, Visions and Landscapes are only referenced as the documentation of the existing situation and architectural context
- In the organizational context, Solution Architects analyze technologies and their features, study relevant areas of the landscape and architectural context and advise on technical questions, but rarely participate in the initial ideation of initiatives
- In the initiative context, Solution Architects serve specific digitalization projects along their entire lifecycle by providing advisory services during the concept step, leading the development of plans during the decision and design steps and ensuring adherence to plans during the delivery step
- In their work, Solution Architects are often assigned by Enterprise Architects to already pre-formed projects to drive these projects to completion through the concept, decision, design and delivery steps of their lifecycle
- Domain specialization of Solution Architects determines their prevalence in organizations, stakeholder circle (business or IT), types of projects (digital transformation or technical rationalization) and the informational contents of their solutions EA artifacts (domain-specific views, models and diagrams)

Chapter 17: Architecture Positions in Organizations

The two previous chapters described in great detail the generic archetypes of Enterprise Architects and Solution Architects respectively. This chapter, based on the foundation laid by these archetypes, discusses specific positions for architects in architecture functions as well as relationships between them. In particular, this chapter begins with introducing the notion of architecture positions and the most general principles of specialization of architects in architecture functions. Then, this chapter discusses the fundamentals of the tier-based and area-based approaches to specialization, describes the most typical structural patterns corresponding to these approaches and explains their applicability in organizations of different sizes and structures. Finally, this chapter addresses the teamwork of architects and describes different patterns of interaction between architects occupying different positions in architecture functions.

Specific Positions for Architects in Organizations

All architects are members of the same common profession and can typically be classified into the two broad archetypes of Enterprise Architects and Solution Architects (see Table 16.2). These generalized representations of the profession and archetypes of architects, though provide adequate high-level views of their occupation, may not exactly correspond to concrete positions for architects existing in organizations and may not accurately describe their job in light of its possible position-specific features and variations.

Administratively, all architects in organizations usually belong to a dedicated architecture function offering its architectural services to other units (see Figure 5.1). To organize their productive work and cooperation, architecture functions define one or more specific positions for architects. **Architecture positions** are characterized by unique titles and delineated circles of duties that architects occupying them have to fulfill. As the successful fulfillment of certain responsibilities requires adequate knowledge, skills and experience, each architecture position is also often associated with requisite position-specific resources that its occupants need to possess. Like all administrative positions, positions for architects in architecture functions can be organized hierarchically, so that lower-ranking architects report to higher-ranking ones, though usually unofficially.

Owing to the existence of specialized architecture positions, in organizations the profession of architects is materialized, or manifested, in various positions that *loosely* fit into the two archetypes of Enterprise Architects and Solution Architects (see Figure 15.8 and Figure 16.5). In other words, in organizational settings, architects actually represent a rich constellation of kindred architecture positions bearing different "something architect"–style titles. However, because positions for architects are always organization-specific, their titles cannot be standardized across the industry and the respective terminology generally remains rather vague and contradictory, resulting in countless inconsistent labels[1]. For this reason, highly similar architecture positions often have different titles in different organizations, while the same job title can refer to different roles in different organizations, or even in different units of one organization[2].

As the number of architects in organizations grows proportionally to the size of their IT department and can be pretty large, there inevitably stands the question of the division of labor and their ensuing professional specialization. The **specialization of architects** implies the separation of their duties into different, non-overlapping but complementary zones of responsibility by establishing multiple architecture positions. For organizations, specialization represents a "double-edged sword" with both beneficial and detrimental effects. On the positive side, it helps concentrate resources, sharpen the focus of attention and reduce irrelevant distractions for individual architects. On the negative side, specialization necessitates tight coordination of efforts between different architects to enable concerted action.

The specialization of architecture positions is subject to the universal rule generally valid for all organizations: the greater the number of people in the organization, the higher their occupational specialization[3]. In other words, the bigger the architecture function, the larger the number of distinct positions for architects it tends to have. Specifically, the specialization of architects in organizations occurs simultaneously along two different lines: vertical tiers and horizontal areas[4]. Tier-based specialization divides architects *vertically*, according to the *levels* of digitalization initiatives that they drive. By contrast, area-based specialization divides architects *horizontally*, according to the *subject areas* of their transformation initiatives[5].

Vertical Tier-Based Specialization of Architects

Vertical, **tier-based specialization** implies defining different positions for architects who work on digitalization initiatives at different levels of the initiative hierarchy, i.e. strategies, programs and projects (see Figure 2.5)[6]. This form of specialization is rather simple, straightforward and intuitive as it closely resembles the classic corporate hierarchy in organizations, where more global, strategic and far-reaching decisions are made at higher levels, while more local, tactical and mundane decisions — at lower levels[7]. Like any hierarchical arrangement, tier-based specialization organizes architects into a multilayer pyramid with lower layers having more people than higher ones. Empirically, every next lower tier of architecture positions tends to include about 3–6 times more architects than the tier above it, depending on their specific responsibilities, workload, degree of independence and other factors.

In practice, the tier-based specialization of architects means that architecture functions can be structured in one, two, three or seldom more tiers of architecture positions. The bigger its size, the greater the number of tiers the architecture function is likely to have[8]. However, three tiers of positions for architects seemingly meet the specialization needs of all but a few exceptionally large companies. In the same sense in which the classification into projects, programs and strategies is adequate to cover the full spectrum of transformation initiatives in organizations, the set of one-, two- and three-tier structural patterns is roughly sufficient to reflect all reasonable design options for architecture functions relevant for the overwhelming majority of organizations.

One-Tier Architecture Functions

In **one-tier architecture functions**, all architects work largely as peers at the same administrative level on all kinds of digital transformation initiatives. In other words, in these functions, the single tier of architecture positions spans all three layers of the initiative hierarchy, from top-level strategies to bottom-level projects. Because in this case architects have to deal with all sorts of global and local, large and small, long and short transformation initiatives, as well as loose project portfolios, in their resources, instruments and activities they combine the archetypes of both Enterprise Architects and Solution Architects, possessing the qualities characteristic of the profession as a whole (see Figure 14.2).

The one-tier pattern represents the simplest possible approach to structuring architecture functions in organizations. Due to its simplicity, this pattern is suitable only for the smallest architecture functions, ranging from sole architects leading all architectural planning efforts in the organization to several architects with an ad hoc, expertise-based separation of responsibilities and assignment to initiatives. Such functions are rather typical for companies with less than a hundred IT staff.

The fact that in one-tier architecture functions digitalization initiatives at all levels are served by a small, tightly knit architecture team, or even by the same architects, has a number of implications for their work. Most importantly, in this model, ensuring the adherence of derivative initiatives to the architectural plans of their parents, or portfolios, becomes largely a matter of personal agreements between architects and is often achieved directly by means of active participation. For example, the same architect can first lead the architectural planning of a transformation strategy, then drive its descending programs and finally switch to their subordinate projects, ensuring the compliance of lower-level initiatives with higher-level plans by own actions.

As a consequence, in one-tier architecture functions, informal individual approaches to achieving adherence to plans (see Table 12.1) are generally more instrumental and effectual than formal governance procedures (see Figure 12.3). Hence, the role of official governance bodies in exercising architectural oversight in these functions tends to be less significant. The logical structure of one-tier architecture functions with the place of architects in their layout is shown schematically in Figure 17.1.

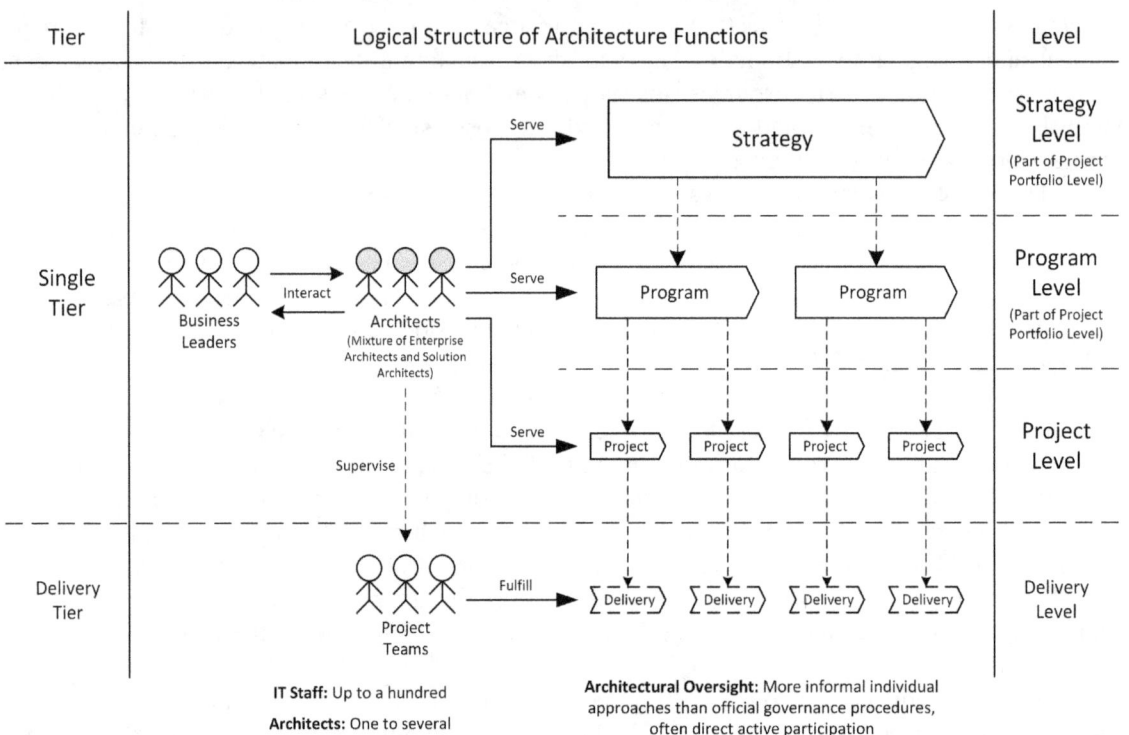

Figure 17.1. The logical structure of one-tier architecture functions

Although the trivial one-tier structure depicted in Figure 17.1 is perfectly appropriate for small architecture functions, larger functions require more complex structures with a pronounced division of labor and an explicit differentiation of architecture positions to organize the collective work of their architects.

Two-Tier Architecture Functions

In **two-tier architecture functions**, architects are clearly stratified into top-tier Enterprise Architects serving all high-level transformation initiatives, or project portfolios, and bottom-tier Solution Architects concentrating exclusively on individual projects, precisely matching the descriptions of these archetypes provided earlier in Chapter 15 (see Figure 15.1 and Figure 15.6) and Chapter 16 (see Figure 16.1) respectively. In other words, in these functions, the top tier of architecture positions covers the strategy and program levels of the initiative hierarchy, or the project portfolio level, while the bottom tier — its project level.

The two-tier pattern represents an approach of moderate complexity to structuring architecture functions in organizations. This pattern is adequate for shaping medium-sized architecture functions whose headcount ranges, say, from several to a few dozen architects, where their responsibilities can no longer be distributed on a case-by-case basis, like in small architecture teams, and a more formal ranking becomes necessary. Such functions are most often found in companies employing from about a hundred to several hundred specialists in their IT departments.

As the number of architects in architecture functions that require two-tier structures is relatively large, personal interactions among all of them cannot be very active and seriously relied upon for the purposes of exercising architectural oversight. Moreover, because in this model high-level digitalization efforts and low-level projects are designedly led by different classes of architects, the opportunities for active participation as a means of ensuring the adherence of derivative initiatives to higher-order architectural plans are limited. For these reasons, in these functions, informal individual approaches to achieving compliance are normally complemented with strong, institutionalized governance procedures to certify that all relevant considerations are taken into account in every important planning decision.

In particular, since the principal decoupling in two-tier architecture functions lies between Enterprise Architects producing high-level architectural plans, whether for coherent initiatives or less coherent portfolios (see Figure 15.4 and Figure 15.7), and Solution Architects having to align their projects with these plans, the role of investment committees and design committees in this model comes to the fore. It is these governance bodies that officially approve all architectural plans for projects (see Figure 16.2), ensuring their connection to parent initiatives or portfolios, as well as to the overall architectural context. In this way, investment committees and design committees help alleviate the imperfections of communication between the two tiers of architects and link strategic architectural plans with their tactical execution. The logical structure of two-tier architecture functions with the place of Enterprise Architects and Solution Architects in their layout is shown in Figure 17.2.

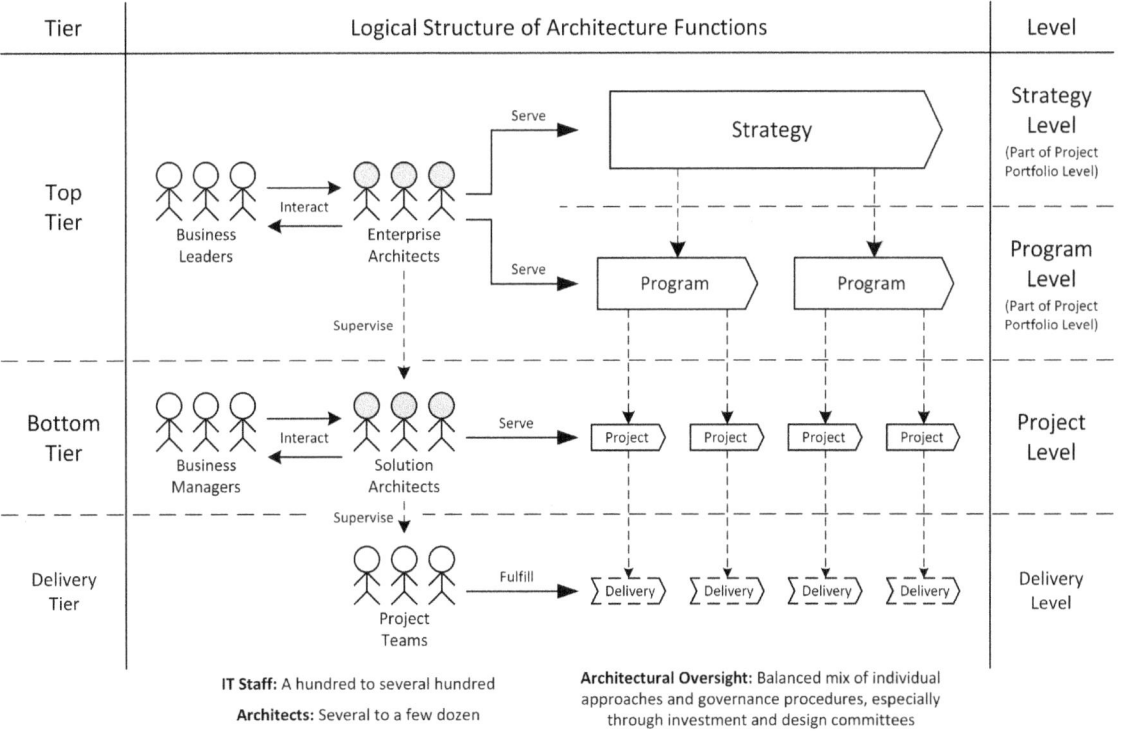

Figure 17.2. The logical structure of two-tier architecture functions

Although the "binary" two-tier structure presented in Figure 17.2 is well suited for mid-size architecture functions, really large functions need even more complicated structures with a more fine-grained separation of duties between different architecture positions and a greater number of vertical tiers to properly organize the collaborative activities of all their numerous architects.

Three-Tier Architecture Functions

In **three-tier architecture functions**, architects are stratified more thinly into top-tier Enterprise Architects focusing primarily on organization-wide digitalization strategies, middle-tier Enterprise Architects dealing with more local transformation programs and bottom-tier Solution Architects working only on individual projects. In other words, in these functions, the three tiers of architecture positions exactly correspond to the three levels of the initiative hierarchy.

The three-tier pattern represents a fairly complex approach to structuring architecture functions in organizations. This pattern is suitable for huge architecture functions measured in numbers ranging from a few dozen to a couple of hundred architects, where even those architects driving high-level transformation efforts can no longer be viewed as peers and need to be ranked. Functions of that size are usually established in very large companies whose IT workforce exceeds several hundred people.

As the number of architects in architecture functions implementing the three-tier pattern is substantial, personal communication within the architecture community tends to be rather weak and highly selective. This problem is often exacerbated by the constant turnover of architects, especially at the bottom tier of the pyramid, where many Solution Architects can be temporary contractors hired for specific projects. Furthermore, in large architecture functions, some groups of architects can be partly disconnected from the rest of the team and operate semi-independently as autonomous "fiefdoms". For these reasons, these functions can be characterized by loose coupling between their members, when different architects try to align their decisions with those of other architects, but at the same time also have a considerable degree of freedom in decision-making.

In these circumstances, effective architectural oversight can hardly be based on ad hoc individual approaches, but only on systematic architecture governance mechanisms, where every significant planning decision undergoes a chain of necessary approvals before being enacted. In other words, to ensure adherence to existing architectural plans, three-tier architecture functions largely resort to bureaucratic governance procedures guaranteeing that some important concerns are not overlooked or neglected in new architectural solutions. For this purpose, they establish a developed system of governance bodies and arrangements permeating virtually all architectural decision-making processes. The logical structure of three-tier architecture functions with the place of strategy-level Enterprise Architects, program-level Enterprise Architects and Solution Architects in their layout is shown schematically in Figure 17.3.

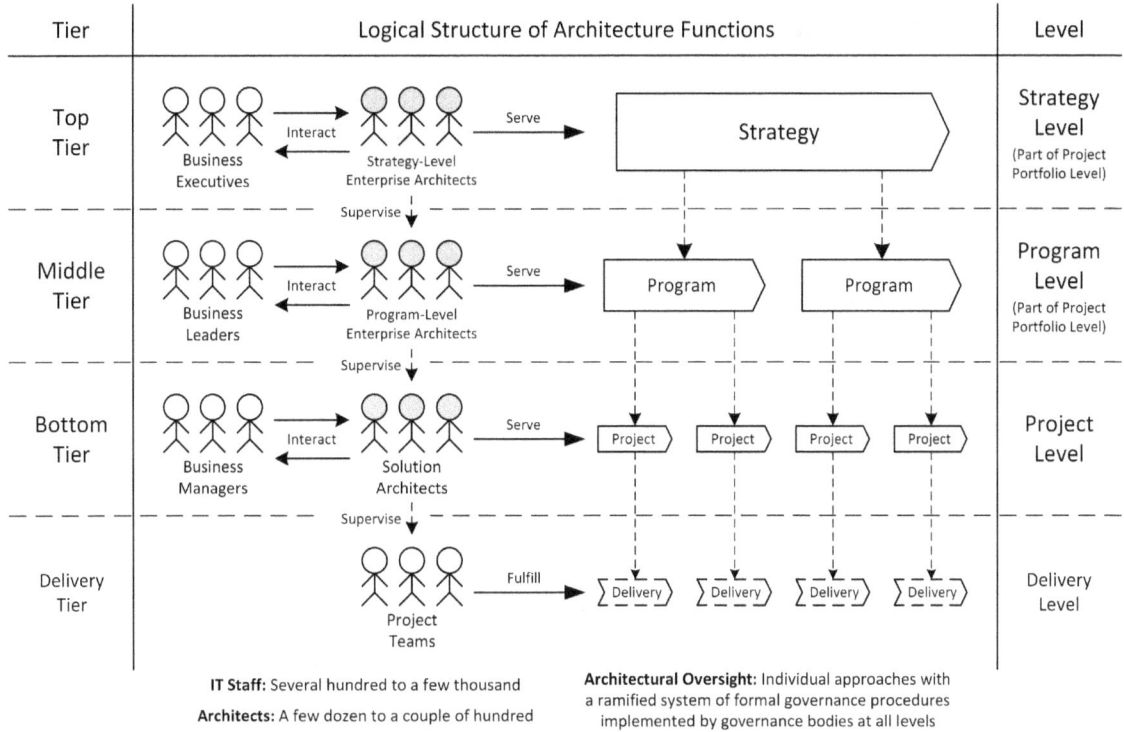

Figure 17.3. The logical structure of three-tier architecture functions

Even though the tripartite three-tier structure demonstrated in Figure 17.3 is adequate for organizing the cooperation of architects in very large architecture functions, some extraordinarily big functions with literally hundreds of architects can be too large even for this model and require more hierarchical tiers of architecture positions. Such functions, however, are rare in the industry and not described in this book.

Importantly, while tier-based specialization was presented as having a discrete number of tiers of architecture positions, it can actually be viewed as *continuous* because the jobs of architects at different tiers can overlap to varying extents, merging the tiers and blurring their boundaries. For example, in a formally two-tier structure, Enterprise Architects can partly perform the work of Solution Architects by serving all projects during their early initiation step, till their passage through the investment decision gate (see Figure 16.2), and only then finally hand them over to Solution Architects, essentially functioning together as a structure with "one and a half" tiers.

Besides vertical, tier-based specialization discussed above, positions for architects in organizations are also specialized horizontally. This horizontal specialization leverages quite different principles to demarcate architecture positions.

Horizontal Area-Based Specialization of Architects

Horizontal, **area-based specialization** implies defining different positions for architects who lead transformation efforts related to different business and IT areas of the organization, e.g. lines of business, locations of operation or classes of technology[9]. With this form of specialization, the organizational context in which architects operate is narrowed from embracing the entire organization with all its drivers, stakeholders and plans to specific organizational areas with their local drivers, stakeholders and plans (see Figure 10.1). This "zoning" of architects' responsibilities cuts through all levels of the initiative hierarchy and sets the spatial boundaries for change initiatives and project portfolios that they serve. In short, it limits their purview to only certain areas of business and IT.

The area-based specialization of architects is somewhat more sophisticated than the tier-based one, less intuitively understandable and largely specific to their profession. Because it blends the division of duties across the realms of both business and IT interwoven in a non-trivial manner, this specialization highly resembles the traditional functional specialization of employees in organizations, but is not fully equivalent to it.

The general idea of the area-based specialization of architects can be best illustrated with three common structural patterns for architecture functions: domain-centric, business-centric and combined. These patterns offer conceptually different approaches to shaping architecture positions suitable for different situations. However, in reality, they represent only basic constructs, or building blocks, from which architecture functions can be composed. In practice, organizations adopt various mixes of these patterns, sometimes rather complex ones, to define the exact structure of their positions for architects corresponding to their needs. Although the choice of appropriate structural patterns arguably does not depend directly on the size of the architecture function, larger functions tend to require more granular focus areas for their architects, necessitating the use of more intricate combinations of these patterns.

Domain-Centric Architecture Functions

In **domain-centric architecture functions**, all architects are closely aligned with the stack of organizational domains, or their narrower subdomains, and drive only those transformation efforts that target these domains. In other words, in these functions, architecture positions at every tier cover the body of the organization "horizontally", according to the typical layers of the corporate landscape — business, applications, data, integration, infrastructure and security (see Figure 3.4).

In domain-centric functions, Enterprise Architects with limited domain coverage are often called simply **domain architects** (see Figure 14.4) and normally titled according to their domains, e.g. "enterprise application architects" and "enterprise integration architects", or, more succinctly, "data architects" and "infrastructure architects". The formal position titles of Solution Architects in these functions are also more likely to reflect the technical categories of their IT solutions, e.g. "application solution architects" and "infrastructure solution architects", or, more precisely, "Java solution architects" and "Juniper solution architects". In this setup, the work specifics of both Enterprise Architects and Solution Architects are strictly determined by their domain specialization, exactly as described in Table 15.1 and Table 16.1 respectively.

The domain-centric pattern concentrates the expertise of architects around specific areas of concern most of which are strongly associated with particular classes of technology. However, as each of these areas has an enterprise-wide scope, this pattern is conducive to their global rationalization, consolidation and optimization across the whole organization. By controlling local variability in every domain, it promotes better utilization of IT assets and technologies and enables higher cost-effectiveness of the organizational landscape.

Due to these compelling benefits, domain-centric architecture functions are very appropriate in situations when local flexibility and diversity are not required. Namely, this model is especially suitable for relatively simple, centralized organizations whose operations are not highly diversified and where strategic decision-making is concentrated in the hands of a single group of business leaders. The logical structure of domain-centric architecture functions with the place of domain-specific architecture positions in their layout is shown in Figure 17.4.

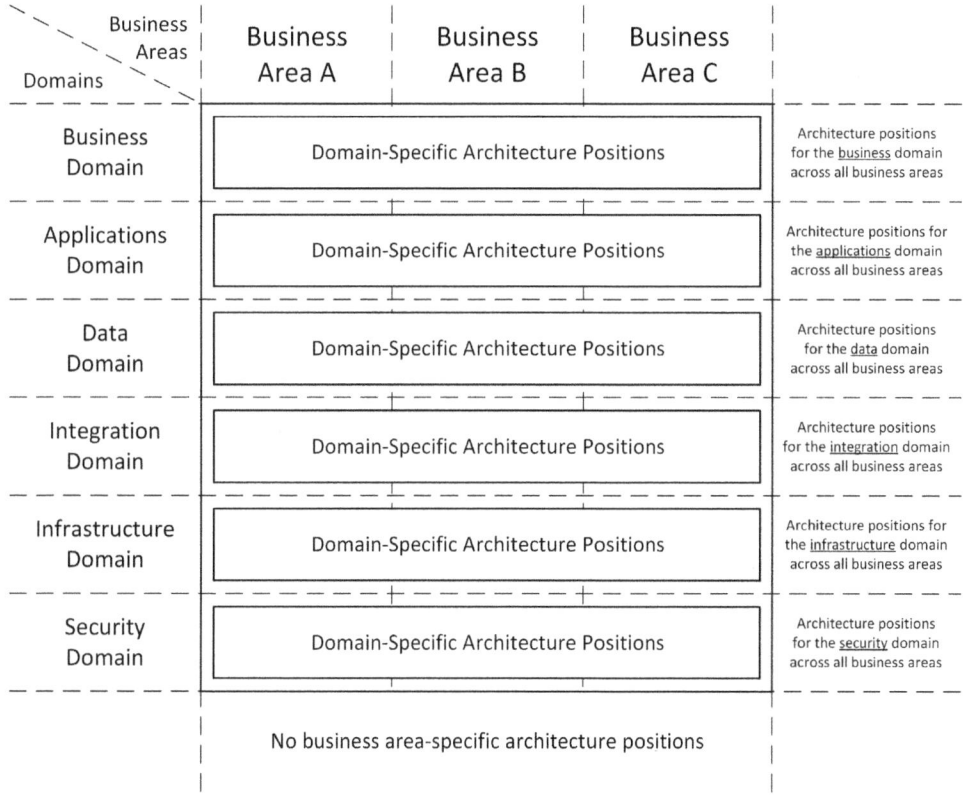

Figure 17.4. The logical structure of domain-centric architecture functions

Even though the horizontal, domain-centric structure depicted in Figure 17.4 has a number of indisputable advantages associated with the global optimization of IT resources and leveraging economies of scale, this structure is unlikely to meet the needs of decentralized organizations, where greater flexibility is a must.

Business-Centric Architecture Functions

In **business-centric architecture functions**, all architects are closely aligned with major business areas[10], whatever they can be (e.g. separate lines of business, business functions or geographic divisions), and drive only those transformation efforts that target these areas, in all organizational domains. In other words, in these functions, architecture positions at every tier cover the organization in a number of verticals that represent semi-independent "islands" of business operations with their supporting IT infrastructure spanning all landscape layers.

In business-centric functions, Enterprise Architects with limited organizational scopes can be called simply **business area architects** (see Figure 14.4) and are often titled according to their areas, e.g. "enterprise architects for mining" and "enterprise architects for Europe", or, more succinctly, "production architects" and "wholesale architects". The formal position titles of Solution Architects in these functions are also more likely to reflect the subject areas of their IT solutions, e.g. "solution architects for mortgages" and "solution architects for sales", or, more concisely, "procurement solution architects" and "retail solution architects". In this setup, the work of Enterprise Architects exhibits little or no signs of domain specialization (see Table 15.1), but the work of Solution Architects is still largely domain-specialized for the necessity to master particular technologies (see Table 16.1).

The business-centric pattern concentrates the expertise of architects around specific business activities with the underlying information systems, databases, platforms and other IT assets. This narrow focus facilitates deeper immersion into their details, better understanding of their specifics and closer personal relationships with their owners. Moreover, as in this pattern architects' attention spans all organizational domains, it allows adjusting the respective elements from all layers of the stack to the needs of particular business areas. By sacrificing organization-wide optimization concerns for the sake of area-specific interests, it boosts local responsiveness and adaptiveness.

By virtue of their ability to react to local interests, business-centric architecture functions are more suitable in situations when high decision-making autonomy is required in different areas across the organization. Specifically, this model is perfectly viable for complex, decentralized, often geographically dispersed organizations where business units are disparate in their needs and activities, governed locally and develop their own strategies[11]. The logical structure of business-centric architecture functions with the place of business area-specific architecture positions in their layout is shown schematically in Figure 17.5.

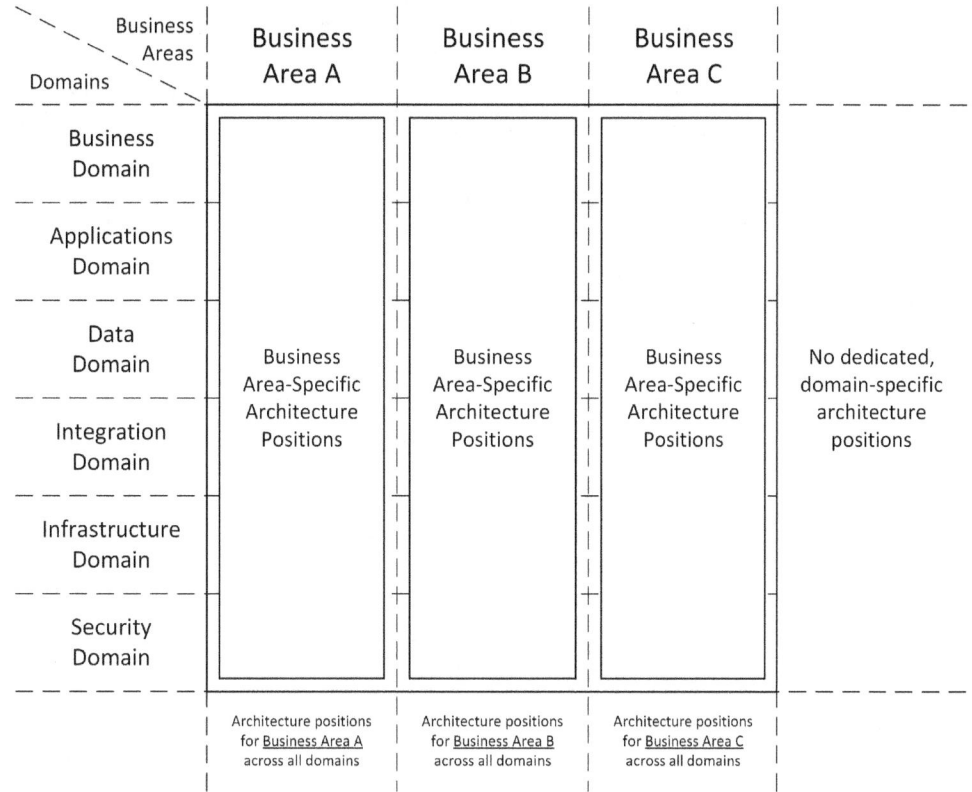

Figure 17.5. The logical structure of business-centric architecture functions

The vertical, business-centric structure presented in Figure 17.5 offers a radically different way of organizing architecture functions whose benefits are strongly associated with local autonomy and responsiveness. In some sense, this structure with its advantages is opposite to the horizontal, domain-centric structure shown in Figure 17.4. However, for many organizations, neither strict centralization nor total decentralization of architectural planning seems appropriate. In these cases, the business-centric and domain-centric patterns can be combined to produce more complicated structures with desirable properties.

Combined Architecture Functions

In **combined architecture functions**, some architects are aligned with typical organizational domains, while others — with specific business areas. In these functions, architecture positions at different tiers cover the body of the organization in a non-linear fashion, mixing both "horizontal" and "vertical" zones of responsibility. In this light, positions for Enterprise Architects with a truly enterprise-wide coverage of all domains and business areas, who can be fairly called enterprise architects in a literal sense (see Figure 14.4), are actually relatively rare in organizations, but when such positions exist, they can be titled as "chief architects", "principal architects" or exactly "enterprise architects".

As discussed earlier, all the organizational domains relevant to architectural planning can be separated into functional ones, which determine the functional capabilities of IT systems (business, applications and data), and non-functional ones, which are largely irrelevant to their functional capabilities (integration, infrastructure and security, see Table 3.2). This separation provides very important considerations for structuring architecture functions and defining positions for architects. On the one hand, functional domains, as they are bound to concrete business activities, are more likely to benefit from decentralization along with the business. On the other hand, non-functional domains, as they tend to be business-agnostic, are more likely to profit from centralization irrespective of the business structure[12]. As a rule, the higher the position of a domain in the stack, the higher the benefits of aligning it with particular business areas, and vice versa.

For these reasons, in combined architecture functions, business area-specific positions for architects usually cover only functional domains, whereas domain-specific positions — only non-functional domains. In other words, these functions often employ a number of architects who focus on the business, applications and data domains for separate business areas together with some architects focusing separately on the integration, infrastructure and security domains for the entire organization. Because of the "perpendicular" orientation of different architecture positions in combined functions, their high-level layout resembles a certain matrix structure.

Combined architecture functions incorporate the business-centric and domain-centric structural patterns discussed above and allow mixing decentralization in business matters with centralization in technical IT infrastructure. They help organizations enjoy the best of two worlds and reap the benefits associated with both of them — local flexibility and global optimization respectively. Unsurprisingly, combined models are very popular across the industry and deployed in the majority of large companies, though their concrete structures in terms of centralization and decentralization of particular domains are organization-specific and depend on the desired balance between local autonomy and global efficiency. The logical structure of combined architecture functions with the place of domain-specific and business area-specific architecture positions in their layout is shown in Figure 17.6.

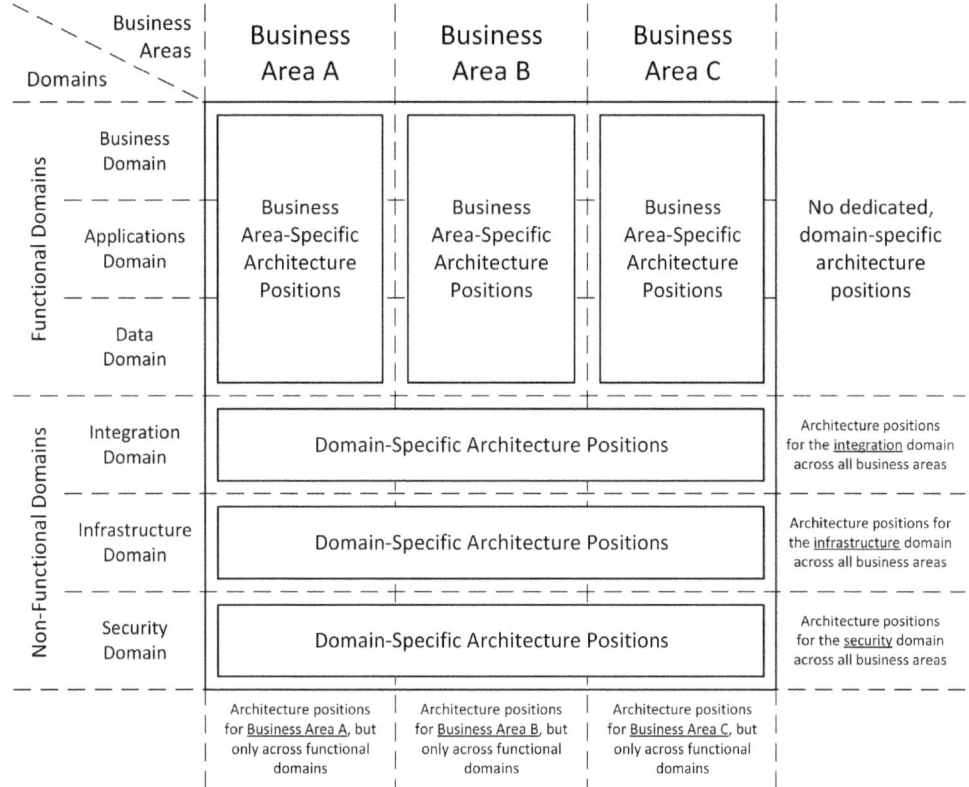

Figure 17.6. The logical structure of combined architecture functions

The matrix-like, combined structure demonstrated in Figure 17.6 illustrates the idea of centralizing non-functional domains to leverage economies of scale and, at the same time, decentralizing functional domains to achieve local agility. However, architecture functions in very large and diversified organizations often establish an even more intricate mosaic of architecture positions to meet their needs. For example, some companies can open positions with "non-rectangular" responsibility zones (i.e. where architects concentrate on different domains for different business areas) or apply different patterns of area-based specialization to different tiers of architecture positions. In other companies, individual architects can be spread across different parts of the organization to work remotely from the core architecture team, or their architecture functions can be highly decentralized around their independent business units to the extent that it would make more sense to talk about *multiple* architecture functions operating separately within their major units.

The Spectrum of Architecture Functions

As noted earlier, the specialization of architects in architecture functions normally goes along vertical and horizontal lines at the same time. Because tier-based separation is orthogonal to area-based separation, these forms of specialization appositely complement each other and are typically used in conjunction. In these cases, area-based specialization applies, in some form or the other, to all tiers of architecture positions defined by tier-based specialization. For example, in two-tier architecture functions, both Enterprise Architects and Solution Architects are often aligned with different business and IT areas (see Figure 17.6), though Solution Architects usually link more strongly with specific technology domains than business areas.

A combination of tier-based and area-based specializations yields complex structures of architecture functions. The larger the function in terms of the number of architects, the more sophisticated its structure tends to be from the standpoint of their positions. In addition, larger functions necessitate a more ramified network of architecture governance bodies and more formalized governance procedures to exercise architectural oversight and coordinate architectural plans at different levels.

For example, in a small single-business organization, the architecture function can employ only a few architects. To organize their work, this function is likely to suffice only one tier of architecture positions (see Figure 17.1) with no formal area-based specialization. It can also host an architecture committee to ratify various important architectural decisions. In this scenario, the architects can contribute in different ways to different transformation initiatives, based on the relevancy of their expertise and time availability. The architecture committee can, for the most part, symbolically legitimize made planning decisions already agreed upon informally among the team.

In a medium-sized diversified company, the architecture function can employ a couple of dozen architects. To organize their work, this function is likely to need two tiers of architecture positions (see Figure 17.2) with their articulate area-based specialization in different lines of business and shared organizational domains. It can also establish a few architecture committees of different ranks to authorize strategic and tactical architectural decisions. In this scenario, the top-tier Enterprise Architects can drive high-level transformation efforts for their lines of business and domains, whereas the bottom-tier Solution Architects assigned to the respective areas can materialize these efforts through descending projects. The architecture committees, in turn, can scrutinize all project-level decisions to ensure their compliance with higher-order plans.

Finally, in a large multinational corporation, the architecture function can employ about a hundred architects in total. To organize their work, this function is likely to require three tiers of architecture positions (see Figure 17.3) with strict area-based specialization, on the one hand, in different geographic regions and their local product lines and, on the other hand, in corporate-wide platform domains and their narrower sub-domains. It can also institute a number of architecture committees at different levels and locations to approve all sorts of architectural decisions. In this scenario, the top-tier Enterprise Architects can develop strategy-level architectural plans for their regions and domains, their subordinate middle-tier Enterprise Architects can derive more detailed program-level plans for their regional products and sub-domains, while the bottom-tier Solution Architects can realize these plans at the project level. The architecture committees can examine all significant decisions to ensure their alignment and consistency across the levels and geographies. The spectrum of architecture functions of different sizes with their possible structures and other properties is presented in Figure 17.7.

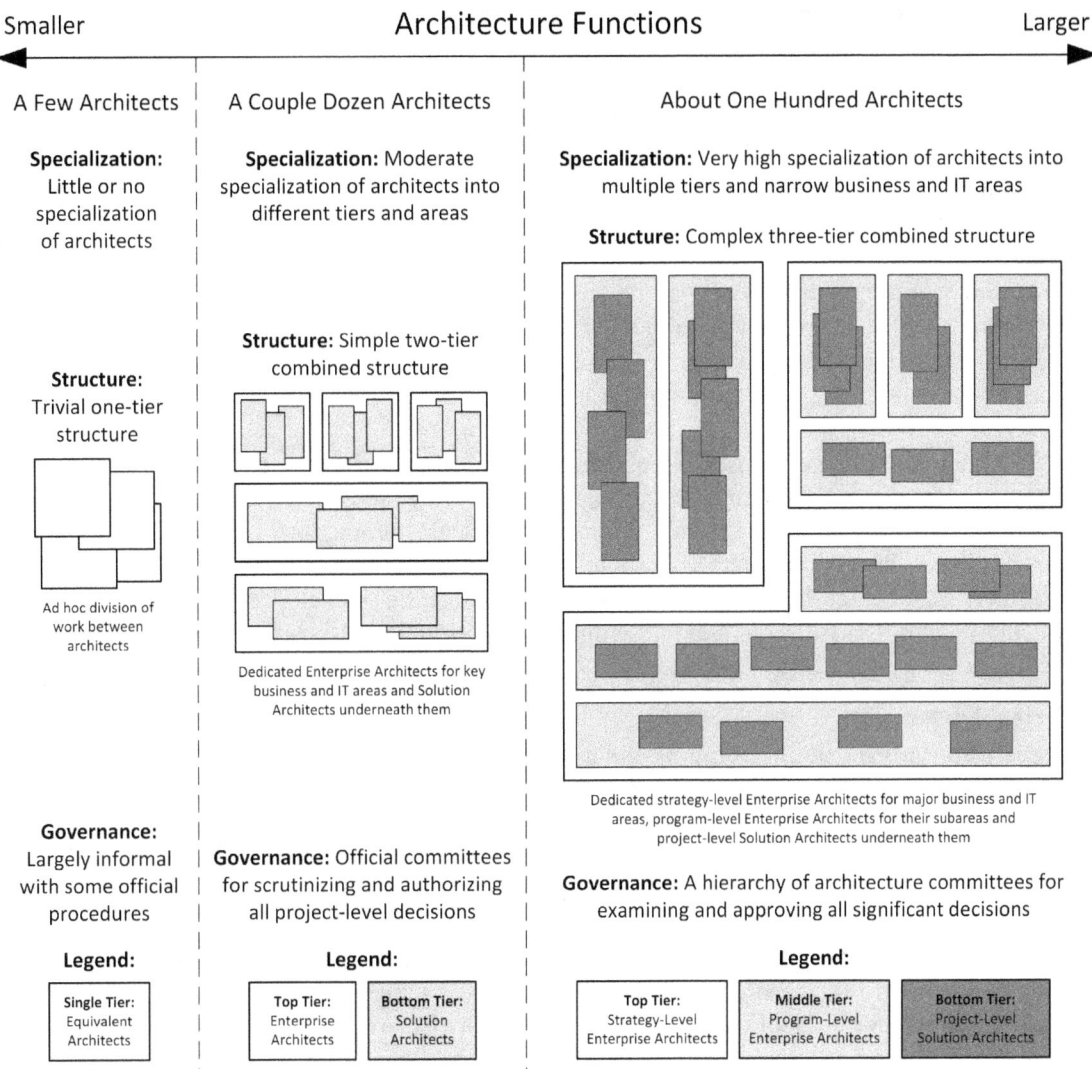

Figure 17.7. The spectrum of architecture functions of different sizes

The progression of architecture functions from simple to complex exemplified in Figure 17.7 illustrates the most fundamental principle of the specialization of positions for architects in organizations. In small functions, architects are more generalists dealing with all kinds of transformation efforts in all areas and combining the archetypes of Enterprise Architects and Solution Architects. By contrast, in large functions, architects are more specialists working only on specific types of initiatives in specific areas and can be clearly classified as either Enterprise Architects or Solution Architects.

Interactions Between Specialized Architects

When architecture functions employ multiple architects with different specializations, each architect has only a partial view of the business and technology landscape, but no one understands the situation as a whole in all its aspects to be able to promote globally optimized architectural decisions for the benefit of the organization. For this reason, the effective performance of architecture functions requires close coordination of the efforts of all their architects across both vertical tiers and horizontal areas to compensate for the narrowness of their expertise and viewpoints[13].

In practical terms, this coordination is manifested in various interactions between architects of different profiles to exchange valuable information or come to some agreements. Because higher specialization of architecture positions causes greater fragmentation of perspectives, the importance and intensity of these interactions grow with the size of architecture functions (see Figure 17.7).

Working interactions between the members of the architecture team can occur in very different circumstances and involve participants from different hierarchical tiers assigned to different business areas and organizational domains. These interactions can also imply different power relations between architects. Despite the wide variety of interactions that can take place within the architecture team, all these interactions can be loosely reduced to five general interaction patterns: offering advice, supervising decisions, co-planning transformations, providing drivers and seeking synergies.

Offering Advice

First, **offering advice** implies helping other architects with competent judgments, opinions or recommendations whenever they are needed. Providing advisory services represents one of the basic activities of architects in the organizational context, and consumers of their unofficial advisory services can be their colleagues from the architecture team seeking their specialized subject-area or technology expertise. These interactions assume no authority relationships whatsoever and can happen between any architects from any tiers and areas. For example, an Enterprise Architect specializing in the data domain can ask an infrastructure Solution Architect about modern hardware capabilities for storing large volumes of information. Or, a Solution Architect specializing in applications can ask an Enterprise Architect from the security domain for the latest approaches to protecting mobile apps from unauthorized access and data theft. Offering advice allows sharing professional knowledge within the architecture team, leveraging everyone's competencies to the maximum and fostering collective intelligence.

Supervising Decisions

Second, **supervising decisions** implies controlling architectural plans developed by other architects, typically for their alignment with some higher-order plans. Ensuring adherence to plans as part of architectural oversight represents an essential activity of architects, which often requires monitoring the architects of descending initiatives. These interactions assume certain authority, whether formal or informal, and normally occur between architects from different vertical tiers, where higher-tier architects supervise lower-tier ones (see Figure 17.2 and Figure 17.3). In the most classic supervision scenario, Enterprise Architects who drive transformation strategies or programs guide subordinate Solution Architects working on their derivative projects.

Or, Enterprise Architects from non-substantive domains (i.e. data, integration and security, see Table 3.3), ordinarily supply Solution Architects with the relevant rules EA artifacts (e.g. Logical Data Models, IT Principles and Guidelines respectively) and control compliance with their prescriptions. Supervising decisions allows linking organizational activities at different levels and translating global intentions into local actions.

Co-Planning Transformations

Third, **co-planning transformations** implies leading the architectural planning of digitalization initiatives, or project portfolios, jointly with other architects. Complex transformative efforts tend to touch *multiple* organizational domains and business areas, so that their architectural solutions can hardly be put together by single architects with narrow specialization. To accomplish these transformations, two or more architects of complementary profiles unite into a team to collaboratively lead the development of their architectural plans. In these interactions, architects work as peers with no subordination relationships and typically belong to the same tier of architecture positions (see Figure 17.6). For instance, large IT solutions that include major application and infrastructure components often necessitate the involvement of both application and infrastructure Solution Architects in their architectural planning. Or, a comprehensive digitalization strategy affecting the operations of several business areas is likely to require the participation of all Enterprise Architects serving these areas and possibly also Enterprise Architects covering the data and integration domains organization-wide. Co-planning transformations allows developing complicated architectural solutions for multi-domain and multi-area transformation efforts crossing the individual specialization boundaries established in architecture functions.

Providing Drivers

Fourth, **providing drivers** implies informing other architects about the existing motives for change relevant to their zones of responsibility. Because in the stack of organizational domains lower layers generally intend to support higher layers, architectural plans for functional domains particularly often act as exogenous *transformation drivers* for the underlying non-functional domains, so that system plans determine platform requirements. For this reason, business-facing architects from functional domains communicate their visions about the future development of these domains to more technically-minded architects from non-functional domains to enable their harmonious co-evolution. These interactions are usually purely informative, assume no formal power relations and happen between architects representing different organizational domains (see Figure 17.4). Most notably, Enterprise Architects for applications announce their anticipated demands for hosting capacity to Enterprise Architects for infrastructure in order to shape their long-range infrastructural plans according to application needs. Through this cross-domain communication channel, agreed business-oriented Roadmaps for applications come as input for producing technical IT Roadmaps for infrastructure. In this way, providing drivers allows aligning and synchronizing changes in the corporate landscape across the entire domain stack, from business and applications down to infrastructure and security.

Seeking Synergies

Lastly, **seeking synergies** implies discussing local goals, drivers and plans with other architects to identify possible opportunities for global optimization. Because business needs emerging in different parts of the organization can interrelate or even largely overlap, considering these needs together can potentially lead to better architectural decisions in terms of reusing assets, avoiding duplication and leveraging economies of scale. For this reason, architects from different business areas constantly exchange information on the situation in their areas to recognize collective needs and think about the most effective ways of addressing them, pursuing enterprise-wide rationalization bottom-up[14]. In these interactions, architects cooperate as equal peers representing different organizational units without mutual subordination (see Figure 17.5). For example, Enterprise Architects responsible for different geographic divisions can meet periodically to explore further opportunities for growing shared IT capabilities. Or, architects serving different lines of business can schedule regular monthly meetings devoted specifically to discussing common problems and demands relevant to more than one line that call for concerted responses from the IT side. Seeking synergies allows making globally optimized planning decisions that take into account various requirements, capabilities and resources of the business as a whole, rather than its separate areas.

The Work of Architects as Teamwork

As it is evident from the diverse scenarios of interaction between architects described above, their occupation is highly collaborative in nature and normally represents *cohesive teamwork*, where they act as part of larger collectivities of architects occupying different positions at different tiers. Therefore, in their job, architects have to build not only an external communication network with business leaders from the outer organization, but also an internal communication network with other members of the architecture team. Their strong affiliation and bonding with the team provide another reason why a collaborative attitude can be fairly regarded among the most critical skills of architects. The five typical interaction patterns of architects with their general meaning, schematic graphical representations and associated benefits are summarized in Figure 17.8.

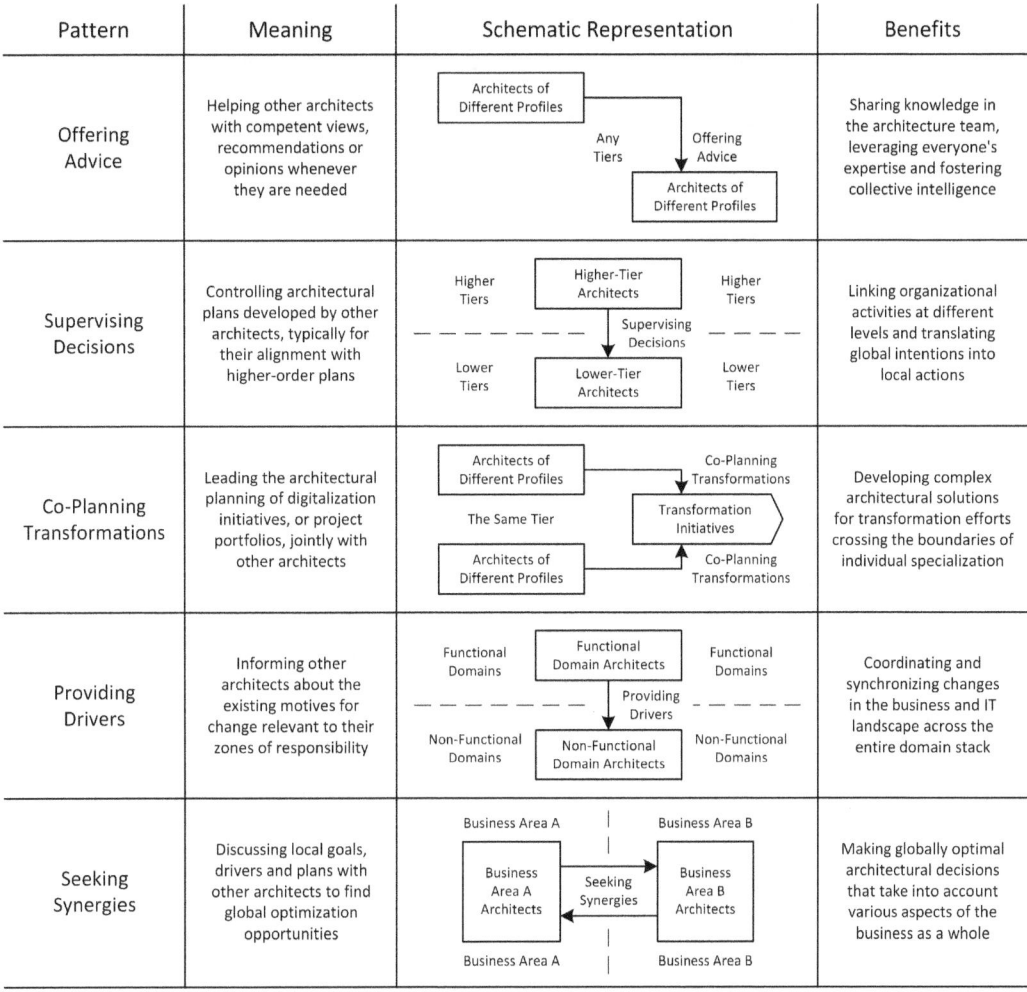

Figure 17.8. Different patterns of interactions between architects of different profiles

Frequent interactions between architects from different hierarchical tiers, organizational domains and business areas illustrated in Figure 17.8 consolidate the architecture function vertically and horizontally, making it operate as one integrated mechanism.

Chapter Summary

This chapter introduced the basic principles of specialization of architecture positions in organizations, explained the tier-based and area-based specializations of architects with their most typical structural patterns, presented the spectrum of possible architecture functions and described different types of interactions between architects of different profiles. The key message of this chapter can be summarized in the following essential points:

- The specialization of architects implies the separation of their duties into different, non-overlapping but complementary zones of responsibility by establishing multiple architecture positions
- The universal rule of occupational specialization in organizations suggests that larger architecture functions in terms of the number of architects require higher specialization of their architecture positions
- Tier-based specialization implies defining different positions for architects who work on digitalization initiatives at different levels of the initiative hierarchy
- Tier-based specialization typically produces one-tier (mixture of Enterprise and Solution Architects), two-tier (separate Enterprise Architects and Solution Architects) or three-tier (strategy-level and program-level Enterprise Architects and Solution Architects) architecture functions
- Area-based specialization implies defining different positions for architects who lead transformation efforts related to different business and IT areas
- Area-based specialization tends to produce domain-centric (positions aligned with organizational domains), business-centric (positions aligned with business areas) or combined (positions aligned with domains and areas) architecture functions
- Depending on the size of organizations, their architecture functions can vary greatly in their complexity, from largely unstructured one-tier functions to very complicated multi-tier functions with ramified arrays of architecture positions
- The work of architects represents cohesive teamwork, where architects with different specializations actively cooperate by offering advice, supervising decisions, co-planning transformations, providing drivers and seeking synergies

Chapter 18: Challenges of Enterprise Architects

The previous chapters thoroughly described numerous aspects of enterprise architects, their activities, work and profession. This chapter concentrates specifically on the challenges faced by enterprise architects as part of their job in organizations and approaches to coping with them. In particular, this chapter starts with discussing the problem of engagement between enterprise architects and business leaders, which represents the crux of their challenges and provides a certain conceptual framework for understanding these challenges. Next, this chapter describes the principal individual challenges of enterprise architects acting as Technology Experts and Change Agents and proposes their potential solutions. Lastly, this chapter describes various organizational challenges of enterprise architects and proposes their possible organizational solutions and individual workarounds.

Engagement Between Enterprise Architects and Business Leaders

The profession of enterprise architects is rather unusual because its members have neither operational nor managerial duties, but act predominantly as internal consultants to real managers taking decisions on behalf of the organization (see Figure 4.4). In this capacity, architects can be called for help by business managers and invited to join decision-making processes, if their participation is desired, or they can be *not* engaged and left out of the stage, if their involvement is not sought after. In the former scenario, architects get busy working with managers on relevant digital transformation issues and assist them with their extensive IT expertise, thereby contributing to organizational success. In the latter scenario, architects, for the most part, have no productive job to do, there is no demand for their services in the organization and they are not given the opportunity to contribute to its success.

Active communication, meaningful collaboration and joint decision-making between enterprise architects and business leaders, for short, can be called **business engagement**, or simply engagement[1]. It is this engagement, or lack thereof, that determines the overall efficacy of the work of architects in organizations. For this reason, the question of their engagement with managers is paramount to their occupation and central to most of their problems. Any serious analysis of challenges faced by architects in their job requires understanding the basics of business engagement.

Engagement between enterprise architects and business leaders, however, is a rather sophisticated, intricate and elusive matter. Effective engagement in organizations is difficult to achieve and maintain. Moreover, the level of engagement is often unsteady and uneven across different business areas, so that the intensity of cooperation between architects and specific management groups in the organization can vary dramatically, from regular collective meetings to the absence of any interactions. Owing to its criticality to the performance of architects, the dynamics of their engagement with business managers deserve a detailed discussion.

Alternatives for Business Leaders Seeking Digitalization

Organizations are governed by business leaders who wield power, control budgets and allocate resources. With their budgets and resources, they are free to decide what to do to achieve their goals and whether to engage enterprise architects as helpers for their purposes. Basically, business managers willing to respond to their transformation drivers with digitalization endeavors and acting as initiative sponsors can go two different ways: implement the respective initiatives without architects or implement them with the involvement of architects. Each of these alternatives has certain advantages and disadvantages, both subjective ones for individual managers and objective ones for the organization as a whole.

The first alternative available to business leaders — implementing digitalization initiatives without enterprise architects — implies making major architectural decisions on their own or with the assistance of some other parties. Specifically, when following this path, nowadays business people generally have at least four viable options at their disposal:

- Plan solutions themselves — develop conceptual architectural solutions themselves based on their own, limited understanding of IT, leaving only technicalities to specialists, e.g. decide to install ERP modules from a particular vendor to automate specific tasks in a specific way and then make IT staff do it
- Create systems themselves — construct primitive "feral" IT systems with own hands, e.g. automate financial calculations using formulas in MS Excel and linked spreadsheets with some manual copy-paste steps and other contraptions
- Go to external providers — approach external partners, service companies, consultancies or other parties to implement change initiatives end-to-end, e.g. sign a contract with Accenture to plan, design and build the required IT solution
- Use cloud applications — purchase existing, ready-to-use SaaS offerings and adopt them for their needs, e.g. subscribe to Salesforce with a personal credit card and start using it immediately to take orders and interact with customers

Pursuing digital transformations without engaging enterprise architects has a number of advantages, primarily subjective to their sponsors. For instance, some options can seem obvious, fast, non-bureaucratic, straightforward and attractively cheap, especially those with cloud-based SaaS solutions. Besides that, proceeding without architects allows initiative sponsors to make planning decisions independently, at their own discretion and gives them full control over what is being implemented and how.

On the flip side, the absence of support from the community of qualified enterprise architects also poses numerous problems, mostly to organizations. For example, the very concepts of initiatives conceived by business leaders not knowledgeable in IT are likely to be suboptimal in too many aspects, e.g. naive, shortsighted, inefficient, unfit for purpose, neglective of the existing IT assets or the latest technological advancements. Various "homemade" Excel-backed calculators concocted by end users tend to be faulty, unreliable and error-prone, at times inflicting direct financial losses[2]. Solutions developed by external parties can be aligned more with the commercial interests of these parties than with the genuine interests of the organization or fail to adequately take into account the unique specifics of its internal environment. Finally, cloud applications can be simply unsafe, insecure, non-compliant with mandatory regulations and not integrable with the rest of the organizational IT landscape[3]. All in all, the systematic creation of IT solutions by business managers bypassing the IT department results in the dangerous spread of "invisible" and uncontrolled shadow IT fraught with all sorts of hazards for organizations[4].

The second alternative available to business leaders — cooperating with enterprise architects — implies inviting professional architects to drive digitalization efforts and delegating the respective duties to them. This alternative comprises all the activities of architects thoroughly described earlier in this book, from participating in the initial ideation of transformation initiatives to serving these initiatives along their lifecycle (see Figure 13.4).

The presence of competent enterprise architects around digitalization initiatives brings multiple indisputable benefits to initiative sponsors as well as to the organization at large. Most importantly, it assures certain diligence in their implementation, reduces their risks, facilitates the choice of the most suitable approaches and ensures the best possible utilization of deployed IT assets and capabilities of modern technology.

Collaborating with enterprise architects, however, is not a "free lunch" and also has some drawbacks associated with the necessity to have more meetings, share more information and balance more concerns. The involvement of architects as additional actors and stakeholders, thus, can slow the process down, cause additional complications and even introduce new obstacles on the way to realizing the change envisioned by the sponsors.

Facing the choice of whether or not to engage enterprise architects for their digitalization aspirations, business leaders can be inclined to one or the other alternative under the influence of various factors that eventually determine their preference. On the one hand, the perceived own knowledge of IT, the abundance of external providers and the accessibility of cloud solutions push managers towards proceeding on their own without architects. On the other hand, the reputation of architects as valuable business partners, their easy availability and administrative pressures to cooperate push managers towards inviting them on board and accepting their services. The two alternative ways for business leaders pursuing digitalization described above, without enterprise architects or with their involvement, with their advantages and disadvantages are illustrated in Figure 18.1.

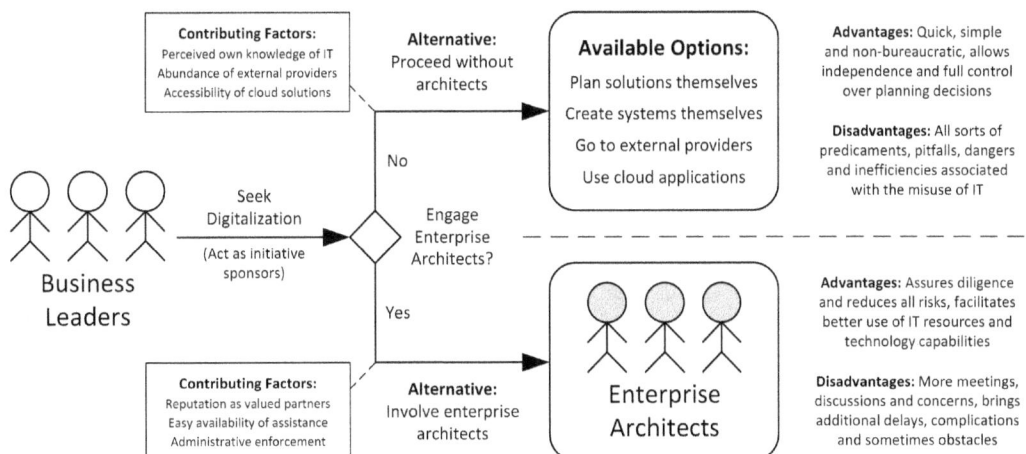

Figure 18.1. Two alternative ways for business leaders pursuing digitalization

As shown in Figure 18.1, for business leaders coming as initiative sponsors, engaging specialized enterprise architects is *not* necessary to attempt their digital transformation efforts. In fact, except for the project level where mandatory interactions with Solution Architects can be imposed administratively (see Figure 16.1), inviting architects is optional and, in many unsuccessful EA practices, their services are not demanded by managers preferring to act alone. Interestingly, the decision to involve architects is not binary, but allows many gradations manifested mainly in the difference of *stages* at which they are asked to join the discussions around initiatives.

Involvement of Enterprise Architects at Different Stages of Initiative Formation
Business leaders acting as initiative sponsors can decide to engage enterprise architects at any stage of initiative formation they consider desirable, e.g. come to architects early with a *problem* to be solved or come to them later with a *solution* to be implemented. In practice, architects can enter a decision-making process for a digitalization initiative at any point before all the necessary decisions are settled and its execution is kicked off, i.e. from the beginning of its initial ideation from transformation drivers till the end of its planning phase finishing all decision-making activities[5]. Once architects join the process at a particular stage, they normally stay in this process for all the subsequent stages as well.

The latest moment when enterprise architects can reasonably join a decision-making process for an initiative is during its planning phase. At this stage of involvement, the concept of the initiative is already formed by its sponsors; its goals, scope and general intent are tightly fixed. In other words, what needs to be done as part of the initiative has already been decided, only *how* to do it is subject to discussion[6]. In this situation, architects can only lead the development of plans for the initiative based on its existing concept (see Figure 11.2), but they cannot change the conception itself by rolling the process back[7]. Their activities in these circumstances are guided by the following question: "What is the best way to materialize the formulated concept with the use of technology?" At this stage, the decision space available to architects is severely limited and confined to the boundaries preset by the initiative concept, so that their potential influence on the future course of the initiative is actually fairly modest. For instance, they can orchestrate architectural planning to reach a consensus view of exactly how to transform the business with IT to meet the stated goals, though without being in a position to modify these goals or cancel the initiative for its suboptimal aims.

The next earlier moment when enterprise architects can join a decision-making process for an initiative is during its conception phase. At this stage of involvement, the very idea of the initiative already exists in the minds of its sponsors, but a more precise vision of its contours does not. In other words, why the initiative is needed is already clear, but *what* it should look like is subject to discussion. In this situation, architects can provide their unofficial advisory services to the initiative sponsors to shape the concept of the initiative in an optimal fashion (see Figure 10.6), but they cannot put forward an entirely new idea for change by rolling the process back. Their activities in these circumstances are guided by the following question: "Are there feasible approaches to realize the proposed idea and which one of them looks better?" At this stage, the decision space available to architects is rather restricted and bound to the original idea for the initiative with the underlying transformation drivers, so that their potential influence on the future course of the initiative is high but not unlimited. For instance, they can perform architectural pre-planning to suggest either reasonable goals, scope and impact appropriate for the basic idea, or to abandon the initiative in the case when the idea itself does not seem promising, though without being able to propose to take radically different actions or address another set of drivers.

However, the earliest possible moment when enterprise architects can join decision-making processes related to digitalization is during the initial ideation of initiatives, even *before* the emergence of specific initiatives as such. At this stage of involvement, only transformation drivers motivating the organization to change are identified by business leaders, but no solid ideas for reacting to these drivers have been formed; decision-making can be started from a "blank sheet". In other words, the very matter of *why* initiatives are needed is subject to discussion. In this situation, architects can provide their unofficial advisory services to driver proponents to generate good ideas for responding to the respective drivers with new initiatives (see Figure 10.5), molding the foundational organizational intentions for digitalization. Their activities in these circumstances are guided by the following question: "What initiatives should be launched by the organization to best react to its transformation drivers?" At this stage, the decision space available to architects is theoretically unrestricted and limited only by the boundaries of rational with respect to the motivational context, so that their potential influence on the future course of the whole organization is maximum. For instance, they can contribute their expertise and creativity to help the organization come up with truly breakthrough initiatives or simply stop the management from wasting their precious resources on initially unpromising ventures.

Generally, because more impactful planning decisions usually happen during earlier stages, the earlier enterprise architects are involved in the formation of digitalization initiatives, the more value they can bring to the organization by shaping its initiatives at more opportune moments. Conversely, the later their involvement in decision-making processes, the higher the risks that non-IT-savvy business leaders have already made some bad decisions about IT that are increasingly difficult to revert as "the train has departed", e.g. agreements with partners were signed, licenses were purchased or equipment was shipped. For example, architects joining the game at the stage of the initial ideation of initiatives with opening "why"-centric discussions represents a perfect scenario, where they can ensure the generation of the most reasonable ideas for given transformation drivers based on collective business and IT wisdom. Architects joining during the conception phase of initiatives with succeeding "what"-centric discussions represents a somewhat worse but relatively good scenario, where they can at least promote the most reasonable concepts for given ideas, even if the ideas themselves can be less than optimal. Finally, architects joining only during the planning phase of initiatives with concluding "how"-centric discussions actually represents a rather poor scenario of involvement, where they can at best develop the most reasonable plans for given concepts, even if the concepts themselves can be inexpedient and problematic. In short, initially ill-conceived transformations are likely to result in meager outcomes for organizations, regardless of the quality of their subsequent architectural planning at later stages.

For example, by the time when business sponsors invited an enterprise architect to lead the architectural planning of a digitalization initiative, they could have already made a number of fundamental decisions to introduce a concrete vendor product they know their competitor is using, to employ this product for improving particular operations they think it should target and to configure it in a specific way they believe is optimal. Furthermore, they could have already reached certain preliminary agreements with the vendor representatives regarding its procurement. However, after joining the initiative, the architect, being more proficient in IT, can conclude that the chosen product itself is far from best-in-class, that it cannot be integrated properly into the corporate IT environment and that its intended use is not fully rational, while the original need that motivated the initiative could have been addressed more easily and cheaply simply by enhancing some of the existing information systems, of which the sponsors were unaware. Nevertheless, in spite of these glaring flaws in its initial conception, the architect has to continue the initiative in line with the settled decisions and cannot renegotiate these decisions as the sponsors have already firmly made up their mind. To summarize, high-impact architecturally significant decisions taken at early stages by business managers without the due assistance of architects, when turn out unwise, often account for numerous inefficiencies during later stages that tend to multiply along with the progress of the respective initiatives[8].

Interestingly, the earlier the stage of initiative formation, the less formal the involvement of enterprise architects at this stage. For instance, the initial ideation of initiatives consists of unstructured conversations about various transformation drivers, the conception phase of initiatives involves more structured discussions around specific ideas, while their planning phase includes prearranged planning sessions (see Table 11.1). Analogously, from the standpoint of material artifacts, the process of initial ideation is purely verbal and typically does not produce any EA artifacts, the conception phase is also mostly verbal, but can generate some ad hoc papers when they are needed (see Figure 10.7), whereas the planning phase normally results in formalized architectural plans with multiple regular artifacts and auxiliary communication materials (see Figure 9.5, Figure 11.6 and Figure 11.7). Possible stages of the involvement of enterprise architects in the formation of digitalization initiatives with their properties described above are shown schematically in Figure 18.2.

Chapter 18: Challenges of Enterprise Architects

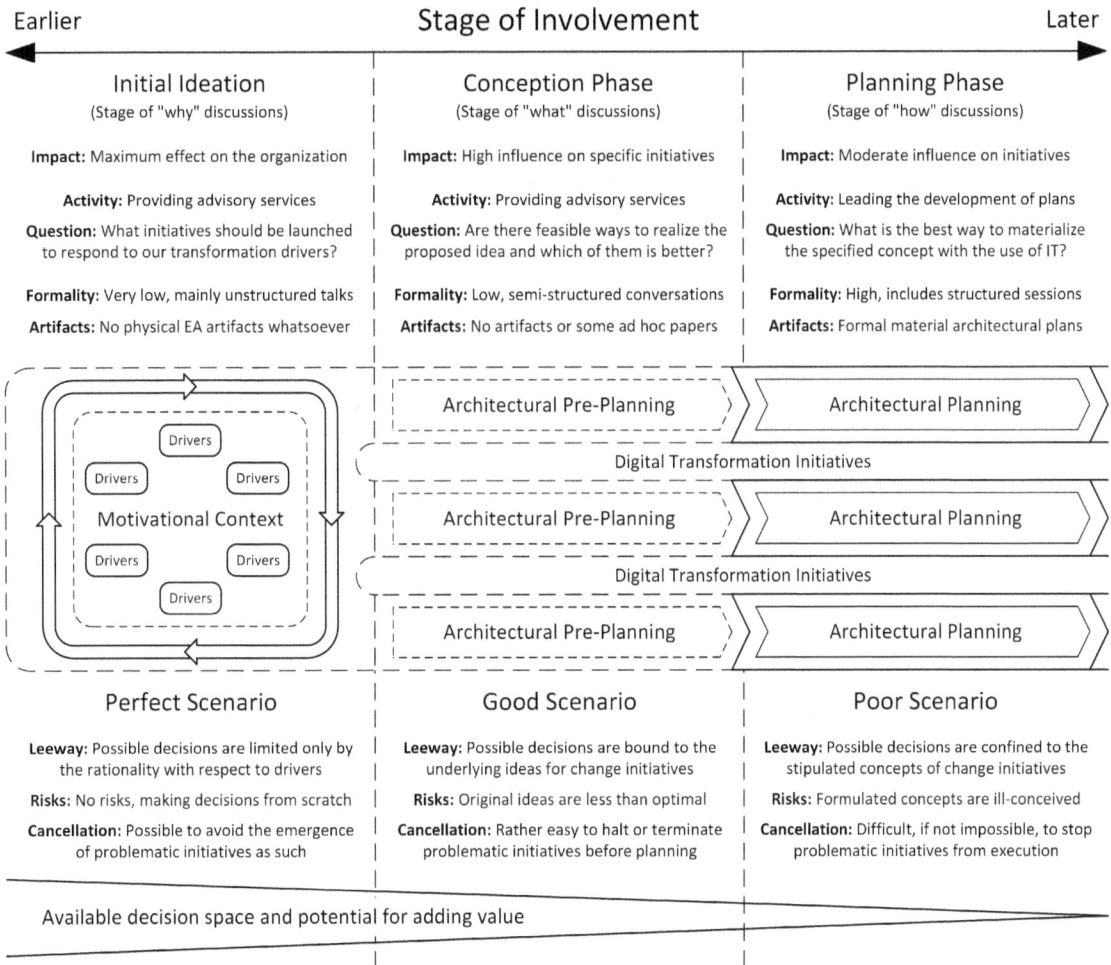

Figure 18.2. Different stages of the involvement of architects in initiative formation

As demonstrated in Figure 18.2, the maximum contribution of enterprise architects is achieved when they participate in decision-making processes around digital transformation initiatives since their earliest "embryonic" stages. For this reason, architects eager to benefit their organization have to struggle to get into the rooms where decisions on initiative formation are made as early as possible.

Early Involvement as a Practical Imperative for Enterprise Architects

As the most far-reaching planning decisions with the greatest impact on the organization and the highest risks of introducing incorrigible defects into its change initiatives are made upstream (see Figure 18.2), *early involvement* in decision-making can be regarded as both a critical success factor and an actionable practical goal for enterprise architects. To attain it, they should expand their communication networks in business groups, keep in touch with various managers to understand what is on their mind, see where new initiatives are germinating and offer their advice in a timely manner to properly frame these initiatives. By achieving wide coverage across the organization and reaching out to the very process of initial ideation that generates seminal ideas for digitalization, effective architects identify and "catch" nascent initiatives *before* they turn into actual initiatives and shape them accordingly. In a word, early involvement is imperative for architects.

As the earliest stages of initiative formation are the least formal ones (see Figure 18.2), the work of enterprise architects during these stages is extremely value-adding but largely *invisible* from an organizational point of view. For instance, for the ultimate outcomes of a transformation initiative, quick spoken advice given by architects to business sponsors in a friendly conversation over a cup of coffee at the beginning of the initiative, by virtue of its high influence on the subsequent course of action, can be as valuable as the heaps of written architectural plans produced towards the end of the process. As an activity of architects performed in the early stages of initiatives, providing advisory services is much less conspicuous organizationally than leading the development of plans, but not at all less important because it is this activity that coarsely forms the initiatives themselves and predetermines their later destiny in terms of detailed planning decisions. Put it simply, despite being a "lightweight", intangible and rather imperceptible activity, the timely provision of unofficial advisory services is crucial for the success of digitalization efforts in organizations.

Because in a personal capacity enterprise architects offer their advisory services informally, on demand of their customers (see Figure 10.5), business leaders cannot be obliged to ask architects for advice or treat their recommendations seriously, but can only choose to do so of their own free will. Whereas within the more officialized planning phase some interactions with architects can be mandated by formal organizational procedures, particularly for administratively assisted projects (see Figure 2.6), during all the earlier, unofficial stages of decision-making, especially for high-level initiatives, these interactions can only be *voluntary* for managers (see Figure 4.4). As a rule, their interactions at later stages and lower levels tend to be more formalized and mandatory, while those at earlier stages and higher levels — more informal and voluntary. For example, compliance of projects with the existing Standards can be enforced by architects administratively through established institutional channels (e.g. mandatory EA artifacts and their approvals at different control gates, see Figure 16.2), but open strategic dialog with architects about future digitalization opportunities can be initiated only from the business side. Fundamentally, the only possible way for architects to influence transformation initiatives at their formative stages is to become sought after *proactively* by their sponsors[9].

For this reason, early involvement is associated with a curious paradox largely defining the work of enterprise architects: the earlier architects are involved in the formation of digitalization initiatives, the more value they can bring, but the more difficult it is for them to get there. To resolve this paradox and secure their early involvement in decision-making, they cannot rely on an official administrative resource, but only on their own unofficial reputation as trusted business partners.

Reputation as a Critical Resource of Enterprise Architects

One of the notable attributes of architects is their public reputation and image. The **reputation of enterprise architects** is their perception in managerial circles that determines the attitude, trust and behavior towards them among decision-makers. From the viewpoint of business leaders, their reputation can be quite varied and range greatly from strongly attractive to harshly repulsive. For example, they can view architects, at best, as valued partners who can help come up with better ideas, less reverentially, as loyal servants who can materialize conceived initiatives or, at worst, as obstinate blockers capable only of creating obstacles to every sensible undertaking.

The positive reputation of enterprise architects as helpful professionals turns them into respectable organizational actors, "activates" them in the eyes of business leaders and evokes their desire to collaborate with architects, thereby inducing engagement between them. Their appealing reputation increases the total demand for their services, intensifies voluntary interactions incoming from managers and lets them enter the meeting rooms where various planning decisions are made[10]. Along with their knowledge, skills and experience, reputation can be regarded as a special, fourth, resource possessed by architects that allows them to do their job in organizations.

In particular, the reputation of enterprise architects represents arguably the most significant factor that determines whether they will be engaged by business sponsors seeking digitalization (see Figure 18.1), as well as the stage of decision-making at which they will be invited to join (see Figure 18.2). Depending on their reputation, architects can be involved as genuine business partners to assist in generating good ideas early on in the process or merely as "order takers" from IT to ensure their proper technical implementation at much later stages of the delivery chain. By contrast, when their reputation is negative or simply nonexistent, managers may not invite architects at all and intentionally reduce communication with them to the required minimum of mandatory interactions prescribed by administrative procedures, turning all cooperation with architects into the bureaucratic burden of passing roadblocks.

For this reason, the reputation of enterprise architects is actually a very dear, much-cherished and critical resource that enables their engagement with business leaders and directly defines the boundaries of potential value that they can provide to the organization. Architects, therefore, must take every available opportunity to enhance their reputation as business partners[11]. However, because different managers can form their own opinions about architects, their reputation often varies across the organization, so that some managers can appreciate their efforts much more than others, which affects the level of their engagement.

Also, the reputation of enterprise architects is not a monolithic construct, but a more complicated concept composed of three different components. Each of these components shapes their perception in the organization, but not all of them depend on the architects themselves. First, their reputation is influenced by the overall reputation of the corporate IT function to which they typically relate. Excellent or poor performance of the IT department as a whole can elevate or tarnish the image of architects as its employees. Second, their reputation is impacted by the general reputation of the architecture function to which they normally belong. The collective perception of the community of architects as sociable fellows or weird nerds naturally influences the individual perception of its separate members. Lastly, their reputation has a major personal component for which they are solely accountable. Their previous successes and failures in collaborating with particular stakeholders certainly determine these stakeholders' opinions about specific architects as welcome or unwelcome companions. Technically, different aspects of the reputation of architects in organizations can be evaluated by running internal surveys with relevant qualitative questions (e.g. asking to describe impressions) and quantitative metrics (e.g. net promoter score) about different units and people.

In any case, reputation is a very reactive and fragile resource, which takes a lot of time and effort to accumulate, but can be easily destroyed. For instance, depending on various factors, it can take up to *two years* of hard work for newly hired enterprise architects to build their reputation, become truly influential, get the necessary traction and "gain altitude". Unlike most other resources of architects, reputation is largely *non-transferable* between different people and from organization to organization. For instance, their positive reputation cannot be taken away with them from one company and then brought to another in a way similar to their skills and experience. Instead, it has to be recreated from nothing each time to achieve deep engagement with business managers in a new place of work.

General Approaches for Starting Engagement with Business Leaders

As explained above, their engagement with business leaders is induced by the reputation of enterprise architects as valuable business partners. Earning this reputation, however, requires engaging with business leaders to prove their value. The reputation, engagement and value of enterprise architects, thus, represent a classic "chicken and egg" situation and form a *positive feedback loop*. On the one hand, the better reputation of architects leads to their earlier informal involvement in initiative formation, which gives them more opportunities to confirm their value and further strengthen their reputation. On the other hand, the worse reputation of architects leads to their later, more formalized involvement in transformation initiatives, which deprives them of any opportunities to demonstrate their full worth and improve their reputation (see Figure 18.2). Due to these virtuous and vicious circles, treating architects as enablers or inhibitors can, in fact, become a self-fulfilling prophecy[12].

A somewhat closed structure of the reputation–engagement cycle makes it rather challenging for enterprise architects to get inside the cycle from the outside to start engaging with business leaders and accumulating their reputation. When no established working relationships exist between them, architects usually cannot simply go to managers for a talk without being invited or expected. Coming as unbidden strangers, they are unlikely to be welcomed and treated warmly by business representatives, so that architects are typically unable to join their inner circle straightforwardly. In short, if their engagement with the business community is lacking, it can hardly be commenced unilaterally by architects.

For this reason, the enclosed reputation–engagement cycle necessitates certain approaches for enterprise architects to start relationships with business leaders from scratch, i.e. initiate engagement in the absence of any positive reputation with them. These approaches allow architects to begin at least some dialog with managers, demonstrate their utility and signal their readiness for productive cooperation, creating a basic reputation and increasing their chances of future engagement. Metaphorically, these approaches provide the initial ignition to rev the engine from the off-state and enter the upward spiral of growing reputation and engagement. Specifically, four different approaches for starting business engagement proved helpful in practice.

First, enterprise architects can get in direct communication with business leaders by escalating the need for this communication through their senior superiors. For example, the CIO, as their most powerful ally, can ask specific business managers, possibly via their bosses, to involve architects in their discussions of particular subjects, issues or initiatives, or even to make them regular members of their discussion forums. This top-down approach to initiating engagement is rather forthright, invasive and bothersome, but effectual and gives architects some official mandate and political weight in decision processes. Unless architects report high enough and have powerful advocates in the organization capable of supporting them from above, it can be very difficult for them to access certain "evasive" stakeholders[13]. As a rule, the higher their position in the corporate hierarchy, the broader their organizational outreach and the more influential decision-makers they can approach[14].

Second, enterprise architects can get into meeting rooms with business leaders by leveraging their networking opportunities through fellow IT leaders. For example, at their request, IT managers can invite architects, as helpful associates, to their meetings with business managers, introduce them to each other and let their working relationships begin. This approach to starting engagement is rather simple, gentle and non-invasive, but does not endow architects with any official authority and can only be used to reach business representatives with whom IT management is in touch.

Third, enterprise architects can get in contact with business leaders via networking through their allies in the business community they already collaborate with. For example, business managers whom they helped previously can be pleased to invite architects, as trusted partners, to their meetings with other managers and acquaint them with architects, or simply recommend their services to colleagues as a kind of "viral marketing". This approach to initiating engagement is rather effective as it inspires trust in architects upfront, but requires having good relationships with some business people and can be used to reach only their "neighbors".

Finally, enterprise architects can take advantage of their mandatory interactions with business leaders imposed by administrative procedures for the purposes of attempting more constructive cooperation. For example, using their official meetings in architecture governance committees as a forum for communication (see Figure 12.3), architects can try to appeal to business managers in a way that piques their interest and persuade them to continue conversations unofficially. Or, during their formal interactions at the project level institutionalized along the project implementation process (see Figure 16.2), architects can try to convince managers that a more open, informal strategic dialog is badly needed. This administratively enabled approach to starting engagement is rather convenient as it does not imply any additional arrangements, but requires excellent oratory skills on the part of architects to captivate business leaders.

All the approaches described above allow initiating engagement between enterprise architects and business leaders when the former do not possess the necessary reputation to make the latter turn to them for advice. Namely, all these approaches provide some fruitful occasions for their engagement and opportunities for interaction which, if seized properly by architects for improving their reputation, can lead to future "unassisted" engagement occasions, launching the self-reinforcing cycle of accumulating reputation and deepening business engagement. However, if during these occasions architects fail to prove themselves, then their reputation can, on the contrary, suffer and this development cycle may never launch.

Generally, to raise the level of their engagement with business leaders, enterprise architects should stay closer to the business, be always present around, constantly visible to them and sincerely interested in their problems, strive for more communication and ask for earlier involvement in decision-making[15]. The conceptual reputation–engagement cycle with the role of approaches for starting engagement from scratch is depicted schematically in Figure 18.3.

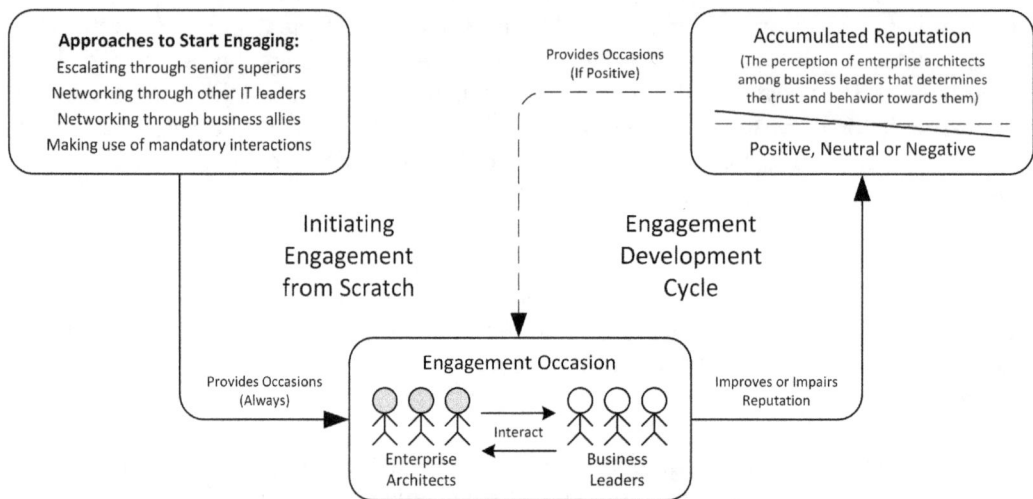

Figure 18.3. The regular cycle of accumulating reputation and developing engagement

The cycle of parallel development of reputation and engagement shown in Figure 18.3 centers around concrete engagement occasions as part of which enterprise architects exercise their capabilities and create their image as valuable business partners. However, to engage productively and bring value, architects must be able to cope with multifarious challenges related to their job.

Individual Challenges of Enterprise Architects

The work of enterprise architects in organizations is associated with numerous challenges of different sorts. Many, but not all, of these challenges closely correspond to the challenges of digital transformation that they have to confront in their job (see Figure 1.5). Some of these challenges are more subjective and attributable mostly to the nature of their occupation, whereas others are more objective and attributable mostly to the specifics of their organization[16].

The challenges of their individual performance, or simply **individual challenges of enterprise architects**, are challenges that relate directly to performing their core duties — leading architectural planning and providing other services to the organization. These challenges are caused by the immanent difficulties of architectural planning, as a multifaceted socio-technical process, and accompanying activities. They are rather obvious, absolutely normal and intrinsic to the job of architects. In some sense, addressing these challenges *is* their job. Individual challenges are subjective and can potentially be resolved by architects themselves. Since their solutions lie in the hands of architects alone, these challenges can be regarded as relatively simple.

Analogously to the resources, instruments and activities of enterprise architects (see Figure 14.2), their individual challenges can be clearly related to one of the two hats that they wear in organizations: Technology Experts and Change Agents (see Figure 4.9). In short, some of these challenges trouble Technology Experts and others — Change Agents.

Challenges of Technology Experts

Challenges encountered by enterprise architects wearing the hat of Technology Experts are primarily technical in nature. These challenges are well-known to all IT specialists, but stand more prominently specifically for architects. Because of their familiarity to everyone working with technologies, they can be viewed as fairly trivial. The challenges of Technology Experts relate mainly, but not only, to understanding complicated landscapes, tracking rapidly developing technologies and maintaining extensive technical documentation.

First, modern IT landscapes are exceedingly complex, heterogeneous and difficult to comprehend. They can be full of entangled cross-layer connections between different assets, non-obvious interdependencies and ancient legacy systems that nobody knows for sure how they work. And yet, enterprise architects need to understand their structure to be able to design robust technical solutions for transformation initiatives that modify them "on the run", without causing operational disruptions and failures. To deal with overwhelming landscape complexity, architects arguably have no other way but to be smarter, think harder and further develop their engineering mindset and systems thinking abilities.

Second, the evolution of technologies goes at a very swift pace, quickly rendering the current IT knowledge inapplicable and obsolete. The technology market constantly offers new, more powerful proprietary and open-source solutions that replace older, less efficient approaches[17]. Accordingly, enterprise architects need to keep abreast of all the pertinent technology innovations and continuously refresh their knowledge of IT to secure their own relevance. To keep up with the galloping speed of technological progress, architects should regularly devote a considerable portion of their time to studying news, reading literature and engaging in other forms of self-education to enable a continual renewal of their technical expertise.

Lastly, large volumes of documentation existing in organizations for various technical purposes, including numerous actualities EA artifacts, are not easy to handle. This documentation is often inaccurate, fragmented, outdated, contradictory, clumsy, laborious to maintain but difficult to reorganize, while specialized software tools and repositories where it is stored can be pretty sophisticated and require proper training. Notwithstanding these and other imperfections, enterprise architects need to use this documentation on a nearly everyday basis, make sense of it and update it to ensure its currency. To work with extensive technical documentation, architects should learn to collate inconsistent information from different sources, master the respective software tools and find the right balance between the granularity of descriptions and the practicality of their maintenance. Typical challenges faced by enterprise architects behaving as Technology Experts and their potential solutions described above are summarized in Table 18.1.

Challenge	Potential solutions
Understanding complex IT landscapes	Be smarter, think harder and further develop the engineering mindset and systems thinking abilities
Tracking rapidly evolving technologies	Systematically allocate time to studying news, reading literature and other forms of self-education
Handling extensive technical documentation	Learn to collate information from different sources, master the necessary tools and find the balance between granularity and maintainability

Table 18.1. Challenges of enterprise architects as Technology Experts and their solutions

The challenges of Technology Experts listed in Table 18.1 are far from specific to the job of enterprise architects, but common to many IT professionals. This conclusion, though, is not valid for the challenges of Change Agents that, of all IT professions, are rather unique to the profession of architects.

Challenges of Change Agents

Challenges encountered by enterprise architects wearing the hat of Change Agents are predominantly social in nature[18]. These challenges are unfamiliar to most IT specialists, but for architects they are truly cardinal. Because of their specificity for architects' trade, they can be viewed as quite novel. The challenges of Change Agents relate mainly, but not only, to communicating with heterogeneous audiences, visualizing complex technical information and resolving conflicting stakeholder interests.

First, in their work, enterprise architects have to communicate directly with many business and IT audiences with diverse specializations. Each audience expects them to speak their language, understand their terminology and be reasonably knowledgeable in their subjects. In spite of their apparent stringency, architects need to meet these demands to be able to develop organizational solutions for transformation initiatives appealing to all relevant audiences[19]. To cope with various communication difficulties, architects should purposefully cultivate their polyglot abilities, learn to imitate the vocabularies of their audiences, invest in studying other people's subject areas and stick to universal discussion points equally meaningful to both business and IT, e.g. business capabilities, needs and processes[20].

Second, to convey architectural decisions to different audiences, it is usually necessary to visualize them in a way intelligible and convincing to these audiences. Effective visualizations of intricate technical or semi-technical concepts, however, are difficult to create, especially when they are intended for mixed, non-specialist audiences incapable of reading sophisticated modeling notations. Nonetheless, enterprise architects need to produce EA artifacts that can be presented and discussed in different circles of decision-makers with disparate backgrounds[21]. To develop intuitive artifacts, architects should learn to shorten, simplify and tailor their message appropriately for particular audience composition, master different diagramming techniques suitable for the task at hand and use semantically transparent graphical representations and visualization patterns that are interpreted naturally by most people, e.g. unidirectional arrows for sequence or causality, containment for subcomponents and trees for hierarchies[22].

Lastly, digitalization efforts in organizations involve numerous diverse stakeholders — representatives of different corporate levels and functional areas, who can come as initiative sponsors or executors. Depending on their organizational roles, their interests in transformation initiatives can be diverging or even incompatible, especially for multi-driver initiatives with different coalitions of stakeholders promoting different drivers. In situations of conflicting, seemingly irreconcilable interests, enterprise architects need to be able to maneuver politically in a skillful fashion to somehow settle the disagreements between different constituencies and devise organizational solutions potentially acceptable to all parties[23]. To satisfy contradictory stakeholder interests, architects should develop their political shrewdness and learn to use proficiently various rhetorical tricks, methods of persuasion and conflict resolution, e.g. leaving proposed architectural plans somewhat ambiguous to allow different people to interpret them differently in their favor and accept them for their own reasons[24]. Typical challenges faced by enterprise architects behaving as Change Agents and their potential solutions described above are summarized in Table 18.2.

Challenge	Potential solutions
Communicating with very diverse audiences	Develop polyglot abilities, learn to imitate vocabularies, study other subject areas and stick to universal discussion points
Visualizing complex technical content	Learn to shorten, simplify and tailor the message, master different diagramming techniques and use highly intuitive visualization patterns
Resolving conflicting stakeholder interests	Develop political shrewdness and learn to use various rhetorical tricks, methods of persuasion and conflict resolution

Table 18.2. Challenges of enterprise architects as Change Agents and their solutions

The challenges of Change Agents listed in Table 18.2 are quite specific to enterprise architects and inherent to their occupation. In addition to these "innate" challenges, many other problems affecting the work of architects are caused by the organizational conditions in which they find themselves.

Organizational Challenges of Enterprise Architects

Individual challenges of enterprise architects can and should be solved by them to operate productively and deserve the title of accomplished architects. Unless architects can "do their homework" and cope with their personal challenges as Technology Experts and Change Agents (see Table 18.1 and Table 18.2), they cannot perform successfully, cannot benefit the organization and no decision-makers will seek their help. Their ability to manage these challenges and facilitate digital transformation efforts, however, does *not* yet automatically guarantee the demand for their services from the business side and their involvement in initiative formation. In short, overcoming individual challenges is necessary but not sufficient for succeeding as architects, achieving business engagement and influencing decision-making.

The challenges of their organizational integration into decision-making processes, or simply **organizational challenges of enterprise architects**, are challenges that do not relate to performing their core duties, but rather to *getting the opportunity* to perform them. These challenges are caused by certain structural features of organizations beyond the control of architects which prevent their participation in initiative formation, so that business leaders pursuing digitalization and acting as sponsors either involve them too late (see Figure 18.2), or do not engage them at all (see Figure 18.1). Unlike their individual challenges, organizational challenges of architects are far from obvious, can be considered abnormal and, owing to their extrinsic character, may not even depend directly on their professional qualities. Essentially, they represent pernicious organizational "pathologies" that eventually result in the exclusion of perfectly capable architects from decision-making, not allowing them to do their job.

Organizational challenges are objective with respect to enterprise architects, typically require complex organizational treatment in a top-down manner and, at an individual bottom-up level, can only be alleviated by finding some workarounds. Because they are rather intractable, often do not have any simple solutions and generally cannot be tackled by architects alone, these challenges can be regarded as really difficult. It is organizational, not individual, challenges that most seriously complicate the work of architects, at least proficient ones, sometimes undermining all their best intentions and strenuous exertions.

All organizational challenges manifest themselves largely identically, in the lack of constructive engagement between enterprise architects and business managers, when the regular reputation–engagement cycle does not start normally, does not develop further, gradually declines, frequently interrupts or even completely discontinues (see Figure 18.3). Their origins, however, can be extremely diverse and include a long list of possible underlying root causes[25]. Despite their diversity, at the highest level, these challenges can be attributed to three different factors: managerial understanding of architects, managerial desire to cooperate with them and managerial distance from them.

Challenges of Managerial Understanding

Most trivially, **challenges of managerial understanding** arise when business leaders do not fully realize who enterprise architects are and what they entail, resulting in their *unintentional* non-inclusion in decision-making. These challenges range widely from not guessing about their existence, to not knowing exactly how they work, to misperceiving their role in the organization.

First, business leaders can be simply unaware of the existence of the architecture function as such in their organization. Even when they desperately need qualified assistance in their digitalization aspirations, they do not go to enterprise architects out of ignorance and do not engage them in transformation initiatives, possibly finding support elsewhere. In these circumstances, architects are unwittingly bypassed by initiative sponsors and not given any opportunities to fulfill their primary responsibility in the organization — drive digitalization efforts. Organizationally, the problem of managerial ignorance can be addressed by advertising the architecture function internally as the right place to go for IT-related consulting services, for example, by IT executives via delivering periodic promotional presentations to the business community[26]. Individually, architects should publicly declare their presence and actively market themselves as competent internal consultants throughout the organization, e.g. send out personal emails directly to business managers inviting them for collaboration[27].

Second, business leaders can know about the existence of the architecture function in their organization, but vaguely understand the purpose of this function relative to their digitalization endeavors. They can meet enterprise architects occasionally here and there, but do not realize exactly who they are, what they do and how they can be helpful to them[28]. This confusion occurs partly because, to most people, their role seems obscure and difficult to comprehend, as mentioned earlier, while the very term "enterprise architect" is hardly intuitive, far from self-explanatory and weakly resonating with business ears[29]. In this situation, architects can also be bypassed by initiative sponsors and left aside from formative decision processes even when their expertise is immediately relevant. Organizationally, this problem can be addressed by communicating to the broader organization precisely what the architecture function does and educating business managers about its specific service offerings, for example, by creating and distributing an itemized catalog of architectural services it can provide, how and when. Individually, to combat managerial unawareness of their role, architects should explain at an interpersonal level what their work implies to introduce more clarity and transparency around their occupation[30].

Third, business leaders can keep away from enterprise architects because they lack the necessary skill set to collaborate with them. Although the bulk of the burden of enabling their collaboration in terms of using the right language and creating intuitive visualizations lies on the shoulders of architects as their individual challenges (see Table 18.2), some skills and habits for dealing with architects and interpreting EA artifacts are required from the business side as well. When these skills and habits are undeveloped or immature, managers can be somewhat afraid to engage architects for their digitalization efforts and opt to proceed without their participation. Organizationally, this problem can be approached, in one way or another, by upskilling business leaders and training them to work with architects and make sense of their artifacts. Individually, on their part, architects should do whatever they can to flatten managers' learning curve, e.g. cater to their needs by adapting to their behavior and flexibly adjusting EA artifacts.

Fourth, business leaders can be uneager to invite enterprise architects because they do not fully recognize their value for digital transformation. In other words, they can understand who architects are, but not how their work can benefit them, or simply do not believe that architects, with all their artifacts and planning exercises, can add any value at all[31]. In some organizations, such as government agencies, architecture functions can be mandated by law, so that their employees are often treated by others more as an obligation than an asset. When managers do not see their value, they will not bother to go to architects and seek their involvement in digitalization endeavors. Organizationally, this issue can be addressed by promulgating the value-adding potential of architects and publicizing various success stories with their participation. Individually, architects should prove their utility to business leaders by helping them achieve what they want, demonstrate the value of their contribution to decision-making and showcase their accomplishments through concrete initiatives.

Lastly, business leaders can have an established perception of enterprise architects and their services, but this perception can be inadequate and detrimental. Pretty often, management views architects as inferior techies, who can aid in implementing their decisions with IT, rather than as complementary equals, who can aid in shaping these decisions. Managers with this "worldview" come to architects to talk about IT solutions, not about business problems, and can be surprised or even confused to hear any broader, contextual questions from their side. In other words, they expect to have IT-centric rather than business-centric conversations[32]. With this perception of architects, business sponsors usually involve them in transformation initiatives, but only at the later stages of their formation, typically during the planning phase, by the time when the most fundamental planning decisions are already made, firmly fixed and cannot be reverted (see Figure 18.2), thereby severely capping the potential contribution of architects to their digitalization efforts. Organizationally, the misperception of architects as mere IT implementers can be corrected by positioning the architecture function specifically as a strategic business consultancy, an equal peer and ally to management. Individually, architects should also present themselves as strategic advisors capable of generating good ideas, not only materializing them, and expressly ask managers to involve them earlier in their digitalization initiatives, start with discussing their original business drivers and provide more background information. Common challenges of managerial understanding, their organizational solutions and individual workarounds described above are summarized in Table 18.3.

Challenge	Organizational solutions	Individual workarounds
No awareness of enterprise architects as such	Advertise the architecture function internally as the right place to go for IT-related consulting services	Declare their presence and market themselves as specialized internal consultants across the organization
No understanding of the role of enterprise architects	Educate the management about what the architecture function does and its specific service offerings	Explain to business leaders what their work implies and introduce more clarity around their occupation
No skills to collaborate with enterprise architects	Upskill business leaders, train them to work with architects and understand EA artifacts	Make learning easier for managers by catering to their needs, adapting to their behavior and adjusting artifacts
No recognition of the value of enterprise architects	Promulgate the value-adding potential of architects and publicize success stories with their participation	Prove their utility to business leaders, demonstrate their value and showcase their concrete accomplishments
Misperception of the role of enterprise architects	Position the architecture function as a strategic business consultancy, equal management peer and ally	Present themselves as strategic advisors, expressly ask for earlier involvement and business drivers

Table 18.3. Challenges of managerial understanding, their solutions and workarounds

Challenges listed in Table 18.3 lead to a largely unconscious exclusion of enterprise architects from decision-making by business leaders. Another group of challenges results in their perfectly conscious expulsion from decision processes.

Challenges of Managerial Desire

Most insidiously, **challenges of managerial desire** emerge when business leaders understand well who enterprise architects are, but *intentionally* prefer not to include them in decision-making. These challenges can ensue from such disparate causes as cognitive biases, time pressures, financial considerations, conflicting interests, historical experiences and attitudinal settings.

First, business leaders can disregard enterprise architects because they overrate their own knowledge of IT and feel rather self-sufficient in IT-related matters. Nowadays, many business people understand IT to varying degrees and some of them tend to exaggerate their competence to the extent that they think they are capable of making wise judgments about the best use of technology[33]. When managers presumptuously believe in their own abilities, they develop high-level architectural solutions for their digitalization initiatives themselves, often suboptimal ones, and either come to architects very late with already formed conceptual solutions in mind, or even do not come to them at all seeking assistance in their technical implementation elsewhere. Organizationally, the excessive self-confidence of business leaders in their IT expertise can be curbed by warning managers through official channels about the intricacies of IT and the dangers of misusing it. Individually, architects should also explain via personal communication with their business counterparts that the world of technology is far more complex than they think and deter them from making naive decisions about IT.

Second, business leaders can be hesitant to go to enterprise architects because architects sound too pessimistic, skeptical and disillusioning compared to external solution providers. Unlike external providers, internal architects fully realize the problems, complexities and limitations of the existing IT landscape and have no selling motive; they are more realistic, do not oversimplify the situation, do not overstate their capabilities and do not promise magical solutions or "silver bullets". For this reason, the expectations created by third parties around their proposals are usually higher than those created by own architects, while the time and cost estimations calculated by third parties are usually lower. A more alluring, "rosy" picture presented to managers by external providers discourages them from engaging internal architects who allegedly "complicate matters", though this picture is often illusory and unrealistic, the associated expectations — inflated, timelines — over-optimistic, and costs — underestimated. Organizationally, the systematic bias towards externally sourced solutions can be rectified by increasing the managerial awareness of its existence, reducing their gullibility and raising the prestige of the corporate architecture function as a more trustworthy source of expertise. Individually, architects should be honest with business leaders, promote candid dialog and do their best to meet expectations and strengthen their credibility in management circles.

Third, for various historical reasons, business leaders can have a bad opinion about enterprise architects and deliberately evade any meaningful contacts with them. Previously accumulated experience and impressions of architects as idealistic dreamers, stubborn naysayers or abstruse technicians naturally kill the desire of managers to deal with them again in the future[34]. When their reputation in the eyes of decision-makers is negative (see Figure 18.3), they are unwilling to involve architects in their digitalization endeavors, preferring to go on their own, even if newly recruited architects can actually turn out very helpful. Moreover, as noted earlier, the reputation of architects represents a three-level construct formed not only by their personal performance, but also by the overall performance of the architecture function and the IT department as a whole, so that it can be damaged by numerous factors beyond their control. Organizationally, these reputational problems can be addressed, in addition to taking other measures to prove their worth, by *renaming* architects to part with the burden of unpleasant reminiscences associated with the discredited title "enterprise architect"[35]. Individually, to restore their good reputation as valuable partners and regain personal trust, architects should always keep their word, deliver on their promise and get things done duly regardless of the circumstances.

Fourth, business leaders can pass over enterprise architects because architects are rarely available for casual talks. As perpetual communicators, they are ordinarily absent from their desks and their calendars can be fully booked with scheduled meetings for a few days ahead (see Figure 13.5). When it is difficult to snatch even a five-minute chat, short consultation or simple "yes or no" opinion from architects, business managers are likely to make decisions without resorting to their advice. The paucity of free slots in their timetables, thus, greatly impairs their informal communication with business representatives so critical for relationship building as well as for the initial formation of proper digitalization initiatives. Organizationally, the timely availability and high responsiveness of architects to those seeking their unofficial advisory services can be ensured by encouraging certain slack in their working schedules to accommodate unexpected requests. Individually, architects should avoid being overbooked and try to leave at least some space in their daily calendars unoccupied for spontaneous conversations with interested managers.

Fifth, business leaders can be disinclined to involve enterprise architects in their digitalization efforts because architects operate too slowly. Business people want to change fast, but IT is very clumsy, reactive and non-agile, so that any additional delays from the IT side are preferably avoided. When architects are overloaded with work, busy with many tasks and limited in their throughput, they cannot act quickly and their participation is likely to slow down the progress of transformation initiatives. In this situation, driven by urgency, business sponsors can reasonably vote against their inclusion in decision-making processes to move faster towards their goals[36]. Organizationally, the sluggishness of the architecture function can be addressed by increasing its capacity and "bandwidth", hiring enough staff to be able to handle the incoming demands quickly and also by prioritizing these demands rationally to ensure that the most critical initiatives are served promptly. Individually, architects should clarify the expectations of their business customers in terms of speed and do their best to respond swiftly.

Sixth, business leaders can be demotivated to ask enterprise architects for assistance because the time spent by architects on serving them is charged to their accounts. Except for the work of Solution Architects on already running projects funded from their allocated budgets (see Figure 16.1), all other architectural services have to be financed from some other sources. In other words, there are typically no dedicated budgets for funding various project-level activities taking place before the official launching of projects (i.e. during their pre-project periods), as well as all higher-order planning activities, but all these works still must be paid for by someone. When the organization obliges business sponsors to pay for the services provided to them by architects from their own pockets, managers prefer to exclude these services from the bills and rely on their own knowledge of IT for initiative formation instead. Put it simply, when architectural services consumed outside of concrete projects are paid partly or fully by their customers, their consumption declines, reducing the quality of engagement between managers and architects. Organizationally, this problem can be solved by offering all advisory and high-level planning services of the architecture function for free to their consumers, largely as a "public good", and funding them from the common IT budget as OPEX, so that business leaders can benefit from using these services whenever they are needed without paying for them. Individually, architects should try to provide their advisory services to managers covertly, making them not chargeable, possibly in their personal time, e.g. during lunches or coffee breaks.

Seventh, because enterprise architects as legitimate IT representatives advocate certain technical interests, business leaders can intentionally avoid involving architects in their transformation initiatives if their interests collide and come in conflict. When vested business interests contradict technical interests, engaging architects becomes an unattractive alternative for managers pursuing digitalization. In fact, the best interests of initiative sponsors and architects can collide in their values, scope or time (see Table 13.1), generating incompatible objectives and causing natural tensions in their possible union[37]. For example, the heads of one business division concerned mostly with their own, immediate customer requests can reasonably argue for purchasing a new CRM product well-suited specifically for their peculiar needs, whereas architects concerned with future landscape-wide efficiency can argue for adapting some of the existing CRM platforms to divisional needs instead. In this conflicting situation, business leaders are likely to choose to proceed without architects according to their valid interests, e.g. go to external providers and buy any CRM solution they wish with no disputes (see Figure 18.1)[38]. Interestingly, architects have to protect technical interests without any official power to assert them, when even their very inclusion in decision-making remains at the discretion of initiative sponsors acting in their own selfish interests, which represents one of the central conundrums of their occupation, as discussed later in Chapter 19 (Other Aspects of Enterprise Architects). Organizationally, bringing together the interests of business leaders and enterprise architects requires a complex set of concerted measures addressing their accountability structure and incentive schemes. On the one hand, positions for architects in the architecture function should be closely aligned with major business areas to minimize the conflicts of interests ensuing from different scopes of concern (see Figure 17.5 and Figure 17.6). On the other hand, incentives for managers and architects should be mutually aligned to minimize the conflicts of interests caused by different foci and time horizons. For example, to put them in the same "boat" and make them share each other's objectives, organizations can include some technical indicators (e.g. total architecture debt) as performance metrics for managers and some business indicators (e.g. annual sales volume) as performance metrics for architects. Individually, architects must, first of all, accept the fact that they can either serve the interests of business managers, or be expelled from their circle; they cannot insist on their interests. Accordingly, architects should comply with managerial demands and reduce their pressure on initiative sponsors in terms of advocating technical interests to avoid their own exclusion from decision-making. Rather, technical interests should be promoted gently, by presenting them through the lens of their positive and negative consequences for the business.

Eighth, business leaders can be reluctant to go to enterprise architects because architects are inflexible and can only propose solutions fully compliant with the existing architectural plans, e.g. included in Target States and conformant to all Standards. All transformation initiatives in the organization are implemented within its architectural context aggregating all previous decisions and plans, and ensuring their alignment with this context is an important part of architects' duties. However, when architects insist on absolute adherence to the enacted plans and permit no deviations, they can hardly meet highly specific or unusual business requirements staying exclusively within the limited zone of authorized IT solutions, for example, by picking one of the few standard applications supplied by the IT department and rejecting any alternative proposals. In these circumstances, business sponsors with non-trivial needs are likely to seek help in other places with a longer "menu" of available options or even order custom IT solutions from external partners[39]. Essentially, the inconsistency between lower-level demands conducive to local responsiveness and higher-level plans promoting global optimization represents a special form of the conflict of interests driving a wedge between managers and architects. Organizationally, the flexibility of the architecture function in reacting to idiosyncratic needs can be enhanced by providing official mechanisms, procedures and forms for handling justified deviations from plans (see Figure 12.6) and loosening the strictness of architectural oversight (see Figure 12.8). Individually, architects should clearly understand the boundaries of possible departures from plans allowed by organizational architectural oversight and act in the best stakeholder interests within these boundaries.

Ninth, business leaders can have difficulties in cooperating with enterprise architects because perfectly rational architectural solutions that architects propose can be unacceptable from the standpoint of some other non-architectural considerations. For example, initiative funding policies in organizations can define different rules as to who pays for what, often introducing additional concerns to decision-making processes, e.g. projects that pioneer the use of new technologies must pay their full price, when later projects can reuse and benefit from these technologies for free[40]. These and similar policies bring another dimension to political games around digitalization initiatives (e.g. some people invest, others enjoy returns), where the reasoning and rationality of more technocratic architects can be inconsistent with those of more organizationally savvy managers, complicating productive collaboration between them[41]. Organizationally, this problem can be addressed by making sensible ideas incoming from the architecture function also sensibly implementable, e.g. providing special funding sources for subsidizing the development of "public" assets, shared platforms and reusable components. Individually, architects should try to understand various non-architectural concerns and hidden agendas of business leaders and adapt to them.

Finally, when they are not acting as original sponsors of digitalization initiatives but their involvement in these initiatives is required as ordinary stakeholders (see Figure 2.3), business managers affected by transformation can be quite happy with the status quo and oppose any attempts to disturb it. For instance, if business owners are conservative and content with the current state of affairs in their operations, they can have no interest in modifying them, no ideas about how they can be improved, no vision for their long-term future, no desire to engage in the respective discussions and, hence, no "time" to meet with enterprise architects. Even worse, if they feel threatened by the impending changes, they can deliberately sabotage their advancement, especially when their power positions or very jobs are at risk[42]. As a result, these people are reluctant to provide their input, share their knowledge, participate duly as stakeholders and play an active role in the process of architectural planning at the invitation of architects, undermining their collaboration efforts and constructive engagement. Organizationally, the resistance to change among personnel can be addressed by fostering an innovative culture of transformation and applying other standard strategies, e.g. creating proper stimuli, securing employment and avoiding layoffs. Individually, architects should push stakeholders more actively and, to overpower their resistance, escalate the issue through senior initiative sponsors to make uncooperative managers collaborate in a top-down manner. Or, they can try to find other, more amenable stakeholders from the same area interested in the initiative and willing to cooperate. Common challenges of managerial desire, their organizational solutions and individual workarounds described above are summarized in Table 18.4.

Challenge	Organizational solutions	Individual workarounds
Overconfidence of managers in their IT expertise	Warn the management through official channels about the intricacies of IT and the dangers of misusing it	Explain to business leaders that IT is very complex and deter them from making naive decisions about it
Disillusioning realism of enterprise architects	Increase managerial bias awareness, reduce their gullibility and raise the prestige of the architecture function	Be honest with business leaders, meet expectations and strengthen their own credibility in management circles
Negative reputation of enterprise architects	In addition to other measures, rename architects to part with the discredited title "enterprise architect"	Always keep their word, deliver on their promise and get things done regardless of the circumstances
Poor time availability of enterprise architects	Encourage certain slack in the working schedules of architects to accommodate unexpected requests	Avoid being overbooked and leave some free space in the calendar for spontaneous conversations
Excessive slowness of enterprise architects	Grow the capacity of the architecture function, hire enough people and better prioritize business demands	Clarify the expectations of business customers in terms of speed and do their best to respond swiftly
Architectural services are paid for by managers	Offer most services of the architecture function for free to their customers as a public good funded by IT	Try to provide advisory services to business leaders covertly, making these services not chargeable
Conflicting interests of managers and architects	Align architecture positions with the business structure and the incentives for managers and architects	Comply with managerial demands and reduce the pressure in terms of advocating technical interests
Architects are inflexible with the existing plans	Provide mechanisms for handling justified deviations from plans and loosen the strictness of oversight	Understand the boundaries of allowed departures from plans and propose solutions within these boundaries
Non-architectural concerns of managers	Make sensible ideas incoming from the architecture function also sensibly implementable organizationally	Understand various non-architectural concerns and hidden agendas of business leaders and adapt to them
Resistance to change among stakeholders	Foster an innovative culture of transformation and apply other strategies for dealing with resistance	Push stakeholders more actively and escalate through initiative sponsors, or find more amenable stakeholders

Table 18.4. Challenges of managerial desire, their solutions and workarounds

Challenges listed in Table 18.4 lead to the exclusion of enterprise architects from decision-making for reasons subjective to business leaders. Another group of challenges results in their exclusion from decision processes for more objective reasons.

Challenges of Managerial Distance

Most excusably, **challenges of managerial distance** arise when business leaders are separated from enterprise architects by various organizational hurdles, *objectively* hindering their inclusion in decision-making. These challenges are associated with different forms of physical, mental, social and cultural detachment between managers and architects in the organization.

First, business leaders can refrain from revealing their true intentions and visions for the future to enterprise architects because they can be strictly confidential. For example, all business plans concerning potential mergers and acquisitions can be market-sensitive and subject to non-disclosure agreements, some plans can contain trade secrets or analogous commercially valuable information, while other plans can include unexpected competitive moves that must not become known to the market. Business plans of this and similar kind are normally kept private within a close circle of people for perfectly valid, often legally required reasons. When their intentions must not be prematurely divulged, business sponsors cannot involve architects as outsiders in the respective "secret" initiatives at their early stages, when various preliminary discussions take place, but only much later, when the time to materialize these initiatives comes. In these cases, architects are often presented with the fact that something important has happened and asked to deal with it, e.g. a major part of the business with the underlying IT infrastructure has been officially sold away and now needs to be disconnected from the rest of the corporate landscape. Organizationally, the problem of secret business plans can be approached by granting selective access to classified information to specific architects, possibly after their formal security clearance. At the level of individual architects, almost nothing can be done with the secrecy of plans, especially when their confidentiality is dictated by law.

Second, business leaders in organizations can frequently rotate, making it impossible for them to maintain long-lasting trustful relationships with enterprise architects. When managers move to another position or leave the company, their established partnerships with architects break off, whereas productive working ties between new management and architects take time to develop. In other words, in case of managerial change, the accumulated reputational capital of architects instantly evaporates, while the positive reputation in the eyes of new managers is slow to build. For this reason, under constant managerial turnover, often fueled by never-ending structural reforms, the chances of engaging architects by newly appointed business leaders seeking digitalization are minimized. For organizations, personnel reshufflings in their leadership teams are often caused by objective necessity and cannot be simply stopped, particularly in governmental organizations whose management can be completely replaced after every election. Individually, to partner with ever-changing leadership, architects should be persistent, incessantly promote their services in management circles and never give up their attempts to "sell" their assistance to decision-makers.

Third, business leaders can be isolated from enterprise architects by invisible communication barriers imposed by the organizational structure. Large organizations have complex structures with multiple branches and hierarchical levels, and their formal communication flows tend to mirror their administrative structure. In organizations with a strong culture of informal communication, their official structure is largely irrelevant, but in organizations without such culture it often creates significant problems for communicating across different branches and levels[43]. In other words, unwritten rules of conduct can limit people's communication circles to their immediate "neighborhood" and discourage any talks with "foreigners". Sometimes these rules can also have quite material manifestations further complicating cross-group interactions, e.g. different departments occupy different floors of the building with no card access to each other, while their management sits separately on the upper floors. In these circumstances, any cooperation between architects and business managers is inhibited, especially when they belong to different ranks of the corporate hierarchy. Organizationally, excessive horizontal compartmentalization and vertical stratification of decision-making can be addressed by embracing an open culture, stimulating informal communication beyond the official reporting structure and removing any material obstacles to free information flows, e.g. moving to open-plan workspaces[44]. Individually, architects can try to penetrate the cultural boundaries of communication formed around the administrative structure by persevering in their efforts to establish connections with the right decision-makers.

Fourth, business leaders can be detached from enterprise architects by their geographical remoteness. In geographically distributed organizations, managers of different areas and architects can be separated physically by a considerable distance, making personal contacts between them problematic and rare, while various electronic means of communication cannot fully substitute for direct face-to-face meetings[45]. Physical dispersion, thus, leads to the "out of sight, out of mind" syndrome that significantly complicates productive collaboration between architects and business stakeholders. Furthermore, if they work in different time zones, difficulties in finding mutually convenient time slots for online communication can also become a serious obstruction on the way to effective engagement. Organizationally, this issue can easily be solved by co-locating architects together with their management clientele in the same cities or even in the same office buildings. Individually, architects can only do their best to communicate through distance and time zones via regular remote calls and occasional in-person visits.

Lastly, business leaders can be unable to cooperate with enterprise architects as they speak different languages, e.g. English and Spanish. In multinational companies, their corporate centers and regional divisions are located in different countries or even continents, where different languages or dialects can be prevalent, making their internal environment multicultural and multilingual. In this setup, the native languages of architects, who tend to concentrate more around the head office, and business managers, who can be spread widely across various geographies, can be different and erect substantial communication barriers, preventing engagement between them. Organizationally, this problem can be solved by adopting an official corporate language mandatory for all senior management or hiring local architects to serve the respective areas. Individually, architects can only try to find some bilingual "translators" in the vicinity of target managers (e.g. their deputies or subordinates) to establish the dialog through them. Common challenges of managerial distance, their organizational solutions and individual workarounds described above are summarized in Table 18.5.

Challenge	Organizational solutions	Individual workarounds
Secrecy of the business intentions of managers	Provide selective access to sensitive information to specific architects through security clearance procedures	Almost nothing can be done with secrecy at an individual level
Frequent rotation of managers in positions	Reshufflings in the leadership team are often necessary and cannot be stopped	Be persistent, untiringly promote their services and never give up attempts to sell their assistance
Managers and architects are separated structurally	Embrace an open culture, stimulate informal communication and remove any obstacles to free information flows	Try to penetrate the boundaries of communication by persevering in their efforts to establish contacts
Managers and architects are separated spatially	Co-locate architects together with the business leaders they are serving in the same cities or even the same offices	Do their best to communicate at a distance via regular remote calls and occasional in-person visits
Managers and architects speak different languages	Promote an official corporate language among all business leaders or hire local architects for serving different areas	Try to find some translators in the neighborhood of target managers to establish the dialog through them

Table 18.5. Challenges of managerial distance, their solutions and workarounds

Organizational challenges of enterprise architects listed in Table 18.3, Table 18.4 and Table 18.5 are very diverse and require highly symptom-specific responses from organizations as well as their individual architects. To address these challenges, management and architects should understand why active engagement between them does not happen, identify the root causes of their condition and then take appropriate measures to eliminate them.

Chapter Summary

This chapter discussed the problem of engagement between enterprise architects and business leaders, explained the importance of their early involvement in decision-making, introduced the reputation of enterprise architects as a critical resource enabling business engagement, described individual and organizational challenges of enterprise architects, as well as approaches to dealing with them. The core message of this chapter can be summarized in the following major points:

- Business leaders pursuing digitalization can either proceed alone by devising solutions themselves, going to external providers or using cloud applications, or engage professional enterprise architects to assist them in their endeavors
- Business leaders can engage enterprise architects at any stage of initiative formation, during the ideation, conception or planning of initiatives, where earlier involvement in decision-making allows architects to bring more value
- The reputation of enterprise architects is their perception in managerial circles, which can be viewed as their special resource that determines the attitude of managers towards them, evokes their desire to cooperate and induces engagement
- In the absence of a positive reputation, enterprise architects have to reach business leaders indirectly through their superiors, colleagues, allies or administrative procedures to start the self-reinforcing reputation–engagement cycle

- Individual challenges of enterprise architects are caused by the immanent difficulties of architectural planning and related to their hats of Technology Experts (complexity issues) and Change Agents (communication issues)
- Challenges of managerial understanding arise when managers do not guess about the existence of enterprise architects, do not know how they work or misperceive their role, resulting in their unintentional non-inclusion in decision-making
- Challenges of managerial desire emerge when managers, because of their cognitive biases, time pressures, conflicting interests, attitudes or other reasons, intentionally prefer not to include enterprise architects in decision-making
- Challenges of managerial distance arise when managers are physically, mentally, socially or culturally detached from enterprise architects by various organizational hurdles, objectively hindering their inclusion in decision-making

Chapter 19: Other Aspects of Enterprise Architects

The previous chapters provided an all-rounded coverage of enterprise architects as the agents of digital transformation with their occupation and paraphernalia. This final chapter addresses a number of important miscellaneous questions pertinent to enterprise architects that remained without proper answers throughout the book. In particular, this chapter begins with describing the typical career paths of enterprise architects in the industry and explaining how one can become an enterprise architect. Then, this chapter discusses several popular topics, including modeling languages, software tools, EA frameworks and professional certifications, and explains their relevance to the work and careers of enterprise architects. Lastly, this chapter analyzes the core conundrums of enterprise architects and proposes possible coping strategies for dealing with them.

Career Paths of Enterprise Architects

To be able to perform their duties in organizations, enterprise architects possess very diversified resources that include broad knowledge, rich skill base and extensive experience. All these resources cannot be possessed by entry-level specialists coming into the labor market, nor can they be acquired quickly on purpose with the view of finding a job as an architect. Instead, the necessary resources have to be accumulated gradually, over long and often branchy career paths eventually leading to employment as architects.

Organizationally, enterprise architects typically reside within the IT department and the bulk of their knowledge relates to IT. Unsurprisingly, their career paths usually start from the positions of ordinary IT specialists of different profiles, e.g. software developers, database administrators, infrastructure engineers and security analysts. After maturing professionally in terms of their technology expertise, they normally progress to more senior IT specialists, such as technical leads, team leads, system designers or subject-matter experts[1].

At the next stage of their career, if IT specialists decide to grow specifically into architects, they need to broaden their IT knowledge, gain some business knowledge, improve disciplined thinking and, most importantly, develop all sorts of communication skills[2]. Following this path, IT specialists reach their first architecture positions, typically corresponding to the archetype of Solution Architects, where they still stay close to technology and interact directly with project teams building IT systems (see Figure 16.1). In this case, their domain specialization as architects reflects, but also widens, their previous technical subject areas, e.g. frontend and backend developers embrace the applications domain, while network and cloud engineers — the infrastructure domain (see Table 16.1).

Then, if Solution Architects decide to continue their professional evolution as architects, they need to extend their business knowledge, master communication skills, enhance political sagacity and, somewhat surprisingly, partly *relinquish* their IT background[3]. Following this path, Solution Architects reach more advanced architecture positions, typically corresponding to the archetype of Enterprise Architects[4], where they deal more with *organizational* rather than technical issues and no longer connect with project teams (see Figure 15.1). In this case, their domain specialization further blurs their original areas of expertise, e.g. architects specializing in one domain uplift their competence in adjacent domains (see Table 15.1).

Interestingly, because the work of Enterprise Architects is pretty distant from technicalities, occasionally these positions can also be reached "from the outside" by IT-savvy *business* managers having no deep technical background, but seriously interested in technology. To make this career leap, they need to invest significant efforts in understanding the realm of IT at the required level[5]. For architects of "business ancestry", their domain specialization usually covers some of the functional domains shaping business capabilities of information systems. However, in practice, the transitions of business managers into architecture positions are rather exotic and happen relatively rarely, so that the overwhelming majority of Enterprise Architects originate squarely from IT[6], growing out of accomplished Solution Architects[7].

Fundamentally, for classic IT specialists passionate about technology, fascinated with complex technical tasks and wearing the hat of Technology Experts, the journey of their transformation into full-fledged architects is the journey of donning the new hat of Change Agents, which is quite alien to them, but absolutely necessary for cooperating with business leaders on the organizational side of architectural planning[8]. For this reason, some people confusingly argue that being an architect "is not about IT at all", presumably meaning only that *converting* into an architect does not imply developing any IT-related proficiencies and, at the same time, forgetting that the existing IT background does not disappear during the conversion and is also equally essential for the job.

The end-to-end transformation journey from junior IT specialists to Solution Architects to Enterprise Architects is neither fast nor easy. To accumulate the necessary resources, they have to pass through a number of technical or semi-technical roles and master each of these roles by spending several years in the role and participating in multiple projects in the respective capacity[9]. On average, it takes about ten years of full-time employment in the industry to reach the positions of Solution Architects and then another ten years for the positions of Enterprise Architects (see Figure 16.5 and Figure 15.8 respectively). No one can expect to turn into an Enterprise Architect quickly, let alone straight after graduating from a university, no matter how smart[10].

Since transforming from mere IT specialists to architects requires profound changes in attitude and reorientation from technology to communication, this transformation journey may not be attractive to everyone. In fact, many IT specialists throughout their entire careers prefer to continue working with technologies, reading documentation and enjoying the inherent rationality of the IT world, rather than switching to working with people, sitting in endless meetings and dealing with the vagaries of organizational decision-making. These people either choose not to transform into architects at all, or go only halfway by evolving into Solution Architects without having any intentions to develop further into Enterprise Architects to keep in touch with technology[11].

As for the next career moves of Enterprise Architects, because their occupation is incredibly versatile, well-paid and offers plenty of opportunities for self-development, many people reaching this stage opt to stay within the profession for long, often till their retirement[12]. However, for those of them who want to continue their career growth, the primary option is to seek senior IT management roles, up to CIOs[13]. If Enterprise Architects decide to progress to IT leaders, they need to acquire or improve a wide range of managerial skills, abilities and competencies. Following this path, Enterprise Architects reach their first IT leadership positions, where they face the whole gamut of IT management problems, much broader than just familiar architectural issues. In this case, they largely exchange their two hats of Technology Experts and Change Agents for other hats relevant to managers, which are out of the scope of this book and not discussed here. The typical and untypical stages in the career paths of enterprise architects described above are depicted schematically in Figure 19.1.

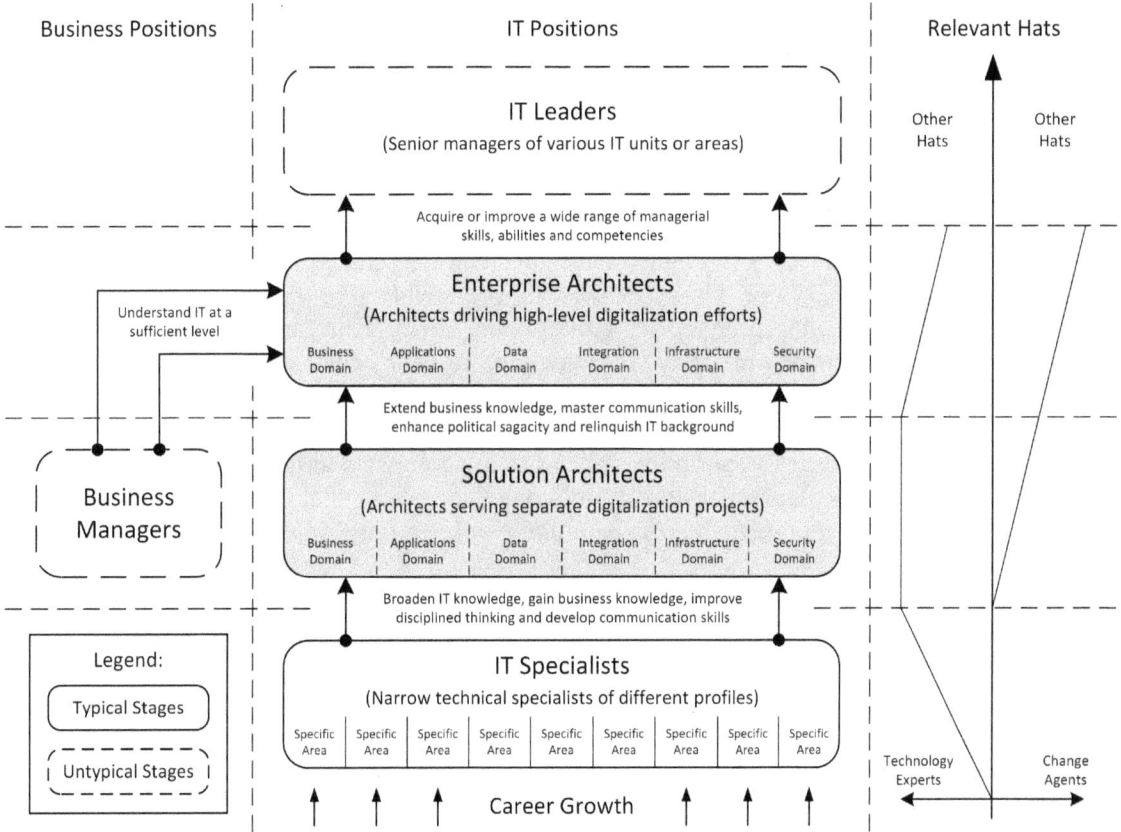

Figure 19.1. Possible stages in the career paths of enterprise architects

All the career steps shown in Figure 19.1 require the acquisition of specific resources by prospective enterprise architects to accomplish the respective transitions. This fact understandably raises questions about the best approaches to acquiring these resources and becoming an architect.

How to Become an Enterprise Architect?

To become a successful enterprise architect, one must gather all the necessary resources by progressing along certain career paths (see Figure 19.1). Gathering these resources, however, is easier said than done because of their two distinctive features that complicate the process. On the one hand, different classes of resources — knowledge, skills and experience — are acquirable by different means and require quite different efforts on the part of aspiring architects (see Figure 6.3). On the other hand, each of these resources is difficult to define precisely, measure the progress in its acquisition and determine when it can be considered acquired.

First, knowledge, as an explicit form of information, is perfectly acquirable in a comparatively straightforward manner through traditional self-education, by reading various materials, attending courses and listening to others. Accumulating this resource is largely equivalent to performing two of the basic activities of architects: analyzing the external environment and studying the internal environment, using the respective means discussed in detail earlier (see Figure 13.3). Accordingly, to turn into architects, ambitious practitioners should persistently invest in learning to deepen and broaden their understanding of different areas of business and IT, e.g. read a lot about technology, actively inquire about their organization's business, network with more senior colleagues, get an MBA degree and some professional certificates discussed later in this chapter[14].

Second, skills, as a tacit form of information, cannot be acquired "theoretically" in a way similar to knowledge, but only through diving into real-life settings, by doing work, imitating others or being coached. For IT specialists in pre-architecture positions external to the community of architects, the primary available option to partly accumulate this resource is to watch seasoned architects at work, pay close attention to their habits and learn the tricks of the trade from their behavior, e.g. how they speak with different audiences, what presentations they give to "sell" solutions and what visualizations they create to explain complex ideas. Besides that, they should always seek opportunities for assisting architects in their work, contributing to EA artifacts and possible apprenticeships to improve their practical skills. In many respects, the architecture community represents a *craftsman guild* with the only way to master their craft is to join the guild[15].

Third, experience, as a heuristic form of information, can only be acquired through long-term practice, by living an active working life and interacting with others doing so. As the famous adage says, "Nothing can substitute experience"[16]; there are no shortcuts to accumulating this resource. Empirically, it can take around 8–12 years of mindful practice for an IT practitioner to qualify for the initial architecture positions of Solution Architects (see Figure 16.5). Nonetheless, to grow into architects, practitioners should try to enrich and diversify their experience by working in different positions, projects, organizations and industries with different technologies, systems and products to avoid repeating the same experience over and over again for many years, delaying the progress in their professional development.

At the same time, none of these three resources can be described with high precision. Although broad categories of knowledge possessed by enterprise architects are easy to outline (see Figure 6.1), it is very difficult, if not impossible, to formulate exactly what should be known within these categories. Analogously, major groups of skills necessary for architects are well-understood (see Figure 6.2), but they can hardly be reduced to a detailed list of testable practical abilities. Even worse, the baggage of experience required for architects can only be characterized by adjectives similar to "extensive", but not broken down into concrete mandatory components; everything is situation-specific. If anything can be stated positively, it is only that their resources are vast, each resource is indistinct, all of them are indispensable, but none of them is dominant.

This ambiguity in the resources of architects does not allow creating any objective criteria, reliable measures or itemized checklists even for clearly specifying these resources, let alone for their quantitative assessment[17]. For this reason, it is never possible to tell for sure whether one is capable of performing as an architect before actually trying to perform.

These features of their resources unequivocally suggest that enterprise architects *cannot* be prepared for real-life work to any satisfactory extent in the classroom, whether in classic universities or specialized training centers[18]. University programs and industry courses can teach practitioners, at best, only relevant explicit knowledge[19], but they cannot teach them skills, or tacit knowledge, that require full immersion in practice, not to mention experience[20]. For architects, the bulk of their profession is an art and craft that must be mastered practically, not a science that can be studied theoretically (see Figure 14.3). Contrary to the irresponsible promises to produce ready-to-work architects straight from the training courses disseminated by various for-profit education providers[21], in reality, proficient architects can only emerge in "natural conditions". Unsurprisingly, most of the pioneering university programs for enterprise architects at first accepted by the industry with great enthusiasm soon withered or were eventually discontinued[22].

From the standpoint of their education, enterprise architects highly resemble general managers, whose job relies mainly on behavioral skills that cannot be acquired in the classroom. Although some theoretical basis and necessary knowledge can (and should) be taught to them in the university, the most important, practical part of their "education" happens hands-on, right at the workplace[23]. As the job of architects is more codifiable than that of managers (see Figure 14.1), a formal educational component in their training can be more significant, but truly competent architects still can only be grown in organizations.

However, unlike managers, enterprise architects are not omnipresent across the industry. Not in every organization can IT specialists observe "live" architects, learn from their behavior, participate in their activities and enjoy their mentorship to be able to develop the respective skills. Moreover, in contrast to administrative hierarchies providing an overall institutional context and specific managerial positions for the work of managers, EA practices and architecture functions that provide an institutional context and architecture positions for the work of architects are also not ubiquitous. In the absence of an established EA practice, IT specialists cannot be appointed as or promoted to architects, even if they gather all the necessary resources in terms of knowledge, skills and experience; an EA practice with its decision processes, governance bodies and supporting tools should be officially instituted in the organization first[24]. Simply put, competent architects can only be grown in the *right* organizations — those with institutionalized EA practices in place.

For all the reasons explicated above, the following general advice can be given to IT specialists eager to become enterprise architects in the future: besides engaging in other forms of professional self-development intended to expand knowledge and enrich experience, find a job in an organization *with a mature EA practice* to see real architects at work, boost the development of skills and have the prospects of transitioning into an architecture position.

What Enterprise Architects Should Know About...

A number of "classic" topics particularly often stand out in the industry discourse surrounding enterprise architects and their occupation. Due to their prominence, they require clarity on their actual relevance to the job of architects. These topics include modeling languages, software tools, EA frameworks and professional certifications.

Modeling Languages

Modeling languages represents a major topic widely discussed in relation to the work of enterprise architects in organizations[25]. Indeed, the use of specialized languages for enterprise architecture (e.g. ArchiMate and ARIS) and partly other "adjacent" languages (e.g. UML and BPMN) is routinely attributed to architects. The reality around the role of formal modeling languages and notations in their work can be summarized in three key facts.

First, because using any non-trivial modeling languages requires special training, they can be understandable only to IT professionals, or even only to architects themselves, and are generally *unsuitable* for communicating with business representatives, e.g. negotiating proposed architectural solutions during the planning process (see Figure 11.3)[26]. For this reason, formalized modeling approaches are simply *irrelevant* to the central duties of architects, especially those pertaining to Change Agents and their typical challenges (see Table 18.2).

Second, because modeling languages offer certain common unambiguous "vocabulary" to educated specialists, they can be used advantageously by architects for communication, storage and exchange of technical or semi-technical information within narrow professional circles, e.g. depicting the existing or planned structure of the IT landscape (see Figure 8.11)[27]. For this reason, standardized graphical notations are relevant to some duties of architects, predominantly those pertaining to Technology Experts and their typical challenges (see Table 18.1).

Third, in practice, most organizations and architects do *not* use any particular "branded" modeling languages in a systematic fashion, though individual architects can certainly choose to utilize some languages in some form for some purposes, e.g. prefer to use simplified UML in their technical Designs when appropriate (see Figure 8.16)[28]. For this reason, using specialized diagramming conventions is always optional, stays at the discretion of architects and cannot be considered necessary for doing their job.

Therefore, the overall importance of "proper" modeling in the occupation of enterprise architects should not be exaggerated. Architects can be highly successful as powerful agents of digital transformation without resorting to any graphical notations more sophisticated than plain "boxes and arrows".

Software Tools

Software tools represents a prominent topic frequently discussed in connection with the work of enterprise architects in organizations[29]. Specialized tools for enterprise architecture (e.g. BOC Group ADOIT and Capsifi Jalapeno) and, to a much lesser extent, general-purpose tools (e.g. Microsoft Office and Google Docs) are often viewed as essential "equipment" of architects. The reality around the role of various software tools and applications in their work can be best summarized in three key facts.

First, because the job of architects is inherently collaborative in nature, the most critical software tools necessary for fulfilling their duties are *collaboration tools* enabling communication and cooperation between multiple people, and particularly MS PowerPoint, or some of its analogs, for supporting collective meetings and decision-making with informative presentation packs[30]. Of their two hats, these tools are indispensable primarily for architects acting as Change Agents and dealing with the respective communication-related challenges.

Second, because the job of architects requires taming the complexity of the business and IT landscape, EA-specific tools with their data repositories and analytical capabilities can be of great value to them, especially in large organizations, though their use is still optional[31]. Of their two hats, these tools are beneficial mainly for architects acting as Technology Experts and dealing with the respective complexity-induced challenges.

Third, in practice, architects employ different software tools for different purposes in their job — most typically simple sketching, drawing and presentation tools for discussing architectural plans and complicated EA-specific tools for managing current-state information[32]. No single tool can satisfy all their needs. For this reason, their toolkits tend to include a wide array of instruments, ranging from commonplace MS Office applications to highly specialized software products, and architects should be skilled with all these tools to operate productively[33].

Therefore, proper tooling is definitely important for the successful performance of enterprise architects. However, tools are only tools and cannot substitute for any of their regular resources, such as knowledge, skills and experience, as well as for their positive reputation with business leaders (see Figure 18.3).

Enterprise Architecture Frameworks

EA frameworks represents a notorious topic very strongly associated with the very discipline of enterprise architecture[34]. In fact, TOGAF, Zachman, FEAF, DoDAF and many other similar frameworks emerged on the wave of hype around enterprise architecture during the 2000s and since then have been permanently present in the industry, causing intense speculations about their relationship to the work of enterprise architects in organizations[35]. The reality around the role of well-known EA frameworks and methodologies in their work can be summarized in three key facts.

First, contrary to their aggressive promotion as "best practices"[36], there is no evidence indicating that any of the famous EA frameworks ever worked successfully anywhere as actionable guidance[37]. Quite the opposite, these frameworks actually have only a documented track record of *failures*, often spectacular ones, even in the organizations for which they were originally developed, e.g. FEAF failed in the U.S. federal government[38] and DoDAF — in the Department of Defense[39]. On this basis, EA frameworks can be fairly regarded as the *antipatterns* of behavior for architects embodying proven *worst* practices.

Second, any observable overlap between the suggestions of EA frameworks and real best practices is purely *coincidental* and unsystematic. However, being "interpreted correctly" in hindsight, their suggestions can fit virtually any sensible activities, in the same way in which vaguely formulated horoscopes can fit any personality[40]. For this reason, it is always possible for framework proponents to argue that whatever was done was done according to their suggestions, but never possible for architects to figure out what needs to be done based on their suggestions.

Third, most organizations and architects do not use EA frameworks even declaratively[41], while those few who declare their usage use them purely symbolically, as labels, markers and badges, without actually following their prescriptions[42]. In either case, their planning efforts do not correlate seriously with the recipes of frameworks. For this reason, in defiance of numerous marketing claims[43], aspiring and practicing architects can safely ignore their existence and avoid studying them.

In summary, despite their amazing popularity in the mainstream discourse, EA frameworks have nothing to offer to enterprise architects, except for accidental good ideas randomly strewn in their texts. They contain no consistent knowledge and resemble architectural planning only haphazardly. Sober architects should not fool themselves, and not let others fool them, with EA frameworks and should not try to stick to their recommendations, viewing them as curious management fads, but never as practical guidance[44].

Professional Certifications

Professional certifications represents a noteworthy topic periodically discussed in relation to the occupation of enterprise architects. These certifications are offered by various bodies and either cover specific subjects relevant to architects, such as concrete technologies (e.g. Professional Cloud Architect from Google), modeling languages (e.g. ArchiMate from The Open Group) and EA frameworks (e.g. TOGAF also from The Open Group), or are based on a general assessment of their practical experience to confirm their professional abilities (e.g. Certified IT Architect from Iasa Global)[45]. The reality around the role of professional courses and certificates in their careers can be best summarized in three key facts.

First, because certification programs in technologies are normally provided by their vendors genuinely interested in their proper use and focus on easily verifiable "hard" skills, they can be considered as both authoritative sources and veritable attestations of general IT-related knowledge necessary for architects. For this reason, from the standpoint of professional growth, technology certifications are undoubtedly valuable to architects, though chiefly to Technology Experts designing technical solutions.

Second, because non-technological certifications are peddled by different parties with questionable interests and often target elusive "soft" skills, they vary greatly in their quality and range from decent but not developmental affirmations (e.g. experience-based assessments) to largely innocuous trinkets (e.g. modeling languages) to deceptive pseudo-education (e.g. EA frameworks). For this reason, in terms of genuine professional growth, these certifications can hardly be valuable in any real sense or teach aspiring architects how to do their work but, if taken naively, can lead to major confusion as to what this work might look like in practice. It is also important to realize that because the conduct of architects is highly contextual and can be codified only loosely (see Figure 14.1), even the most "ideal" (currently nonexistent) developmental certifications cannot possibly ensure their proficiency, which requires years of practice, as discussed earlier.

Third, in the labor market for architects, being certified is *not* a necessary condition for finding a job[46]. Nonetheless, any officially recognized certificates, irrespective of their quality and actual educational value, can benefit architects symbolically, by signaling their desire to grow professionally and their willingness to engage in self-development, increasing their chances of promotion or salary premium. Or, certificates can make job candidates look more attractive to hiring managers and help them pass through initial screening procedures, enhancing their odds of good employment. For example, the most sought-after TOGAF certification[47], despite giving no meaningful knowledge but only emblematic badges in resumes[48], still provides certain pragmatic advantages to its holders[49] and, in some circles, is even regarded as an expensive "entry ticket" to the profession[50]. Unsurprisingly, certifications are often pursued by architects for multiple valid reasons unrelated to becoming more competent.

Therefore, getting certified is *not* required for enterprise architects as they can succeed in effecting digital transformation as "autodidacts", without any formal professional education or degrees[51]. However, various certificates can be obtained selectively: some for genuine technical expertise, some for prestige among colleagues and others for the sake of purely rational career-building purposes.

Conundrums of Enterprise Architects

The work of enterprise architects is associated with a number of inescapable conundrums — irresolvable contradictions intrinsic to their occupation[52]. Due to their pervasive influence on architects, they need to be clearly articulated, acknowledged as a perfectly normal part of their job and discussed from the standpoint of possible strategies for dealing with them. These conundrums include reasoning through superficiality, deciding under uncertainty and influencing without power.

Reasoning Through Superficiality

First, as enterprise architects advance in their careers (see Figure 19.1), their knowledge becomes broader and broader in both business and IT aspects. At the same time, on the flip side, their knowledge also inevitably becomes more and more *superficial*, so that they gradually lose touch with the details of whatever they handle[53]. Moreover, because the IT domain evolves very quickly, by the time they reach professional maturity as architects, even those technologies that they mastered in the past as practicing IT specialists are likely to become obsolete, breaking their last solid connection with technicalities.

Fundamentally, the knowledge horizon of enterprise architects is so extensive and the pace of change is so fast that nobody can expect to learn everything that can be important or has enough time to keep up with all the relevant updates. As a result, for their inability to be omniscient, sooner or later architects have to leave their comfort zone of in-depth understanding and, in their judgments, start *somehow* relying on increasingly incomplete, approximate or purely conceptual knowledge, if not sheer speculations, while realizing the concomitant dangers (though, their understanding of IT still remains much deeper compared to other people of their rank).

The meaning of the conundrum of superficiality can be summarized in the following question: "How to reason sensibly when available knowledge is superficial?" This question has no good answer, but all enterprise architects face it. As a possible coping strategy, they can try to set a certain internal threshold of confidence in their own knowledge, where all knowledge above this threshold can be considered reliable for making judgments and all knowledge below it — unreliable and subject to further studies.

Deciding Under Uncertainty

Second, because the lifecycles of systems and especially technologies in corporate IT landscapes often exceed a decade, any decisions concerning their introduction represent serious long-term commitments for organizations with potentially critical implications. At the same time, the future in terms of both business demands and technology developments is very *uncertain*, unknown and unknowable; all the risks associated with adopting, or not adopting, new technologies cannot be assessed.

In these circumstances, enterprise architects are forced to make "fateful", far-reaching technical choices in spite of the unpredictability of their ultimate consequences[54]. For example, technologies, products and vendors selected today can put the organization in a very disadvantageous position in five years' time (e.g. turn into a burdensome, toxic legacy) or, on the contrary, prove remarkably successful (e.g. become truly strategic IT assets), but these scenarios cannot be foreseen at the time of their selection. And yet, architects have to decide now, *somehow*, in a non-random, intendedly rational manner, as to what solutions should be preferred without knowing what surprises the future will bring.

The meaning of the conundrum of uncertainty can be summarized in the following question: "How to make future-proof decisions when the future is uncertain?" This question has no definite answer, but all enterprise architects confront it. As a possible coping strategy, they can try to make decisions based solely on the best presently available information and the extrapolation of current trends, treating other factors as pure luck and safely ignoring them as completely unpredictable.

Influencing Without Power

Third, as part of their work in organizations, enterprise architects must advocate technical interests, such as simplification, harmonization and deduplication, to enable the sustainable evolution of their IT landscapes in the long run — interests that too often contradict immediate business interests in many ways (see Table 13.1). At the same time, they are largely *powerless* actors and even their very inclusion in decision-making is mostly a prerogative of business leaders pursuing their own interests (see Figure 18.1).

To be involved in decision processes, enterprise architects need to serve business interests, whereas any attempts to insist on technical interests on their part are likely to result in their conflict with management and subsequent expulsion from decision-making circles as undesirable assistants (see Table 18.4). Put it simply, either they cater to the interests of business managers, or they are not invited to participate at all, so that they cannot claim their technical interests upfront. In this predicament, architects have to balance *somehow* their service to business interests and their advocacy of technical interests to stay within decision processes but promote technically optimal solutions.

The meaning of the conundrum of powerlessness can be summarized in the following question: "How to protect technical interests without official power to assert them?" This question has no specific answer, but all enterprise architects encounter it. As a possible coping strategy, they can try to walk the thin line between, on the one hand, gratifying business interests at the expense of neglecting technical interests and, on the other hand, defending technical interests up to their exclusion from decision-making. In other words, they can respect business interests strongly enough to secure their involvement in decision processes and simultaneously push technical interests mildly enough to avoid their removal from these processes.

Enterprise Architects as an Intriguing Profession

These and other, less prominent conundrums make the job of enterprise architects nothing like dull routine. Their fundamental insolubility offers an inexhaustible source of puzzles, challenges and quandaries, as well as a vast field for personal ingenuity and creativity of all sorts. The irresolvable conundrums of enterprise architects and their potential coping strategies described above are summarized in Table 19.1.

Conundrum	Meaning	Possible coping strategy
Reasoning through superficiality	How to reason sensibly when available knowledge is superficial?	Set an internal threshold of confidence in their knowledge and consider all knowledge above this threshold as reliable, otherwise — as unreliable
Deciding under uncertainty	How to make future-proof decisions when the future is uncertain?	Make decisions based solely on the best currently available information, treating other factors as luck and ignoring them as unpredictable
Influencing without power	How to protect technical interests without official power to assert them?	Respect business interests strongly enough to secure their involvement in decision-making and push technical interests mildly enough to avoid their exclusion

Table 19.1. Irresolvable conundrums of enterprise architects and their coping strategies

All the conundrums listed in Table 19.1 are integral to the work of enterprise architects in organizations[55]. Because these conundrums are conceptually unsolvable and the respective questions have no "right" answers, architects should invent their own individual approaches to (somehow) dealing with them and succeeding with digitalization efforts despite their presence. Perhaps, these conundrums provide yet another reason why their profession is so interesting, intriguing and exciting!

Chapter Summary

This chapter described the most typical career paths of enterprise architects in the industry, explained how to become an enterprise architect, discussed the role of modeling languages, software tools, EA frameworks and professional certifications in the occupation and careers of enterprise architects and introduced their existential conundrums. The key message of this chapter can be summarized in the following essential points:

- Usually, architects begin their careers as IT specialists, then progress to Solution Architects and finally to Enterprise Architects by going through a series of technical or semi-technical positions and accumulating the necessary resources
- To become enterprise architects, besides engaging in other forms of professional self-development intended to expand knowledge and enrich experience, aspiring IT specialists should get a job in an organization with a mature EA practice
- Modeling languages with formal semantics are completely useless for enterprise architects as Change Agents, but can be rather helpful for architects as Technology Experts, though generally their use is always discretionary

- Software tools most critical for enterprise architects are collaboration tools, especially for Change Agents, and EA-specific tools can also be very useful, mostly to Technology Experts, whereas in practice they use many different tools
- EA frameworks never worked successfully as actionable guidance, any overlap between their suggestions and real best practices is coincidental and their use is always purely declarative, so that enterprise architects can safely ignore them
- Professional certifications in technologies are valuable to enterprise architects, mainly to Technology Experts, while non-technological certifications can hardly be valuable for genuine professional growth, but any official certificates can still bring symbolic benefits to architects for the purposes of career-building
- The work of enterprise architects is associated with a number of conundrums, including reasoning through superficiality, deciding under uncertainty and influencing without power, that cannot be resolved, but only somehow alleviated

Afterword

This book represents a determined effort to close a long-standing gap in the literature and provide a comprehensive, end-to-end description of enterprise architects, as highly relevant and demanded industry professionals driving digital transformation in organizations. The book covered in fair detail arguably all important aspects of their occupation and directly answered the most central questions about them: who they are as personalities, what resources they possess, what instruments they employ, what activities they perform, how they work in different contexts and what challenges they face. Hopefully, the book has shed some light on their shadowy craft and greatly elucidated its meaning to the readers.

At the time of writing, this book has no analogs on the bookshelves and represents essentially the first systematic, evidence-based and exhaustive information source devoted specifically to enterprise architects and their job in organizations. The very act of its publication marks a significant milestone in their profession and intends, among other things, to acknowledge the starring role of architects in the age of digital transformation and put them right in the limelight of public attention. Therefore, it is also my hope that the book will cause a new wave of interest in enterprise architects, revitalize the industry discourse around their occupation, boost their professional education and otherwise do a good service to the generations of aspiring and experienced practitioners.

As this book was completed in parallel with ongoing research activities, it can actually be viewed as a work in progress and subject to future enhancements. In other words, it represents only the current snapshot of knowledge on enterprise architects that is likely to be enriched and extended along with the advancement of my studies. For this reason, any kind of feedback from the architecture community, whether critical or appreciative, is very welcome. Negative feedback will reveal existing flaws, highlight unintended omissions and suggest opportunities for improvement. Positive feedback will strengthen my morale, increase my enthusiasm and motivate me to prepare the second updated edition of this book!

Best regards,
Svyatoslav Kotusev (kotusev@kotusev.com)

Notes

Foreword

[1] As Unde (2008, p. 7) explains, "What architects do is a mystery to much of the world — this is hardly surprising since an architect's work is intangible — "thought-ware", if you will — and it happens in the background. That makes many wonder about the architect's role in an organization". Interestingly, the same observation is also made by McBride (2007, p. 75) even about the simpler role of software architects: "In teaching software architecture and working as a software architect, database architect, and chief architect, I have often found that an unfortunate lack of knowledge surrounds the architect's role. Even experienced software practitioners are often unable to define what exactly the architect does or adds to the software development process"

[2] For instance, as Woods and Rozanski (2012, p. 5) point out, "While today architects appear to be in every organization, and there is some similarity in what they call themselves, there is still widespread confusion over what IT architecture is, what IT architects do (or should do) and what types of IT architect exist". Gellweiler (2019, p. 1) agrees: "The role of the IT architect is vague in the literature and in practice". Likewise, Paras (2011, p. 2) reports that "the overall findings of [our] survey suggest diversity in interpretation of the EA [enterprise architect] role by the practitioners and by their leadership. Looking broadly across the results, it appears that some respondents interpret the role of EA to be strategic and transformational, while others see it as biased to expedite the delivery of infrastructure and solutions". Ylinen and Pekkola (2020, p. 9) conclude that "there is no shared understanding of what EA work is or what skills are required. This can be extrapolated to the organizational level where each organization recruits enterprise architects to very different duties". In a similar vein, Hoberman (2007) notes the variety of interpretations of the data architect's role in different organizations

[3] As Olsen (2017, p. 642) reports, "What is rather astounding in [our] study, is that even enterprise architects do not have clear conceptions of their role"

[4] For instance, in the survey of Network World (2016, p. 5), "one challenge architects reported was difficulty in finding information relevant to their job [...]. Just 26% said their need for information and community resources about their role were being met to a great extent". Moreover, enterprise architects also experience professional loneliness: "Just one in five said they agreed to a great extent that they had the opportunity to connect with peers in a similar role to the one they occupied" (Network World, 2016, p. 5)

[5] The search for practitioner books about enterprise architects yields only five results that seem relevant: Tinsley (2009), Potts (2010), Evans (2010), Hohpe (2020) and Bowman (2023). However, of these five books, two actually discuss somewhat different subjects (Bowman, 2023; Tinsley, 2009)

[6] See Hohpe (2020)

[7] See Potts (2010)

[8] See Evans (2010)

[9] See Bowman (2023)

[10] See Tinsley (2009)

[11] For instance, by the end of 2015, of 1075 mostly academic publications constituting the corpus of literature on enterprise architecture, only 32 (less than 3%) were relevant specifically to enterprise architects (Kotusev, 2017b). Following the same search methodology, by the end of 2023, of 1781 available publications on enterprise architecture, only 74 (about 4.2%) are relevant to architects

[12] Knowledge, skills, capabilities, personalities and worldviews of enterprise architects are rather widely studied and their consensus understanding is largely reached (Besker et al., 2015; du Preez et al., 2014;

Frampton, 2006; Frampton et al., 2005; Frampton and Ho, 2009; Frampton et al., 2006b; Gellweiler, 2020; Mapingire et al., 2018; Steghuis and Proper, 2008; Sultanow et al., 2020; Ullrich et al., 2021; Wagter et al., 2012; Ylimaki and Halttunen, 2005; Ylinen and Pekkola, 2018; Ylinen and Pekkola, 2020)

[13] Conduct, roles, activities, tasks and responsibilities of enterprise architects are addressed by only a limited number of studies that, taken together, fail to provide a rich and consistent view of the matter (Besker et al., 2015; du Preez et al., 2018; Gellweiler, 2020; Nsubuga et al., 2014; Steghuis and Proper, 2008; Strano and Rehmani, 2007; Ullrich et al., 2021)

[14] For example, Strano and Rehmani (2007, p. 383) came to the following conclusion: "In summary, a review of the literature raised more questions than it answered. Most of the information on the role of the enterprise architect was anecdotal and was not supported by details of analytical studies. [...] Theory that defined the role of the enterprise architect was sparse and inconsistent. It raised questions about whether the role of enterprise architect is an extension of the systems architect role or a unique discipline, if the role is mostly technical or managerial, and what competencies are required to perform the daily tasks of practicing architects". This conclusion, for the most part, is still valid today

[15] The world's first business information system, the Lyons Electronic Office (LEO), initiated in 1949 and completed in 1953 was propelled by a man named John Simmons whose competencies and activities highly resembled those of contemporary enterprise architects (Mason, 2004). During the 1960s, full-time positions for dedicated information systems planners, direct predecessors of modern architects, emerged in many large organizations (McFarlan, 1971; McLean and Soden, 1977)

[16] See, for example, CAEAP (2010a), Lane (2010), Uppal (2013) and Walrad et al. (2013)

[17] See, for example, Gotze (2013), Bloomberg (2016), Bontinck et al. (2016), LeanIX (2017), Izard (2019) and Bossert and van der Wildt (2021)

[18] The expression "jack-of-all-trades" is quite often used to characterize enterprise architects (Mapingire et al., 2018; Steghuis and Proper, 2008; Theuerkorn, 2004; Ylimaki and Halttunen, 2005; Ylinen and Pekkola, 2020). As Ylimaki and Halttunen (2005, p. 29) explain, "An architect should ideally be a jack-of-all-trades. (S)he should for example be able to communicate with various stakeholder groups using the language his/her audience can easily understand, be capable of abstract thinking, be able to see the big picture, have a strong expertise in information technology, and be able to sell ideas to other people". Mapingire et al. (2018, p. 161) come to the same conclusion: "In summary, it emerged that the enterprise architect is a jack-of-all-trades as evidenced by the range of skills and competencies that they should possess. Enterprise architects should possess interpersonal, personal, technical, business, legal, project management, EA skills etc.". Even more radically, Ylinen and Pekkola (2020, p. 9) conclude that "there is no all-inclusive skill portfolio that suites for every enterprise architect. [...] This means that the enterprise architects need to be jacks-of-all-trades in order to survive with different EA related tasks"

[19] Some authors compare enterprise architects to superhumans (Bittler, 2008; Ylinen and Pekkola, 2018)

[20] Ylinen and Pekkola (2018, p. 1) compare enterprise architects to five-legged sheep: "Our results indicate that the range of skills [essential for architects] is great, and finding an expert with all appropriate competencies is like looking for a five-legged sheep"

[21] The metaphor of enterprise architects as management consultants is elaborated, most of all, by Blosch et al. (2016)

[22] The metaphor of enterprise architects as city planners is routinely used in the literature (Akenine, 2008; Daniel, 2007; FEAPO, 2013; Jung and Fraunholz, 2021; Luo, 2014; McDowall, 2019; Murer et al., 2011; Schmidt and Buxmann, 2011; Sessions, 2007; Sessions and de Vadoss, 2014; The Open Group, 2022; Wierda, 2015; Worthen, 2005; Ziemann, 2022)

[23] The metaphor of enterprise architects as wedding planners is proposed by Madhav Naidu: "Transformation itself is more like a wedding, and EA [enterprise architect] is more like a wedding planner. I know we have seen many weddings without a wedding planner, but getting married is much easier if you have a

wedding planner because of the planner's experience. A planner walks us through a series of processes, methods, and approaches, which makes things easier" (Gardner et al., 2012, p. 285)

[24] The metaphor of enterprise architects as diplomats is proposed by Network World (2016, p. 3): "Using an analogy to statecraft, architects are like diplomats within a technology-dependent organization, moving between different groups and fostering conversation, information exchange and (hopefully) agreement"

[25] Although enterprise architects are rather often compared to translators (Abraham et al., 2013; Apthorp, 2011; Jiang et al., 2024; Ziemann, 2022), or interpreters (Ylinen and Pekkola, 2020), in the most explicit form, this metaphor is formulated by Worthen (2005, p. 49): "In fact, it's best to think of the enterprise architect as a translator. The businesspeople tell the architect what they need to do. The architect in turn designs an IT project that will meet those needs and is consistent with the IT department's overall strategy"

[26] The metaphor of enterprise architects as salesmen is proposed by Levine (2014, p. 36): "An important metaphor for the architect function is as a salesman — for ideas! In order to be successful, the architect must consider himself or herself as a salesman for the concepts and understanding that they have developed"

[27] The metaphor of enterprise architects as tour guides is proposed by Erik Dornenburg: "Erik likens an architect to a tour guide, someone who has been to a certain place many times, can tell a good story about it, and can gently guide you to pay attention to important aspects and avoid unnecessary risks. This is a guiding role: tour guides cannot force their guests to follow their advice, except maybe those who drop off a bus load of tourists at a tourist-trap restaurant in the middle of nowhere" (Hohpe, 2020, p. 18)

Preface

[1] The problem of defining business information systems, or enterprise applications, relevant to the subject of this book and clearly distinguishing them from the rest of the IT universe is also noted and addressed in the same way by Fowler (2002, pp. 2-3): "What do I mean by the term "enterprise application"? I can't give a precise definition, but I can give some indication of my meaning. [...] Enterprise applications include payroll, patient records, shipping tracking, cost analysis, credit scoring, insurance, supply chain, accounting, customer service, and foreign exchange trading. Enterprise applications don't include automobile fuel injection, word processors, elevator controllers, chemical plant controllers, telephone switches, operating systems, compilers, and games"

[2] The first edition of this book was released in 2018 (Kotusev, 2018c), and its second updated edition — in 2021 (Kotusev, 2021c)

[3] See, for example, Richards and Ford (2020), Shrivastava and Srivastav (2024), Bass et al. (2021), Fowler (2002) and Hohpe and Woolf (2004)

[4] See, for example, Rao et al. (2011), Rao et al. (2018), Harrison and Josey (2018b) and Harrison and Josey (2018a)

[5] This conclusion refers only to *valid* interpretations of the term having reasonable empirical justification and ignores, for example, *metaphorical* interpretations of enterprise architects as senior business executives (Allaire and Howard, 1992; Nadler and Gerstein, 1992; Potts, 2010) and *fictional* interpretations of enterprise architects as nonexistent designers of enterprises (Coghill, 2016; Graves, 2007; Graves, 2008)

[6] For instance, Markus and Rowe (2023, p. 331) point out that "in the English language, the word transformation both denotes and connotes something different from mere change". As Hohpe (2020, p. 272) explains, "Not every kind of change deserves to be called "transformation". You change the layout of the furniture in your living room, but you transform [...] your house into a club, retail store, or place of worship. [...] When we speak of IT transformation, we therefore imply not an incremental evolution, but a fundamental restructuring of the technology landscape, the organizational setup, and the culture"

[7] The lack of conceptual clarity, potential redundancy and other flaws of the term "digital transformation" are noticed by many authors (Markus and Rowe, 2023; Vial, 2019; Wessel et al., 2021)

Chapter 1: Digital Transformation

[1] A comprehensive historical discussion of IT innovations is provided, for example, by Haigh and Ceruzzi (2021)

[2] See, for instance, Diebold (1952), Canning (1956) and Hoos (1960)

[3] See, for instance, Parsons (1983), McFarlan (1984) and Wiseman (1988)

[4] See, for instance, Coltman et al. (2001), Earl and Khan (2001) and Weill and Vitale (2001)

[5] See, for instance, Westerman et al. (2014), Siebel (2019) and Woerner et al. (2022)

[6] In fact, the term "digital transformation" is very elusive, all-encompassing, problematic in many aspects and used in the literature rather loosely, usually without any particular definition (Markus and Rowe, 2023; Vial, 2019). As Markus and Rowe (2023, p. 328) summarize, "The digital transformation label has been applied to the evolution of technology, as well as to the evolution of organizations and society. It has been used to refer to change in entities or processes and to processes of change. It has been used to refer to particular technological artifacts and to particular kinds of data and processing power". To a large extent, digital transformation can be viewed merely as the latest industry buzzword for using IT in organizations

[7] For example, since the early 1990s, various authors have been discussing "IT-enabled transformation" (Markus and Benjamin, 1997; Scott Morton, 1991; Venkatraman, 1994), whose differences from current "digital transformation" are far from obvious (Wessel et al., 2021), while the very transformative potential of IT for organizations was recognized by many much earlier (Diebold, 1965; Leavitt and Whisler, 1958)

[8] Currently, digital transformation invariably ranks among the most important IT management issues (Johnson et al., 2024)

[9] As McSweeney (2019, p. 28) puts it, "The [IT] solution is intrinsically concerned with solving one problem"

[10] For example, Beijer and de Klerk (2010) propose a somewhat simpler classification scheme with three general types of transformation drivers: pain, directive and opportunity

[11] See Kotusev (2022)

[12] The distinction between deliberate and emergent strategies was famously made by Mintzberg and Waters (1985)

[13] These problems with business strategy as the driver of digital transformation are discussed in more detail by Kotusev et al. (2020b), Kotusev (2022) and Kotusev (2021c) (Chapter 5)

[14] For example, the strategic business goal to "increase corporate revenue to one billion dollars by 2027" and the like are perfectly SMART-compatible, but still fail to provide any meaningful guidance for organizational digitalization efforts

[15] For example, Gartner Magic Quadrants cover more than a hundred distinct categories of systems, technologies and IT-related services, where each category usually includes more than ten different offerings, vendors or providers. The current list of Gartner Magic Quadrants can be found here: https://www.gartner.com/en/research/magic-quadrant

[16] For instance, the survey of Bizzdesign (2024, p. 26) shows that "forty-two percent of organizations have poor or very poor visibility of data flows and application links, making it potentially risky to remove an application"

[17] Over the past decade, security has become the paramount concern of IT management (Johnson et al., 2024)

[18] As Hohpe (2020, p. 10) observes, "Nowadays, [...] the linkage between business goals and technology choices has become much more direct, even for "traditional" businesses. For example, the desire for faster time-to-market to meet competitive pressures translates into the need for an elastic cloud approach to computing, which in turn requires applications that scale horizontally and thus should be designed to be stateless. Targeted

content on customer channels necessitates analytical models, which are tuned by churning through large amounts of data via a Hadoop cluster, which in turn favors local hard-drive storage over shared-network storage"

[19] In the literature, business and IT alignment is usually conceptualized as the mutual consistency between four key elements: business strategy, IT strategy (strategic alignment), organizational infrastructure and processes, and IT infrastructure and processes (operational alignment) (Henderson and Venkatraman, 1993)

[20] Historically, business and IT alignment persistently tops among the most important IT management issues (Johnson et al., 2024; Kappelman et al., 2014; Luftman and McLean, 2004)

[21] In organizational theory, organizations are often conceptualized as loosely coupled systems (March, 1994; Orton and Weick, 1990; Weick, 1976)

[22] A comprehensive discussion of planning horizons, task complexity and other aspects of managerial work at different levels of the administrative hierarchy is provided, for instance, by Jaques and Clement (1994)

[23] As March (1987, p. 154) explains, "The fundamental idea of conflict of interest is that an organization is a coalition of individuals and groups pursuing different objectives". Organizations, thus, can be best viewed as political coalitions (Cyert and March, 1992; March, 1962)

[24] See, for example, Argyris (1957)

[25] These estimates of the lifespan of information systems in the organizational IT landscape are provided by a number of authors (Mocker, 2012; Ross, 2011; Wierda, 2015). As Wierda (2015, p. 140) asserts, "Systems have an average life time of fifteen years"

[26] Presently, compliance with regulations consistently features among the most important IT management issues (Johnson et al., 2024)

Chapter 2: Digital Transformation Initiatives

[1] For example, in the survey of Preisker et al. (2020), the respondents classify 29% of their IT investments as operational tasks, 39% — as tactical improvements, and 32% — as strategic transformations

[2] By contrast, Kotusev (2021c) views all IT initiatives mainly as projects because larger initiatives, such as programs and strategies, are out of the discussion

[3] As McSweeney (2019, p. 28) explains, "[IT] solutions are implemented individually by separate projects or as a collection of solutions implemented as a program"

[4] See, for example, Luehrman (1998)

[5] As Bente et al. (2012, p. 88) explain, "[High-level] initiatives are expressed as intentions and work streams. They are coarsely defined at a high level with work packages and ballpark estimates. In contrast, projects are more concrete. They are defined in a formal way using a statement of work, a project charter, or a project proposal"

[6] The classic step-wise waterfall approach to system development is often mistakenly credited to Royce (1970)

[7] See Kruchten (2003) and Martin (1991) respectively

[8] Agile software development is discussed in numerous sources, for example, by Martin (2003) and McConnell (2019)

[9] See Schwaber and Beedle (2002), Beck and Andres (2004), Cockburn (2004) and Stapleton (1997) respectively

[10] Industry surveys demonstrate that different waterfall and agile methodologies and used in practice (Dahalin et al., 2010; Schekkerman, 2005)

[11] For instance, the survey of Manwani and Bossert (2016) shows that 49.5% of organizations use agile methodologies mainly for fast-moving applications

[12] For example, regarding the waterfall and some other sequential models of software development, Humphrey (1989, p. 249) observed that "the real world of software development doesn't conform neatly to [any]

of these models". A realistic discussion of the applicability of popular agile methodologies and a critical analysis of their ideas is provided, for instance, by Meyer (2014)

[13] See, for example, Thummadi and Lyytinen (2020)

[14] As Armour et al. (1999b, p. 39) explain, "Reaching agreement on a target architecture definition in a large, changing, multicultural organization with competitive groups is difficult. The larger the organization, the more difficult it will be"

Chapter 3: Architectural Planning

[1] The distinction between factual and value components of planning decisions corresponding to their means and ends respectively was first made by Simon (1943, p. 5): "Each decision involves the selection of a goal, and a behavior relevant to it. [...] In so far as decisions lead toward the selection of final goals, they will be called "value judgments". In so far as they involve the implementation of such goals they will be called "factual judgments""

[2] As Beijer and de Klerk (2010, p. 46) explain, "IT architecture needs to perform a balancing act by listening to [its] stakeholders, discovering their concerns, and coming to a consensus among stakeholders to decide on the best way forward to realize the business goals. That is, we want to set up an IT architecture that provides a solution that fits all stakeholders. This will be done with some give and take from all sides, but at least with a mutual understanding and consensus about the way forward"

[3] Architectural planning as the process of negotiation, reconciliation and mutual alignment of the interests of multiple actors is analyzed, for instance, by Sidorova and Kappelman (2010), Sidorova and Kappelman (2011b) and Sidorova and Kappelman (2011a)

[4] As Boster et al. (2000, p. 44) explain, "The process [of architectural planning] will almost certainly be both political and technical", where a technical perspective is about "how we do it" and a business perspective is about "what we want to get from all this". "The need for a technical perspective is clear, but a business perspective is equally valuable. Anyone who has led an [architectural planning] effort knows negotiations for world peace pale by comparison"

[5] As Boster et al. (2000, p. 44) put it, "In the architecture dimension, a system that is technically flawless but useless from a business perspective fails just as grandly as a system that would be wonderful if it ever ran more than a day without errors"

[6] For example, McSweeney (2019) proposes the following six domains: location and offices, business processes, organization and structure (three business-oriented change areas), technology, infrastructure and communications, applications and systems, information and data (three technology-oriented change areas). Traditionally, business, data, applications and technology (BDAT) are viewed as the four key domains in the mainstream EA literature, but this structuring dates back to the 1980s (PRISM, 1986) and now is patently obsolete (FEAPO, 2018)

[7] The same domain structure is proposed, for instance, by Behara and Paradkar (2015)

[8] Unsurprisingly, the three substantive domains (business, applications and infrastructure) exactly correspond to the three core layers of the ArchiMate modeling language (business, application and technology) intended for describing the landscape structure (Lankhorst, 2017; Wierda, 2017)

[9] The translation of higher-level architectural decisions into lower-level ones through the initiative hierarchy on both the technical and organizational sides follows the general principles of hierarchical decision-making in organizations explained, for example, by Simon (1997, p. 107): "In reality, the process [of translating decisions] involves [...] a whole hierarchy of steps, the decisions at any given level of generality providing the environment for the more particular decisions at the next level below. The integration of behavior at the highest level is brought about by decisions that determine in very broad terms the values, knowledge, and possibilities that will receive consideration. The next lower level of integration, which gives greater specificity to these very general determinants, results from those decisions that determine what activities shall be undertaken. Other levels follow, each one determining in greater detail a subarea lying within the area of the level above"

¹⁰ For instance, as Sauer and Willcocks (2002, p. 42) report, "Among companies that were successfully aligning business and technology, we identified a series of bridging activities that amounted to the creation of what we call the organizational architect, someone who is neither all strategist nor all technologist, who guides the translation of a strategic vision to a flexible, integrated [IT] platform. Organizational architects sustain a dialogue between visionaries and technologists as they define and design the right combination of structures, processes, capabilities and technologies — one that has a greater chance of being responsive to the organization's goals. [...] Organizational architects work with both strategists and technologists to identify and grow the organizational and technical capabilities needed to see a vision through to its supporting platform"

Chapter 4: Welcome, Enterprise Architects

¹ For example, Florentine (2017, p. 1) notices that "large organizations are increasingly turning to enterprise architects to help bridge the divide between IT and the business and drive digital transformation". In a similar vein, Edwards (2020, p. 1) makes the following observation: "With digital transformation challenging businesses worldwide, a growing number of companies are placing their future into the hands of an enterprise architect, someone who can take disruption and turn it into a competitive advantage". Violino (2020, p. 1) asserts that "the enterprise architect is one of the most pivotal IT positions at an organization, and especially for a company that is embarking on a digital transformation". Some authors even call enterprise architects "digital transformers" (Preiss, 2017; Suer, 2018). Bossert and Laartz (2016) argue that architects can push digitalization efforts in organizations forward by reducing the concomitant complexity of their IT landscapes

² As Network World (2016, p. 2) reports, "The most vexing and persistent question about the "architect" role within organizations is about its focus. To put it simply, is the architect a tech person who interfaces with business, or a businessperson who talks to IT? The answer, according to our survey, is that the role is much more the former than the latter"

³ As Strano and Rehmani (2007, pp. 386-387) summarize, "The competencies that are most needed to be effective in the role of enterprise architect are analytical change management, communication, interpersonal, leadership, management, modeling and problem solving skills as well as business acumen and technical acumen". Or, Beijer and de Klerk (2010, p. 144) provide the following summary: "Knowledge and experience of the business domain, knowledge and experience of the IT domain, experience in consulting and communication, and skills in using modern methodologies and techniques are just a few aspects that would characterize the competent IT architect today". Likewise, Violino (2020, p. 1) argues that "an enterprise architect needs to have skills such as knowledge of the business and how it relates to architecture; the ability to communicate and collaborate with others in IT and on the business side, and to translate complex technical concepts for non-technical executives; knowledge of IT governance and operation; and expertise in hardware, software and systems engineering". Ylinen and Pekkola (2018, p. 7) conclude that there is no unified set of skills for all enterprise architects: "In general, the range of [necessary] skills is great. Finding a smaller subset of key skills and competencies is difficult. Our experts seem to emphasize different skills from their own perspectives. Consequently a general list of skills that every enterprise architect should know and master cannot be composed"

⁴ For example, in the survey of Network World (2016, p. 3), enterprise architects express rather different opinions about their primary responsibilities: "Eighty two percent of survey respondents identified converting business strategies into IT strategies as their primary job responsibility. A slightly smaller share said their primary responsibility was providing product roadmaps and specifications to engineers (73%), and helping align the company's "infrastructure strategy" with its information technology (72%). Other common responsibilities were specifying vendors and technology solutions for purchase (60%) and ensuring that solutions are built according to agreed upon specifications and product roadmaps (54%)". Gellweiler (2020) distinguishes 37 diverse task categories associated with the job of architects. As for the contacts and communication networks of architects, "Every enterprise implements enterprise architecture in different ways [...]. Unfortunately, this diversity of interaction styles and methods makes it difficult to describe the common interactions between any particular architectural role and other roles in an enterprise" (FEAPO, 2018, p. 15). Interestingly, an enormous variety of duties and competencies is identified by Clements et al. (2007) even for the simpler role of software

architects: "Our survey resulted in over 400 duties, skills, and knowledge areas, each of which somebody thinks is important for software architects to master. The result was about 200 separately cataloged duties, about 100 skills, and about 100 areas of knowledge"

[5] For instance, in the survey of Preisker et al. (2020, p. 10), "according to the survey participants, 95 percent of enterprise architects are already actively involved in transformation initiatives and major IT decisions [...]. Moreover, 68 percent see enterprise architects as a critical success factor in these transformations"

[6] The very term "enterprise architecture" is extremely ambiguous, notoriously difficult to define and has numerous incompatible meanings among both academics and practitioners (Fehskens, 2015b; Saint-Louis et al., 2019)

[7] The connection between enterprise architecture and digital transformation is widely discussed in both academic studies (Hafsi and Assar, 2016; Korhonen and Halen, 2017; van de Wetering et al., 2021) and industry publications (Blumberg et al., 2018; Newman, 2018; Preisker et al., 2020). Some even argue that "enterprise architecture is critical to digital transformation" (Suer, 2018, p. 1) and that "EA is a key enabler for digital transformation" (Manwani and Bossert, 2016, p. 8)

[8] As Tamm et al. (2022, p. 9) observe, "Enterprise architects rarely have the mandate to decide which major IT investments their organization makes, and even the level of control they have over project execution varies greatly from organization to organization. Therefore, in practice the primary way in which enterprise architects can drive business value or organizational benefits is by informing and positively influencing decisions taken by others". Similarly, Besker et al. (2015, p. 35) point out that "the architect has a large degree of freedom and full mandate to make decisions concerning architectural issues but less power to implement their recommendations"

[9] As FEAPO (2018, p. 9) explains, "Most enterprise architects work with other teams, but have no authority. Therefore, enterprise architects must be able to convince or positively influence other people into cooperation or compliance with recommendations. There are no sticks, only carrots"

[10] In the industry literature, the work of enterprise architects is often viewed as the provision of specialized services to the organization in many respects resembling traditional management consultancy (Blosch et al., 2016; Faber, 2010; Robertson, 2008) and some academic studies even conceptualize an EA practice as an internal organizational capability for providing architectural services (Frampton et al., 2015; Shanks et al., 2018; Tamm et al., 2022). For instance, Tamm et al. (2022, p. 9) argue that "it may be useful to think of the EA team as an internal advisory service function focused on guiding organizational IS decision-making". As Worthen (2005, p. 50) points out, "In fact, many architects consider themselves internal consultants, with the exception that they stick around to make sure the project gets done properly"

[11] In the existing literature, enterprise architects are very often compared to city planners (Akenine, 2008; Daniel, 2007; FEAPO, 2013; Jung and Fraunholz, 2021; Luo, 2014; McDowall, 2019; Murer et al., 2011; Schmidt and Buxmann, 2011; Sessions, 2007; Sessions and de Vadoss, 2014; The Open Group, 2022; Wierda, 2015; Worthen, 2005; Ziemann, 2022). As Akenine (2008, p. 24) points out, "A classic analogy is to compare the enterprise architect to a city planner who, using strategy, planning, and regulations, is responsible for different functions in a city that must work together effectively". Likewise, Daniel (2007, p. 1) also notices that "an oft-used metaphor for the enterprise architect's role is that of the city planner, since he also provides the road maps, zoning, common requirements, regulations and strategy-albeit for a company, rather than a city"

[12] In the EA literature, organizations are routinely compared to cities and their separate IT systems — to buildings (Ahlemann et al., 2012; Burke, 2003; Burke, 2004; FEAPO, 2013; Jung and Fraunholz, 2021; Laartz et al., 2000; Longepe, 2003; Rehring et al., 2019; Robertson, 2010; Schmidt and Buxmann, 2011; Schulte, 2002; Sessions, 2007; Sessions and de Vadoss, 2014)

[13] As Ziemann (2022, p. 2) explains, "Like a city planner, an enterprise architect must think strategically and plan a complete landscape of systems. Naturally, instead of quarters, train stations, urban residences, and parks, the enterprise architect designs a landscape consisting of business domains, large applications, middleware, and IT infrastructure"

[14] A rather elaborate collation of the work of enterprise architects and city planners is provided by Murer et al. (2011, p. 36): "In a very large information system, the architect's work at the highest level is very similar to the work of a city planner. The architect defines guidelines and IT standards comparable to city zoning plans, setting constraints for building in certain areas. Reviews and approvals of designs are comparable to implementation permits, just as city planners issue building permits for construction projects. The architect plans and builds the necessary infrastructure to allow for a managed evolution of the city — via IT strategy and architecture driven investment programs"

[15] Enterprise architects are often compared with traditional architects (Beijer and de Klerk, 2010; Fez-Barringten, 2010; Strano and Rehmani, 2005) and the very discipline of enterprise architecture — with traditional architecture (Kerr, 1989; Pavlak, 2006; Rerup, 2018; von Halle, 1992; von Halle, 1996). As Beijer and de Klerk (2010, p. 143) point out, "In discussions about the IT architecture profession, it is not uncommon to reflect on the concepts and profession of physical architecture. There is a very simple reason for this: in essence they both pursue similar goals and need similar skills to achieve these goals". Strano and Rehmani (2005, p. 7) even conclude that "the profession of enterprise architect may be an extension of the roles of a traditional architect". These misleading analogies are seemingly inspired largely by the famous but flawed ideas of Zachman (1987)

[16] As Potts (2013, p. 29) explains, "From an architectural perspective, enterprises offer a particular challenge because they are self-determining. Enterprises can constantly re-design their own architectures in ways that other kinds of entities cannot. This process may be deliberate or by accident, obvious or unseen"

[17] As Worthen (2005, p. 48) explicates, "With a title like architect, you'd expect the job to be about building things, but a more accurate analogy might be city planner. Unlike a building, a company's IT architecture is never complete. Furthermore, an enterprise architect needs a high-level view that takes into account applications, data formats and hardware platforms, and how these three parts of IT interact much the way a city planner has to consider a new building's impact on sewers, traffic and the electrical grid"

[18] For instance, Isenberg (1984, p. 82) finds that senior managers "seldom think in ways that one might simplistically view as "rational", i.e., they rarely systematically formulate goals, assess their worth, evaluate the probabilities of alternative ways of reaching them, and choose the path that maximizes expected return. Rather, managers frequently bypass rigorous, analytical planning altogether, particularly when they face difficult, novel, or extremely entangled problems"

[19] See, for example, March (1991b), March (1994) and March (1997). As March (1991b, p. 97) elucidates, "To say that decisions "happen" instead of "are made" is to suggest that the organizational processes that result in decisions may be poorly comprehended by a conception of intentional, future-oriented choice"

[20] As Potts (2013, p. 29) explains, "To be an effective enterprise architect means being an influential participant in the enterprise's ongoing journey of self-redesign. [...] Through their participation in the enterprise, each enterprise architect must impact people's ideas, decisions, and actions whenever these might materially affect the enterprise's architectural performance". Potts (2013, p. 30) continues: "For enterprise architects, the most significant challenge that differentiates their role from other architects is that they are working within an entity that can redesign itself, every minute of every day. They are part of the structure they are there to design, part of the enterprise's capability at "self-architecture""

[21] As Madhav Naidu explains, "It is not just the enterprise architects who will be solely responsible for transforming the enterprise. Almost everybody in the enterprise is engaged in one way or another. The enterprise architect plays a facilitator role. The architect brings people together and aligns them with the vision for the transformation, drives the transformation" (Gardner et al., 2012, p. 285). Bente et al. (2012, p. 100) formulate the same idea metaphorically: "A good enterprise architect is not a solo artist — maybe the first violinist but always an orchestra musician". Unfortunately, some authors portray architects largely as "solo artists" working on their own: "We can sum up an EA effort in this broad statement: An architect follows some process and produces some architecture" (Boster et al., 2000, p. 44)

[22] This expression is used for describing some aspects of the job of architects, for example, by Correa (2013), Hohpe (2020) and Bowman (2023)

[23] See, for example, Brunsson (1982) and Brunsson (1985)

[24] As Bolton (2003, p. 12) puts it, "Remember, the "right" strategy may not be the best technology or even the best answer. The right strategy is the one that has commitment from those responsible for delivering business results"

[25] As noted by Lindblom (1959, p. 84), in political contexts with multiple constituencies and heterogeneous interests, any objective criteria of decision correctness are absent and "agreement on policy thus becomes the only practicable test of the policy's correctness". Woods (2014, p. 11) argues that "there's rarely a right answer in architecture work [...]. Owing to the number of concerns that must be balanced, a truly optimal solution often does not exist". As Hohpe (2020, p. 61) puts it, "Architecture is a matter of trade-offs: there rarely is one single "best" architecture"

[26] As Buckl et al. (2009, p. 20) put it, "If the decisions are made in an ivory tower and are only handed over to the people there will be no acceptance"

[27] The fact that the meaning of the job of enterprise architects is extremely difficult to explain, even to IT people, is widely acknowledged in the industry (Blosch et al., 2016; Bowman, 2023; Unde, 2008). For example, Bowman (2023, p. 3) notices that "laypeople are not alone in their bewilderment about the role of enterprise architects. Indeed, much of the software industry is also awash in confusion". As Blosch et al. (2016, p. 5) point out, "One of the hardest questions any enterprise architect can get asked is, "What do you do?" Just like some of the attendees at our CIO event, many people both in the business and in IT don't understand EA and how it adds value"

[28] The mantle of enterprise architects as organizational change agents is recognized, for instance, by Brockbank (1987), Bredemeyer and Malan (2002), Strano and Rehmani (2007) and Evans (2010). As Hohpe (2020, p. 4) explains, "Today's successful architects aren't just IT specialists, they're also major change agents. Architects must therefore possess a special set of skills beyond just technology". EACOE (2023, p. 1) agrees: "Enterprise architects are change agents who need to work with both business people and technology people to be effective. Therefore, enterprise architects should have the necessary soft skills in addition to technology acumen to work successfully in this profession"

[29] As Levine (2014, p. 36) explains, "An important metaphor for the architect function is as a salesman — for ideas! In order to be successful, the architect must consider himself or herself as a salesman for the concepts and understanding that they have developed"

[30] As Strano and Rehmani (2007, p. 385) put it, "As a change agent, the enterprise architect supports enterprise leaders in establishing and promoting the best strategy to accomplish business goals and objectives"

[31] As Levine (2014, p. 36) puts it, "The architect must be able not only to understand a (technical) concept, but also to convey that understanding to the people who will decide and execute on it"

[32] The duality of the occupation of enterprise architects combining distinct engineering and political dimensions is also noticed by Chuang and van Loggerenberg (2010, p. 9): "One can state in brief that there are two essential dimensions to the role of enterprise architect: [first,] a technical, engineering side which focuses on delivering technically accurate, reliable architecture [and, second,] a non-technical side that focuses on delivering services to remediate the value deficiencies of the stakeholders based on the social structure of the organization. [...] The two aspects are intertwined, and have a symbiotic relationship. Enterprise architects must demonstrate the capacity to effectively fulfill these two dimensions when delivering architectural service"

[33] For example, Chuang and van Loggerenberg (2010, p. 7) report that "many architects with a technical background [i.e. senior techies] expect the business to provide them with a set of functional requirements and this often results in disappointments in the expectations of the business and the architects. Some interviewees blamed the problem on the 'engineering mindset' of the architect meaning that many enterprise architects generally are not interested in business concepts"

Chapter 5: Enterprise Architects in Context

[1] For instance, Preisker et al. (2022, p. 8) report that "96% of the [surveyed] respondents which have EA as an established corporate function, mostly agreed that [it] is involved into digitalization initiatives and is considered an essential function to enable collaboration between IT and business units". Similarly, in the survey of Preisker et al. (2023, p. 28), "78% of the participants state that their EA function is integrated into digitalization initiatives and is considered essential to enable collaboration between IT and business units"

[2] This estimate comes from the recent statistics on the number of enterprise architects in organizations (Kotusev et al., 2024; Preisker et al., 2020)

[3] This observation is supported by a number of surveys consistently demonstrating that architecture functions most often report to CIOs or other similar IT executives, e.g. CTOs, CDOs, vice presidents or directors of IT (Aziz and Obitz, 2005; Aziz and Obitz, 2007; Carr and Else, 2018; Manwani and Bossert, 2016; Obitz and Babu, 2009; Planview, 2018; Schekkerman, 2005). For example, Carr and Else (2018, p. 13) conclude that "the EA function is still viewed strongly as an IT discipline, with more than 75% of respondents reporting to IT leadership positions". Likewise, Manwani and Bossert (2016, p. 6) discover that "two out of three EA groups report to the CIO/CTO"

[4] As discussed later in this chapter, in small organizations that employ no specialized enterprise architects, architectural planning is typically accomplished by their IT executives, so that they actually fulfill the role of architects on a part-time basis

[5] As Sauer and Willcocks (2002, p. 42) explain, "The shifting competitive landscape is creating a larger gap between strategists and technologists. Executives are busy creating and refining visions and have little time to focus on technology. Technologists are busy keeping the platform current and have little time to understand the business in depth"

[6] In fact, IT leaders can be fairly regarded as the closest organizational "relatives" of enterprise architects: "Asked whom they consider their closest peers within their organization, 59% [of the 271 surveyed architects] identified IT management, compared with just 39% who identified the CIO as their closest peer. Within enterprises (1,000 or more employees) the percentage of respondents who cite close ties to IT management is even higher (71%), compared to SMB organizations (less than 1,000 employees) (38%). The explanation for the close identification with IT is pretty clear as well: many individuals occupying the architect role have emerged from development and IT departments" (Network World, 2016, p. 3)

[7] For instance, as Sauer and Willcocks (2002, p. 42) report, "Some companies [in our study] looked to the CEO or CIO to bridge interests, but rarely did either role have the right combination of skills and mind-set. The "believer" CEO, who sees IT as central to business management, was rare. Even a CIO who had the trust of the CEO's inner circle typically had a shallow understanding of organizational design"

[8] As Hohpe (2020, p. 211) points out, "Architects in the enterprise live at the intersection of the technical and business worlds. In fact, getting these two pieces to work together seamlessly is one of an architect's key contributions". Likewise, Preisker et al. (2023, p. 15) observe that "the challenge with [finding] the "rare breed" of enterprise architects is that they are positioned between tech-savvy experts who often lack a comprehensive understanding of business context and the soft skills necessary for business communication on the one side and those with this understanding and the required soft skills, [...] often lacking in-depth technical knowledge on the other side"

[9] As Network World (2016, p. 2) puts it, "The power behind the IT throne, architects are more important than ever before: acting as liaisons between technology-focused engineers focused on discrete technical problems and business leaders who take the long view: focusing on strategy and execution". Similarly, Planview (2018, p. 2) concludes that "enterprise architects are uniquely qualified to be a vital link between business strategy and IT, enabling their organizations to digitally transform all functions and deliver innovative products and services". As Hohpe (2020, p. 4) explains, "IT's purpose is to support the business strategy. Architects establish this linkage by translating business needs into technical drivers"

[10] As Hohpe (2020, p. 8) explains, "Architects can fill an important void in large enterprises: they work and communicate closely with technical staff on projects, but are also able to convey technical topics to upper management without losing the essence of the message. Conversely, they understand the company's business strategy and can translate it into technical decisions that support it". In a similar vein, Apthorp (2011, p. 6) argues that "one of the roles of an enterprise architect is as a translator: [...] between the language of business, information, and technology, [...] between high-level management decisions and concrete design decisions [and] between a vision and the concrete actions to realize it"

[11] For instance, Figueiredo et al. (2014, p. 1239) report that "some of the organizations observed have the architect roles [...] formally defined and institutionalized, while in others these roles are informal. In some organizations these roles are not called architects, despite performing architecture-related activities"

[12] As Hohpe (2020, p. 1) points out, "Ironically, though, many of the most successful digital companies have a world-class software and systems architecture, but don't have architects at all"

[13] The specifics of enterprise architects employed by IT service providers are out of the scope of this book and not discussed further

[14] High demand for enterprise architects in the industry is noted, for example, by Woldt (2017). Likewise, Hohpe (2020, p. 1) observes that "IT architects have become some of the most sought-after IT professionals as traditional enterprises are looking to transform their IT landscape to compete with digital disruptors"

[15] Historically, the deficiency of skilled enterprise architects has been widely reported (GAO, 2002; GAO, 2003; GAO, 2006; GAO, 2015; Lucke et al., 2010). For example, in the survey of Preisker et al. (2023, pp. 12-13), "98% of the participants agree that the availability of enterprise architects in the job market is limited" and "companies that do not employ [architects] state that one of the main reasons is the lack of (fitting) applicants". In the survey of Hauder et al. (2013), 87% of participants agreed that the lack of experienced architects on the job market represents a challenge for their EA practices. Gartner (2013) reports that, of all IT roles, the skills gap related to enterprise architecture has the greatest negative business impact. As Hohpe (2020, p. 32) explicates, "The translation between business needs and IT architecture remains a domain that's perennially short of talent. It appears that most folks find comfort on one or the other side of the fence, but only a few can, and choose to, credibly play in both worlds. It's a good time to be an enterprise architect"

[16] For example, Gibson (2008) reports that enterprise architects consistently top among hardest-to-fill positions. In the survey of Bizzdesign (2023, p. 4), "seventy percent of respondents described hiring and retaining EA talent as a challenge". In a similar vein, in the survey of Preisker et al. (2023, p. 14), "52% of survey participants state that finding a suitable enterprise architect for a vacant position takes about 5–8 months. For 39% of companies, it takes even longer"

[17] For instance, in the survey of Bizzdesign (2023, p. 9), "twenty percent of respondents said their organization was severely under-resourced", "44 percent said they were under-resourced" and only "a third of respondents said that their EA resources were about right"

[18] As Levine (2014, p. 36) explains, "While most of the roles contribute directly to an easily identified end result, enterprise architects make contributions that are not easy to identify. Engineers build products; operators run products; managers direct the people doing work. What is the contribution of an architect?". Hohpe (2020, p. 3) expresses a similar view: "Articulating an architect's value isn't always easy. I often explain to people that if an IT system can still absorb high rates of change after many years, the project team probably included a good architect"

[19] For instance, in the study of Besker et al. (2015, p. 32), "a great number of [enterprise architects] state that their organizations have no specific measurement tools to determine how efficient their work is carried out. One of the respondents is measured on the primarily cost-saving basis while the majorities are evaluated by vague EA performance indicators only". As Paras (2011, p. 3) reports, "When actually measuring success, the respondents [of our survey] identified several key performance indicators (KPIs) as critical. These were split evenly between process, programmatic, and financial measures, as expected. Unexpectedly, 32% did not have any measures at all, and it isn't clear how to interpret that result. In today's typical IT environment, it is unusual to find any functional unit that isn't managed against a set of measures"

[20] These statistical figures on the salary of enterprise architects come from various online job services, including Glassdoor, PayScale, Indeed, Salary.com, Talent.com and SimplyHired. Some earlier estimates of their salaries are also provided in the literature. For example, as Bernard (2004, p. 70) reports, "From an informal survey of EA salaries in 2003 conducted by the author, a senior enterprise architect's position can command over $100,000 per year. Mid-level positions (3–5 years of experience) can earn in the range of $50,000 to $80,000.00 per year, and the junior positions for beginning architects can earn in the range of $30,000 to $50,000 per year". Or, according to Gibson (2008, p. 49), "Enterprise data architects earn in the top 25 percent of IT salaries — between $100,000 to $160,000 for a large financial services firm [...]. Factoring in incentives such as stock options, [...], the median pay totals about $150,000, although in high-cost locations such as Manhattan, compensation could go as high as $180,000". Their current compensation rates can be found, for example, here: https://www.indeed.com/career/enterprise-architect/salaries

[21] As Strano and Rehmani (2007, p. 386) explain, "The unique role that the enterprise architect provides is aligning technology with the business goals and objectives by managing the complex set of interdependencies to communicate a common or shared vision of the strategic direction of the enterprise. The impact of not having the role filled is the increased potential for chaos and confusion, inadequate information to support key decisions, increased complexity, local versus enterprise optimization, reduced efficiency and effectiveness, and increased risk of finding the wrong solution"

[22] As Jiang et al. (2024, p. 11) explain, "Enterprise architects' strong technical background and solid business domain knowledge empower them to be the translator for both sides. They help achieve mutual understanding and enable smooth communication. For business stakeholders, enterprise architects get to know their concerns and struggles and elicit their requirements and expectations. They then translate those into IT language to communicate with the technical team to define the solutions' scope and the final deliverables' criteria. By effectively engaging with both parties, architects can bridge the communication gap and become the glue to stick IT solutions with business requirements". Buckl et al. (2009, p. 20) concur: "Enterprise architects are simply communicating people. They have to translate between the business and IT people. What implications does a business decision have for the IT behind the scene and vice visa?". In a similar vein, Network World (2016, p. 3) provides the following, somewhat metaphorical explanation: "Using an analogy to statecraft, architects are like diplomats within a technology-dependent organization, moving between different groups and fostering conversation, information exchange and (hopefully) agreement. Forty-three percent of architects [in our survey] strongly agreed with the notion that their role was to be an IT liaison within their organization [...]. As with statecraft, it helps if these employees are 'bilingual' — able to communicate in terms that both IT and non-IT stakeholders understand. Fifty-eight percent of the professionals we surveyed said it was critical to have such a skill, and another 30% said it was very important to their job"

[23] For instance, Hohpe (2020, p. 8) actively promotes the metaphor of an *elevator* that enterprise architects use to travel between the top and bottom levels of the organization and link them: "If you picture the levels of an organization as the floors in a building, architects can ride what I call the architect elevator: they ride the elevator up and down to move between a large enterprise's board room and the engine room where software is being built. Such a direct linkage between the levels has become more important than ever in times of rapid IT evolution and digital disruption". Niemann (2006, p. 183) proposes another metaphorical explanation for architects linking the top and bottom levels: "Architects must work with their heads in the clouds and their feet on the ground"

[24] For example, Bowman (2023) describes enterprise architects, for the most part, merely as large-scale software architects

[25] For example, Bredemeyer and Malan (2004, pp. 13-14) provide a quite unrealistic description of enterprise architects in terms of their knowledge, activities and personalities more resembling superheroes who, among performing many other duties, "influence business leaders at the highest level in the organization", "identify avenues to create unique and sustainable value to create strategic advantage", "lead teams to identify entirely new markets and business opportunities", "identify strategic themes and help create synergies across groups to accomplish the associated strategic objectives" and "coach others on achieving organizational effectiveness and dealing with political situations". As Hohpe (2020, p. 1) jokes, "In the case of architects,

exaggerated expectations can paint a picture of someone who solves intermittent performance problems in the morning and then transforms the enterprise culture in the afternoon". Hohpe (2020, p. 19) continues: "A common expectation of an architect is that of the superhero: if you believe some job postings, enterprise architects can single-handedly catapult companies into the digital age, solve just about any technical problem, and are always up to date on the latest technology. These are tough expectations to fulfill, so I'd caution any architect against taking advantage of this common misconception"

[26] As Hohpe (2020, p. 30) observes, "The recurring challenge with the title enterprise architect tends to be that it could describe a person who architects the enterprise as a whole (including the business strategy level) or someone doing IT architecture at the enterprise level". In fact, some authors indeed use the term "enterprise architect", or analogous terms, in reference to senior executive officers defining business strategy for their organizations (Allaire and Howard, 1992; Potts, 2010)

[27] Some sources introduce enterprise architects largely as generalists, or universal strategy executors, who can lead any business transformations and execute any strategies, whether with or without an IT component. For example, CAEAP (2010a, pp. 7-8) in its professional practice guide provides the following description: "An enterprise architect is a professional who brings together rational business views with logical blueprints enabling the transformation from business strategy to operational execution. [...] The professional enterprise architect uses certain capabilities and duties to bridge the gap between the business model, which focuses on the revenue generating parts of the business, and the operating model, which focuses on production and reducing costs". CAEAP (2010b, p. 3) further explains that "enterprise architects use specialized practices to determine where the company is today, scenarios for where it will be tomorrow, and they provide roadmaps that lead from one stage in the journey to the next". Similarly, du Preez et al. (2018, p. 96) state that "the role of the enterprise architect is enhancing the designing and redesigning of the goals and objectives of the enterprise into architected reality thereby promoting proactive enterprise development". Graves (2008) even proposes a perfectly speculative methodology and framework for such "real", not IT-centric enterprise architects

[28] In fact, many authors recognize system, software or technical architects as a major archetype of architects akin to enterprise architects (Akenine, 2008; Banger and Barnes, 2010; Beijer and de Klerk, 2010; Figueiredo et al., 2014; Gellweiler, 2020; Gellweiler, 2021; Unde, 2008)

[29] As discussed earlier, enterprise architects can be compared metaphorically to city planners, but system architects, or software architects, can only be compared to classic building architects. As Jung and Fraunholz (2021, p. 3) observe, "This metaphor [of enterprise architects as town planners] is very common in the literature [...]. It explains the point of view of the software architect as being the one in charge of building a house or a group of houses. By contrast, enterprise architect is more like the town planner. The town planner is responsible for defining the infrastructure of a town, [...] or even a metropolitan area (e.g. Melbourne). He or she ensures that we have for example streets, public transport and water supplies. Town planning also includes the definition of rules for building houses — i.e. rules that the architect of an individual house needs to follow"

[30] The image of enterprise architects largely as draftsmen obsessed with a proper modeling notation and viewpoints is promoted, for instance, by Lankhorst (2017) touting the ArchiMate language

[31] As Fehskens (2015a, p. 12) explains, "Enterprise architects often make a big deal about an enterprise being a system of systems, but, really, everything that we as enterprise architects are likely to think of as a system is likely to be a system of systems"

[32] See Kotusev (2020a)

[33] As Hohpe (2020, p. 16) jokingly observes, "The enterprise architect is sometimes seen as [the Architect from "The Matrix" movie] — the all-knowing decision maker. Some even wish themselves into such a role, partly because it is neat to be all-knowing and partly because it gets you a lot of respect. Naturally, this role model has some issues: all-knowingness turns out to be a little too ambitious for humans, leading to poor decision-making and all sorts of other problems. Even if the architect is a super-smart person, they can base decisions on only those facts that are known to them. In large companies with a complex IT, it would be impossible to stay in touch with all technology that is in place". Hohpe (2020, p. 18) adds: "Architects can

sometimes be seen as wizards who can solve just about any technical challenge. Although that can be a short-term ego boost, it's not a good job description and expectation to live up to"

[34] See, for example, Coghill (2016). Likewise, Bernard (2005, p. 2) argues that the "vision of enterprise architects as "designers of enterprises" is the highest, most far reaching and compelling vision of [architects'] future", ascribing this vision to John Zachman, whom he mistakenly calls the "father of enterprise architecture" (Kotusev, 2021c)

[35] For example, David Knott fairly observes that "architects are sometimes accused of "not making anything"" (Hohpe, 2020, p. ix). As Hohpe (2020, p. 1) sarcastically points out, "Some managers and technical staff might consider [architects] to be overpaid ivory tower residents who, detached from reality, bestow their thoughts upon the rest of the company with slides and wall-sized posters, while their quest for irrelevant ideals causes missed project timelines". Bossert and Manwani (2021, p. 11) confirm: "We have seen many organizations in which the EA department was considered an "ivory tower"". Generally, enterprise architects are often perceived in the industry as dwellers of ivory towers (Perry, 2015)

[36] For instance, in the study of Tamm et al. (2022, p. 9), "lack of engagement and relevance (also referred to as an "ivory tower" approach) were among the most frequently mentioned failures of less-effective EA teams, reflecting a mindset where producing EA artifacts, rather than providing advice to decision-makers, had become the end-game"

Chapter 6: Resources of Enterprise Architects

[1] Due to their great variety, the resources of enterprise architects can be organized in many different ways. However, irrespective of their specific organization, the qualities of architects described in this chapter are highly congruent with their knowledge, skills, competencies, traits, characteristics, personality types, talents and profiles described in numerous academic studies (Besker et al., 2015; Clements et al., 2007; Frampton et al., 2005; Frampton and Ho, 2009; Gellweiler, 2020; Steghuis and Proper, 2008; Strano and Rehmani, 2007; Wagter et al., 2012; Ylimaki and Halttunen, 2005; Ylinen and Pekkola, 2018; Ylinen and Pekkola, 2020) and industry publications (Banger and Barnes, 2010; Beijer and de Klerk, 2010; Bente et al., 2012; Bittler, 2008; Bredemeyer Consulting, 2002; Bredemeyer and Malan, 2002; Bredemeyer and Malan, 2004; Coghill, 2016; Collins, 2014; EACOE, 2023; Edwards, 2020; Evans, 2010; FEAPO, 2018; Gibson, 2008; Hofstader, 2008; Krishnamurthy, 2017; Lambert, 2018; McSweeney, 2019; Nash, 2010; Network World, 2016; Preisker et al., 2023; Shirey, 2008; Shrivastava and Srivastav, 2024; The Open Group, 2022; Unde, 2008; Violino, 2020; Walker, 2007; Weiss et al., 2008; White, 2020; Wierda, 2015; Worthen, 2005)

[2] The official information about the GDPR (General Data Protection Regulation) can be found here: https://eur-lex.europa.eu/eli/reg/2016/679

[3] A brief overview of information privacy laws adopted in different jurisdictions can be found, for example, on Wikipedia: https://en.wikipedia.org/wiki/Information_privacy_law

[4] The official information about the PMBOK (Project Management Body of Knowledge) Guide can be found here: https://www.pmi.org/pmbok-guide-standards/foundational/pmbok

[5] The official information about the PRINCE2 (PRojects IN Controlled Environments) method can be found here: https://www.axelos.com/certifications/propath/prince2-project-management

[6] The official information about the ITIL (Information Technology Infrastructure Library) can be found here: https://www.axelos.com/certifications/itil-service-management

[7] The official information about the COBIT (Control Objectives for Information and Related Technologies) framework can be found here: https://www.isaca.org/resources/cobit

[8] The official information about the Scrum framework can be found here: https://scrumguides.org

[9] The official information about the HIPAA (Health Insurance Portability and Accountability Act) can be found here: https://www.hhs.gov/hipaa/index.html

[10] The official information about the PCI DSS (Payment Card Industry Data Security Standard) can be found here: https://www.pcisecuritystandards.org

[11] The latest version of the Business Process Framework (eTOM) can be found here: https://www.tmforum.org/oda/business/process-framework-etom/

[12] The latest version of the BIAN (Banking Industry Architecture Network) Service Landscape can be found here: https://bian.org/deliverables/bian-standards/

[13] The latest version of the ACORD (Association for Cooperative Operations Research and Development) Reference Architecture can be found here: https://acord.org/standards-architecture/reference-architecture

[14] The latest version of the SCOR (Supply Chain Operations Reference) model can be found here: https://scor.ascm.org

[15] The latest version of HL7 (Health Level Seven) standards can be found here: https://www.hl7.org/implement/standards/

[16] The latest version of the LEDES (Legal Electronic Data Exchange Standard) can be found here: https://ledes.org

[17] The latest version of the AIDX (Aviation Information Data Exchange) messaging standard can be found here: https://www.iata.org/en/publications/info-data-exchange

[18] The latest version of railML (Railway Markup Language) can be found here: https://www.railml.org

[19] See, for example, Lave and Wenger (1991)

[20] For example, Krishnamurthy (2017) proposes a somewhat similar classification scheme with four major skill areas: collaborator, stimulator, expert and thinker

[21] The enormous diversity of the potential stakeholder audiences of enterprise architects, as well as the necessity for architects to adapt their communication approaches to each of these audiences, are widely recognized in the literature (Besker et al., 2015; Mapingire et al., 2018; Schulenklopper and Rommes, 2016; Shirey, 2008; Unde, 2008). As Unde (2008, p. 8) explains, "The architects need to adapt their communication style when interfacing with different stakeholders. For example, when they deal with the senior management, brevity is important, whereas when they deal with the developers, clarity is more important. The different stakeholders have different expectations — the executives require a business view of the solution explaining the investments, returns, and benefits, whereas the developers are interested in nitty-gritty of the technology implementation. The architect must understand the needs of these different stakeholders and change the articulation style and content of each interface accordingly". Schulenklopper and Rommes (2016, p. 15) concur: "Effective communication means adapting the message to the audience, speaking their language, and selecting only the relevant information and presenting it accessibly. To make matters more interesting, architects communicate with a diverse set of stakeholders: end users, developers, operators, financial professionals, and business managers, to name a few. Each of them speaks a slightly different language, has his or her own interests, and has a different level of understanding of the system". Similarly, Mapingire et al. (2018, p. 158) conclude that "communication should be done effectively and tailored to all managerial levels. Other participants emphasized that communication has many facets and that the enterprise architect as a professional who deals with diverse audiences should be able to communicate and tailor their message appropriately to each audience". As Shirey (2008, p. 28) reports, "Some of the best architects I've known have the ability to meet with executives and discuss topics in business terms, then walk down the hall to the development team and dive deep into technology discussions"

[22] In fact, communication skills are unanimously acknowledged as the single most important competency by most studies of the necessary competencies of enterprise architects (Besker et al., 2015; Frampton and Ho, 2009; Mapingire et al., 2018; Ylimaki and Halttunen, 2005). For example, as Frampton and Ho (2009, p. 46) report, "Communication is the key capability for enterprise architects. Oral, visual, and written communication skills, and presentation skills are all thought to be essential to the role. As one interviewee said, "If they can't communicate nothing else matters"". Likewise, Mapingire et al. (2018, p. 158) come to a similar conclusion: "The skill to communicate is like a golden thread that joins and complements all the other skills that the enterprise architect must have. Communication emerged as a natural skill that needs to be honed and perfected to make one a well-polished professional. [...] In comparison to all other competencies and skill sets that were

highlighted by research participants, communication was by far the most popular skill that every participant mentioned, pointing to the importance of this competence". In the study of Besker et al. (2015, p. 35), "architects describe communication as the single most important core competence for the enterprise architect's profession". In another study, analogously, "the informants saw the ability to communicate as one of the most important capabilities of enterprise architects" (Olsen, 2017, p. 642). In the same spirit, in the study of Jiang et al. (2024, p. 8), "almost all participants agree that architects need to be good at communication, especially the ability to communicate with people coming from different backgrounds to join the dots and to become translators for both business and IT sides for resolving communication difficulties and achieving mutual understanding". The industry survey conducted by Capgemini Invent shows that being good communicators between business and IT is the top success factor for architects (Preisker et al., 2023). Another survey by McKinsey and Henley Business School demonstrates that interpersonal skills represent the most important development area for architects with 86% of the participants selecting this area among the top three high-priority development areas (Bossert and Manwani, 2021; Bossert and van der Wildt, 2021). As Hohpe (2020, p. 141) explains, "Architects don't live in isolation. It's their job to gather information from disparate departments, articulate a cohesive strategy, communicate decisions, and win supporters at all levels of the organization. Communication skills are therefore paramount for architects". Unsurprisingly, Apthorp (2011, p. 6) gives the following advice to aspiring enterprise architects: "Communicate, communicate, communicate"

[23] As FEAPO (2018, p. 15) stresses, "A key requirement for any enterprise architect is the ability to collaborate effectively with that role's unique stakeholders, set appropriate expectations, and build consensus towards a desired or intended solution". Moreover, "a skilled enterprise architect is a negotiator. He or she must have the skills to find a win-win situation for the enterprise. Not to underestimate the other competencies, any enterprise architect lacking in interpersonal skills is unlikely to succeed, regardless of their ability to understand and communicate complex systems" (FEAPO, 2018, p. 10). Wright (2011, p. 72) agrees: "Technical skills are no panacea — they're extremely important, but they do you no good if you can't collaborate with others". As Krishnamurthy (2017, p. 10) points out, "As highly accomplished individuals, architects sometimes might have traces of arrogance and the desire to show that they're right. This will create unnecessary friction"

[24] As Network World (2016, p. 4) reports, "In fact, most of the architects we surveyed saw [technological] evangelism as a core part of their role within their organization. An impressive majority (87%) agreed that they could beneficially change the way the organization views IT, and almost half of those we asked strongly agreed with that idea"

[25] As Strano and Rehmani (2007, p. 386) describe it metaphorically, "The enterprise architect has the maestro view of the enterprise. Just as the symphony orchestra conductor understands how each family of instruments adds value to the complete symphony sound and how each musician contributes to the composition, the enterprise architect understands how each capability supports the organizational goals and objectives and how each of the processes, roles, and technologies must be integrated to achieve the desired results"

[26] Interestingly, it is this ability that gave the title to the book of Evans (2010, p. 83): "It's time to explain the original premise of this book. One of the biggest differentiators between most IT resources and architects is the architects' ability to think in an abstract manner. Excellent architects who become EAs [enterprise architects] also possess what I've named the Zoom Factor. [...] It is the ability to zoom in and out while you are speaking and listening, and to see the big picture in the back of your mind while you process the finer details at the very same time. The ability to focus is highly regarded in most professions. The ability to focus on two perspectives at the same time is rare". Krishnamurthy (2017, p. 11) agrees: "Being able to zoom in or out as required is important. Being extremely detail oriented yet having an abstraction capability is perhaps the distinguishing quality of a successful architect". Unde (2008, p. 7) offers a similar explanation: "Architects interact with many stakeholders — CIOs, project managers, business users, and developers — and each expects them to work differently. While the CIO expects an architect to derive a solution roadmap for implementing the company's IT vision, the developer expects the architect to provide direction on the technical problem. The architect needs to have a bird's eye view in one scenario, while in some other scenarios, the architect needs to dive deep into the problem area. The architect is expected to be both a generalist and a specialist"

[27] See, for example, Chase and Simon (1973)

[28] As Unde (2008, p. 9) asserts, "Architects need exposure to projects of varying scope and scale on a range of technology platforms. [...] I believe aspiring architects should deliberately try to get into the assignments that offer a range of experiences rather than sticking to the assignments of similar nature"

[29] A good deal of personal experience and practical wisdom accumulated over the years of working as an enterprise architect is provided by Hohpe (2020)

[30] As Unde (2008, p. 9) explains, "The size of the project does matter in enhancing your architectural skills. For example, the architectural considerations for a small, local application for a limited number of users will be totally different than those for a large application being accessed by a large user base across the globe"

[31] As Hohpe (2020, p. 100) observes, "One item routinely missing from [product selection] "features" lists is planned obsolescence: how easy is it to replace the system? Can the data be exported in a well-defined format? Can business logic be extracted and reused in a replacement system to avoid vendor lock-in? During the new product selection honeymoon, this can feel like discussing a prenup before the wedding — who likes to think about parting ways when you are about to embark on a lifelong journey? In the case of an IT system, you better hope the journey isn't lifelong; systems are meant to come and go. So better to have a prenup in place than being held hostage by the system (or vendor) you are trying to part with"

[32] As Hohpe (2020, p. 133) explains, "Because it's difficult for a vendor to change its product philosophy, you will likely encounter old products with a new coat of paint on it. Your job as an architect is to look through the shiny new paint and see whether there's any rust or filler underneath"

[33] A number of alternative competency frameworks for enterprise architects were proposed in the industry, for instance, by Bredemeyer Consulting (2002), Tambouris et al. (2012), FEAPO (2018) and The Open Group (2022). However, the quality of these frameworks in terms of their accurate reflection of real architects' roles and competencies is debatable. For example, Gellweiler (2020, p. 27) concludes that "the widely used TOGAF framework [...] does not mirror the roles [of architects] as searched on labor markets. [...] Even the set of 76 skills in the TOGAF framework [...] was not suitable as the coding scheme for analyzing the job ads [for architects]"

Chapter 7: Instruments of Enterprise Architects

[1] For instance, Hohpe (2020, pp. 142-143) describes six ways in which material EA artifacts provide value: coherence, validation, clarity of thought, education, history and stakeholder communication

[2] See Kotusev (2021b) and Kotusev (2021c) (Chapter 2)

[3] In sociological terminology, EA artifacts represent *boundary objects* between diverse business and IT communities (Abraham, 2013; Kotusev and Kurnia, 2021; Kotusev et al., 2023)

[4] Actualities and plans EA artifacts introduced here closely correspond to facts and decisions artifacts respectively discussed by Kotusev (2019b) and Kotusev (2021c) (Chapter 2)

[5] Initiative-specific and general EA artifacts introduced here closely correspond to temporary and permanent artifacts respectively discussed by Kotusev (2021c) (Chapter 2)

[6] Solutions, structures and rules EA artifacts introduced here are identical to changes, structures and rules artifacts respectively discussed by Kotusev (2016e), Kotusev (2019e) and Kotusev (2021c) (Chapter 8)

[7] IT-focused and business-focused EA artifacts introduced here are identical to IT-focused and business-focused artifacts respectively discussed by Kotusev (2016e), Kotusev (2019e) and Kotusev (2021c) (Chapter 8)

[8] The six general types of EA artifacts (Considerations, Standards, Visions, Landscapes, Outlines and Designs) are discussed in great detail by Kotusev (2021c) (Part II) and in other related sources (Kotusev, 2017c; Kotusev et al., 2020a; Kotusev et al., 2022)

[9] For the sake of contextual fit, the CSVLOD taxonomy for EA artifacts presented here is rotated clockwise relative to its presentation in other sources (Kotusev, 2016e; Kotusev, 2017a; Kotusev, 2019e; Kotusev, 2021c)

[10] See Lankhorst (2017) and Scheer (1992) respectively

[11] See White and Miers (2008) and Marca and McGowan (2005) respectively

[12] See Fowler (2003) and Richards and Ford (2020) respectively

[13] See, for example, the recent analyses of the EA tool market provided by Gartner (Gianni et al., 2023) and Forrester (Barnett et al., 2023)

Chapter 8: The Catalog of Enterprise Architecture Artifacts

[1] A more detailed, comprehensive discussion of different subtypes of EA artifacts is provided by Kotusev (2021c) (Part II), while the underlying research is described by Kotusev (2019a)

[2] A brief overview and comparison of popular reference models for different industries is provided, for instance, by Paradkar (2024)

[3] A comprehensive description of core diagrams is provided by Ross et al. (2006)

[4] A detailed description of the concept of business model canvas is provided by Osterwalder and Pigneur (2010)

[5] See Kotusev (2017a)

Chapter 9: Using Enterprise Architecture Artifacts

[1] The process of modifying EA artifacts for documenting the existing situation described here is identical to the process of developing facts artifacts by enterprise architects discussed by Kotusev (2019b) and Kotusev (2021c) (Chapter 2)

[2] The mapping of EA artifacts to the space of architectural solutions presented here, though rotated clockwise, is largely identical to the mapping of artifacts to the continuous CSVLOD taxonomy presented by Kotusev (2021c) (Chapter 15)

Chapter 10: Basic Activities of Enterprise Architects

[1] For instance, Woods (2014, p. 10) fairly points out that "one intriguing aspect [of architects' profession] is the sheer diversity of work that people with "architect" in their job titles perform". As Bente et al. (2012, p. 40) explain at the beginning of their chapter on the activities of enterprise architects, "Because of the many facets of [enterprise architects], any compilation of [their] activities will probably be incomplete, but the selection we lay out in this chapter lists the situations we most frequently encounter in both practice and literature"

[2] For example, in the study of Besker et al. (2015, p. 32), "almost all [enterprise architects] describe continuous acquisition of knowledge through academic studies, participate in forums, read trade magazines, visiting fairs and collegial networking as important to be able to develop themselves and the business within the EA field"

[3] See, for example, Hohpe (2020) (Chapter 14)

[4] As Krishnamurthy (2017, p. 11) puts it, "An architect must be prepared to acquire new knowledge, which might require shaking off established understanding and assumptions"

[5] For instance, Jiang et al. (2024, p. 8) conclude that "architects should have market sensitivity to recognize and understand technological trends and market demands in a timely and effective way. A competent architect must be sensitive to major technological trends and market changes to guide organizations to equip strong adaptability to changes and surpass competitors"

[6] For example, the survey of Network World (2016, p. 5) identifies virtually identical sources of information on the external environment used by enterprise architects: "The architects we surveyed pointed to common — but not specialized — sources of information about both strategy and technical matters: search engines, analyst firms, and of course, information provided by technology vendors through web sites, white papers, in-person discussions and more. Social media sites including LinkedIn (66%), YouTube (yes, YouTube

— 38%) and Facebook (29%), were listed among the community sources most often visited by architects in a given week"

[7] The official information about Thoughtworks Technology Radar can be found here: https://www.thoughtworks.com/radar

[8] The official information about Gartner Magic Quadrant can be found here: https://www.gartner.com/en/research/methodologies/magic-quadrants-research

[9] The official information about Forrester Wave can be found here: https://www.forrester.com/policies/forrester-wave-methodology/

[10] As Hohpe (2020, p. 28) explains, "When you sit near a large IT budget that's being vied for by vendors, you'll have many folks wanting to update you on new technologies [...]. However, neutrality is an architect's major asset, so they're expected to cut through the buzzword fog to discern what's really new and what's just clever repackaging of old concepts"

[11] See Fenn and Raskino (2008)

[12] For instance, the decreasing dependence between the time spent by enterprise architects on studying their transformation drivers and their tenure in the organization is confirmed by the survey of Network World (2016, p. 5): "On average, architects spend around 9 hours a week educating themselves about problems and business needs within their organization. Among new (<3 years tenure) and younger employees (18-34 years old) in the enterprise architect role, time spent coming up to speed on business needs and problems within their organization was even greater. On average, new architects spend an average of 10 hours per week on this task, and younger architects spend 13 hours per week"

[13] For example, the survey of Kleehaus and Matthes (2019) identifies very similar sources of information on the internal IT environment used by enterprise architects, in order of decreasing importance: project documentation, CMDBs, knowledgeable people, IT management tools and monitoring tools

[14] For example, the survey of Bizzdesign (2024, p. 14) shows that information about the internal environment in organizations is most typically spread across multiple different systems, where "only a quarter of organizations have their enterprise architecture data created and mastered in a single source", and their EA tools, therefore, are frequently integrated with many other systems, including CMDBs, IT service management, project management, portfolio management and GRC (governance, risk and compliance) management tools, data governance and modeling systems, business process and innovation management platforms

[15] For instance, Jiang et al. (2024, p. 8) observe that architects "need to demonstrate their leadership and decisiveness when making strategic decisions. Indecisiveness or hesitation when coming to decision-making is often detrimental to maintaining credibility and deeper collaboration [with managers]"

Chapter 11: Leading the Development of Plans

[1] This terminological distinction is made specifically to accentuate the difference between the general organizational responsibilities of enterprise architects (i.e. leading architectural planning) and their concrete daily activities (i.e. leading the development of plans), though both these terms ultimately refer to the same physical actions

[2] For instance, the research of Pentland (2012, p. 65) comes to the following conclusions: "The most valuable form of communication is face-to-face. The next most valuable is by phone or videoconference, but with a caveat: Those technologies become less effective as more people participate in the call or conference. The least valuable forms of communication are e-mail and texting"

[3] The three-step process of architectural planning described here is identical to the process of developing decisions artifacts by enterprise architects discussed by Kotusev (2019b) and Kotusev (2021c) (Chapter 2)

[4] As Hohpe (2020, p. 142) emphasizes, "Architects must help close the gap between technical knowledge holders and high-level decision makers by clearly communicating the ramifications of technical decisions on the business; for example, through development and operational cost, flexibility, or time-to-market. It's not only the "business types" who face challenges in understanding complex technology, though. Even architects and

developers cannot possibly keep up with all aspects of intricate technical solutions, forcing them to also rely on easy-to-understand but technically accurate descriptions of architectural decisions and their implications"

⁵ In practice, developing architectural solutions can require many cyclical iterations of discussions between stakeholders. For example, Ross (2004, p. 1) reports that the CIO of Delta Air Lines, "who led the development of the enterprise architecture, estimated that the management team needed about 60 iterations before everyone agreed on Delta's [core diagram]"

⁶ As Woods and Rozanski (2012, p. 5) explain, "Architectural design tends to involve searching for an acceptable solution amongst a range of possible options, which meet the concerns of different stakeholders to a different degree. It is often a case of achieving the least bad option, given stakeholder needs and biases, rather than the optimal engineering solution". Woods (2014, p. 11) even jokes that "architecture normally involves selecting the least worst option". Conceptually, the development of architectural solutions for transformation initiatives corresponds to the "satisficing" model of rational choice by groups of people with different preferences described by Simon (1955)

⁷ A more sophisticated example of architectural planning at the highest level, where a strategic business vision is translated into an abstract IT platform by balancing what is organizationally desirable and what is technically achievable, is described by Sauer and Willcocks (2002, pp. 43-44)

⁸ Many experience-based practical recommendations for creating engaging architectural presentations are provided, for instance, by Hohpe (2020) (Part III)

⁹ These two modes of working highly correlate with the observations of architectural planning by Ross et al. (2006, pp. 65-66): "We have seen two successful strategies to involve senior executives: IT-facilitated senior management discussions and senior management approval of IT-led designs"

Chapter 12: Ensuring Adherence to Plans

¹ As in the case of leading the development of plans, this terminological distinction is necessary to differentiate between the general organizational responsibilities of enterprise architects (i.e. exercising architectural oversight) and their concrete daily activities (i.e. ensuring adherence to plans), though both these terms ultimately refer to the same physical actions

² As Walker (2007, p. 1) puts it, "When there are no management ties between you and the personnel you wish to influence, it becomes increasingly challenging for EAs [enterprise architects] to accomplish their goals"

³ As Besker et al. (2015, p. 32) explain, "When an architect becomes aware of a lacking project that does not conform to the agreed architecture, most architects have not the power to alone stop such a project. In these cases, a discrepancy report is created and escalated to decision-makers with more power"

⁴ This adage is typically ascribed to Helmuth von Moltke, a Prussian field marshal of the 19th century

⁵ For instance, Haag and Eckhardt (2017, p. 469) define shadow IT as "hardware, software, or services built, introduced, and/or used for the job without explicit approval or even knowledge of the organization". In the survey of Schneider et al. (2015, p. 17), 56% of respondents confirmed the statement that "the higher the standardization degree of the applied IT, the higher the danger of generating shadow IT by the business departments"

⁶ As Faber (2010, p. 37) explains, "Keeping the rules isn't the goal; the goal is the overall system's quality. Also, architects can't inhibit rule breaking completely, even if they try. The pressure of requirements and the project schedule is too high. Rather, architects must help break the rules correctly. If they don't, developers under stress break rules without notice, likely ignoring the quality balance, thereby leading to inconsistencies or even flaws in the architecture". In a similar vein, in the study of Besker et al. (2015, p. 34), "several respondents clarify that the area of responsibility and power should not be associated with an organizational police permitting authorization or actively searching for scapegoats who violate the architectural guidelines"

⁷ See, for example, Levitt and March (1988) and Denrell and Le Mens (2020)

⁸ See, for example, March (1991a) and Levinthal and March (1993)

Chapter 13: The Work of Enterprise Architects

[1] For instance, Sauer and Willcocks (2002, p. 42) stress that "the support of key executives is critical, and the architect must be trusted by the CEO's inner circle. Someone who has directed a strategic change is a good candidate as an [enterprise] architect"

[2] For example, in the survey of Network World (2016, p. 4), "85% [of the surveyed enterprise architects] said they had been the source of ideas that have directly impacted their company's business model or go to market strategy"

[3] For example, in the survey of Network World (2016, p. 3), "47% [of the surveyed enterprise architects] strongly agreed with the notion that cultivating strong relationships with senior business stakeholders was a core component of their job"

[4] For instance, as Besker et al. (2015, p. 32) report, "The results of [our] study show that it is not uncommon that [enterprise architects] have other parallel assignments besides direct EA and some respondents estimate that they periodically work more than half their time on non-direct EA activities"

[5] As Erder and Pureur (2016, p. 32) argue, "Architects can't overcommunicate. More than 50 percent of architects' time must focus on effective communication and collaboration"

[6] This and related discussions are inspired by the famous study of the work, activities and schedule of managers by Mintzberg (1973)

[7] A similar sample of the timetable of an enterprise architect specializing in the security domain is provided by Collins (2014) (Chapter 7)

[8] In fact, most organizations spend more than half of their IT budget on keeping the existing systems up and running rather than developing new systems for digital transformation: "We asked respondents to estimate what percentage of their IT resources were devoted to new capabilities and innovations rather than maintaining the status quo. The average response was 39 percent" (Bizzdesign, 2021, p. 22). Various industry surveys provide different estimates of the portion of IT budget spent by organizations on "keeping the lights on" usually falling within the range of about 40–65% (Johnson et al., 2024; Kappelman et al., 2019; Weill and Ross, 2009; Weill and Woerner, 2010; Weill et al., 2009; Weill et al., 2008; Weiss and Rosser, 2008), with a recorded maximum of 71% (Weill and Ross, 2009) and a recorded minimum of 36.8% (Johnson et al., 2024)

Chapter 14: The Profession of Enterprise Architects

[1] The fact that managerial work is intractable to codification and cannot be treated as a profession is widely acknowledged in the management literature (Barker, 2010; Mintzberg, 2004; Whitley, 1989). As Mintzberg (2004, p. 11) explains, "Engineering does apply a good deal of science, codified and certified as to its effectiveness. And so it can be called a profession, which means it can be taught in advance of practice, out of context. [...] But that cannot be said of management [...]. Little of its practice has been reliably codified, let alone certified as to its effectiveness. So management cannot be called a profession or taught as such"

[2] Some authors argue for universal certification or even mandatory licensing of enterprise architects in a way similar to other professionals (CAEAP, 2010a; Lane, 2010; Preiss, 2008; Strano and Rehmani, 2005; Walrad et al., 2013), but because their profession can be defined only loosely, these calls do not seem realistic

[3] The validity, legitimacy and status, values, principles and ethics, qualifications, accreditations and certifying bodies, as well as some other aspects of the profession of enterprise architects, are discussed by many authors (CAEAP, 2010a; Fehskens, 2016; Lane, 2010; Preiss, 2008; Strano and Rehmani, 2005; Uppal, 2013; Walrad et al., 2013)

[4] This question and the ensuing discussion are inspired by a similar analysis of the practice of management by Mintzberg (2009, pp. 9-13)

[5] The multifaceted nature of the profession of enterprise architects is also noticed by Beijer and de Klerk (2010, p. 144): "Clearly, [...] the IT architecture profession is an interdisciplinary field that draws upon science,

technology, sociology, politics, art, etc. and is often governed by the architect's own personal experience, approach, and philosophy"

[6] The story of LEO is thoroughly documented from different perspectives by direct project participants, science journalists and technology historians (Bird, 1994; Caminer et al., 1998; Ferry, 2003; Hendry, 1987; Simmons, 1962) and its groundbreaking achievement is widely acknowledged in the academic community (Baskerville, 2003; Hirschheim and Klein, 2012; Mason, 2004)

[7] The original master plan for LEO is provided by Simmons (1962) (Chapter 5)

[8] As Caminer et al. (1998, p. 15) recollect, "Simmons set up [the Systems Research Office] to ensure that the most suitable machines were installed and that they were incorporated into comprehensive systems aimed at producing, in a secure and timely way, the information needed by management at all levels to run the business". And "when more advanced office machinery became available, the Systems Research responsibility was not merely to speed up what was being done already. Its job was to examine whether the business needs could now be met in new ways, yielding more help to management along the way" (Caminer, 2003, p. 268)

[9] For instance, McFarlan (1971, p. 80) provides a job description for the position titled "Manager of Divisional EDP [IT] Planning" whose tasks clearly correspond to the activities of enterprise architects (see Figure 13.3) and include, among others, "to keep abreast of developments in information technology" (i.e. analyzing the external environment), "to help corporate planning management optimize cost/effectiveness" (i.e. providing advisory services), "to develop and maintain [...] short- and long-range objectives and plans for systems" (i.e. leading the development of plans) and "to review all proposals and requisitions for consistency with established short- and long-range plans" (i.e. ensuring adherence to plans)

[10] See McFarlan (1971), McLean and Soden (1977), Sporn (1978), Rush (1979), van Rensselaer (1979) and McNurlin (1979). As McFarlan (1971, p. 76) reports, "Only one company of those [15 large companies] we examined had been planning its CBIS [computer-based information systems] systematically for as long as four years". Nevertheless, "of the 15 companies studied, 9 use a well-defined, formal planning structure to write and update their plans annually" (McFarlan, 1971, p. 84). In the survey of 20 large organizations conducted in 1974 by McLean and Soden (1977, p. 66), all the participants launched their formal systems planning efforts during the last ten years: two in 1964–1965, two in 1966–1967, four in 1968–1969, four in 1970–1971, six in 1972–1973 and two in 1974. The very problem of information systems planning has been discussed in the industry since the 1950s (Canning, 1956; Evans and Hague, 1962; Levin, 1957)

[11] For example, in IBM, "the corporate information systems planning function was officially instituted in 1966. A formal organizational structure evolved, beginning with corporate and group information systems planning activities in 1966; division and major location information systems planning activities followed in 1967, as the processes became better defined. [...] During the first 15 months the activity's staff increased from three to eight professionals [...]. In 1969 the architecture staff expanded to 14 members. [...] In 1974 20 people were concerned with information systems control and planning, exercising worldwide responsibility for maintaining the information system in a manner consistent with the architectural design" (McLean and Soden, 1977, pp. 174-176). In Trans World Airlines, "the first comprehensive long-range plan for information systems was prepared in 1968. It was the result of a substantial effort by the planning group within the corporate systems and data services department. It had a horizon of seven years and consisted of two massive volumes, covering projects that had a total price tag of $300 million!" (McLean and Soden, 1977, p. 197). Or, in Mobil Oil, "long-range planning for information systems was first begun in 1969, with the creation of the first five-year and one-year plans; each of these plans has been revised or redone every succeeding year. As an indication of the amount of attention devoted to information systems planning at Mobil, in 1973 an estimate was made that the creation of that year's five-year plan absorbed more than 200 man-months" (McLean and Soden, 1977, p. 106)

[12] Numerous industry surveys conducted yearly since 1980 (Ball and Harris, 1982) till the present days (Johnson et al., 2024) consistently demonstrate that improving information systems planning and their alignment with business needs represents the single biggest concern, or one of the biggest concerns, for IT executives

[13] For instance, the survey of 334 organizations conducted in 1982 by Hoffman and Martino (1983, pp. C-1) demonstrates that "14 per cent of respondents overall have a dedicated IS [information systems] planning staff"

[14] For instance, in the survey of 105 organizations conducted in 1991 by Finnegan and Fahy (1993, p. 132), "a permanent IS [information systems] planning group was found to exist in only 43.6% of organizations. Such a group is more likely to be found in larger organizations and where there are close links between business and IS planning". Also, "IS planning was found to be a relatively recent phenomenon for the majority of the organizations studied, with over 82% of those studied having less than ten year's experience in the area"

[15] All these and some other, more exotic titles (e.g. data processing planners and information resource planners) had been used in the industry from the 1950s till the 1990s (Boynton and Zmud, 1987; Brathwaite, 1992; Canning, 1957; Cheung, 1990; Evans and Hague, 1962; King, 1978; Lederer and Sethi, 1991; Levin, 1957; McFarlan, 1971; McNurlin, 1979; Periasamy, 1994; Segars and Grover, 1996; Seiler and Boockholdt, 1983; Selig, 1982; Sullivan, 1988). Historically, in different epochs, IT and information systems themselves had different, rather peculiar names that determined the titles of their planners, e.g. electronic data processing (EDP) (Kami, 1958), automatic data processing (ADP) (Diebold, 1964) and information resource management (IRM) (Holmes, 1977).

[16] As Dietz (2008, p. 1) fairly observes, "Somewhere in the eighties, the terms "architect" and "architecture" became 'hot' in the practice of building, implementing, and using ICT applications in enterprises. The proliferation of both terms went quickly. By the beginning of the nineties, designers of e.g., information systems, infrastructural networks, and business processes called themselves architects. Likewise, the global design of a system was commonly called its architecture". Woods and Rozanski (2012, p. 5) make an analogous observation: "[Despite originating much earlier,] the idea of a software or IT architect did not become widespread until the 1990s, when it became more common to hear of people described as "architects" [...]. Since then, awareness and understanding of the role has accelerated, to the point where today you can find architects in almost any enterprise with a significant IT capability"

[17] Although the very buzzword "architects" emerged in the 1980s (Ben-Nathan, 1980; Brockbank, 1987; Huff, 1982; Mills, 1985; Tsichritzis, 1980), the origins of the term "enterprise architects" are difficult to trace; it is not clear who and when initially coined it. However, the first use of this term in the mainstream literature can be traced to Armour et al. (1999a) and, by the mid-2000s, the term became deeply ingrained in the industry discourse (Daniel, 2007; Parsons, 2005; Strano and Rehmani, 2007; Worthen, 2005)

[18] The same conclusion is also valid for the discipline of enterprise architecture as a whole, which historically "re-emerged" in the mainstream discourse several times under different labels: first, as information systems planning in the 1960s–1970s, then as information architecture in the early 1980s, next as information engineering in the late 1980s and, finally, as enterprise architecture in the 1990s (Kotusev, 2016d; Kotusev, 2018f; Kotusev, 2021c). Interestingly, the first sources using the label "enterprise architecture" do not call the respective practitioners "enterprise architects", but still apply the older term "planners" (Richardson et al., 1990; Spewak and Hill, 1992)

[19] For instance, recent surveys by Capgemini Invent demonstrate that corporate architecture functions are established in about 68% (Karmann et al., 2019), 67% (Preisker et al., 2020), 61% (Preisker et al., 2022) and 73% (Preisker et al., 2023) of predominantly large organizations in Europe, North America and Australia. Earlier surveys of different years and origins provide rather similar numbers (Alaeddini et al., 2017; Ambler, 2010; Aziz and Obitz, 2005; Aziz and Obitz, 2007; Obitz and Babu, 2009). As van der Raadt et al. (2007, p. 1) observe, "Almost every self-respecting organization (private or public) of considerable size has at least one, but often various, architecture functions". Bente et al. (2012, p. 279) agree: "There is hardly any large company in the world that does not have an EA team, whatever it is called in the respective organization"

[20] The official website of the AEA is located here: https://www.globalaea.org

[21] The official website of the Architectural Thinking Association is located here: https://architectural-thinking.com

[22] Currently, the official website of the FEAPO is available only in the Internet Archive: https://web.archive.org/web/20230402020757/https://feapo.org/

[23] The official website of Gartner is located here: https://www.gartner.com

[24] The official website of Forrester is located here: https://www.forrester.com

[25] The official website of Cutter Consortium is located here: https://www.cutter.com

[26] The official website of The Open Group is located here: https://www.opengroup.org

[27] The official website of the OMG is located here: https://www.omg.org

[28] The official website of the FEAC Institute is located here: https://www.feacinstitute.org

[29] The official website of the EACOE is located here: https://www.eacoe.org

[30] The global pioneers of higher education in the discipline of enterprise architecture include the Pennsylvania State University in the United States, the Delft University of Technology in Europe, the National University of Singapore in Asia and the RMIT University and Griffith University in Australia (Bittler, 2010; Bittler, 2012). A broader overview of notable EA programs in colleges and universities is provided by Calnan (2017)

[31] The official website of the CISR is located here: https://cisr.mit.edu

[32] The official website of SEBIS is located here: https://wwwmatthes.in.tum.de

[33] Currently, the official website of the IFEAD is available only in the Internet Archive: https://web.archive.org/web/20190607134830/http://www.enterprise-architecture.info/

[34] Currently, the official website of the ZIFA is available only in the Internet Archive: https://web.archive.org/web/20081002000034/http://www.zifa.com/

[35] The official website of the JEA is located here: https://www.globalaea.org/page/JEA_Overview

[36] The official website of EAPJ is located here: https://eapj.org

[37] The official website of Architecture & Governance Magazine is located here: https://www.architectureandgovernance.com

[38] The official website of Bizzdesign is located here: https://bizzdesign.com

[39] The official website of LeanIX is located here: https://www.leanix.net

[40] The official website of the BCS EASG is located here: https://www.bcs.org/membership-and-registrations/member-communities/enterprise-architecture-specialist-group/

[41] Currently, the official website of the NAF is available only in the Internet Archive: https://web.archive.org/web/20220411094844/https://www.naf.nl/

[42] The Enterprise Architecture Network group is located here: https://www.linkedin.com/groups/36781/

[43] Enterprise Architecture Forum group is located here: https://www.linkedin.com/groups/36248/

[44] Australasian Architecture Network group is located here: https://www.linkedin.com/groups/1822816/

[45] The official website of Iasa Global is located here: https://iasaglobal.org

[46] The official website of DAMA International is located here: https://www.dama.org

[47] The official website of the Business Architecture Guild is located here: https://www.businessarchitectureguild.org

[48] For instance, the survey of Schekkerman (2005) shows that enterprise architects consume information relevant to their trade from a very wide range of sources, including websites, newsletters, books, brochures, courses, seminars, workshops and presentations, as well as meetings with experienced colleagues

[49] See, for example, Tetlock (2005). As March (2007, p. 16) puts it, "Forecasting the future is a fool's conceit"

[50] For instance, in the survey of Bizzdesign (2023, p. 4), "sixty-two percent of respondents said that demand for EA services had increased in the past year. Of these, 17 percent said that demand had increased significantly"

[51] As Network World (2016, p. 6) reports, "The results of our survey and our in-depth interviews with enterprise architects suggest that these professionals recognize the growing importance of their role and skillset in the workplace. As companies become more reliant on technology, enterprise architects occupy a critical role of facilitating conversations between business and technical leaders, synthesizing technical capabilities and strategic goals and forging a path forward"

[52] For instance, over the period from 2005 to 2023, the average IT budgets of organizations have increased from 3.6% to 6.8% of their revenue (Johnson et al., 2024; Kappelman et al., 2014), which roughly corresponds to a compound annual growth rate of 3.6%

[53] This conclusion can be made from the analysis of various estimates of the ratio of enterprise architects in the IT workforce provided by different sources over the years (Akella and Barlow, 2004; Aziz and Obitz, 2005; Keller, 2005; Kotusev et al., 2024; Manwani and Bossert, 2016; Niemann, 2006; Obitz and Babu, 2009; Preisker et al., 2020; Short and Burke, 2010). For example, as Short and Burke (2010, p. 1) report, "From 2006 to 2007, Gartner conducted research based on approximately 500 companies and determined that the average size of an EA team surveyed was 2.2% [...] of the IT head count. Subsequent surveys and discussions with clients have yielded similar information". In the survey of Akella and Barlow (2004, p. 1), "the architecture groups were small — 2 to 3 percent of the IT group size". As Niemann (2006, p. 181) points out, "Our own figures [from 2003] show that the area of architecture accounts for an average of around 3.4% of total HR capacity in IT". In the survey of Aziz and Obitz (2005, p. 16), "as a weighted average, the enterprise architect ratio is about 3.8%. [However,] removing [the outliers] from the statistics dropped the average from 3.8% to 2.4%". Based on their survey conducted in 2008, Obitz and Babu (2009, pp. 13-14) concluded that "enterprise architecture teams are 2–4% of IT staff [...]. We have asked how many FTEs [full-time employees] are working in IT, and how many are enterprise architects [...]. The median [ratio] was 2.4%. [...] The arithmetical average [...] was 3.5%". Later, in the survey conducted in 2015 by Manwani and Bossert (2016, p. 6), the ratio of enterprise architects was around 3.5% in total: "EA-dedicated resource (internal/external) is about 1% of total IT FTE [full-time equivalent], supplemented by 2.5% outside of EA". In the data gathered by Kotusev et al. (2024) during the period from 2014 to 2021, "the precise ratio of architects was ~4.74%". The survey of Preisker et al. (2020, p. 10) indicates that "on average, 5 percent of employees in IT organizations are enterprise architects". This gradual growth of the ratio of enterprise architects across the industry during the last two decades can arguably be attributed to the emergence and progressing adoption of cloud-based IT solutions, which require roughly the same effort to plan, but less effort to build and maintain, increasing the relative numbers of architects among IT personnel

[54] For example, the survey of Preisker et al. (2020, p. 14) shows that cloud computing (voted for by 79% of respondents), microservices and containerization (68%), APIs and integration technologies (65%), data analytics and business intelligence (61%) and artificial intelligence (53%) are among the most needed future competencies of enterprise architects

[55] The collation of current EA best practices existing in the industry and various historical prescriptions on the subject provided by Kotusev (2021c) (Appendix A) reveals virtually no correlation

[56] For instance, Preisker et al. (2023) already call enterprise architects "digital architects"

[57] For example, in the survey of Paras (2011), 42% of respondents characterized the future of their EA practice as bright and another 32% of respondents — as very bright

[58] The ambiguity of the term "enterprise architect" is clearly manifested, for instance, in job ads: "Searching at the Swiss job market for 'enterprise architect' lists 156 hits. Checking the details reveals that there is no common understanding of what enterprise architecture is, which roles belong to it" (Thonssen and von Dewitz, 2018, p. 410). Steghuis and Proper (2008, p. 94) make an analogous observation: "The requirements put on an enterprise architect seem to range from very specific programming skills to broad leadership qualities as well as the ability to develop a business strategy. Tasks and responsibilities differ per job ad: there is no one set of tasks and responsibilities for the role of enterprise architect". Unsurprisingly, FEAPO (2018, p. 4) reports a reciprocal problem with resumes: "It is no longer difficult to find two people who both have the title of "enterprise architect" on their resume. What has emerged as the next-order problem for organizations hiring an architect is simple: two resumes are highly unlikely to contain similar descriptions of the jobs performed, even

though they have the same title. [...] This diversity of needs and qualifications, all under the title of "enterprise architect", creates an issue for organizations and companies trying to implement a mature EA program. Now that many companies have decided that they want to either hire or develop enterprise architects, there's no standard description of what an enterprise architect should know"

[59] Enterprise architects and solution architects are unanimously recognized as the two main archetypes of architects (Akenine, 2008; Banger and Barnes, 2010; Beijer and de Klerk, 2010; FEAPO, 2018; Figueiredo et al., 2014; Gellweiler, 2020; Gellweiler, 2021; Preisker et al., 2023; The Open Group, 2022; Unde, 2008)

[60] The difference between enterprise architects as a position and other related positions is explained, for instance, by Steghuis and Proper (2008, p. 94): "Besides an enterprise architect, there are many other types of architects, such as business architects, information architects, process architects, IT architects, software architects, application architects, etcetera. The difference between these types of architects and the enterprise architect is that the enterprise architect covers the breadth of business and IT, while domain architects focus on one aspect of the enterprise (business, IT, information) and solution architects on one small part of the implementation of the architecture (applications, software, business processes)"

[61] This metaphor is sometimes used in the specialized EA literature (Finkelstein, 2006; Potts, 2010) and even in the general management literature (Allaire and Howard, 1992; Nadler and Gerstein, 1992). As Potts (2010) explains, "Business executives are, in practice, the architects of their enterprise". Moreover, "business leaders have been the architects of their enterprise, whether they knew it or not, for as long as enterprises have existed" (Potts, 2010). Goebl (2020, p. 1) argues that this is "certainly true" because "decisions made by (senior) executives have the biggest impact on the architecture of an enterprise". Likewise, Finkelstein (2006, p. 19) argues that "the real architects of an enterprise are the senior business managers who set strategic directions for the future, based on business plans and strategies, and processes designed for that future and its technologies". Finkelstein (2006, p. 471) continues: "Enterprise architects are the senior managers who set the directions for the future", "Senior managers establish the business plans and are the true architects of the enterprise" (Finkelstein, 2006, p. 480)

[62] This fiction is promoted, most prominently, in multiple works of Tom Graves: "Real enterprise-architecture requires us [i.e. enterprise architects] to deal with a much broader scope than the familiar comfort-zone of IT-architecture. We do need our architecture to address that full scope — the entire enterprise" (Graves, 2008, p. 1), "Enterprise architecture can't be solely about IT, but about how every aspect of the enterprise interacts with everything else — including security, marketing, business-models, value-flows, and much, much more. And it also can't be centered on IT: in fact, it isn't centered anywhere, other than on that guiding theme, the "defined business scope and mission"" (Graves, 2023, p. 8), "Real enterprise-architecture isn't much about IT at all. Or rather, although IT is significant, it's only one small part. Turns out instead that that blurry 'business architecture' isn't something that can be skipped in a headlong rush down to the technical minutiae: it's actually the core of enterprise-architecture" (Graves, 2007, p. 1), "To make it work, enterprise architecture must be a literal 'architecture of the enterprise': anything less will guarantee the fragmentation and failure of the respective architecture" (Graves and Fehskens, 2015, p. 24), "Enterprise architecture is about the structure and story of the enterprise — how everything fits together in support of the enterprise vision, values, and goals" (Graves, 2023, p. 1), "The scope of enterprise architecture is always the whole of the enterprise – the enterprise as a whole" (Graves, 2023, p. 8)

[63] As Network World (2016, p. 2) puts it, "The "architect" has many modifiers: enterprise architect, infrastructure architect, and solution architect. But the idea is always the same, translating business needs into information technology strategies that help businesses succeed when executed properly". Specifically regarding the archetypes of enterprise and solution architects, FEAPO (2018, p. 7) provides the following explanation: "The relationship between an enterprise architect and a solution architect is not so much a distinction between jobs as it is an understanding of the scope of each architect's work. Whereas the enterprise architect's focus is on formulation of strategy, the focus of the solution architect is on execution of that strategy to solve a particular, tangible, problem". Woods and Rozanski (2012) and Woods (2014) formulate six core characteristics shared by all varieties of architects that can be considered definitive for their profession: design-centric activity, system-wide concerns, stakeholder focus, balancing concerns, lifecycle involvement and technical leadership

Chapter 15: The Archetype of Enterprise Architects

[1] See Kotusev (2022)

[2] In the industry, people with uneven knowledge profiles, and Enterprise Architects in particular, are often called "T-shaped" or "V-shaped" professionals (FEAPO, 2018). "Why "V-shaped"? Because the result is a person whose skills may [resemble the letter "V"], with some skills going far "deeper" than the others" (FEAPO, 2018, p. 7)

[3] As FEAPO (2018, p. 7) puts it, "An effective Enterprise Architect must be able to perform in each [domain] at a "surface" level, and with depth in at least one"

[4] For instance, in the survey of Network World (2016, p. 5), "more than 7 in 10 Enterprise Architects agreed that a technology architecture roadmap was a core deliverable that they owed to their organization"

[5] For example, in the survey of Preisker et al. (2023, pp. 26-27), "50% of the companies [...] state that their enterprise architecture function plays an important role in the development of the future business strategy", "91% of companies agree that integrating EA into the strategy definition results in strong synergies, improved decision making and sustainable strategic change", and "59% of the participants agree that strategic decision-making is based on enterprise architecture information and takes the disruptive forces of new technologies and increasing architectural complexity into account"

[6] As FEAPO (2018, p. 9) explains, "EA decisions can become personal to their stakeholders. Often, two or more business leaders, each with their own "measure of success", are pulling on an initiative: creating subtle conflicts in scope, cost, and expectations. Conflicts such as these have the effect of grinding progress to a halt"

[7] The difficulties of completing major change initiatives under fluid leadership are analyzed, for instance, by Denis et al. (1996)

[8] In this flow of digitalization, high-level architectural planning represents the unity of the interrelated Strategic Planning and Technology Optimization processes discussed by Kotusev (2019d) and Kotusev (2021c) (Chapters 6 and 7)

[9] By contrast, the organization-centric view of digital transformation is adopted by Kotusev (2021c) to discuss enterprise architecture at large, as an organizational practice, without distinguishing programs and strategies as separate change initiatives

[10] For instance, FEAPO (2018) identifies four common patterns of organizing architecture teams: by project, by domain, by strategy and by segment. In this classification, organizing by project and by strategy reflect the initiative-centric view of digitalization (i.e. architects are assigned to individual change initiatives), whereas organizing by domain and by segment reflect the organization-centric view of digitalization (i.e. architects are assigned to different organizational areas)

[11] For example, Figueiredo et al. (2014, p. 1239) report that "our analysis did not identify the [separate] role of the business architect in any of the [nine] studied organizations. What we observed was that when there is an [IT-centric] enterprise architect, this role encompasses business architect activities". Besides that, because the business domain is non-technical (see Table 3.1), architects specializing exclusively in this domain (i.e. pure business architects) do not wear the hat of Technology Experts and, therefore, do *not* qualify as enterprise architects constituting the subject of this book (see Figure 4.10). Generally, the status of business architects in the industry seems questionable and deserves separate in-depth research

Chapter 16: The Archetype of Solution Architects

[1] FEAPO (2013) uses the analogy of Solution Architects as *building architects* concerned with meeting specific needs in contrast with Enterprise Architects as *urban planners* concerned with the broader landscape structure. This analogy is not entirely correct because Solution Architects are also concerned with the broader landscape structure in terms of fitting their IT solutions into the existing landscape while maintaining its overall consistency

[2] This observation relates only to organizations with *mature* EA practices, where dedicated Enterprise Architects exist to drive high-level architectural planning and suggest concrete projects to be implemented. However, in immature EA practices, where Enterprise Architects are absent as such and no high-level planning takes place, Solution Architects actively participate in the initial ideation of new digitalization projects. A detailed discussion of the maturity of EA practices is out of the scope of this book and provided by Kotusev (2021c) (Chapter 19)

[3] As van den Berg and van Vliet (2016, p. 121) explain, "The formalization of the IT decision-making process impacts the involvement of the enterprise architect. The more formalized the process, the more the enterprise architect can rely on standard ways of involvement with standard deliverables"

[4] As Hofstader (2008, p. 3) describes, "The problem domain for a [Solution Architect] can be horizontal or vertical. A horizontal domain is applicable across industries, like workflow automation. Vertical domains are specific to a particular industry, like telecommunications"

[5] The project implementation process described here is identical to the Initiative Delivery process discussed by Kotusev (2019d) and Kotusev (2021c) (Chapter 6)

[6] As McSweeney (2019, p. 112) observes, "Every organization will have a solution delivery process based on project management standards such as PRINCE2 or PMBOK or a local variant of one of these. [...] Note that the project management process does not necessarily imply a specific approach to the implementation of solution components, such as agile or waterfall"

[7] The realization step of the project implementation process described here is identical to the implementation step of the Initiative Delivery process discussed by Kotusev (2019d) and Kotusev (2021c) (Chapter 6)

[8] Specific methodologies for implementing digital transformation projects from an architectural point of view are offered, for instance, by Beijer and de Klerk (2010) and McSweeney (2019)

[9] Specific lists of EA artifacts and other related deliverables that can be produced during the project implementation process are provided, for instance, by Beijer and de Klerk (2010) and McSweeney (2019)

[10] The distinction and exact boundary between "architecture" and "design" are elusive and subject to perpetual debates in the IT community. Some cogent criteria for differentiating architecture from design are proposed, for instance, by Rivera (2007) and Beijer and de Klerk (2010)

[11] The concept of architecture debt, or technical debt, represents a metaphor for tactically beneficial actions that have to be redeemed later (Cunningham, 1992). A detailed discussion of this concept is out of the scope of this book and provided by Kotusev (2021c) (Chapter 18)

[12] As Wright (2011, p. 71) explains, "A strong focus on achieving consensus when evaluating candidate architectures will help smooth the path to a successful implementation. That said, I've found it can be a struggle to achieve consensus for several reasons, the most important one being that people have personal concerns and agendas — an architect must sometimes play psychologist to understand and cater to these while keeping architectural goals in mind. For example, project managers tend to be driven predominantly by relatively short-term considerations of delivery dates and budget. Developers are driven by technology interests and feature delivery. Architects typically have a longer-term orientation on nonfunctional requirements that (hopefully) shape their vision"

[13] As Hohpe (2020, p. 110) jokes, agile development "is still widely misinterpreted as doing random stuff and hoping for the best"

[14] Some other benefits and associated drawbacks of working directly with code for architects are discussed by Woods (2017)

[15] As Wright (2011, p. 72) explains, "Unfortunately, sometimes you won't be able to build consensus [within the project team]. When this happens, you have no choice but to assert yourself in your role as architect. Do this as a last resort. [...] When empowerment, persuasion, reasoning, and asserting yourself fail, you might have to take even more drastic action to break the impasse. On your recommendation, the project manager might have to consider shuffling teams and replacing staff"

¹⁶ Although there are no formal statistics available on the distribution of Solution Architects across different domains, this distribution pattern is arguably widely observed in the industry

¹⁷ As FEAPO (2018, p. 18) puts it, "It is unusual to see a business architect assigned to a project team"

¹⁸ For instance, in the survey of Preisker et al. (2023, p. 18), "most participants state that their Enterprise Architects have a generalist orientation (73%)", whereas "Solution Architects [...] are [...] mostly described as specialists (89%)". In terms of their skill sets, "a strong business-oriented thinking is particularly important for Enterprise [Architects]", while "Solution Architects on the other hand should have a higher technical orientation" (Preisker et al., 2023, p. 22). Figueiredo et al. (2014) argue that Enterprise Architects and Solution Architects operate in different knowledge domains

¹⁹ As FEAPO (2018, p. 7) observes, "The Solution Architect will often have a single, clear business leader whose metrics are driving the need for change. An Enterprise Architect often has to work with many senior business and technology stakeholders, and many competing measures of success"

²⁰ In many respects, the "endless" job of Enterprise Architects resembles the open-ended job of managers, as described by Mintzberg (2009, p. 20): "Every manager is responsible for the success of the unit, yet there are no tangible mileposts where he or she can stop and say, "Now my job is finished". The engineer completes the design of a bridge on a particular day; the lawyer wins or loses a case at some moment in time. The manager, in contrast, must always keep going, never sure when success is truly assured [...]. As a result, managing is a job with a perpetual preoccupation: the manager can never be free to forget the work, never has the pleasure of knowing, even temporarily, that there is nothing left to do"

Chapter 17: Architecture Positions in Organizations

¹ As Akenine (2008, p. 23) fairly points out, "The first problem you encounter when you start discussing different roles [of architects] is the number of perspectives and roles out there. IASA found more than 50 different roles: Although many roles were more or less equivalent, many organizations have created their own roles with unique deliverables". Analogously, in the study of Gellweiler (2020, p. 23), "the sampled IT architect ads had various titles that reflect the inconsistency of the IT architect's role in general. The search term Architect provided 59 different titles out of 66 job ads", where "titles, tasks, and skills within job ads were numerous and did not adhere to any framework or standard" (Gellweiler, 2020, p. 26). In a similar vein, Woods and Rozanski (2012, p. 1) make the following observation: "The architect takes a high-profile role in many IT departments today. In fact, it can be quite difficult in some organizations to find a senior member of IT technical staff whose job title does not include the word "architect". However there is little consensus in the academic community or amongst practitioners as to the responsibilities of the many different types of architect we encounter — or indeed, what they should even be called". Woods (2014, pp. 10-11) continues: "I've stopped counting the architecture job titles I've encountered over the years: enterprise architects, network architects, storage architects, software architects, application architects, solution architects, Oracle architects, data architects, information architects, consultant architects, user-interface architects, and so on. The list seems to go on forever". Wierda (2017, p. 13) concurs: "Now, the enterprise architecture function has proliferated and also fragmented. There are now business architects, security architects, application architects, data architects, information architects, integration architects, enterprise architects, infrastructure architects, domain architects, IT architects, solution architects, integration architects, the list seems endless". As Preiss (2022, p. 1) jokes, "The world is full of architect titles"

² As FEAPO (2018, p. 6) reports, "In numerous discussions with various international organizations, FEAPO has found a wide array of "architect roles" described. This creates some confusion, since these roles are inconsistent between organizations and even within a single enterprise". Unde (2008, p. 7) makes a similar observation: "Many companies try to reduce the ambiguity [around the role of architects] by introducing different flavors of the role, such as enterprise architect or solution architect. Ironically, differentiation within the role can add to the confusion since there is no standardization of the designations across companies". Likewise, Wierda (2017, p. 13) observes that "the same job name may mean quite something different depending on whom and where you ask for the definition. What one company calls a business architect, the other company calls an

enterprise architect or a lead architect and what one company calls an enterprise architect another may call information architect". Akenine (2008, p. 23) argues that "this [confusion with role titles] causes a lot of problems", such as "the same architect role has different deliverables between organizations" and "organizations may have different roles but they produce the same deliverables". Unsurprisingly, Gellweiler (2020, p. 24) concludes that "the titles of architects alone are not only insufficient but also misleading for capturing the particular architect role". Woods and Rozanski (2012, p. 4) confirm this conclusion: "The problem we have often faced is someone introducing themselves using one of the many of architect titles that are in common use, but this not helping to define the key characteristics of their role". Worst of all, even "the term "architect" at one company can mean a radically different role from an architect at another company" (Shirey, 2008, p. 28)

[3] Professional specialization of their members represents one of the most fundamental structural properties of organizations (March and Simon, 1993; Mintzberg, 1983; Simon, 1997)

[4] Both vertical and horizontal specializations are not at all specific to the profession of architects (Simon, 1944; Simon, 1997). However, their application to the work of architects has numerous important profession-specific features. The principles of structuring architecture functions and defining positions for architects are also discussed by Kotusev (2020b), Kotusev et al. (2024) and Kotusev (2021c) (Chapter 17)

[5] A somewhat simpler but conceptually similar two-dimensional taxonomy for architecture positions is described by Woods and Rozanski (2012) and Woods (2014): "To help explain the differences between [architecture] roles, we classify them along two axes, namely their business/technology focus [i.e. area-based specialization] (the extent to which they focus on the problem domain as opposed to the solution domain), and the breadth of their architectural portfolio [i.e. tier-based specialization] (the number of systems that they have architectural responsibility for)" (Woods and Rozanski, 2012, p. 6). As Woods (2014, p. 11) reports, "I [...] realized that two aspects of an architect's job dictated how I dealt with them: whether they primarily had expertise in the problem domain (business) or solution domain (technology) [i.e. area-based specialization], and whether they were concerned about one or many systems [i.e. tier-based specialization]. These characteristics shape how you interact with architects because they drive their primary concerns and level of abstraction (which shapes factors like their style of involvement and time horizons)"

[6] The tier-based specialization applies only to *mature* architecture functions, which include positions for architects covering all levels of the initiative hierarchy. By contrast, immature architecture functions can employ only Solution Architects working exclusively at the project level, leaving the program and strategy levels unattended. A detailed discussion of the maturity of architecture functions is out of the scope of this book and provided by Kotusev (2021c) (Chapter 19)

[7] The same principles of the tier-based specialization of architects based on the breadth and depth of their coverage are formulated, for instance, by Woods and Rozanski (2012, p. 7): "When considering the breadth dimension, some architects are responsible for a large number of systems (possibly all of the applications in the organization), but at a necessarily shallow level, whereas other architects are responsible for a single application, but at a very deep level of involvement. We also find that the number of systems that an architect is responsible for determines the time horizon and abstraction level that she works at. Architects that work across many systems tend to have a longer term, more abstract focus than those architects responsible for a small number of systems, who are involved in shorter term single-system change and many more of the details of how a system works and is operated"

[8] Mathematically, the number of tiers in a hierarchy, at least with a constant degree of branching at each tier, can be calculated as a logarithm of the number of elements in the hierarchy

[9] The same principles of the area-based specialization of architects based on different business and IT domains that they cover are also formulated by Woods and Rozanski (2012, p. 6): "Some architects focus primarily on the business of the organization that they work for (the problem domain) being experts on one or more aspects of the business that they are helping to automate. Other architects focus primarily on the technology used to solve business problems (the solution domain), and are experts in one or more broad technology areas, such as messaging, networking, user interface development or data storage and retrieval"

[10] In the industry, different business areas of the organization are often called business domains. This book, however, does not use the term "domains" for business areas to avoid possible confusion and clearly distinguish them from the six classic domains of the EA discipline — business, applications, data, integration, infrastructure and security (see Figure 3.4)

[11] As Preisker et al. (2023, p. 31) explain, "A diverse IT environment necessitates a federal or decentralized configuration of the enterprise architecture management (EAM) function. This approach ensures that the distinct needs of various departments or applications are served appropriately". In their survey, "67% of the participants have heterogeneous requirements for their IT systems, of which 50% have a central, 38% a federal and 12% a decentral [EA] governance. In comparison 33% have homogeneous requirements for their IT systems, of which 70% have a central, 20% a federal and 10% a decentral governance" (Preisker et al., 2023, p. 30)

[12] For instance, the survey of Schneider et al. (2015) demonstrates that business processes, applications and data (functional domains) are much less standardized in organizations than their infrastructure and technical components (non-functional domains)

[13] For example, in the study of Chuang and van Loggerenberg (2010, p. 5), "interviewees claimed that enterprise architects tend to rigorously focus on their own domains. For example, different architects often communicate independently of each other with the business representatives. This often results in discrepancies in the architectural messages. [...] The [internal] communication challenge comes from different EA teams who tend to operate, and therefore communicate, in 'silos'"

[14] See Kotusev (2022)

Chapter 18: Challenges of Enterprise Architects

[1] See Kotusev and Kurnia (2019), Kurnia et al. (2020), Kurnia et al. (2021) and Jiang et al. (2024). As Kurnia et al. (2021, p. 3) summarize, "Engagement implies working together, rather than working separately"

[2] See, for example, Chartis Research (2016) and Panko (1998)

[3] See, for example, Stadtmueller (2013) and Gozman and Willcocks (2015)

[4] For instance, in the survey of Coles and Yeoh (2015, p. 8), "71 percent of respondents were somewhat to very concerned over shadow IT", but "only 8 percent of companies know the scope of shadow IT at their organizations, and an overwhelming majority (72 percent) of companies surveyed said they did not know the scope of shadow IT but wanted to know"

[5] For example, the survey of Preisker et al. (2023, p. 29) shows that "57% of the companies get the enterprise architecture function involved before the project starts [and 17%] at the beginning of the project. Another 18% add them to the project while it is on-going. Only 3% involve it at the end and 5% never"

[6] For instance, in the survey of Preisker et al. (2023, p. 28), "for 43% of the surveyed companies the involvement of enterprise architecture in strategic decision-making [...] is prevented, as the enterprise architecture function is only involved in projects when they are already running or even finished"

[7] For example, Chuang and van Loggerenberg (2010, p. 7) report that "business executives frequently have made up their minds about a specific solution before the architecture is designed. The result is that they unwilling to be convinced otherwise even if it is to protect their ego's"

[8] For instance, the survey of Preisker et al. (2023, p. 33) demonstrates that "almost 40% of businesses struggle to incorporate the EA function early in decision-making and thereby significantly increase the risk of accumulating technical debt"

[9] For example, some interviewees in the study of Tamm et al. (2022, p. 9) suggested that "the strongest indicator of EA success is when the EA team becomes an integral part of key decision processes and when the decision-makers themselves start proactively turning to the EA team for advice". In the survey of Preisker et al. (2023, p. 28), "53% of respondents state that their business organization is proactively asking their enterprise architecture function for advice regarding technology decisions"

¹⁰ For instance, one interviewee in the study of Tamm et al. (2022, p. 9) expressed the following opinion: "The first sign that [enterprise architects are] doing something right is that they are being invited to lots of discussions, that they are trusted adviser on many issues. The second attribute [is] that they don't stand out as something separate but that they are a natural part of the process of creating plans"

¹¹ As Jiang et al. (2024, p. 8) point out, "Being able to build partnership and trust with stakeholders is vital [for enterprise architects] to achieve long-term engagement. Stakeholders are more willing to accept [architects'] advice and engage in EA practice when they trust architects"

¹² Various factors conducive to the formation of virtuous and vicious circles in the work of enterprise architects are analyzed by Kotusev (2021d). Another possible form of vicious circle in their work caused by communicating with business leaders through intermediaries is identified by Bossert and Laartz (2016, p. 4): "Some enterprise architects told us that, during the course of their work assignments, they are actually more likely to interact with suppliers than with internal business executives and C-level leaders. When this happens, the EA group can enter into an unproductive cycle: its capability and process models won't accurately reflect business needs and therefore won't be used by the business to make critical technology decisions"

¹³ For instance, Paras (2011, p. 3) concludes that "an important element of EA success is awareness and support from enterprise leadership. [...] When asking what is important for EA success in your organization, [...] 27% [of respondents] identified that executive sponsorship is critical"

¹⁴ As Besker et al. (2015, p. 34) report, "A distinctive feature of the respondents is their desire to be positioned higher up in the organizational hierarchy. Thereby, their role might be strengthened as a strategic capability"

¹⁵ For instance, Jiang et al. (2024, p. 8) conclude that "a good architect is expected to be open-minded and empathetic to business problems. A genuine interest in understanding and solving difficulties faced by stakeholders is helpful in bringing the two sides closer together to initiate cooperation"

¹⁶ For example, in the survey of Network World (2016, pp. 5-6), enterprise architects express rather different opinions about their biggest challenges: "Among the top-ranked challenges, merging multiple departments and objectives into one technology roadmap ranked the highest with 62% of the enterprise architects identifying this as extremely or very challenging. Being the point person for those new standards and practices was also a source of stress. The professionals we surveyed said that rolling out new business standards across multiple projects within their organization was a key challenge (62% said extremely or very challenging.) Sixty percent said that about the job of making or proposing business process changes. [...] Forty-three percent said they were very or extremely challenged in educating themselves about various, siloed business problems within their organization. An identical percentage said they were very or extremely challenged by the lack of available information from subject matter experts within the organization concerning infrastructure strategy and upgrades"

¹⁷ For instance, in the survey of Network World (2016, p. 6), "half of those surveyed [architects] said that keeping up with the pace of technology change, in itself, was a challenge"

¹⁸ As Chuang and van Loggerenberg (2010, p. 7) conclude, "In summary, whilst there are some technical issues relate to the specific domains of EA [...], one can see that the major challenges [of enterprise architects] are, as described by the interviewees, largely non-technical. Many of these problems are associated with the social structure of an organization"

¹⁹ For instance, Chuang and van Loggerenberg (2010, p. 5) report that "communication is considered one of the biggest challenges by all of the interviewees. One of the interviewees commented: 'We are trained to design perfect architectures, so we are technically competent... but we lack the ability to communicate those architectures to the organization'. This statement points to the communication problem in the overall architecting process: the challenge of getting the message across to the stakeholders". Likewise, Olsen (2017, p. 642) concludes that "communication is an essential success factor and a critical challenge related to [...] the enterprise architect role. [Architectural planning] involves many stakeholders in various parts of the enterprise. Communication is essential to achieve a common understanding, which is instrumental for obtaining an agreement about scope, goals and vision". As Apthorp (2011, p. 6) points out, "Enterprise architecture has its own unique vernacular, but we need to communicate with our stakeholders in the language they understand, not

the language of "artifacts"". Tamm et al. (2022, p. 9) concur: "Many of our interviewees emphasized the need to communicate EA-related information tailored to the understanding and information needs of specific stakeholders. This suggests a need for a more personalized, interactive approach for conveying this information"

[20] See Kotusev (2021c) (Chapter 5)

[21] As Hohpe (2020, p. 141) explains, "Conveying technical content to a diverse audience is challenging [...] because many classical presentation or writing techniques don't work well for highly technical subjects. For example, slides with single words superimposed on dramatic photographs may draw the audience's attention, but they aren't going to convey the intricacies of your cloud computing platform strategy. Instead, architects need to focus on a communication style that emphasizes content, but in an engaging and approachable manner"

[22] The discussion of semantic transparency and some examples of intuitively understandable graphical relationships are provided, for instance, by Moody (2009). Hohpe (2020) offers more general advice for architects on visualizing and presenting technical information to managerial audiences

[23] As Chuang and van Loggerenberg (2010, p. 7) explain, "Enterprise architects [...] require the skills to deal with organizational politics if they want to be successful in their EA efforts. [Architectural planning] is being perceived as a political game and unless the architects are skilled in playing the game, their chances of success are seriously jeopardized"

[24] Contrary to the popular intuitive opinion, ambiguity of goals and plans is not only a problem for organizations, but also a *powerful discursive resource* widely used in decision-making processes for dealing with conflicting interests (Eisenberg, 1984; Jarzabkowski et al., 2010). As Baier et al. (1986, p. 206) explain, "Difficult issues [in politicized situations] are often "settled" by leaving them unresolved or specifying them in a form requiring subsequent interpretation. [...] Particularly where an issue is closely contested, success in securing support for a program or policy is likely to be associated with increasing, rather than decreasing ambiguity. Policy ambiguity allows different groups and individuals to support the same policy for different reasons and with different expectations". Specifically in relation to the work of enterprise architects, Wierda (2017, p. 49) fairly notes that "one of the 'nice' aspects of [informal] modeling is that it is often ambiguous enough for all stakeholders to see their own preferred reality in it. A more vague and ambiguous approach enables this often 'politically' expedient modeling"

[25] Some factors preventing effective engagement between enterprise architects and business leaders are discussed by Kotusev and Kurnia (2019) and Kurnia et al. (2021)

[26] For example, in the study of Jiang et al. (2024, p. 9), "architects emphasized that influential EA leader is an essential enabler for [their] stakeholder engagement success. The influential CIO managed to introduce the EA concept to senior leadership and get the executive team on board quickly, laying a good foundation [...] and getting support from the rest of the business"

[27] For example, as Besker et al. (2015, p. 34) report, "The empirical study shows that the architect's responsibility extends beyond the direct EA issues and concerns responsibilities such as promoting [...] EA as an organizational service offering"

[28] For instance, the studies of McKinsey and Henley Business School demonstrate that in more than 40% of companies, business leaders are not aware of what the architecture function does (Bossert and Laartz, 2016; Bossert and Manwani, 2021; Manwani and Bossert, 2016). As Bossert and Laartz (2016, p. 2) summarize, "Unfortunately, most business executives don't understand what the enterprise architecture group does and how it can help". Analogously, in the study of Olsen (2017, p. 642), "all stakeholders had unclear conceptions of EA and the EA value propositions"

[29] As Bird (2013, p. 5) notes, "Sadly the term EA is neither descriptive, nor comprehensive. So the fall-back is "oh you are one of those IT propeller heads that I don't understand, so I will have someone else explain it to me" from business leadership"

[30] For instance, Blosch et al. (2016, p. 5) recommend explaining the role of enterprise architects as that of internal management consultants (see Figure 4.4): "Because most people understand the concept of management

consulting and what it does, applying that label to EA immediately demystifies it. The conversation then moves to defining the type of consultancy, its focus and the services it offers"

[31] As Bird (2013, p. 5) points out, "Even if one can describe the role [of enterprise architects] sensibly, getting the value proposition of EA explained properly is difficult. Especially if you are pigeon-holed into the technology realm"

[32] Interestingly, dissociating enterprise architects from IT also has its downsides for their perception and credibility in the organization: "[One company] learned that positioning the [EA] function purely within the business domain also brings some disadvantages, in particular in terms of the perception of business stakeholders regarding IT knowledge of the architects. After shifting the [EA] function from the business domain to the IT domain, the architects receive more trust regarding their IT knowledge from business stakeholders — they are now perceived to be better able to consult on IT-related matters" (Labusch et al., 2018, p. 20)

[33] Systematic exaggeration of their own understanding of IT by business managers can be explained by the well-known Dunning–Kruger effect, when people with limited competence tend to overestimate their abilities (Dunning, 2011; Kruger and Dunning, 1999)

[34] For instance, Chuang and van Loggerenberg (2010, p. 6) discover that "when organizations or individuals have had previous unsuccessful experiences, the stakeholders tend to be quite reluctant to offer their support to the EA initiative. It is often very difficult to overcome such negative perceptions. [...] There are therefore a number of perceptions that the enterprise architects must understand, appreciate, and effectively address before they can expect buy-in from the stakeholders". As Ross et al. (2014, p. 1) observe, "In fact, architecture has become a bad word in some companies, mostly because architects in those companies are seen as more of an obstacle than a problem solver"

[35] For example, Bittler and Burton (2011, p. 4) report that "many restarted [EA] programs find that the negative "baggage" associated with the term "EA" is too strong to overcome, and it is simply easier and more effective to call it something else". Likewise, James (2008, p. 1) observes that "architecture is not a well-regarded practice in many [organizations]. Attendees [of our summit] reported that terms, such as "business transformation imperatives", were more helpful in garnering support"

[36] For instance, the survey of Stadtmueller (2013, p. 7) shows that 32–38% of respondents adopt non-approved SaaS applications because "IT approval process for new software applications is too slow or cumbersome"

[37] As Wierda (2015, p. 153) explains, "Basically, all stakeholders must see enterprise architecture as part of their own interests. This is not automatically the case. [...] For instance, if department managers are rewarded purely on their 'local' results and not on the 'overall landscape' or on collaboration with central functions, the chance is that they are only interested in what happens in their own domain. Taking the rest of the organization into account is not their problem, worse even, they will not voluntarily spend time on those other domains by working with/on enterprise architecture. They might support enterprise architecture in speech, but not in deed". Walker (2007, p. 1) agrees: "Localized interest — asking "What's in it for me?" on a personal or team level — is a common organizational barrier [to involving architects]. EAs [enterprise architects] are typically individual contributors and have little or no organizational powers. When working with teams whose incentives are based on their own organizational goals, it can be difficult to propose ideas that span the organizational unit"

[38] As Minaz Sarangi reports, "I have [...] seen EA initiatives fail because they don't realize the importance of the [stakeholder interests] analysis and propose a strategy that cannot be successful. For example, if the lines of business (LOB) heads are compensated mostly on the performance of their own business results versus the entire enterprise's results, proposing an enterprise application consolidation strategy as a starting point will fail" (van Gils and van Dijk, 2014, p. vii)

[39] For instance, the survey of Stadtmueller (2013, p. 7) shows that 24% of respondents adopt non-approved SaaS applications because "the non-approved software I use better meets my needs than IT-approved equivalent", 14–18% — because "IT did not approve the application I need to do my job", and 12–18% — because "IT restrictions on approved applications make it difficult to do my job"

⁴⁰ Or, Walker (2007, p. 1) provides another example of non-architectural resourcing concerns: "Even if a LOB [line of business] manager buys in on a strategy, shelling out the cash or personnel to support it can be a different story altogether. In many cases, since [strategies] span across the enterprise, there are resource needs not only from that business owner but from multiple functional areas"

⁴¹ Some theoretical analysis of the problem of public goods relevant to enterprise architects is provided by Beese et al. (2019)

⁴² As Chuang and van Loggerenberg (2010, p. 6) explain, "Because EA often causes major changes in an organization, stakeholders (such as system champions, data owners and policy owners) often resist the EA initiative because EA affects their status in the business hierarchy. This causes some individuals to behave defensively in order to protect their ownership of that space"

⁴³ By contrast, in the study of Jiang et al. (2024, p. 9), "most participants mentioned that organizations with small and flat structures find it easier to keep stakeholders engaged. Such organizations tend to have more informal communication which is sometimes more effective for supporting production work and social connection than formal communication"

⁴⁴ For example, Jiang et al. (2024, p. 9) conclude that "an open working environment can […] encourage collaboration and informal communication to improve stakeholder engagement. For example, [one bank] achieved this by implementing hot desking and setting up physical and online chat rooms for discussion anytime"

⁴⁵ Despite the active development of electronic media for remote meetings, personal face-to-face conversations still remain the most effective form of communication in organizations (Mintzberg, 2009; Pentland, 2012)

Chapter 19: Other Aspects of Enterprise Architects

¹ As one respondent in the study of Network World (2016, p. 3) reports, "Most of the architects I've come across have done development in the past. You need to start out with the very basics, doing the development, then working your way into design and analysis, on up into architecture". FEAPO (2018, p. 14) makes an analogous observation: "As most existing Enterprise Architects rose out of technology ranks, it would be uncommon to find an Enterprise Architect without serious technical skills, typically in software development, systems operations, project management, or business analysis". In the study of Jiang et al. (2024, p. 8), "the majority of the participants believe that a strong technical background is an essential requirement for architects. It enables architects to provide solid technical guidance for stakeholders and enhances their credibility when developing technical solutions. Stakeholders intend to get in touch with architects early if architects can demonstrate their technical competence and leadership"

² As FEAPO (2018, p. 15) reports, "When moving from technical roles to architecture roles, the ability to succeed in the new role is highly dependent upon interpersonal skills and often leadership skills. For technologists, this is a frequent cause for struggle and retraining, as those skills are not often initially taught or required"

³ As FEAPO (2018, p. 14) observes, "The role of Enterprise Architect is often not a technical one, and very technical people may find that their deep technology skills will become less relevant while broad technical and organizational skills become more important"

⁴ For instance, in the study of Besker et al. (2015, p. 32), "several respondents consider the Enterprise Architect profession as superior to other architectural roles" and FEAPO (2018, p. 7) points out that "it is quite common for a Solution Architect to grow into an Enterprise Architect"

⁵ As FEAPO (2018, p. 15) reports, "When moving from non-technical roles to architecture roles, the ability to succeed in the new role is highly dependent upon a broad technical grasp of issues such as integration, hosting, core data concepts, and software lifecycle. For non-technologists, this is a frequent cause for struggle and retraining"

[6] For example, Carr and Else (2018, p. 13) observe that "there is no single career path into an EA [Enterprise Architect] role, although most are of a technical nature". Similarly, in the study of Chuang and van Loggerenberg (2010, p. 6), "all the interviewees had an IT or engineering background. They confirmed that it seems to be true of most other enterprise architects in their organizations". In the survey of Preisker et al. (2023, p. 21), "78% of participants state that the academic/professional background of their [...] architects is mostly technical" and "although the business orientation is clearly a focus topic, only 5% of [...] architects have a business background and 17% bring experiences and competencies from both the technical and business side"

[7] For instance, in the survey of Carr and Else (2018, p. 9), all the participating Enterprise Architects previously performed some other architecture-related roles, where "solution architecture, information architecture and application architecture occupied nearly 70% of all responses"

[8] As Besker et al. (2015, p. 33) find out, "Commonly, the architects emanate from the IT domain, with a previous clear IT role, but have progressively adopted the role as part of the business domain"

[9] For example, FEAPO (2018, p. 15) illustrates possible career paths leading to the role of Enterprise Architects through various IT-related roles and warns that "a person attempting to "move" through this matrix [of roles] towards a role in enterprise architecture should expect to spend several years in a role in order to build proficiency before moving on"

[10] As FEAPO (2018, p. 14) reports, "It is generally accepted across the industry that the actual skills and experiences needed to be effective as an EA [Enterprise Architect] develop through experience over an extended period of time. Even with degree programs and certification courses, it would be exceptionally rare to find a person who is capable of switching from a non-[architectural] role directly into Enterprise Architect". Bird (2013, p. 6) confirms: "It is pretty hard to be a young EA [Enterprise Architect]. I don't see the career path as starting as an apprentice EA and working up. [...] It is one of those fields that does require a little (or in my case a lot of) grey hair. You have to be able to [do many different things]. Your skill base needs to be very broad"

[11] Unsurprisingly, in the survey of Preisker et al. (2023, p. 13), "48% of survey participants state that Enterprise Architects are hardest to find in the job market, while [...] Solution Architects (10%) are easier to find in comparison". Similarly, in the survey of Bizzdesign (2023, p. 12), 79% of respondents "said that Enterprise Architects were difficult or somewhat difficult to hire", but only 70% said the same about Solution Architects

[12] As Hohpe (2020, p. 43) explicates, "Even though architects have one of the most exciting jobs, some people might be sad to see that being an architect implies that you'll likely remain one for most of your career. I am not so worried about that. First, this puts you in a good peer group of CEOs, presidents, doctors, lawyers, and other high-end professionals. Second, in technically minded organizations, software engineers should feel the same: your next career step should be to remain a software engineer, except a senior one, or staff engineer or perhaps a principal engineer"

[13] For example, in the study of Besker et al. (2015, p. 32), "a substantial part of the interviewed architects regard a CIO's position as a natural next step in their career"

[14] For instance, the survey of Schekkerman (2005) shows that enterprise architects in organizations are educated in different ways, including self-education, internal trainings, external trainings, online courses, certification programs and university studies

[15] For instance, the survey of Schekkerman (2005) shows that most organizations practice coaching of their enterprise architects by more experienced colleagues

[16] This adage is typically ascribed to Paulo Coelho, a contemporary Brazilian writer

[17] For example, as a viable workaround, IASA (2014) provides a comprehensive set of competency areas with the associated expectations and exemplary questions for assessing the proficiency of enterprise architects, while FEAPO (2018) offers an approximate list of interview questions that can be used to evaluate job candidates

[18] Full-fledged degree programs and individual courses relevant to enterprise architects have long been offered, in some form or the other, by many universities (Frampton and Ho, 2009; Tambouris et al., 2012), let alone by commercial education providers

[19] Although many different approaches to teaching the discipline of enterprise architecture have been proposed by academics and industry experts (BCS, 2023; Frampton, 2005; Gamble, 2011; Kudryavtsev et al., 2018; Seppanen et al., 2020; Steenkamp et al., 2013; Stewart, 2004; Stewart, 2006; Wegmann et al., 2007), they are all mostly theoretical and weakly resemble the actual work of architects in practice

[20] As Kudryavtsev et al. (2018, p. 76) fairly point out, "Teaching enterprise architecture in universities is a difficult task because of the interdisciplinary nature of the subject, its generalized character and close connection with practical experience". Rao et al. (2018) concur: "Since communication skills and analytical skills are difficult to teach and are gained mainly through experience, most EA education focuses either general concepts or on architecture frameworks". At the same time, Frampton et al. (2006a, p. 8) report that the experiment intended to enhance some practical capabilities of architects as part of a relevant university subject was "not successful in producing a measurable positive difference in those capabilities"

[21] Most egregiously, EACOE (2018, p. 2) promises that after attending their four-day workshop, "you will return to your organization with a proven, step-by-step methodology and project plan to begin immediately!" and "we ensure that you are able to demonstrate your ability to develop an enterprise architecture based on real-world issues and events" (EACOE, 2018, p. 3). "The EACOE workshop is the only EA learning experience available in which you actually create an enterprise architecture that is ready to be implemented "on Monday morning" when you return to your organization", continues their advertisement (EACOE, 2018, p. 6)

[22] For example, all the early degree programs for enterprise architects celebrated by Gartner have lost their prominence or even disappeared (Bittler, 2010; Bittler, 2012)

[23] As Mintzberg (2009, p. 12) explains about the job of managers, "What does exist about managing [instead of explicit knowledge] is a good deal of tacit knowledge. But tacit means not easily accessible, which is why the practice [of managing] has to be learned on the job, through apprenticeship, mentorship, and direct experience"

[24] The question of establishing EA practices in organizations from scratch is out of the scope of this book and discussed by Kotusev (2021c) (Chapter 19)

[25] For instance, Kotusev (2017b) identifies modeling as the single most popular topic in the EA literature

[26] As Schulenklopper and Rommes (2016, p. 13) explain, "Common architecture languages favor correctness and completeness over expressiveness and clarity. The models and descriptions created using these languages fulfill the architect's needs well but can be understood only by those with a similar mindset and background. Other stakeholders are often dazzled by the abstract symbols and terminology". As Wierda (2017, p. 201) reports, "I know no enterprise architect who uses a modeling language (UML, ArchiMate, etc.) that really makes communication with the decision makers easier. [...] So, the most effective way of communicating to the decision makers is often still simple graphics with those ambiguous lines and boxes"

[27] As Wierda (2017, p. 201) explains, "There is an obvious place where rigor, structure and logic really help: when the situation to model becomes very large and complex and you still want to get to grips with it. Then, using structured [modeling] approaches (especially if applied in a disciplined fashion) helps. But those are models that are definitely not for management. They are complex instruments that require a high level of 'engineering attitude' to set up and that can be used by those actually working in the detailed reality of those complex domains"

[28] As Wierda (2017, p. 49) fairly observes, "Sometimes, some modeling for projects is done in UML, but most of the time, you will look at some non- or semi-standardized use of boxes, arrows, dotted lines, nesting, etc.". The available industry statistics generally show that some organizations and architects use some modeling languages, such as ArchiMate, BPMN and UML, but their adoption rates are rather low (Ambler, 2010; Carr and Else, 2018; Schekkerman, 2005; Schneider et al., 2015; Scholtz et al., 2013). For example, in the survey of Schneider et al. (2015), only eleven out of 47 participants (or about 23%) indicated that they use ArchiMate and, in the survey of Carr and Else (2018), only 19% of respondents stated that they used ArchiMate at any point in their career

[29] For instance, Kotusev (2017b) identifies tools among the most popular topics in the EA literature

[30] For example, the survey of Preisker et al. (2023) identifies collaboration tools as the single most important category of tools for enterprise architects. Many surveys also demonstrate that standard MS Office applications are by far the most popular software tools used in EA practices (Aziz and Obitz, 2005; Aziz and Obitz, 2007; Bizzdesign, 2024; Dahalin et al., 2010; GAO, 2003; Obitz and Babu, 2009; Schekkerman, 2005)

[31] All industry surveys show that many organizations do not use any EA-specific tools (Aziz and Obitz, 2005; Aziz and Obitz, 2007; Carr and Else, 2018; Dahalin et al., 2010; GAO, 2003; GAO, 2006; Obitz and Babu, 2009; Preisker et al., 2020; Schekkerman, 2005; Walker, 2007). For example, in the survey of Preisker et al. (2020, p. 10), only "44 percent of participants stated that enterprise architects are using tools such as LeanIX, Alfabet, Mega HOPEX, and Bizzdesign"

[32] As Nowakowski et al. (2017, p. 4851) observe, "[EA-specific] tools are mostly used for capturing the current architecture. The actual planning and discussion of scenarios is mostly done by hand with the help of flipcharts, whiteboards, MS PowerPoint, and MS Visio"

[33] Industry surveys generally reveal a broad spectrum of software tools used in EA practices (Aziz and Obitz, 2005; Aziz and Obitz, 2007; Bizzdesign, 2024; Carr and Else, 2018; GAO, 2003; GAO, 2006; Kleehaus and Matthes, 2019; Obitz and Babu, 2009; Preisker et al., 2023; Schekkerman, 2005; Walker, 2007). For example, in the survey of Kleehaus and Matthes (2019), 58 respondents provided, in total, 32 different tools used in their organizations, including EA-specific tools, MS Office applications, CMDBs and even some homemade tools. Analogously, in the survey of Bizzdesign (2024, p. 15), respondents indicated popular EA-specific tools, MS Office applications, web-based diagramming software and "other" tools, where "respondents who selected Other [category] named 24 tools, with many of them not shared by any other respondents to our survey". In a similar vein, the survey of Preisker et al. (2023) identifies six categories of tools relevant to enterprise architects, in order of decreasing importance: collaboration, visualization, reporting, simulation, project management and testing tools

[34] For instance, Kotusev (2017b) identifies frameworks analysis among the top most popular topics in the EA literature

[35] The most comprehensive and perfectly speculative overviews of the existing EA frameworks are provided by Schekkerman (2004) and Matthes (2011) (in German)

[36] Most egregiously, Hornford et al. (2022) use the phrase "best practice" in reference to TOGAF 33 times

[37] A comprehensive analysis of the curious situation with EA frameworks is provided by Kotusev (2021c) (Appendix A) and in other related sources (Kotusev, 2016a; Kotusev, 2016b; Kotusev, 2016c; Kotusev, 2016f; Kotusev, 2018a; Kotusev, 2018b; Kotusev, 2018d; Kotusev, 2018e; Kotusev, 2018f; Kotusev, 2019c; Kotusev, 2021a; Kotusev, 2023; Kotusev and Kurnia, 2021)

[38] See, for instance, Gaver (2010)

[39] See, for instance, GAO (2015)

[40] See Forer (1949)

[41] All industry surveys show that many organizations do not use any specific EA frameworks (Ambler, 2010; Aziz and Obitz, 2007; Buckl et al., 2009; Cameron and McMillan, 2013; Carr and Else, 2018; Dahalin et al., 2010; de Vries and van Rensburg, 2009; Gall, 2012; Lange and Mendling, 2011; Obitz and Babu, 2009; Schekkerman, 2005; Schneider et al., 2015; Scholtz et al., 2013)

[42] See, for instance, Smith et al. (2012) and Kotusev (2018d)

[43] Most egregiously, EACOE (2023, p. 1) makes the following, obviously false statement: "Finally, and key to this position, the enterprise architect should have demonstrated skills, and actual examples of models built using [our] The Enterprise Framework"

[44] As Allega (2011, p. 5) fairly observes, "Enterprise architecture methodology and framework debates have been ratholes for enterprise architecture practitioners to argue over; rather than focusing upon the needs of their key stakeholders, many have become enamored with completing a method or framework"

[45] An overview of popular certifications for enterprise architects is provided by Tittle and Lindros (2018), White (2022) and Berner (2024)

[46] For example, the study of Gellweiler (2020) shows that only 8.9% of all job ads for architects include certification requirements. Likewise, the survey of Schekkerman (2005, p. 24) demonstrates that certification is not an issue for 72% of organizations, "there is no real demand for certification of enterprise architects" and "most organizations that are using and implementing enterprise architecture are today not interested in certification for their own people". As for EA framework certification, Gellweiler (2020, pp. 26-27) notes that "only a few jobs required knowledge of or certificates for a particular framework, such as [PMBOK] or [TOGAF]". Similarly, in the study of Besker et al. (2015, p. 33), "the respondents state [...] that during the recruitment of a new enterprise architect, a certification or experience in a particular framework is not essential"

[47] For instance, the analysis of job posts conducted by Tittle and Lindros (2018) shows that the TOGAF certification is the most popular of all certifications relevant to enterprise architects. The total number of TOGAF-certified individuals exceeds 140 thousand globally. The current number of TOGAF-certified people can be found here: https://togaf-cert.opengroup.org/certified-individuals

[48] As Moore (2018) explains, "Earning a [TOGAF] Credential leads to the award of an Open Badge from The Open Group, which can be displayed in locations such as your LinkedIn profile, or email signature. The badge features a link to material itemizing the actions necessary to earn it, and demonstrates to your peers your accomplishments"

[49] For example, TOGAF certifications historically generated an average pay premium of up to 10% of base salary equivalent (Foote, 2019)

[50] The two-part TOGAF certification examination fee alone exceeds 600 U.S. dollars, not to mention various preparatory courses and trainings usually priced at a few thousand dollars. The current examination rates from The Open Group can be found here: https://certification.opengroup.org/examinations/exam-fees

[51] For instance, in the survey of Carr and Else (2018, p. 13), "one third [37%] of practitioners do not have a formal certification in EA, with some comments suggesting that real-world experience is of much higher value". Similarly, in the study of Besker et al. (2015, p. 32), "none of the respondents states certification requirement within a framework as a core competence". As Carr and Else (2018, p. 5) conclude, "It appears that a lack of certification is not a barrier to entry in EA roles", but "anecdotal evidence in reviewing job advertisements on online job-boards shows a high prevalence of the need for major framework certification, suggesting a disconnect between advertisers/agencies and the experience of practitioners"

[52] This discussion is inspired by a similar analysis of the work of managers by Mintzberg (2009) (Chapter 5). Mintzberg (2009, p. 158) defines the conundrums of managing simply as "concerns that cannot be resolved"

[53] Exactly the same problem is also typical for managers: "A major occupational hazard of managing is to know more and more about less and less until finally the manager knows nothing about everything" (Mintzberg, 2009, p. 167)

[54] A somewhat similar problem is also typical for managers: "Managers have to be decisive. [...] They have to take stands, make certain decisions, and provoke actions that move their units forward. The problem is that much of this has to be done under difficult circumstances, full of ambiguities" (Mintzberg, 2009, p. 187)

[55] As Mintzberg (2009, p. 192) explains about the conundrums of managing, "These paradoxes and predicaments, labyrinths and riddles [i.e. conundrums], are built into managerial work — they are managing — and there they shall remain. They can be alleviated but never eliminated, reconciled but never resolved"

References

Abraham, R. (2013) "Enterprise Architecture Artifacts as Boundary Objects - A Framework of Properties", In: van Hillegersberg, J., van Heck, E. and Connolly, R. (eds.) *Proceedings of the 21st European Conference on Information Systems*, Utrecht, The Netherlands: Association for Information Systems, pp. 1-12.

Abraham, R., Niemietz, H., de Kinderen, S. and Aier, S. (2013) "Can Boundary Objects Mitigate Communication Defects in Enterprise Transformation? Findings from Expert Interviews", In: Jung, R. and Reichert, M. (eds.) *Proceedings of the 5th International Workshop on Enterprise Modelling and Information Systems Architectures*, St. Gallen, Switzerland: Gesellschaft fur Informatik, pp. 27-40.

Ahlemann, F., Legner, C. and Schafczuk, D. (2012) "Introduction", In: Ahlemann, F., Stettiner, E., Messerschmidt, M. and Legner, C. (eds.) *Strategic Enterprise Architecture Management: Challenges, Best Practices, and Future Developments*, Berlin: Springer, pp. 1-33.

Akella, J. and Barlow, C. (2004) "EA on the Baseline", Enterprise Architect, URL: http://archive.visualstudiomagazine.com/ea/magazine/summer2004/columns/businesscase/default_pf.aspx.

Akenine, D. (2008) "A Study of Architect Roles by IASA Sweden", *The Architecture Journal*, Vol. 1, No. 15, pp. 22-25.

Alaeddini, M., Asgari, H., Gharibi, A. and Rad, M. R. (2017) "Leveraging Business-IT Alignment Through Enterprise Architecture - An Empirical Study to Estimate the Extents", *Information Technology and Management*, Vol. 18, No. 1, pp. 55-82.

Allaire, P. and Howard, R. (1992) "The CEO as Organizational Architect: An Interview with Xerox's Paul Allaire", *Harvard Business Review*, Vol. 70, No. 5, pp. 106-113.

Allega, P. (2011) "Architect in the Spotlight: Philip Allega", *Journal of Enterprise Architecture*, Vol. 7, No. 1, pp. 5-6.

Ambler, S. W. (2010) "Enterprise Architecture: Reality Over Rhetoric", Dr. Dobb's Journal, URL: https://web.archive.org/web/20201020205941/http://www.drdobbs.com/architecture-and-design/enterprise-architecture-reality-over-rhe/224600174.

Apthorp, A. (2011) "Architect in the Spotlight: Adrian Apthorp", *Journal of Enterprise Architecture*, Vol. 7, No. 2, pp. 5-6.

Argyris, C. (1957) *Personality and Organization: The Conflict Between System and the Individual*, New York, NY: Harper and Row.

Armour, F. J., Kaisler, S. H. and Liu, S. Y. (1999a) "A Big-Picture Look at Enterprise Architectures", *IT Professional*, Vol. 1, No. 1, pp. 35-42.

Armour, F. J., Kaisler, S. H. and Liu, S. Y. (1999b) "Building an Enterprise Architecture Step by Step", *IT Professional*, Vol. 1, No. 4, pp. 31-39.

Aziz, S. and Obitz, T. (2005) "Infosys Enterprise Architecture Survey 2005", Bangalore, India: Infosys.

Aziz, S. and Obitz, T. (2007) "Infosys Enterprise Architecture Survey 2007", Bangalore, India: Infosys.

Baier, V. E., March, J. G. and Saetren, H. (1986) "Implementation and Ambiguity", *Scandinavian Journal of Management Studies*, Vol. 2, No. 3-4, pp. 197-212.

Ball, L. and Harris, R. (1982) "SMIS Members: A Membership Analysis", *MiS Quarterly*, Vol. 6, No. 1, pp. 19-38.

Banger, D. R. and Barnes, J. (2010) "Characteristics, Roles and Responsibilities of the Modern Day Systems Architect: Lessons from the Field", *Journal of Enterprise Architecture*, Vol. 6, No. 1, pp. 17-23.

Barker, R. (2010) "No, Management Is Not a Profession", *Harvard Business Review*, Vol. 88, No. 7-8, pp. 52-60.

Barnett, G., Betz, C., Sjoblom, S. and Barton, J. (2023) "The Forrester Wave: Enterprise Architecture Management Suites, Q1 2023", Cambridge, MA: Forrester.

Baskerville, R. (2003) "The LEO Principle: Perspectives on 50 Years of Business Computing", *Journal of Strategic Information Systems*, Vol. 12, No. 4, pp. 255-263.

Bass, L., Clements, P. and Kazman, R. (2021) *Software Architecture in Practice (4th Edition)*, Boston, MA: Addison-Wesley Professional.

BCS (2023) "BCS Practitioner Certificate in Enterprise and Solution Architecture: Syllabus", London: British Computer Society (BCS).

Beck, K. and Andres, C. (2004) *Extreme Programming Explained: Embrace Change (2nd Edition)*, Boston, MA: Addison-Wesley Professional.

Beese, J., Haki, K., Aier, S. and Winter, R. (2019) "Enterprise Architecture as a Public Goods Dilemma: An Experimental Approach", In: Aveiro, D., Guizzardi, G. and Borbinha, J. (eds.) *Advances in Enterprise Engineering XIII*, Cham, Switzerland: Springer, pp. 102-114.

Behara, G. K. and Paradkar, S. S. (2015) *Enterprise Architecture: A Practitioner's Handbook*, Tampa, FL: Meghan-Kiffer Press.

Beijer, P. and de Klerk, T. (2010) *IT Architecture: Essential Practice for IT Business Solutions*, Raleigh, NC: Lulu.com.

Ben-Nathan, E. A. (1980) "The Information Systems Architect and Systems Development", In: Lucas, H. C., Land, F. F., Lincoln, T. J. and Supper, K. (eds.) *The Information Systems Environment: Proceedings of the IFIP TC 8.2 Working Conference on the Information Systems Environment, Bonn, West Germany, 11-13 June 1979*, Amsterdam: North-Holland Publishing, pp. 275-290.

Bente, S., Bombosch, U. and Langade, S. (2012) *Collaborative Enterprise Architecture: Enriching EA with Lean, Agile, and Enterprise 2.0 Practices*, Waltham, MA: Morgan Kaufmann.

Bernard, S. (2005) "Editor's Corner", *Journal of Enterprise Architecture*, Vol. 1, No. 1, p. 2.

Bernard, S. A. (2004) *An Introduction to Enterprise Architecture*, Bloomington, IN: AuthorHouse.

Berner, M. (2024) "Best IT Certifications for 2024", Business News Daily, URL: https://www.businessnewsdaily.com/10953-best-it-certifications.html.

Besker, T., Olsson, R. and Pessi, K. (2015) "The Enterprise Architect Profession: An Empirical Study", In: Pimenidis, E. and Odeh, M. (eds.) *Proceedings of the 9th European Conference on Information Management and Evaluation*, Bristol, UK: Academic Conferences and Publishing International Limited, pp. 29-36.

Bird, C. (2013) "Architect in the Spotlight: Chris Bird", *Journal of Enterprise Architecture*, Vol. 9, No. 2, pp. 5-6.

Bird, P. J. (1994) *LEO: The First Business Computer*, Wokingham, UK: Hasler.

Bittler, R. S. (2008) "Guide for Recruiting and Interviewing Enterprise Architects" (#G00154945), Stamford, CT: Gartner.

Bittler, R. S. (2010) "Innovative, New Enterprise Architecture Degree Programs Are Under Development" (#G00208044), Stamford, CT: Gartner.

Bittler, R. S. (2012) "Penn State's Degree in Enterprise Architecture Advances the EA Profession" (#G00234540), Stamford, CT: Gartner.

Bittler, R. S. and Burton, B. (2011) "How to Restart and Re-Energize an Enterprise Architecture Program" (#G00214385), Stamford, CT: Gartner.

Bizzdesign (2021) "State of Enterprise Architecture 2021", Enschede, The Netherlands: Bizzdesign.

Bizzdesign (2023) "State of Enterprise Architecture 2023", Enschede, The Netherlands: Bizzdesign.

Bizzdesign (2024) "State of Enterprise Architecture 2024", Enschede, The Netherlands: Bizzdesign.

Bloomberg, J. (2016) "Change as Core Competency: Transforming the Role of the Enterprise Architect", Forbes, URL: https://www.forbes.com/sites/jasonbloomberg/2016/06/16/change-as-core-competency-transforming-the-role-of-the-enterprise-architect/.

Blosch, M., Burton, B. and Walker, M. J. (2016) "Rethink EA as an Internal Management Consultancy to Rapidly Deliver Business Outcomes" (#G00291300), Stamford, CT: Gartner.

Blumberg, S., Bossert, O. and Sokalski, J. (2018) "Five Enterprise-Architecture Practices That Add Value to Digital Transformations", Hong Kong: McKinsey & Company.

Bolton, P. (2003) "Governing Enterprise Architecture: Lessons Learned from Implementing Federal Government EAs", *Cutter IT Journal*, Vol. 16, No. 7, pp. 11-19.

Bontinck, G., Cumps, B., Viaene, S., Bille, W. and Vanden Brande, J. (2016) "From Enterprise Architect to Opportunity Architect: The Changing Role of Enterprise Architecture in a Digital Transformation Context", *Journal of Enterprise Architecture*, Vol. 12, No. 4, pp. 32-41.

Bossert, O. and Laartz, J. (2016) "How Enterprise Architects Can Help Ensure Success with Digital Transformations", London: McKinsey & Company.

Bossert, O. and Manwani, S. (2021) "Enterprise Architecture and Digital Leaders: A Survey Report Based on Research with McKinsey & Company and Henley Business School", *Journal of Enterprise Architecture*, Vol. 17, No. 1, pp. 1-20.

Bossert, O. and van der Wildt, N. (2021) "How Enterprise Architects Need to Evolve to Survive in a Digital World", San Francisco, CA: McKinsey & Company.

Boster, M., Liu, S. and Thomas, R. (2000) "Getting the Most from Your Enterprise Architecture", *IT Professional*, Vol. 2, No. 4, pp. 43-51.

Bowman, C. F. (2023) *Confessions of an Enterprise Architect*, Boca Raton, FL: CRC Press.

Boynton, A. C. and Zmud, R. W. (1987) "Information Technology Planning in the 1990's: Directions for Practice and Research", *MIS Quarterly*, Vol. 11, No. 1, pp. 59-71.

Brathwaite, K. S. (1992) *Information Engineering (Volume I: Concepts, Volume II: Analysis and Administration, Volume III: Development Issues)*, Boca Raton, FL: CRC Press.

Bredemeyer Consulting (2002) "Architect Competency Framework", Bloomington, IN: Bredemeyer Consulting.

Bredemeyer, D. and Malan, R. (2002) "The Role of the Architect", Bloomington, IN: Bredemeyer Consulting.

Bredemeyer, D. and Malan, R. (2004) "What It Takes to Be a Great Enterprise Architect", *Cutter Consortium Executive Report*, Vol. 7, No. 8, pp. 1-21.

Brockbank, R. T. (1987) "An Architect on Architecture", *Stage by Stage*, Vol. 7, No. 2, pp. 14-16.

Brunsson, N. (1982) "The Irrationality of Action and Action Rationality: Decisions, Ideologies and Organizational Actions", *Journal of Management Studies*, Vol. 19, No. 1, pp. 29-44.

Brunsson, N. (1985) *The Irrational Organization: Irrationality as a Basis for Organizational Action and Change*, Chichester, UK: Wiley.

Buckl, S., Ernst, A. M., Lankes, J., Matthes, F. and Schweda, C. M. (2009) "State of the Art in Enterprise Architecture Management", Munich, Germany: Software Engineering for Business Information Systems (SEBIS), Technical University of Munich.

Burke, B. (2003) "Enterprise Architecture or City Planning?" (#Delta 2638), Stamford, CT: META Group.

Burke, B. (2004) "City Planning: A Metaphor for Enterprise Architecture", CIO, URL: https://web.archive.org/web/20160211185121/http://www.cio.com.au/article/180920/city_planning_metaphor_enterprise_architecture/.

CAEAP (2010a) "Enterprise Architecture: A Professional Practice Guide", Austin, TX: Center for the Advancement of the Enterprise Architecture Profession (CAEAP).

CAEAP (2010b) "Enterprise Architecture: A Strategic Differentiator", Austin, TX: Center for the Advancement of the Enterprise Architecture Profession (CAEAP).

Calnan, C. (2017) "Ten Leading Colleges and Universities Preparing Tomorrow's Enterprise Architects", *Architecture and Governance Magazine*, Vol. 13, No. 2, pp. 10-13.

Cameron, B. H. and McMillan, E. (2013) "Analyzing the Current Trends in Enterprise Architecture Frameworks", *Journal of Enterprise Architecture*, Vol. 9, No. 1, pp. 60-71.

Caminer, D., Aris, J., Hermon, P. and Land, F. (1998) *LEO: The Incredible Story of the World's First Business Computer*, New York, NY: McGraw-Hill.

Caminer, D. T. (2003) "LEO and the Computer Revolution", *Journal of Strategic Information Systems*, Vol. 12, No. 4, pp. 265-284.

Canning, R. G. (1956) *Electronic Data Processing for Business and Industry*, New York, NY: Wiley.

Canning, R. G. (1957) "Planning for the Arrival of Electronic Data Processing", *Journal of Machine Accounting*, Vol. 7, No. 1, pp. 22-30.

Carr, D. and Else, S. (2018) "State of Enterprise Architecture Survey: Results and Findings", *Enterprise Architecture Professional Journal*, Vol. 6, No. 1, pp. 1-17.

Chartis Research (2016) "Quantification of End User Computing Risk in Financial Services", London: Chartis Research.

Chase, W. G. and Simon, H. A. (1973) "Perception in Chess", *Cognitive Psychology*, Vol. 4, No. 1, pp. 55-81.

Cheung, S. C. (1990) "Avoiding the Pitfalls of Information Systems Planning", *Data Resource Management*, Vol. 1, No. 3, pp. 16-22.

Chuang, C.-H. and van Loggerenberg, J. (2010) "Challenges Facing Enterprise Architects: A South African Perspective", In: Sprague, R. H. (ed.) *Proceedings of the 43rd Hawaii International Conference on System Sciences*, Kauai, HI: IEEE, pp. 1-10.

Clements, P., Kazman, R., Klein, M., Devesh, D., Reddy, S. and Verma, P. (2007) "The Duties, Skills, and Knowledge of Software Architects", In: Paulish, D., Gorton, I., Tyree, J. and Soni, D. (eds.) *Proceedings of the 2007 Working IEEE/IFIP Conference on Software Architecture (WICSA)*, Mumbai, India: IEEE, pp. 1-4.

Cockburn, A. (2004) *Crystal Clear: A Human-Powered Methodology for Small Teams*, Boston, MA: Addison-Wesley Professional.

Coghill, C. (2016) "Enterprise Architect as Enterprise Designer", CIOReview, URL: https://enterprise-architecture.cioreview.com/cxoinsight/enterprise-architect-as-enterprise-designer-nid-14699-cid-102.html.

Coles, C. and Yeoh, J. (2015) "Cloud Adoption Practices & Priorities Survey Report", Seattle, WA: Cloud Security Alliance.

Collins, J. (2014) *Security Architect: Careers in Information Security*, Swindon, UK: BCS Learning & Development.

Coltman, T., Devinney, T. M., Latukefu, A. and Midgley, D. F. (2001) "E-Business: Revolution, Evolution, or Hype?", *California Management Review*, Vol. 44, No. 1, pp. 57-86.

Correa, B. (2013) "How Are Architects Made?", *IEEE Software*, Vol. 30, No. 5, pp. 11-13.

Cunningham, W. (1992) "Experience Report - The WyCash Portfolio Management System", *ACM SIGPLAN OOPS Messenger*, Vol. 4, No. 2, pp. 29-30.

Cyert, R. M. and March, J. G. (1992) *A Behavioral Theory of the Firm (2nd Edition)*, Cambridge, MA: Blackwell.

Dahalin, Z. M., Razak, R. A., Ibrahim, H., Yusop, N. I. and Kasiran, M. K. (2010) "An Enterprise Architecture Methodology for Business-IT Alignment: Adopter and Developer Perspectives", In: Soliman, K. S. (ed.) *Proceedings of the 14th International Business Information Management Association (IBIMA) Conference*, Istanbul, Turkey: IBIMA, pp. 1-14.

Daniel, D. (2007) "The Rising Importance of the Enterprise Architect", CIO, URL: https://www.cio.com/article/272268/it-organization-the-rising-importance-of-the-enterprise-architect.html.

de Vries, M. and van Rensburg, A. C. J. (2009) "Evaluating and Refining the 'Enterprise Architecture as Strategy' Approach and Artifacts", *South African Journal of Industrial Engineering*, Vol. 20, No. 1, pp. 31-43.

Denis, J.-L., Langley, A. and Cazale, L. (1996) "Leadership and Strategic Change Under Ambiguity", *Organization Studies*, Vol. 17, No. 4, pp. 673-699.

Denrell, J. and Le Mens, G. (2020) "Revisiting the Competency Trap", *Industrial and Corporate Change*, Vol. 29, No. 1, pp. 183-205.

Diebold, J. (1952) *Automation: The Advent of the Automatic Factory*, New York, NY: D. Van Nostrand.

Diebold, J. (1964) "ADP - The Still-Sleeping Giant", *Harvard Business Review*, Vol. 42, No. 5, pp. 60-65.

Diebold, J. (1965) "What's Ahead in Information Technology", *Harvard Business Review*, Vol. 43, No. 5, pp. 76-82.

Dietz, J. L. G. (2008) *Architecture: Building Strategy into Design*, The Hague, The Netherlands: Academic Service.

du Preez, J., van der Merwe, A. and Matthee, M. (2014) "Enterprise Architecture Schools of Thought: An Exploratory Study", In: Grossmann, G., Halle, S., Karastoyanova, D., Reichert, M. and Rinderle-Ma, S. (eds.) *Proceedings of the 9th Trends in Enterprise Architecture Research Workshop*, Ulm, Germany: IEEE, pp. 3-12.

du Preez, J., van der Merwe, A. and Matthee, M. (2018) "Understanding Enterprise Architects: Different Enterprise Architect Behavioral Styles", In: Tjoa, A. M., Raffai, M., Doucek, P. and Novak, N. M. (eds.) *Proceedings of the 12th International Conference on Research and Practical Issues of Enterprise Information Systems (CONFENIS)*, Poznan, Poland: Springer, pp. 96-108.

Dunning, D. (2011) "The Dunning-Kruger Effect: On Being Ignorant of One's Own Ignorance", In: Olson, J. M. and Zanna, M. P. (eds.) *Advances in Experimental Social Psychology (Volume 44)*, San Diego, CA: Elsevier, pp. 247-296.

EACOE (2018) "Taking Enterprise Architecture Beyond Theory... Into Action", Pinckney, MI: Enterprise Architecture Center of Excellence (EACOE).

EACOE (2023) "The EACOE Enterprise Architect Position Description", Pinckney, MI: Enterprise Architecture Center of Excellence (EACOE).

Earl, M. and Khan, B. (2001) "E-Commerce Is Changing the Face of IT", *MIT Sloan Management Review*, Vol. 43, No. 1, pp. 64-72.

Edwards, J. (2020) "7 Traits of Successful Enterprise Architects", CIO, URL: https://www.cio.com/article/201541/7-traits-of-successful-enterprise-architects.html.

Eisenberg, E. M. (1984) "Ambiguity as Strategy in Organizational Communication", *Communication Monographs*, Vol. 51, No. 3, pp. 227-242.

Erder, M. and Pureur, P. (2016) "What's the Architect's Role in an Agile, Cloud-Centric World?", *IEEE Software*, Vol. 33, No. 5, pp. 30-33.

Evans, M. K. and Hague, L. R. (1962) "Master Plan for Information Systems", *Harvard Business Review*, Vol. 40, No. 1, pp. 92-103.

Evans, S. C. (2010) *Zoom Factor for the Enterprise Architect: How to Focus and Accelerate Your Career*, Winnipeg, Canada: Firefli Media.

Faber, R. (2010) "Architects as Service Providers", *IEEE Software*, Vol. 27, No. 2, pp. 33-40.

FEAPO (2013) "A Common Perspective on Enterprise Architecture", University Park, PA: The Federation of Enterprise Architecture Professional Organizations (FEAPO).

FEAPO (2018) "The Guide to Careers in Enterprise Architecture", University Park, PA: The Federation of Enterprise Architecture Professional Organizations (FEAPO).

Fehskens, L. (2015a) "Book Review: "Composite/Structured Design" by Glenford J. Myers", *Journal of Enterprise Architecture*, Vol. 11, No. 3, pp. 12-15.

Fehskens, L. (2015b) "Len's Lens: Eight Ways We Frame Our Concepts of Architecture", *Journal of Enterprise Architecture*, Vol. 11, No. 2, pp. 55-59.

Fehskens, L. (2016) "A Conceptual Framework for a Professional Code of Ethics for Enterprise Architects", *Journal of Enterprise Architecture*, Vol. 12, No. 4, pp. 49-55.

Fenn, J. and Raskino, M. (2008) *Mastering the Hype Cycle: How to Choose the Right Innovation at the Right Time*, Boston, MA: Harvard Business School Press.

Ferry, G. (2003) *A Computer Called LEO: Lyons Teashops and the World's First Office Computer*, London: Fourth Estate.

Fez-Barringten, B. (2010) "Architect in the Spotlight: Barie Fez-Barringten", *Journal of Enterprise Architecture*, Vol. 6, No. 1, pp. 5-6.

Figueiredo, M. C., de Souza, C. R. B., Pereira, M. Z., Prikladnicki, R. and Audy, J. L. N. (2014) "Knowledge Transfer, Translation and Transformation in the Work of Information Technology Architects", *Information and Software Technology*, Vol. 56, No. 10, pp. 1233-1252.

Finkelstein, C. (2006) *Enterprise Architecture for Integration: Rapid Delivery Methods and Technologies*, Boston, MA: Artech House.

Finnegan, P. and Fahy, M. J. (1993) "Planning for Information Systems Resources?", *Journal of Information Technology*, Vol. 8, No. 3, pp. 127-138.

Florentine, S. (2017) "Why You Need an Enterprise Architect", CIO, URL: https://www.cio.com/article/230031/why-you-need-an-enterprise-architect.html.

Foote, D. (2019) "Why Pay for Tech Certifications Is Declining", CIO, URL: https://www.cio.com/article/219709/why-pay-for-tech-certifications-is-declining.html.

Forer, B. R. (1949) "The Fallacy of Personal Validation: A Classroom Demonstration of Gullibility", *Journal of Abnormal and Social Psychology*, Vol. 44, No. 1, pp. 118-123.

Fowler, M. (2002) *Patterns of Enterprise Application Architecture*, Boston, MA: Addison-Wesley Professional.

Fowler, M. (2003) *UML Distilled: A Brief Guide to the Standard Object Modeling Language (3rd Edition)*, Boston, MA: Addison-Wesley Professional.

Frampton, K. (2005) "Master of Enterprise Architecture", Melbourne, Australia: RMIT University.

Frampton, K. (2006) "Information Technology Architects: Can We Improve Their Capabilities?", In: Kaiser, K. and Ryan, T. (eds.) *Proceedings of the 2006 ACM SIGMIS CPR Conference on Computer Personnel Research*, Claremont, CA: Association for Computing Machinery (ACM), pp. 348-350.

Frampton, K., Carroll, J. and Thom, J. A. (2005) "What Capabilities Do IT Architects Say They Need?", In: Wainwright, D. (ed.) *Proceedings of the 10th Annual Conference of the UK Academy for Information Systems*, Newcastle, UK: Northumbria University Press, p.?

Frampton, K. and Ho, S. Y. (2009) "Skills Analysis for Enterprise Architects: Implications for University Education and Curriculum Design", *Journal of Enterprise Architecture*, Vol. 5, No. 4, pp. 44-54.

Frampton, K., Shanks, G., Tamm, T., Kurnia, S. and Milton, S. (2015) "Enterprise Architecture Service Provision: Pathways to Value", In: Becker, J., vom Brocke, J. and de Marco, M. (eds.) *Proceedings of the 23rd European Conference on Information Systems*, Munster, Germany: Association for Information Systems, pp. 1-9.

Frampton, K., Thom, J. A. and Carroll, J. (2006a) "Enhancing IT Architect Capabilities: Experiences Within a University Subject", In: Spencer, S. and Jenkins, A. (eds.) *Proceedings of the 17th Australasian Conference on Information Systems*, Adelaide, Australia: Association for Information Systems, pp. 1-11.

Frampton, K., Thom, J. A., Carroll, J. and Crossman, B. (2006b) "Information Technology Architects: Approaching the Longer View", In: Kaiser, K. and Ryan, T. (eds.) *Proceedings of the 2006 ACM SIGMIS CPR Conference on Computer Personnel Research*, Claremont, CA: Association for Computing Machinery (ACM), pp. 221-229.

Gall, N. (2012) "Gartner's 2011 Global Enterprise Architecture Survey: EA Frameworks Are Still Homemade and Hybrid" (#G00226400), Stamford, CT: Gartner.

Gamble, M. T. (2011) "Teaching Enterprise Integration and Architecture - Tools, Patterns, and Model Problems", In: Sambamurthy, V. and Tanniru, M. (eds.) *Proceedings of the 17th Americas Conference on Information Systems*, Detroit, MI: Association for Information Systems, pp. 1-9.

GAO (2002) "Information Technology: Enterprise Architecture Use Across the Federal Government Can Be Improved" (#GAO-02-6), Washington, DC: Government Accountability Office.

GAO (2003) "Information Technology: Leadership Remains Key to Agencies Making Progress on Enterprise Architecture Efforts" (#GAO-04-40), Washington, DC: Government Accountability Office.

GAO (2006) "Enterprise Architecture: Leadership Remains Key to Establishing and Leveraging Architectures for Organizational Transformation" (#GAO-06-831), Washington, DC: Government Accountability Office.

GAO (2015) "DOD Business Systems Modernization: Additional Action Needed to Achieve Intended Outcomes" (#GAO-15-627), Washington, DC: Government Accountability Office.

Gardner, D., Fehskens, L., Naidu, M., Rouse, W. B. and Ross, J. (2012) "Point-Counterpoint: Enterprise Architecture and Enterprise Transformation as Related but Distinct Concepts", *Journal of Enterprise Transformation*, Vol. 2, No. 4, pp. 283-294.

Gartner (2013) "Hunting and Harvesting in a Digital World: Insights from the 2013 Gartner CIO Agenda Report", Stamford, CT: Gartner.

Gaver, S. B. (2010) "Why Doesn't the Federal Enterprise Architecture Work?", McLean, VA: Technology Matters.

Gellweiler, C. (2019) "Collaboration of Solution Architects and Project Managers", *International Journal of Human Capital and Information Technology Professionals*, Vol. 10, No. 4, pp. 1-15.

Gellweiler, C. (2020) "Types of IT Architects: A Content Analysis on Tasks and Skills", *Journal of Theoretical and Applied Electronic Commerce Research*, Vol. 15, No. 2, pp. 15-37.

Gellweiler, C. (2021) "IT Architects and IT-Business Alignment: A Theoretical Review", In: Cruz-Cunha, M. M., Martinho, R., Rijo, R., Domingos, D. and Peres, E. (eds.) *Proceedings of the 2021 Conference on Enterprise Information Systems (CENTERIS)*, Braga, Portugal: Elsevier, pp. 13-20.

Gianni, A., Frangou, A., Steinmetz, A. and Jhawar, A. (2023) "Magic Quadrant for Enterprise Architecture Tools" (#G00784483), Stamford, CT: Gartner.

Gibson, S. (2008) "Wanted: Enterprise Data Architect", *eWeek*, Vol. 25, No. 33, pp. 48-49.

Goebl, W. (2020) "Enterprise Architects Are Dead. Long Lives Enterprise Architecture Management!", Architectural Thinking Association, URL: https://architectural-thinking.com/at42-enterprise-architects-are-dead-long-live-enterprise-architecture-management-2/.

Gotze, J. (2013) "The Changing Role of the Enterprise Architect", In: Bagheri, E., Gasevic, D., Halle, S., Hatala, M., Nezhad, H. R. M. and Reichert, M. (eds.) *Proceedings of the 8th Trends in Enterprise Architecture Research Workshop*, Vancouver, Canada: IEEE, pp. 319-326.

Gozman, D. and Willcocks, L. (2015) "Crocodiles in the Regulatory Swamp: Navigating the Dangers of Outsourcing, SaaS and Shadow IT", In: Carte, T., Heinzl, A. and Urquhart, C. (eds.) *Proceedings of the 36th International Conference on Information Systems*, Fort Worth, TX: Association for Information Systems, pp. 1-20.

Graves, T. (2007) *Real Enterprise-Architecture: Beyond IT to the Whole Enterprise*, Colchester, UK: Tetradian Books.

Graves, T. (2008) *Bridging the Silos: Enterprise Architecture for IT-Architects*, Colchester, UK: Tetradian Books.

Graves, T. (2023) *The Service-Oriented Enterprise: Learn Enterprise Architecture and Its Viable Services*, New York, NY: Apress.

Graves, T. and Fehskens, L. (2015) "Talking Shop: A Conversation with Tom Graves", *Journal of Enterprise Architecture*, Vol. 11, No. 2, pp. 19-24.

Haag, S. and Eckhardt, A. (2017) "Shadow IT", *Business and Information Systems Engineering*, Vol. 59, No. 6, pp. 469-473.

Hafsi, M. and Assar, S. (2016) "What Enterprise Architecture Can Bring for Digital Transformation? An Exploratory Study", In: Kornyshova, E., Poels, G., Huemer, C., Wattiau, I., Matthes, F. and Sanz, J. (eds.) *Proceedings of the 18th IEEE Conference on Business Informatics*, Paris: IEEE, pp. 83-89.

Haigh, T. and Ceruzzi, P. E. (2021) *A New History of Modern Computing*, Cambridge, MA: MIT Press.

Harrison, R. and Josey, A. (2018a) *TOGAF 9 Certified Study Guide (4th Edition)*, Hertogenbosch, The Netherlands: Van Haren Publishing.

Harrison, R. and Josey, A. (2018b) *TOGAF 9 Foundation Study Guide (4th Edition)*, Hertogenbosch, The Netherlands: Van Haren Publishing.

Hauder, M., Roth, S., Matthes, F. and Schulz, C. (2013) "An Examination of Organizational Factors Influencing Enterprise Architecture Management Challenges", In: van Hillegersberg, J., van Heck, E. and Connolly, R. (eds.) *Proceedings of the 21st European Conference on Information Systems*, Utrecht, The Netherlands: Association for Information Systems, pp. 1-12.

Henderson, J. C. and Venkatraman, N. (1993) "Strategic Alignment: Leveraging Information Technology for Transforming Organizations", *IBM Systems Journal*, Vol. 32, No. 1, pp. 4-16.

Hendry, J. (1987) "The Teashop Computer Manufacturer: J. Lyons, LEO and the Potential and Limits of High-Tech Diversification", *Business History*, Vol. 29, No. 1, pp. 73-102.

Hirschheim, R. and Klein, H. K. (2012) "A Glorious and Not-So-Short History of the Information Systems Field", *Journal of the Association for Information Systems*, Vol. 13, No. 4, pp. 188-235.

Hoberman, S. (2007) "Role of the Data Architect", *DM Review*, Vol. 17, No. 1, p. 24.

Hoffman, J. and Martino, C. (1983) "Information Systems Planning to Meet Business Objectives: A Survey of Practices", New York, NY: Cresap, McCormick and Paget.

Hofstader, J. (2008) "We Don't Need No Architects!", *The Architecture Journal*, Vol. 1, No. 15, pp. 2-6.

Hohpe, G. (2020) *The Software Architect Elevator: Redefining the Architect's Role in the Digital Enterprise*, Sebastopol, CA: O'Reilly Media.

Hohpe, G. and Woolf, B. (2004) *Enterprise Integration Patterns: Designing, Building, and Deploying Messaging Solutions*, Boston, MA: Addison-Wesley Professional.

Holmes, F. W. (1977) "Information Resource Management", *Journal of Systems Management*, Vol. 28, No. 9, pp. 6-9.

Hoos, I. R. (1960) "When the Computer Takes Over the Office", *Harvard Business Review*, Vol. 38, No. 4, pp. 102-112.

Hornford, D., Hornford, N., Lambert, M. and Street, K. (2022) "An Introduction to the TOGAF Standard, 10th Edition" (#W212), Reading, UK: The Open Group.

Huff, S. L. (1982) "A Methodology for Supporting System Architects During Preliminary Design", *Information and Management*, Vol. 5, No. 4-5, pp. 259-268.

Humphrey, W. S. (1989) *Managing the Software Process*, Reading, MA: Addison-Wesley.

IASA (2014) "Certified IT Architect - Professional: Candidate Overview Manual", Austin, TX: International Association of Software Architects (IASA).

Isenberg, D. J. (1984) "How Senior Managers Think", *Harvard Business Review*, Vol. 62, No. 6, pp. 81-90.

Izard, S. (2019) "The Changing Role of the Enterprise Architect", Computer Weekly, URL: https://www.computerweekly.com/opinion/The-changing-role-of-the-enterprise-architect.

James, G. A. (2008) "Findings: Elements for Successful EA in Government Agencies" (#G00157190), Stamford, CT: Gartner.

Jaques, E. and Clement, S. D. (1994) *Executive Leadership: A Practical Guide to Managing Complexity*, Arlington, VA: Wiley-Blackwell.

Jarzabkowski, P., Sillince, J. A. and Shaw, D. (2010) "Strategic Ambiguity as a Rhetorical Resource for Enabling Multiple Interests", *Human Relations*, Vol. 63, No. 2, pp. 219-248.

Jiang, X., Dilnutt, R. and Kurnia, S. (2024) "Improving Business-IT Alignment Through Enterprise Architecture Stakeholder Engagement", In: Constantiou, I., Fitzgerald, B. and Seidel, S. (eds.) *Proceedings of the 32nd European Conference on Information Systems*, Paphos, Cyprus: Association for Information Systems, pp. 1-16.

Johnson, V., Maurer, C., Torres, R., Guerra, K., Mohit, H., Srivastava, S. and Chatterjee, S. (2024) "The 2023 SIM IT Issues and Trends Study", *MIS Quarterly Executive*, Vol. 23, No. 1, pp. 83-124.

Jung, J. and Fraunholz, B. (2021) *Masterclass Enterprise Architecture Management*, Cham, Switzerland: Springer.

Kami, M. J. (1958) "Electronic Data Processing: Promise and Problems", *California Management Review*, Vol. 1, No. 1, pp. 74-80.

Kappelman, L., McLean, E., Johnson, V. and Gerhart, N. (2014) "The 2014 SIM IT Key Issues and Trends Study", *MIS Quarterly Executive*, Vol. 13, No. 4, pp. 237-263.

Kappelman, L., Torres, R., McLean, E., Maurer, C., Johnson, V. and Kim, K. (2019) "The 2018 SIM IT Issues and Trends Study", *MIS Quarterly Executive*, Vol. 18, No. 1, pp. 51-84.

Karmann, G., Preisker, N., Hell, D. N. and Assmann, J. (2019) "Digital Architecture Management Study 2019", Paris: Capgemini Invent.

Keller, W. (2005) "Germania Versus the Timeless Way of Building: A Few Episodes on How to Sell Enterprise IT Architecture to Your Peers and Bosses", Munich, Germany: objectarchitects.

Kerr, J. M. (1989) "A Blueprint for Information Systems", *Database Programming and Design*, Vol. 2, No. 9, pp. 60-67.

King, W. R. (1978) "Strategic Planning for Management Information Systems", *MIS Quarterly*, Vol. 2, No. 1, pp. 27-37.

Kleehaus, M. and Matthes, F. (2019) "Challenges in Documenting Microservice-Based IT Landscape: A Survey from an Enterprise Architecture Management Perspective", In: Cherfi, S. S.-S. and Dijkman, R. (eds.) *Proceedings of the 23th IEEE International Enterprise Distributed Object Computing Conference*, Paris: IEEE, pp. 11-20.

Korhonen, J. J. and Halen, M. (2017) "Enterprise Architecture for Digital Transformation", In: Loucopoulos, P., Manolopoulos, Y., Pastor, O., Theodoulidis, B. and Zdravkovic, J. (eds.) *Proceedings of the 19th IEEE Conference on Business Informatics*, Thessaloniki, Greece: IEEE, pp. 349-358.

Kotusev, S. (2016a) "The Critical Scrutiny of TOGAF", British Computer Society (BCS), URL: https://www.bcs.org/articles-opinion-and-research/the-critical-scrutiny-of-togaf/.

Kotusev, S. (2016b) "Enterprise Architecture Frameworks: The Fad of the Century", British Computer Society (BCS), URL: https://www.bcs.org/articles-opinion-and-research/enterprise-architecture-frameworks-the-fad-of-the-century/.

Kotusev, S. (2016c) "Enterprise Architecture Is Not TOGAF", British Computer Society (BCS), URL: https://www.bcs.org/articles-opinion-and-research/enterprise-architecture-is-not-togaf/.

Kotusev, S. (2016d) "The History of Enterprise Architecture: An Evidence-Based Review", *Journal of Enterprise Architecture*, Vol. 12, No. 1, pp. 29-37.

Kotusev, S. (2016e) "Six Types of Enterprise Architecture Artifacts", British Computer Society (BCS), URL: https://www.bcs.org/articles-opinion-and-research/six-types-of-enterprise-architecture-artifacts/.

Kotusev, S. (2016f) "Two Worlds of Enterprise Architecture", Melbourne, Australia: Unpublished manuscript.

Kotusev, S. (2017a) "Enterprise Architecture on a Single Page", British Computer Society (BCS), URL: https://www.bcs.org/articles-opinion-and-research/enterprise-architecture-on-a-single-page/.

Kotusev, S. (2017b) "Enterprise Architecture: What Did We Study?", *International Journal of Cooperative Information Systems*, Vol. 26, No. 4, pp. 1-84.

Kotusev, S. (2017c) "The Relationship Between Enterprise Architecture Artifacts", British Computer Society (BCS), URL: https://www.bcs.org/articles-opinion-and-research/the-relationship-between-enterprise-architecture-artifacts/.

Kotusev, S. (2018a) "Enterprise Architecture: A Reconceptualization Is Needed", *Pacific Asia Journal of the Association for Information Systems*, Vol. 10, No. 4, pp. 1-36.

Kotusev, S. (2018b) "Fake and Real Tools for Enterprise Architecture", British Computer Society (BCS), URL: https://www.bcs.org/articles-opinion-and-research/fake-and-real-tools-for-enterprise-architecture/.

Kotusev, S. (2018c) *The Practice of Enterprise Architecture: A Modern Approach to Business and IT Alignment*, Melbourne, Australia: SK Publishing.

Kotusev, S. (2018d) "TOGAF-Based Enterprise Architecture Practice: An Exploratory Case Study", *Communications of the Association for Information Systems*, Vol. 43, No. 1, pp. 321-359.

Kotusev, S. (2018e) "TOGAF Version 9.2: What's New?", British Computer Society (BCS), URL: https://www.bcs.org/articles-opinion-and-research/togaf-version-92-whats-new/.

Kotusev, S. (2018f) "TOGAF: Just the Next Fad That Turned into a New Religion", In: Smith, K. L. (ed.) *TOGAF Is Not an EA Framework: The Inconvenient Pragmatic Truth*, Great Notley, UK: Pragmatic EA Ltd, pp. 27-40.

Kotusev, S. (2019a) "Enterprise Architecture and Enterprise Architecture Artifacts: Questioning the Old Concept in Light of New Findings", *Journal of Information Technology*, Vol. 34, No. 2, pp. 102-128.

Kotusev, S. (2019b) "Enterprise Architecture Artifacts: Facts and Decisions", British Computer Society (BCS), URL: https://www.bcs.org/articles-opinion-and-research/enterprise-architecture-artifacts-facts-and-decisions/.

Kotusev, S. (2019c) "Fake and Real Tools for Enterprise Architecture: The Zachman Framework and Business Capability Model", Enterprise Architecture Professional Journal (EAPJ), URL: https://eapj.org/fake-and-real-tools-for-enterprise-architecture/.

Kotusev, S. (2019d) "The Process View of Enterprise Architecture Practice", British Computer Society (BCS), URL: https://www.bcs.org/articles-opinion-and-research/the-process-view-of-enterprise-architecture-practice/.

Kotusev, S. (2019e) "Yet Another Taxonomy for Enterprise Architecture Artifacts", *Journal of Enterprise Architecture*, Vol. 15, No. 1, pp. 1-5.

Kotusev, S. (2020a) "Enterprise Architecture: Forget Systems Thinking, Improve Communication", British Computer Society (BCS), URL: https://www.bcs.org/articles-opinion-and-research/enterprise-architecture-forget-systems-thinking-improve-communication/.

Kotusev, S. (2020b) "Sizing, Structuring, and Fine-Tuning Your EA Function", *Cutter Consortium Executive Update*, Vol. 23, No. 1, pp. 1-8.

Kotusev, S. (2021a) "A Comparison of the Top Four Enterprise Architecture Frameworks", British Computer Society (BCS), URL: https://www.bcs.org/articles-opinion-and-research/a-comparison-of-the-top-four-enterprise-architecture-frameworks/.

Kotusev, S. (2021b) "The Most Important Property of Enterprise Architecture Artifacts", British Computer Society (BCS), URL: https://www.bcs.org/articles-opinion-and-research/the-most-important-property-of-enterprise-architecture-artifacts/.

Kotusev, S. (2021c) *The Practice of Enterprise Architecture: A Modern Approach to Business and IT Alignment (2nd Edition)*, Melbourne, Australia: SK Publishing.

Kotusev, S. (2021d) "Vicious and Virtuous Circles in Enterprise Architecture Practice", British Computer Society (BCS), URL: https://www.bcs.org/articles-opinion-and-research/vicious-and-virtuous-circles-in-enterprise-architecture-practice/.

Kotusev, S. (2022) "Enterprise Architecture Is Based on Business Strategy, Is It Not?", British Computer Society (BCS), URL: https://www.bcs.org/articles-opinion-and-research/enterprise-architecture-is-based-on-business-strategy-is-it-not/.

Kotusev, S. (2023) "The TOGAF Standard, 10th Edition: What's New?", Melbourne, Australia: SK Publishing.

Kotusev, S. and Kurnia, S. (2019) "The Problem of Engagement in Enterprise Architecture Practice: An Exploratory Case Study", In: Boh, W. F., Leimeister, J. M. and Wattal, S. (eds.) *Proceedings of the 40th International Conference on Information Systems*, Munich, Germany: Association for Information Systems, pp. 1-17.

Kotusev, S. and Kurnia, S. (2021) "The Theoretical Basis of Enterprise Architecture: A Critical Review and Taxonomy of Relevant Theories", *Journal of Information Technology*, Vol. 36, No. 3, pp. 275-315.

Kotusev, S., Kurnia, S. and Dilnutt, R. (2020a) "Roles of Different Artifacts in Enterprise Architecture Practice: An Exploratory Study", In: Karahanna, E., Oestreicher-Singer, G. and Sarker, S. (eds.) *Proceedings of the 41st International Conference on Information Systems*, Hyderabad, India: Association for Information Systems, pp. 1-17.

Kotusev, S., Kurnia, S. and Dilnutt, R. (2022) "The Practical Roles of Enterprise Architecture Artifacts: A Classification and Relationship", *Information and Software Technology*, Vol. 147, No. 1, pp. 1-22.

Kotusev, S., Kurnia, S. and Dilnutt, R. (2023) "Enterprise Architecture Artifacts as Boundary Objects: An Empirical Analysis", *Information and Software Technology*, Vol. 155, No. 1, pp. 1-18.

Kotusev, S., Kurnia, S., Dilnutt, R. and Taylor, P. (2020b) "Can Enterprise Architecture Be Based on the Business Strategy?", In: Bui, T. X. (ed.) *Proceedings of the 53rd Hawaii International Conference on System Sciences*, Maui, HI: University of Hawaii at Manoa, pp. 5613-5622.

Kotusev, S., Kurnia, S., Dilnutt, R. and van de Wetering, R. (2024) "The Structuring of Enterprise Architecture Functions in Organizations: Towards a Systematic Theory", *Business and Information Systems Engineering*, Vol. 66, No. 4, pp. 465-488.

Krishnamurthy, R. (2017) "Breezing My Way as a Solution Architect: A Retrospective on Skill Development and Use", *IEEE Software*, Vol. 34, No. 3, pp. 9-13.

Kruchten, P. (2003) *The Rational Unified Process: An Introduction (3rd Edition)*, Boston, MA: Addison-Wesley Professional.

Kruger, J. and Dunning, D. (1999) "Unskilled and Unaware of It: How Difficulties in Recognizing One's Own Incompetence Lead to Inflated Self-Assessments", *Journal of Personality and Social Psychology*, Vol. 77, No. 6, pp. 1121-1134.

Kudryavtsev, D., Zaramenskikh, E. and Arzumanyan, M. (2018) "The Simplified Enterprise Architecture Management Methodology for Teaching Purposes", In: Pergl, R., Babkin, E., Lock, R., Malyzhenkov, P. and Merunka, V. (eds.) *Proceedings of the 14th International Workshop on Enterprise and Organizational Modeling and Simulation*, Tallinn: Springer, pp. 76-90.

Kurnia, S., Kotusev, S. and Dilnutt, R. (2020) "The Role of Engagement in Achieving Business-IT Alignment Through Practicing Enterprise Architecture", In: Newell, S., Pouloudi, N. and van Heck, E. (eds.) *Proceedings of the 28th European Conference on Information Systems*, Marrakech, Morocco: Association for Information Systems, pp. 1-12.

Kurnia, S., Kotusev, S., Shanks, G., Dilnutt, R. and Milton, S. (2021) "Stakeholder Engagement in Enterprise Architecture Practice: What Inhibitors Are There?", *Information and Software Technology*, Vol. 134, No. 1, pp. 1-23.

Laartz, J., Sonderegger, E. and Vinckier, J. (2000) "The Paris Guide to IT Architecture", *McKinsey Quarterly*, Vol. 36, No. 3, pp. 118-127.

Labusch, N., Aier, S. and Winter, R. (2018) "A Major Transformation at a Global Insurance Company", In: Proper, H. A., Winter, R., Aier, S. and de Kinderen, S. (eds.) *Architectural Coordination of Enterprise Transformation*, Cham, Switzerland: Springer, pp. 15-20.

Lambert, D. (2018) "7 Compelling Qualities of Business and Enterprise Architects", CIO, URL: https://web.archive.org/web/20220405120754/https://www.cio.com/article/222146/7-compelling-qualities-of-business-and-enterprise-architects.html.

Lane, M. (2010) "To Be or Not to Be: Recognize Enterprise Architecture as a True Profession?", In: Kappelman, L. A. (ed.) *The SIM Guide to Enterprise Architecture*, Boca Raton, FL: CRC Press, pp. 52-60.

Lange, M. and Mendling, J. (2011) "An Experts' Perspective on Enterprise Architecture Goals, Framework Adoption and Benefit Assessment", In: Kutvonen, L., Johnson, P., Chi, C.-H. and Grossmann, G. (eds.) *Proceedings of the 6th Trends in Enterprise Architecture Research Workshop*, Helsinki: IEEE, pp. 304-313.

Lankhorst, M. (2017) *Enterprise Architecture at Work: Modelling, Communication and Analysis (4th Edition)*, Berlin: Springer.

Lave, J. and Wenger, E. (1991) *Situated Learning: Legitimate Peripheral Participation*, New York, NY: Cambridge University Press.

LeanIX (2017) "The Enterprise Architect of Tomorrow", Bonn, Germany: LeanIX.

Leavitt, H. J. and Whisler, T. L. (1958) "Management in the 1980's", *Harvard Business Review*, Vol. 36, No. 6, pp. 41-48.

Lederer, A. L. and Sethi, V. (1991) "Guidelines for Strategic Information Planning", *Journal of Business Strategy*, Vol. 12, No. 6, pp. 38-43.

Levin, H. S. (1957) "Systems Planning for Computer Application", *The Controller*, Vol. 25, No. 4, pp. 165-186.

Levine, A. (2014) "The Architect as a Salesman within the Enterprise", *Journal of Enterprise Architecture*, Vol. 10, No. 1, pp. 36-41.

Levinthal, D. A. and March, J. G. (1993) "The Myopia of Learning", *Strategic Management Journal*, Vol. 14, No. S2, pp. 95-112.

Levitt, B. and March, J. G. (1988) "Organizational Learning", *Annual Review of Sociology*, Vol. 14, No. 1, pp. 319-340.

Lindblom, C. E. (1959) "The Science of "Muddling Through"", *Public Administration Review*, Vol. 19, No. 2, pp. 79-88.

Longepe, C. (2003) *The Enterprise Architecture IT Project: The Urbanisation Paradigm*, London: Kogan Page Science.

Lucke, C., Krell, S. and Lechner, U. (2010) "Critical Issues in Enterprise Architecting - A Literature Review", In: Santana, M., Luftman, J. N. and Vinze, A. S. (eds.) *Proceedings of the 16th Americas Conference on Information Systems*, Lima: Association for Information Systems, pp. 1-11.

Luehrman, T. A. (1998) "Strategy as a Portfolio of Real Options", *Harvard Business Review*, Vol. 76, No. 5, pp. 89-100.

Luftman, J. and McLean, E. (2004) "Key Issues for IT Executives", *MIS Quarterly Executive*, Vol. 3, No. 2, pp. 89-104.

Luo, H. (2014) "Navigating Complexity with Enterprise Architecture Management", In: Saha, P. (ed.) *A Systemic Perspective to Managing Complexity with Enterprise Architecture*, Hershey, PA: Business Science Reference, pp. 392-432.

Manwani, S. and Bossert, O. (2016) "EA Survey Findings: The Challenges and Responses for Enterprise Architects in the Digital Age", *Journal of Enterprise Architecture*, Vol. 12, No. 3, pp. 6-9.

Mapingire, K., van Deventer, J. P. and van der Merwe, A. (2018) "Competencies and Skills of Enterprise Architects: A Study in a South African Telecommunications Company", In: van Niekerk, J. and Haskins, B. (eds.) *Proceedings of the 26th Annual Conference of the South African Institute of Computer Scientists and Information Technologists*, Port Elizabeth, South Africa: Association for Computing Machinery (ACM), pp. 154-163.

Marca, D. A. and McGowan, C. L. (2005) *IDEF0 and SADT: A Modeler's Guide*, Auburndale, MA: OpenProcess, Inc.

March, J. G. (1962) "The Business Firm as a Political Coalition", *Journal of Politics*, Vol. 24, No. 4, pp. 662-678.

March, J. G. (1987) "Ambiguity and Accounting: The Elusive Link Between Information and Decision Making", *Accounting, Organizations and Society*, Vol. 12, No. 2, pp. 153-168.

March, J. G. (1991a) "Exploration and Exploitation in Organizational Learning", *Organization Science*, Vol. 2, No. 1, pp. 71-87.

March, J. G. (1991b) "How Decisions Happen in Organizations", *Human-Computer Interaction*, Vol. 6, No. 2, pp. 95-117.

March, J. G. (1994) *A Primer on Decision Making: How Decisions Happen*, New York, NY: The Free Press.

March, J. G. (1997) "Understanding How Decisions Happen in Organizations", In: Shapira, Z. (ed.) *Organizational Decision Making*, New York, NY: Cambridge University Press, pp. 9-32.

March, J. G. (2007) "The Study of Organizations and Organizing Since 1945", *Organization Studies*, Vol. 28, No. 1, pp. 9-19.

March, J. G. and Simon, H. A. (1993) *Organizations (2nd Edition)*, Cambridge, MA: Blackwell.

Markus, M. L. and Benjamin, R. I. (1997) "The Magic Bullet Theory in IT-Enabled Transformation", *MIT Sloan Management Review*, Vol. 38, No. 2, pp. 55-68.

Markus, M. L. and Rowe, F. (2023) "The Digital Transformation Conundrum: Labels, Definitions, Phenomena, and Theories", *Journal of the Association for Information Systems*, Vol. 24, No. 2, pp. 328-335.

Martin, J. (1991) *Rapid Application Development*, New York, NY: Macmillan.

Martin, R. C. (2003) *Agile Software Development: Principles, Patterns, and Practices*, Upper Saddle River, NJ: Prentice Hall.

Mason, R. O. (2004) "The Legacy of LEO: Lessons Learned from an English Tea and Cake Company's Pioneering Efforts in Information Systems", *Journal of the Association for Information Systems*, Vol. 5, No. 5, pp. 183-219.

Matthes, D. (2011) *Enterprise Architecture Frameworks Kompendium: Uber 50 Rahmenwerke fur das IT-Management*, Berlin: Springer.

McBride, M. R. (2007) "The Software Architect", *Communications of the ACM*, Vol. 50, No. 5, pp. 75-81.

McConnell, S. (2019) *More Effective Agile: A Roadmap for Software Leaders*, Bellevue, WA: Construx Press.

McDowall, J. D. (2019) *Complex Enterprise Architecture: A New Adaptive Systems Approach*, Berkeley, CA: Apress.

McFarlan, F. W. (1971) "Problems in Planning the Information System", *Harvard Business Review*, Vol. 49, No. 2, pp. 75-89.

McFarlan, F. W. (1984) "Information Technology Changes the Way You Compete", *Harvard Business Review*, Vol. 62, No. 3, pp. 98-103.

McLean, E. R. and Soden, J. V. (1977) *Strategic Planning for MIS*, New York, NY: Wiley.

McNurlin, B. C. (1979) "What Information Do Managers Need?", *EDP Analyzer*, Vol. 17, No. 6, pp. 1-12.

McSweeney, A. (2019) *Introduction to Solution Architecture*, Dublin: Independently Published.

Meyer, B. (2014) *Agile!: The Good, the Hype and the Ugly*, Zurich, Switzerland: Springer.

Mills, J. A. (1985) "A Pragmatic View of the System Architect", *Communications of the ACM*, Vol. 28, No. 7, pp. 708-717.

Mintzberg, H. (1973) *The Nature of Managerial Work*, New York, NY: Harper and Row.

Mintzberg, H. (1983) *Structure in Fives: Designing Effective Organizations*, Englewood Cliffs, NJ: Prentice Hall.

Mintzberg, H. (2004) *Managers Not MBAs: A Hard Look at the Soft Practice of Managing and Management Development*, San Francisco, CA: Berrett-Koehler Publishers.

Mintzberg, H. (2009) *Managing*, San Francisco, CA: Berrett-Koehler Publishers.

Mintzberg, H. and Waters, J. A. (1985) "Of Strategies, Deliberate and Emergent", *Strategic Management Journal*, Vol. 6, No. 3, pp. 257-272.

Mocker, M. (2012) "2012-07 Enterprise Architecture Research at MIT", MIT Sloan CIO Symposium, Boston, MA, URL: https://www.youtube.com/watch?v=9IGQm4-HheA.

Moody, D. (2009) "The "Physics" of Notations: Toward a Scientific Basis for Constructing Visual Notations in Software Engineering", *IEEE Transactions on Software Engineering*, Vol. 35, No. 6, pp. 756-779.

Moore, R. (2018) "Introducing TOGAF Credentials", *Journal of Enterprise Architecture*, Vol. 14, No. 1, p. 67.

Murer, S., Bonati, B. and Furrer, F. J. (2011) *Managed Evolution: A Strategy for Very Large Information Systems*, Berlin: Springer.

Nadler, D. A. and Gerstein, M. S. (1992) "What Is Organizational Architecture?", *Harvard Business Review*, Vol. 70, No. 5, pp. 120-121.

Nash, K. S. (2010) "What CIOs Look for in an Enterprise Architect", CIO, URL: https://www.cio.com/article/282987/careers-staffing-what-cios-look-for-in-an-enterprise-architect.html.

Network World (2016) "Enterprise Architects: The Power Behind the IT Throne", Needham, MA: Network World.

Newman, D. (2018) "6 Tips to Frame Your Digital Transformation with Enterprise Architecture", Forbes, URL: https://www.forbes.com/sites/danielnewman/2018/11/20/6-tips-to-frame-your-digital-transformation-with-enterprise-architecture/.

Niemann, K. D. (2006) *From Enterprise Architecture to IT Governance: Elements of Effective IT Management*, Wiesbaden: Vieweg.

Nowakowski, E., Farwick, M., Trojer, T., Hausler, M., Kessler, J. and Breu, R. (2017) "Enterprise Architecture Planning: Analyses of Requirements from Practice and Research", In: Bui, T. X. (ed.) *Proceedings of the 50th Hawaii International Conference on System Sciences*, Big Island, HI: Association for Information Systems, pp. 4847-4856.

Nsubuga, W. M., Magoulas, T. and Pessi, K. (2014) "Understanding the Roles of Enterprise Architects in a Proactive Enterprise Development Context", In: Devos, J. and De Haes, S. (eds.) *Proceedings of the 8th European Conference on Information Management and Evaluation*, Ghent, Belgium: Academic Conferences and Publishing International Limited, pp. 172-180.

Obitz, T. and Babu, M. (2009) "Infosys Enterprise Architecture Survey 2008/2009", Bangalore, India: Infosys.

Olsen, D. H. (2017) "Enterprise Architecture Management Challenges in the Norwegian Health Sector", In: Hammoudi, S., Smialek, M., Camp, O. and Filipe, J. (eds.) *Proceedings of the 19th International Conference on Enterprise Information Systems*, Porto, Portugal: SciTePress, pp. 637-645.

Orton, J. D. and Weick, K. E. (1990) "Loosely Coupled Systems: A Reconceptualization", *Academy of Management Review*, Vol. 15, No. 2, pp. 203-223.

Osterwalder, A. and Pigneur, Y. (2010) *Business Model Generation: A Handbook for Visionaries, Game Changers, and Challengers*, Hoboken, NJ: Wiley.

Panko, R. R. (1998) "What We Know About Spreadsheet Errors", *Journal of Organizational and End User Computing*, Vol. 10, No. 2, pp. 15-21.

Paradkar, S. S. (2024) "Frameworks & Reference Architectures: Pillars of Industry Modernization & Transformation", Medium, URL: https://medium.com/oolooroo/frameworks-reference-architectures-pillars-of-industry-transformation-a5dba3b6f970.

Paras, G. S. (2011) "A&G 2011 Annual Survey Yields Provocative Trends", *Architecture and Governance Magazine*, Vol. 7, No. 2, pp. 1-4.

Parsons, G. L. (1983) "Information Technology: A New Competitive Weapon", *MIT Sloan Management Review*, Vol. 25, No. 1, pp. 3-14.

Parsons, R. J. (2005) "Enterprise Architects Join the Team", *IEEE Software*, Vol. 22, No. 5, pp. 16-17.

Pavlak, A. (2006) "Enterprise Architecture: Lessons from Classical Architecture", *Journal of Enterprise Architecture*, Vol. 2, No. 2, pp. 20-27.

Pentland, A. (2012) "The New Science of Building Great Teams", *Harvard Business Review*, Vol. 90, No. 4, pp. 60-69.

Periasamy, K. P. (1994) *Development and Usage of Information Architecture: A Management Perspective*, PhD Thesis: University of Oxford, UK.

Perry, M. (2015) "How Far Up the Tower Should Enterprise Architects Climb?", *Journal of Enterprise Architecture*, Vol. 11, No. 1, pp. 21-22.

Planview (2018) "Elevating an Enterprise Architect's Strategic Impact in Transforming the Business: Six Recommendations to Develop Your Strategic Edge", Austin, TX: Planview.

Potts, C. (2010) *recrEAtion: Realizing the Extraordinary Contribution of Your Enterprise Architects*, Bradley Beach, NJ: Technics Publications.

Potts, C. (2013) "Enterprise Architecture: A Courageous Venture", *Journal of Enterprise Architecture*, Vol. 9, No. 3, pp. 28-31.

Preisker, N., Haffner, A., Effmert, M., Maiwald, M., Koster, P. and Hegering, H. (2022) "How Scaling Technologies Challenge Digital Architecture: Digital Architecture Study 2022", Paris: Capgemini Invent.

Preisker, N., Klassen, H., Hell, D. N., Assmann, J. and Kanngiesser, L. (2020) "Enterprise Architecture as Success Factor in Digital Transformations: Digital Architecture Study 2020", Paris: Capgemini Invent.

Preisker, N., Zeeb, S., Reimann, G., Peters, P., Koster, P., Hegering, H., Koch, S. and Kunz, C. (2023) "Why Digital Architects Are Hard to Find but Create the Impact You Need!: Digital Architecture Study 2023 (How the Role of Digital Architects and Their Organizational Function Changes)", Paris: Capgemini Invent.

Preiss, P. (2008) "Architecture Journal Profile: Paul Preiss", *The Architecture Journal*, Vol. 1, No. 15, pp. 10-12.

Preiss, P. (2017) "Becoming Digital Transformers", Medium, URL: https://medium.com/iasa-global/becoming-digital-transformers-9c11f56ccf2c.

Preiss, P. (2022) "How to Stop Screwing Up Architect Titles", Architecture and Governance Magazine, URL: https://www.architectureandgovernance.com/elevating-ea/how-to-stop-screwing-up-architect-titles/.

PRISM (1986) "PRISM: Dispersion and Interconnection: Approaches to Distributed Systems Architecture", Cambridge, MA: CSC Index.

Rao, P. C., Reedy, A. and Bellman, B. (2011) *FEAC Certified Enterprise Architect CEA Study Guide*, New York, NY: McGraw-Hill Education.

Rao, P. C., Reedy, A. and Bellman, B. (2018) *Certified Enterprise Architect All-in-One Exam Guide*, New York, NY: McGraw-Hill Education.

Rehring, K., Bree, T., Gulden, J. and Bredenfeld, L. (2019) "Conceptualizing EA Cities: Towards Visualizing Enterprise Architectures as Cities", In: Johannesson, P., Agerfalk, P. J. and Helms, R. (eds.) *Proceedings of the 27th European Conference on Information Systems*, Stockholm: Association for Information Systems, pp. 1-17.

Rerup, N. (2018) "The Parallels Between Architecture and the Building Industry", *Architecture and Governance Magazine*, Vol. 14, No. 2, pp. 7-9.

Richards, M. and Ford, N. (2020) *Fundamentals of Software Architecture: An Engineering Approach*, Sebastopol, CA: O'Reilly Media.

Richardson, G. L., Jackson, B. M. and Dickson, G. W. (1990) "A Principles-Based Enterprise Architecture: Lessons from Texaco and Star Enterprise", *MIS Quarterly*, Vol. 14, No. 4, pp. 385-403.

Rivera, R. (2007) "Am I Doing Architecture or Design Work?", *IT Professional*, Vol. 9, No. 6, pp. 46-48.

Robertson, B. (2008) "Organize Your Enterprise Architecture Effort: Services" (#G00160689), Stamford, CT: Gartner.

Robertson, B. (2010) "Use Analogies to Market Enterprise Architecture" (#G00129426), Stamford, CT: Gartner.

Ross, J. W. (2004) "Enterprise Architecture: Depicting a Vision of the Firm", Cambridge, MA: Center for Information Systems Research (CISR), MIT Sloan School of Management.

Ross, J. W. (2011) "Gaining Competitive Advantage from Enterprise Architecture (Executive Seminar: Enabling IT Value Through Enterprise Architecture)", Case Western Reserve University, Cleveland, OH, URL: https://www.youtube.com/watch?v=ScHG63YmJ2k.

Ross, J. W., Mocker, M. and Sebastian, I. (2014) "Architect Your Business - Not Just IT!", Cambridge, MA: Center for Information Systems Research (CISR), MIT Sloan School of Management.

Ross, J. W., Weill, P. and Robertson, D. C. (2006) *Enterprise Architecture as Strategy: Creating a Foundation for Business Execution*, Boston, MA: Harvard Business School Press.

Royce, W. W. (1970) "Managing the Development of Large Software Systems", In: Unknown (ed.) *Proceedings of the 26th IEEE Western Electronic Show and Convention (WESCON)*, Los Angeles, CA: IEEE, pp. 328-338.

Rush, R. L. (1979) "MIS Planning in Distributed Data-Processing Systems", *Journal of Systems Management*, Vol. 30, No. 8, pp. 17-25.

Saint-Louis, P., Morency, M. C. and Lapalme, J. (2019) "Examination of Explicit Definitions of Enterprise Architecture", *International Journal of Engineering Business Management*, Vol. 11, No. 1, pp. 1-18.

Sauer, C. and Willcocks, L. P. (2002) "The Evolution of the Organizational Architect", *MIT Sloan Management Review*, Vol. 43, No. 3, pp. 41-49.

Scheer, A.-W. (1992) *Architecture of Integrated Information Systems: Foundations of Enterprise Modelling*, Berlin: Springer.

Schekkerman, J. (2004) *How to Survive in the Jungle of Enterprise Architecture Frameworks: Creating or Choosing an Enterprise Architecture Framework (2nd Edition)*, Victoria, BC: Trafford Publishing.

Schekkerman, J. (2005) "Trends in Enterprise Architecture 2005: How Are Organizations Progressing?", Amersfoort, The Netherlands: Institute for Enterprise Architecture Developments (IFEAD).

Schmidt, C. and Buxmann, P. (2011) "Outcomes and Success Factors of Enterprise IT Architecture Management: Empirical Insight from the International Financial Services Industry", *European Journal of Information Systems*, Vol. 20, No. 2, pp. 168-185.

Schneider, A. W., Gschwendtner, A. and Matthes, F. (2015) "IT Architecture Standardization Survey", Munich, Germany: Software Engineering for Business Information Systems (SEBIS), Technical University of Munich.

Scholtz, B., Calitz, A. and Connolley, A. (2013) "An Analysis of the Adoption and Usage of Enterprise Architecture", In: Gerber, A. and van Deventer, P. (eds.) *Proceedings of the 1st Enterprise Systems Conference*, Cape Town: IEEE, pp. 1-9.

Schulenklopper, J. and Rommes, E. (2016) "Why They Just Don't Get It: Communicating About Architecture with Business Stakeholders", *IEEE Software*, Vol. 33, No. 3, pp. 13-19.

Schulte, W. R. (2002) "Enterprise Architecture and IT 'City Planning'" (#COM-17-2304), Stamford, CT: Gartner.

Schwaber, K. and Beedle, M. (2002) *Agile Software Development with Scrum*, Upper Saddle River, NJ: Prentice Hall.

Scott Morton, M. S. (1991) "Introduction", In: Scott Morton, M. S. (ed.) *The Corporation of the 1990s: Information Technology and Organizational Transformation*, New York, NY: Oxford University Press, pp. 3-23.

Segars, A. H. and Grover, V. (1996) "Designing Company-Wide Information Systems: Risk Factors and Coping Strategies", *Long Range Planning*, Vol. 29, No. 3, pp. 381-392.

Seiler, R. E. and Boockholdt, J. L. (1983) "Creative Development of Computerized Information Systems", *Long Range Planning*, Vol. 16, No. 5, pp. 100-106.

Selig, G. J. (1982) "Approaches to Strategic Planning for Information Resource Management (IRM) in Multinational Corporations", *MIS Quarterly*, Vol. 6, No. 2, pp. 33-45.

Seppanen, V., Pulkkinen, M., Taipalus, T. and Nurmi, J. (2020) "Information Systems Students' Impressions on Learning Modeling Enterprise Architectures", In: Unknown (ed.) *Proceedings of the 2020 IEEE Frontiers in Education Conference*, Uppsala, Sweden: IEEE, pp. 1-8.

Sessions, R. (2007) "A Comparison of the Top Four Enterprise-Architecture Methodologies", Microsoft, URL: https://web.archive.org/web/20170310132123/https://msdn.microsoft.com/en-us/library/bb466232.aspx.

Sessions, R. and de Vadoss, J. (2014) "A Comparison of the Top Four Enterprise Architecture Approaches in 2014", Redmond, WA: Microsoft.

Shanks, G., Gloet, M., Someh, I. A., Frampton, K. and Tamm, T. (2018) "Achieving Benefits with Enterprise Architecture", *Journal of Strategic Information Systems*, Vol. 27, No. 2, pp. 139-156.

Shirey, J. (2008) "The Softer Side of the Architect", *The Architecture Journal*, Vol. 1, No. 15, pp. 26-28.

Short, J. and Burke, B. (2010) "Determining the Right Size for Your Enterprise Architecture Team" (#G00206390), Stamford, CT: Gartner.

Shrivastava, S. and Srivastav, N. (2024) *Solutions Architect's Handbook: Kick-Start Your Career with Architecture Design Principles, Strategies, and Generative AI Techniques (3rd Edition)*, Birmingham, UK: Packt Publishing.

Sidorova, A. and Kappelman, L. (2011a) "Realizing the Benefits of Enterprise Architecture: An Actor-Network Theory Perspective", In: Hammami, O., Krob, D. and Voirin, J.-L. (eds.) *Proceedings of the 2nd International Conference on Complex Systems Design and Management*, Paris: Springer, pp. 317-333.

Sidorova, A. and Kappelman, L. A. (2010) "Enterprise Architecture as Politics: An Actor-Network Theory Perspective", In: Kappelman, L. A. (ed.) *The SIM Guide to Enterprise Architecture*, Boca Raton, FL: CRC Press, pp. 70-88.

Sidorova, A. and Kappelman, L. A. (2011b) "Better Business-IT Alignment Through Enterprise Architecture: An Actor-Network Theory Perspective", *Journal of Enterprise Architecture*, Vol. 7, No. 1, pp. 39-47.

Siebel, T. M. (2019) *Digital Transformation: Survive and Thrive in an Era of Mass Extinction*, New York, NY: RosettaBooks.

Simmons, J. R. M. (1962) *LEO and the Managers*, London: Macdonald.

Simon, H. A. (1943) *A Theory of Administrative Decision*, PhD Thesis: University of Chicago, IL.

Simon, H. A. (1944) "Decision-Making and Administrative Organization", *Public Administration Review*, Vol. 4, No. 1, pp. 16-30.

Simon, H. A. (1955) "A Behavioral Model of Rational Choice", *Quarterly Journal of Economics*, Vol. 69, No. 1, pp. 99-118.

Simon, H. A. (1997) *Administrative Behavior: A Study of Decision-Making Processes in Administrative Organizations (4th Edition)*, New York, NY: The Free Press.

Smith, H. A., Watson, R. T. and Sullivan, P. (2012) "Delivering an Effective Enterprise Architecture at Chubb Insurance", *MIS Quarterly Executive*, Vol. 11, No. 2, pp. 75-85.

Spewak, S. H. and Hill, S. C. (1992) *Enterprise Architecture Planning: Developing a Blueprint for Data, Applications and Technology*, New York, NY: Wiley.

Sporn, D. L. (1978) "Designing an ADP Planning Process", *Long Range Planning*, Vol. 11, No. 1, pp. 43-46.

Stadtmueller, L. (2013) "The Hidden Truth Behind Shadow IT: Six Trends Impacting Your Security Posture", Mountain View, CA: Stratecast | Frost & Sullivan.

Stapleton, J. (1997) *DSDM: Dynamic Systems Development Method (The Method in Practice)*, Harlow, UK: Addison-Wesley.

Steenkamp, A. L., Alawdah, A., Almasri, O., Gai, K., Khattab, N., Swaby, C. and Abaas, R. (2013) "Teaching Case: Enterprise Architecture Specification Case Study", *Journal of Information Systems Education*, Vol. 24, No. 2, pp. 105-119.

Steghuis, C. and Proper, E. (2008) "Competencies and Responsibilities of Enterprise Architects: A Jack-of-All-Trades?", In: Dietz, J. L. G., Albani, A. and Barjis, J. (eds.) *Advances in Enterprise Engineering I*, Berlin: Springer, pp. 93-107.

Stewart, G. (2004) "Developing a Systemic Understanding of Information Systems in Emerging IT Professionals Using an Enterprise Architecture Approach", In: Romano, N. C. (ed.) *Proceedings of the 10th Americas Conference on Information Systems*, New York, NY: Association for Information Systems, pp. 4368-4373.

Stewart, G. (2006) "Reflections on Teaching Enterprise Architecture to Graduate Students", In: Romano, N. C. (ed.) *Proceedings of the 12th Americas Conference on Information Systems*, Acapulco, Mexico: Association for Information Systems, pp. 2407-2413.

Strano, C. and Rehmani, Q. (2005) "The Profession of Enterprise Architecture", *Journal of Enterprise Architecture*, Vol. 1, No. 1, pp. 7-15.

Strano, C. and Rehmani, Q. (2007) "The Role of the Enterprise Architect", *Information Systems and e-Business Management*, Vol. 5, No. 4, pp. 379-396.

Suer, M. F. (2018) "Enterprise Architects as Digital Transformers", CIO, URL: https://www.cio.com/article/221861/enterprise-architects-as-digital-transformers.html.

Sullivan, C. H. (1988) "The Changing Approach to Systems Planning", *Journal of Information Systems Management*, Vol. 5, No. 3, pp. 8-13.

Sultanow, E., Duane, J.-N. and Chircu, A. (2020) "Skills for Sustainable Enterprise Architectures in a VUCA World", In: Unknown (ed.) *Proceedings of the 15th International Conference on Wirtschaftsinformatik*, Potsdam, Germany: GITO, pp. 1-16.

Tambouris, E., Zotou, M., Kalampokis, E. and Tarabanis, K. (2012) "Fostering Enterprise Architecture Education and Training with the Enterprise Architecture Competence Framework", *International Journal of Training and Development*, Vol. 16, No. 2, pp. 128-136.

Tamm, T., Seddon, P. B. and Shanks, G. (2022) "How Enterprise Architecture Leads to Organisational Benefits", *International Journal of Information Management*, Vol. 67, No. 1, pp. 1-22.

Tetlock, P. E. (2005) *Expert Political Judgment: How Good Is It? How Can We Know?* , Princeton, NJ: Princeton University Press.

The Open Group (2022) "TOGAF Series Guide: Architecture Skills Framework" (#G198), Reading, UK: The Open Group.

Theuerkorn, F. (2004) *Lightweight Enterprise Architectures*, Boca Raton, FL: Auerbach Publications.

Thonssen, B. and von Dewitz, M. (2018) "A Label Is Not Enough - Approach for an Enterprise Architecture Role Description Framework", In: Varajao, J. E., Cruz-Cunha, M. M., Martinho, R., Rijo, R., Domingos, D. and Peres, E. (eds.) *Proceedings of the 2018 Conference on Enterprise Information Systems (CENTERIS)*, Lisbon: Elsevier, pp. 409-416.

Thummadi, B. V. and Lyytinen, K. (2020) "How Much Method-in-Use Matters? A Case Study of Agile and Waterfall Software Projects and Their Design Routine Variation", *Journal of the Association for Information Systems*, Vol. 21, No. 4, pp. 864-900.

Tinsley, T. A. (2009) *Enterprise Architects: Masters of the Unseen City*, Charleston, SC: BookSurge Publishing.

Tittle, E. and Lindros, K. (2018) "Best Enterprise Architect Certifications", *Business News Daily*, URL: https://web.archive.org/web/20190331050308/https://www.businessnewsdaily.com/10758-best-enterprise-architect-certifications.html.

Tsichritzis, D. (1980) "The Architects of System Design", *Datamation*, Vol. 26, No. 9, pp. 201-202.

Ullrich, A., Bertheau, C., Wiedmann, M., Sultanow, E., Korppen, T. and Bente, S. (2021) "Roles, Tasks and Skills of the Enterprise Architect in the VUCA World", In: Pufahl, L., Karastoyanova, D. and Gill, A. (eds.) *Proceedings of the 25th IEEE International Enterprise Distributed Object Computing Conference Workshops*, Gold Coast, Australia: IEEE, pp. 261-270.

Unde, A. (2008) "Becoming an Architect in a System Integrator", *The Architecture Journal*, Vol. 1, No. 15, pp. 7-9.

Uppal, J. (2013) "A Blueprint for Professionalization of Enterprise Architecture", *Journal of Enterprise Architecture*, Vol. 9, No. 4, pp. 26-28.

van de Wetering, R., Kurnia, S. and Kotusev, S. (2021) "The Role of Enterprise Architecture for Digital Transformations", *Sustainability*, Vol. 13, No. 4, pp. 1-4.

van den Berg, M. and van Vliet, H. (2016) "The Decision-Making Context Influences the Role of the Enterprise Architect", In: Franke, U., Lapalme, J. and Aier, S. (eds.) *Proceedings of the 11th Trends in Enterprise Architecture Research Workshop*, Vienna: IEEE, pp. 114-121.

van der Raadt, B., Slot, R. and van Vliet, H. (2007) "Experience Report: Assessing a Global Financial Services Company on Its Enterprise Architecture Effectiveness Using NAOMI", In: Sprague, R. H. (ed.) *Proceedings of the 40th Hawaii International Conference on System Sciences*, Big Island, HI: IEEE, pp. 1-10.

van Gils, B. and van Dijk, S. (2014) *The Practice of Enterprise Architecture: Experiences, Techniques, and Best Practices*, Enschede, The Netherlands: BiZZdesign Academy.

van Rensselaer, C. (1979) "Centralize? Decentralize? Distribute?", *Datamation*, Vol. 25, No. 7, pp. 88-97.

Venkatraman, N. (1994) "IT-Enabled Business Transformation: From Automation to Business Scope Redefinition", *MIT Sloan Management Review*, Vol. 35, No. 2, pp. 73-87.

Vial, G. (2019) "Understanding Digital Transformation: A Review and a Research Agenda", *Journal of Strategic Information Systems*, Vol. 28, No. 2, pp. 118-144.

Violino, B. (2020) "Career Roadmap: Enterprise Architect", *IDG Insider Pro*, URL: https://web.archive.org/web/20200810203257/https://www.idginsiderpro.com/article/3488866/career-roadmap-enterprise-architect.html.

von Halle, B. (1992) "Leap of Faith", *Database Programming and Design*, Vol. 5, No. 9, pp. 15-18.

von Halle, B. (1996) "Architecting in a Virtual World", *Database Programming and Design*, Vol. 9, No. 11, pp. 13-18.

Wagter, R., Proper, H. A. and Witte, D. (2012) "Enterprise Architecture: A Strategic Specialism", In: Ma, S. R., Sanz, J. and Bai, X.-Y. (eds.) *Proceedings of the 14th IEEE Conference on Commerce and Enterprise Computing*, Hangzhou, China: IEEE, pp. 1-8.

Walker, M. (2007) "A Day in the Life of an Enterprise Architect", Microsoft, URL: https://web.archive.org/web/20081007062837/http://msdn.microsoft.com/en-us/library/bb945098.aspx.

Walrad, C. C., Lane, M., Jeffrey, W. and Hirst, D. V. (2013) "Architecting a Profession", *IT Professional*, Vol. 16, No. 1, pp. 42-49.

Wegmann, A., Regev, G., de la Cruz, J. D., Le, L.-S. and Rychkova, I. (2007) "Teaching Enterprise Architecture and Service-Oriented Architecture in Practice", In: Lankhorst, M. M. and Johnson, P. (eds.) *Proceedings of the 2nd Trends in Enterprise Architecture Research Workshop*, St. Gallen, Switzerland: Telematica Instituut, pp. 13-22.

Weick, K. E. (1976) "Educational Organizations as Loosely Coupled Systems", *Administrative Science Quarterly*, Vol. 21, No. 1, pp. 1-19.

Weill, P. and Ross, J. W. (2009) *IT Savvy: What Top Executives Must Know to Go from Pain to Gain*, Boston, MA: Harvard Business School Press.

Weill, P. and Vitale, M. (2001) *Place to Space: Migrating to eBusiness Models*, Boston, MA: Harvard Business School Press.

Weill, P. and Woerner, S. L. (2010) "What's Next: Learning from the Most Digital Industries", Cambridge, MA: Center for Information Systems Research (CISR), MIT Sloan School of Management.

Weill, P., Woerner, S. L. and McDonald, M. (2009) "Managing the IT Portfolio (Update Circa 2009): Infrastructure Dwindling in the Downturn", Cambridge, MA: Center for Information Systems Research (CISR), MIT Sloan School of Management.

Weill, P., Woerner, S. L. and Rubin, H. A. (2008) "Managing the IT Portfolio (Update Circa 2008): It's All About What's New", Cambridge, MA: Center for Information Systems Research (CISR), MIT Sloan School of Management.

Weiss, D., Blanton, C. E. and Allega, P. (2008) "Building the Enterprise Architecture Team" (#G00156818), Stamford, CT: Gartner.

Weiss, D. and Rosser, B. (2008) "Focus Enterprise Architecture Metrics on Business Value" (#G00155631), Stamford, CT: Gartner.

Wessel, L., Baiyere, A., Ologeanu-Taddei, R., Cha, J. and Blegind-Jensen, T. (2021) "Unpacking the Difference Between Digital Transformation and IT-Enabled Organizational Transformation", *Journal of the Association for Information Systems*, Vol. 22, No. 1, pp. 102-129.

Westerman, G., Bonnet, D. and McAfee, A. (2014) *Leading Digital: Turning Technology into Business Transformation*, Boston, MA: Harvard Business School Press.

White, S. A. and Miers, D. (2008) *BPMN Modeling and Reference Guide: Understanding and Using BPMN*, Lighthouse Point, FL: Future Strategies.

White, S. K. (2020) "What Is an Enterprise Architect? A Vital Role for IT Operations", CIO, URL: https://www.cio.com/article/193329/what-is-an-enterprise-architect-a-vital-role-for-it-operations.html.

White, S. K. (2022) "Top 15 Certifications for Enterprise Architects", CIO, URL: https://www.cio.com/article/222483/12-certifications-for-enterprise-architects.html.

Whitley, R. (1989) "On the Nature of Managerial Tasks and Skills: Their Distinguishing Characteristics and Organization", *Journal of Management Studies*, Vol. 26, No. 3, pp. 209-224.

Wierda, G. (2015) *Chess and the Art of Enterprise Architecture*, Amsterdam: R&A.

Wierda, G. (2017) *Mastering ArchiMate (Edition III): A Serious Introduction to the ArchiMate Enterprise Architecture Modeling Language* Amsterdam: R&A.

Wiseman, C. (1988) *Strategic Information Systems*, Homewood, IL: Irwin.

Woerner, S. L., Weill, P. and Sebastian, I. M. (2022) *Future Ready: The Four Pathways to Capturing Digital Value*, Boston, MA: Harvard Business School Press.

Woldt, R. (2017) "Enterprise Architecture: The Scarce Skillset in Big Demand", CIO, URL: https://www.cio.com/article/230703/enterprise-architecture-the-scarce-skillset-in-big-demand.html.

Woods, E. (2014) "Return of the Pragmatic Architect", *IEEE Software*, Vol. 31, No. 3, pp. 10-13.

Woods, E. (2017) "Should Architects Code?", *IEEE Software*, Vol. 34, No. 5, pp. 20-21.

Woods, E. and Rozanski, N. (2012) "Relating Enterprise, Application, and Infrastructure Architects", In: Mistrik, I., Tang, A., Bahsoon, R. and Stafford, J. A. (eds.) *Aligning Enterprise, System, and Software Architectures*, Hershey, PA: Business Science Reference, pp. 1-22.

Worthen, B. (2005) "Wanted: Enterprise Architects", *CIO Magazine*, Vol. 18, No. 10, pp. 46-50.

Wright, A. (2011) "Lessons Learned: Architects Are Facilitators, Too!", *IEEE Software*, Vol. 28, No. 1, pp. 70-72.

Ylimaki, T. and Halttunen, V. (2005) "Perceptions on Architecture Management and Architect's Profession", In: Soliman, K. S. (ed.) *Proceedings of the 4th International Business Information Management Association (IBIMA) Conference*, Lisbon: Citeseer, pp. 23-31.

Ylinen, M. and Pekkola, S. (2018) "Looking for a Five-Legged Sheep: Identifying Enterprise Architects' Skills and Competencies", In: Zuiderwijk, A. and Hinnant, C. C. (eds.) *Proceedings of the 19th International Conference on Digital Government Research*, Delft, The Netherlands: Association for Computing Machinery (ACM), pp. 1-8.

Ylinen, M. and Pekkola, S. (2020) "Jack-of-All-Trades Torn Apart: Skills and Competences of an Enterprise Architect", In: Newell, S., Pouloudi, N. and van Heck, E. (eds.) *Proceedings of the 28th European Conference on Information Systems*, Marrakech, Morocco: Association for Information Systems, pp. 1-13.

Zachman, J. A. (1987) "A Framework for Information Systems Architecture", *IBM Systems Journal*, Vol. 26, No. 3, pp. 276-292.

Ziemann, J. (2022) *Fundamentals of Enterprise Architecture Management: Foundations for Steering the Enterprise-Wide Digital System*, Cham, Switzerland: Springer.

Index

A

Active participation, 255, *See also* Individual approaches

Activities of enterprise architects, 197-224, 271-78, 316-18, 318-28, 335-37, 350-52, 352-65

Actualities EA artifacts, 125-27

Ad hoc demands, 7, *See also* Transformation drivers

Ad hoc papers, 142, *See also* Auxiliary artifacts

Agile methodologies, 35-37, *See also* Project delivery process

Amendment forms, 264-65, *See also* Meta-EA artifacts

Analytical papers, 168, *See also* Outlines

Analytical quadrants, 204-5, *See also* Ad hoc papers

Analytical Reports, 148-49, *See also* Considerations

Analytical techniques, 141-42, *See also* Instruments of enterprise architects

Analyzing the external environment, 199, 201-7, 316, 350, *See also* Activities of enterprise architects

Application architects. *See* Domain architects

Applications domain, 50, *See also* Organizational domains

Approval step of the architectural planning process, 235, *See also* Architectural planning process

ArchiMate, 140, 302, 426, 428

Architectural context, 190-95

Architectural decisions, 41, *See also* Architectural planning

Architectural directions for Designs, 169, *See also* Designs

Architectural directions for Outlines, 168, *See also* Outlines

Architectural oversight, 74-75

Architectural planning, 41-50, 58-61, 79-81

Architectural planning process, 73-74, 231-36, *See also* Architectural planning, *See also* Leading the development of plans

Architectural plans, 42, 65, *See also* Architectural planning

Architectural pre-planning, 72-73, *See also* Architectural planning

Architectural solutions, 42, 55-56, 57-58, 65, *See also* Architectural planning

Architectural Thinking Association, 302

Architecture & Governance Magazine, 302

Architecture change requests, 264, *See also* Amendment forms

Architecture debt, 359, 413

Architecture decision papers, 241-43, *See also* Communication materials

Architecture functions, 85-87, 373-92, *See also* Architecture positions

Architecture governance bodies, 66, 75, 248-50, 256-58

Architecture of Integrated Information Systems (ARIS), 140, 426

Architecture positions, 373-92, *See also* Specialization of architects

Architecture Strategies, 65, 147-48, *See also* Considerations

Area-based specialization of architects, 380-85, *See also* Specialization of architects

Art, 297, *See also* Profession of enterprise architects

Artifact approvals, 257, *See also* Governance procedures

Artifact templates, 238-39, *See also* Meta-EA artifacts

Artifacts. *See* Enterprise architecture artifacts

Assessment reports, 220-22, *See also* Ad hoc papers

Asset Inventories, 160-61, *See also* Landscapes

Asset Roadmaps, 163-64, *See also* Landscapes

Association for Cooperative Operations Research and Development (ACORD), 103
Association of Enterprise Architects (AEA), 302
Autonomous initiatives, 29, *See also* Initiative hierarchy
Auxiliary artifacts, 142-43, *See also* Instruments of enterprise architects
Aviation Information Data Exchange (AIDX), 104

B

Banking Industry Architecture Network (BIAN), 103
Basic activities, 200-201, *See also* Activities of enterprise architects
Building step of the project delivery process, 34, *See also* Project delivery process
Business and IT alignment, 15
Business architects, 462, *See also* Domain architects
Business Architecture Guild, 303
Business area architects, 305, 382, *See also* Enterprise Architects (archetype), *See also* Specialization of architects, *See also* Business-centric architecture functions
Business Capability Models, 157-58, *See also* Visions
Business case, 353
Business cases, 360
Business domain, 50, *See also* Organizational domains
Business engagement, 393-404
Business executives, 44, 87, 89
Business interests, 15, 286, *See also* Conflicts of interests
Business managers, 44, 87
Business model canvases, 160, *See also* Visions
Business motivation models, 150, *See also* Considerations
Business Process Framework (eTOM), 103
Business Process Model and Notation (BPMN), 140, 302, 426
Business requirements documents, 170, *See also* Designs
Business specialists, 44, 87

Business strategy, 9-10, 89-90, *See also* Transformation drivers
Business-centric architecture functions, 381-83, *See also* Architecture functions
Business-focused EA artifacts, 132-35

C

C4 model, 140
Capturing architectural solutions, 119-21, 179-86, 186-90, *See also* Functions of EA artifacts, *See also* Architectural solutions
Career of enterprise architects, 421-23
Center for Information Systems Research (CISR), 302
Challenges of digital transformation. *See* Technical challenges of digital transformation, *See* Organizational challenges of digital transformation
Challenges of enterprise architects. *See* Individual challenges of enterprise architects, *See* Organizational challenges of enterprise architects
Challenges of managerial desire, 410-15, *See also* Organizational challenges of enterprise architects
Challenges of managerial distance, 415-18, *See also* Organizational challenges of enterprise architects
Challenges of managerial understanding, 408-10, *See also* Organizational challenges of enterprise architects
Change activists, 81
Change Agents, 78-79, 88, 406-7
City planners, xx, 69-70, 76
Cloud-native organizations, 51
Collaborative attitude, 107, *See also* Skills of enterprise architects
Combined architecture functions, 383-85, *See also* Architecture functions
Communication materials, 142, *See also* Auxiliary artifacts
Communication skills, 106-7, *See also* Skills of enterprise architects
Compliance checklists, 261-62, *See also* Meta-EA artifacts

Concept step of the project implementation process, 354, 358-59, *See also* Project implementation process

Conception phase of the initiative implementation process, 22, 72-73, 321-22, *See also* Initiative implementation process

Conceptual Data Models, 148-49, *See also* Considerations

Conflicts of interests, 15-18, 24-26, 37, 288, 412, 430

Considerations, 135-36, 146-50, 315, 349, *See also* CSVLOD taxonomy for EA artifacts

Context diagrams, 160, *See also* Visions

Control Objectives for Information and Related Technologies (COBIT), 103

Conundrums of enterprise architects, 429-31

Co-planning transformations, 389

Core diagrams, 160, *See also* Visions

Craft, 297, *See also* Profession of enterprise architects

Crystal, 36

CSVLOD taxonomy for EA artifacts, 135-40, *See also* Enterprise architecture artifacts

D

DAMA (Data Management Association) International, 303

Data architects. *See* Domain architects

Data domain, 50, *See also* Organizational domains

Data portfolio models, 165, *See also* Landscapes

Decision approvals, 257, *See also* Governance procedures

Decision step of the project implementation process, 355, 359-60, *See also* Project implementation process

Deliberate intentions, 7, *See also* Transformation drivers

Delivery functions, 86, *See also* Project delivery process

Delivery level, 30-33, *See also* Initiative hierarchy

Delivery phase of the initiative implementation process, 31, *See also* Execution phase of the initiative implementation process

Delivery step of the project implementation process, 355, 362-63, *See also* Project implementation process

Department of Defense Architecture Framework (DoDAF), 427

Deployment step of the project delivery process, 34, *See also* Project delivery process

Derivative initiatives, 29, *See also* Initiative hierarchy

Design alteration forms, 264, *See also* Amendment forms

Design committees, 249, *See also* Architecture governance bodies

Design step of the project implementation process, 355, 360-62, *See also* Project implementation process

Designs, 137, 168-70, 316, 349-50, *See also* CSVLOD taxonomy for EA artifacts

Detailed design documents, 356

Digital transformation, 5-6

Digital transformation efforts, 6, *See also* Digital transformation

Digital transformation initiatives, 21-26, *See also* Technical rationalization initiatives

Digitalization. *See* Digital transformation

Disciplined thinking, 108-9, *See also* Skills of enterprise architects

Discussion step of the architectural planning process, 231, *See also* Architectural planning process

Documentation review, 255, *See also* Individual approaches

Documenting the existing situation, 118-19, 175-79, *See also* Functions of EA artifacts

Domain architects, 305, 380, *See also* Enterprise Architects (archetype), *See also* Specialization of architects, *See also* Domain-centric architecture functions

Domain stack, 51-52, *See also* Organizational domains

Domain-centric architecture functions, 380-81, *See also* Architecture functions, *See also* Organizational domains

Driver proponents, 6, 289, *See also* Transformation drivers

Drivers of digital transformation. *See* Transformation drivers

Duality of EA artifacts, 121-24

Dynamic Systems Development Method (DSDM), 36

E

Elaboration step of the architectural planning process, 232, *See also* Architectural planning process

Emergent opportunities, 7, *See also* Transformation drivers

Ensuring adherence to plans, 200, 247-69, *See also* Activities of enterprise architects

Enterprise architects, 63-70

Enterprise Architects (archetype), 304-5, 311-43, 370-71

Enterprise architecture, 64

Enterprise architecture artifacts, 64-65, 145-73, *See also* Instruments of enterprise architects

Enterprise Architecture Center of Excellence (EACOE), 302

Enterprise architecture frameworks, 427-28

Enterprise Architecture on a Page, 172-73

Enterprise architecture practice, 66-67

Enterprise Architecture Professional Journal (EAPJ), 302

Enterprise Architecture Specialist Group (EASG), 302

Epoch of digital transformation, 4

Epoch of electronic business, 4

Epoch of process automation, 3

Epoch of strategic systems, 3

Exception forms, 262-64, *See also* Meta-EA artifacts

Execution phase of the initiative implementation process, 23, 74-75, 325-26, *See also* Initiative implementation process

Experience of enterprise architects, 110-13, 315, 348-49, 424, *See also* Resources of enterprise architects

Explicit duality, 122-23, *See also* Duality of EA artifacts

Extended inventories, 164, *See also* Landscapes

Extreme Programming (XP), 36

F

Federal Enterprise Architecture Certification (FEAC) Institute, 302

Federal Enterprise Architecture Framework (FEAF), 427

Federation of Enterprise Architecture Professional Organizations (FEAPO), 302

Functional domains, 53, *See also* Organizational domains

Functions of EA artifacts, 117-21, *See also* Enterprise architecture artifacts

Future of enterprise architects, 303-4

G

General Data Protection Regulation (GDPR), 102, *See also* Normative acts

General EA artifacts, 127-29, 182-84

Goals of digital transformation initiatives. *See* Initiative goals

Governance procedures, 256-58, *See also* Ensuring adherence to plans

Guidelines, 152-53, *See also* Standards

H

Hats of enterprise architects, 76-82, *See also* Technology Experts, *See also* Change Agents

Health Insurance Portability and Accountability Act (HIPAA), 103, *See also* Normative acts

Health Level Seven (HL7), 104

Hierarchy of digital transformation initiatives. *See* Initiative hierarchy

History of enterprise architects, 300-301

History of IT. *See* Information technology (IT)

Hype cycle for technologies, 206

I

Iasa Global, 303, 428

Ideation of digital transformation initiatives. *See* Initial ideation

IDEF0, 140

Implementation of digital transformation initiatives. *See* Initiative implementation process

Implicit duality, 123-24, *See also* Duality of EA artifacts

Individual approaches, 254-56, *See also* Ensuring adherence to plans

Individual challenges of enterprise architects, 404-7

Industry reference models, 159, *See also* Visions

Information inventories, 165, *See also* Landscapes

Information technology (IT), 3-5
Information Technology Infrastructure Library (ITIL), 103
Infrastructure architects. *See* Domain architects
Infrastructure domain, 50, *See also* Organizational domains
Infrastructure portfolio models, 165, *See also* Landscapes
Initial ideation, 21-22, 71-72, 318, 351-52
Initiation step of the project implementation process, 354, *See also* Project implementation process
Initiative approval gate, 320, 324
Initiative context, 279
Initiative context of activities, 198-99, 318-28, 352-65, *See also* Activities of enterprise architects
Initiative executors, 25, *See also* Initiative stakeholders
Initiative goals, 21, 29
Initiative hierarchy, 29-30, 37-39, 181-82, 194-95, *See also* Digital transformation initiatives
Initiative implementation process, 22-24, 319-21, 396-99
Initiative sponsors, 24, *See also* Initiative stakeholders
Initiative stakeholders, 24-26, 287-89
Initiative-specific EA artifacts, 127-29
Innovative mindset, 107-8, *See also* Skills of enterprise architects
Institute for Enterprise Architecture Developments (IFEAD), 302
Instruments of enterprise architects, 117-43, 315-16, 349-50
Integration architects. *See* Domain architects
Integration domain, 50, *See also* Organizational domains
Interface definitions, 155, *See also* Standards
Investment committees, 249, *See also* Architecture governance bodies
Investment decision gate, 353, 359
IT analytical reports, 155, *See also* Standards
IT architecture strategies, 155, *See also* Standards
IT capability models, 165, *See also* Landscapes
IT executives, 87
IT functions, 85-87
IT initiatives. *See* Digital transformation initiatives
IT managers, 87
IT Principles, 152-53, *See also* Standards
IT Roadmaps, 163-64, *See also* Landscapes
IT solutions, 6, 26
IT specialists, 88
IT target states, 165, *See also* Landscapes
Item registers, 142, *See also* Auxiliary artifacts
IT-focused EA artifacts, 132-35
Ivory tower, 97

J

J. Lyons & Co., 300, *See also* History of enterprise architects
Journal of Enterprise Architecture (JEA), 302

K

Keeping in touch, 256, *See also* Individual approaches
Key design decisions (KDDs), 241-43, *See also* Communication materials
Knowledge of enterprise architects, 101-6, 314, 347-48, 424, 429, *See also* Resources of enterprise architects

L

Landscape Diagrams, 160-61, *See also* Landscapes
Landscape Maps, 161-63, *See also* Landscapes
Landscapes, 136-37, 160-65, 315, 349, *See also* CSVLOD taxonomy for EA artifacts
Leading the development of plans, 200, 225-45, *See also* Activities of enterprise architects
Legal Electronic Data Exchange Standard (LEDES), 104
Logical Data Models, 153-54, *See also* Standards
Lyons Electronic Office (LEO), 300, 436, *See also* History of enterprise architects

M

Management consultants, xx, 67-69, 76
Mandatory interactions, 68, 346, 403
Meta-EA artifacts, 142, *See also* Auxiliary artifacts
Mini-designs, 170, *See also* Designs

Modeling languages, 140, 426, *See also* Instruments of enterprise architects

Motivational context, 10-12, *See also* Transformation drivers

N

Netherlands Architecture Forum (NAF), 302

Non-functional domains, 53, *See also* Organizational domains

Non-substantive domains, 54, *See also* Organizational domains

Non-technical domains, 53, *See also* Organizational domains

Normative acts, 18

O

Object Management Group (OMG), 302

Offering advice, 388

Official advisory services, 215-19, *See also* Providing advisory services

One-on-one meetings, 229-31, *See also* Leading the development of plans

One-tier architecture functions, 374-76, *See also* Architecture functions

Operational problems, 7, *See also* Transformation drivers

Operations specialists, 44

Organizational challenges of digital transformation, 14-18, 37-39

Organizational challenges of enterprise architects, 407-18

Organizational context of activities, 198-99, 278-79, 316-18, 335-37, 350-52, *See also* Activities of enterprise architects

Organizational domains, 50-56, 170-72, 339-41, 367-69

Organizational side of architectural planning, 46-48, *See also* Architectural planning

Organizational solutions, 46, *See also* Organizational side of architectural planning

Organizational structures, 160, *See also* Visions

Organization-centric view of digital transformation, 331-33, *See also* Digital transformation initiatives

Outlines, 137, 165-68, 316, 349-50, *See also* CSVLOD taxonomy for EA artifacts

P

Passive observation, 255, *See also* Individual approaches

Patterns, 153-54, *See also* Standards

Payment Card Industry Data Security Standard (PCI DSS), 103, *See also* Normative acts

Permanent imperatives, 7, *See also* Transformation drivers

Pipeline of initiatives, 284

Plan approvals, 257, *See also* Governance procedures

Planning by talking, 73, 78, 107, 141, 229, 282, *See also* Architectural planning

Planning phase of the initiative implementation process, 23, 73-74, 323-24, *See also* Initiative implementation process

Planning sessions, 229-31, *See also* Leading the development of plans

Plans EA artifacts, 125-27

Policies, 146-47, *See also* Considerations

Position papers, 220-22, *See also* Ad hoc papers

Preliminary Solution Designs, 168-69, *See also* Designs

Presentation packs, 239-41, *See also* Communication materials

Primary stakeholders of architectural planning, 43, *See also* Stakeholders of architectural planning

Principles, 146-47, *See also* Considerations

Process Maps, 158-59, *See also* Visions

Process models, 168, *See also* Outlines

Product catalogs, 160, *See also* Visions

Product inspection, 254, *See also* Individual approaches

Profession of enterprise architects, 293-99, 304

Professional certifications, 428-29

Programs, 26-33, *See also* Digital transformation initiatives

Project delivery process, 34-35, *See also* Delivery step of the project implementation process

Project dispensation cards, 263, *See also* Exception forms

Project evaluation worksheets, 261, *See also* Compliance checklists

Project implementation process, 352-57, *See also* Initiative implementation process

Project Management Body of Knowledge (PMBOK), 103

Project management plans, 353, 362

Project portfolio, 331, *See also* Organization-centric view of digital transformation

Project portfolio level, 334, *See also* Organization-centric view of digital transformation

Project team members, 44, *See also* Project teams

Project teams, 34, 90, *See also* Project delivery process

Projects, 26-33, *See also* Digital transformation initiatives

PRojects IN Controlled Environments (PRINCE2), 103

Proponents of transformation drivers. *See* Driver proponents

Providing advisory services, 200, 214-23, 317-18, 351, *See also* Activities of enterprise architects

Providing drivers, 389

Pyramid of resources, 113-14, *See also* Resources of enterprise architects

R

Railway Markup Language (railML), 104

Rapid Application Development (RAD), 35

Rational Unified Process (RUP), 35

Realization step of the project implementation process, 355, *See also* Project implementation process

Release designs, 170, *See also* Designs

Reputation of enterprise architects, 215, 272, 276, 400-402, 402-4, *See also* Resources of enterprise architects

Resources of enterprise architects, 101-15, 313-15, 347-49

Revision phase of the initiative implementation process, 320, 326-27, *See also* Initiative implementation process

Roadmaps, 155-56, *See also* Visions

Robust decisions, 92, *See also* Value of enterprise architects

Rules EA artifacts, 129-32

S

Salary of enterprise architects, 91

Schedule of enterprise architects, 281-85

Scheduled meetings, 282, *See also* Schedule of enterprise architects

Science, 296, *See also* Profession of enterprise architects

Scrum, 36

Secondary stakeholders of architectural planning, 44, *See also* Stakeholders of architectural planning

Security architects. *See* Domain architects

Security domain, 51, *See also* Organizational domains

Seeking synergies, 389-90

Senior techies, 81

Shadow IT, 266, 395

Simmons, John, 300-301, 436, *See also* History of enterprise architects

Skills of enterprise architects, 106-10, 314, 348, 424, *See also* Resources of enterprise architects

Software architects. *See* System architects

Software Engineering for Business Information Systems (SEBIS), 302

Software tools, 140-41, 426-27, *See also* Instruments of enterprise architects

Solution Architects (archetype), 305, 307, 345-72

Solution Briefs, 166-67, *See also* Outlines

Solution Designs, 168-69, *See also* Designs

Solution diagrams, 168, *See also* Outlines

Solution exemption forms, 263, *See also* Exception forms

Solution Options, 166-67, *See also* Outlines

Solution Overviews, 65, 165-66, *See also* Outlines

Solutions EA artifacts, 129-32

Space of architectural solutions, 120, 184-86

Space of descriptive representations, 118, 176-79

Specialization of architects, 308, 339-41, 367-69, 373-92

Stakeholder diversity, 37

Stakeholders of architectural planning, 43-45

Stakeholders of digital transformation initiatives. *See* Initiative stakeholders

Standalone initiatives. *See* Autonomous initiatives

Standards, 136, 150-55, 315, 349, *See also* CSVLOD taxonomy for EA artifacts

Standards conformance checklists, 262, *See also* Compliance checklists

Strategic alignment, 93, *See also* Value of enterprise architects

Strategies, 26-33, *See also* Digital transformation initiatives

Strategy committees, 248, *See also* Architecture governance bodies

Strategy maps, 150, *See also* Considerations

Structures EA artifacts, 129-32

Studying the internal environment, 200, 207-14, 317, 350-51, *See also* Activities of enterprise architects

Subject-matter experts, 44

Subordinate initiatives. *See* Derivative initiatives

Substantive domains, 54, *See also* Organizational domains

Supervising decisions, 388-89

Supplementary materials, 170, *See also* Designs

Supply Chain Operations Reference (SCOR), 103

Support functions, 86

System architects, 94-95

System Portfolio Models, 161-63, *See also* Landscapes

Systems thinking, 95, 109, *See also* Disciplined thinking

T

Target States, 65, 155-56, *See also* Visions

Taxonomy of instruments. *See* CSVLOD taxonomy for EA artifacts

Technical challenges of digital transformation, 12-14, 37-39

Technical concerns, 8, *See also* Transformation drivers

Technical design gate, 353, 361

Technical domains, 53, *See also* Organizational domains

Technical granularity, 37

Technical interests, 16, 285-91, *See also* Conflicts of interests

Technical rationalization initiatives, 289-91, *See also* Digital transformation initiatives

Technical side of architectural planning, 45-46, *See also* Architectural planning

Technical solutions, 45, *See also* Technical side of architectural planning

Technology committees, 249, *See also* Architecture governance bodies

Technology Experts, 77-78, 88, 405-6

Technology Inventories, 151-52, *See also* Standards

Technology radars, 204-5, *See also* Ad hoc papers

Technology Reference Models, 150-51, *See also* Standards

Technology Roadmaps, 151-52, *See also* Standards

Testing step of the project delivery process, 34, *See also* Project delivery process

The Open Group, 302, 428

The Open Group Architecture Framework (TOGAF), xix, 302, 303, 427, 428

Three-tier architecture functions, 378-79, *See also* Architecture functions

Tier-based specialization of architects, 374-79, *See also* Specialization of architects

Traditional architects, 70

Transformation drivers, 6-12

Transformational context, 192-94, *See also* Motivational context, *See also* Architectural context

Translation capability, 92, *See also* Value of enterprise architects

Two-tier architecture functions, 376-78, *See also* Architecture functions

U

Unified Modeling Language (UML), 140, 302, 426

Unofficial advisory services, 215-19, *See also* Providing advisory services

Updates approval gate, 320, 326

V

Value Chains, 158-59, *See also* Visions

Value of enterprise architects, 91-93

Value stream of activities, 276-78, *See also* Activities of enterprise architects

Visions, 136, 155-60, 315, 349, *See also* CSVLOD taxonomy for EA artifacts

Voluntary interactions, 68, 312, 400

W

Waterfall methodologies, 35-37, *See also* Project delivery process

Work of enterprise architects, 278-81, 329-30, 337-39, 366-67

Z

Zachman Framework, xix, 427

Zachman Institute for Framework Advancement (ZIFA), 302

About the Author

Svyatoslav Kotusev is an independent researcher, educator and consultant. Since 2013, he has been studying enterprise architecture practices in organizations. Besides this book, he is an author of the book *The Practice of Enterprise Architecture: A Modern Approach to Business and IT Alignment* (now in its second edition), more than 50 articles and other materials on enterprise architecture that appeared in various academic journals and conferences, industry magazines and online outlets (visit https://kotusev.com for more information). Svyatoslav received his PhD in information systems from RMIT University, Melbourne, Australia. Prior to his research career, he held various software development and architecture positions in the industry. He can be reached at kotusev@kotusev.com.

www.ingramcontent.com/pod-product-compliance
Lightning Source LLC
LaVergne TN
LVHW081523060526
838200LV00044B/1977